Endorsement Statement

In order to ensure that this resource offers high-quality support for the associated Pearson qualification, it has been through a review process by the awarding body. This process confirms that this resource fully covers the teaching and learning content of the specification or part of a specification at which it is aimed. It also confirms that it demonstrates an appropriate balance between the development of subject skills, knowledge and understanding, in addition to preparation for assessment.

Endorsement does not cover any guidance on assessment activities or processes (e.g. practice questions or advice on how to answer assessment questions), included in the resource nor does it prescribe any particular approach to the teaching or delivery of a related course.

While the publishers have made every attempt to ensure that advice on the qualification and its assessment is accurate, the official specification and associated assessment guidance materials are the only authoritative source of information and should always be referred to for definitive guidance.

Pearson examiners have not contributed to any sections in this resource relevant to examination papers for which they have responsibility..

Examiners will not use endorsed resources as a source of material for any assessment set by Pearson.

Endorsement of a resource does not mean that the resource is required to achieve this Pearson qualification, nor does it mean that it is the only suitable material available to support the qualification, and any resource lists produced by the awarding body shall include this and other appropriate resources.

Praise for this edition

ESSENTIALS OF UK POLITICS AND GOVERNMENT

EDEXCEL A-LEVEL

Kathy Schindler

Andrew Heywood

SIXTH EDITION

BLOOMSBURY ACADEMIC

LONDON · NEW YORK · OXFORD · NEW DELHI · SYDNEY

BLOOMSBURY ACADEMIC
Bloomsbury Publishing Plc, 50 Bedford Square, London, WC1B 3DP, UK
Bloomsbury Publishing Inc, 1359 Broadway, New York, NY 10018, USA
Bloomsbury Publishing Ireland, 29 Earlsfort Terrace, Dublin 2, D02 AY28, Ireland

BLOOMSBURY, BLOOMSBURY ACADEMIC and the Diana logo
are trademarks of Bloomsbury Publishing Plc

Previous editions published in Great Britain by Palgrave

Fifth edition first published by Red Globe Press 2021,
reprinted by Bloomsbury Academic 2022

This edition first published 2026

Copyright © Kathy Schindler and Andrew Heywood, 2026

Kathy Schindler and Andrew Heywood have asserted their right
under the Copyright, Designs and Patents Act, 1988,
to be identified as Authors of this work.

Cover design: Eleanor Rose
Cover image © Adobe Stock

A catalogue record for this book is available from the British Library.

A catalog record for this book is available from the Library of Congress.

ISBN: HB: 978-1-350-54012-5
           PB: 978-1-350-54011-8
         ePDF: 978-1-350-54014-9
        eBook: 978-1-350-54013-2

Typeset by Integra Software Services Pvt. Ltd.
Printed and bound in Great Britain by Bell and Bain Ltd, Glasgow

For product safety related questions
contact productsafety@bloomsbury.com.

To find out more about our authors and books visit
www.bloomsbury.com and sign up for our newsletters.

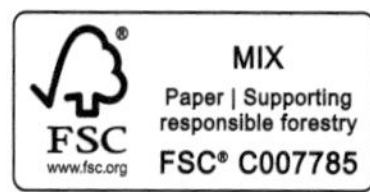

Brief Contents

Contents

Key Topic Debates

About the Authors

KATHY SCHINDLER has been teaching Politics for over 30 years, working in a large comprehensive school in London for most of that time. Kathy is part of the Senior Examination Team for a large exam board and was involved in the development of the linear Politics specification. Subsequently, she led many training sessions for the exam board around the country, helping teachers to get to grips with the demands of the new specification as well as supporting individual politics departments and holding student revision conferences in schools. In addition to this book, Kathy has also written textbooks published by Pearson. You can also find Kathy on Facebook (search for the page Politics_Tutor) and on X @politics_tutor.

ANDREW HEYWOOD is author of such best-selling textbooks as *Politics, Political Ideologies, Global Politics* and *Political Theory*, used by hundreds of thousands of students around the world and translated into over 20 languages. He was Vice Principal of Croydon College, having previously been Director of Studies at Orpington College and Head of Politics at The Sixth-Form College Farnborough. Andrew had many years' experience as an A-Level Chief Examiner for Government and Politics, and Principal Examiner for Political Ideologies and Global Politics. He currently works as a freelance author.

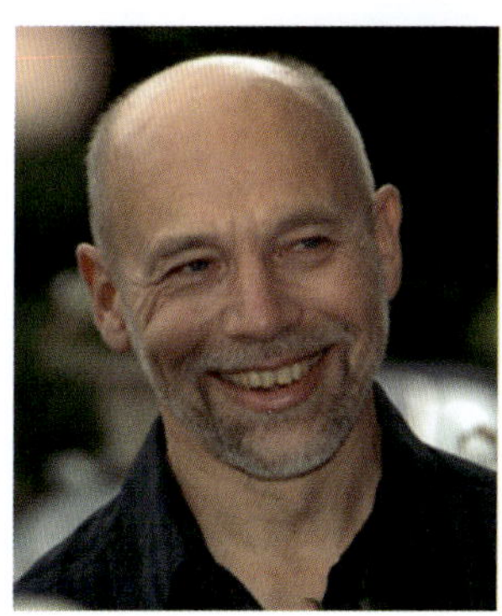

Acknowledgments

Thank you to everyone at Bloomsbury who have worked with me on this book, especially to Aléta Bezuidenhout, who helped me to navigate the conflicting needs of getting the book published in time and a crazy, ever changing period in British politics!

And of course, to my husband, Danny, who makes everything I do possible with his unswerving support and pride in everything I do – thank you.

For Nigel, an inspiration to me and so many others

Tour of the Book

Chapter Preview
These offer a broad outline of what each chapter will cover.

Chapter Preview
Democracy is one of those rare issues over which everyone seems to agree: we are all democrats. Very few of us are prepared to say that we are against democracy. But what is it that we all support?

Democracy is, in fact, a difficult issue. On the one hand, it seems simple. Democracy is 'government by the people'; however, there is no agreement about the form it should take. There are various models of democracy, the most common being 'direct democracy' and 'representative democracy'. Not only do these models offer quite different ways in which rule of the people can and should take place, but each has its own supporters and critics. What is the best form of democracy?

If democracy is popular rule, then participation must be the lifeblood of democracy. In the UK, participation has become highly problematic with low levels of party memberships and voter turnout across elections. Ensuring that there is increased participation is therefore a major issue facing British politics.

Key Questions and Debates
» What is democracy and why is participation central to democratic politics in the UK?
» Is the UK suffering from a participation crisis?
» How could UK democracy be improved?
» How was universal suffrage achieved and what does the future hold for expanding the vote?

Key Questions and Debates
At the start of every chapter there is a list of the key questions and debates addressed by the chapter.

Specification Checklist
A short checklist of the points from the Edexcel specification that will be covered by each chapter.

Specification Checklist
1.1. Current systems of representative democracy and direct democracy
» The features of direct democracy and representative democracy.
» The similarities and differences between direct democracy and representative democracy.
» Advantages and disadvantages of direct democracy and representative democracy and consideration of the case for reform.

1.2. A wider franchise and debates over suffrage
» Key milestones in the widening of the franchise in relation to class, gender, ethnicity and age, including the 1832 Great Reform Act and the 1918, 1928 and 1969 Representation of the People Acts.
» The work of the suffragists/suffragettes to extend the franchise.
» The work of a current movement to extend the franchise.

Synoptic Link
The concept of whether constitutions should be codified or un-codified is directly linked to the core political ideas of Conservatism and Liberalism.

Synoptic link
In Component 2 chapters only you will find suggestions of how you can make synoptic links back to Component 1 topics.

Definitions
Definitions of important terms to help you deepen your understanding of political concepts.

Definition
Partisan dealignment: The process where individuals no longer identify themselves on a long-term basis as being associated with a certain political party.

MILESTONES: WIDENING SUFFRAGE IN THE UK

1832 Great Reform Act – This abolished 'rotten boroughs', which had either no electors or a few electors and were controlled by a single powerful patron. The Act enfranchised almost all male middle-class property owners. Although it increased the electorate by about two-thirds, it still meant that fewer than 6% of the total population could vote.

1867 Second Reform Act – This Act gave the vote to all settled tenants (men only) in the boroughs, creating a substantial working-class franchise for the first time.

1884 Third Reform Act – This extended the franchise to rural and mining areas, and enfranchised virtually all male householders and tenants.

1918 Representation of the People Act – This Act widened suffrage by abolishing almost all property qualifications for men (effectively establishing universal manhood suffrage) and by enfranchising women over 30 who met a minimum property qualification.

Milestones
Timelines of key historical events in UK history with clear explanations to provide the context for the political debates of today.

Election Results
Key information on the General Elections in 2017, 2019 and 2024 laid out in a clear and helpful way.

Case Studies
Relevant case studies to illustrate key issues in UK politics and enhance your understanding of them.

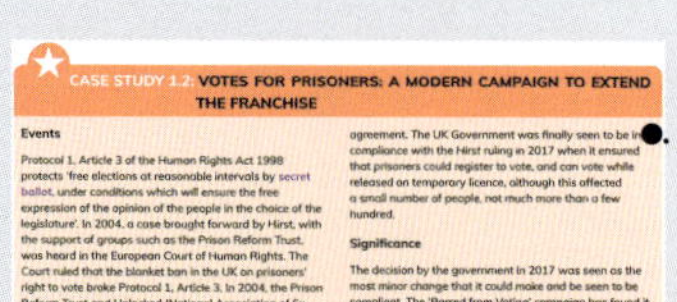

KEY TOPIC DEBATE: HOW EFFECTIVELY DOES THE UK PROTECT RIGHTS?

Rights in the UK are effectively protected by the courts via judicial review which allows citizens to challenge decisions made by public bodies, including the government, which they believe may contravene rights. (See Chapter x on the Supreme Court.)

» This allows the courts in the UK to protect the rights of the individual, even when it's unpopular, since judges are unelected. The court's protection of the rights of prisoners, suspected terror suspects and migrants seem to back this up.

1. In 2023, the UK Supreme Court ruled that the government's plan to send asylum seekers to Rwanda was unlawful, citing potential breaches of human rights obligations under the HRA.

2. The Illegal Migration Act 2023 has faced several significant legal challenges. The Act has been challenged for its incompatibility with the UK's human rights obligations under the ECHR; the UK Government could not say, when introducing the bill, whether it was compatible with the HRA. The High Court in Belfast identified sections of the Act that violated both the ECHR and the Windsor Framework.

3. In 2022, the case of Leigh v. Commissioner of the Metropolitan Police addressed the right to protest during the Covid-19 pandemic. The court found that the Metropolitan Police Service failed to conduct a proper proportionality assessment when making decisions about a planned vigil for Sarah Everard. This case underscored the importance of balancing public health measures with fundamental rights protected by the HRA.

Key Topic Debate
Throughout the book, we have selected the most important debates within each topic and outlined the arguments for and against. We have paired these arguments up, which is crucial for success in essay writing.

Chapter Summary
Bullet lists summarising the key points covered by the chapter, so you can check your understanding.

Chapter Summary

» The role of a constitution is to organise a political system and keep all players in check.

» The UK's constitution is uncodified and made up of a number of sources which work together.

» There is a debate as to whether the UK constitution works effectively.

» Since 1997 there has been a plethora of constitutional changes which have transformed the UK's political system, some more than others.

» Devolution has had a transformative effect on almost all parts of the UK.

Key Debate Summaries
Two-column table summaries with a bulleted list of the for and against points from the preceding topic debates. Useful for quick revision.

Key Debate Summary: Is direct democracy superior to representative democracy?

For	Theme	Against
✓ Direct democracy is genuine democracy with direct, immediate and continuous participation.	Is full participation more important than practicality?	✗ Representative democracy is the only practicable form of democracy in modern societies.
✓ The continuous participation of direct democracy allows for the personal development of citizens.	Is continuous participation more important than efficiency?	✗ Representative democracy creates a division of labour which is far more efficient than continuous participation.
✓ Direct democracy ends the reliance on a political class by returning power to the people to ensure decisions are in the public interest not the interest of the political class.	Is 'people power' better than government by experts?	✗ Representative democracy allows for government by experts; it is the sensible way to make complex decisions in the public interest.
✓ Legitimacy and political stability are both created by the direct involvement of citizens in decision making.	Does direct involvement of citizens provide greater stability or governing by compromise?	✗ Representative democracy is built on compromise, helping to maintain political stability.

Companion Website
Throughout the text there are directions to find further content related to the topic at hand on the book's extensive companion website.

Visit the companion website for a case study from the previous fifth edition on the work of the Suffragettes.

Exam Style Questions

● Evaluate the view that human rights are well protected in the United Kingdom (30).

● Evaluate the view that the largest pressure groups in the UK are the most powerful (30).

● Evaluate the view that group politics promotes pluralist democracy in the UK (30).

● Evaluate the view that think tanks, lobbyists and pressure groups have a significant impact on political decision making in the UK (30).

Exam Style Questions
A list of exam-style essay and source questions at the end of every chapter.

Source Question

Elections are the key method for citizens to have a say in who governs them and to hold politicians to account. Elections in the UK are free, fair and regular, with fraud being rare. The results of elections are respected, and voting is simple. Since 2022, voters need to present a relevant form of ID at the polling station which improves the security of elections. The franchise is based on universal suffrage and a secret ballot upholding its democratic nature. However, elections in the UK are undermined by First Past the Post. Voters who live in safe seats find that their vote does not matter as much as those who live in marginal seats. Additionally, FPTP undermines legitimacy by giving governments huge majorities on a small percentage of the vote. The introduction of Voter ID in 2022 has made voting harder, which suppresses turnout. Lastly, the Lords is unelected, which fundamentally undermines democracy in the UK.

Exam Focus Chapter
Unique to this book, a whole chapter devoted to exam skills and detailed step-by-step instructions on how to structure essays and sources.

Spec Key Term

Left wing: Political ideas that are based on the belief that the state can be used to deliver social change; they tend to prioritise equality over liberty.

Right wing: Political ideas that favour order, authority and also liberty, they favour free market economics.

Tips
Short bits of advice to help you maximise your understanding of what you need to do to develop your skills.

Tip: When preparing plans for parties questions, it is useful to keep a grid of policies throughout the time you are studying, so that you are always updating the information. Go to our online resources to find a template to use.

Spec Key Term
These are named Key Terms from the Edexcel Specification. It is important to know what they are because they can be used in exam questions.

Digital Resources

Accompanying this book is a suite of supportive online resources to help you get the most out of your learning.

Go online to the companion website **https://bloomsbury.pub/essentials-of-uk-politics-and-government-6e** to access further learning materials to support each chapter.

 A QR code to access the website is also provided throughout the book.

You can access the following:

Bonus case studies – Access fascinating bonus case studies and deepen your insights on key topics and events.

Flashcards of key terminology – Check your understanding of key specification terms and other important political concepts.

Tips for planning and organising revision – Get expert tips from the authors on how to plan and organise your revision effectively.

Specification matching table – A handy chart that will help you to target your revision by mapping the specification directly on to pages in the textbook.

How to Use the Book

Welcome to the latest edition of *Essentials of UK Politics and Government*, which has been fully revised and updated. Between us we have decades of experience in teaching politics and extensive knowledge of the Pearson Edexcel specification. We wanted to outline for you the changes we have made to this edition of the book and why we think it's in a good position to help you do well in this subject.

The book has been **fully updated** with the 2024 General Election and also analyses the three (yes … three!) Prime Ministers who have been and gone since the last edition. We have significantly developed the Devolution section and added lots about the different committees in the House of Commons. Almost **every case study is new** and as you would expect in a Politics textbook, **all the content in every chapter has been fully updated to provide you with the very latest examples**, to help you stay current when writing your essays.

As with the fifth edition, all the chapters in the book relate directly to a part of the Pearson Edexcel specification for A-Level Politics. You will see in the Tour of the Book (pages xii-xiii) that we have listed the relevant parts of the specification at the beginning of each chapter. This allows you to see clearly how the content of each chapter relates to the specification. In addition, the page design is also organised to help you identify content and features that are related to the specification, the exam and the skills needed. For example, you will notice that the key debate summaries, the spec terms, the tips and the specification checklists are all presented in the same colour (light green) throughout the book.

A unique and exciting aspect of the book is that it offers **an entire chapter** to help you understand the skills needed to write good answers. The Exam Focus chapter at the end of the book is packed full of helpful advice on how to write essays, use comparative language, develop your synoptic skills and ensure you're fully prepared for the A-Level Politics exams.

Another distinctive feature of this book is the way the chapters have been organised to help you **get to grips with the key debates in each topic**. As well as covering the relevant subject knowledge for each topic, we have also provided for and against points and examples for the key debate areas. We have organised these in a paired format, meaning that each argument on one side of a debate is paired with an opposing argument on the other side. The reason for this is that we want this book to do more than just provide you with the essential content. We have gone beyond the content traditionally found in textbooks to help you understand the debates that will form the basis of the essay and source questions you will be set, and to help you understand how to bring the content together to answer essay questions.

A final thing to note is that throughout the book you will find links to our companion website. You will find it packed with case studies as well as downloadable templates and some useful revision tips.

We really hope you find this book helpful. We have put all our experience and expertise together to make it the ideal guide for all students of A-Level Politics.

Kathy Schindler

Andrew Heywood

1 DEMOCRACY AND SUFFRAGE

Chapter Preview

Democracy is one of those rare issues over which everyone seems to agree: we are all democrats. Very few of us are prepared to say that we are against democracy. But what is it that we all support?

Democracy is, in fact, a difficult issue. On the one hand, it seems simple. Democracy is 'government by the people'; however, there is no agreement about the form it should take. There are various models of democracy, the most common being 'direct democracy' and 'representative democracy'. Not only do these models offer quite different ways in which rule of the people can and should take place, but each has its own supporters and critics. What is the best form of democracy?

If democracy is popular rule, then participation must be the lifeblood of democracy. In the UK, participation has become highly problematic with low levels of party memberships and voter turnout across elections. Ensuring that there is increased participation is therefore a major issue facing British politics.

Specification Checklist

1.1. Current systems of representative democracy and direct democracy

» The features of direct democracy and representative democracy.

» The similarities and differences between direct democracy and representative democracy.

» Advantages and disadvantages of direct democracy and representative democracy and consideration of the case for reform.

1.2. A wider franchise and debates over suffrage

» Key milestones in the widening of the franchise in relation to class, gender, ethnicity and age, including the 1832 Great Reform Act and the 1918, 1928 and 1969 Representation of the People Acts.

» The work of the suffragists/suffragettes to extend the franchise.

» The work of a current movement to extend the franchise.

Source: vm / iStock

Democracy

What is democracy?

Democracy is rule by the 'demos' – the people as a whole – rather than by any class or group within it. Most political systems throughout history have been based either on rule by one person (monarchies, empires and dictatorships) or rule by a small group of people (elites and oligarchies). As such, democracy was a revolutionary idea and was largely spoken about in critical language until the twentieth century. Democracy means giving power to the people. In its simplest sense, democracy is 'people power' and involves the concept of popular participation.

In order to think about whether a political system is democratic or not, we need to establish some criteria to judge it by. In his book, *On Democracy* (1998), Robert A. Dahl used five key measures of democracy:

1. **Participation:** All must have an equal and effective opportunity to make their opinions known.

2. **Voting equality:** Every member must have an equal opportunity to vote, and all votes must be counted as equal.

3. **Understanding:** Each person must have equal and effective opportunities for learning about the choices available and their likely outcomes.

4. **Agenda setting:** Each person must have the opportunity to decide how to set and what to place on the agenda so that past decisions are always open to be revisited.

5. **Universal:** All adults should have the same rights, as citizens, that are necessary for participation, voting equality, understanding and setting the agenda.

While the UK has democratic roots that go back as far as the Magna Carta of 1215, it can be argued that the UK system can only be seen as democratic since the granting of **universal suffrage** by the Equal Franchise Act of 1928. It was at this moment that the democratic rights for effective **political participation** became universal.

Legitimacy

Democracy is of central importance in politics because it provides the basis for legitimacy, the right to rule. Democracy provides those in power with the permission of the people to rule over them and places an obligation on the people to obey the law in several ways.

1. First, it does so through **consent**. Citizens implicitly give the 'right to rule' each time they participate in the political process. Democracy thus underpins **legitimacy** by allowing for effective political participation, most importantly through the act of voting, but also through joining a political party or pressure group, or serving in public office.

2. Second, democracy ensures that political power is widely dispersed, each group having a political voice of some kind. As such, it gives rise to a process of compromise and negotiation that allows people with different interests to live together in conditions of relative peace and order.

3. Finally, democracy ensures that the political system fairly reflects the views of the people.

Types of democracy

The task of understanding democracy is made more difficult by the fact that democracy comes in such a variety of shapes and forms. However, the two main types of democracy are:

1. Direct democracy

2. Representative democracy.

Direct democracy

Direct democracy is associated with the origins of democracy itself, which are usually traced back to Ancient Greece, and notably to its famous city-state, or polis, Athens. From about 500 to 322 BCE, a form of democracy operated in Athens that has served ever since as the model of 'classical' democracy.

Athenian democracy, however, was a very particular form of democracy, quite different from the forms that are found in the modern world. In particular, it relied on the participation of all citizens in open assemblies which made all the key decisions.

The key features of direct democracy are:

» Popular participation is *direct* in that the people 'make' policy decisions – they do not merely choose who will rule on their behalf.

» Popular participation is *immediate* in that the people 'are' the government – there are no professional politicians.

» Popular participation is *continuous* in that people engage in politics on a regular and ongoing basis – all decisions are made by the people.

Athenian democracy was built upon three important institutions:

1. The *Ekklesia*, or Assembly, which was the main governing body. Any male citizen could attend, debate and vote on all the major decisions such as declaring war, foreign policy, and making and revising laws. Decisions were made by majority vote. In the Assembly, all male citizens had the rights that were necessary for participation, voting equality, understanding and setting the agenda. However, only the very best speakers, such as Demosthenes, could hold the attention of the demanding crowd so a small elite of the best orators often dominated the Assembly.

Photo 1.1 Demosthenes, a Greek orator and statesman

Source: Nastasic / Getty Images

2. The Boule, or Council, was made up of 500 men and met every day to do the hands-on work of running the state. Council members were chosen by lot and only served for a term of one year. Drawing by lot, or **sortition**, was seen as more democratic than elections because it could not be affected by money or popularity and would not lead to a professional class of politicians separate from the people.

3. The Dikasteria, or popular courts, made up of 501 jurors chosen each day by lot from male citizens over the age of 30, resolved court cases brought by the people. This principle can still be seen as active in the UK, where juries are randomly selected from those between 18 and 70, who are on the electoral register. The aim is to ensure a justice system that is fair, democratic and independent.

Representative democracy

Representative democracy is the dominant form of democracy in the modern world because it solves the problem inherent in direct democracy that only a small percentage of people can spend their time learning about, debating and voting on political issues. Representative democracy is a way of voters electing a small group of representatives who work full-time on getting informed, debating and voting on political issues on behalf of the people. In a representative democracy, people acquire the power to make political decisions by means of a competitive struggle for the people's vote. Those who win elections can claim to 'represent' the people and the legitimate right to govern.

The key features of representative democracy are:

» Popular participation is *indirect* – the public do not exercise power themselves; they elect who will rule on their behalf.

» Popular participation is *mediated* – the people are linked to government through representative institutions.

» Popular participation in government is *limited* – it is infrequent and brief, being restricted to the act of voting every few years.

Whereas direct democracy is based on the principle of popular participation, representative democracy is based on popular control – ways of ensuring that professional politicians represent the people and not themselves. This is the role of elections and relies on the people exercising their right to vote. Therefore, the basic condition for representative democracy is the existence of democratic elections. These are elections that are based on the following rules:

» **Freedom, fairness and regularity:** voters can participate freely and express their own views.

» **Universal suffrage:** all adults can vote and there is voting equality, based on the principle of one person, one vote.

» **Party and candidate competition:** voters have a choice and effective opportunities for learning about alternative choices and their likely outcomes.

Historically in the UK, participation in representative democracy has been limited to voting in **general elections** to select MPs and in local elections to select local councillors. However, the number of opportunities for participation has increased with voters now also able to vote in a wide range of elections, depending on where they live, including:

» Elections in Scotland, Wales and Northern Ireland for the devolved governments since the first elections in 1998.

» Elections for the London Mayor and Greater London Authority since 2000.

» Elections for metro mayors, such as the Mayor of Greater Manchester, since 2017.

» Elections for Police Crime Commissioners, who make sure that local police meet the needs of the community, since 2012, although the Starmer Government announced the scrapping of them in 2025.

Spec Key Term

Representative democracy: A limited and indirect form of democracy. It operates through the ability of representatives to speak for, or act on behalf of, the people. At the heart of representative democracy is the process through which representatives are chosen and can be removed. In practice, this is usually done through regular and popular elections.

Definition

General elections: Full parliamentary elections, in which all 650 seats in the House of Commons come up for re-election. They traditionally take place within a five-year maximum term.

KEY TOPIC DEBATE: IS DIRECT DEMOCRACY SUPERIOR TO REPRESENTATIVE DEMOCRACY?

In the Athenian model, democracy meant putting power in the hands of ordinary people, giving them time and information so they would come up with effective solutions to the problems of the day and doing it frequently to increase understanding and participation. However, the strength of representative democracy is that it places ultimate power in the hands of the public – the power to decide who governs – while leaving day-to-day policymaking in the hands of experts. It is therefore based on a compromise between the need for 'government by the people' and the need for 'government for the people' (government in the public interest).

Genuine democracy:

 **Direct democracy is the only pure form of democracy.**

» This is because it ensures that people only obey laws that they make themselves. Direct participation in government is the very stuff of freedom: it is how the people determine their collective destiny.

✓ **Representative democracy always means that there is a gap between government and the people.**
  » This can lead to political apathy because citizens feel powerless when they want to make a change. Governments therefore govern in the name of the people, but, in practice, the people may have little meaningful control over government. This certainly appears to be a common attitude in the UK (see Figure 1.1).

Practical democracy:

✗ **Representative democracy is the only form of democracy that can operate in large, modern societies like the UK.**
  » It is therefore a practical solution to the problem of rule by the people. This does not mean that representative democracy cannot be enhanced by aspects of direct democracy.

✗ **Direct democracy is only achievable in relatively small communities, especially in the form of government by mass meeting.**
  » Such a form of democracy is unworkable in the modern world. Athenian citizens devoted a great deal of time and energy to political activity. They were also able to meet together in a single place. This is unrealistic in societies that are composed of tens or hundreds of millions of people.

Figure 1.1 Levels of political engagement in the UK

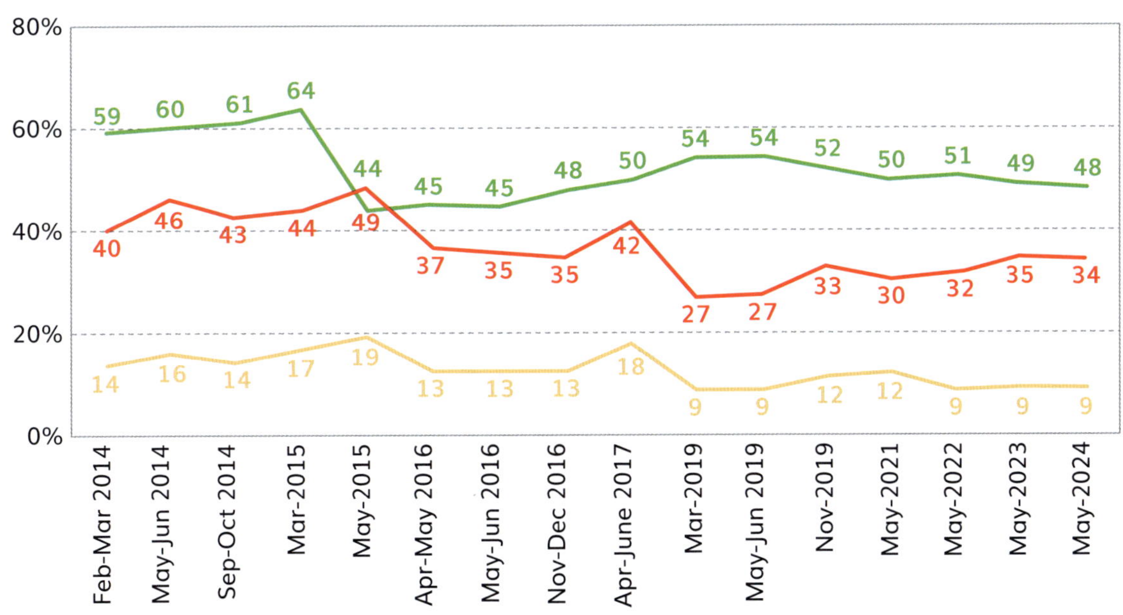

Source: Contains parliamentary information licensed under the Open Parliament Licence v3.0

Personal development:

✓ **Direct democracy creates better informed and more knowledgeable citizens.**
  » In this sense, it has educational benefits. Direct and regular participation in government encourages people to take more interest in politics and to better understand their own society.

✓ **In representative democracy, with votes taking place so infrequently, people can easily switch off from politics.**
  » As a result, political understanding decreases. This reduces the ability of people to learn about alternatives, which is necessary for effective participation.

Division of labour in politics:

- ❌ **Representative democracy is more efficient because citizens are relieved of the burden of day-to-day decision making.**
  - » They simply choose who they want to govern them.
- ❌ **One of the drawbacks of direct democracy is that it means that politics is a job for all citizens, restricting their ability to carry out other duties and activities.**
  - » Although the idea of Athenian democracy sounds egalitarian, in reality it was deeply undemocratic. The 'citizens' of Athens who were able to participate constituted only a tiny minority of those who lived in the city-state. Women, men classified as 'immigrants' and slaves, who made up at least three-fifths of the population of Athens, were excluded from participation and voting. The remaining men needed the time to be involved, and these were invariably the well off in society who did not work.

End of professional politics:

- ✅ **Direct democracy reduces, or removes, the public's dependence on self-serving professional politicians.**
  - » This increases public trust and political understanding while decreasing corruption, which means that decisions have real legitimacy in the eyes of the people.
- ✅ **Representative democracy places too much faith in politicians, who are always liable to distort public opinion by imposing their own views and preferences on it.**
  - » It therefore amounts to 'government by politicians', acting only in the name of the people. Also, this political class won't be representative of the wider public, and is more interested in winning elections than arriving at long-term solutions. In the UK, this is increasingly a widely held attitude; as Figure 1.2 shows below, in 2023 only 5% trust politicians to tell the truth when they're in a tight corner always or most of the time.

Figure 1.2   Levels of trust in politicians to tell the truth, 1994–2023

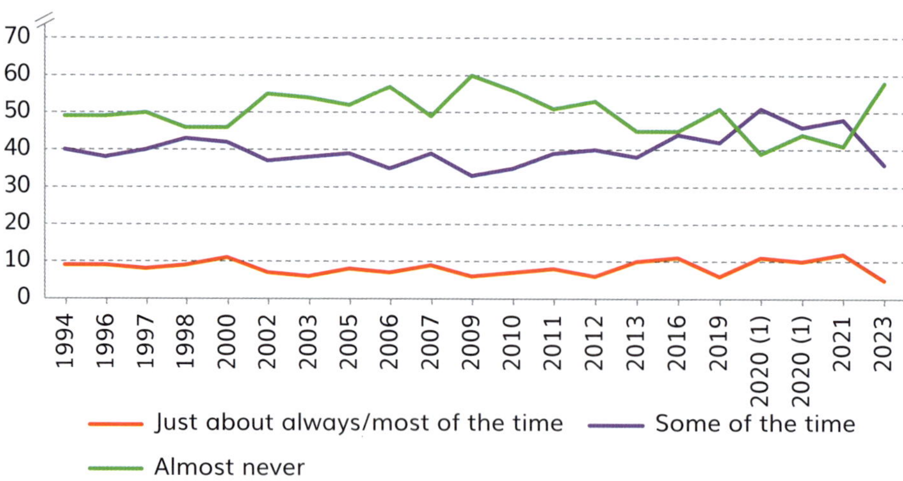

Source: British Social Attitudes. National Centre for Social Research Damaged Politics *report 2024, John Curtice, Ian Montagu and Chujan Sivathasan*

Government by experts:

- ❌ **Representative democracy places decision making in the hands of politicians who have better education and greater expertise than the mass of the people.**
  - » They can therefore govern for the people using their expertise to act in the public interest.

❌ **Direct democracy is not a sensible way to make complex decisions**.
  » This is because many of the big issues facing the UK don't have easy or clear solutions. Citizens are not always best placed to make complex decisions and may do so based on personal benefit rather than what is good for the country as a whole.

Legitimate government:

✅ **Direct democracy ensures that rule is legitimate, in the sense that people are more likely to accept decisions that they have made themselves.**
  » When citizens make political decisions directly, they take responsibility for them – there is no one else to blame. This helps to ensure political stability and legitimacy for decisions.

✅ **Representative democracy in the UK is experiencing something of a crisis.**
  » Voter turnout remains low and people feel increasingly disengaged from politicians and institutions. Figure 1.3 outlines a clear lack of satisfaction with governance. Overall satisfaction with the system of governing in the UK has been on a downward trend from 36% in the first Hansard *Audit* in 2004 to 25% in 2019. More recently, the National Centre for Social Research's Damaged Politics Report 2024 showed that 79% felt that the way the UK was governed could be improved quite a lot/a great deal. This was up from 61% in 2021.

Figure 1.3 Attitudes towards how Britain is governed, 2020–2023

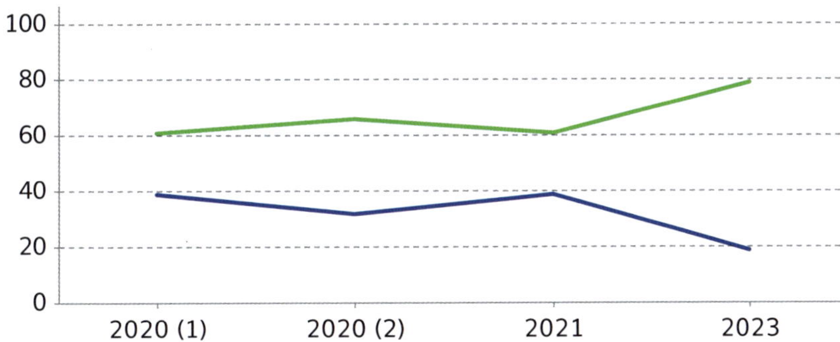

Source: British Social Attitudes. National Centre for Social Research Damaged Politics *report 2024, John Curtice, Ian Montagu and Chujan Sivathasan*

Political stability:

❌ **Representative democracy maintains political stability by helping to distance ordinary citizens from politics, thereby encouraging them to accept compromise.**
  » A certain level of apathy is helpful in maintaining political stability. The more involved in decision making citizens are, the more passionate and uncompromising they may become.

❌ **Direct democracy can engage people too much, which may create deep divisions in society.**
  » In cases where direct democracy creates clear winners and losers over a political choice, it will be very hard for the losers to see the political choice as legitimate. It may feel that there are only winners and losers.

Key Debate Summary: Is direct democracy superior to representative democracy?

For	Theme	Against
✓ Direct democracy is genuine democracy with direct, immediate and continuous participation.	Is full participation more important than practicality?	✗ Representative democracy is the only practicable form of democracy in modern societies.
✓ The continuous participation of direct democracy allows for the personal development of citizens.	Is continuous participation more important than efficiency?	✗ Representative democracy creates a division of labour which is far more efficient than continuous participation.
✓ Direct democracy ends the reliance on a political class by returning power to the people to ensure decisions are in the public interest not the interest of the political class.	Is 'people power' better than government by experts?	✗ Representative democracy allows for government by experts; it is the sensible way to make complex decisions in the public interest.
✓ Legitimacy and political stability are both created by the direct involvement of citizens in decision making.	Does direct involvement of citizens provide greater stabilty or governing by compromise?	✗ Representative democracy is built on compromise, helping to maintain political stability.

KEY TOPIC DEBATE: IS THE UK SUFFERING FROM A PARTICIPATION CRISIS?

Spec Key Term

Participation crisis: The idea that there is a crisis in citizen involvement in the processes aimed at influencing the government and shaping politics due to the lack of interest by a significant number of citizens. This creates a serious issue for democracy as it undermines the legitimacy of elected institutions.

Perhaps the main modern concern about democracy in the UK stems from evidence of growing political apathy. Some have seen this as nothing less than a **participation crisis**. How can democracy be healthy when, despite increasing opportunities for participation, more and more citizens seem to be uninterested in political life? This has been most evident in:

» Not voting

» Not joining political parties

» Not engaging with politics due to high levels of dissatisfaction with the current political system.

However, the idea of a participation crisis in UK politics has also been criticised. The problem may not so much be a decline in the overall level of political participation but, rather, that there has been a shift from one kind of participation to another. In particular, as disillusionment and cynicism with conventional party politics have grown, new forms of participation have developed to compensate for low voter turnout and declining party membership.

Voting

Low turnout is a growing cause for concern in the UK. The slow collapse in voter turnout in general elections and the low turnouts in other UK elections suggest there is a growing participation crisis in the UK. However, the increasing number of voting opportunities and the recent signs of life in voter turnout suggest that the crisis is being exaggerated.

✓ **Voter participation is slowly on an upward trajectory.**
» Since 2001, there has been a slow rise in the voter turnout, up to a high of 69% in 2017 from the low of 59% in 2001 (see Figure 1.4).
» Low turnouts in 2024 and 2001 can be explained by the expectation of a predictable result. In 2024, opinion polls widely indicated a clear win for Labour, and this was also true in 2001. Interestingly, in elections after 2001, turnout climbed back to 69%.

✗ **Participation is very poor compared to elections during the twentieth century.**
» The UK 2024 General Election recorded a hugely disappointing 60% turnout, which was even more surprising as it was considered a 'change' election, which normally sees high levels of turnout, yet Labour's large majority in 2024 was achieved on an exceptionally low turnout.

» Typically, general elections in the UK since 1928 and in the period between 1945 and 1992 saw turnouts above 75%, with a post-war high of 84% being achieved in 1950. The 2024 and 2001 election turnouts of 60% and 59% respectively, are the lowest since 1918.

» Given that 40% of the voting population didn't cast a vote in 2024, this means that only 20% of eligible voters voted for Labour. One must wonder what this says about the legitimacy of the win and Labour's mandate to carry out their manifesto?

Figure 1.4 Turnout across elections between 1918 and 2024

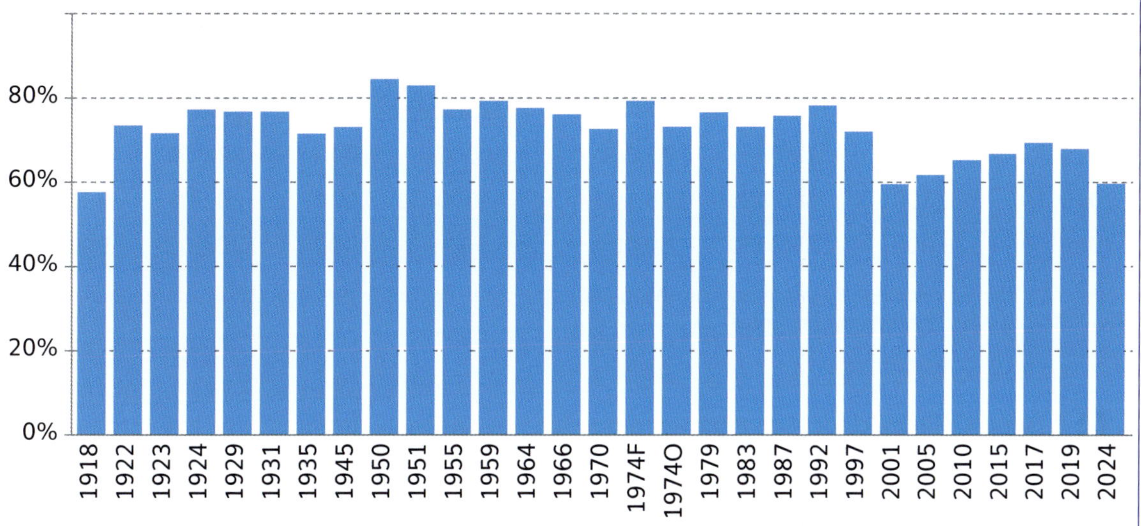

Source: Contains parliamentary information licensed under the Open Parliament Licence v3.0

✅ **However, the number of opportunities to vote has been increasing.**

» Since 1979, there has been a widening in the number of voting opportunities in the UK, with elections to the devolved assemblies in Northern Ireland, Wales and Scotland, Mayors across England and Police and Crime Commissioners, although the latter are now to be abolished.

❌ **But turnout is even lower in these elections.**

» The turnout in these elections has remained consistently lower than for general elections during the same period (see Figure 1.4). This could be attributed to voter fatigue from too many opportunities to engage or down to the institutions themselves not engaging the people's interest. In the 2024 mayoral elections in England, the overall turnout for the metro mayor elections averaged around 30%, which represents a decline from the 35% turnout recorded in 2021.

✅ **As well as elections, there is increased use of referendums.**

» There has also been a widening of participation opportunities since 1997 with the increased use of referendums across the UK. The turnout figures where matters have been of considerable historical importance have been very high. For example, in the Northern Ireland 1998 referendum on the Good Friday Agreement the turnout was 81%, which was topped by a turnout of 85% for the Scottish Independence Referendum of 2014.

❌ **However, there is also low turnout in many referendums.**

» Unlike the Scottish independence vote, the referendum on devolution in Wales saw a turnout of 50% while the referendum on the creation of the London Mayor and Assembly saw a turnout of just 33%. The Alternative Vote referendum had a turnout of 42%.

» Referendums for Mayors and PCCs were even lower. The turnout for the 2022 referendum to abolish the directly elected mayor in Bristol was 28.6%. This was slightly higher than the 24% of the previous referendum a decade earlier to introduce a mayor.

Party membership

In the early twentieth century, political parties had mass memberships with very strong party loyalty. Table 1.1 shows that since the 1950s there has been a large collapse in party membership as the public appeared to move away from this type of participation, although in recent times, there has been a slow increase suggesting a revival of participation.

Table 1.1 Party membership figures in the UK

Year	Conservative	Labour	Liberal democrat	Green	SNP	UKIP/ Reform	Total
1953	2,806,000	1,005,000					3,811,000
2003	248,000	215,000	71,000	5,300	9,500	16,000	564,800
2013	149,000	190,000	43,000	14,000	25,000	32,000	453,000
2019	180,000	485,000	115,000	49,000	125,000	29,000	983,000
2025	123,000	250,000	60,000	216,000*	56,000*	270,000	903,149

Source: Contains parliamentary information licensed under the Open Parliament Licence v3.0. Reform figure from https://www.reformparty.uk/counter
* 2026 figure

❌ **It is increasingly clear that mass membership has seriously declined, as have strong party loyalties, as shown in Table 1.1.**

» The Labour Party was traditionally seen as the party of the working class and the Conservatives the party of the middle class, and the 1950s and 1960s were associated with times of strong partisan alignment. Some argue that the decline reflects the fact that the political parties no longer reflect the modern UK, where age, ethnicity, education and income divides are more important than class. (See Chapter 5 for a detailed analysis of this issue.)

✅ **However, there have been periods of resurgence in party membership, reflecting changing political circumstances; it is not a linear decline. Also, as the major parties lose members, often the smaller parties gain them.**

» This is true particularly within the smaller parties such as Reform UK, the Scottish National Party (SNP) and the Green Party as people turned to them and away from the Labour and

Photo 1.2 Nigel Farage has overseen a huge increase in Reform UK membership

Conservative Parties. In 2025 Nigel Farage announced that they now had more members than the Conservative Party.

» Historically, members joined parties to enjoy the social facilities provided rather than for political purposes. Nowadays, members tend to be the most engaged supporters, joining to have a say in policy and a vote for the leader. This was shown in 2024 when Kemi Badenoch was elected leader of the Conservative Party with 56% of the votes based on a turnout of 73% of party members.

Group participation

A further traditional route for participation in UK politics has been to engage by joining groups to campaign on issues. This allows citizens to express their views on particular issues as well as in between elections.

The decline of the trade union movement.

» Pressure Groups (See Chapter 2), can be seen to be headed in the same direction as political parties. The largest and most influential of all groups in the UK are **trade unions** who reached their peak in 1979 with around 13.2 million members. By 2016, trade union membership had dropped to an all-time low of 6.2 million, and currently it is slightly higher at 6.4 million. This has largely come about due to the decline in manual jobs in large, traditional industries like coal mining and ship building. Moreover, even though membership of trade unions may be in the millions, often members are joining for non-political reasons, e.g. the National Union of Students has 6.3 million members, but many students join for the membership perks available, not political reasons.

The rise of new groups around issues.

» At the same time, there has been an explosion in the number of charities and campaigning groups. This growth has come about as it is felt that groups built around single issues are more effective at representing their interests and ensuring that policies are shaped to meet their views. According to the Association Management's Top 100 Membership Organisations 2025, total membership of the top 100 groups is 40 million people (although it's worth noting that many people may belong to multiple groups).

A recent trend that has transformed participation is the rise of social movements. Most social movements involve the use of **direct action**; mostly through mass peaceful protest, but also **civil disobedience** such as obstruction of roads, sometimes accompanied by violence to property.

» These movements are loosely organised and flexible, seeming to emerge quickly in response to issues as they appear on the political agenda, and have mass participation.

» The numbers of people taking part are very large, as can be seen in the Gaza marches of 2024, often engaging younger people, who have switched off from voting and party membership.

» Just Stop Oil is also an example of a social movement that focuses on civil disobedience to get media attention to focus on the climate emergency as shown in Photo 1.3 below. Their tactics are controversial.

Direct action is seen as a real challenge to democracy and traditional forms of participation.

» Social movements seek to challenge the traditional politics of working through elections, parties and Parliament with a new form of direct action politics. This raises the question as to whether they are undermining democratic participation and reducing legitimacy, or are part of a transformation in the way that people participate and the way that UK democracy works.

» In 2023 Dale Vince stopped funding Just Stop Oil as he felt their tactics (see Photo 1.3) were undermining the message and they were alienating the very people whom they needed support from. Instead, he donated £1 million to the Labour Party. Consequently in March 2025, Just Stop Oil announced that, after three years of disruptive protests, they were ending their campaign of civil resistance.

Individual participation

It has been argued that, in place of the more traditional forms of participation, the UK is experiencing a rise in individual rather than collective acts of participation. Individuals are sparked into action by issues that concern them, finding ways to engage on that particular issue rather than joining a formally organised group or party. This helps to explain the rise of the new forms of protest politics and why these movements appear so quickly, only to disappear at the same speed. This form of individual action can only be seen in a number of other political actions which are becoming increasingly commonplace:

Definition

Trade unions: Groups of employees who join together to maintain and improve their conditions of employment.

Direct action: Political action in the form of protest that aims at forcing change but does not go through the usual channels such as Parliament.

Civil disobedience: Law breaking that is justified on the grounds it is being used to create a more just and fair society.

Photo 1.3 Just Stop Oil protesters threw soup over Van Gogh's *Sunflowers* to gain media attention for their cause

»   **Petitions** – Signing petitions online has become a very common online activity. Change.org has over 150 million users globally and 38 Degrees claims to have a community of more than a million people who take action on issues they care about. In 2025 465,000 people signed a change.org petition to improve the awareness and diagnosis of cancer in young adults – known as Jess's Rule – which was then rolled out across the NHS in England.

»   **E-petitions** – The introduction of e-petitions by the government allows the public to petition the House of Commons and press for action from the government. In 2025 the UK Parliament e-petition "Do not introduce digital ID cards", reached 2,984,193 signatures. This led to a U-turn in the Government's position early in 2026. The rapid accumulation of signatures highlighted the strong public sentiment surrounding the demand for a new election.

»   **Social Media Activism** – As social media platforms have become endemic, a wider culture of 'clicktivism' has emerged that allows individuals to use platforms like X, TikTok and Instagram to promote a cause, or pressure MPs to act in a certain way rather than voting.

✓   This type of participation allows individuals to easily and quickly express their views.

»   Essentially, the individual can express their concerns directly, rather than through pressure groups or parties. These forms of individual participation engage people in politics in new and innovative ways that may revive democracy's flagging fortunes.

✗   However, it can lead to engagement without sufficient knowledge and fake news being shared.

»   It has been suggested that political campaigns become 'fashionable', encouraging individuals to jump on the bandwagon of a cause without having any understanding of the complex issues. Online platforms have become cesspits of hate and fake news which is quickly shared, causing significant problems for democracy. Moreover, the power wielded by 'tech barons' like Elon Musk, and to a lesser extent Mark Zuckerberg, is also a cause for concern.

Key Debate Summary: Is the UK suffering from a participation crisis?

For	Theme	Against
✓ There has been a long-term decline in voter turnout in the UK in general elections, with low turnout also a persistent issue in other types of election and many referendums.	Does voter turnout show that there is a crisis?	✗ There has been an increase in the opportunities to vote in the UK, with some revival of turnout in elections and referendums.
✓ There has been a long-term decline in party membership since the 1950s in the UK, in particular for the two major parties.	Does declining party membership suggest a crisis?	✗ There has been a recent revival in party membership, particularly for smaller parties.
✓ There has been a decline in the membership and power of the largest and most influential organisation in group politics: the trade union movement.	Does group participation suggest a crisis or an improvement?	✗ There has been an explosion in single issue groups, which now have mass membership and engagement.
✓ Social movements can undermine the key aspects of representative democracy and reduce the legitimacy of elected institutions.	Does group participation suggest a crisis or an improvement?	✗ Social movements have been a vehicle of mass engagement in politics in an era of protest politics. These forms of participation are replacing the more traditional methods.
✓ Individual participation on social media platforms can encourage individuals to jump on the bandwagon of a cause without having any understanding of the complex issues.	Do new forms of individual engagement indicate an increase in participation?	✗ Individual online participation has become a way for people to engage in politics in new and innovative ways. These methods are very democratic as they are open to all. The nature of participation is changing not declining.

A wider franchise and debates over suffrage

Universal suffrage

Elections in the UK became democratic through the progressive extension of the franchise throughout the nineteenth and twentieth centuries, first on the basis of social class, then on the basis of gender, and finally on the basis of age. Voting equality was achieved largely through Parliament responding to pressure from below to widen the franchise. The main steps on the UK's road to universal suffrage are shown below.

Spec Key Term

Franchise/ Suffrage: Franchise and suffrage are both terms that refer to the right to vote in public elections, such as the general election.

MILESTONES: WIDENING SUFFRAGE IN THE UK

1832 **Great Reform Act** – This abolished 'rotten boroughs', which had either no electors or a few electors and were controlled by a single powerful patron. The Act enfranchised almost all male middle-class property owners. Although it increased the electorate by about two-thirds, it still meant that fewer than 6% of the total population could vote.

1867 **Second Reform Act** – This Act gave the vote to all settled tenants (men only) in the boroughs, creating a substantial working-class franchise for the first time.

1884 **Third Reform Act** – This extended the franchise to rural and mining areas, and enfranchised virtually all male householders and tenants.

1918 **Representation of the People Act** – This Act widened suffrage by abolishing almost all property qualifications for men (effectively establishing universal manhood suffrage) and by enfranchising women over 30 who met a minimum property qualification.

These changes saw the electorate triple in size, reaching over 21 million, about 43% of whom were women (a figure inflated by the loss of men in the First World War).

1928 **Equal Franchise Act** – By lowering the voting age for women from 31 to 21 and abolishing property qualifications, this created equal voting rights for women and men, and established universal adult suffrage in the UK.

1969 **Representation of the People Act** – This lowered the voting age from 21 to 18, enfranchising 18–20-year-olds.

2014 **Scotland** – Following the precedent set by the Scottish Independence Referendum, the Scottish Parliament unanimously approved the proposal to reduce the voting age from 18 to 16 for Scottish Parliament elections (in 2016) and Scottish local elections (in 2017). The Welsh Senedd (Parliament) lowered the voting age in Wales to 16 in 2020 in Welsh Senedd elections.

Visit the companion website for a case study from the previous fifth edition on the work of the Suffragettes.

The right to vote in the twenty-first century

The extension of the franchise in the UK has moved over 200 years in the direction of widening the number of people who can vote to achieve voting equality. In the twenty-first century you can vote in the general election if you are over 18, are a British, Irish or qualifying Commonwealth citizen, resident at an address in the UK and have not been legally disqualified from voting. The following individuals cannot vote in a UK parliamentary election:

- ❌ **Members of the House of Lords**
- ❌ **EU citizens resident in the UK and anyone other than British, Irish and qualifying Commonwealth citizens**
- ❌ **Convicted people detained in prison**
- ❌ **Anyone found guilty within the last five years of corrupt or illegal practices in relation to an election.**

In 2022 the Conservative Government passed the controversial Elections Act 2022 which introduced a requirement for voters at polling stations in Great Britain to show photo identification (Voter ID) to prevent fraud.

Critics point to the fact that there is no real evidence of voter fraud undermining trust in UK elections and democracy, with only 33 allegations of voter fraud out of over 45 million votes in the 2019 General Election. Instead, opponents argue that Voter ID laws suppress the vote, particularly among already marginalised groups – the low paid and unemployed, disabled people, ethnic minorities and young people – because they are the least likely to have access to any form of photographic ID. According to the Electoral Commission, approximately 16,000 individuals across Great Britain were unable to vote in person due to not possessing the required ID in 2024, although the actual number is probably considerably higher.

Should the franchise be extended to 16- and 17-year-olds?

In July 2025, the Labour Government announced that as of the next general election (due by July 2029), the vote would be extended to 16–17-year-olds. When announcing, then Deputy Prime Minister Angela Rayner said, 'I was a mum at 16, you can go to work, you can pay your taxes and I think that people should have a vote at 16.' However, Conservative shadow minister Paul Holmes said the government's position was 'hopelessly confused'. 'Why does this government think a 16-year-old can vote but not be allowed to buy a lottery ticket, an alcoholic drink, marry or go to war, or even stand in the elections they're voting in?' Currently in the UK, only young people in Scotland and Wales have the right to vote in elections to their Parliaments.

✅ **Responsibilities without rights.**
»   The UK has a blurred 'age of majority', with the minimum age for various activities being lower than 18. Young people can leave full-time education to start an apprenticeship or work while in part-time education, pay direct tax, consent to sexual relationships, and (with parental consent) join the army, and give full consent to medical treatment. Some 16-year-olds are paying taxes, so arguably, if they contribute to society financially, they should have a voice in how those taxes are spent.

❌ **Immature voters.**
»   The main argument against lowering the voting age is that until 18 most young people are in full-time education and continue to live with their parents. This means that they are not full citizens, and their educational development, even though they can leave school, remains incomplete. The right to marry and enter a civil partnership was recently raised to 18, so it is odd to suggest that they should be able to vote at 16. They lack the life experience necessary to understand complex political issues fully.

✅ **Youth interests ignored.**
»   The lack of political representation for young people between 16 and 18 means that their needs, views and interests are routinely marginalised or ignored. Lowering the voting age may therefore give greater attention to, and stimulate fresher thinking on, issues such as education, drugs policy and social morality generally.

❌ **Deferred representation.**
»   To regard the lack of representation of 16–18-year-olds as a political injustice is absurd. Unlike women and the working classes of old, young people are not permanently denied political representation. Their representation is only delayed or deferred. Moreover, 18-year-olds are also likely to be broadly in touch with the interests of 16- and 17-year-olds.

✅ **Stronger political engagement.**
»   Lowering the voting age would engage young voters in two ways. Firstly, it would strengthen their interest and understanding, and secondly, it would help to refocus politics around issues that are meaningful to young voters. The evidence from the Scottish Independence Referendum shows that estimated turnout for 16–17-year-olds was 75%, much higher than the 54% for 18–24-year-olds. The earlier a person has the chance to vote, the more likely they are to use it and to continue to use it, helping to tackle the participation crisis.

❌ **Undermining turnout.**
»   There is a possibility that, by lowering the voting age, turnout rates may decline. As young voters are less likely to vote than older voters, many 16–17-year-olds may choose not to vote. As voters who do not vote in their first eligible election are the most unreliable voters, this may create a generation of abstainers.

✅ **Consistency.**
»   In Scotland and Wales, 16-year-olds can vote in local and devolved elections. Lowering the voting age across the entire UK would create consistency in voting rights, ensuring that young people are treated equally regardless of where they live.

❌ **Arbitrary Age.**
»   Some argue that if 16-year-olds are granted the right to vote, it raises questions about why not lower the age further. This could lead to calls for even younger individuals to participate in elections, complicating the debate about what constitutes an appropriate age for voting.

Should voting be compulsory?

The debate centres on whether compulsory voting would increase engagement in the political process across social classes and ages. The question was investigated by the House of Commons Political and Constitutional Reform Committee in November 2014 and February 2015, but the idea is seen as lacking widespread public support.

✅ **Increased participation.**
»   The almost certain consequence of introducing compulsory voting would be that turnout rates would increase. At a stroke, the UK's 'participation crisis' would be resolved. Citizens are already made to do things for the public good, such as jury duty and paying taxes, and compulsory

voting would be no different. When they get to the ballot box, voters would still have the option to spoil their ballot paper rather than vote for a party or candidate.

❌ **Abuse of freedom.**
» Compulsion, even in the name of democracy, remains compulsion, a violation of individual freedom. The right not to vote may be as significant as the right to choose whom to vote for. Non-voting may, indeed, be entirely rational, reflecting, for instance, the absence of choice between parties or a principled rejection of the political system.

✅ **Greater legitimacy.**
» Governments formed by compulsory voting would be much more likely to rest on a majority of votes, or at the very least, a much larger percentage of the total electorate, not just a majority of seats. This has never occurred in a UK general election, and in 2024 the winning Labour Party's popular support was just 21% of eligible voters, which includes those who voted and those who did not vote. Compulsory voting would therefore strengthen the democratic legitimacy of UK governments.

❌ **Cosmetic democracy.**
» Compulsory voting addresses the symptom but not the cause of the problem. Making voting compulsory would undoubtedly increase electoral turnout, but it would not address the deeper problems that account for the accelerating decline in political engagement. Higher turnout levels brought about through compulsion may simply mask these problems.

✅ **Civic duty.**
» Making voting compulsory would have wider educational implications in emphasising that political participation is a civic duty. The more people participate in politics, the more they will think and act as full citizens, as members of a political community.

❌ **Worthless votes.**
» Generally, those who do not vote have the least interest in and understanding of politics. Forcing people to vote would simply increase the number of random and unthinking votes that are cast rather than in line with policy preferences. Forcing people who are sceptical about the democratic system in the UK to vote may intensify their negative attitudes to democracy.

> **Definition**
>
> **Secret ballot:** A ballot in which the casting of votes is private and protected from public scrutiny.

⭐ CASE STUDY 1.1: VOTES FOR PRISONERS: A MODERN CAMPAIGN TO EXTEND THE FRANCHISE

Events

Protocol 1, Article 3 of the Human Rights Act 1998 protects 'free elections at reasonable intervals by **secret ballot**, under conditions which will ensure the free expression of the opinion of the people in the choice of the legislature'. In 2004, a case brought forward by Hirst, with the support of groups such as the Prison Reform Trust, was heard in the European Court of Human Rights. The Court ruled that the blanket ban in the UK on prisoners' right to vote broke Protocol 1, Article 3. In 2004, the Prison Reform Trust and Unlocked (National Association of Ex-Offenders) launched the 'Barred from Voting' campaign to argue that the ban on prisoners' voting undermined the principle of voting equality.

David Cameron described the idea of giving prisoners the vote as making him feel 'physically ill' and every time the issue has arisen in Parliament since 1970, the ban on prisoners' voting has been supported by cross-party agreement. The UK Government was finally seen to be in compliance with the *Hirst* ruling in 2017 when it ensured that prisoners could register to vote, and can vote while released on temporary licence, although this affected a small number of people, not much more than a few hundred.

Significance

The decision by the government in 2017 was seen as the most minor change that it could make and be seen to be compliant. The 'Barred from Voting' campaign has found it is almost impossible to cut through to the public with their arguments.

These arguments include:

- voting is a human right
- voting equality is central to democracy
- voting would promote rehabilitation and reintroduce prisoners into society

The last one is particularly important because social exclusion is a major cause of crime and reoffending. Additionally, it would perhaps ensure that politicians would take the rights, needs and interests of prisoners more seriously. However, politicians have remained steadfast in their opposition.

The key argument for opponents has been the idea that if you break the law, you cannot make the law; prisoners have broken their contract with society so they should lose their rights. The issue in Parliament is further complicated by that fact that many feel the *Hirst* ruling involves the European Court of Human Rights overextending its powers in telling the UK how to run its own country. The position of politicians is mirrored by the position in wider society where there remains widespread opposition to granting prisoners the right to vote. The wider situation across Europe shows the UK to be in a minority position: there are currently 18 countries in Europe where prisoners have the right to vote, including Denmark and the Netherlands, while there are another 12 where the right is partially restricted, including France. In only 13 countries do prisoners have no right to vote at all. In France and Germany, courts have the power to impose loss of voting rights as an additional punishment as part of a sentence for a convicted person.

However, the situation in the UK remains unlikely to change despite the Court ruling and the 'Barred from Voting' campaign because the main political parties and the public remain opposed to granting the vote to prisoners.

Democracy in the UK – problems and solutions?

The **democratic deficit** in the UK can be understood through three different but linked issues:

> » Voters are dissatisfied and disengaged so are not voting in large numbers, undermining the support for democratic institutions.
> » Elected representatives are seen as unaccountable for their actions and not widely trusted.
> » There has been a widespread recognition among politicians that there are problems with political participation, yet they have struggled to reform democratic institutions and processes to increase voter engagement.

Spec Key Term

Democratic deficit: The democratic deficit is a flaw in the democratic process whereby decisions are taken by people who lack legitimacy.

KEY TOPIC DEBATE: HOW DEMOCRATIC IS THE UK?

The nature of democracy in the UK needs to be judged in terms of whether there is real political equality for all to equally participate in the political process and how far that participation allows for the people to exercise popular controls over politicians.

Participation

 **Elections are the key method for citizens to have a say in who governs them** and to hold politicians to account and so are crucial to democracy in the UK. Elections in the UK are free, fair and regular, with electoral fraud being extremely rare, and are overseen by the Electoral

Photo 1.4 Voters going to the polls in UK elections

Source: NurPhoto / Contributor / Getty Images

Commission. The public and political parties respect the results of these elections and in general the process of voting is relatively simple: voters need to present a relevant form of ID at the polling station or register to have a postal vote. The vote is based on the principle of political equality, with universal suffrage and the secret ballot ensuring the adult public of the UK can vote in a range of elections.

❌ Although there is the principle of one person, one vote in UK elections, this is severely undermined by the First Past the Post (FPTP) electoral system. If a voter lives in a 'safe' seat, their vote is unlikely to matter as much as those who live in marginal seats. Additionally, FPTP undermines the principle of legitimate government. In 2024, the Labour Government was elected with a huge majority of seats on only 34% of the vote. Additionally, critics argue that the introduction of Voter ID in 2022 has created a significant barrier to voting. It also remains the case in the UK that the House of Lords is unelected, restricting popular control and accountability.

> **Tip:** See Chapter 4 for a detailed analysis of FPTP.

Group politics

✅ Politicians recognise the importance of pressure groups and there are multiple access points for groups to engage in dialogue and consultation with elected politicians in between elections. Pressure groups encourage participation in the political system and disperse power across society and ensure there is a channel of communication for minority groups in society. Social media has made it easier for groups and individuals to express their views and participate in politics.

❌ Group politics in the UK is seen to be politically unequal, amplifying the voice of the wealthy, well organised and strategically important groups at the expense of other groups in society. This concentrates power, rather than dispersing it, and can lead to democracy being undermined by giving too much unaccountable influence to some groups to shape policy in their own interest rather than the public interest. Concerns remain that pressure groups are internally undemocratic, and the use of tactics that break the law by some groups undermines democracy.

> **Tip:** See Chapter 2 for detailed coverage of the activities of pressure groups.

Rights

✅ In order for individuals to be free to participate effectively in the political process, democracy must be built on respect for basic rights. In the UK, the Human Rights Act 1998, the Freedom of Information Act 2005 and the Equalities Act 2010 have created a strong legal framework to protect rights. Parliament has shown a willingness to accept rulings of the Supreme Court when it judges rights to have been infringed.

❌ Successive governments have introduced legislation to curtail human rights in the UK, particularly in relation to national security issues. There is a growing debate about the role of Judicial Review, the Human Rights Act and the European Court of Human Rights in UK democracy. Critics have argued that the balance has been tilted too far in favour of rights and the courts, limiting the ability for efficient and effective government to deliver in the public interest.

> **Tip:** See Chapter 2 for detailed coverage of rights protection in the UK.

Key Debate Summary: How democratic is the UK?

For	Theme	Against
✔ Elections in the UK are free, fair and regular delivering popular control and accountability.	Do elections in the UK enhance democracy?	✘ There are considerable problems with FPTP as well as the introduction of Voter ID.
✔ Group politics disperses power across society and provides a key channel for political participation; citizens can express their opinions in between elections.	Does group politics promote pluralism and therefore democracy in the UK?	✘ Group politics acts as a potential threat to democracy by concentrating power, with decision making hidden behind closed doors, reducing accountability.
✔ Human rights are well protected in the UK, providing citizens with the freedom to participate in democracy.	Are rights protected effectively enough in the UK democracy?	✘ Rights have been breached by successive governments and there has been a growing debate about the balance between rights and effective government in the public interest.

Enhancing democracy in the UK

As criticisms of the UK's democratic system have increased, a growing debate has emerged about how democracy can best be protected or enhanced.

KEY TOPIC DEBATE: WHICH REFORMS CAN ENHANCE DEMOCRACY IN THE UK?

Recent years have witnessed a steady trend, evident in the UK and elsewhere, towards the wider use of direct involvement. This has occurred because representative democracies have been seen to suffer from increased political apathy and growing popular disillusionment with politics. The great advantage is that it strengthens popular participation in politics by placing power directly into the hands of the people.

Initiatives

Initiatives allow people to propose a new law by gathering the required number of signatures from the public. If the proposal is then passed by the voters, it becomes part of the law of that country. Initiatives are not currently used in the UK but are used in other democracies such as Switzerland and certain states in the USA. The key difference to a referendum is that initiatives allow the people to put the measure on the ballot paper themselves without any role for elected politicians.

✔ **The UK could introduce the use of initiatives to give the public more direct control over making law.** Essentially, the UK could allow the public to put new laws on the ballot paper and then vote on it themselves removing the role of politicians in the process.

✘ **However, initiatives would undermine UK democracy by removing politicians from making decisions** and potentially create a situation where the majority could undermine the rights of minority groups.

Citizens' assemblies

Citizens' assemblies are made up of a representative group who are chosen using sortition. Certain criteria such as age, gender, ethnicity, region and social background are used as part of the selection process to ensure that the group is broadly representative of wider society. The assembly is then given the job of carrying out an in-depth analysis of a particular policy issue; this process involves analysing the problem, deliberating on potential solutions, then making informed recommendations for action.

The *2022 Report of the Citizens' Assembly on Democracy in the UK* proposed stronger standards rules, reduced executive dominance, more empowered parliament, better civic education, and wider use of advisory citizens' assemblies. The report was written after bringing together members of the public from across the UK in a citizens' assembly. It explored what roles should be played by the government, parliament, the courts, and the general public.

✔ **Citizens' assemblies are a way of exploring the views of the public on a policy issue and coming up with concrete solutions.**
  » Citizens' assemblies can reinforce and add to representative democracy, not only by giving elected politicians an understanding of informed public viewpoints on complex issues, but also by building trust in the political process through participation and engagement.

✘ **However, there must be key elements in place for assemblies to be successful:**
  » There would need to be a clear focus, sufficient time and a large enough budget to cover the topic in the appropriate detail. There would also need to be the political will, probably backed by cross-party support, to implement rather than ignore the recommendations made.

Automatic voter registration

In 2024, the **Electoral Commission** found that more than 8 million people were not registered to vote, limiting their ability to participate in elections. Their investigation also found clear differences in registration levels between younger people, renters, low-income and ethnic minorities, compared with older white people who own their homes. Automatic voter registration would resolve this immediately. In July 2025, the government announced it was working towards creating an automated voter registration scheme. Currently people in the UK need to register in order to vote. The Electoral

Definition

Initiatives: Give people the power to propose a new law or constitutional amendment and then vote on it.

Definition

Electoral Commission: An independent body charged both with reviewing the operation of the UK's democratic processes and with making recommendations for strengthening democracy. It was established by the Political Parties, Elections and Referendums Act 2000 (PPERA).

Commission estimates that nearly 8 million people are incorrectly registered or missing from the electoral register entirely, with the issue disproportionately affecting private renters and young people. The government said its plans would mean eligible voters could be directly added to the electoral register through better sharing of data between government agencies.

✓ **Automatic voter registration simplifies the registration process,** making it easier for eligible citizens to register without having to navigate complex forms or procedures. This can particularly benefit underrepresented groups, including young people and low-income individuals.

✗ **There may be apprehensions regarding the security of voter registration data** and the potential for misuse of personal information. Citizens might worry about their data being exposed or mishandled. Consequently, implementing it could face legal and political challenges, particularly from those who argue it may favour one political party over another.

Other reform options which are explored in other sections of the book are:

- » Change the voting system from FPTP (see Chapter 4)
- » Compulsory voting (see page 19)
- » Lower the voting age (see page 16)
- » Improve recall elections (see Chapter 7)
- » Referendums (see Chapter 4)
- » State funding for political parties (see Chapter 3)
- » Elect the House of Lords (see Chapter 7)

Key Debate Summary: Which reforms could enhance democracy in the UK?

For	Theme	Against
✓ Initiatives allow the people to put the measure on the ballot paper and then vote on it themselves without any role for elected politicians.	Would initiatives enable citizens to reconnect with politics?	✗ Initiatives would undermine UK democracy by removing politicians from making decisions.
✓ Citizens' Assemblies benefit representative democracy by creating higher levels of engagement and participation, increasing legitimacy while also making politicians more accountable.	Would citizens' assemblies enable citizens to reconnect with politics?	✗ However, without enough commitment from politicians, it could result in greater frustration and increase political apathy.
✓ Automatic voter registration would ensure that all citizens were ready and able to vote, increasing participation across all sections of society.	Would automatic voter registration enhance turnout?	✗ Concerns remain about fraud, accuracy and the cost of automatic registration.

Exam Style Questions

- Evaluate the view that the UK is suffering from a participation crisis (30).
- Evaluate the view that direct democracy can be considered superior to representative democracy (30).
- Evaluate the view that a wider franchise will only enhance democracy (30).
- Evaluate the view that democracy in the UK is in need of reform (30).
- Evaluate the view that UK democracy is suffering from a democratic deficit (30).

Source Question

Elections are the key method for citizens to have a say in who governs them and to hold politicians to account. Elections in the UK are free, fair and regular, with fraud being rare. The results of elections are respected, and voting is simple. Since 2022, voters need to present a relevant form of ID at the polling station which improves the security of elections. The franchise is based on universal suffrage and a secret ballot upholding its democratic nature. However, elections in the UK are undermined by First Past the Post. Voters who live in safe seats find that their vote does not matter as much as those who live in marginal seats. Additionally, FPTP undermines legitimacy by giving governments huge majorities on a small percentage of the vote. The introduction of Voter ID in 2022 has made voting harder, which suppresses turnout. Lastly, the Lords is unelected, which fundamentally undermines democracy in the UK.

Pressure groups are very important in UK democracy and there are many ways for groups to engage with politicians in between elections. Pressure groups encourage participation and ensure there is a way for minority groups to be heard. Social media has made it easier for groups and individuals to express their views. However, some pressure groups are much more influential than others, Think tanks and lobbyists can amplify the voice of the wealthy, and well-organised and strategically important groups succeed at the expense of others, concentrating power, rather than dispersing it. Law breaking by some groups undermines democracy.

Democracies must be built on respect for basic rights. In the UK, we have the Human Rights Act 1998, the Freedom of Information Act 2005 and the Equalities Act 2010, which have created a strong legal framework to protect rights. Parliament has shown a willingness to accept rulings of the Supreme Court when it judges rights to have been infringed. However, successive governments have introduced legislation to limit rights. Additionally, there is a growing debate about the role of Judicial Review, the Human Rights Act and the European Court of Human Rights in UK democracy by some who argue that the balance has been tilted too far in favour of individual rights and the courts, limiting the ability of the government to protect the public.

Using the source, evaluate the view that the UK is suffering from a democratic deficit.

In your response you must:

» *Compare and contrast different opinions in the source*

» *Examine and debate these views in a balanced way*

» *Analyse and evaluate **only** the information presented in the source.*

Chapter Summary

» Democracy is of central importance in politics because it provides the basis for legitimacy, the right to rule, and so is the key to political stability.

» Democracy requires high levels of political participation, yet in the UK there appears to have been a decline in traditional methods of participation such as voter turnout and party membership, creating a participation crisis.

» The UK has seen the rise of alternative methods of participation based around group politics, new social movements and individual politics, which some argue has counterbalanced the fall in traditional forms of participation.

» In light of the perceived participation crisis, multiple reforms have been suggested to re-energise UK democracy.

Further Resources

Dahl, R. (2015) *On Democracy* (2nd edn) (New Haven, CT: Yale University Press).

Extending the voting age to 16, Electoral Reform Society https://www.electoral-reform.org.uk/campaigns/votes-at-16/

Goodhind, W. (2023) Why the UK's e-petitions platform is not living up to its democratic potential, LSE Blog. https://blogs.lse.ac.uk/politicsandpolicy/why-the-uks-e-petitions-platform-is-not-living-up-to-its-democratic-potential/

Griffiths, S. and Leach, R. (2018) *British Politics* (3rd edn) (London: Bloomsbury Academic): Chapter 16.

Heffernan, R., Hay, C., Russell, M. and Cowley, P. (2016) *Developments in British Politics* (10th edn) (London: Bloomsbury): Chapter 8.

Moran, M. (2017) *Politics and Governance in the UK* (3rd edn) (London: Bloomsbury): Chapter 14.

Why it's time for Automatic Voter Registration (2020) Electoral Reform Society *based on 'Is it time for Automatic Voter Registration in the UK?' Report, funded by the UK Democracy Fund.* https://www.electoral-reform.org.uk/why-its-time-for-automatic-voter-registration/ https://www.lse.ac.uk/assets/richmedia/channels/government/slides/20131209_week9_policyMakingInfluence_sl.pdf

Visit the companion website to access the Further Resources Booklet to explore a range of useful web links related to: political engagement, membership of political parties, electoral registration, electoral turnout, voter engagement, voting at age 16, compulsory voting and votes for prisoners.

2

DEMOCRACY AND PARTICIPATION: PRESSURE GROUPS AND RIGHTS

Chapter Preview

Viewing political participation as simply about party membership and voter turnout gives only a limited understanding of participation in the UK. There has been an increased role for pressure groups with a highly diverse and growing number of groups looking to represent their interests. Beyond these formal groups, the UK has also seen a return to its long history of public protest, with a rise in marches, demonstrations and direct action. This has raised questions as to whether group politics is enhancing UK democracy or undermining it.

The link between rights and democracy is founded on the belief that political participation is only meaningful when it is carried out by individuals who can think and act for themselves. UK citizens are entitled to certain liberties, such as freedom of speech and the right to vote, which act as an effective check on the power of the state. This raises the question as to how effectively rights are protected in the UK, and whether they act as a building block or a stumbling block to democracy.

Key Questions and Debates

» What is group politics?

» Why are some groups more successful than others?

» How much influence do groups exert on UK politics and how far does group politics enhance democracy?

» What are rights and how well protected are they in the UK?

Specification Checklist

1.3. Pressure groups and other influences

» How different pressure groups exert influence and how their methods and influence vary in contemporary politics.

» Case studies of two different pressure groups, highlighting examples of how their methods and influence vary.

» Other collective organisations and groups including think tanks, lobbyists and corporations, and their influence on government and Parliament.

1.4. Rights in context

» Major milestones in their development, including the significance of Magna Carta and more recent developments, including the Human Rights Act 1998 and Equality Act 2010.

» Debates on the extent, limits and tensions within the UK's rights-based culture, including consideration of how individual and collective rights may conflict, the contributions from civil liberties pressure groups – including the work of two contemporary civil liberties pressure groups.

Source: Henry Nicholls / Contributor / Getty Images

What are pressure groups?

When people are asked to name a pressure group, certain groups come to mind; for example, Black Lives Matter, trade unions such as UNISON and Unite, Just Stop Oil or Extinction Rebellion. These are groups that have a high public profile by getting the attention of the media. However, the pressure group universe is much broader than just pressure groups and includes other collective organisations – corporations such as Amazon UK or CITIBANK, think tanks such as the Institute of Economic Affairs and Labour Together, and lobbying firms such as Arden Strategies.

Types of groups

<table>
<tr><td>

Definition

Interest group: A pressure group that exists to advance or protect the interests of its members.

Peak group: An umbrella group which represents and speaks on behalf of its members who share common interests, who pool resources and work together to achieve their aims.

Cause group: A pressure group that is based on shared values, ideals and principles.

</td><td>

Pressure groups

Pressure groups are defined by three key features:

- They seek to exert *influence* from outside, rather than to win or exercise government power.
- They typically have a *narrow* issue focus. In some cases, they may focus on a single issue.
- Their members are *united* by either a shared belief in a particular cause or a common set of interests.

Pressure groups are categorised as interest or cause groups.

Interest and cause groups

The interest/cause distinction is based on the *purpose* of the group in question:

- **Interest groups** are groups that represent and defend the interests of a particular section of society: workers, employers, consumers, an ethnic or religious group, and so on. Trade unions, business corporations, trade associations and professional bodies are the prime examples of this type of group. They are called interest groups because they represent the interests of a particular section of the population. Specific examples include the National Education Union (NEU), representing nearly 450,500 teachers and education workers, and so-called **peak groups** such as the National Farmers' Union (NFU) which acts as a peak group for farmers in England and Wales, and speaks on behalf of over 50,000 businesses, and the Trades Union Congress (TUC), bringing together 48 unions and over 5.5 million workers.
- **Cause groups** are groups that are based on shared values, usually on a specific topic, rather than the common interests of their members. The causes they seek to advance are many and varied, and so the range of cause groups is infinite: from charity activities and poverty reduction to human rights and the environment. Specific examples of cause groups include Liberty, a human rights organisation which has been influential in protecting civil liberties and promoting human rights in the UK, the Child Poverty Action Group (CPAG), working on behalf of children growing up in poverty in the UK, which successfully influenced several policies including the uprating of benefits by 10% in 2022/23, and the first-ever increase to the benefit cap, and Shelter, who bring people together to fight homelessness, has 400,000 supporters and has helped over 30,000 people with their housing.
- Social movements are a type of pressure group, which, while not new (we could consider the Suffragettes and the civil rights movement to be examples), have dominated the landscape in recent years due to the ease of mobilising people through mobile phones. Social movements are large groups of people aiming to promote or change society. These movements often emerge in response to perceived injustices and seek to mobilise individuals towards a common goal, typically involving protests or organised campaigns. Examples are Just Stop Oil, Black Lives Matter, Extinction Rebellion or the Gaza protests. Social movements differ from pressure groups in that they are very loosely organised, lacking clear leadership structures and they also have very wide aims, not usually seeking to change a specific, individual policy. These movements often have a global presence due to social media, which allows people to follow movements in many different countries.

</td></tr>
</table>

Insider and outsider groups

The insider/outsider distinction is valuable because it is based on a group's *relationship to government*. It therefore affects the strategies that a group can adopt.

- **Insider groups** are groups that are consulted on a regular basis by government. They operate 'inside' the decision-making process, using their influence rather than direct action. The degree, regularity and level of their insider status vary. 'Core insider' groups have regular and meaningful consultation at ministerial or senior official level within the government while 'peripheral insiders' may have regular but only cosmetic consultation with government that doesn't really bring them into the corridors of power.

- **Outsider groups**, by contrast, have no special links to government. They are kept, or choose to remain, at arm's length from government. They therefore try to exert influence indirectly via the mass media, through public opinion campaigns and protests. Many outsider groups have been attracted to a type of politics which turns away from traditional methods of political engagement towards more theatrical forms of protest politics. This style of politics has been closely associated with social movements that emerged in the late twentieth and early twenty-first centuries – the women's movement, the green movement, the peace movement and the anti-capitalist or anti-globalisation movement.

Think tanks

Think tanks are organisations that provide advice and policy proposals on political, economic and social problems. They carry out research to provide evidence about an issue and use their links with politicians, the media and political parties to present evidence to shape policy. It is their expertise and reputation that gives them access to politicians and the media. Think tanks can be left wing or right wing, but many claim to be politically neutral and academic so they can shape policy without being tied directly to party politics. For instance, the Institute of Economic Affairs (IEA) states that it is a free market think tank, 'entirely independent of any political party or group' and that its ideas are 'consistent with a wide range of political positions, including no political position at all'. However, during the brief premiership of Liz Truss, we saw just how close they were to the Conservative Party.

✅ **Many see think tanks as enriching democracy by carrying out policy research, developing policy options and aiding public debate.**

» By providing different ideas and the evidence to back them up, think tanks are using their expertise to enable the public and politicians to weigh up different ideas, make decisions about what they believe and inform their choices. Their expertise is crucial to improving political decision making in the UK.

» Recently the Resolution Foundation has shaped minimum wage policy mainly by providing evidence, and working with the Low Pay Commission.

» The Institute for Government (IfG) is a think tank that aims to make government more effective through research and analysis, and support for ministers, officials and policymakers. It has long criticised UK spending reviews as opaque, short term and prone to unrealistic savings assumptions, and has published detailed proposals for a more strategic process. In 2025, the government said it would adopt key IfG recommendations on reforming the spending review, including clearer objectives, earlier engagement with departments and better links between capital and resource spending.

❌ **Critics argue that think tanks push policies and evidence that favour the powerful corporate interests who fund them, undermining democracy.**

» These concerns focus on the lack of transparency around think tanks since they do not have to declare the sources of their funding and politicians do not need to declare meetings with think tanks in the same way as they do with corporations. According to Open Democracy the IEA boasted of securing access to 75 cross-party parliamentarians in its annual accounts for the financial year ending March 2022.

» The IEA lists the five main areas its money comes from (see Figure 2.1) but (due to privacy concerns) does not reveal the names of the companies or individuals who donate. Critics argue it is not possible for politicians or the public to have confidence in the independence and objectivity of a think tank report if they do not know who funded it. In 2018, the IEA received a legal warning from the Charity Commission for publishing a report calling for a hard Brexit that the Commission said constituted 'political activity' in breach of its status as an educational charity.

CASE STUDY 2.1: THE INSTITUTE OF ECONOMIC AFFAIRS AND THEIR INFLUENCE ON THE LIZ TRUSS PREMIERSHIP

Liz Truss's brief tenure as Prime Minister was marked by a controversial economic agenda that culminated in her resignation after just 49 days in office. Central to her economic philosophy was the influence of the Institute of Economic Affairs (IEA), a libertarian think tank advocating free-market policies. This case study examines the relationship between the IEA, Truss and the controversial mini-budget that led to her downfall.

Liz Truss started working with the IEA shortly after she was elected to Parliament in 2010 with some suggesting the IEA 'incubated' Truss and her key ally, Kwasi Kwarteng, when they were junior MPs. The IEA's emphasis on deregulation, tax cuts and minimal state intervention resonated with Truss's vision of economic growth driven by individual enterprise and market freedom. In 2011, Truss co-founded the Free Enterprise Group in Parliament, a group of over 30 Thatcherite Conservative MPs and over the next 12 years, she spoke at IEA events more frequently than any other politician as she rose through the ranks of the Conservative Party. The IEA's policy papers and publications, which championed low taxes and a smaller state, became key aspects of her economic worldview and her speeches often echoed the IEA's rhetoric, emphasising the need to 'unleash Britain's potential'. Truss reportedly had a standing Monday lunch date at the IEA's offices, demonstrating her deep engagement with the organisation's ideas. But it was when she became Prime Minister in September 2022 that the scale of their influence was revealed.

The mini-budget fiasco

Within weeks of taking office, Truss and her Chancellor, Kwasi Kwarteng, presented the government's 'growth plan' to Parliament. The plan included £45 billion of unfunded tax cuts, including the abolition of the 45% income tax rate for high earners; the cancellation of the planned corporation tax increase; reduction in National Insurance contributions and the removal of the cap on bankers' bonuses. These policies closely mirrored the IEA's recommendations, reflecting its belief in supply-side economics as a driver of growth. It was largely prepared by IEA members Julian Jessop and Andrew Lilico, along with former Boris Johnson aide Gerard Lyons, known as 'the three Trussketeers'. However, the mini-budget's lack of a plan to address ballooning public debt spooked financial markets. The pound fell to record lows, government borrowing costs soared, and the Bank of England was forced to intervene to stabilise pension funds. It later transpired that Truss and Kwarteng had ignored advice from senior civil servants and had also declined an independent growth forecast from the Office for Budget Responsibility.

Consequently, Truss was forced to abandon most of the mini-budget proposals and ultimately resigned after just 49 days in office. The IEA's director general, Mark Littlewood, expressed being 'distraught' over the abandonment of their championed ideas. Another think tank, the Resolution Foundation, estimated that Truss and Kwarteng's decisions cost the UK Treasury £30 billion. The whole episode raised questions about the influence of think tanks on government policy, especially those that do not disclose their funding sources.

Figure 2.1 IEA funding breakdown (2020)

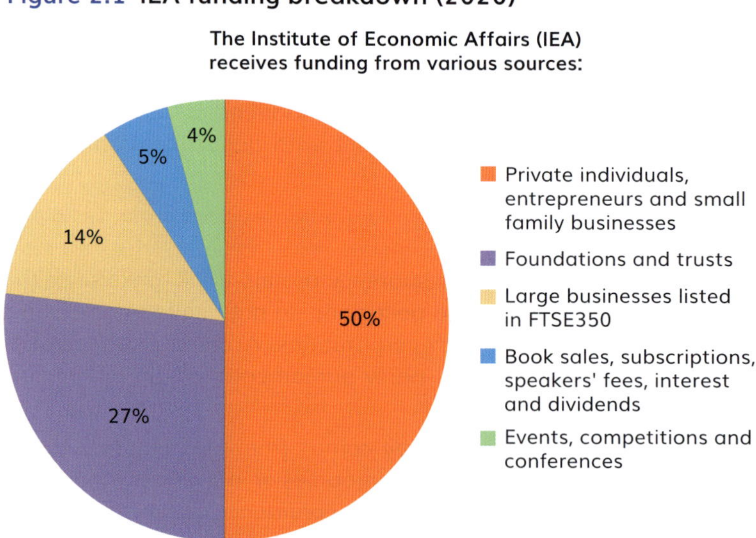

Source: Compiled using data from IEA report 'Who Funds You: FAQ' (2020)

Corporations

Corporations have a huge impact on modern democratic societies. Corporations, such as Tesco and Shell as well as the financial services industry, are so vital to the running of the economy that it is little wonder they expect a say in the making of laws and regulations in a wide range of areas from tax and the environment to trade deals with other countries and workers' rights.

✅ **Clearly, as corporations play such a crucial role in the economy, it is important for democracy that their voice is heard.**

» The success of the economy depends largely on firms investing their money and employing workers. As corporations have such a big stake in society, it is only right that they should seek to have their opinions heard in policy matters that will directly impact them. They tend to be organised into highly effective blocs – like the British Bankers' Association (BBA) whose tag line is 'the voice of banking', or UK Finance which represents around 300 member firms across the banking and financial services industry. These corporations have built up strong ties with government, have high levels of expertise in their area that can be used by government to improve decision making, and many are wealthy enough to employ their own lobbyists or hire lobbying firms. The financial and related professional services sector contributed the most to the UK's tax revenue in 2023, a record £110.2 billion, representing 12.3% of all UK tax receipts.

❌ **However, the role of corporations invites the question whether the world of group politics is a level playing field.**

» Corporations possess the wealth, central economic role, organisation and expertise to ensure that they have a head start to influence government. There is therefore a risk of **'corporate state capture'**, where private interests undermine legitimate political processes. This can lead to policies that favour corporations at the expense of public interest, as seen in instances where government contracts are awarded to companies with political connections rather than through fair competition, for example when VIP lanes were used during Covid to procure PPE equipment.

» As corporations gain more access to policymakers, there can be a tendency for regulations to become less stringent or to favour business interests, which may undermine consumer protections and public welfare.

» The natural counterbalance to the corporations are trade unions, but their membership and power has been in decline since the end of the 1970s, with only around 22% of all workers being members of a trade union.

> **Definition**
>
> **Corporate state capture** refers to the idea that private interests subvert legitimate channels of political influence and shape the rules of the legislative and institutional game.

Lobbyists

Lobbyists are firms who are paid by organisations or individuals to help them to influence government policy. Lobbying in the UK is an industry worth an estimated £2 billion per year and employing over 4,000 people. In 2010, David Cameron warned that lobbying was the next big scandal waiting to happen and decided to legislate to remove any undue influence with the Transparency of Lobbying, Non-Party Campaigning and Trade Union Administration Act 2014.

✅ **The Act puts transparency at the heart of the political agenda to increase trust in politics by ensuring that lobbyists have to sign up to an official register and disclose a list of clients four times a year.**

Former ministers in the UK are subject to specific rules regarding lobbying after leaving office, as outlined in the Business Appointment Rules:

» Former ministers are prohibited from lobbying the government for a period of two years after leaving office. This ban applies to any communication intended to influence government decisions, policies or contracts related to their interests or those of their new employers.

» Former ministers must seek advice from the Advisory Committee on Business Appointments (ACOBA) regarding any appointments or employment they wish to pursue within this two-year period. They are required to abide by the advice provided by the committee.

» The ban on lobbying includes all forms of communication with government officials, including ministers and civil servants. However, it does not prohibit general social or party political contacts that are unrelated to lobbying activities.

» ACOBA has the discretion to reduce the two-year lobbying ban if they consider it justified based on individual circumstances.

» For Cabinet Ministers and senior civil servants, there is a minimum waiting period of three months before they can take up new employment, in addition to the two-year lobbying ban.

> **Spec key term**
>
> **Lobbyists:** Individuals and firms that are paid by clients to influence government and/or MPs and members of the House of Lords to act in their client's interests, particularly when legislation is under consideration.

CASE STUDY 2.2: DELIVEROO

Deliveroo is a food delivery platform which relies on gig workers, whose employment status has sparked debate on workers' rights and economic inequality. Deliveroo connects consumers, restaurants and delivery riders through a phone app. Its success has dramatically increased the gig economy in the UK, creating flexible job opportunities for thousands. However, these jobs often lack traditional benefits, such as sick pay, pensions and job security. These employment practices have been criticised by trade unions, putting pressure on governments to address the balance between business innovation and workers' rights.

Deliveroo has faced lawsuits from riders demanding employee status, and Labour MPs, such as Angela Rayner, have been vocal in advocating for stronger employment laws; the Labour Party has traditionally aligned with unions and championed worker protections. When Deliveroo and similar gig economy platforms, like Uber, became prominent, Labour increased its focus on ensuring fair conditions for gig workers. The 2024 manifesto included commitments to introduce an Employment Rights Act to redress the balance. The Employment Rights Act 2025 gave some "day one" rights to sick pay, paternity leave and flexible working, however, unfair dismissal was dropped as a "day one" right and the qualifying period was cut from two years to six months instead. In response, Deliveroo has engaged in public relations campaigns highlighting its contribution to job creation and community support, such as offering free meals to NHS workers during the Covid-19 pandemic.

Deliveroo's lobbying efforts to prevent such measures reveal its influence in shaping government deliberations, and it has been actively attempting to influence the UK Labour Government through several lobbying efforts:

- Deliveroo has been invited to and attended Labour Party Conferences, establishing a direct line of communication with party leadership.

- The company has been 'intensively lobbying the party', according to Ben Wray, coordinator of The Gig Economy Project.

- Deliveroo was among the companies hosting events at the 2023 Labour Party Conference, seeking to influence party policy.

- Deliveroo has recruited former Labour Party insiders into senior policy and communications roles. Joe Carberry, who has been director of corporate communications for Deliveroo since June 2017, was previously head of research for the Labour Party and a special adviser to David Miliband. He is the godson of Peter Mandelson, and his mother, Kay Carberry, is on the board of Progressive Britain, a Blairite think tank.

As a consequence, there are concerns that Deliveroo's lobbying efforts contributed to Labour watering down its policies on gig economy worker rights. The party reportedly scaled back plans to create a single 'worker' status that would have included app-based couriers. Critics argue this lobbying could lead to policies that favour companies like Deliveroo at the expense of workers' protections.

» These rules aim to prevent conflicts of interest and ensure that former public officials do not exploit their previous positions for private gain, thereby maintaining public trust in government processes.

✖ However, the Act has come under heavy criticism.

» Current lobbying rules only apply to a very small group of lobbyists – mainly those working for private consultancy firms – who make up around 1% of all UK lobbyists. Lobbyists employed directly by large companies do not have to register, which leaves a major gap and allows much lobbying to happen without oversight.

» The enforcement mechanisms are weak. ACOBA lacks the authority to enforce compliance effectively. For instance, they can express concerns about breaches but cannot compel individuals to follow the rules.

» Meetings between lobbyists and government officials below the level of Permanent Secretaries are not required to be reported, meaning that a vast amount of lobbying remains hidden.

» There has been a historic lack of political will to strengthen lobbying regulations, resulting in a system that falls short of international standards for transparency and integrity. Efforts to reform have often been stalled or insufficiently implemented.

» These weaknesses contribute to public distrust in government and elected officials, as many citizens believe that corporate interests unduly influence political decisions without adequate oversight.

Addressing these weaknesses would require comprehensive reforms aimed at expanding the scope of regulation, enhancing transparency, strengthening enforcement mechanisms, and ensuring that all forms of lobbying are subject to appropriate oversight.

✅ **Lobbying is a central part of any democracy because it allows groups who are likely to be impacted by a particular decision to engage with the government and Parliament.**

» Lobbying allows groups, representing a wide array of interests, to provide detailed evidence to the government prior to a decision being made and focus on problems with current policies. This improves the quality of the decisions being made. There are many lobbying firms such as Arden Strategies that can be hired by groups, while wealthy and well-organised groups have their own in-house lobbying teams.

❌ **Critics argue that lobbying in the UK can be abused by those seeking to further their own private interests.**

» In particular, the focus is on the fact that the wealthiest groups can afford to spend vast sums on lobbying and can rely on who they know to influence policy, no matter the consequence to the wider public. The row very early on in Starmer's Government in 2024 over access to 10 Downing Street for Lord Alli and Ian Corfield, significant Labour donors, highlighted this.

» The **revolving door** between lobbying firms and public office suggests that influence is more about whom you know than what you know, undermining the idea of equal participation. The perception of the misuse of public office for private gain is very damaging to trust in politics, and there has been a history of lobbying scandals:

> **Definition**
>
> **Revolving door:** A process whereby former, high-level public officials move into the private sector and vice versa.

- In August 2025, a *Times* newspaper investigation found that Labour officials arranged parties for MPs, including ministers, and invited lobbyists and their staff to attend as "part of a commercial deal" costing £15,000. In the leaked email, lobbying firms were told that there would be no need for public disclosure as "this is a commercial transaction and not a gift to the party, it is not a recordable donation." In the *Times* report, the Chartered Institute of Public Relations (CIPR), the industry body for lobbyists, said the UK's lobbying rules were "not fit for purpose". Jon Gerlis, from the CIPR, said: "The loopholes that exist are not tight loopholes … it means the majority of lobbying activity in this country is not captured."

- Scott Benton 2023/24 – The UK betting lobbying scandal primarily revolved around Scott Benton, the former Conservative MP for Blackpool South, who was caught in an undercover investigation by *The Times*. Benton was secretly filmed offering to lobby on behalf of the gambling industry in exchange for financial compensation. He discussed his willingness to leak confidential information, including a forthcoming White Paper on gambling reform, to an undercover reporter posing as an investor. Following the revelations, Benton was suspended from the House of Commons for 35 days, triggering a recall petition. In March 2024, Benton resigned as an MP, and the by-election was won by Chris Webb for Labour.

- Owen Paterson 2021 – Owen Paterson MP, a former Cabinet Minister, was found by the Parliamentary Commissioner for Standards to have lobbied on behalf of two companies (Randox Laboratories and Lynn's Country Foods) for financial remuneration. This violated the parliamentary Code of Conduct, which prohibits MPs from accepting paid lobbying work. Ultimately, Paterson resigned from Parliament amid the scandal.

- The Greensill Scandal 2021 – The Greensill Capital scandal was one of the most high-profile lobbying-related scandals in the UK in recent years, which implicated senior politicians and raised questions about the revolving door between government and business. Greensill Capital, a financial services firm, became embroiled in controversy after it collapsed in early 2021. It was revealed that David Cameron, the former Prime Minister, had lobbied the government on behalf of Greensill after leaving office. Cameron had taken a paid role as an adviser for Greensill and reportedly texted the Chancellor Rishi Sunak and other ministers urging them to support Greensill by securing access to government-backed financial schemes. This led to widespread criticism of the cosy relationship between former politicians and powerful corporations.

- Covid-19 Contracts (2020–21) – The handling of government contracts during the Covid-19 pandemic attracted attention regarding potential lobbying and the awarding of contracts to companies with close ties to the Conservative Party. Several companies with political connections were awarded contracts for the supply of PPE, raising questions about the transparency of the process. One of the most notable cases was the awarding of contracts to PPE Medpro, which was given a contract worth over £200 million despite having no prior experience in medical supplies. The company was linked to Baroness Mone, a Conservative

CASE STUDY 2.3: LOBBYING COMPANY ARDEN STRATEGIES AND ITS INFLUENCE ON THE LABOUR GOVERNMENT

Arden Strategies, a lobbying firm led by former Labour Cabinet Minister Jim Murphy, has emerged as a significant power broker under Sir Keir Starmer's Labour Government. The firm's activities, client list and sponsorships have highlighted its growing influence over government policies and political operations.

Background

Founded in 2017, Arden Strategies has positioned itself as a bridge between Labour and the private sector. With Murphy's political background – including roles under Tony Blair and Gordon Brown – the firm has deep connections within the Labour Party. Arden's declared mission is to support corporate clients in navigating Labour's policies while fostering a partnership between business and government. Although it's early on in Starmer's Government, it is evident that Arden Strategies is deeply connected to the Labour Government.

Key Clients

Arden Strategies represents many clients spanning a range of industries including defence, oil and gas, energy, transportation, sport and higher education sectors.

They represent Northrop Grumman, a defence giant supplying weapons to militaries globally. The firm hosted an event for Northrop Grumman at the Labour Party Conference in Liverpool in 2025, underscoring its alignment with defence clients.

- In the energy sector, they represent NEO Energy, Equinor, Jersey Oil and Gas, and Serica Energy. Many of these companies have been critical of Labour's National Insurance policies, and Arden has questioned the 'punitive' taxation proposals and promoted dialogue between business and policymakers. Arden's portfolio extends to Centrica, Cadent and INEOS, further consolidating its influence across the energy sector.

- In the sports and recreation sector, Arden represents the Premier League and has opposed Labour's plans for a football regulator. The Premier League and clubs have provided significant perks to politicians, including high-value gifts like Taylor Swift concert tickets.

Arden also includes as clients Universities UK and the British Soft Drinks Association.

Fundraising

Arden Strategies has sponsored Labour Party Conferences, fundraisers and events, spending tens of thousands of pounds annually.

Arden has been instrumental in Labour's electoral efforts, supporting over 30 aspiring MPs, and involved in sponsorship of events and dinners for parliamentary candidates, often in collaboration with corporate sponsors like Budweiser.

- Financial support for constituency fundraisers, with individual contributions often falling below public declaration thresholds.

- Two Labour MPs elected in 2024, Anna Turley and Blair McDougall, have previous affiliations with Arden, highlighting the revolving door between the firm and Labour politics.

Access

Arden's influence extends to government premises, as was evidenced by its involvement in a private roundtable at the Treasury. Attendees included business leaders and Arden clients who met with Ian Corfield, the controversial Labour donor, who had to step down from his role as a civil servant, against allegations that ministers were giving preferential treatment to their donors. In 2026, Arden Strategies was inviting clients to sponsor an event for £30,000, including a photo opportunity with a minister and access to a VIP dinner with top advisers to Keir Starmer and Rachel Reeves. Through events like these, Arden facilitates direct dialogue between its clients and government officials, offering businesses access to key decision makers. This exemplifies Arden's ability to secure privileged access for its clients, sparking concerns over transparency and fairness.

Ethical Concerns

Critics argue that Arden's lobbying prioritises corporate interests over public concerns. Moreover, Arden is absent from the Public Relations and Communications Association's register, which limits public scrutiny. While it is too early to see how much influence Arden Strategies will have over Labour policies going forward, it is clear that the company's deep integration within Labour's operations blurs the line between lobbying and governance.

peer, whose business associates, including her husband, were involved with PPE Medpro. In October 2025 a judge ruled that MedPro must pay back £122m for breaching their contract, after the PPE equipment provided was faulty. There were concerns that companies with political connections were given preferential treatment or were able to bypass usual procurement procedures through 'VIP lanes' that were set up to fast-track suppliers during the pandemic. It led to allegations of cronyism in the awarding of contracts and raised questions about transparency and the role of lobbying in public procurement.

Methods used by pressure groups to exert influence on both government and Parliament

Who do pressure groups seek to influence? What methods do they use? Pressure groups are confronted by a wide range of 'points of access', such as ministers and civil servants, the courts and public opinion. Their choice of targets and methods, however, depends on two factors. First, how *effective* is a particular strategy likely to be? Second, given the group's aims and resources, which strategies are *available*?

KEY TOPIC DEBATE: ARE INSIDER METHODS MORE EFFECTIVE THAN OUTSIDER METHODS?

✔ Insider method – Working with government and civil servants

» It is easy to understand why pressure groups want to influence ministers and civil servants. They work at the heart of the decision-making process. This is where power lies. Many groups therefore aspire to insider status, and those who have it are reluctant to lose it.

» Governments also seek to consult pressure groups, lobbying firms, think tanks and corporations as they have specialised knowledge to inform the policy process; therefore governments will want to work with these groups to gauge the reaction of affected parties to proposed policies.

» A very wide range of groups therefore stalk the 'corridors of power', under both Labour and Conservative Governments, and much of the work that goes on here is hidden away from the gaze of the media and the public. Group objectives are to apply influence before the government has taken a public position because this gives them the ability to shape the policy and, even if they can't shift the government position, to help shape the details as much in their interest as possible.

✖ Outsider method – Engaging the public

» However, most groups do not have access to the corridors of power, and neither can they afford to pay for lobbying companies to help them get it. As a consequence, they seek to influence government *indirectly* by pushing issues up the political agenda and demonstrating both the strength of commitment and the level of public support for a particular cause. The hope is that government will pay attention for fear of suffering electoral consequences. The classic strategies include public petitions, marches and demonstrations, such as the mass demonstrations for Gaza in 2023/24, which was effective in shaping public opinion and putting pressure on the UK Government.

✔ Insider method – Working with Parliament

Groups that cannot gain access to the government may look to exert influence through Parliament. Groups can look to influence legislation as it passes through Parliament in several ways:

» Working with MPs and peers to draft and introduce amendments to legislation

» Influencing the way that MPs and peers vote on a bill

» Drafting **Private Members' Bills**. Groups will work with MPs to draft bills and to persuade MPs to vote in a particular way. In November 2024, the campaigning group Dignity in Dying worked hard to persuade MPs to back Kim Leadbeater's Assisted Dying Bill, which would have allowed terminally ill adults, expected to die within six months, to seek help to end their own life. Although the bill passed the Commons, it ran into many concerns in the Lords and ran out of time, and so the bill failed to pass.

» Contributing to Select Committee reports. Groups can provide evidence to Committees and aim to influence the reports they produce. The Justice Select Committee was influenced by the Howard League for Penal Reform's efforts to reform Imprisonment for Public Protection (IPP) sentences. IPPs were open-ended sentences for dangerous offenders whose crimes did not warrant life imprisonment. Although abolished in 2012 after being used far more widely than expected, around 946 people sentenced under IPPs remain in prison as of January 2026.

> The Justice Select Committee conducted a year-long inquiry into IPP sentences, to which the Howard League submitted lengthy evidence. In September 2022, the committee published its report and concluded that IPP sentences were 'irredeemably flawed' and called on the government to re-sentence all people in prison subject to them. The committee's report cited evidence provided by the Howard League about the impact of IPP sentences.

❌ Outsider method – Direct action

> However, all of these methods are likely to be unsuccessful if they don't have government support. In many cases it would be more effective to be more overt in working to persuade the government via the people. Civil disobedience tactics that are non-violent but disruptive are utilised by more radical campaigning groups.

> For example, Just Stop Oil (JSO) was a non-violent direct action movement challenging inaction over climate change. They targeted major public events, including Wimbledon and the World Snooker Championship, as well as performances of *Les Miserables* and throwing soup on Van Gogh's *Sunflowers*, which sparked widespread media coverage. JSO argue that these actions were intended to create dramatic moments to capture media headlines, overshadowing more traditional forms of protest. They claim to have achieved 92% name recognition, successfully placing the issue of new oil, gas and coal projects at the forefront of national discussions.

✅ Insider method – Working with political parties

> If groups are unable to access the government, they can work with the other political parties. They do this in the hope that the party will become the next government, or that parties will work together to make life difficult for the current government in Parliament. The most obvious way in which groups influence parties is through funding and donations.

> The Labour Party receives money from trade unions, like the GMB, UNISON and Unite, who donated approximately £2 million to the party in 2024. They also received significant funding from individuals; for example Dale Vince, founder of Ecotricity, donated £1 million, stopping his previous funding for Just Stop Oil. The Conservatives are funded largely by donations from individuals and businesses, for example Lord John Sainsbury of the supermarket chain donated £10.85 million and Frank Hester, the healthcare entrepreneur and founder of The Phoenix Partnership, contributed £10.17 million in 2024.

CASE STUDY 2.4: THINK TANK: LABOUR TOGETHER

Labour Together is a think tank closely associated with the Labour Party which has played a significant role in shaping the policies of Keir Starmer's Government since Labour's victory in the 2024 General Election. Regarded as an 'incubator' for Labour's 2024 election manifesto, the organisation gained support from prominent Labour MPs and raised substantial funds, including £4 million since Starmer became leader. Jonathan Ashworth, former Labour MP for Leicester. South, serves as the Chief Executive of Labour Together and its board members include Rachel Reeves, Wes Streeting and Shabana Mahmood as well as Baroness Sally Morgan. Morgan McSweeney, who previously directed the think tank, became a powerful figure within the Labour Party and government, serving as head of political strategy and Chief of Staff to Starmer. McSweeney was instrumental in Labour's victorious 2024 General Election campaign. The New Statesman ranked him number 1 on a list of most influential progressive figures in the UK.

Labour Together has shaped the party's approach to economic issues, emphasising economic security and a more activist state. The organisation has also influenced Labour's move towards more centrist positions, recommending the dropping of certain nationalisation policies to appeal to specific voter demographics. Labour Together has contributed to the party's move away from more left-wing positions, with policies developed with electability in mind.

However, as the Labour Government's popularity plummeted post-2024, Labour Together was criticised from the left for pushing Labour more right-wing, especially on migration, by advocating for a "Farage-flavoured approach" that leans into anti-migrant rhetoric and policies associated with the far right. Critics argued that this risked destroying the progressive electoral coalition that helped bring Labour to power in 2024, undermining the party's identity.

In late 2025, the think tank caused a stir when it reportedly commissioned polling of Labour members about who they would support to replace Starmer, leading to accusations that Labour Together was already planning to undermine or replace the Prime Minister.

» Many think tanks have also developed close ties to political parties, helping to inform their process of designing new policies. The think tank Common Wealth, established in 2019 with the previous Labour leader Ed Miliband on their board, developed strong links with the Labour Party and has been instrumental in developing the concept of Great British Energy, which aims to create a publicly owned energy company to facilitate the transition to renewable energy in the UK. Starmer has endorsed this policy as a central part of Labour's manifesto, highlighting its potential to reduce energy bills and promote clean energy. However, arguably the most significant think tank under Starmer's Labour Government is Labour Together.

✖ Outsider method – Using technology

» However, working too closely with a particular party can also mean that the pressure group narrows its appeal. Groups might be more effective by harnessing the powers of technology to achieve their aims. Strategies to influence public opinion have been transformed by the arrival of modern technology. Pressure groups have used TikTok, X and Instagram to create hashtag campaigns to generate media focus and shape the political agenda.

» The #MeToo movement began on X in 2017 when actress Alyssa Milano tweeted asking women who had been sexually harassed or assaulted to reply 'me too' which came in response to sexual abuse allegations against Hollywood producer Harvey Weinstein. Within 24 hours, Milano's tweet received 12 million responses on social media and the hashtag spread globally, with 1.7 million tweets in 85 countries within days. The movement empowered many famous survivors to speak out, including Reese Witherspoon and Lady Gaga. Consequently, Weinstein faced numerous allegations of sexual harassment, assault and rape from over 80 women in the film industry, leading to his arrest, conviction and imprisonment. His case was central to the #MeToo movement; however, the ramifications of this hashtag were felt for years after, empowering victims of sexual abuse to speak up with growing confidence that they would be heard and believed. Allegations resurfaced about Jeffrey Epstein leading to his arrest, which then linked him to then Prince Andrew, who was stripped of all his royal titles and duties in October 2025 as a consequence of allegations made by Virginia Giuffre which was settled out of court in 2022. #MeToo managed to change the culture across the world around sexual abuse and harassment which is the ultimate aim of any group.

✔ Insider method – Wider access points

» The creation of devolved institutions in Scotland, Wales and Northern Ireland has provided new targets for lobbying by creating many more access points, with the British Medical Association, the National Farmers Union, the CBI and the Trades Union Congress having offices in Scotland and Wales as well as their London headquarters. With the growing powers of the devolved governments, this method has been seen as increasingly effective. The NFU in Scotland successfully lobbied for the continuation of direct payments and subsidies for Scottish farmers in 2024, emphasising the importance of maintaining support for food production.

✖ Outsider method – The courts

» However, this may only result in being able to impact very small groups of people, with there being only 17,000 farmers in Scotland, for example. A better way of affecting policy would be to use the courts to challenge government decisions which may have nationwide consequences. This is evidenced by the substantial increase in the use of **judicial review** (See Chapter 10) in recent years by a growing number of campaigning groups. This usually involves attempts to challenge government policy on the grounds that ministers or officials have exceeded, or breached, their legal powers.

» For Women Scotland's successful Supreme Court ruling in 2025 had far-reaching consequences for the entire UK, when the Supreme Court ruled that the terms "man" and "woman" in the Equality Act 2010 referred to biological sex. Subsequently, many decisions have been made across the UK as a result of this ruling. In 2026 a tribunal ruled that hospital bosses had violated the dignity of a group of female nurses who complained about a transgender woman using their changing room.

» Asylum Aid's persistent legal action played a crucial role in exposing flaws in the government's Rwanda policy, leading to policy amendments and ultimately contributing to the decision to repeal the Safety of Rwanda Act.

> **Definition**
>
> **Judicial review:** A type of legal action which every citizen, as well as organisations, can use to challenge decisions made by public bodies, including the government, which they feel to be unlawful or contravene rights.

Visit the companion website for a case study of the For Woman Scotland Supreme Court ruling

Insider	Theme	Outsider
✓ Influence with ministers and civil servants is seen as the most effective method, as this is where most power lies in UK politics.	Is working within government always more effective than engaging the public?	✗ Engaging public opinion can shift the political agenda and force government into action out of fear of the electoral consequences.
✓ Parliament has become more powerful and lobbying more sophisticated, increasing the effectiveness of this method.	Can Parliament provide more influence than powerful direct action?	✗ Direct action has become more common as it can be used to set the agenda for the 24-hour, 7-day-a-week news media.
✓ Influence inside a political party can impact on government policy when that party wins power.	Can social media campaigns be as powerful as working with a political party?	✗ The arrival of new technology has enabled groups to generate media attention, set the agenda and force political parties to adopt their position.
✓ Insider status with the devolved assemblies has become more important as these institutions have grown in power.	Is it more effective to try to change policy via devolved assemblies or the Supreme Court?	✗ Judicial review, which can apply across the whole of the UK, is being used more frequently to challenge policy and/or generate media coverage.

KEY TOPIC DEBATE: ARE SOME GROUPS MORE SUCCESSFUL THAN OTHERS?

Some groups are clearly more powerful than others. Some succeed while others fail. But what does 'success' mean? How can we weigh up group power or influence? These are difficult questions because success may be measured in different ways. Success may mean:

- » *Influencing* government policy
- » *Pushing* an issue up the political agenda
- » *Changing* people's values, perceptions and behaviour.

Wealth

✓ **The most powerful groups in the country are the ones that have financial and economic power – they are wealthy and government listens to them because of the influence they have over the economy.**

- » This largely explains the power of corporations, business groups and their peak organisations.
- » All governments, regardless of party, must seek the cooperation and support of key business groups and corporations as they are the main source of employment and investment in the economy.
- » These groups possess knowledge and expertise that are essential to the formulation of effective economic policies.
- » They possess the financial strength to employ professional lobbyists and public relations consultants, and to make donations to political parties. According to Transparency International, a Global Witness investigation revealed that government officials met with oil and gas lobbyists an average of 1.4 times per working day in 2023 and UK government ministers met with representatives from the oil and gas sector at least 343 times in 2023. In 2025 the most frequent lobbyists engaging with the UK government were the CBI, the BBC, banks, energy companies and defence companies.

✗ **Wealth does not always buy success, particularly where wealthy groups' aims are out of touch with the party in power or where they run up against hostile public opinion.**

- » Wealth matters less in the modern world where internet technology and social media have made it far cheaper and easier for people to express their opinions to elected politicians using X, TikTok, likes and shares of political stories and online campaigns as well as e-petitions.
- » The BMA, despite frequent, high-level meetings with government, were unable to agree a satisfactory deal regarding the pay and conditions of junior doctors, going on strike several times between 2019 and 2024. It was only a change of government in 2024 that led to a pay increase from the Labour Government. Their wealth and status did not help them before this.

Size

✅ **Are the largest groups the most powerful? This is one of the assumptions that is made by pluralist theorists, who believe that pressure-group power is democratically based.**

» Large groups can claim to represent public opinion. Government listens to them because, ultimately, their members can have an electoral impact. Groups such as the National Trust has around 5.75 million members and has significant influence on the UK's conservation policies. It actively lobbies the government on planning and environmental protections. For example, in 2011 and 2025, it publicly opposed a proposal to make it easier to build on low-quality green belt land which they argued 'raised alarms about potential impacts on biodiversity and landscape integrity'. The Trust's advocacy in 2011 led to modifications in national planning policy after gathering public support through petitions.

» Age UK, which represents millions of pensioners, campaigned successfully in 2025 for changes to the government's Winter Fuel Payments abolition, which returned the payment to 9 million pensioners.

» National Society for the Prevention of Cruelty to Children (NSPCC) ensure that their membership levels remain high, with hundreds of thousands of supporters. Their 'Wild West Web' campaign, which urged the government to introduce new laws to regulate big tech companies and protect children from sexual abuse online, was successful and the Online Safety Act 2023 was passed which placed a legal duty of care on tech companies to protect young people on their platforms.

» *More members mean more subscriptions and donations.* Large groups tend to be wealthy groups. This enables groups to employ full-time professionals to carry out research and run campaigns. In 2024, the NSPCC had a total income of £124 million, with most of that coming directly from supporters.

❌ **However, it would be a mistake to believe that big groups are always the most powerful.**

» Membership size cannot usually compensate for a lack of insider status. The National Trust may have been successful in 2011 under a Conservative Government but in 2025, it was unable to persuade Angela Rayner that the Labour Government's planning proposals should be altered. The trade union movement has the largest membership base, has huge economic resources, can organise large campaigns and protests, and makes large donations to the Labour Party yet it has lacked insider status under Conservative-led governments and does not appear to be particularly influential under Prime Minister Starmer.

» Small membership groups, which are highly specialised, can exert influence through their expertise. Think tanks and lobbying firms may lack size, but their insider connections to government and political parties can provide them with high levels of influence.

Good organisation and effective leadership

✅ **Organisation helps groups to mobilise their resources effectively and to take concerted action. Effective organisation also requires financial resources and high-quality leadership.**

» Surfers Against Sewage (SAS) are an example of how a small but well-organised and committed organisation can be highly effective. Their slogan is 'From a handful of activists to a nationwide movement' and they number no more than 40 people working full-time. They argue that being both highly strategic and well resourced means they can stay responsive, independent and agile, making a difference without compromising their beliefs. They successfully campaigned for legal obligations on real-time sewage pollution reporting from water companies. As a result, all storm overflow pipes in England are monitored, providing better data on pollution. Moreover, they have engaged hundreds of thousands of people on the issue of sewage and plastic pollution, further advancing their cause. In July 2025, the government announced that OFWAT was to be abolished due to its failure to effectively regulate the water companies, and it will be replaced by a new, single water regulator in England and in Wales.

» Well-known figures who are supportive of a campaign can help bring much-needed publicity, for example Chris Packham has been very supportive of SAS and former lead singer of the undertones Feargal Sharkey is also an active campaigner on this issue. Sharkey joined the Save Windermere campaign which has been severely affected by sewage discharges from water companies. He participated in protests against United Utilities and demonstrates alongside various environmental groups, including River Action, to demand urgent action from the government regarding sewage dumping practices.

Photo 2.1 Many pressure groups have been campaigning against sewage and waste dumped by water companies

Source: Robert Brook / Science Photo Library

❌ **However, organisation and leadership can only go so far.**

» The Women Against State Pension Inequality (WASPI) campaign advocates for women born in the 1950s who have been adversely affected by changes to the state pension age. After increases to the state pension age for women, to align them with men, WASPI argued that the government failed to adequately communicate the changes, leaving many women with little or no notice about their delayed pensions. Approximately 3.6 million women were affected, with many facing financial hardship and emotional distress. The primary aim of WASPI is to secure compensation for these women. However, after reconsidering the issue in 2026, the Starmer Government decided not to compensate the WASPI women, arguing that it would place an unfair burden on taxpayers when the government was facing a difficult fiscal situation. No matter how well organised a group is, if their aims don't correspond with the government's, they will find it hard to achieve their aims.

Compatibility with the government

✅ **Groups are far more likely to succeed when the government is broadly sympathetic towards their aims or goals.**

» The think tank Labour Together had very little influence on government when it was set up in 2015 until the 2024 General Election; however, since July 2024 it is the think tank most closely associated with the Starmer project and has significant influence. (See Case Study page 36.)

» Equally, groups like Refugee Action, City of Sanctuary and Safe Passage, who seek to create a culture of welcome for refugees and asylum seekers across various local communities in the UK, will be unlikely to gain government support.

❌ **However, if groups can mobilise public opinion and clearly illustrate the depth of opposition to a view, they can still influence policy even if they are ideological outsiders.**

» Asylum Aid's aims were not compatible with the government's, yet their persistent legal action played a crucial role in exposing flaws in the Rwanda policy, leading to policy amendments and ultimately contributing to the decision to repeal the Safety of Rwanda Act. In 2025, the National Farmers' Union lobbied hard against the Government's planned inheritance tax on farms over £1 million which, they argued, would force families to sell up. Farmers staged mass protests, including a large tractor convoy into Westminster on Budget Day. In 2026, the

Government watered down the rules, so that most ordinary family farms would keep their full tax relief, effectively U-turning on the original plan.

Popular support

✅ **Pressure groups that enjoy high levels of public support have greater political influence than ones with only minority support.**

» Crudely, governments calculate how much electoral damage may be caused by *not* acceding to a group's demands.

» The Gaza demonstrations throughout 2023/24 put enormous pressure on all political parties to support this cause. Alongside it, a highly effective and orchestrated social media campaign helped to pressurise MPs and celebrities to support its aims. Many Labour MPs voted against their party when a ceasefire was debated in the Commons, including Jess Phillips who was sacked as Shadow Minister for Domestic Violence and Safeguarding as a consequence.

❌ **Nevertheless, public support is not always reflected in political influence.**

» Despite this relentless campaigning, Prime Minister Sunak did not make any real changes to his policy towards Israel, broadly supporting their war against Hamas. And even though Prime Minister Starmer adjusted his language and banned the sale of some weapons to Israel, this meant in practice that there was very little difference between the parties in terms of substance and the protests did not significantly change the policies of the two main parties.

» Think tanks, corporations and lobbying firms do not rely on public support, rather on their political connections, the revolving door and party donations for their influence.

> **Tip:** In judging the influence of groups, it is worth considering which types of group are most influential – is it lobbying firms, think tanks, corporations or pressure groups?

Key Debate Summary: Are some groups more successful than others?

For	Theme	Against
✔ Wealthy groups which are central to the economic success of the government hold huge influence. This influence is strengthened by the revolving door, donations and lobbying.	How influential is wealth in pressure group success?	✖ Wealthy groups lack one thing elected politicians need: votes. Where wealthy groups' aims clash with public opinion, their influence is limited.
✔ Groups with large memberships have real influence as they represent large numbers of voters and can run effective campaigns.	How influential is large membership in pressure group success?	✖ The large membership of a group does not make up for wealth and insider status with government.
✔ Groups with highly effective leaderships can win the battle of ideas and gain high-level access within government.	How influential is effective leadership in pressure group success?	✖ High levels of organisation and effective leadership can only go so far.
✔ Where groups are compatible with the government, they have a real chance to impact on decision making.	How influential is compatibility with government in pressure group success?	✖ Ultimately, the party in power wants to win re-election; if public opposition is too strong then the government has to be sensitive to that opinion.
✔ Groups backed by high levels of public support will naturally influence the government due to the electoral implications.	How influential is public support in pressure group success?	✖ Where groups backed by public opinion clash with the policy commitments made by the government, their influence will be limited.

KEY TOPIC DEBATE: DOES GROUP POLITICS PROMOTE DEMOCRACY IN THE UK?

Questions about group power are closely related to debates about the implications of group politics for democracy. There is considerable debate about how power is distributed among pressure groups. There is disagreement about whether groups tend to *widen* the distribution of power, giving power to the people, or whether they tend to *concentrate* it, strengthening the already powerful. This is often portrayed as a battle between two rival theories of political power: **pluralism** and **elitism**. Pluralist theorists argue that group politics is the very stuff of democracy, advancing the idea of **pluralist democracy.**

Democracy

✅ **Supplementing electoral democracy.**

» Pressure groups supplement electoral democracy, making up for its defects and limitations, allowing for representation in between elections.

» In July 2025, the government announced it was lowering the voting age to 16. This is as a result of a coalition of influential pressure groups known as the Votes at 16 Coalition. This coalition consisted of a large alliance of youth organisations, civil society groups and democratic reform advocates that actively campaigned for years to extend the franchise to 16- and 17-year-olds. Their coordinated campaigns, evidence-based advocacy and ability to build cross-party and cross-societal support were crucial to this policy change.

» Pressure groups offer alternative viewpoints and widen the information available to the public. This allows groups to change the political agenda, as social movements like Just Stop Oil have shown, and force political parties to take notice.

❌ **Holding unaccountable power.**

» Regardless of which groups are most powerful, influence is exerted in a way that is not subject to scrutiny and public accountability, and so undermines democracy. Pressure groups usually exert influence 'behind closed doors'.

» This particularly applies in the case of think tanks, lobbyists or corporations who stalk the 'corridors of power' unseen by the public or media. No one knows who said what to whom, who influenced whom, and why. This is unaccountable power, and it undermines democracy. It highlights the weakness of the Lobbying Act of 2014 to offer the sort of transparency and accountability required in a democracy, while the hidden funding of highly influential think tanks, like the IEA, further undermines transparency.

» Groups are never held to account publicly for the influence they exert, which is undemocratic. Moreover, their leaders are very rarely elected, and when they are (as in the case of trade unions) this is often on the basis of very low turnouts.

» Some groups use strikes, blockades and even intimidation and violence, to 'hold the country to ransom', which is unacceptable in a democracy. Once groups operate outside the legal and constitutional framework, they are also operating outside – and arguably against – democracy.

Participation

✅ **Widening participation.**

» Pressure groups have become increasingly effective agents of political participation as they allow new and previously excluded groups a voice in society. The global grassroots activism and decentralised organisation of many campaigning groups have proved to be attractive to many young people and those who may be disillusioned with conventional politics.

Photo 2.2 **Black Lives Matter protest assembled near the US embassy in London on 7 June 2020**

Source: Becky Mutton

» This participation has been amplified by the growth of new access points in UK politics through the devolved administrations, meaning that with so many decisions taken elsewhere, it is no longer so crucial to be an insider at Westminster.

» The rise of global social movements has seen a massive increase in the politics of protest such as the Black Lives Matter protests, the Gaza protests and the direct action of Just Stop Oil, while the rise of technology and online activism has created new ways for the public to participate in politics.

❌ Narrowing participation.

» Far from dispersing power more widely, group politics tends to empower the already powerful. They therefore increase, rather than reduce, political inequality leading to elitism.

» In practice, the most powerful groups tend to be the ones that possess money, expertise, institutional leverage and privileged links to government.

» Equally, there are significant and large sections of society that are excluded from the pressure-group universe. This is usually because they are difficult to organise and so rely on others to protect them. Examples of such groups include children, asylum seekers, the homeless and prisoners.

» Participation in some groups is purely 'chequebook membership', where signing up to groups like the National Trust is more about the membership benefits than their campaign objectives, while online engagement is more 'slacktivism' than real activism and so provides very superficial political engagement.

Power

✅ Widening power.

» Pressure groups help to promote democracy by widening the distribution of political power. This is because groups compete against one another, ensuring that no group or interest can dominate permanently.

» Pluralists would argue that there is no such thing as a 'power elite'. Instead, as one group becomes influential, other groups come into existence to combat them and offer rival viewpoints; these rival groups through their actions promote debate, educate the public and improve decision making.

» Trade unions developed in response to the growth of business power. The tobacco lobby used to be influential, but its power waned in the face of an effective campaign by health campaigners. The fossil fuel corporations are now faced by a growing environmental movement. In this way, public policy is developed through an ongoing debate between rival groups which ensures that political influence is widely and evenly dispersed. Group politics is therefore characterised by a rough balance of power. This is the essence of pluralist democracy.

❌ Concentrating power.

» Pressure groups increase inequality by strengthening the voice of the wealthy and the privileged, who have access to financial, educational and organisational resources. Other groups are ignored by government.

» Group politics gives core insiders real power due to their economic importance to the government, and their ability to offer donations to parties, afford lobbying and gain access to power through the revolving door. In 2023, Andrew Bridgen MP was found guilty of breaching lobbying rules 'on multiple occasions and in multiple ways' by the Commissioner for Standards. He failed to declare a relevant interest in Mere Plantations on numerous occasions and did not disclose receiving a funded visit to Ghana and a £12,000 contract as their adviser. He committed a 'significant litany of errors'.

» In June 2025, a scandal arose regarding Conservative MP George Freeman which centred on allegations that Freeman sought help from GHGSat, a green technology firm, for drafting parliamentary questions for the company while being paid £60,000 as an adviser. The Parliamentary Commissioner for Standards reviewed the matter.

» As a result, sectional interests may prevail at the expense of the interests of the public, and elected governments may find it more difficult to serve the public interest and to do what is best for society as a whole because of the power of, for example, the financial services corporations in relation to the interests of the consumer.

» It is hard to see the government acting as a neutral umpire between competing groups as governing parties clearly have their own ideological outlook, which naturally aligns with the interests of particular pressure groups.

Key Debate Summary: Does group politics promote democracy in the UK?

For	Theme	Against
✓ Group politics supplements electoral politics.	Is lack of pressure group accountability more significant than the important role they play in supplementing democracy?	✗ The unaccountable power of groups is a threat to democracy.
✓ Group politics allows increased participation and reaches those who have previously been disengaged or excluded.	Do pressure groups promote greater participation or narrow it?	✗ Group politics narrows participation by placing power in the hands of the few.
✓ Group politics disperses political power away from the centre.	Do pressure groups spread power more widely (pluralism) or concentrate it (elitism)?	✗ Group politics is the preserve of insiders, channelling political power into the hands of a narrow elite.

Rights in context

What are rights?

Human rights are rights which are common to all people. They are based on a moral view of what all human beings deserve wherever they live and whatever government they live under. Human rights are:

- » *Universal* in that they belong to all humans everywhere, regardless of nationality, ethnic or racial origin, and social background.
- » *Fundamental* in that they are inalienable – a human being's entitlement to them cannot be removed.
- » *Absolute* in that, as the basic grounds for living a genuinely human life, they must be fully upheld in all circumstances.

Civil liberties, which include many human rights, are the rights and freedoms that are recognised within a particular country and protect the individual from the state. A key principle of any democracy is the effectiveness with which civil liberties that clearly set the boundaries to the power of the state are guaranteed. This link between rights and democracy is founded, most importantly, on the belief that political participation is only meaningful when it is carried out by free individuals.

As the UK emerged as a democracy, there was a growing consensus that Parliament should respect basic civil liberties. The civil liberties that emerged were built around the basic principle that the individual was free to do whatever they wanted as long as it was not forbidden by law. This basic principle was reinforced gradually over time by constitutional events such as the Magna Carta, the passage of legislation such as the Representation of the People Act 1928 establishing universal suffrage, and in **common law**, such as fundamental rights of access to justice and to the courts.

Development of a rights-based culture in the UK

The UK's rights-based culture traces back to medieval milestones like the Magna Carta of 1215, which first asserted legal rights against the Crown and introduced trial by jury. Subsequent acts, including the Habeas Corpus Act 1679 and English Bill of Rights 1689, advanced fair trials, limited monarch power, and banned cruel punishments. These laid the groundwork for civil liberties through common law, predating modern codification.

Post-WWII, the UK ratified the European Convention on Human Rights (ECHR) in 1951. The pivotal Human Rights Act (HRA) 1998, brought ECHR rights back home, obliging public bodies to comply and courts to consider a law's compatibility. It is suggested that this marked a shift from parliamentary sovereignty to judicial oversight, promoting rights compliance in legislation.

The HRA empowered individuals to seek redress via judicial review; cases like post-9/11 terror detentions were struck down for discrimination, prompting the 2005 Prevention of Terrorism Act. Judicial reviews surged from 4,240 in 2000 to an all-time peak in 2013 with 15,594 applications. However, this changed dramatically when immigration and asylum cases were transferred to the Upper Tribunal in November 2013. Since then, the figures dropped significantly and have only recently begun rising again.

In the UK, a rights-based culture emerged as judges were able, via the HRA to declare laws incompatible and quash government decisions, significantly raising the profile of rights protection in the UK. Critics argue it hampers security, yet groups like Liberty credit it for aiding vulnerable people's rights, embedding rights in public services. Overall, the HRA transformed UK law into a positive rights framework.

Visit the companion website for a list of the milestones in the development of rights in the UK.

How are rights protected in the UK?

The consensus around rights in the UK began to change in the second half of the twentieth century with the UK involved in drafting the Universal Declaration of Human Rights (1948) and **European Convention on Human Rights (ECHR)** (1950) while lacking any equivalent legislation domestically. From the 1960s onwards, concerns were raised that the powers of public bodies were open to abuse, particularly in the treatment of immigrants, minorities and other groups without political power. This coincided with a period of lobbying by pressure groups to reform the law in light of growing evidence that civil liberties were being restricted.

In the 1970s, the European Court of Human Rights began to show up large gaps in the UK's civil liberties legislation with court decisions affecting UK law in areas such as freedom of expression, freedom from discrimination and the right to a fair trial. These different influences all came together in the Labour Party manifesto of 1997, which pledged that UK citizens should have statutory rights to enforce their rights in the UK courts. Labour saw the Human Rights Act as establishing a floor for human rights, not a ceiling, and that rights could be enhanced further by Acts of Parliament such as the Equalities Act to tackle discrimination.

Human Rights Act

The Human Rights Act of 1998 is seen as the key symbol and protection of civil liberties in the UK.

Before the passing of the Human Rights Act, taking a case to the ECtHR was very lengthy and expensive, and law passed in the UK did not need to make any reference to the Convention. The passing of the Human Rights Act had three key aims:

1. **Bringing rights back home.** The HRA made rights much more readily available by ensuring that British citizens could bring rights cases to British courts, although once raised in UK courts, citizens could still ask the ECtHR to look at the case. It is possible to use the HRA to challenge an Act of Parliament, and the Supreme Court can issue a declaration of incompatibility if a law is incompatible with rights in the Convention. This is a formal legal statement that the law contravenes the HRA, but does not invalidate or strike down the law; instead, it encourages Parliament to take action to amend or remove the law in question. The Supreme Court recently ruled that a law was incompatible with the Human Rights Act in April 2024. In the case of *Secretary of State for Business and Trade v. Mercer* (2024), the Supreme Court issued a declaration of incompatibility under section 4 of the Human Rights Act, which protects the right to freedom of assembly and association. This ruling was significant as it affirmed the 'right to strike', marking the first time the UK Supreme Court explicitly recognised such a right. In response, the Labour Government, elected after the ruling, introduced the Employment Rights Bill 2024, which includes provisions to address the incompatibility identified by the Supreme Court. The Bill aims to introduce new protections for workers against being subjected to detriments for participating in industrial action.

2. **Creating a culture of respect for human rights.** The HRA placed a legal duty on all public organisations, such as NHS bodies, the police, central government departments and local councils but not Parliament, to respect and protect the rights listed. This meant that human rights should inform the everyday practices and actions of these bodies, and any action, or failure to act, in line with rights can be challenged. Mersey Care NHS Trust worked with Barnardo's and the British Institute of Human Rights to pioneer a 'rights-based' approach to their services, known as the HOPES model. They developed safe spaces for relatives to visit children in secure mental health settings that complied with Article 8. The wider aim was to reduce long-term segregation and restrictive practices for autistic adults, adults with learning disabilities, and children and young people in hospital settings.

3. **Increasing public awareness of human rights.** By placing civil liberties in one document, it helps to make people aware of and understand their rights so they can challenge decisions that do not treat them equally, with fairness, dignity and respect.

Freedom of Information Act 2000

The Freedom of Information Act allows the public access to information held by public authorities. Public authorities are required to publish certain information about their activities, and the public can request further information from them. The aim of the Act was to create a more open government, where decisions taken by public authorities should be open to scrutiny. This would build trust and confidence in the authorities, and make it easier to hold them to account for their actions. In 2023, there were around 70,000 requests under the Act which represented a 30% increase from the previous year. Of these, 34% were granted in full, down from 39% in 2022, and 34% were withheld in full, down from 35% in 2022. In 2024, FOI disclosures exposed that UK police forces, backed by the Home Office, had been running mass facial recognition searches against the UK's passport and immigration photo databases for years, without parliament's approval. Previous revelations showed inadequate government preparation for the Covid-19 pandemic, revealed safety issues with smart motorways, showed the extent of untreated sewage being released into waterways, threatening public health, and revealed that half of all unlawful sexual contacts with children involve apps owned by Meta, raising concerns about child protection rights online. These revelations demonstrate the crucial role FOI requests play in exposing threats to various rights.

CASE STUDY 2.5:   THE UK AND THE ECHR

The UK helped to create the European Convention on Human Rights (ECHR), but its relationship with the Convention and the Strasbourg Court has become increasingly uneasy, with a growing current in politics arguing that the UK should leave in order to regain control over immigration and sovereignty.

Background

The UK was central to drafting the ECHR after the Second World War; Churchill publicly called for a binding European human rights charter and British lawyers played a leading role in negotiating the text. The UK signed in 1950 and was the first state to ratify in 1951, but initially refused both the Strasbourg Court's jurisdiction and the right of individual petition, seeing the Convention as broad principles that could not override Acts of Parliament. In 1966 the UK accepted the Court's jurisdiction and individual petition, allowing people in the UK to take cases to Strasbourg, and in 1998 the Human Rights Act (HRA) incorporated Convention rights into domestic law, making it possible to enforce most rights in UK courts. Under this model, UK courts must "take into account" Strasbourg case law, but Parliament remains sovereign and the UK Supreme Court is not formally bound to follow every Strasbourg judgment.

A controversial Rwanda ruling

In June 2022, a single Strasbourg judge issued an urgent interim measure under Rule 39 to stop the first deportation flight taking asylum seekers from the UK to Rwanda, on the basis that UK courts had not yet fully examined the risks. The order required the removal of the last passenger from the aircraft and effectively grounded the flight, after which claimants pursued their case in the UK courts. The delay created by that interim measure allowed litigation to reach the UK Supreme Court, which in November 2023 ruled the Rwanda scheme unlawful because of a real risk of refoulement and systemic defects in Rwanda's asylum system. Ministers responded politically by promising not to let a "foreign court" block flights and then legislating to declare Rwanda safe and to instruct civil servants that ministers could choose to ignore future Rule 39 orders in removal cases.

Political backlash and the movement to leave

The Rwanda ruling crystallised long-running criticisms that the ECHR and Strasbourg judges undermine democratic control over borders and crime policy. Critics argue that Convention rights have been stretched beyond their original post-war intent, making it harder to deport foreign offenders and failed asylum seekers and to run deterrent policies such as offshore processing. Within the Conservative Party this has moved from a fringe position to an explicit pledge: Kemi Badenoch has stated that a future Conservative government would take the UK out of the ECHR because it is said to obstruct migration reform and the treatment of veterans. Reform UK has made leaving the ECHR a core part of its identity, helping to normalise withdrawal as a mainstream option in parts of the political debate.

Polling suggests public opinion is ambivalent and often poorly informed; awareness of what the ECHR actually does is low, but withdrawal has become a salient dividing line between parties, with Conservatives and Reform UK more favourable to exit and Labour, Liberal Democrats and others warning of serious legal and diplomatic costs.

Visit the companion website for a case study on the pressure group Liberty.

Equality Act 2010

The Equality Act 2010 brought 116 separate pieces of legislation on discrimination together into one Act to make the law easier to understand and to enhance protection in certain areas. The Act laid out the different ways in which it was unlawful to treat someone in the workplace and in wider society. There are nine characteristics that are protected from discrimination under the Act: age, disability, gender reassignment, marriage and civil partnership, pregnancy and maternity, race, religion or belief, sex and sexual orientation.

The Act lays out what an individual can do if they feel that they have been discriminated against and also requires public bodies to pay attention to eliminating discrimination, advancing equality of opportunity and fostering good relations between different people in carrying out their work.

The limits and tensions of rights protection in the UK

The focus on rights since the introduction of the HRA in 1998 has raised a number of key issues about how rights work in practice within a democracy.

Rights and responsibilities

Rights are commonly viewed as the other side of the coin from **responsibilities**, on the grounds that having an entitlement to act or be treated in a particular way entails an obligation to respect the entitlement of others to do the same. Citizenship is thus normally seen to be composed of a combination of rights and responsibilities.

Conservatives, in particular, have seen the growth of a human rights culture as a threat to the moral fabric of society, with people being more concerned with what society owes them than with what they owe society. Rights have thus become divorced from responsibilities, especially when these rights are seen as fundamental, meaning that they do not have to be 'earned'.

Can rights be restricted?

The UK Parliament has the power to 'derogate' from (set aside) certain articles in the ECHR when passing law during a state of emergency or at a time of war. The only time this has happened was during the Labour Government of Tony Blair when they derogated from Article 5, the right to liberty and security, in the passing of the Anti-Terrorism, Crime and Security Act 2001, which included the power to detain foreign nationals who were suspected international terrorists because they believed they represented a threat to the UK. Also, regarding the Illegal Migration Act, Suella Braverman indicated that 'our approach is robust and novel, which is why we can't make a definitive statement of compatibility under section 19(1)(a) of the Human Rights Act. Of course, the UK will always seek to uphold international law and I am confident that this bill is compatible with international law.' This is seen as a clear example of the common good overriding the rights of the individual, but raises the question as to whether rights really are universal, fundamental and absolute.

However, there are four exceptions to this rule: the UK Parliament cannot derogate from Articles 2, 3, 4 and 7 as these rights are considered absolute. All other rights within the HRA can all be compromised in times of crisis, provided the action is proportionate and lawful, to protect the public. A clear example can be found in the Coronavirus Act 2020, which massively increased state power and was backed by emergency regulations that allowed the police to prevent people from leaving their homes without a 'reasonable excuse', which could be argued to restrict Article 5 in order to protect public health.

Clash of rights – individual vs collective rights

It is by no means clear that rights belong only to individuals, as they are also claimed by collective bodies, ranging from trade unions and political parties to cultural or religious groups. Collective rights nevertheless often clash with individual rights, as the former tend to place restrictions on freedom of choice. These issues are generally resolved via the courts rather than by elected politicians and many of the decisions receive widespread publicity as they can be controversial:

> » In *R v. Michaela School* (2024), a Muslim student challenged the school's ban on prayer rituals, claiming it was discriminatory. The school had implemented a ban on all prayer rituals after some students began praying during lunchtime. The school argued that this practice fostered division among students and disrupted school activities. The ban affected all students regardless of faith. The court upheld the school's policy and found that the prayer ban did not interfere with the student's right to manifest her religious beliefs. It noted that she had options to attend another school that allowed prayer and also that she could perform missed prayers at a later time. While

---

Definition

Responsibilities: Obligations or duties towards others or the larger society. This includes paying tax, jury duty, abiding by the law and voting.

acknowledging that the ban placed Muslim pupils at a disadvantage, the court ruled that this disadvantage was justified as it served a legitimate aim of promoting inclusion and preventing division within the school community.

» *In Ashers v. Lee* (2018): In this case it was decided by the Supreme Court that a Belfast bakery run by evangelical Christians did not have to make a cake with the message 'support gay marriage' on it. The court ruled the bakery did not refuse to make the cake because of Lee's sexual orientation and so there was no discrimination on these grounds. Under Article 10, the court ruled that freedom of expression includes the right not to express an opinion that one does not hold. The decision was welcomed by some as a victory for free speech, while gay rights groups, such as Stonewall and the Rainbow Project, as well as the Equality Commission for Northern Ireland, saw it as a backward step for equality.

However, the biggest conflict arises between individual rights and the collective rights expressed by the state such as national security, public health and keeping the public safe. These clashes often pit the government, backed by the will of those who elected them, against individual rights and the courts are left to resolve the dispute. This often brings the courts into direct conflict with the government and according to critics could put the safety of the country at risk and undermine the trust of the public in the legal system.

Photo 2.3 Supreme Court rules in favour of a Belfast bakery under Article 10 of the Human Rights Act

Source: Leon Neal / Getty Images

Individual rights have come into conflict with the priorities of government in four main areas:

1. **Sentencing laws:** In *R v. D* (2024), the case involved a defendant who was convicted of multiple sexual offences against minors. The sentencing raised significant questions about the appropriate length of custodial sentences and the rights of the victims versus the rights of the offender. The court had to consider the rights of the offender to a fair sentence while also weighing the need to protect the public, particularly vulnerable children, from future harm. The court ultimately imposed a lengthy custodial sentence, reflecting both the severity of the crimes and the necessity to safeguard potential victims. The decision emphasised that while individual rights are important, they must be balanced against collective rights to safety and security within society.

2. **Treatment of prisoners:** In *Hirst v. UK* (2005) the ECtHR ruled that a blanket ban on prisoners voting violated Article 3 in a case that David Cameron described as making him feel physically ill. Although the case was resolved in 2017, it was done in the most limited way possible with the following prisoners being able to vote: prisoners on remand, those convicted but not yet sentenced, those imprisoned for civil matters and for contempt of court, and lastly, those prisoners on home detention curfew or released on temporary licence. In 2018 the Council of Europe said these were sufficient to signify compliance with the 2005 ruling and finally closed the case in 2018.

3. **Terrorism:** This has perhaps been the most controversial area of all, especially in light of an increased terrorist threat since 9/11.

   » In the *Malakai Wheeler Case* (2023) where an 18-year-old was convicted of multiple offences of possession and dissemination of terrorist material, and the *Jacob Graham Case* (2024) where a 20-year-old from Liverpool was convicted of preparing for acts of terrorism, both cases have raised issues about how young people are prosecuted for online terrorist activities regarding freedom of expression versus public safety, especially concerning young offenders.

   » *Morgan and Others v. Ministry of Justice* (2022), involved several defendants who had pleaded guilty to terrorism offences and were sentenced under the Counter-Terrorism and Sentencing Act 2021. The defendants challenged their sentence conditions, arguing that it was a violation of their rights. The Supreme Court ruled that they were not in violation of Articles 5 or 7 of the ECHR, emphasising that the sentence was a legitimate response to public safety concerns regarding terrorism and reflected the government's responsibility to protect society from individuals convicted of serious terrorist offences.

   » While over 20 years old, the Belmarsh ruling is still significant today. *A and others v. Secretary of State for the Home Department* (2004), saw the Law Lords rule that the Labour policy of indefinite detention of foreign terror suspects without charge broke the Human Rights Act. The court ruled that laws like this were 'the real threat to the life of the nation'. Charles Clarke, the Home Secretary, did not release the suspects until the following year, having passed new legislation that allowed him to place the suspects under control orders that impose strict restrictions on suspects, including electronic tagging and limits on whom they can meet.

4. **Right to privacy and family life versus the need to protect others:**

   » In *R (on the application of M) v. the Home Department* (2024), a mother challenged her deportation order, arguing that it would disrupt her family life with her British children. The court ruled in favour of the government, stating that the need to maintain public safety and prevent potential threats justified the deportation, despite its impact on her family life.

   » In *R v. B* (2024), a convicted terrorist sought to challenge his prison sentence and restrictions on contact with his family. The court upheld the restrictions, determining that public safety concerns justified limitations on his family interactions, emphasising that protecting society from further harm was paramount.

   » *KO (Nigeria) and Others v. the Home Department* (2018) involved a challenge to the government's immigration policy regarding children. The court dismissed the appeal and found that decisions affecting children's rights must consider their family life and welfare. The ruling emphasised that public safety measures must be proportionate and not infringe excessively on family rights, particularly when children are involved.

KEY TOPIC DEBATE: HOW EFFECTIVELY DOES THE UK PROTECT RIGHTS?

✓ **Rights in the UK are effectively protected by the courts** via judicial review which allows citizens to challenge decisions made by public bodies, including the government, which they believe may contravene rights. (See Chapter 10 on the Supreme Court.)

   » This allows the courts in the UK to protect the rights of the individual, even when it's unpopular, since judges are unelected. The court's protection of the rights of prisoners, suspected terror suspects and migrants seem to back this up.

   » In 2025 the Supreme Court ruled that the definition of a woman in the Equality Act should be based on biological sex. This ruling was cheered by women's groups who saw this ruling as clarifying and protecting their rights as women.

   » In 2023, the UK Supreme Court ruled that the government's plan to send asylum seekers to Rwanda was unlawful, citing potential breaches of human rights obligations under the HRA.

   » The Illegal Migration Act 2023 faced several significant legal challenges. The Act was challenged for its incompatibility with the UK's human rights obligations under the ECHR; the UK Government could not say, when introducing the bill, whether it was compatible with the HRA. The High Court in Belfast identified sections of the Act that violated both the ECHR and the Windsor Framework.

» In 2022, the case of *Leigh v. Commissioner of the Metropolitan Police* addressed the right to protest during the Covid-19 pandemic. The court found that the Metropolitan Police Service failed to conduct a proper proportionality assessment when making decisions about a planned vigil for Sarah Everard. This case underscored the importance of balancing public health measures with fundamental rights protected by the HRA.

Visit the companion website for a case study on the Supreme Court Ruling For Women Scotland vs Scottish Ministers

❌ **However, the courts have also handed down judgements that may be seen to limit rights protection.** This may be because the HRA, ECHR and Judicial Review are increasingly coming under attack from the media, think tanks and politicians for undermining the balance between individual rights and collective rights and the need for effective government to act in the public interest.

» The 2025 Supreme Court ruling that the definition of a woman should be based on biological sex, left trans rights groups despondent, seeing the ruling as a major setback that increases the risk of trans people being challenged, denied access, or harassed. It is clear that rights protection is not a simple thing to define.

» In *Shamima Begum v. the Home Department* (2024), the Supreme Court ruled against Shamima Begum on all counts regarding the removal of her British citizenship on national security grounds, noting that Begum would not be allowed to return to the UK to pursue her appeal. The court agreed that national security concerns outweighed Begum's right to a fair and effective hearing.

» In *AM (Belarus) v. the Home Department* (2024), the Supreme Court upheld the Home Secretary's decision to deny leave to remain to an illegal immigrant, identified as AM, who had multiple criminal convictions and had obstructed deportation efforts by providing false information. The court determined that the Home Secretary's actions were lawful and pursued legitimate aims, including economic wellbeing, and protection of others' rights and freedoms.

» In 2024, five Just Stop Oil climate campaigners were sentenced to lengthy jail terms by a judge who told them they had 'crossed the line from concerned campaigner to fanatic'. They were found guilty of conspiracy to cause a public nuisance for coordinating direct action protests on the M25 over four days in November 2022. The sentences are considered to be the longest sentences given for non-violent protest.

✅ **Rights in the UK are protected by Parliament.**

» Parliament enhanced rights protection fundamentally when it passed the Human Rights Act in 1998 (see page 44). Parliament also established a Joint Committee on Human Rights to scrutinise every government bill for its compatibility with human rights.

» In the case of *R (HM, MA and KH) v. the Home Department (2022), the court ruled against the Home Office's blanket policy of seizing phones from asylum seekers arriving by small boats. The court found that this policy violated rights under the HRA, concerning unlawful search and seizure.*

» In 2024, the court ruled that part of Westminster Council's Housing Allocation Scheme was unlawful due to indirect discrimination against women and girls escaping violence. This case illustrates how the HRA can be used to challenge discriminatory policies and protect vulnerable groups.

» In 2024, Bloomberg lost an appeal over naming an executive under criminal investigation, with the Supreme Court ruling it violated the individual's privacy rights under Article 8 of the HRA.

» Parliament also passed the Freedom of Information Act (FOIA) in 2000 to enhance transparency and openness in government (see page 45).

» The FOIA played a significant role in uncovering details about the Post Office Horizon scandal, which involved wrongful convictions of sub-postmasters due to faults in the Horizon IT system.

» Another significant use of FOIA was related to the Hillsborough disaster. Requests for information about the police's actions during the tragedy led to the release of documents that revealed failures in the investigation and cover-ups.

» Parliament subsequently passed the Equalities Act in 2010 (see page 46) and incorporated an Equality and Human Rights Commission to promote and uphold equality and human rights laws.

- » *Macken v. BNP Paribas*: In 2022, a female broker successfully claimed £2 million in damages for sexual discrimination after humiliating treatment from male colleagues. The tribunal's ruling emphasised the importance of addressing gender-based discrimination and highlighted the role of the Equality Act in securing justice for victims.
- » A pregnant policewoman won a sex discrimination case against Devon and Cornwall Police after she was forced to move from the front line to a desk-bound position. Her employers believed this was 'safe and suitable for a pregnant woman' despite receiving advice that she was fit to carry out her regular role. The employment tribunal ruled that she was a victim of indirect sex discrimination.

❌ **However, the strong culture of respect for rights appears more as lip service, with Parliament also passing laws which limit and restrict rights.**

- » In response to *R (HM, MA and KH) v. Secretary of State for the Home Department (2022)*, the Border Security, Asylum and Immigration Act 2025 created specific powers for police, Border Force and immigration officers to search for and seize electronic devices (including phones and SIMs) from people who have entered or arrived in the UK illegally, with the aim of gathering intelligence on smuggling networks. These powers came into force in January 2026 showing that Parliament can overrule rights rulings by passing new laws.
- » In October 2025 the Home Secretary, Shabana Mahmood, announced that police would be given broader powers to restrict "repeat" protests by taking into account their cumulative impact. It was tied to plans to amend sections 12 and 14 of the Public Order Act 1986. She announced that they would also ban pyrotechnics at protests, climbing on war memorials, and prohibit face coverings at designated demonstrations. This is as well as the previous government passing the Public Order Act 2023, which created new protest-related offences (including obstructing major transport works and interfering with key national infrastructure), and suspicion-less stop-and-search powers. Critics argue that it poses a threat to the right to protest by criminalising certain forms of dissent and expanding police power.
- » The Safety of Rwanda Act 2024 mandates decision makers, including courts and immigration officials, to treat Rwanda as a safe country for the removal of asylum seekers. It did this by disapplying sections 2, 3, and 6 to 9 of the Human Rights Act. This declaration overrides previous judicial findings that deemed Rwanda unsafe for asylum processing due to systemic defects. The Starmer Government passed the Border Security, Asylum and Immigration Act 2025 which repealed in full the Safety of Rwanda (Asylum and Immigration) Act 2024.
- » The Illegal Migration Act 2023 has been criticised for its human rights violations on vulnerable populations seeking asylum in the UK. When introducing the Bill, the Home Secretary used section 19(1)(b) of the Human Rights Act to state that she was unable to confirm compatibility with rights and the Act expressly disapplies section 3 of the HRA, which normally requires courts and public authorities to interpret legislation compatibly with Convention rights where possible. This removed a key protection against human rights violations.
- » The Police, Crime, Sentencing and Courts Act 2022 introduced several provisions that critics argue limit individual rights regarding protest and public assembly. Critics argue that it creates an environment where dissent is more easily suppressed and there are severe penalties for exercising their rights to protest and assemble.
- » The Elections Act 2022 has been criticised for disenfranchising voters, altering electoral systems in ways that may favour one party, and undermining independent electoral oversight. The *Guardian* suggested that at the 2024 General Election, as many as 400,000 voters could have been disenfranchised.
- » The Safety of Rwanda Act 2024 mandates decision makers, including courts and immigration officials, to treat Rwanda as a safe country for the removal of asylum seekers. It did this by disapplying sections 2, 3, and 6 to 9 of the Human Rights Act. This declaration overrides previous judicial findings that deemed Rwanda unsafe for asylum processing due to systemic defects. The Starmer Government passed the Border Security, Asylum and Immigration Act 2025 which repealed in full the Safety of Rwanda (Asylum and Immigration) Act 2024.

The FOIA also has significant weaknesses:

- » After the Hillsborough disaster, there was significant resistance to disclosing information, with authorities citing exemptions to withhold documents. The Hillsborough panel's findings highlighted how previous investigations had been hampered by incomplete disclosures and attempts to manipulate narratives about fan behaviour on that tragic day.

» Despite its importance in the sub-postmasters' Horizon scandal, there were instances where FOI requests were denied or met with resistance from government departments, raising concerns about transparency and accountability in handling such significant issues.

There have also been concerns expressed about the **Equality Act:**

» The ability to claim discrimination on multiple grounds (e.g. as both a woman and a disabled person) was eliminated, significantly undermining its effects. UNISON advocates for increased protections against sexual harassment in the workplace and stronger protections for pregnant workers in the Act.

» The Equality and Human Rights Commission (EHRC), responsible for enforcing the Act, has faced funding cuts and capacity issues, which hinder its ability to effectively monitor compliance and support individuals facing discrimination.

✅ **In the UK, rights are also protected and promoted by pressure groups.** There is now a far greater awareness of civil liberties and a strong commitment to fighting for and protecting rights.

» Liberty has been vocal in campaigning against any weakening of rights. In May 2024, the courts found government anti-protest legislation unlawful after Liberty's legal challenge. The court ruled that the former Home Secretary Suella Braverman acted unlawfully in making it easier for the police to criminalise peaceful protests. It found that government did not have the power to create the legislation, and as such it was unlawful. Hundreds of protesters had been arrested since the government redefined the sort of protest that could be restricted by the police. Liberty called the ruling 'a huge victory for democracy'.

» Stonewall is renowned for its campaigning. Some major successes include helping achieve the equalisation of the age of consent, lifting the ban on LGB people serving in the military, securing legislation which allowed same-sex couples to adopt, and the repeal of Section 28. More recently, Stonewall has helped secure civil partnerships and then same-sex marriage and ensured that the recent Equality Act protected lesbian, gay and bi people. Stonewall's advocacy has significantly influenced the UK government's stance on conversion therapy.

» The union for senior civil servants, the FDA, launched a legal challenge to the Rwanda plan in 2024, fearing the scheme would force officials to break the law. Under the law, ministers could ignore the ECtHR and direct officials to organise flights. The union wanted to protect civil servants in a difficult legal position.

❌ **Nonetheless, pressure groups have not been successful in protecting rights.**

» Despite Amnesty's huge 'Kill the Bill' protests, which opposed the Police, Crime, Sentencing and Courts Act, the Act was passed.

» Despite Stonewall influencing bans on conversion therapy, the government eventually announced that it would proceed with a ban on gay and bisexual conversion therapy but would not extend this protection to transgender people. This was criticised by Stonewall but ultimately made no difference to the government's plans.

» The FDA's challenge to the Rwanda scheme was unsuccessful with the guidance for civil servants deemed lawful by the courts.

Key Debate Summary: How effectively does the UK protect rights?

For	Theme	Against
✓ In the UK, the courts take a strong interest in rights protection.	Are the courts able to withstand government pressure to effectively protect rights?	✗ However, possibly under pressure from politicians, the courts have also been responsible for some questionable rulings on rights.
✓ Parliament is at the forefront of rights protection, passing the HRA, the FOIA and the Equalities Act.	Does government dominance of Parliament limit their ability to protect rights?	✗ However, Parliament has also introduced a number of pieces of legislation that restrict rights.
✓ There is a strong commitment to human rights within wider civil society, with pressure groups using the HRA and Equalities Act to further human rights.	Are pressure groups strong enough to uphold rights protection?	✗ Pressure groups lack resources and power to do enough to protect rights and are at the whim of Parliament and the courts.

CASE STUDY 2.6: THE ILLEGAL IMMIGRATION ACT, THE RWANDA PLAN AND THE SAFETY OF RWANDA ACT

Background

The UK Government, under Prime Minister Johnson, introduced two plans as a response to the increasing numbers of asylum seekers crossing the English Channel in small boats. The government argued that these initiatives would deter dangerous journeys facilitated by human traffickers and reduce the backlog of asylum claims in the UK.

- The Rwanda immigration scheme was a controversial approach by the UK Government to manage asylum seekers. Announced in April 2022, the scheme allowed for the relocation of individuals who arrived in the UK illegally to Rwanda, where their asylum claims would be processed. The plan involved significant financial commitments, including an initial £120 million investment in Rwanda's development fund and additional costs for each relocated asylum seeker.

- The Illegal Migration Act also addressed concerns regarding irregular migration, particularly small boat crossings of the Channel. The Act aimed to deter unlawful migration by preventing individuals who arrive in the UK through unauthorised routes from claiming asylum or protection. The Act mandated that such individuals could be detained indefinitely and removed either to their home country or a designated 'safe third country', such as Rwanda. The Home Secretary is required to ensure the removal of individuals who enter the UK unlawfully.

Legal Challenges

The Rwanda scheme faced substantial legal opposition. In November 2023, the UK Supreme Court ruled that Rwanda could not be considered a safe third country for asylum seekers for the following reasons:

1. Human Rights Violations: Evidence highlighted Rwanda's poor human rights record, including reports of extrajudicial killings, torture and restrictions on political freedoms. The court emphasised that these conditions raised serious concerns about the treatment asylum seekers would face if relocated.

2. Risk of Refoulement: The Supreme Court found substantial grounds to believe that individuals sent to Rwanda could be returned to their home countries where they might suffer persecution or harm (refoulement), violating UK and international obligations.

3. Inadequate Asylum Processing: The court noted systemic defects in Rwanda's asylum system, which would likely prevent fair and accurate assessments of asylum claims.

The Supreme Court's decision raised critical questions about the future of the UK's broader immigration policy, particularly in relation to the Illegal Migration Act. Critics argued that this Act created a legal limbo for many asylum seekers, leaving them without protection or support in the UK.

Government Response

In response to the Supreme Court ruling, Prime Minister Sunak introduced emergency legislation aimed at reaffirming Rwanda's status as a safe country. The Safety of Rwanda (Asylum and Immigration) Act was passed in 2024 designed to facilitate the removal of asylum seekers to Rwanda. This Act responded to legal challenges against the government's Rwanda asylum plan, following a Supreme Court ruling that deemed the plan unlawful.

The Act explicitly declared Rwanda a safe third country for the removal of individuals seeking asylum in the UK, despite the Supreme Court ruling to the contrary. This designation allowed the government to proceed with deportations despite previous judicial findings questioning Rwanda's safety for asylum seekers. The legislation was linked to a treaty between the UK and Rwanda, which guaranteed that individuals sent to Rwanda would not face risks upon return to their home countries.

Rights Implications

- By designating Rwanda as a processing country, the UK denied individuals arriving illegally from accessing asylum procedures within its borders. This undermined their right to seek protection as guaranteed under international law.

- Provisions within the Safety of Rwanda Act limited judicial review over decisions related to removals, effectively stopping individuals from challenging their deportation based on human rights grounds.

- Critics argue that externalising asylum responsibilities contravened established international refugee protection systems. The UN High Commissioner for Refugees (UNHCR) consistently warned that such arrangements pose serious risks for refugees' safety and wellbeing.

However, in 2025 the Starmer Government passed the Border Security, Asylum and Immigration Act 2025, which repealed in full the Safety of Rwanda (Asylum and Immigration) Act 2024.

Visit the companion website for case studies on the CBI, Tesco and Hanbury Strategy.

Exam Style Questions

- Evaluate the view that human rights are well protected in the United Kingdom (30).

- Evaluate the view that the largest pressure groups in the UK are the most powerful (30).

- Evaluate the view that group politics promotes pluralist democracy in the UK (30).

- Evaluate the view that think tanks, lobbyists and pressure groups have a significant impact on political decision making in the UK (30).

Source Question

Pressure groups enhance democracy by making up for its defects, allowing for representation in between elections; they also ensure that minority voices are represented. Pressure groups offer alternative viewpoints and widen the information available to the public which allows groups to change the political agenda and force political parties to take notice. Pressure groups also allow new and previously excluded groups a voice in society. The grassroots activism of many campaigning groups have proved to be attractive to many young people and those who may be disillusioned with conventional politics. This participation has been amplified by the growth of new access points in UK politics through the devolved administrations, meaning that, with so many decisions taken elsewhere, it is no longer so crucial to be an insider at Westminster. Pressure groups help to promote democracy by widening the distribution of political power because groups compete against one another, ensuring that no group or interest can dominate permanently.

However, pressure groups have been accused of holding unaccountable power as they exert influence in a way that is not subject to any scrutiny and public accountability, and so undermine democracy. Pressure groups usually exert influence 'behind closed doors', and this particularly applies in the case of think tanks, lobbyists or corporations who stalk the 'corridors of power' unseen by the public or media. Moreover, their leaders are not well known and very rarely elected, and when they are (as in the case of trade unions) this is often on very low turnouts. Moreover, far from dispersing power more widely, group politics tends to empower the already powerful, increasing, rather than reducing, inequality leading to elitism. In practice, the most powerful groups tend to be the ones that possess money, expertise, leverage and privileged links to government. Group politics gives core insiders real power due to their economic importance to the government, their ability to offer donations to parties, afford lobbying and gain access to power through the revolving door. As a result, sectional interests may prevail at the expense of the interests of the public, and elected governments may find it more difficult to serve the public interest and to do what is best for society as a whole.

Using the source, evaluate the view that pressure groups enhance democracy.

In your response you must:

» *Compare and contrast different opinions in the source*

» *Examine and debate these views in a balanced way*

» *Analyse and evaluate **only** the information presented in the source.*

 # Chapter Summary

» Group politics allows for the public to be more directly involved in politics, with pluralists arguing that groups disperse power in society and promote democracy.

» Group politics remains contentious, with critics arguing that group politics concentrates power, narrows participation and undermines democracy.

» Democracy relies on the respect for rights, to allow people to freely and effectively participate in the political process.

» The UK has seen a strengthening of the protection of rights since 1998. However, the role of the courts in protecting rights remains contentious.

 # Further Resources

Casey, C. The Critic (2024): What's wrong with the Human Rights Act? https://thecritic.co.uk/whats-wrong-with-the-human-rights-act/

Griffiths, S. and Leach, R. (2018) *British Politics* (3rd edn) (London: Bloomsbury): Chapter 16.

Heffernan, R., Hay, C., Russell, M. and Cowley, P. (2016) *Developments in British Politics* (10th edn) (London: Bloomsbury): Chapter 8.

Innes, A. (2021) LSE Blog: Corporate state capture: the degree to which the British state is porous to business interests is exceptional among established democracies https://blogs.lse.ac.uk/politicsandpolicy/corporate-state-capture/

Institute for Government Explainer (2024): Jobs after government: rules for ex-ministers and civil servants https://www.instituteforgovernment.org.uk/explainer/jobs-after-government-rules

Moran, M. (2015) *Politics and Governance in the UK* (3rd edn) (London: Bloomsbury): Chapter 14.

Politics.eu (2024): Inside Labour Together: The project behind Keir Starmer https://www.politico.eu/newsletter/westminster-insider/inside-labour-together-the-project-behind-keir-starmer/

Shadowy think tanks are a risk to the UK's democratic integrity (2019). Unlock democracy https://unlockdemocracy.org.uk/blog1/2023/7/19/shadowy-think-tanks-are-a-risk-to-the-uks-democratic-integrity

The Week (2022): High stakes: how much sway does gambling lobby have in Westminster? https://theweek.com/news/uk-news/960365/high-stakes-how-much-sway-does-gambling-lobby-have-in-westminster

UNISON (2024): Feargal Sharkey brings star quality – and rage – to conference https://www.unison.org.uk/news/article/2024/06/feargal-sharkey-brings-star-quality-and-rage-to-conference/

Visit the companion website to access the Further Resources Booklet to explore a range of useful web links related to: how democratic the UK is, how well the UK protects human rights and civil liberties, and the nature of protest politics. You can also find links to various pressure group websites such as Black Lives Matter, Extinction Rebellion, the TUC and more.

3 POLITICAL PARTIES

Chapter Preview

UK politics is party politics. When we vote, we vote for a political party. When governments are formed, they are formed by parties, and they govern largely as parties: that is, through a process of party discipline. If parties did not exist, we would have to invent them to fulfil the key functions they currently carry out in our representative democracy.

Since the introduction of universal suffrage, the Labour and Conservative Parties have dominated the UK political landscape and shaped the political debate around the role of the state versus the role of the market in managing the economy. In recent years, this division has become less dominant with the rise of Scottish and Welsh nationalism, as well as the rise of the Green Party and Reform UK.

And yet, party politics in the UK appears to be in a sorry state. Somehow, the established parties seem to be failing in one of their basic functions: getting people involved in political life. Turnout levels at elections have fallen; there has been a decline in party membership and fewer voters claim to 'identify' with a party. The decline of the mass party has impacted their funding at the very time parties have moved to centrally organised, expensive national campaigns in elections. This has led critics to talk of a crisis in party funding and the need for funding reform.

Specification Checklist

2.1 Political parties

» The functions and features of political parties in the UK's representative democracy.

» How parties are currently funded and debates on the consequences of the current funding system.

2.2 Established political parties

» The origins and historical development of the Conservative Party, the Labour Party and Liberal Democrat Party, and how this has shaped their ideas and current policies on the economy, law and order, welfare and foreign policy.

2.3 Emerging and minor UK political parties

» The importance of other parties in the UK.

» The ideas and policies of two other minor parties.

2.4 UK political parties in context

» The development of a multi-party system and its implications for government.

» Various factors that affect party success – explanations of why political parties have succeeded or failed, including debates on the influence of the media.

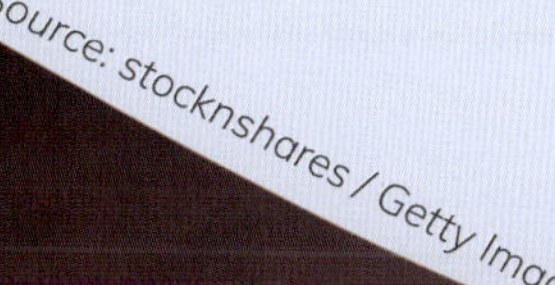

Source: stocknshares / Getty Images

What is a political party?

A political party is a group of people that is organised for the purpose of winning power at a national and local level. In a democratic system, parties do this by putting candidates up for election, in the hope of gaining support and winning and exercising power. Political parties have three main features:

1. **Parties aim to exercise power by winning political office**; historically only the Labour and Conservative Parties could hope to win power in a general election, with smaller parties like the Green Party, which won four seats in 2024, using general elections more to gain a political platform than to win power. At a devolved level and local level, there has been a far wider range of parties that can realistically expect to win and exercise power.

2. **Parties typically adopt a broad issue focus**, addressing each of the major areas of government policy. Prior to an election, parties produce a manifesto that sets out their policies, covering all that they hope to implement in the period until the next election if they win power.

3. **Members of political parties are usually united by a shared ideology**, although these are often broadly defined. For example, ideologically the Labour Party is a socialist party, with a broadly defined commitment to creating a more equal society.

KEY TOPIC DEBATE: HOW EFFECTIVELY DO POLITICAL PARTIES SUPPORT DEMOCRACY IN THE UK?

Parties carry out a wide range of functions; however, in many cases these have come under pressure in recent years, even allowing some commentators to speak of a 'crisis' in party politics.

Policy formulation

The main role of political parties is to create a coherent policy programme that can be placed before voters at election so they have an effective choice.

✓ **Political parties are one of the key means through which policy is formulated and the voters offered an effective choice.**
  » In the process of seeking power, parties develop programmes for government. Not only does this mean that parties often come up with policy proposals, but the major parties have clear ideological convictions and develop rival programmes of government, giving the electorate a meaningful choice between potential governments.
  » By offering a manifesto at election time and by accepting that they will be judged on that platform, parties can be held responsible for their performance in government, ensuring accountability within UK democracy.

✗ **However, the effectiveness of parties in formulating policies has also been questioned.**
  » As the major parties have distanced themselves from their traditional ideologies in recent years, they have become less interested in formulating larger goals for society, and generally less interested in ideas. Parties have moved from presenting an ideological choice about where society should be headed to a choice between which 'team' will run the country more effectively or a choice between leaders based on their personalities. Parties have become more eager to follow public opinion than to try to shape it.
  » Where parties lack a clear ideological identity and where there is a lack of choice for the voter, this can contribute to political apathy and low voter turnout (see Table 3.1).
  » Given that the Conservative and Labour Parties dominate the seats won in general elections, there is a lack of real choice for voters between potential governments.

Table 3.1 Voter turnout and perceived differences between parties

Year	General election turnout	Percentage of voters who perceived a great difference between the parties (%)
2024	60	17
2015	66	27
2010	65	23
2005	61	13
2001	59	17
1997	71	33
1992	78	56
1987	75	85

Recruitment of leaders

Political parties train and recruit people for elections, political office and government posts.

✅ **All senior political careers start with the decision to join a political party, and it is almost impossible to think of a major politician in the UK who is not associated with a party.**

» Thus, parties control the process of who is chosen as a candidate to stand for election and therefore who is elected. Through this process, parties provide the candidates for elections and help fill the seats in elected bodies, from local councils to devolved parliaments to the House of Commons.

» Parties also act as a training ground for future party leaders because a budding politician can gain experience of canvassing, debating issues and helping to run a constituency party. This local activity trains people in the values and processes of their party, allows them to test and grow their political skills, and to work their way up the party.

❌ **However, the effectiveness of parties in recruiting and training leaders has also been questioned.**

» Parties are likely to choose leaders who are the most expert at winning elections, choosing the most popular rather than the most competent. The skills for winning elections are not necessarily the same skills needed to run the country, especially when difficult decisions need to be made. It is suggested that Boris Johnson is a good example of this.

» The selection of party leaders has moved away from MPs to the party membership. The membership of parties is only about 2% of the population and is not democratically accountable, yet has disproportionate power in that it chooses leaders. The consequence has been leaders, such as Jeremy Corbyn, who were widely out of touch with the ideology of a majority of the party's MPs and, as in the case of Liz Truss in 2022, who were chosen as party leader (and Prime Minister) by a small band of membership-paying Conservatives, thereby undermining the democratic principle of equal participation.

Organisation of government

Political parties take control of government in the UK, and are held accountable for their actions in government.

✅ **The operation of government relies on parties.**

» Traditionally, a single party with a majority of seats in the House of Commons forms the government and implements its manifesto (see Table 3.2). They give governments a degree of stability and coherence, especially as the members of the government are usually drawn from a single party and are therefore united by common views.

> » They organise the legislative programme for government and ensure that it is passed in the legislature.

> » They provide a source of opposition and criticism, helping to scrutinise government policy and provide a 'government in waiting'.

Table 3.2 Size of majority for the government from 1970 to 2024

Year	Party in government	Prime minister	Size of majority in the house of commons
1970	Conservative	Edward Heath	31
1974 February	Labour	Harold Wilson	No majority
1974 October	Labour	Harold Wilson	4
1979	Conservative	Margaret Thatcher	44
1983	Conservative	Margaret Thatcher	144
1987	Conservative	Margaret Thatcher	101
1992	Conservative	John Major	21
1997	Labour	Tony Blair	178
2001	Labour	Tony Blair	166
2005	Labour	Tony Blair	65
2010	Conservative–Liberal Democrat coalition	David Cameron	80
2015	Conservative	David Cameron	12
2017	Conservative	Theresa May	No majority
2019	Conservative	Boris Johnson	80
2024	Labour	Keir Starmer	172

❌ **However, the effectiveness of parties in organising government has also been questioned.**

> » The decline in party unity since the 1970s has tended to weaken the majority party's control of the Commons.

> » Instability can occur, even where a single party in power has a majority, if there are clear internal party splits. This was seen throughout 2025 and 2026 during Starmer's leadership, where so many backbench Labour MPs were prepared to vote against government proposals that many U-turns were made. This led to significant instability and discussions of leadership changes.

Participation and mobilisation

Political parties play a key role in encouraging voters to turn out at election time; taking an active role in a party is a key route for ordinary people to participate in democracy.

✅ **Political parties promote participation in two ways.**

> » They provide opportunities for citizens to join a group of like-minded people and therefore help to shape party policy.

> » They help to educate and mobilise the electorate through a range of activities – canvassing, public meetings, advertising and poster campaigns, party broadcasts, and so on, building up loyalty and identification among the electorate.

❌ **However, the effectiveness of parties in ensuring participation and mobilisation has also been questioned.**

> » Voters' loyalty towards, and identification with, parties has declined. This is known as **partisan dealignment**. Whereas 44% of voters claimed to have a 'very strong' attachment to a party in 1964, this had fallen to a mere 11% by 2024. The consequences have been that people are less likely to vote and that voting patterns are far more unpredictable.

Definition

Partisan dealignment: The process where individuals no longer identify themselves on a long-term basis as being associated with a certain political party.

» Turnout in general elections has fallen sharply since 1997, with only 59% voting in 2001, the lowest turnout since 1918, and 60% in 2024.

» The membership of the three traditional major parties in the UK has fallen significantly. This suggests parties are not only less able to mobilise the public to participate more widely in politics, but also unable to mobilise people to participate in their own party.

» Party leaders have increasingly taken over running election campaigns based around centralised messaging, using the media and online platforms to replace the role of local activists.

Representation

Political parties exist to articulate the interests of the electorate.

✅ **Representation is often seen as the primary function of parties in liberal democracies.**

» Parties link government to the people by responding to the demands of public opinion and turning them into deliverable policy positions. The winning party in an election can thus claim a popular **mandate** to carry out its policies.

» The Labour Party emerged from the trade unions and socialist societies to represent working-class interests, while the Conservatives have been associated with representing the interests of private businesses and the middle classes.

» With the increasing wealth of UK society in the second half of the twentieth century and the move away from a heavy industry economy, parties have distanced themselves from their traditional interests and ideology by developing policies that appeal to the mass of the electorate. This suggests that UK parties are now 'catch-all parties'. This can be seen with Starmer's right-wing stance on immigration, and Reform UK's position against welfare cuts.

❌ **However, the effectiveness of parties in ensuring representation has also been questioned.**

» By moving away from representing their traditional groups, such as Labour looking to reduce its links with trade unions to attract the uncommitted voter, the ability of parties to represent interests has been reduced.

» In modern society, pressure groups (see Chapter 2) have been seen by some as more effective than parties in articulating interests to policymakers.

Definition

Mandate: An instruction or command that gives authority to a person or body to act in a particular way; a mandate therefore confers legitimacy on a political actor.

Catch-all party: A party that develops policies that will appeal to the widest range of voters, by contrast with a more ideological party.

Key Debate Summary: How effectively do political parties support democracy in the UK?

For	Theme	Against
✓ Parties provide a mechanism to formulate policies and offer the voters a choice.	Are parties effective in presenting a wide range of policies to the electorate?	✗ Questions remain over whether there is enough difference between parties and a real choice for voters.
✓ Parties select candidates to contest elections and train future leaders.	Are parties effective in finding political leaders or does their limited internal democracy hinder it?	✗ There is concern that the new selection processes for choosing party leaders is undermining democracy.
✓ Parties are necessary for the effective working of government and Parliament.	Are parties effective in enhancing the way Parliament works?	✗ The decline of party unity and discipline has increased instability.
✓ Parties play a key role in educating and mobilising the electorate to ensure wider participation.	Are parties effective in encouraging the electorate to engage in politics?	✗ Falling voter turnout, party identification and party membership reflect a failure of parties to engage people in politics.
✓ Parties play a key role in representation, linking together the people and the government.	Are parties effective in representing the electorate?	✗ As parties have become catch-all parties, this representation function has weakened and pressure groups have challenged the role of parties in this area.

Party funding

The funding of political parties has become an increasingly controversial issue in the UK. Parties have seen a decline in their memberships and the subscription fees that come with it, while they have moved to more centrally organised, media-based and expensive campaigning methods. This has meant that political parties are increasingly reliant on donations from individuals, corporations and trade unions, raising a key question for democracy: to what extent are political party donors effectively buying influence and power?

There is a long history of allegations of money buying power in the UK. David Lloyd George, Liberal leader and Prime Minister between 1916 and 1922, was alleged to have sold around 100 peerages in return for party donations. In 1997, under Blair, the Labour Party was embarrassed when a large donation from Formula One boss Bernie Ecclestone was linked by critics to the exemption for Formula One events from the ban on any tobacco advertising. The party was caught up in a cash for peerages scandal in 2006. In 2020, the SNP called for a public inquiry into cash for honours after Prime Minister Boris Johnson raised 26 people to the House of Lords, including several Conservative Party donors.

How are parties funded in the UK?

There are four main sources of funding for political parties in the UK:

Membership fees

Parties receive funding from membership subscriptions. This has been in decline with the collapse of party membership (see Table 3.3).

Table 3.3 **Membership income**

Party	Membership figures (2025)	Estimated membership income (2024)
Labour	309,000	£12–15 million
Reform UK	220,000+	Up to £5.5 million
Conservative	131,680	£1.5 million+
Liberal Democrats	90,000+	£2–3 million
Green Party of England and Wales	215,000	£1,485,907*
Scottish National Party (SNP)	58,940	£1–2 million
Plaid Cymru	10,000	£268,290

* denotes 2023 figure

Donations

These can be donations from individuals, corporate donations from businesses and institutional donations from pressure groups such as trade unions. There is no upper limit on the size of donations, but only 'permissible sources' are allowed – these include individuals on the UK electoral register, UK-registered companies conducting business in the UK, UK trade unions and certain UK-based associations. Critics have long alleged that Labour has, in effect, been controlled by the trade unions while the Conservatives are similarly open to the allegation that their major business backers (such as finance, insurance and real estate) exert undue influence over the process of policy development.

The total income for each major UK political party for the whole of 2024, according to official Electoral Commission accounts, is shown in Table 3.4. These figures reflect all sources of party income, including donations, membership fees and public funds for the 2024 calendar year as follows:

Grants

There is a limited amount of public money made available to the parties in the form of grants.

» There is 'Short money' available to opposition parties to help them with their parliamentary duties, but not with election or campaigning expenses. It is based on the number of seats and votes won at the last election with additional income for the Leader of the Opposition's office to assist them with their key constitutional role of holding the government to account.

» 'Cranborne money' is a similar scheme that operates for the largest and second largest opposition party in the House of Lords.

» The Electoral Commission has £2 million in money from the UK Parliament to allocate to parties with at least two sitting MPs, to develop policies to include in their election manifestos.

Loans

Parties can borrow money, but loans over £500 must come from 'permissible sources' and be reported to the Electoral Commission.

Table 3.4 Party income (2025)

Party	Total income (2025)
Conservative and Unionist Party	£50,174,000
Labour Party	£57,996,000
Liberal Democrats	£12,580,154
Scottish National Party (SNP)	£4,506,027
Reform UK	£10,832,716
Green Party	£5,217,767
Plaid Cymru	£1,033,111
Scottish Green Party	£544,939
Democratic Unionist Party (DUP)	£441,985
Social Democratic & Labour Party (SDLP)	£474,574
Alliance Party of Northern Ireland	£475,562

The rules

After the 1997 Ecclestone Affair, the Committee on Standards in Public Life made a number of proposals which were adopted in the Political Parties, Elections and Referenda Act (PPERA) of 2002, which was updated further in 2009. The Act aimed to manage party finance by regulating donations and spending and increasing the transparency about where parties got their funding.

PPERA established the Electoral Commission to oversee the laws relating to party finance. All parties must submit audited annual accounts, which are made public, while the Commission monitors and publishes details of party spending during elections.

- All donations over £11,180 to national parties (and over £2,230 to local parties) must be reported to the Electoral Commission, which publishes this information for public scrutiny.

- MPs must also report loans and donations over £500 related to their parliamentary activities.

- During election campaigns, there are strict limits on how much parties can spend nationally and in each constituency. For a party contesting all 650 seats, the national limit is just over £34 million for the regulated period before a general election.

- Finally, election spending is capped at £30,000 per constituency contested during an election to stop parties attempting to outspend each other.

- Foreign individuals and companies (not on the UK electoral register or not UK-registered and trading) are banned from donating to UK parties. This is to prevent foreign influence in UK politics. In 2025, the government announced plans to tighten political donation rules to tackle foreign interference. These have been developed into the Representation of the People Bill 2026, including tougher tests on company and association donors, stronger "know your donor" due-diligence requirements, and higher fines of up to £500,000 for breaches. Currently, political parties can only accept donations from individuals registered on a UK electoral register or UK-registered companies which carry out business in the country.

- The Act also increased the amount of Short money available for opposition parties and introduced the policy development grant.

KEY TOPIC DEBATE: SHOULD UK PARTIES BE STATE FUNDED?

The 2007 Phillips Review looked into the state of party funding and made eight major recommendations, one of which was an extension of state funding of political parties to make a fairer, more sustainable system of party politics in the UK. However, both parties have studiously avoided the debate around state funding of parties, which is one of the major issues that concerns minor parties in the UK, and state funding remains highly controversial with the public. It is worth exploring the issues around the state funding of political parties in more depth.

✅ **State funding would reduce parties' dependence on vested interests.**
  » State funding would lessen parties' dependence on wealthy individuals, corporations and trade unions, reducing the risk or perception that large donors can 'buy' influence or policy favours (see Figure 3.1). This would help restore public trust in the political process.
  » State funding would allow parties to be more responsive to the views of party members and voters, making parties more democratically responsive and increasing public trust in politics.

Figure 3.1 shows how donations shifted from Conservative to Labour from 2019 to 2024.

Figure 3.1 Donations received by Labour and Conservatives in the first three weeks of campaigning

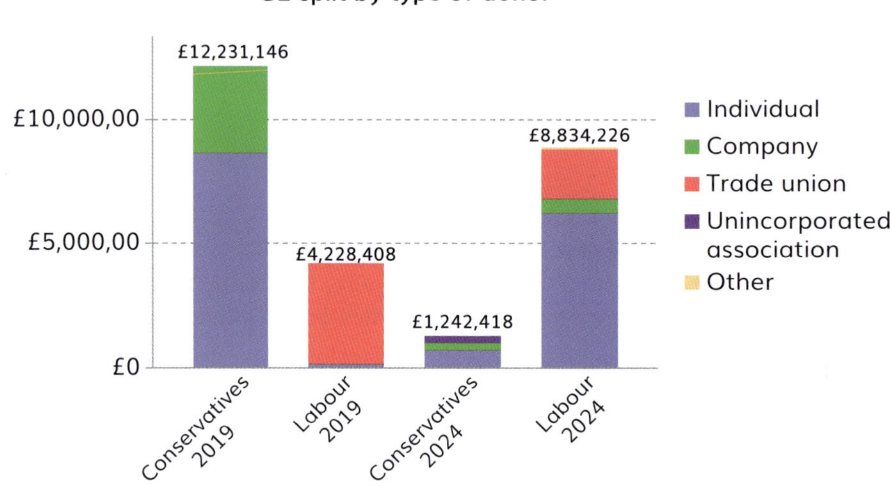

Source: Electoral Reform Society

❌ **The provision of a reliable income stream to parties from the state may weaken their links to larger society.**
  » If parties rely on state funds, they may become less connected to their members, supporters and wider society, potentially making them less responsive and more insular. Parties currently need to reach out to society to seek donations; this means they have to listen and be responsive to a range of interests and groups.
  » The Labour Party under Tony Blair and more recently under Keir Starmer looked to reduce its reliance on trade union money by attracting a wider range of donors. During the official campaign period in 2024, Starmer received £9.5 million. Under Jeremy Corbyn, the party generated a very healthy membership income stream due to the large increase in membership.

» The Conservative Party has also looked to reach out to society by expanding its base, increasing its membership from 124,000 in 2018 to 160,000 in 2019 as new members joined to have a say in the leadership election.

✅ State funding creates a level playing field

» Public funding would help smaller and newer parties compete with established ones, who often benefit from large private donations. This would make elections fairer and encourage a more pluralist democracy.

» Public funds could be allocated based on an agreed measure of parties' popularity and democratic engagement. This might include votes won across a range of different elections (especially as smaller parties are far more successful in local and regional elections) and the size of party membership. Reform, for example, boasted in 2025 that it had more members than the Conservative Party.

» This would create a more level playing field for the parties, removing the unfair advantages that some parties derive from the simple fact that they have wealthy backers. This would provide a far healthier party system in the UK.

❌ It may create a bias in favour of existing parties if the level of state funding reflects past party performance measured in terms of votes cast in preceding elections.

» This would further entrench the power of the Labour and Conservative Parties and leave minor parties behind.

» State funding cannot equalise resources as larger parties with more members and support will still have advantages.

✅ The current regulatory framework is inadequate – state funding is the only solution.

» Since passing PPERA in 2000, allegations that donations secure peerages and political influence have continued.

» The regulations have also failed to create a level playing field for smaller parties and are out of date due to the rise of social media.

» State funding provides the solution and the cost to the taxpayer would be relatively small, with the parties requiring around £25 million per year of taxpayers' money to carry out their functions.

» Public funds are 'clean' and transparent, reducing the risk of hidden or questionable sources of income

❌ State funding is unpalatable. The public already distrusts politicians with public money following the many financial scandals and the public do not like the idea of their money going to parties they do not support.

» This problem is exacerbated by the fact the state funding measure may end up allocating funds to parties that much of the public consider to be extremists.

» In a free democratic society, it is the right of the individual to financially support whichever party or political cause they like, and this right should not be restricted.

» The answer is not state funding, but more transparency on party funding so the public can scrutinise the political parties before making a choice on whether to join or vote for one.

Key Debate Summary: Should UK parties be state funded?

For	Theme	Against
✓ State funding would reduce parties' reliance on their donors.	Would state funding reduce reliance on donors or reduce parties' connection to their voters?	✗ Reliance on state funding might reduce parties' links to wider society.
✓ State funding would create a level playing field and healthier party system.	Would state funding reduce or reinforce the two-party system?	✗ State funding could lead to reinforcing the existing two-party dominance.
✓ A reliable income would allow parties to fulfil their democratic functions.		✗ Reliance on state funding might reduce the independence of parties.
✓ State funding is needed to replace the failed existing framework.	Is the current system bad enough to justify state funding?	✗ State funding is unpopular with the wider public.

CASE STUDY 3.1: PARTY FUNDING IN THE 2024 UK GENERAL ELECTION

The 2024 UK General Election saw a record £97.8 million in donations accepted by political parties, driven by heightened campaigning and public engagement. However, the surge in funding also exposed vulnerabilities in the regulatory framework, controversies over permissible donors, and stark disparities in the financial power between parties.

Record donations and key players

The Labour Party emerged as the dominant financial force, raising £58.6 million in 2024. Over a third of Labour donations were from donors who previously gave money to other parties, with only £2.4 million coming from the party's 11 affiliated trade unions. This was the lowest figure since 2015. Others like Unite, once the party's largest donor – donating £3 million in 2019 – refused to donate to the party or endorse its manifesto. Its largest donations included:

» **£2.5 million** from Lord David Sainsbury, a former minister and supermarket heir

» **£1.5 million** from Dale Vince's green energy firm Ecotricity

» Over **£1 million** from trade unions, including GMB and UNISON

» £700,000 from Martin Taylor, hedge fund manager

» £250,000 from Transilluminate Limited

» £250,000 from Danny Luhde-Thompson

» £250,000 from Derek Webb

» £239,000 from Gary Lubner

» £200,000 from Laura Bailey

» £180,000 from Mr Grayson Perry CBE

» £166,567 from Labour Together Limited

In April 2024, *openDemocracy* revealed that Starmer, Reeves and other senior party figures met with the Bloomberg Group, a major media and financial information multinational, weeks after it donated £150,000 to the party. They were given detailed information about Labour's policy plans for the financial services sector, sparking concerns of 'cash for access'. Reeves was also criticised for appointing a party donor, former banker Ian Corfield, to a senior role at the Treasury. Corfield was a senior business adviser to the party in opposition and donated more than £20,000 to Labour in the run-up to the election.

The Conservative Party reported £59.4 million in total income, though its donation intake dropped sharply post-election. Key sources included:

• £16.1 million in 2024, primarily from high-net-worth individuals and businesses.

• A £225,000 donation from the National Conservative Draws Society.

• Frank Hester, whose company The Phoenix Partnership has received £427.7 million from the NHS and Department for Health since 2016 and who donated £15.3 million to the Conservatives since 2023. The businessman, mired in a row about comments condemned as racist and misogynistic, gave the Conservative Party £5 million in January 2024.

• Richard Harpin, who has donated £2.7 million between 2016 and 2024. His firms Harmony Bridge Limited and Liberty House (Hull) Ltd received a combined £730,980 from Homes England between May 2019 and August 2021. Homes England is a public body that funds new affordable housing in England.

The Lib Dems' funding included £2.6 million in donations, largely from small donors and businesses.
Other parties like **Reform UK** (£2.6 million) and the **SNP** (£4.75 million) relied on small donors, businesses, grassroots donations and public funds, while the **Green Party** (£3.8 million) drew support from environmental advocates.

Controversies

• The Electoral Commission fined the Conservative Party £1,500 for late and inaccurate reporting of nine donations and two loans. This followed earlier criticism of the party's financial transparency, including a 2023 investigation into undeclared loans.

• A 2024 Bureau of Investigative Journalism sting revealed five major parties – Conservatives, Reform UK, Lib Dems, Greens and SNP – accepted illegal donations from a foreign national. Only Labour flagged and rejected the funds. The incident highlighted gaps in monitoring aggregated small donations.

The Electoral Commission urged stricter rules to prevent foreign interference, including:

- Limiting company donations to UK-generated profits.

- Mandating 'know your donor' checks.

- Closing loopholes allowing unincorporated associations to channel foreign funds.

Impact on the Election

» Outspending rivals, Labour targeted marginal seats with extensive advertising and grassroots campaigns, contributing to its landslide victory.

» The Conservative Party's funding decline mirrored its electoral collapse, with donors shifting to Reform UK or withholding support amid internal chaos.

» Despite limited resources, Reform UK's anti-establishment messaging and Nigel Farage's social media prominence amplified its influence, splitting the right-wing vote and damaging Tory prospects.

» Representation of the People Bill 2026, including tougher tests on company and association donors, stronger "know your donor" due-diligence requirements, and higher fines of up to £500,000 for breaches.

Conclusion

The 2024 Election emphasised the role of money in the UK: vital for campaigning yet a source of controversy.

While Labour's financial clout secured its victory, systemic flaws – such as inadequate safeguards against foreign donations and inconsistent enforcement – left the system vulnerable. The Electoral Commission's proposed reforms, if adopted in the 2026 Representation of the People Bill, could bolster transparency. However, with parties like Reform UK and the Green Party gaining popularity and global figures eyeing political influence, the UK's party funding regime faces unprecedented challenges in maintaining public trust.

Visit the companion website for a case study on party funding and the 2019 General Election.

Established political parties

Left and Right

Political ideas and beliefs are often categorised on the basis that they are either **left wing** or **right wing**. Although the terms 'left' and 'right' do not have exact meanings, they tend to summarise different attitudes to the individual, society, the economy and the role of the state. This can be illustrated by the traditional, linear left/right political spectrum (see Figure 3.2).

Figure 3.2 The left/right political spectrum

LEFT   RIGHT

COMMUNISM   SOCIALISM   LIBERALISM   CONSERVATISM   FASCISM

Table 3.5 Left and right characteristics

Left wing	Right wing
Supports higher taxes on the wealthy and robust welfare for the poor	Supports lower taxes, limited government and free-market capitalism
Advocates for universal healthcare and public services	Favours private sector solutions and individual responsibility in welfare and healthcare
Promotes government intervention in the economy and regulation of business	Prefers deregulation and minimal state interference in the economy
Champions multiculturalism, lenient immigration and internationalism	Prioritises nationalism, stricter immigration and cultural cohesion
Seeks environmental protection and action on climate change	More sceptical of environmental regulation and climate policy

In the UK, the left/right divide has traditionally been portrayed as a battle between two contrasting ideologies – socialism and conservatism – with liberalism somehow standing between them. In turn, these ideologies have been represented by political parties that have dominated UK politics since the early twentieth century – the Labour and Conservative Parties. Socialism has traditionally been viewed as the ideology of the Labour Party, and conservatism has traditionally been seen as the ideology of the Conservative Party. This vision was always defined in very general terms, allowing both major

Spec Key Term

Left wing: Political ideas that are based on the belief that the state can be used to deliver social change; they tend to prioritise equality over liberty.

Right wing: Political ideas that favour order, authority and also liberty, they favour free market economics.

parties to be 'broad churches' and, when in power, to respond more to practical pressures than to ideological beliefs. Nevertheless, both parties had a sense of what they 'stood for' (see Table 3.5). This was underpinned by the basis of their support: working-class voters tended to vote Labour and middle-class voters tended to vote Conservative.

However, in recent years, British politics has undergone some significant shifts in what issues have become politically 'acceptable'.

Shifts in the Overton Window in UK politics

Since 2015, the Overton Window – the range of politically acceptable ideas in UK public discourse – has experienced significant shifts on multiple issues. The Overton Window has shifted in two major ways: previously unthinkable ideas entered mainstream debate (most notably Brexit and radical party platforms), while other progressive causes (environmental policy, LGBT+ rights) became broadly acceptable or established policy.

- **Brexit moved from a fringe idea to mainstream, then reality:** Leaving the EU was considered radical or unthinkable pre-2015. By 2016–19, Brexit dominated political debate, and policies once seen as extreme became central.
- **Rise of identity politics:** The importance of issues around Britishness, sovereignty and immigration has intensified, and these identity questions are now a persistent divide alongside the traditional left/right economic spectrum.
- **Fragmentation and radicalism:** The rise of new parties, e.g. Reform UK, and increased popularity of other smaller parties like the Greens, led to growing hostility to centrism, and surges in both left- and right-wing populism which expanded what was discussed in the mainstream. Radically progressive or conservative ideas became more visible, challenging norms in both directions.
- **End of two-party dominance:** Local and national elections have seen Labour and Conservatives lose ground to smaller parties, reflecting public appetite for alternatives and shifting what policies are considered acceptable.
- **Centrism and ambivalence:** While the debate has grown more intense at the margins, many policies have moved closer to the centre, with mainstream parties focusing on pragmatic economic solutions and technology-driven change.
- **Social progressivism:** Demands for climate action, LGBT+ rights, feminism and environmentalism have moved rapidly towards mainstream acceptance.

The Conservative Party

The origins of conservatism

The Conservative Party emerged in the first half of the nineteenth century. Conservatism established itself with a **pragmatic** view of the world, sceptical about radical change and favoured **tradition**. This allowed it to emerge as the party of gradual reform to benefit all classes and of furthering British national interests abroad. Two main strands of conservatism have been observed in the UK: One Nation conservatism and Thatcherism.

One Nation conservatism

One Nation conservatism is generally traced back to Benjamin Disraeli, Prime Minister in 1867 and 1874–80. Disraeli warned of the dangers of the divisions between two nations – the rich and the poor – and therefore believed that the conditions of the working class needed to be improved to bring together the two nations into one. One Nation conservatism strived to create social unity by using the state to provide a safety net for the least well off. However, the role of the state was to remain small, with individuals and the wider community also encouraged to provide support to the least well off.

After 1945, One Nation conservatives, such as Harold Macmillan (Prime Minister from 1957 to 1963) and Edward Heath (Prime Minister from 1970 to 1974), used the state to promote economic growth, providing a welfare state and recognising trade unions as playing a role in society.

Thatcherism

During the 1970s, the UK suffered renewed economic problems. Unemployment rose and prices also increased, creating the problem of 'stagflation' (a combination of economic stagnation and inflation).

This brought about the 'Thatcherite revolution', initiated by the Thatcher Governments of 1979–90. What became known as the **New Right**, and in the UK was more commonly called 'Thatcherism', amounted to a kind of counter-revolution against both the post-war drift towards state intervention and the spread of liberal social values.

The New Right adopted a more ideological approach driven by a belief in the benefits of free markets, private property and competition which would incentivise hard work, creativity and self-reliant individuals to generate greater wealth and prosperity. Famously, Margaret Thatcher argued that 'there is no such thing as society, there are individual men and women and their families.' These ideals translated into a policy programme that included:

- the sale of council houses
- **privatisation** of the nationalised industries
- reduction of trade union power
- cutting back of the role of the state
- cuts to public spending and taxation

The rolling back of the state also targeted the 'nanny state' – a welfare system that undermines hard work and initiative by creating a culture of dependency.

When it came to other areas, Thatcherism was described as 'neoconservative'; Thatcher was deeply committed to a strong but **minimal state** in order to:

- maintain law and order by increasing the use and length of prison sentences.
- defend the traditional values associated with the nuclear family and the Christian faith, by introducing Section 28 which banned the promotion of homosexuality in schools.
- strengthening national identity; this came increasingly to be expressed as Euroscepticism.

Critics argued it introduced a foreign, ideological element that broke with the Conservative Party's commitment to pragmatism. Thatcherism replaced a worldview that aimed to heal divisions with a view that revelled in an uncaring, selfish and greedy individualism, which placed the 'I' over the 'we'.

Spec Key Term

New Right: In the UK, this refers to an economic policy of neoliberalism, which is an updated version of the classical liberal belief in the free market and self-reliant individual tied to a neoconservative view of society, with the emphasis on order, discipline and authority.

Definition

Privatisation: The selling off of nationalised industries and other state assets, transferring them from the public to the private sector.

KEY TOPIC DEBATE: IS ONE NATION CONSERVATISM THE MAIN IDEOLOGICAL INFLUENCE ON THE CURRENT PARTY?

The modern Conservative Party remains a broad church with a range of views and influences that drive its outlook.

Economy

When it comes to the economy, the party remains wedded to the market and private property to drive wealth creation. The 2024 Manifesto emphasised that 'The Conservative Party will always be the party of business. It is the private sector which will unlock the investment, growth and opportunities of the future.'

Tip: This section uses the 2024 manifestos to analyse the parties. In order to stay up to date, regularly add to this with current policy announcements.

Thatcherite influences

The 2024 Conservative Manifesto contained several economic policies that were clearly Thatcherite reflecting her legacy of free-market economics, tax cuts, deregulation and a strong private sector.

Thatcherite economic policies in the 2024 Conservative Manifesto

Policy	Thatcherite characteristic
Tax cuts, no rise in corporation tax, incentives for investment	Lowering taxes to stimulate investment
Reducing business regulation, Brexit freedoms	Deregulation to transform the economy
Business support, business rates relief, focus on enterprise	Entrepreneurship to create growth
Reducing borrowing/debt, opposing unfunded spending	Reducing public borrowing
Private sector-led growth, limited government role	Keeping the size of government under control

One Nation influences

The 2024 Conservative Manifesto also included several economic policies that can be seen as reflecting One Nation conservatism, even though the overall tone is more free-market and Thatcherite.

One nation economic policies in the 2024 Conservative Manifesto

Policy	One Nation characteristic
Maintain National Living Wage	Reduces in-work poverty, supports social cohesion
Business rates support	Sustains communities, protects local jobs
Fiscal responsibility	Economic security for all
Triple Lock Plus for pensioners	Protects vulnerable elderly
Free childcare expansion	Supports working families, promotes opportunity

Welfare

The Conservative Party remains united in its commitment to make sure that it pays to work.

Thatcherite influences

Several welfare reforms in the 2024 Conservative Manifesto are **clearly Thatcherite** in character, reflecting her emphasis on reducing welfare dependency and prioritising individual responsibility over state support.

Thatcherite welfare reforms in the 2024 Conservative Manifesto

Policy	Thatcherite characteristic
Large-scale reduction in benefit spending	Reducing the size and cost of welfare
Stricter tests for sickness/disability benefits	Reducing 'dependency culture'
Harsher penalties for fraud	Individual responsibility over state support

One Nation influences

While the 2024 Manifesto is largely focused on welfare cost-cutting, its pledges on social care, childcare, family support and help for carers reflect One Nation conservative values of social duty, protection for the vulnerable and fostering national cohesion.

One nation welfare policies in the 2024 Conservative Manifesto

Policy area	One nation characteristic
Social care cap	Protects elderly/disabled from large costs
Support for carers	Recognises duty to support those caring for others
Child Benefit reform	Broadens support for families
Free childcare	Support for working families

Law and Order

The Conservative Party remains strongly committed to its principles of law and order, and this binds the party together.

Thatcherite influences

Several law and order policies in the 2024 Conservative Manifesto are strongly Thatcherite in character, echoing her 'tough on crime' stance, emphasis on authority and belief in deterrence and strong policing.

Thatcherite law and order policies in the 2024 Conservative Manifesto

Policy	Thatcherite characteristic
Harsher penalties, mandatory life orders, three-strikes eviction	Tough sentencing as a deterrent
More officers, visible policing, new powers	Strong belief in law enforcement
More prison places, tougher community sentences	'Prison works'
Evictions, Respect Orders, community payback, crackdown on anti-social behaviour	Restore order and discipline in communities

One Nation influences

Several law and order policies in the 2024 Conservative Manifesto can be seen as One Nation conservative in spirit, reflecting a concern for social cohesion, community safety, support for victims, and rebuilding public trust in policing and justice.

One nation law and order policies in the 2024 Conservative Manifesto

Policy area	One nation characteristic
Neighbourhood policing	Community safety, visible policing, local trust
Victim support and protection	Justice for victims, support for vulnerable groups
Rehabilitation/reintegration of offenders	Break reoffending cycles, support for second chances

Foreign policy

The Conservative Party has always been patriotic and strongly committed to the union of nations within the United Kingdom. In particular, the party is united by its commitment to investing in the armed forces, maintaining the Trident nuclear deterrent and continuing to be a leading partner within NATO.

Thatcherite influences

Several foreign policies in the 2024 Conservative Manifesto are strongly Thatcherite in character, reflecting her legacy of national sovereignty, strong defence, close relations with the US, assertive action against adversaries, and scepticism towards supranational constraints.

Thatcherite foreign policy themes in the 2024 Conservative Manifesto

Policy area	Thatcherite characteristic
Boost defence spending to 2.5% of GDP	Increased defence spending, nuclear deterrent, strong military alliances
Cap legal migration and continue Rwanda deportation scheme	Hard-line immigration/asylum, border control
Stand up against 'axis of authoritarian states' (Russia, China, Iran) via sanctions and alliances	Confront authoritarian states

One Nation

Several foreign policies in the 2024 Conservative Manifesto can be seen as One Nation conservative in character, reflecting a commitment to international cooperation, upholding democratic values, supporting global institutions and protecting vulnerable communities.

One nation foreign policy elements in the 2024 Conservative Manifesto

Policy area	One nation characteristic
International alliances (NATO, UN, G7)	Commitment to multilateralism and global cooperation
Sanctions for human rights abuses	Upholding democratic values and international law
Protecting Overseas Territories	Defending self-determination

Kemi Badenoch as Leader

Photo 3.1 Kemi Badenoch became leader of the Conservative Party after it suffered a landslide defeat in 2024

Source: Carl Court / Staff / Getty Images

Kemi Badenoch inherited a party shattered by its 2024 general election defeat and framed her mission as "revitalising" a historically dominant party that risked long-term marginalisation.

Strategically, Badenoch positioned the Conservatives clearly on the right, arguing that centrist and one-nation ideas had "had their time" and telling sceptical MPs to "get out of the way". Policy signals on immigration, welfare, tax and net-zero were deliberately sharper and closer to Reform UK's platform, aimed at recapturing voters who had defected to the populist right. This reorientation, combined with a combative style at Prime Minister's Questions, helped secure her grip over the parliamentary party despite persistent poor polling.

Electorally, the 2025 local elections were grim, with heavy Conservative losses and further defections to Reform UK, prompting Badenoch to apologise to members while stressing the depth of the post-general-election hole the party was in. Her position was further undermined in January 2026 with the defections of Robert Jenrick, Suella Braverman and Nadim Zahawi to Reform UK. The May 2026 local elections again saw large-scale losses across England, Scotland and Wales, as the party continued to cede ground to both Reform and the Liberal Democrats. However, Badenoch's team highlighted a small improvement in their national vote share, the symbolic recapture of Westminster council and strength in some London boroughs as evidence that the party might have "bottomed out".

Crucially, there was no serious leadership challenge after May 2026, with many MPs judging that replacing Badenoch again would worsen the party's reputation for chaos. Interestingly, her personal poll ratings put her consistently ahead of her party's, which may have been a significant factor for her party.

Going forward, Badenoch must navigate a fragmented right-of-centre vote, deciding whether to keep competing with Reform UK through a harder line on issues like immigration and welfare, or risk a more centrist pivot that could alienate parts of the base. At the same time, she has to hold together a restless parliamentary party and demoralised activist base.

Key Debate Summary: Is One Nation conservatism the main ideological influence on the current party?

For	Theme	Against
✓ The party remains One Nation in its commitment to tackling the cost of living issues and wider environmental problems.	Which faction is stronger today when considering the economy?	✗ The party still holds fiscally conservative views, favouring a minimal state, free market and low tax economy.
✓ The party has stated its aim of protecting the welfare state to ensure work pays and providing a safety net for those unable to work.	Which faction is stronger today when considering welfare?	✗ Reducing welfare dependency and prioritising individual responsibility over state support is a key platform of the party.
✓ The party remains largely united on law and order, seeing it as of central importance to stability and order.	Which faction is stronger today when considering law and order?	✗ The need to balance the books limited the party's law and order with cuts to the Police Service.
✓ One Nation favours a pragmatic approach to foreign affairs, with an emphasis on building bridges.	Which faction is stronger today when considering welfare?	✗ The party supports a tough stance on defence and standing up to authoritarian states.

The Labour Party

Origins of the Labour Party

The Labour Party emerged from the trade union movement at the start of the twentieth century with the aim of representing the newly enfranchised working class. The party was built around the moderate strands of socialism and it seeks to achieve change via Parliament. Typically, the Labour Party has been associated with:

- the pursuit of greater equality in society
- minimising divisions between classes
- state ownership of industry, known as **nationalisation**

Capitalism was accepted as the only reliable means of generating wealth, but it was seen as a very poor means of distributing it. The party is associated with two traditions:

Old Labour

The Labour Party was deeply influenced by the Attlee Government reforms of 1945–51. These gave rise to a brand of socialism, known as **Old Labour (social democracy)**. It was an attempt to create greater equality within a capitalist society by redistributing wealth.

Old Labour came to be associated with three key policies:

1. **A mixed economy** made up of both publicly and privately owned industries. The Attlee Government nationalised the 'commanding heights' of the economy – industries including coal, steel, shipbuilding, the railways, gas and electricity.

2. **Economic management** – an economy regulated by the government, based on the ideas of economist John Maynard Keynes (1883–1946). Keynesianism reflects the belief that governments achieve full employment and stimulate growth by 'reflating' the economy through higher levels of public spending.

3. **Comprehensive social welfare.** Under Attlee, the welfare state was expanded to provide 'cradle to grave' care based on the Beveridge Report (1942), written by the economist and social reformer William Beveridge (1879–1963). The Beveridge Report set out to attack the so-called 'five giants' of want, disease, ignorance, squalor and idleness.

New Labour

By 1992, the Labour Party had suffered four consecutive election defeats and looked to modernise its policies. New Labour ideas formed around the '**Third Way**', believing the old politics of the left and right were obsolete in the modern world.

This period of change culminated in the new look Labour Party under Tony Blair in 1995; the commitment to nationalisation in Clause IV of the Labour Party constitution was abandoned in what was seen as a symbolic break with Labour's past. The Third Way looked to marry together aspects of liberalism with aspects of social democracy:

> » **Market economics.** The economy should be regulated by the market, not the state, accepting the Thatcherite policies of privatisation, reduced union power, lower taxes and deregulation. This included use of the private sector in delivering public services.

> » **Social justice.** The party remained committed to social justice, but equality was reinterpreted to mean social inclusion, with a strong emphasis on education and training to create a competitive workforce and tackling environmental issues as a matter of justice.

> » **Social investment state.** The welfare state needed to be redesigned from universal to targeted benefits to give the individual the means to be independent and to tackle inequality and poverty; welfare was seen as 'a hand up, not a handout'.

> » **Community, not class.** New Labour emphasised that individuals needed to balance their rights with their responsibilities to others based on the ideas of communitarianism.

KEY TOPIC DEBATE: IS THE MODERN LABOUR PARTY MORE INFLUENCED BY OLD LABOUR THAN NEW LABOUR?

Economy

The Labour Party remains united around the idea of economic justice for working people.

Old Labour influences:

Old Labour is traditionally associated with support for public ownership of key industries, state intervention in the economy, and a focus on reducing inequality and protecting workers' rights.

Old Labour economic policies in the 2024 Labour Manifesto

2024 manifesto	Old Labour characteristic
Rail nationalisation, Great British Energy and public control of buses	Nationalisation of key industries
Stronger regulation of utilities and intervention in the water industry	State intervention to protect public interest
Ban on zero-hours contracts and strong employment rights	Support for trade unions and workplace rights
Abolish non-dom status and close loopholes	Progressive taxation and reduce inequality
Investment in childcare, housing and affordable energy	Expansion of welfare state and social justice

New Labour influences:

'New Labour' is marked by a centrist, pro-market approach, fiscal discipline and a focus on social justice through market mechanisms rather than traditional state intervention.

New Labour economic policies in the 2024 Labour Manifesto

2024 manifesto	New Labour characteristics
Tax lock, tough spending rules, focus on stability	Economic competence, avoid 'tax and spend'
Corporation tax cap, business-friendly reforms	Market efficiency, partnership with business
National Wealth Fund to encourage private investment	PFIs, public-private partnerships
'Make Work Pay', childcare support, employment focus	Welfare to work

Welfare

In terms of welfare, the Labour Party comes together around the principle of social justice, although differences remain about how to interpret what social justice means.

Old Labour influences:

Old Labour was characterised by a strong commitment to universal welfare, expansion of public services, robust support for trade unions, and tackling poverty and inequality through state intervention.

Old Labour welfare policies in the 2024 Labour Manifesto

2024 manifesto policy	Old Labour characteristic
Strengthened union rights, fair pay agreements, day-one rights	Collective bargaining and union rights
National Care Service	Cradle to grave welfare
Commitment to reducing child poverty	Collective action against poverty

New Labour influences:

New Labour's centrist approach combining social justice aims with market mechanisms, and a focus on making work pay rather than expanding unconditional welfare.

New Labour welfare policies in the 2024 Labour Manifesto

2024 manifesto policy	New Labour characteristic
Rights and responsibilities, 'people who can work, should work' consequences for non-compliance	Welfare to work
Living wage, free childcare, breakfast clubs	Incentivise employment over welfare
Support into work, Access to Work reforms	Welfare to work*

** There is a suggestion that these welfare reforms are further to the right of New Labour.*

Law and order

The party remains committed to the idea of building a stronger, fairer society and that focusing on crime prevention and rehabilitation is the key to tackling crime.

Old Labour influences:

The central plank of their policy is to focus on social justice: tackling poverty, inequality and rebuilding public services as the key way to make society safer.

Old Labour law and order policies in the 2024 Labour Manifesto

2024 manifesto policy	Old Labour characteristic
Youth hubs, mental health and job support for young people	Prevention, early intervention
Focus on cutting reoffending, reforming prisons	Rehabilitation over punishment
Targeting antisocial behaviour in poorest communities	Protecting vulnerable groups
Rebuilding police and justice system	Strong, well-funded public services

New Labour influences:

New Labour's centrist stance: 'tough on crime, tough on the causes of crime', combining increased police resources, tougher sentencing and community-based prevention, alongside a willingness to use state authority to reassure the public.

New Labour law and order policies in the 2024 Labour Manifesto

2024 manifesto policy	New Labour characteristic
Guarantee of extra officers and named contacts	Emphasis on visible policing and community reassurance
Respect Orders, tough penalties	ASBOs, 'tough on crime'
Youth hubs, knife crime plan	'Tough on the causes of crime' early intervention and support for at-risk youth
Increased powers for the Victims' Commissioner	Victims at the centre of the justice system
Strengthen security at public venues and update counter-extremism rules	Anti-terror laws, expanded police powers
Establishment of a new Border Security Command	Robust approach to illegal immigration*

*There is a suggestion that these immigration reforms are further to the right of New Labour.

Foreign policy

The Labour Party continues to unite around the idea that foreign policy should be based on the aim of making foreign policy about international peace and justice.

Old Labour influences:

Old Labour supports ethical internationalism, support for collective security, anti-militarism, a focus on international development and solidarity with oppressed peoples.

Old Labour foreign policies in the 2024 Labour Manifesto

2024 manifesto policy	Old Labour characteristic
Strengthen UN, NATO, remain in ECHR, uphold international law	Collective security, ethical internationalism
Restore UK leadership, partner with Global South, climate action	Humanitarianism, anti-colonialism
Focus on ceasefires, conflict prevention, peacebuilding	Anti-militarism, diplomacy over force

New Labour influences:

New Labour foreign policy is marked by a strong commitment to multilateralism, the transatlantic alliance, economic globalisation and a blend of values-driven and interest-based diplomacy.

New Labour foreign policies in the 2024 Labour Manifesto

2024 manifesto policy	New Labour characteristic
Unshakeable NATO commitment, nuclear deterrent, defence review	Atlanticism, strong defence
Special relationship, reset with EU, security pacts	Transatlanticism, pragmatically pro-European
Reforming UN, G7, G20, remain in ECHR	Multilateral engagement, human rights
Strategic trade partnerships	Economic globalisation, commercial focus

The Premiership of Keir Starmer

Photo 3.2 Keir Starmer became leader of the Labour Party in 2020 and Prime Minister in 2024

Source: Alishia Abodunde / Stringer / Getty Images

The premiership of Keir Starmer began in July 2024 after Labour won a landslide (in seats at least, but with only 35% of the vote), ending fourteen years of Conservative government. Starmer entered office promising national renewal, economic stability, and a more disciplined style of government after years of turbulence under Boris Johnson, Liz Truss, and Rishi Sunak. His government initially benefited from public exhaustion with Conservative rule, however, by mid-2026, Starmer's leadership had become deeply uncertain, with falling poll ratings, internal Labour unrest, and huge electoral losses triggering significant speculation about his leadership.

Policy profile

- One of Starmer's government's earliest achievements was introducing workers' rights reforms, including stronger protections against unfair dismissal, expanded sick-pay rights, and restrictions on exploitative employment practices. However, 'day-one' rights were delayed to six months after pressure from business.
- Housing and planning reform became another major focus, by relaxing planning restrictions in some areas and accelerated housebuilding targets, although critics argued progress remained too slow.
- In transport, Labour began bringing rail services back into public ownership and expanded powers for local authorities over bus services.

- Starmer also established "Great British Energy," a publicly owned clean energy company intended to encourage investment in renewable energy.
- On social policy, Starmer and Reeves initially refused to abolish the controversial two-child benefit cap, but after significant unrest on the backbenches, Starmer U-turned and it was removed.
- In the economy, Rachel Reeves pursued a strategy aimed at reassuring financial markets while increasing public investment. The 2024 budget introduced major tax rises, intended to stabilise public finances and fund improvements to public services, which were welcomed by the bond markets. However, opponents argued this increased the tax burden to historically high levels and would lead to job losses. Although inflation fell during parts of 2025 and interest rates gradually declined, economic growth remained sluggish. The 2026 Iran war resulted in huge increases in oil prices, triggering another cost-of-living crisis.
- One controversial move involved cuts to winter fuel payments for many pensioners, which critics argued undermined Labour's claim to protect vulnerable groups. After heavy criticism, this was watered down.
- In May 2025, Starmer sparked controversy after warning that Britain risked becoming an "island of strangers" unless immigration was reduced. Critics accused Starmer of echoing the rhetoric of Enoch Powell and attempting to imitate Reform UK's anti-immigration language. Polling suggested the speech failed to win over Reform UK voters while damaging support among Labour's own base, forcing Starmer to later admit he "deeply regretted" the phrase.
- With immigration, the Government, via Home Secretary Shabana Mahmood pursued the so-called Danish Model – a tough asylum system with temporary, not permanent refugee status, stricter family reunion rules, and policies aimed at deterring arrivals and speeding up deportations.
- The government's failure to deliver its key welfare reform bill, aimed at saving £5 billion, through Parliament in July 2025 damaged its standing among its own MPs and contributed to the erosion of Labour's opinion poll lead.
- Foreign policy was an area where Starmer gained praise. He maintained strong support for Ukraine against Russia, improved relations with European allies after years of Brexit tensions and attempted to rebuild Britain's international reputation. In 2025, his government formally recognised Palestine, and in 2026, after a public fallout with President Trump, Starmer refused to be involved in offensive strikes against Iran.

When assessing the Labour Party under Starmer, it is clear that he was politically to the right of much of his party, prioritising fiscal stability, illegal immigration, and reducing the welfare bill. However, his government's focus on workers' rights, housebuilding, improving the NHS, and bringing key industries back under government control also indicated a more left-wing approach.

In office, but not in power

Starmer's popularity declined rapidly during 2025. By early 2026, polling suggested Starmer had become one of the most unpopular prime ministers in modern British history.

- Labour suffered a very poor performance in the 2025 local elections; its vote and seat totals fell sharply. The party lost overall control of one council and failed to gain any new councils, while Reform UK and the Liberal Democrats made large advances.
- In the February 2026 Gorton and Denton by-election, Labour suffered a historic defeat in one of its safest seats, falling to third place behind the Greens and Reform UK. The Greens won with 40.7% of the vote, while Labour's vote share collapsed by over 25%. The result was a major political blow for Starmer and intensified criticism that Labour was losing both left-wing voters to the Greens and working-class voters to Reform UK.
- One of the most damaging events during Starmer's time in office was the Mandelson scandal, involving Starmer's decision to appoint a person with links to Jeffrey Epstein as ambassador to Washington. When the 'Epstein Files' revealed the full depth of their friendship, it triggered intense media scrutiny and calls for Starmer to resign, deepening concern among Labour MPs already uneasy about sliding poll numbers. It resulted in the resignation of Morgan McSweeney and the sacking of several high-profile civil servants. Although he survived, the episode tarnished his reputation and reinforced the view that, once again, others had taken the fall for his errors.
- Consequently, Starmer faced constant speculation about leadership challenges from his former deputy Angela Rayner and former Health Secretary Wes Streeting. An attempt by Andy Burnham to return to Westminster in the Denton & Gorton by-election, potentially enabling him

to challenge Starmer, was blocked, with many unhappy that this resulted in a Green victory when Burnham may well have retained the seat for Labour.

Crisis, what crisis?

By mid-2026, Starmer's leadership was engulfed in extraordinary uncertainty, with the May 2026 local and devolved elections crystallising doubts that had been building for months. Opinion polls at the start of the year already showed his net approval deep in negative territory with a majority of voters telling pollsters he should resign following the Mandelson appointment. The elections – widely billed as a referendum on his leadership – delivered some of Labour's worst results in modern times, with the party losing hundreds of councillors, control of dozens of councils, and seeing Reform UK and the Greens surge in many of its former strongholds. Those knocking on doors for Labour were repeatedly given one message: "Starmer needs to go."

In the aftermath of the election, Starmer insisted he would not "walk away and plunge the country into chaos," but the scale of the losses triggered open talk of a leadership challenge amongst Labour MPs, with many Cabinet ministers privately urging Starmer to set out a timeline for his resignation to allow an orderly transition to new leadership. Streeting resigned, and Burnham found a seat to contest in the North-West – courtesy of Josh Simons, then Labour MP for Makerfield. Starmer, however, continued to argue that "no leadership contest had been triggered," leaving many in the party confounded by his stance.

Starmer's premiership became defined by a perceived lack of competence, and political turmoil. Although his government introduced significant reforms, persistent economic difficulties, controversial policy decisions, and repeated political crises steadily eroded public and party confidence in his leadership. By mid-2026, Starmer was an increasingly weakened, isolated, and vulnerable Prime Minister.

Key Debate Summary: Is the modern Labour Party more influenced by Old Labour than New Labour?

For	Theme	Against
✓ The party emphasises the importance of economic justice.	Which faction is stronger today when considering the economy?	✗ The party still values the role of the market and individual aspiration.
✓ The party supports social justice in its policies on the welfare state.	Which faction is stronger today when considering welfare?	✗ This interpretation still owes much to the idea of social inclusion rather than the concept of the redistribution of wealth.
✓ Tackling poverty and rebuilding public services are the key way to make society safer.	Which faction is stronger today when considering law and order?	✗ There remains a commitment to tackling crime with more police officers and more prisons planned to deal with overcrowding.
✓ There is a wider acceptance of ethical internationalism and support for collective security.	Which faction is stronger today when considering law and order?	✗ The party favours a strong commitment to multilateralism, the transatlantic alliance, economic globalisation and are committed to patriotism and national security.

The Liberal Democrats

Origins

The Liberal Democrats were formed in 1987 through the merger of the Liberal Party and the Social Democratic Party (SDP), which had broken away from the Labour Party in 1981. The Liberal Democrats have drawn on a range of ideological traditions and their liberalism has encompassed both a **classical liberal** belief in a minimal state and the free market, and a **modern liberal** belief in government intervention to deliver the freedom that is needed for individuals to grow and flourish. In foreign policy, the Liberal Democrats come together around a liberal internationalist approach that works through global institutions such as the EU and UN to tackle global issues like climate change and human rights abuses.

Social Liberals – Centre Left

In electoral terms, the Liberal Democrats set out to provide a centrist alternative to the left and the right. However, ideologically they are generally viewed as a centre-left party, based around a Keynesian economic approach, and a larger role for the state in delivering equality of opportunity so everyone can lead fulfilling lives.

Orange Book Liberals – Centre Right

Associated with *The Orange Book*, published in 2004, which contained significant contributions from Nick Clegg, Ed Davey and David Laws, there was growing support within the Liberal Democrats for a stronger free market with a free trade economic strategy. This aimed to shift the Liberal Democrats from the centre left to the centre right. The advent of a Conservative–Liberal Democrat coalition in 2010, although surprising, was only possible with Clegg (a keen Orange Book liberal) as their leader.

The Liberal Democrat 2024 Manifesto

Economy

The Liberal Democrats unite around the idea that individuals should have good, fulfilling and well-paid jobs, while businesses and entrepreneurs who are creative, invest in their workforce and behave responsibly to their employees and to the environment should be supported.

Social liberalism

- Green industrial strategy: £9 billion investment in renewable energy, home insulation and green infrastructure to create jobs and tackle climate change.
- Pro-EU pragmatism: Commitment to repair UK–EU relations and rejoin the Single Market to boost trade and investment.

Orange Book liberalism

- Fiscal responsibility: Reduce national debt as a share of GDP and fund policies through 'careful economic management' rather than borrowing.
- Pro-business stance: Support for small businesses, entrepreneurs and tax reforms to stimulate private-sector growth.

Verdict: Social liberalism dominates in climate and regional policies, but fiscal caution and pro-market reforms reflect Orange Book priorities.

Welfare

The party is united around the belief in delivering welfare that supports people in the hardest of times and delivers equal opportunities across the whole country.

Social liberalism

- Anti-poverty measures: Scrap the two-child benefit cap and abolish the bedroom tax.
- Carer support: Raise the Carer's Allowance, expanding eligibility and ending punitive overpayment clawbacks.
- Disability rights: Reform assessments and involve disabled people in policy design.

Orange Book liberalism

- Work incentives: Replace benefit sanctions with 'incentive-based schemes' to encourage employment.
- Fiscal caution: No commitment to universal basic income or major tax hikes for welfare expansion, despite progressive rhetoric.

Verdict: Overwhelmingly social liberal, with bold redistributive policies.

Law and order

The Liberal Democrats are united around the idea that law and order policy involves being willing to take the preventative measures that actually work to stop crime.

Social liberalism

- Police reform: Ambitious diversity targets, ending disproportionate stop and search, and improving mental health responses.
- Scrap Police and Crime Commissioners.

Orange Book liberalism

- Border security: Create a Border Security Command with expanded powers to tackle smuggling gangs and 'restore order'.
- Online crime agency: Centralised tech-focused policing to combat cybercrime, prioritising efficiency over civil liberties debates.

Verdict: Mixed. Social liberal emphasis on fairness and community policing co-exists with Orange Book-style centralised security measures.

Foreign policy

The Liberal Democrats believe in international liberalism and wants the UK to play an active role, working with the UN, and World Trade Organization to tackle issues like climate change and human rights abuses. Rejoining the European Union is their longer-term objective.

Social liberalism

- Pro-Ukraine stance: Strong support for President Zelensky, and opposition to Trump–Putin negotiations.
- Climate leadership: Pledges to make the UK a 'world leader' in green tech and align pension funds with Paris Agreement goals.

Orange Book liberalism

- Economic pragmatism: Emphasis on EU trade ties and security partnerships as drivers of UK prosperity.
- Defence: Focus on diplomatic and economic alliances.

Verdict: Leans to social liberal on human rights and climate, but pragmatic economic framing of EU relations hints at Orange Book priorities.

The Liberal Democrats under the leadership of Ed Davey

Ed Davey became leader of the Liberal Democrats in 2020 and his leadership has been marked by a distinctive blend of social liberal and Orange Book liberalism, culminating in a record-breaking 2024 general election campaign that restored the party as the third force in British politics. However, his 2024 general election success now sits alongside more mixed local election results and some disillusionment within the party over strategy and direction.

The 2024 general election campaign was defined by Davey's unconventional media stunts such as bungee jumping, paddle boarding, and waterslide rides, that captured public attention and delivered serious messages about party priorities, which helped the Liberal Democrats break through the media dominated by Labour and the Conservatives, making Davey the only major party leader to see a significant improvement in personal favourability during the campaign. The results of the 2024 election vindicated Davey's strategy: the Liberal Democrats won 72 seats, their highest ever in the party's history and the largest number for a third party since the 1920s. The party's gains were concentrated in southern England, particularly in the Conservative "blue wall", thanks to a disciplined, targeted campaign and effective tactical voting.

However, the May 2026 local elections exposed limits, with only small advances in vote share and Reform UK and the Greens surged beyond the Lib Dems. This fuelled disillusionment among activists who argued that his leadership lacked a strong national vision and relied too heavily on electoral tactics rather than a clear ideological message. Some Liberal Democrat MPs and commentators believe the party is effective at targeting and winning specific seats with its large network of supporters, but less successful at presenting itself as a convincing nationwide alternative to either Labour or Reform UK.

There was also criticism that, despite declining support for Labour across the UK, the Liberal Democrats failed to achieve the major national breakthrough that many expected, leaving it open to the resurgent

Green Party, under Zack Polanski, to benefit from Labour's decline. After the 2026 local elections, critics noted that although the Lib Dems made advances, much of the political attention was dominated by the rise of Nigel Farage's Reform UK and growing support for the Green Party.

How ideologically similar are the main political parties?

Table 3.6 Similarities and differences between the political parties

	Similarities	Differences
Economy	Economically, all parties remain committed to the market and aspiration as central to the generation of wealth, higher levels of public spending and a commitment to the economically insecure.	Key divisions remain over tax policy, the role of the state in the economy, especially nationalisation and the need to balance the books.
Welfare	All parties support higher levels of spending on welfare, especially on the NHS and education.	There are differences over the levels of spending and how they are paid for. It is clear that there are wider differences over the role of competition in the delivery of public services and the workings of the benefit system.
Law and order	All parties favour an increase in the number of police officers on the street and investment in law and order.	Differences remain over how to tackle crime, in particular the causes of crime.
Foreign policy	The parties remain committed to an open and outward-facing UK playing a key role in the world. The gap between the parties in relation to defence policy appears to have narrowed following the 2019 Election.	There are clear differences over the relationship with the EU, the wider world and immigration policies, and the free movement of people.

Emerging and minor UK political parties

What is an emerging or 'minor' party?

The 2015 and 2024 General Elections emphatically demonstrated what has gradually become apparent since the 1970s, which is that it is no longer possible to confine a discussion of political ideas and policies in the UK to the ideological positions of the traditional major parties. In 2024 and 2015, minor parties gained, collectively, one-third of the popular vote. These parties may not yet be 'major' parties, in the sense that they have a realistic possibility of winning government power, but reflect the increasing fragmentation of UK politics.

The Scottish National Party (SNP)

The SNP has had a profound impact on UK politics. As well as its central goal of independence from the UK, it has reshaped the political landscape both within Scotland and across the United Kingdom.

Its historic majority in the 2011 Scottish Parliament Election gave it the mandate to hold the 2014 Scottish Independence Referendum - the first in UK history. Although the `no' side prevailed (55% to 45%), the campaign fundamentally changed UK politics, putting the question of Scottish independence at the heart of national debate.

Its long-time leader, Alex Salmond, resigned after the 2014 no vote, and under its new leader, Nicola Sturgeon, the party emerged strengthened, buoyed by a significant decline in Labour's Scottish vote. In 2016 and 2021 the SNP returned to government in the Scottish Parliament for successive terms. In the 2026 Scottish Parliament election, the SNP won 58 seats, 7 short of a majority, on a combined vote share of 33%, which is significantly less than the 49.6% of 2021. Nonetheless as the largest party by a significant margin, they once again returned to Government.

While the party won the vast majority of the 59 Scottish seats in UK general elections in 2015, 2017 and 2019, in 2024, following the demise of Nicola Sturgeon and the ensuing financial scandals and leadership turbulence, the party dropped to only 9 out of 57 seats with Labour winning 37. (See online Case Study for a detailed look at the impact of the SNP on UK politics.)

Visit the companion website for a detailed study of the SNP and a case study on the rise of Plaid Cymru.

CASE STUDY 3.2: THE IMPACT OF REFORM UK

Reform UK, led by Nigel Farage, has become a disruptive force in British politics. While its parliamentary representation remains modest, its influence on parties, public opinion and policy has been significant, reshaping the political landscape and challenging the dominance of the traditional parties.

Impact on parties

Reform UK's most dramatic impact has been on the Conservative Party. By attracting disillusioned Tory voters, Reform UK split the right-wing vote. In 2026, Reform UK secured major Conservative defections including former Home Secretary Suella Braverman, former Immigration Minister Robert Jenrick, and ex-Chancellor Nadhim Zahawi, significantly boosting the party's parliamentary credibility and ministerial experience. In the 2024 General Election, it secured 14% of the vote and five seats, contributing to the Conservatives' worst-ever result and a Labour landslide. This trend continued into the May 2026 local elections in England, where Reform UK made substantial gains winning an astonishing 1,453 council seats, and control of 10 more councils, in some areas pushing the Conservatives into third place.

Reform UK has also challenged Labour, particularly in 'Red Wall' areas and parts of Wales. In 2024, it came second in 89 constituencies, signalling a growing threat to Labour's working-class base. This pressure became clearer in the 2026 Welsh Senedd elections, where Reform UK achieved around 30% of the vote and a third of the seats, cutting into Labour's dominance. Similarly, in the 2026 Scottish Parliament elections, Reform UK gained visibility and support, winning 17 seats and around 16% of the vote, highlighting dissatisfaction with both Labour and SNP voters. In response, Labour MPs – especially in vulnerable constituencies – have pushed for tougher stances on immigration and cost of living policies.

Impact on public opinion

Reform UK has tapped into widespread disaffection with the political establishment, appealing to voters who feel ignored by mainstream parties. Its support base includes older, working-class voters and former Conservatives, but it has also attracted Labour voters. By 2026, consistent polling above 20% and strong performances in local and devolved elections reinforced its status as a credible political force rather than a fringe protest party. This demonstrated organisational growth and the ability to convert national polling into real electoral gains. Media coverage, especially via social media, has amplified its messaging on immigration, national identity and political distrust.

Impact on policy

Reform UK's platform remains populist and right wing, advocating tax cuts, reduced state intervention, a rollback of net zero policies, and withdrawal from the ECHR. Although widely criticised as economically unrealistic, these proposals have shifted the terms of political debate. Its hard-line stance on immigration – calling for strict limits and reduced legal constraints on deportations – has pressured both Labour and the Conservatives to adopt tougher rhetoric and policies. Following Reform UK's advances in the 2026 elections, this policy influence has deepened. Both major parties have increasingly emphasised border control and some scepticism toward rapid net zero targets.

Criticism

Criticism of Reform UK are that it is a 'one man band' dominated by Farage, rather than a credible political party. Moreover, concerns have been raised about some Reform UK candidates posting racist and homophobic social media posts, exposing poor vetting processes and unsavoury attitudes amongst supporters.

CASE STUDY 3.3: THE GREEN PARTY UNDER ZACK POLANSKI

In August 2025 Zack Polanski, the Green Party's deputy leader since 2022 and a London Assembly member, campaigned and won the leadership election on an "eco-populist" platform that linked the climate emergency directly to the cost-of-living crisis. He argued that the Greens must be bolder in challenging both Labour and Reform UK, and called for the party to learn from Nigel Farage's communication style while rejecting his politics.

Polanski won 85% of the votes with the largest ever turnout in a Green leadership contest. He pledged to replace the first-past-the-post system, renationalise water, introduce a wealth tax on the "super-rich", and framed the Greens as the genuine left alternative to the Labour government.

Policy profile

Economic justice and "eco-populism": Polanski's signature policy is a progressive wealth tax funded by extreme-wealth levies, intended to finance universal free childcare, expanded SEND education, green jobs, and a modest Universal Basic Income. He argues that people cannot prioritise climate action while struggling with high rents, energy bills, and food prices; therefore, economic redistribution is a prerequisite for ecological transition.

Public services and housing: The party committed to renationalising water companies, ending private profit in essential utilities, and launching a massive programme to deliver warm, affordable homes. Polanski pledged to tackle the housing crisis through public investment rather than austerity-driven cuts.

Foreign policy: Polanski has been unequivocal in describing the UK government as complicit in the "genocide" in Gaza, calling for an immediate arms embargo on Israel. He has advocated eventual UK withdrawal from NATO, citing concerns over militarism and the threat posed by Donald Trump's foreign adventures. He also criticised the government's immigration policy.

Electoral strategy and gains

Within six months of taking office, Polanski led the Greens to their first ever Westminster by-election victory: Hannah Spencer won Gorton and Denton on 29 January 2026, defeating both Labour and Reform UK with a majority of 4,402. The win was framed as a "Reform–Green battle" and attracted left-leaning, especially Muslim, voters disillusioned by Labour's Gaza policy. Shortly after, party membership surged past 200 000 – three times the figure at the start of his term.

May 2026 elections

The Greens achieved historic success in the May 2026 local elections, securing their best-ever performance with a suggested national vote share of 18% and winning control of four councils and gaining 550 new councillors. The party won its first-ever elected mayors, in Hackney and Lewisham, which Polanski described as "historic victories" that signal Labour's dominance was over.

Criticism

Polanski's popularity suffered a dramatic collapse in the days before the election, falling 14 points to -27 in just one week when Polanski shared a post suggesting heavy-handed police treatment during an arrest, prompting public criticism from Met Police Commissioner Sir Mark Rowley, condemnation from party members, and Starmer labelling his actions "disgraceful". Further, as Zack Polanski became a significant figure on the political scene, he faced scrutiny over falsely claiming to be a British Red Cross spokesperson, his past hypnotherapy "breast enlargement" claims, and failing to pay council tax while living on an east London houseboat, all of which he has now admitted and apologised for. Moreover, concerns have been raised about some Green candidates' antisemitic social media posts, exposing poor vetting processes and unsavoury attitudes amongst supporters.

Visit the companion website for earlier case studies from the Conservatives, Labour, Liberal Democrats and UKIP.

In July 2025, Jeremy Corbyn and Zarah Sultana launched Your Party to challenge wealth inequality and corporate power, rejecting Labour's right-wing drift and Reform UK's divisiveness. Corbyn said: "It's time for a new kind of political party – one that belongs to you", targeting child poverty and war spending. Factional infighting soon erupted: Sultana's unilateral membership launch sparked significant infighting; two MPs quit. Over 200,000 signed up for updates, though only 50,000 became paid members as supporters lost faith amid the chaos. In February 2026's leadership election, Corbyn's faction won the majority of executive seats, making him parliamentary leader, amid accusations of "witch hunts".

KEY TOPIC DEBATE: DO MINOR PARTIES HAVE A BIG IMPACT IN THE UK?

The success of minor parties in recent years is driven by partisan and class dealignment. This has seen attachment to the main political parties decline, creating a fragmentation of the electorate and much higher levels of electoral volatility. Added to this is the failure of the main political parties to clearly represent issues important to certain voters. This is particularly true where there has been a rise of issues that cut across the traditional left–right spectrum such as Brexit, Scottish independence and the environment. These divides have created new political tribes that do not fit neatly into the traditional voting blocks that back the main political parties.

✅ **Minor parties have changed the electoral landscape in the United Kingdom, both in Westminster and other elections.**

» In the 2024 UK General Election, Reform UK received a record vote share and seats receiving 4,117,620 votes (14.3% of the national vote), its highest ever, making it the third-largest party by vote share. It won a record five seats, all gained from the Conservatives, and came second in 98 constituencies. In the 2026 local elections, Reform UK gained 1,453 councillors and took control of 14 councils, with a vote share of approximately 27%. This built on their 2025 results where they won 31% of the vote, took control of 10 councils and won two Metro Mayor elections in Greater Lincolnshire, and in Hull and East Yorkshire, The Greens took control of 4 councils and won 2 Mayoralties in Hackney and Lewisham, achieving 18% vote share.

» In the 2024 General Election, the Greens had their best-ever result receiving 1.94 million votes (6.7% UK vote share), their highest ever in a general election, up from 3% in 2019. In the 2026 local elections, the first under Zack Polanski, the Greens had a net gain of 550 new councillors, smashing their 2025 gain of 43 councillors. Most significantly, in February 2026, they won the Gorton and Denton by-election, polling 40% of the vote, their largest ever share of the vote in a Westminster election. This sent shockwaves through the established parties.

» The SNP was the largest party in the Scottish Parliament following the elections in 2007, 2011, 2016, 2021 and 2026 and went on to form the government on each occasion. It was also the largest party in Scotland in the general elections of 2015, 2017 and 2019, and was the third largest party in the Commons from 2019 to 2024.

» Minor and emerging parties have challenged FPTP's ability to deliver strong, stable one-party governments based on clear majorities. In two of the five elections between 2010 and 2024, FPTP delivered hung parliaments.

» Following the 2017 election, the DUP propped up Theresa May's Government via a 'confidence and supply' deal with the Conservative Party. As part of the negotiations, the DUP secured additional annual spending commitments for Northern Ireland.

❌ **General elections, and therefore the Commons, remains dominated by the main parties as a result of FPTP.**

» The main issue facing minor parties is the use of FPTP for Westminster elections. Whilst minor parties may poll well between elections, when it comes to general elections, their votes get squeezed as it is clear that only the main political parties have a realistic chance of winning, and both 2019 and 2024 saw results that delivered a strong, one-party government with large majorities.

» In the 2024 General Election, Reform UK won 14.3% of votes (4.1 million) but secured just 5 seats (0.8% of MPs), while the Greens gained 6.7% of votes (1.9 million) for 4 seats (0.6%). Labour's 34% vote share delivered a 412-seat landslide, underscoring FPTP's disproportionality.

» Minor parties' support, which is spread nationally rather than concentrated, fails to translate into seats, for example, Reform came second in 98 constituencies. This disparity, where Labour needed 23,500 votes per seat versus Reform's 820,000, illustrates FPTP's bias against minor parties. Only parties with a concentrated, regional vote, such as the SNP, can really breakthrough in general elections due to this limitation.

✅ **Minor parties have a huge impact by introducing issues on to the political agenda that have been neglected by the main political parties.**

» In 2024, Reform UK focused on immigration during the general election campaign, ensuring that it was one of the most important issues of the election.

» Also in 2024, the Green Party adopted a very tough stance on the Gaza conflict, giving a voice to those who were unhappy with Starmer's approach. This was also done by a number of independent MPs.

» The SNP brought the issue of Scottish independence to the table, leading to the 2014 Independence Referendum and pressure for IndyRef2 because of its dominance of Scottish elections.

» UKIP's concern with the EU and immigration during the 2010s brought these issues on to the agenda, when none of the main parties were discussing them.

❌ **Where emerging and minor parties place issues on the agenda, their policies are often adopted by the main parties, limiting their chances of long-term success. This is known as co-optation.**

» Minor and emerging parties often raise issues that are distinctive; however, where these issues offer a threat to the voter base of one of the main parties, this policy is poached by the main party, limiting the political space for minor parties to gain votes.

» Because of the success of Reform in the 2024 General Election, the Starmer Government adopted a very strong approach to immigration to challenge Reform.

» They also toughened up their rhetoric on the Gaza conflict to win back voters.

» The Brexit strategy and immigration proposals of the 2019 Conservative Party manifesto effectively collapsed the political space for either UKIP / Brexit Party to operate in.

» In response to UKIP's success in the 2010s, the Conservatives and Labour produced policies to introduce immigration controls in the 2015 Election, and the Tories pledged the EU referendum to counter UKIP's electoral threat.

✅ **Minor parties have provided an alternative route of political participation for many that feel unrepresented by the main political parties.**

» Reform UK and the Green Party are the only parties with rapidly increasing membership, while Labour, Conservatives, Lib Dems and SNP have all seen declines.

» In February 2025, Nigel Farage announced Reform had exceeded 200,000 members, overtaking the Conservative Party's 131,680, and as of May, it had surpassed 230,000. In contrast, Labour's membership fell below 400,000 for the first time since 2015, standing at 370,450 at the end of 2023, down from a peak of 564,443 in 2017.

» The Green Party surpassed 200,000 members in March 2026, tripling from 68,000 in 2025. This surge stems from leader Zack Polanski's "eco-populist" appeal, capturing disillusioned Labour voters amid Keir Starmer's rightward shift. The Gorton and Denton by-election win and consistent 15% polling boosted momentum, making the Greens the third-largest UK party behind Reform UK and Labour.

» Liberal Democrat membership also dropped to 63,000 in early 2025, and the SNP's membership fell from a peak of 125,000 in 2019 to roughly 65,000 in 2023.

» Reform's surge has also boosted its finances, with estimates suggesting an increase of about £3.5 million in membership revenue since 2022. Green membership tripling to 200,000 has boosted their subscriptions to £10–20m/year, with a five-fold increase in small donations and total income up by 200–300%. This dramatic rise signals the Greens and Reform UK's growing grassroots strength and their new role as a major force in UK politics, as the established parties' memberships shrink.

❌ **Minor and emerging parties face obstacles in building up the resources to develop their vote and to get their voices heard.**

» Minor parties need to build up and keep a strong membership base to campaign for the party between elections and during election campaigns.

» Minor parties need to raise enough finances to fund their organisation and campaigns, which is extremely difficult given the lack of state funding for parties in the UK. Given that there is a £500 deposit needed for each candidate standing in a general election, parties need significant funds to compete in a large number of seats. Only if the party achieves more than 5% of the vote is the deposit returned; in 2024, 250 Green candidates lost their deposit, costing the party a total of £125,000. This was the highest number for any party in 2024.

» Minor parties can find it difficult to find enough high-quality candidates to stand at elections. This has been an issue for Reform after their 2024 success.

» Minor and emerging parties are now a permanent feature of the UK's political landscape, however their fortunes fluctuate. The SNP has become less significant in Westminster since 2024 and only time will tell if Reform UK and the Greens suffer the same fate as UKIP.

Key Debate Summary: How much impact have minor parties had on UK politics?

For	Theme	Against
✓ Minor parties have changed the electoral landscape, both in Westminster and other elections.	Have minor parties broken the two-party system?	✗ General elections, and therefore the Commons, remain dominated by the main parties because of FPTP.
✓ Minor parties have a huge impact by introducing political issues on to the political agenda that have been neglected by the main political parties.	Can minor parties challenge the role of main parties by changing the agenda?	✗ Where emerging and minor parties place issues on the agenda, their policies are often adopted by the main parties, known as co-optation.
✓ Minor parties have provided an alternative route of political participation for many that feel unrepresented by the main political parties.	Do minor parties have significant impact beyond Westminster?	✗ Minor and emerging parties face obstacles in building up the resources to develop their vote and to get their voices heard.

Party systems in the UK

Political parties are important, not only because of the range of functions they carry out, but also because the relationships between and among them are crucial in structuring the way the political system works in practice. These relationships are called a **party system**.

Two-party system

The traditional view of UK politics is that it is dominated by a **two-party system**. The epitome of the two-party system existed between 1945 and 1970. During this period, Conservative and Labour Parties consistently won over 90% of the vote and also dominated the House of Commons with over 90% of MPs. However, even during this period, two-partyism was called into question during the 13 years of continuous Conservative rule between 1951 and 1964; this looked more like a **dominant party system**.

Two-party politics' key advantage is that it makes possible a system of party government, characterised by stability, choice and accountability. The two major parties offer the electorate a straightforward choice between rival programmes and alternative governments. It is built on two key foundations. The system is supported by stable party loyalties. During the period of 1945 to 1970, around 80% of the public identified with either the Conservative or the Labour Party; with voters' party identification being strongly linked to that of their parents. This was linked to the class-based division within society, with working-class voters identifying with Labour and upper- and middle-class voters identifying with the Conservative Party.

Two-and-a-half-party system

The two-party system started to break down from 1974 onwards, with vote share for the two main parties slipping from 89.4% in 1970 to averaging around the mid-70s until 2015. Despite the lower voter share, thanks to FPTP, the two parties still received over 90% of the seats in the Commons from 1974 to 1992 and 86.7% between 1997 and 2024.

In the 1970s, the main beneficiary of this change was the Liberal Party, achieving 19% of the vote in 1974. Their position as the third party continued throughout the period of 1974 to 2015. However, since 2015, there have been other parties who have challenged them for this position, notably the SNP between 2015 and 2019. Additionally, UKIP in 2015 and Reform UK in 2024 achieved 12% and 14% share of the vote respectively.

Spec Key Term

Party system: The number of parties in a political system, and how those parties compete and cooperate.

Definition

Two-party system: Two parties win most of the votes and seats, and power alternates between the two parties.

Dominant party system: Where one party dominates the government and Parliament, with limited chance of any change in the short term.

Dominant-party systems

A **dominant party system** is where several parties compete for power, but only one wins elections over several years. In such systems, opposition parties may win seats and influence debate but rarely form governments. The UK is usually described as a two-party or two-and-a-half-party system, yet it has shown dominant tendencies at times. From 1979–1997 and 2010–2024 the Conservatives governed continuously (in coalition with the Liberal Democrats from 2010–2015), leading some to see this as a Conservative-dominant phase. Labour's 1997–2010 rule, with three successive victories, is similarly cited as a Labour-dominant era.

> **Definition**
>
> **Multi-party system:** Multiple parties are competing for votes and seats, with the likelihood of minority governments or coalition governments being formed.

Multi-party systems

Since 1997, the UK has started to give way to multi-party systems, which operate in different ways at different levels. This has happened for a number of reasons:

- » Devolution has made nationalist parties more prominent, turning them from being 'minor' Westminster parties into 'major' parties in Scotland and Wales.

- » The use of proportional electoral systems for newly created bodies since 1997 has improved minor and emerging party representation.

- » New issues have emerged that cut across traditional party political battle lines, such as Europe, immigration, the environment and Scottish independence. This has fragmented traditional voting blocs and given impetus to parties such as UKIP, Reform UK, the Green Party and the SNP.

KEY TOPIC DEBATE: IS THE UK A TWO-PARTY SYSTEM?

 **In terms of general elections, the UK remains a two-party system.**

- » All the governments formed since 1945 have been led by either a Conservative or Labour Prime Minister.

- » The Conservative and Labour Parties continue to dominate in terms of the percentage of votes (see Figure 3.3) and more emphatically in terms of the number of seats, although there was a significant dip in 2024.

- » The two main parties continue to dominate due to their clear advantage in terms of party funding.

- » First-past-the-post favours the main two parties.

Figure 3.3 The vote share for the main two parties

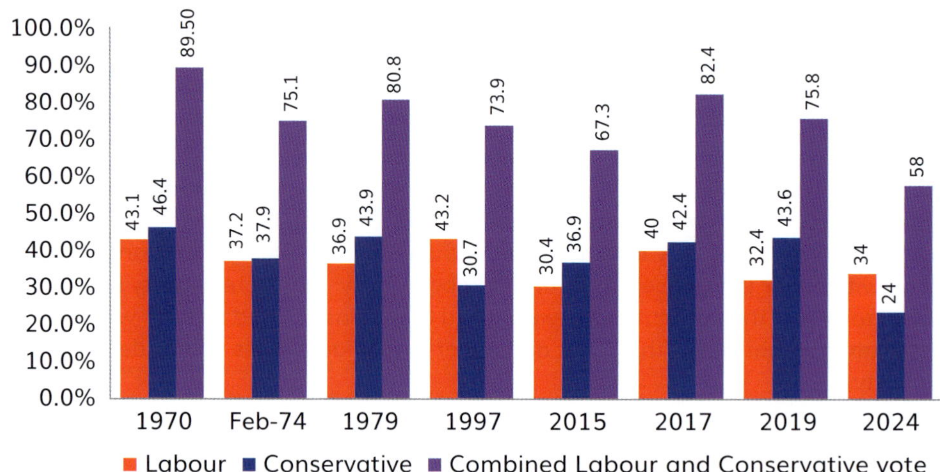

The evidence shows that a two-party system has not been the case in the UK since 1974 due to the breakdown of strong party identification, class-based voting and the emergence of new political issues that have fragmented the party system.

- » Between 1974 and 2015, the Liberal Democrats secured around 18% of votes cast and held a significant number of seats in the Commons. In 2024 it received 72 seats, its highest amount ever.

- » Labour was the dominant party in Scotland until the independence debate in 2014. In 2010, Labour won 41 of the 59 seats, but post referendum in 2015, Labour won only one seat, with the SNP picking up 56 of the 59 seats. This was followed by 35 seats in 2017 and 48 in 2019.

» In two of the five elections between 2010 and 2024, they did not deliver a majority government for one of the two main parties.

✅ **The two main parties still set the political agenda and dominate the media.**
» The key policy ideas are still generated by the main parties, while the main parties are the only parties that can realistically win power and deliver on their promises.
» Media coverage remains focused on the main parties, and their leaders in particular.

❌ **Increasingly the political agenda is being shaped by minor and emerging parties.**
» The potential of UKIP (then) and Reform UK (currently) to take voters from both main parties has seen policy shifts by both the Conservatives and Labour.
» Thoughout 2026 the Green Party has shown itself to be very effective at taking votes from the Labour Party since the election of Zack Polanski as its leader.
» Both the EU Referendum in 2016 and the Scottish Independence Referendum of 2014 emerged from the policy platforms of minor parties.

✅ **While other elections are important, the key elections take place for Westminster as this is the seat of power in the UK.**
» At Westminster, the two big parties continue to dominate, winning 82% of the seats in 2024.
» Westminster sets the direction; while the minor parties seek to influence policy, ultimately the government (usually Labour or Conservative) will make the decisions.

❌ **Outside of Westminster, the two-party system has fragmented into a multi-party system.**
» The Scottish Parliament was controlled until 2007 by a Labour–Liberal Democrat coalition, but since then it has been dominated by the SNP who have been the government since 2011.
» The Welsh Parliament has had four different types of government since 1998: a majority Labour administration, a minority Labour administration, a Labour–Liberal Democrat coalition and a coalition between Labour and Plaid Cymru.

Key Debate Summary: Is the UK a two-party system?

For	Theme	Against
✓ At general elections, the UK remains a two-party system in terms of winning power and winning seats.	Does the two party system still exist in Westminster?	✗ Since 1974, the two-party system has been breaking down, creating a more fragmented system in terms of votes and seats.
✓ The main parties still dominate the political agenda, policymaking and the media.	Do major parties still dominate the political agenda?	✗ Increasingly minor and emerging parties are shaping the agenda, forcing the main parties to change their policies.
✓ Power lies at Westminster, where the main parties dominate.	Do minor parties have significant impact beyond Westminster?	✗ Beyond Westminster, the UK is increasingly a multi-party system with minor and emerging parties winning votes, seats and power.

KEY TOPIC DEBATE: WHAT ARE THE MAIN FACTORS THAT DRIVE PARTY SUCCESS?

Leaders

Party leaders are the most important political figures in the UK; for many of the public, they are the recognisable public face of the party. Providing strong and effective leadership is therefore crucial if the leader is to become an electoral asset for the party.

A leader that can communicate the party's message effectively, bring their party with them and offer a clear sense of purpose and direction can ensure that the party is effective when in power or in opposition, and will deliver election victories.

Tip: This content is very similar to that of Chapters 5 and 6. Use the detailed information provided there to illustrate the points below.

Campaigns

Electoral campaigns have become increasingly centralised, focused on the party leaders and expensive. They are seen as critical to getting the party's supporters out to vote and to convince those who are undecided to vote for the party. In the modern era, campaigns are considered even more important because the electorate has become increasingly likely to switch their votes (see Figure 3.4).

Media

The media support for a political party and its leadership can be important in shaping perceptions in the wider public (see Chapter 6). The more effective their media presence, the easier it is for parties to project their message to the public.

Policy

The right policies, both in terms of manifesto commitments and in terms of delivery when in office, are important for ensuring the success of political parties.

Figure 3.4 Increasing volatility in UK elections

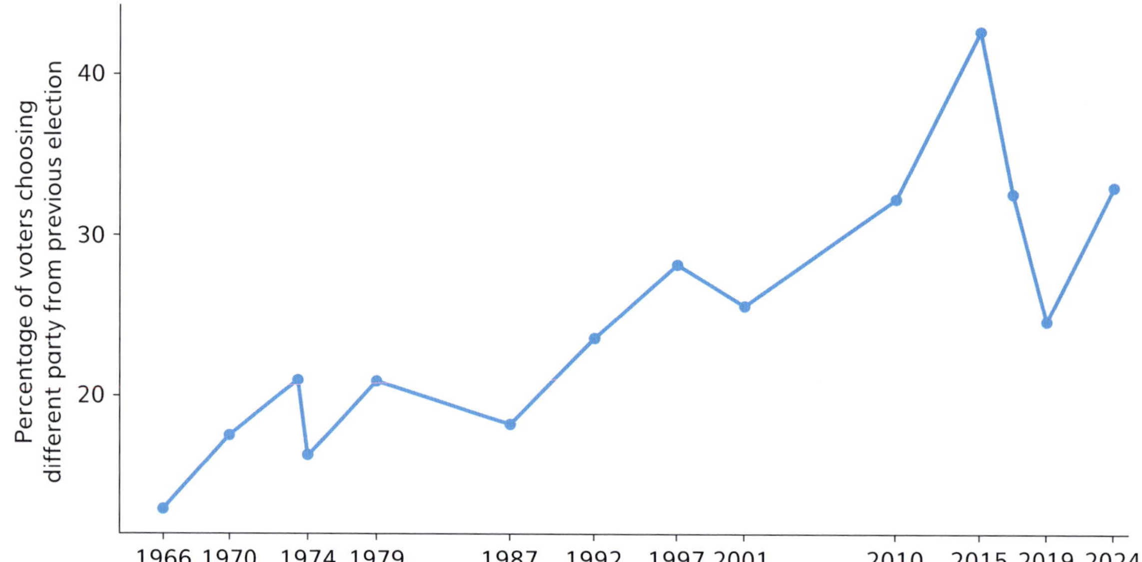

Source: Reproduced from the report Explaining Voter Volatility (2019) by the British Election Study

Party unity

One of the established rules of UK politics is that divided parties appear weak, unable to lead or to deliver on their policy promises. This problem is particularly important where the leadership of a party is openly at war with its members and the party is unable to focus on the key issues of the day.

Opposition

The nature of the opposition faced by a political party is important, both in terms of winning elections and of delivering on its manifesto when in office.

Wider political context

One of the main influences on the success of political parties is events, and how the party responds to those events, particularly when the party is in power.

Key Debate Summary: What are the main factors that drive party success?

For	Theme	Against
✓ Effective leadership can ensure the party is successful when in power or in opposition, and will deliver election victories.	Are party leaders the most important factor in party success?	✗ A party leader may appear strong in public; however, a difficult relationship with their own party can undermine the chances of success.
✓ Effective campaigns are needed to get out the vote and deliver electoral success.	Are campaigns the most important factor in party success?	✗ Generally campaigns in the run-up to elections have limited impact on the result.
✓ A strong relationship with the media and good media image are crucial to success.	Is the media the most important factor in party success?	✗ Media support is no guarantee of success.
✓ The right policies are important for ensuring the success of political parties.	Are policies the most important factor in party success?	✗ Even with the right policies, parties can be unsuccessful without the right leader or media image.
✓ United parties are able to lead, appear strong and can deliver on their policy promises.	Is unity the most important factor in party success?	✗ Despite clear divisions over the EU, the Conservatives were the largest party in the 2010, 2015, 2017 and 2019 elections.
✓ A weaker political opponent increases the chance of party success.	Are weaker opponents an important factor in party success?	✗ In some years a party can face a weak opponent yet still lose the election.
✓ The success of political parties depends on events and how they respond to them.	Are events the most important factor in party success?	✗ Whilst events can shape success, the importance of a united party, with a strong leader and the right policies, remains more important.

Exam Style Questions

- Evaluate the view that political parties no longer fulfil their functions in UK democracy (30).

- Evaluate the view that the time has come for state funding for political parties in the UK (30).

- Evaluate the view that the current Conservative Party is no longer a Thatcherite party (30).

- Evaluate the view that the current Labour Party is still a New Labour Party (30).

- Evaluate the view that the two main political parties are no longer defined by the terms 'left' and 'right' (30).

- Evaluate the view that minor parties now have huge significance in UK politics (30).

- Evaluate the view that there are no significant policy differences between the established political parties in the UK (30).

- Evaluate the view that the UK no longer has a two-party system (30).

- Evaluate the view that the success of political parties now depends more on their leaders than any other factor (30).

Source Question

State funding would lessen parties' dependence on wealthy individuals, corporations and trade unions, reducing the perception that large donors can 'buy' influence or policy favours. This would help restore public trust in the political process. It would also help smaller and newer parties compete with established ones, who often benefit from large private donations. This would create a more level playing field for the parties, removing the unfair advantages that some parties derive from the simple fact that they have wealthy backers. Another argument in favour of state funding is that current regulations are inadequate – state funding is the only solution. Since passing the Political Parties, Elections and Referenda Act in 2000, allegations that donations secure peerages and political influence have continued. Public funds are 'clean' and transparent, reducing the risk of hidden or questionable sources of income. State funding provides the solution, and the cost to the taxpayer would be relatively small, with the parties requiring around £25 million per year of taxpayers' money to carry out their functions.

Parties currently need to reach out to society to seek donations; this means they must listen and be responsive to a range of interests and groups. If parties rely on state funds, they may become less connected to them and wider society. If the level of state funding reflects votes cast in previous elections, it could create a bias in favour of existing parties, which would further entrench the power of the main parties, leaving minor parties behind. State funding is unpalatable as the public already distrusts politicians with public money following the many financial scandals, and they don't like the idea of their money going to parties they do not support, especially if much of the public consider the party to be extremists. In a free democratic society, it is the right of the individual to financially support whichever party or political cause they like, and this right should not be restricted.

Using the source, evaluate the view that state funding of political parties needs to be introduced.

In your response you must:

» *Compare and contrast different opinions in the source*

» *Examine and debate these views in a balanced way*

» *Analyse and evaluate **only** the information presented in the source.*

Chapter Summary

» Political parties fulfil important roles in the UK's representative democracy. However, questions have been raised about whether there is a crisis in party politics.

» Political parties need money to compete effectively and questions have been raised over whether the state funding of parties is now required.

» Political parties in the UK are broad churches, and the three main parties all contain competing ideological influences.

» The Conservative Party was transformed by the rise of Thatcherism while Labour was transformed under Blair as it responded to the challenge of Thatcherism.

» The relationship between these influences within parties influences what they stand for today and how united they appear.

» The rise of minor and emerging parties in the UK have had a major impact on politics and the party system in the UK.

» The relationships between the various factors that ensure party success in the UK remain hotly contested.

Further Resources

Clark, A. (2018) *Political Parties in the UK* (2nd edn) (London: Bloomsbury).

Griffiths, S. and Robert, L. (2018) *British Politics* (3rd edn) (London: Bloomsbury): Chapter 14: Political Parties and Chapter 15: Ideology.

Visit the companion website to access the Further Resources Booklet to explore a range of useful web links related to: Conservatism and Thatcherism, Labour and the Third Way, party funding and the party system.

4 ELECTIONS AND REFERENDUMS

Chapter Preview

Elections are representative democracy in action. When voters cast their ballots, they, rather than politicians or government, are taking control. The task of electing representatives can be done in a wide variety of ways, and each has its strengths and weaknesses. In this chapter, we will look at the role elections play in our democracy, as well as the different electoral systems in use in the UK. We will explore the ways in which the different systems work and the consequences in the way they reflect voters' wishes. We will then analyse the impact of the newer electoral systems and how they have changed the nature of representation in the component nations of the UK.

Following the 2024 General Election, the Electoral Reform Society (ERS) published a report on the systemic flaws of the election, arguing that, 'The way we elect our MPs is bad for voters, bad for governance and bad for democracy.' The ERS was also critical about the general elections of 2019, 2017 and 2015, referring to the latter as 'the most disproportionate in UK history'. By the end of this chapter, you will be able to decide if you agree or disagree with their damning indictment of the first-past-the-post electoral system.

The issue of referendums has been at the forefront of British politics since 2014. Initially, there was the Scottish Independence Referendum in 2014, which was followed by the in/out referendum on the UK's membership of the EU in 2016. Both of these referendums rocked the British political system to its core by challenging the consensus of the UK and its place in Europe. The outcomes of these referendums have caused immense change for the foreseeable future, if not forever.

Key Questions and Debates

» What is the role of elections in UK democracy and are they effective at fulfilling their democratic functions?

» Is the first-past-the-post electoral system fit for purpose in the twenty-first century?

» What has been the impact of the electoral systems introduced into the UK since 1997, and do they make the case for reform?

» Why have referendums been used, and have they had a positive impact on democracy in the UK?

Specification Checklist

3.1. Different electoral systems

» First-past-the-post (FPTP), Additional Member System (AMS), Single Transferable Vote (STV), Supplementary Vote (SV).

» The advantages and disadvantages of these different systems.

» Comparison of first-past-the-post (FPTP) to a different electoral system in a devolved parliament/assembly.

3.2. Referendums and how they are used

» How referendums have been used in the UK and their impact on UK political life since 1997.

» The case for and against referendums in a representative democracy.

3.3. Electoral system analysis

» Debates on why different electoral systems are used in the UK.

» The impact of the electoral system on the government or type of government appointed.

» The impact of different systems on party representation and of electoral systems on voter choice.

Source: Leon Neal / Staff / Getty Images

Elections in the UK

Elections are central to the practice of democracy. The UK's claim to be a democracy is largely based on the nature of its electoral system, and the fact that its elections are based on:

- » Universal adult suffrage
- » One person, one vote
- » A secret ballot
- » Competition between candidates and parties.

Elections are therefore the main link between government and the people, meaning that voting is the most important form of political participation. The opportunities to vote in the UK have, in fact, increased significantly in recent years.

The main elections in the UK are:

- » **General elections** – These are parliamentary elections, in which all the seats in the House of Commons come up for re-election. They must take place within five years of the last election, although within this timeframe, the choice remains with the Prime Minister.
- » **Devolved assembly elections** – These are elections to the Scottish Parliament, the Welsh Parliament and the Northern Ireland Assembly. They are fixed-term elections that take place every four years (first held in 1998 in Northern Ireland and in 1999 in Scotland and Wales).
- » **Local elections** – These are elections to district, borough and county councils. They include elections to the Greater London Assembly, the London Mayor and mayoral elections also taking place in other local authorities. They are fixed-term elections that take place usually every four or five years.

KEY TOPIC DEBATE: DO ELECTIONS ENHANCE OR HINDER UK DEMOCRACY?

Elections fulfil a number of roles in a democracy. They serve to:

- » Remove unwanted governments and form new ones
- » Ensure representation
- » Enable participation and uphold legitimacy
- » Educate the electorate.

Forming governments

✅ **General elections transfer power from one government to the next in a peaceful and stable way.**

- » In the UK, governments are usually formed by the leading members of the majority party in the House of Commons. As the results of general elections are usually clear, governments are generally formed the day after the election, with the leader of the majority party becoming the Prime Minister.
- » Elections in the UK are very effective at removing unwanted governments as can be seen in 1979, 1997 and 2024. These were clear 'change' elections.

❌ **However, elections may not always be successful in forming governments.**

- » FPTP has been less successful at enabling a single 'winning' party to emerge, as the general elections in 2010 and 2017 demonstrated. Governments may therefore be formed through deals negotiated among two or more parties after the election has taken place. These deals may take days (five days in 2010) to negotiate and lead to instability and uncertainty.
- » Also, although FPTP removes unwanted governments, sometimes it removes 'wanted' governments. In February 1974, more people voted for Heath's government, but FPTP provided Wilson's Labour Party with more seats. This was also true in 1951.

Representation

✅ **Elections are a vital channel of communication between government and the people.**

» They create a link between elected politicians and their constituents. This helps to ensure that constituents' concerns are properly articulated and addressed.

» Elections make politicians publicly accountable and ultimately removable. When the public are dissatisfied with their government, elections are the tool to express this; for example, the dismissal of the Conservative Party from government in 2024 was a clear example of this.

» Elections also offer the electorate choice. In the UK, the electorate can choose between many different parties. For example, in every constituency the electorate usually have the opportunity to choose between at least four candidates.

❌ **However, doubts have also been raised about the effectiveness of elections in ensuring representation.**

» General elections in the UK have come under huge criticism because of FPTP. Governments are elected on less than 50% of the vote. In 2019, 229 out of 650 MPs were elected with less than 50% support in their constituencies, and in 2024 this number rocketed to 554 out of 650 MPs. In other words, only 96 MPs won their seat with a majority of votes as shown in Figure 4.1. Here we can see to the left of the dotted line MPs who won with less than 50% of the vote in their constituency.

Figure 4.1 Percentage of the vote won by winning candidates in each constituency, 2024 General Election

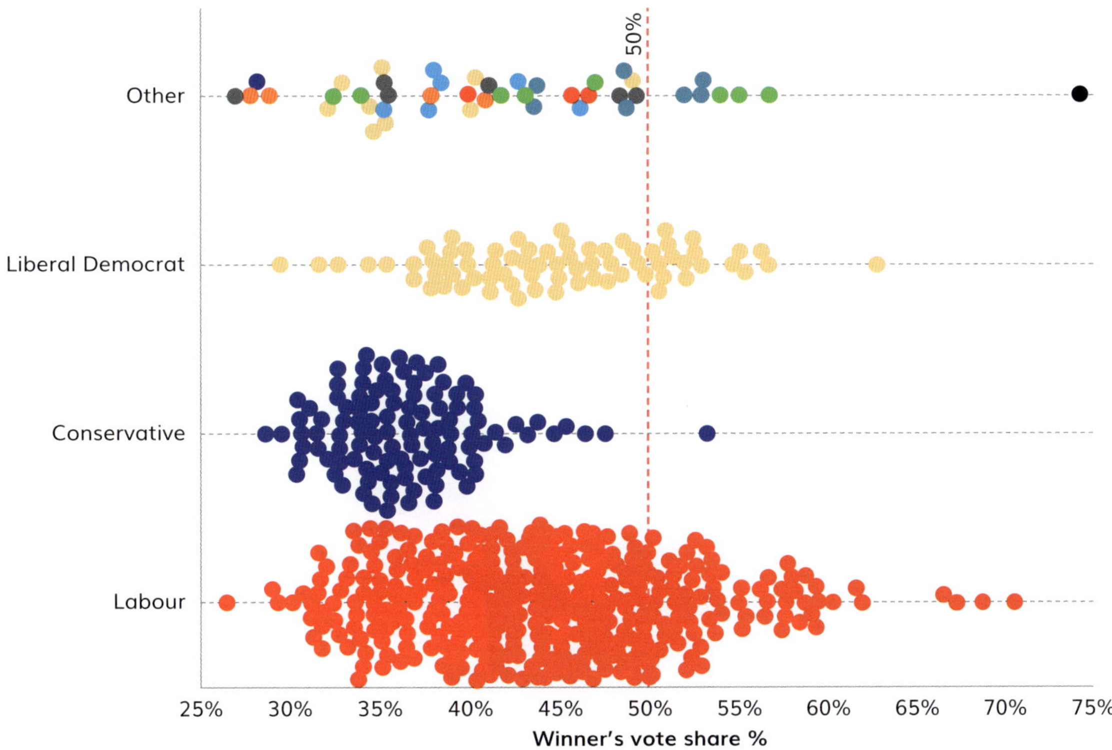

Source: The Electoral Reform Society

» Elections in Britain limit choice. Voters have very little say about which candidates are selected to stand in their constituencies and if they live in **safe seats** their vote can be almost worthless. According to the ERS, 73.7% of votes did not directly affect the outcome in 2024 – 21.2 million votes in total.

» Elections in a representative democracy can lead to a lack of trust in the representative process because there is no guarantee that elected representatives will abide by their mandate. For example, the Liberal Democrats fought the 2010 General Election with a promise to abolish tuition fees and then joined a coalition government that raised them.

Spec Key Term

Safe seat: A seat in which the incumbent has a considerable majority over their closest rival and which is largely immune from swings in voting choice. The same political party retains the seat from election to election.

Participation and legitimacy

✓ **Elections play a crucial role in enabling participation which in turn makes elections legitimate.**

» Participation is a core feature of democracy and elections encourage participation at various levels. Participation is promoted by voting at local, general or mayoral elections and also through joining a political party and actively campaigning for it during elections.

» Elections uphold legitimacy by providing a means through which citizens 'consent' to being governed: the act of voting.

» Legitimacy is maintained by regular, free and fair elections which are held at agreed maximum intervals in which there is a secret ballot and wide adult franchise. Freedom of speech and association help to ensure that elections are 'free and fair'.

✗ **However, elections may not always be successful in upholding legitimacy.**

» Low turnout in general elections has cast doubt on the legitimacy of the UK political system. Voter apathy may be a way in which disillusioned citizens are withholding consent. In 2024, turnout dropped to 59.7%, significantly less than the 69% achieved in 2017.

» The devolved governments' electoral systems, despite using more proportional elections, have failed to advance the levels of turnout. In 2026, the Senedd election achieved a turnout of just 51.4%.

» Falling support for the two 'governing' parties may indicate declining levels of popular satisfaction with the UK political system. In 2024, support for Labour and Conservative stood at just 58% – a historic low.

Education

✓ **Elections educate the public as one of their key functions.**

» As political parties seek to explain current issues and why their way of dealing with them is better than the other parties, they educate the public on the key political issues of the day.

» New ideas and policies are proposed, explained and discussed during campaigns, and parties inform the electorate about current issues and their views on them.

Photo 4.1 Boris Johnson poses after hammering a 'Get Brexit Done' sign into the garden of a supporter, 11 December 2019

Source: Ben Stansall / Getty Images

❌ **However, elections can also misinform the public with half-truths and 'fake news'.**

» Due to the adversarial nature of politics, parties rarely acknowledge the positive aspects of opposition policies, so instead they seek to convince the electorate that other parties aren't telling them the truth.

» In the modern age of social media, politicians resort to repetitive sound bites which oversimplify very complicated issues. For example, 'Get Brexit Done' was a very snappy election slogan in 2019, whereas the reality was more complicated than this. This undermines the electorate's faith and trust in politicians.

Key Debate Summary: Do elections enhance or hinder UK democracy?

For	Theme	Against
✓ General elections serve to transfer power from one government to the next in a peaceful and stable way.	Do elections promote stability?	✗ Elections may not always be successful in forming governments in a stable way.
✓ Elections are a vital channel of communication between government and the people.	How effectively do elections ensure representation of the people?	✗ Doubts have also been raised about the effectiveness of elections in ensuring representation.
✓ Elections play a crucial role in enabling participation which in turn makes elections legitimate.	How effectively do elections enhance participation?	✗ Elections may not always be successful in upholding legitimacy due to FPTP and turnout.
✓ Elections educate the public as one of their key functions.	How effectively do elections educate voters?	✗ Elections can also miseducate the public with half-truths and 'fake news'.

Electoral systems in the UK

Different electoral systems have different political outcomes. It is possible for a party to win an election under one set of rules, but to lose it under another. Similarly, one electoral system may produce a single-party government, while another would lead to coalition government. Electoral systems have a major impact on political parties, on government, and also on the quality of representation and effectiveness of democracy. Which electoral system is used really matters.

For general purposes, the voting systems that are used in the UK can be divided into two broad categories on the basis of how they convert votes into seats:

1. **Non-proportional systems** – This is when larger parties typically win a higher proportion of seats than the proportion of votes they gain in the election. This increases the chances of a single party gaining a parliamentary majority and being able to govern on its own. These can then be divided into:

   » Plurality systems – the party or candidate who polls more votes in their constituency than any other is elected.

   » Majority systems – the party or candidate winning more than 50% of the vote (a majority) in their constituency is elected.

2. **Proportional systems** – These guarantee a close and reliable relationship between the seats won by parties and the votes they gained in the election.

Plurality systems

Plurality systems are electoral systems where the winner of a constituency is the candidate that received the highest number of votes – more than anyone else. The candidate need not win an outright majority in their constituency to be elected.

First-past-the-post

The main voting system used in the UK is **first-past-the-post (FPTP)**, sometimes called the single-member simple plurality system. It is undoubtedly the most important electoral system used in the UK as it is the system that is used for elections to the House of Commons and therefore it serves to form the government, and was also used in mayoral elections in 2024. To stand in elections under FPTP, a deposit has to be paid and this is returned if 5% of the vote is obtained. All citizens aged 18 or over are allowed to vote.

FIRST-PAST-THE-POST

Used for elections to the House of Commons and in England and Wales, for Mayors, Police and Crime Commissioners (since 2024) and for local government elections.

Features:

» It is a constituency system. For UK general elections, there are 650 single-member parliamentary constituencies in the UK. The aim of FPTP in the UK is for a party is to achieve a majority of seats in order to form a government.

» Voters select a single candidate in their constituency by marking the candidate's name with an 'X' on the ballot paper. This reflects the principle of 'one person, one vote'.

» Constituencies are of roughly equal population size, which is ensured by reviews by the Electoral Commission and the Boundary Commission, most recently reviewed for the 2024 Election.

» Each constituency returns a single candidate. This is often seen as the 'winner-takes-all' effect.

» The winning candidate in a constituency needs only to achieve a plurality of votes (one more than their nearest rival). The winner is thus the candidate with the most votes in their constituency. This may not be above 50% of votes cast. Hence, it is possible for the winning candidate to have fewer votes than the other candidates combined.

Example:

» In the example of this constituency from 2024, Sarah Sackman won despite not winning 50% of the votes. There were only 96 MPs out of 650 who won their constituency with more than 50% of the vote in 2024.

Finchley & Golders Green 2024 results

		Votes share	Change compared with 2019
Labour	Sarah Sackman	44.3%	▲ +19.9
Conservative	Alex Deane	35.1%	▼ −8.7
Liberal Democrat	Sarah Hoyle	6.8%	▼ −25.0
Green	Steve Parsons	6.3%	▲ +6.3
Reform UK	Bepi Pezzulli	5.3%	▲ +5.3
Rejoin EU	Brendan Donnelly	1.0%	▲ +1.0
Party of Women	Katharine Murphy	0.6%	▲ 0.6% +0.6
Independent	Michael Shad	0.6%	▲ +0.6

Vote concentration and FPTP

The reason for big disproportionality under FPTP is to do with how votes are spread across the country. Look at three constituencies from 2024:

Party	Southend West & Leigh Votes	%	Peterborough Votes	%	Clacton Votes	%
Labour	16,739	36	13,418	32	7,448	16
Conservative	14,790	32	13,330	32	12,820	28
Reform	8,273	18	5,379	13	21,225	46

Over the three seats, Labour won nearly 38,000 votes and 2 seats, yet Reform only won 1 seat despite winning nearly 35,000 votes, and the Conservatives won no seats at all despite winning over 40,000 votes across the three constituencies.

The key to winning under FPTP is to have a vote concentration which is enough to win you a seat comfortably, but not too comfortably as you pile up too many votes that are meaningless. It was the secret to the SNP's success in Westminster elections between 2015 and 2019. In 2019, they won 81% of the Scottish seats with 45% of the Scottish vote, by having a small margin of votes in many constituencies. However, in 2024 they then lost the vast majority of them, going down to 9, precisely because their 2019 winning margin was so narrow.

Safe and marginal constituencies/seats

A safe seat is one which is seen as secure. In such seats, there is very little chance of the seat changing hands because of the political leanings of the electorate in the constituency concerned and/or the popularity of the incumbent MP. Table 4.1 shows the 20 safest seats in the UK in 2024.

The opposite type of seat is a **marginal seat**, which is one held with a very small majority. They only require a small swing to change hands and therefore are typically the focus of most election campaigns. The 2024 General Election produced a large rise in the number of very marginal seats – 115 seats were won by a margin of 5% or less, 48 more than the 67 seats won by this margin in the 2019 election. Table 4.2 shows the 20 most marginal seats in the UK in 2024, with the most marginal being Hendon, with only 15 votes separating the candidate coming first and the candidate coming second, at the time of the general election. (In May 2025, Runcorn and Helsby was won by Reform by only six votes.)

FPTP was also used for Mayoral and Police and Crime Commissioner Elections in 2024. Figures 4.1 and 4.2 show that, like in general election constituencies all around the UK, results can be extremely close, or easily won.

Table 4.1 Top 20 safest seats in the 2024 General Election

Rank	Constituency	Country/region	Winner/result	Second party	Majority (%)	Majority (votes)
1	Chorley	North West	Spk hold	Green	60.58%	20,575
2	Bootle	North West	Lab hold	RUK	56.54%	21,983
3	Liverpool Walton	North West	Lab hold	RUK	54.89%	20,245
4	Liverpool West Derby	North West	Lab hold	RUK	53.74%	20,423
5	Knowsley	North West	Lab hold	RUK	50.82%	18,319
6	Liverpool Garston	North West	Lab hold	RUK	47.87%	20,104
7	Liverpool Riverside	North West	Lab hold	Green	45.68%	14,793
8	Lewisham East	London	Lab hold	Green	44.47%	18,073
9	York Central	Yorkshire and The Humber	Lab hold	Con	44.21%	19,154
10	Hornsey and Friern Barnet	London	Lab hold	Green	44.15%	21,475
11	Westmorland and Lonsdale	North West	LD gain from Con	Con	43.35%	21,472
12	Widnes and Halewood	North West	Lab hold	RUK	43.09%	16,425
13	Greenwich and Woolwich	London	Lab hold	Green	42.99%	18,366
14	Clapham and Brixton Hill	London	Lab hold	LD	42.13%	18,005
15	Wallasey	North West	Lab hold	RUK	42.10%	17,996
16	Nottingham East	East Midlands	Lab hold	Green	41.65%	15,162
17	Mitcham and Morden	London	Lab hold	Con	41.46%	18,761
18	Dulwich and West Norwood	London	Lab hold	Green	41.41%	18,789
19	Liverpool Wavertree	North West	Lab hold	Green	40.95%	16,304
20	Blaenau Gwent and Rhymney	Wales	Lab hold	PC	40.72%	12,183

Source: Contains parliamentary information licensed under the Open Parliament Licence v3.0

Table 4.2 Top 20 marginal seats in the 2024 General Election

Rank	Constituency	Country/region	Winner/result	Second party	Majority (%)	Majority (votes)
1	Hendon	London	Lab gain from Con	Con	0.04%	15
2	Poole	South West	Lab gain from Con	Con	0.04%	18
3	Basildon and Billericay	East of England	Con hold	Lab	0.05%	20
4	North West Cambridgeshire	East of England	Lab gain from Con	Con	0.09%	39
5	Central Devon	South West	Con hold	Lab	0.11%	61
6	Havant	South East	Con hold	Lab	0.22%	92
7	Exmouth and Exeter East	South West	Con hold	Lab	0.24%	121
8	South Basildon and East Thurrock	East of England	RUK gain from Con	Lab	0.25%	98
9	Beverley and Holderness	Yorkshire and The Humber	Con hold	Lab	0.28%	124
10	Peterborough	East of England	Lab gain from Con	Con	0.28%	118
11	Chelsea and Fulham	London	Lab gain from Con	Con	0.32%	152
12	Blackburn	North West	Ind gain from Lab	Lab	0.34%	132
13	East Londonderry	Northern Ireland	DUP hold	SF	0.43%	179
14	Middlesbrough South and East Cleveland	North East	Lab gain from Con	Con	0.56%	214
15	Forest of Dean	South West	Lab gain from Con	Con	0.58%	278
16	Bromley and Biggin Hill	London	Con hold	Lab	0.65%	302
17	Derbyshire Dales	East Midlands	Lab gain from Con	Con	0.68%	350
18	Sittingbourne and Sheppey	South East	Lab gain from Con	Con	0.87%	355
19	Ely and East Cambridgeshire	East of England	LD gain from Con	Con	0.95%	495
20	North Antrim	Northern Ireland	TUV gain from DUP	DUP	1.09%	450

Source: Contains parliamentary information licensed under the Open Parliament Licence v3.0

Figure 4.2 Mayoral results in the UK in 2024 using first-past-the-post

Sadiq Khan re-elected London Mayor
Vote share by candidate, after all 14 constituencies counted

			Vote share		Change
	Labour	Sadiq Khan	43.8%		▲ +3.8
	Conservative	Susan Hall	32.7%		▼ −2.6
	Lib Dem	Rob Blackie	5.8%		▲ +1.4
	Green	Zoë Garnett	5.8%		▼ −2.0
	Reform UK	Howard Cox	3.2%		▲ +3.2

Greater Manchester mayor result
Vote share by candidate

			Vote share		Change
	Labour	Andy Burnham	63.4%		▼ −3.9
	Conservative	Laura Evans	10.4%		▼ −9.2
	Independent	Nick Buckley	7.6%		▲ +7.6
	Reform UK	Dan Barker	7.5%		▲ +4.8
	Green	Hannah Spencer	6.9%		▲ +2.5
	Lib Dem	Jake Austin	4.2%		▲ +1.1

West Midlands mayor result
Vote share by candidate

			Vote share		Change
	Labour	Richard Parker	37.8%		▼ −1.9
	Conservative	Andy Street	37.5%		▼ −11.2
	Independent	Akhmed Yakoob	11.7%		▲ +11.7
	Reform UK	Elaine Williams	5.8%		▲ +3.6
	Green	Siobhan Harper-Nunes	5.2%		▼ −0.6
	Lib Dem	Sunny Virk	2.0%		▼ −1.5

KEY TOPIC DEBATE: IS FIRST-PAST-THE-POST FIT FOR PURPOSE?

The first-past-the-post electoral system is used for Westminster elections. It has come under criticism for alleged faults and defects. It has, however, survived and distinct advantages have been cited in its favour.

✓ **First-past-the-post delivers strong, single-party government with a clear electoral mandate.**

» With FPTP, voters get what they vote for: winning parties have the ability to carry out their manifesto promises. Under **proportional representation (PR),** policies are decided in post-election deals not endorsed by the electorate.

» FPTP helps to ensure that governments can govern. This happens because the government of the day enjoys majority control of the House of Commons, for example Labour won 411 out of the 650 constituencies at the 2024 Election. Coalition governments, by contrast, are weak and ineffective because they must seek legislative support from two or more parties.

» Single-party governments are stable and cohesive, and so are generally able to survive for a full term in office. This is because the government is united by common ideological loyalties and is subject to the same party disciplines. Coalition governments, by contrast, are often weak and unstable.

❌ **However, strong government comes at the expense of unrepresentative government.**

» FPTP is unfair *because* it discriminates in favour of the two main parties. Both Labour and the Conservatives have benefitted from a 'winner's bonus' under FPTP. For example, in 2024, Labour achieved 34% of the vote and 65% of the seats.

» FPTP is primarily concerned with the election of individual MPs (as opposed to representing political parties); therefore, it is possible with FPTP for the 'wrong' party to win an election. This is what happened in 1951 when the Conservatives achieved a majority but won fewer votes than Labour. In February 1974, the tables were turned, with Labour being the largest party in the Commons with fewer votes than the Conservatives.

» Critics argue that Parliament should mirror the opinion of the electorate, and that a party should get seats in proportion to its votes. The distortion between votes cast and seats won under FPTP is too great to go unnoticed. Figure 4.3 shows this distortion in elections over the post-war era. It is broadly proportionate when there are only two main parties competing, but when more than two parties are popular, it is hugely unfair.

» Proportionality underpins the basic democratic principle of political equality. With PR, everyone's vote has the same value, regardless of the party they support.

» Moreover, it is important to challenge the idea that stable government can only come from FPTP. The Additional Member System (AMS) (see page 118) provided stable, single-party government in 2011 in Scotland. Coalitions and minority governments in the devolved assemblies and parliaments almost always lasted the full term. Similarly, the coalition provided by FPTP in 2010 in Westminster lasted the full five-year term and was very stable, whereas the 2019 single party government resulted in three different PMs in five years.

✅ **The close relationship between MPs and constituencies is a vital feature of the current system.**

» Under FPTP, MPs have a close relationship with constituents. They meet them regularly at 'surgeries', represent their concerns in Parliament and deal with their grievances. This is worth preserving.

Figure 4.3 FPTP proportionality in the post-war era

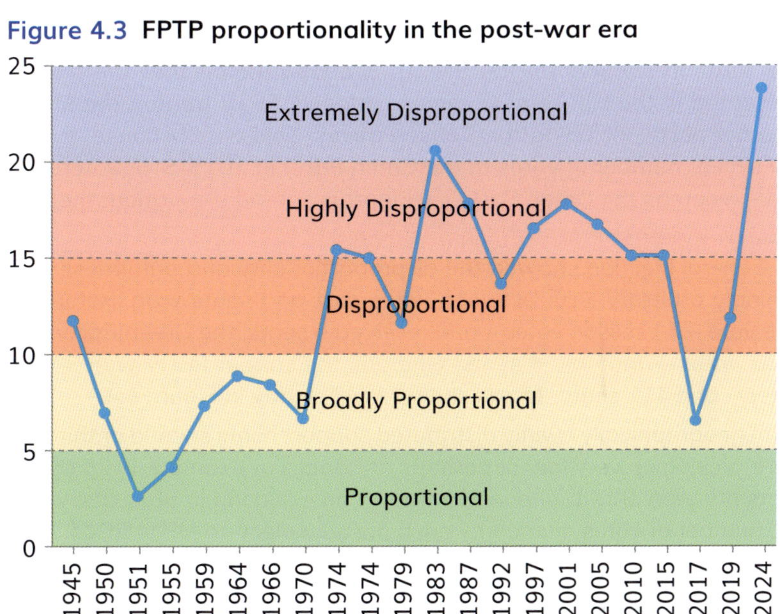

Source: Data from www.makevotesmatter.org.uk

» This means voters can have a direct effect on issues and it also means MPs must be accountable to their constituents come the next election.

✖ **Other systems also have good MP–constituency links. FPTP is not unique in this feature.**

» The Additional Member System (AMS) (see page 118) preserves the MP–constituency link because it includes a large FPTP element.

» The Single Transferable Vote (STV) (see page 122) gives constituents a choice of members to represent them in multi-member constituencies.

» Supplementary Vote (SV) (see page 116) ensures that those elected are chosen by 50% or more of their constituents.

» Because under FPTP most MPs are elected on a plurality, not a majority, they are not truly representative of their constituency. Table 4.3 shows the seven smallest vote shares in the 2024 General Election.

Table 4.3 **The seven smallest majorities of the 2024 General Election**

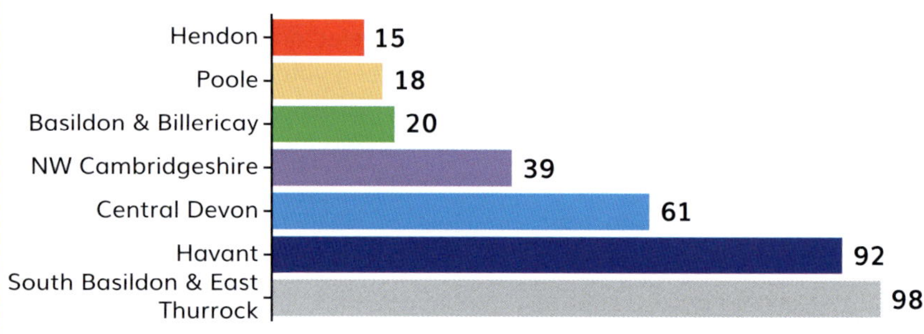

✔ **First-past-the-post has the effect of keeping out extremist parties by giving one of the larger parties a 'winner's bonus'.**

» In order to win a seat under FPTP, candidates need to win a large number of votes in each constituency. This concentration of votes is realistically only achievable by a few parties.

» A 'winner's bonus' occurs as small shifts in votes between the two main parties lead to dramatic changes in their seats. Parties can win 'landslide' victories on the basis of relatively modest electoral support. For example, in 2024, Labour won a landslide of 411 seats – 65% of the total seats based on 34% of the total vote.

» The 2015 and 2017 General Elections produced results that were biased *in favour* of a small party. The surge in support for the SNP in Scotland meant that the party ended up being over-represented in the House of Commons. Indeed, FPTP treated the SNP more favourably than any other party, including the Conservatives. This was because, even though the SNP received a similar number of votes to the Green Party in 2015, SNP voters live in a small area – Scotland – whereas the Green Party's support is spread throughout the country.

✖ **Opponents say it discriminates against almost ALL small parties.**

» The 2024 General Election showed the disproportionality and unfairness of the FPTP system with seemingly arbitrary links between votes cast and seats won. Reform UK received over 14% of the vote – 4.1 million votes – and received 5 seats; the Green Party won 7% of the vote – 1.9 million votes – and only 4 seats; whereas the Labour Party won 34% of the vote – 9.7 million votes – and 411 seats. This is shown most clearly in Figure 4.4.

» Parties with geographically evenly distributed support come second or third in elections almost everywhere, picking up very few or perhaps no seats. For example, in 2015, UKIP came second in 190 seats but won only 1, and in 2024 they came second in 98 seats, winning 5. Figure 4.5 shows the number of votes needed by each party to elect an MP in 2024.

» Under PR, fewer votes are 'wasted', which should strengthen electoral turnout and promote civic engagement.

Figure 4.4 Difference between votes cast and seats won in UK general elections in 2024

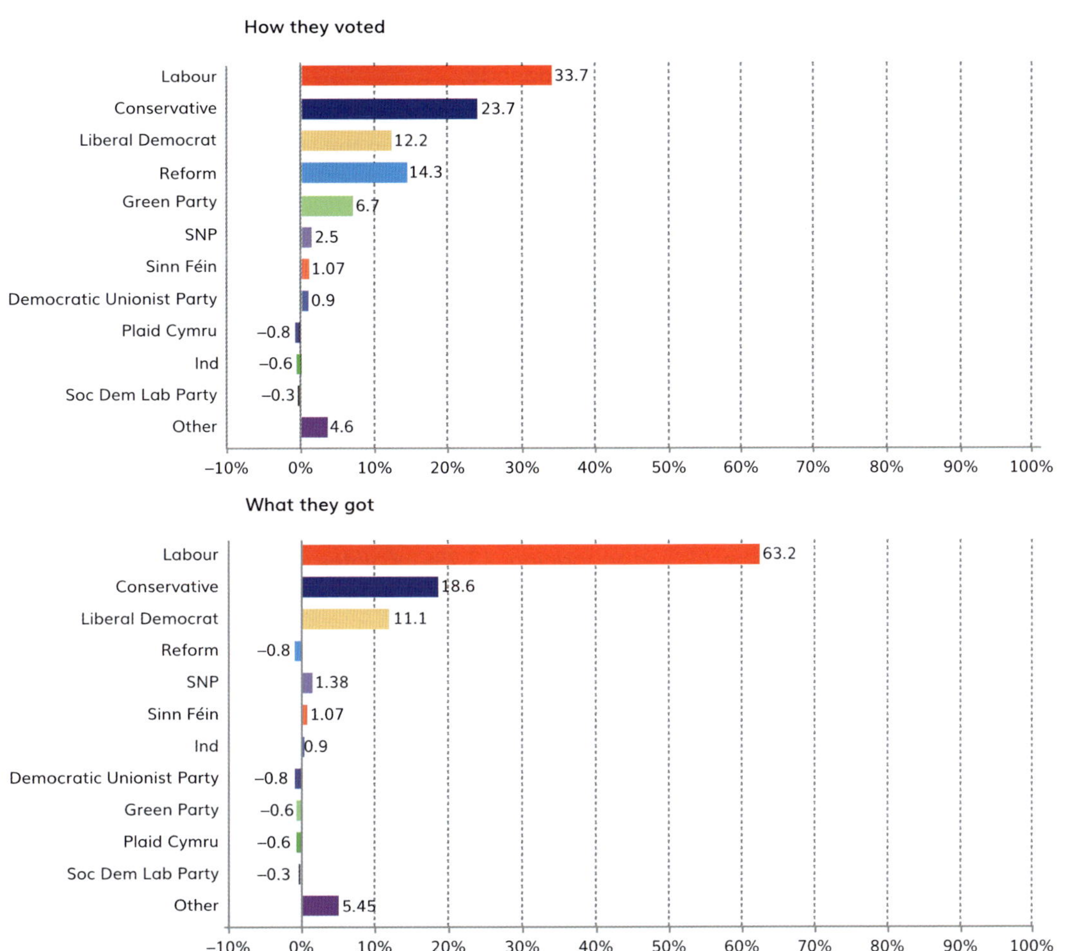

Source: Data from FairVote Canada

Figure 4.5 Votes needed per MP

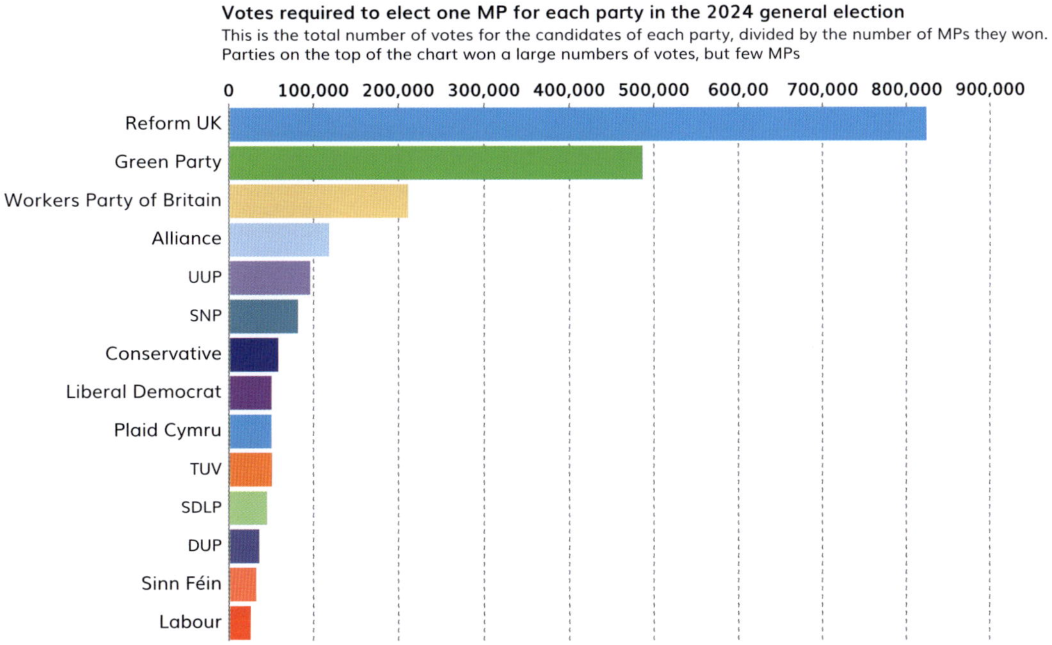

Votes required to elect one MP for each party in the 2024 general election
This is the total number of votes for the candidates of each party, divided by the number of MPs they won.
Parties on the top of the chart won a large numbers of votes, but few MPs

Source: © Electoral Reform Society

✓ **The system provides a clear choice and the two-party format mirrors the natural divide in society, also making governments accountable.**

» FPTP offers voters a clear and simple choice between potential parties of government, each committed to a different policy or ideological agenda.

» Although the proportion of votes gained by the two main parties has fallen – from over 95% to a low of 58% in 2024 – they have continued to have a hold on the House of Commons. Even in 2024, *82% of MPs belonged to either the Labour or Conservative Parties.*

» FPTP also has the big advantage of enabling the electorate to get rid of unwanted governments and make a clear break with the past. This can be seen in 2024, 2010, 1997 and 1979. Under coalitions, the electorate have a limited say in how the next government is formed; it is decided by the parties in private after the election.

✗ **The two-party dominance created by FPTP is hard for minor parties to break, making the party choice on offer an illusion.**

» Two-party politics restricts choice, lacks representation and places too much power in the hands of the executive.

» It discourages potential supporters of smaller parties from voting for them because their vote would be 'wasted' as it would not affect the outcome of the election.

» According to analysis by the ERS, a whopping 73.7% of votes did not directly affect the outcome in 2024 – 21.2 million votes in total. In Figure 4.6 this is shown by the unrepresented

Figure 4.6 Votes cast in 2024

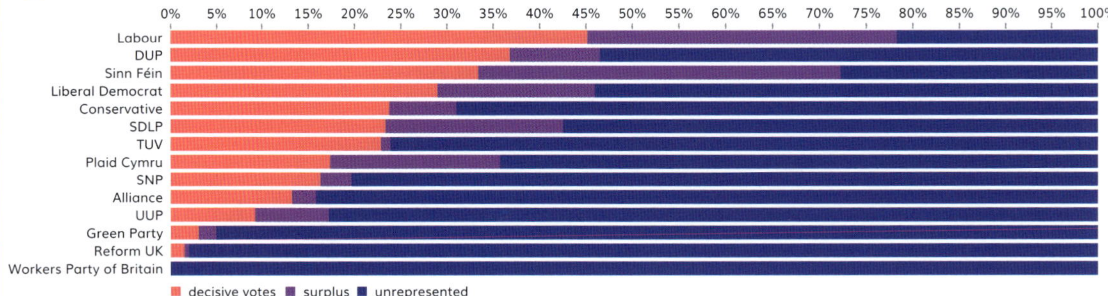

Source: © Electoral Reform Society

votes, which were cast for unsuccessful candidates, and surplus votes, which were not needed to help the winning candidate secure the seat.

» The problem of **wasted votes** is all the greater because Labour and the Conservatives traditionally have 'heartlands' in which seats are 'safe'. The outcome of a general election is therefore determined by what happens in 'marginal' seats.

» In safe seats, votes are wasted on losing candidates, or on huge majorities; hence, not everybody's vote is 'worth' the same.

» PR electoral systems distribute political power more widely. Because a wider range of parties are involved in the formulation of policy, decision making becomes a process of consultation, negotiation and compromise. Partnership politics therefore replaces adversarial politics.

✓ **FPTP is simple, easy to operate, and quick to produce a result.**

» It is a tried-and-tested system with a certain amount of public acceptance. All that's required is an 'X' in the relevant box. It is uncomplicated and gives citizens clarity and confidence in use. Other electoral systems appear cumbersome and complex.

» It is quick to produce a result; there is no delay and elected members and governments are soon in place.

» PR systems can take some time for the final outcome to be calculated, whereas FPTP results are very quick. Houghton and Sunderland South claimed the honours in 2024 declaring their result at 11:13pm. However, the quickest a result has been declared was in 2001, when Sunderland South declared at 10:43pm, just 43 minutes after polls closed.

❌ **However, one could counter the arguments above not as significant, but as opposing arguments.**

» The electorate can cope with listing a numerical choice and preferences. This happens in other developed nations and there is no evidence that the UK is less educated than our European counterparts, who use a variety of other electoral methods. Northern Ireland uses Single Transferable Vote (STV) for its Assembly elections and this has been a success.

» Some suggest that the 'speed' attribute is overrated. Although speed is valued, accuracy and fairness are more desirable outcomes. Also, if electronic voting was introduced, other systems would be equally swift.

Key Debate Summary: Is first-past-the-post fit for purpose?

For	Theme	Against
✓ FPTP delivers strong, single-party government with a clear electoral mandate.	Is single party government more important than representation?	✗ Strong government comes at the expense of unrepresentative government.
✓ The close relationship between MPs and constituencies is vital.	How effectively do systems provide close relationships with MPs?	✗ Other systems also have good MP–constituency links. FPTP is not unique in this feature.
✓ FPTP keeps out extremist parties by giving one of the larger parties a 'winner's bonus'.	Is keeping out extremist parties more important than representing all smaller parties?	✗ It discriminates against almost all small parties.
✓ The two-party format mirrors the natural divide in society.	Is it a positive of FPTP that it reinforces the two-party system?	✗ The two-party dominance is hard for minor parties to break, limiting party choice.
✓ FPTP is simple and easy to operate and quick to produce a result.	Is being easy to work, and quick with a result a strong reason to keep FPTP?	✗ The argument that FPTP is simple to use is not a good enough reason to keep it. PR systems are also capable of producing results quickly these days.

Visit the companion website for case studies of the 2015 and 2010 General Elections from the previous fifth edition.

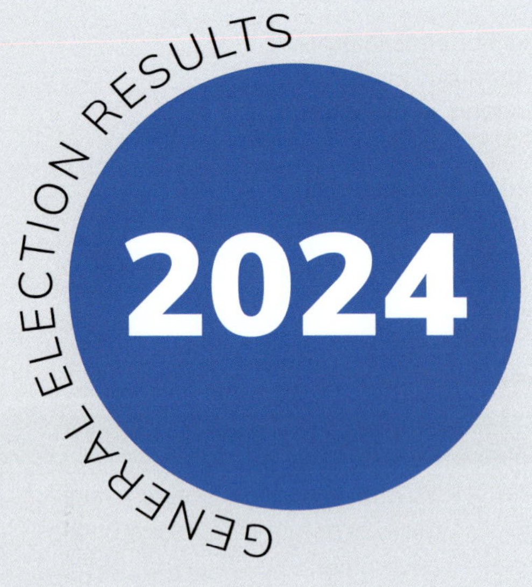

KEY STATISTICS

		Seats won out of 650	Change	Share of seats won (%)	Votes won	Share Change
Seats contested	650					
Turnout	59.9%					
Overall Outcome	Labour majority government					
	Labour	411	+211	33.7	9,708,716	+1.6
	Conservative	121	-251	23.7	6,828,925	-19.9
	Lib Dem	72	+64	12.2	3,519,143	+0.7
	SNP	9	-39	2.5	724,758	-1.4
	Sinn Féin	7	0	0.7	210,891	+0.1
	Independent	6	+6	2.0	564,042	+1.4
	Reform UK	5	+5	14.3	4,117,610	12.3
	DUP	5	-3	0.6	172,058	-0.2
	Greens	4	+3	6.7	1,944,501	+4.0
	Plaid Cymru	4	+2	0.7	194,811	+0.2
	SDLP	2	0	0.3	86,861	-0.1
	Alliance Party	1	0	0.4	117,191	0.4
	UUP	1	+1	0.3	94,779	0.0
	TUV	1	+1	0.2	48,685	+0.2

Compared with the results of the 2019 election:

OTHER KEY FACTS

 **42.6%** 42.6% of the vote went to parties other than the Conservatives, Labour or Liberal Democrats.

 **208** Labour gained 208 seats and increased their vote share by 2%.

244 Conservatives lost 244 seats and decreased their vote share by 13%.

 **61** The Liberal Democrats gained 61 seats to 72 seats (their highest amount ever) yet only increased their vote share by 0.5%.

 **5** Reform received 4.1 million votes and 5 seats; previously they had 1 seat.

 **9** The SNP lost 39 seats, down to 9 and nearly half of their vote share (1.2 million to 724,000).

 **263** Following the July 2024 Election, 263 women MPs were elected – 40% of MPs, compared to 34% in 2019, the highest-ever number.

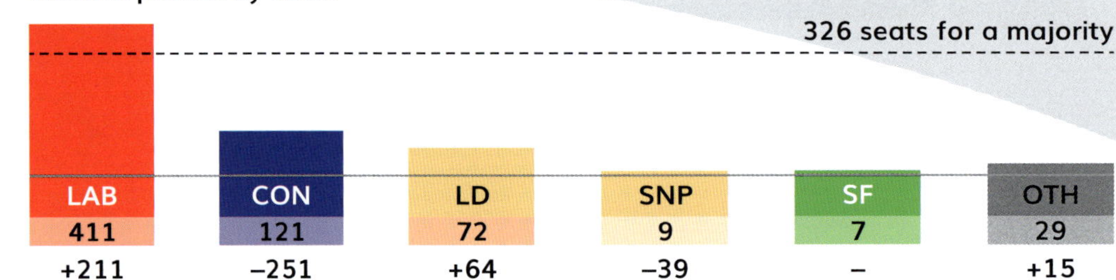

Figure 4.7 Parliament in 2024

Results: parties by seats

Change since 2019

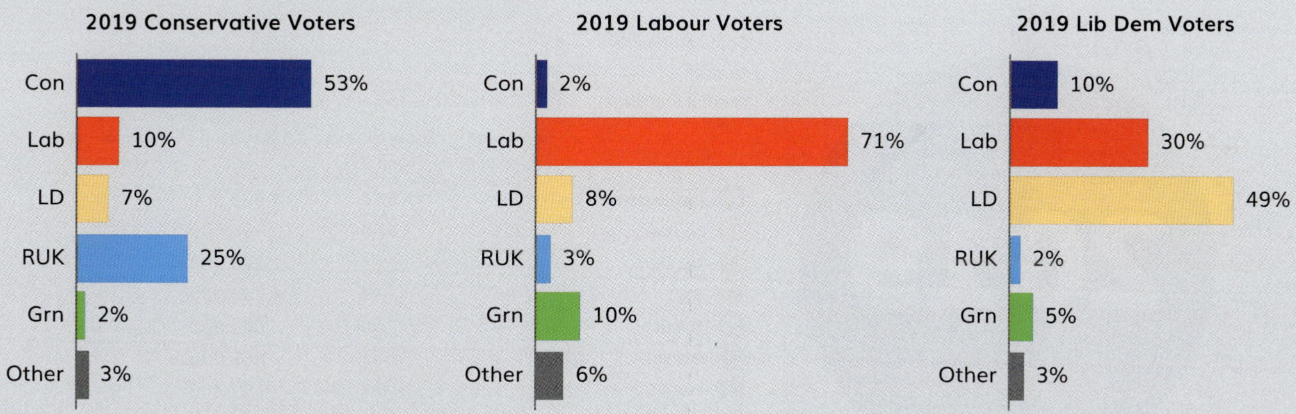

Source: YouGov, How Britain voted in the 2024 General Election

KEY STATISTICS

Seats contested   650
Turnout   67%
Overall Outcome   Conservative majority government

	Seats won out of 650	Share of seats won (%)	Votes won	Share of total vote (%)
Conservative	365	56.0	13,900,000	45.0
Labour	203	31.0	10,300,000	32.0
Lib Dem	11	1.7	2,370,000	7.4
SNP	48	7.4	1,240,000	3.9
Brexit	0	0	642,000	2.0
Greens	1	0.15	866,000	2.7
Plaid Cymru	4	0.6	153,265	0.5
DUP	8	1.2	244,127	0.8
Sinn Féin	7	1.0	181,853	0.6
SDLP	2	0.3	118,737	0.4

Compared with the results of the 2017 election:

OTHER KEY FACTS

11.5%
11.5% of the vote went to parties other than the Conservatives, Labour or Liberal Democrats.

47
The Conservatives gained 47 seats and increased their vote share by 3%.

59
Labour lost 59 seats and decreased their vote share by 8%.

1
The Liberal Democrats lost 1 seat.

13
The SNP gained 13 seats.

82%
Despite winning only 45% of the Scottish vote, the SNP won 82% (48 of 59) of the seats in Scotland.

220
Following the December 2019 Election, 220 women MPs were elected – 34% of MPs, compared to 32% in 2015, the highest-ever number.

Figure 4.9   Parliament in 2019

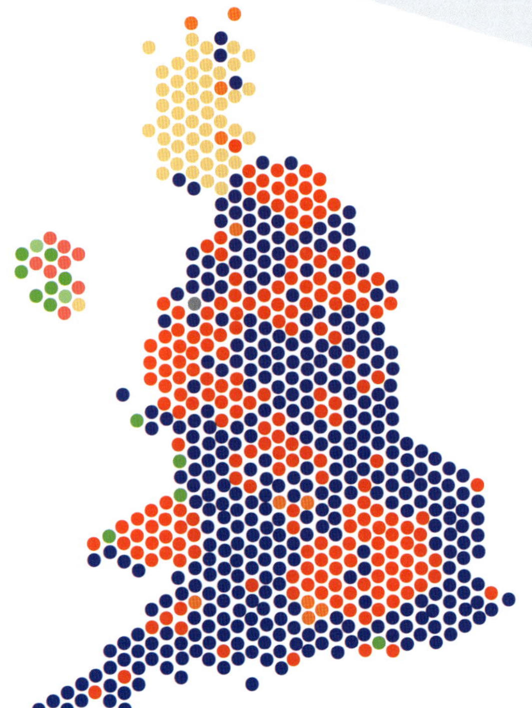

Figure 4.10   How we voted in 2019

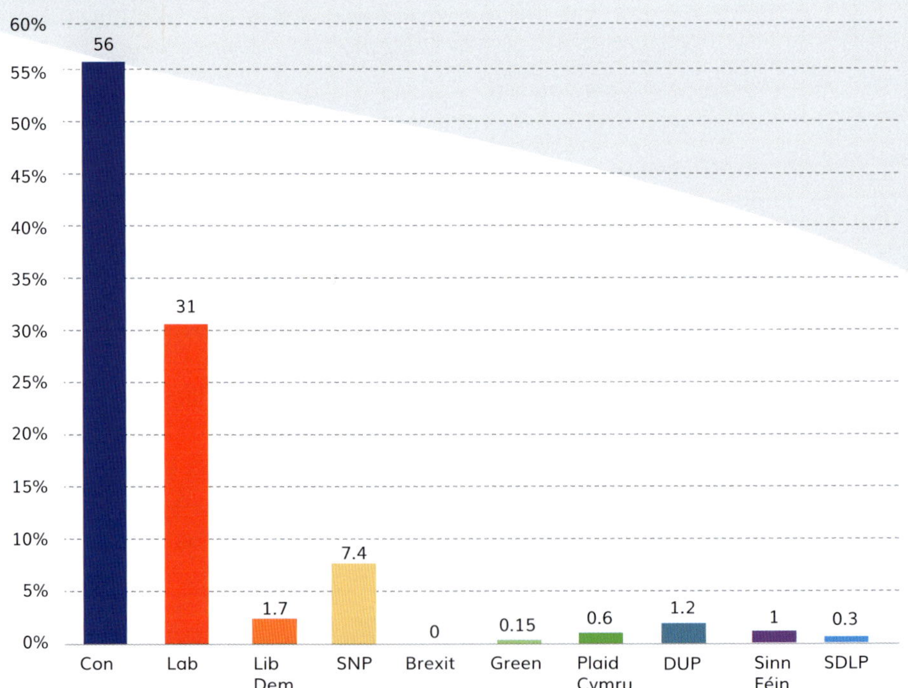

Figure 4.11 Swing analysis since 2017 Election

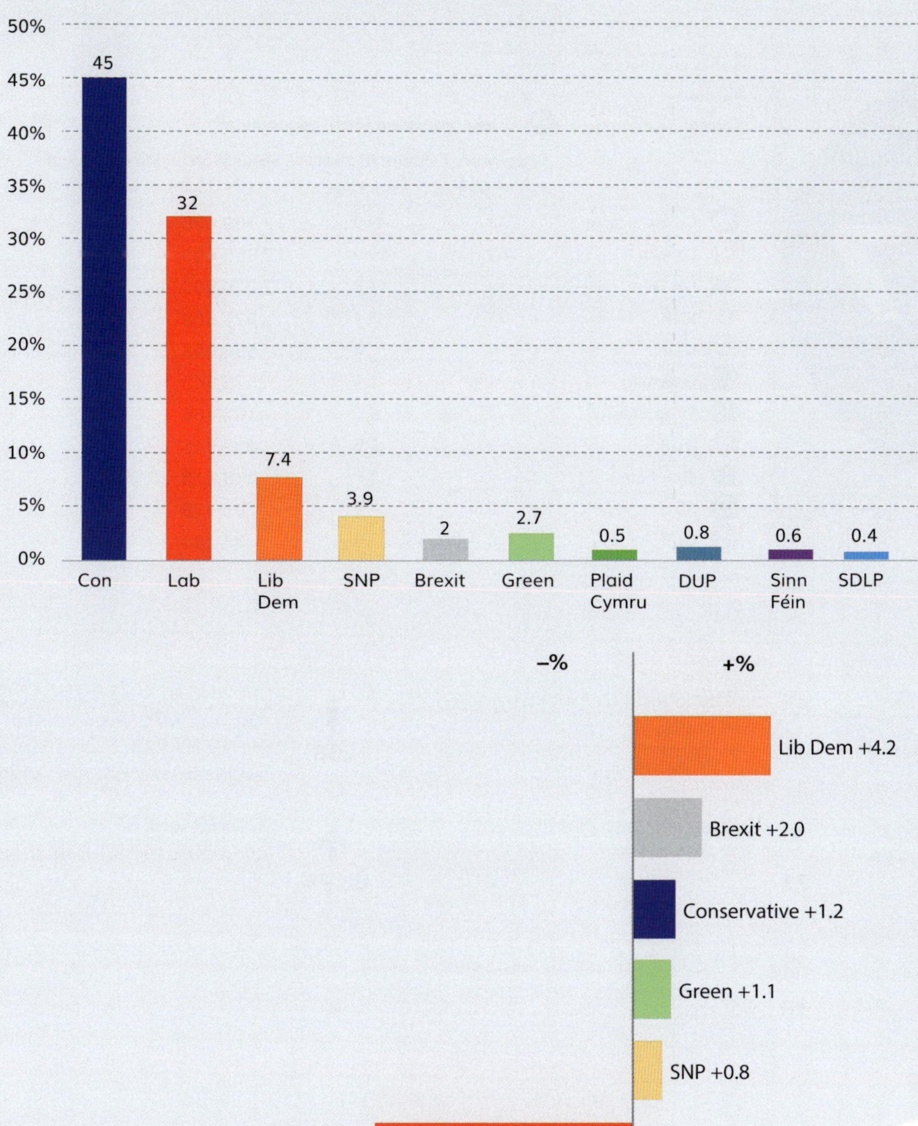
50%
45%
40%
35%
30%
25%
20%
15%
10%
5%
0%
45
32
7.4
3.9
2
2.7
0.5
0.8
0.6
0.4
Con
Lab
Lib Dem
SNP
Brexit
Green
Plaid Cymru
DUP
Sinn Féin
SDLP
–%
+%
Lib Dem +4.2
Brexit +2.0
Conservative +1.2
Green +1.1
SNP +0.8
-7.9 Labour

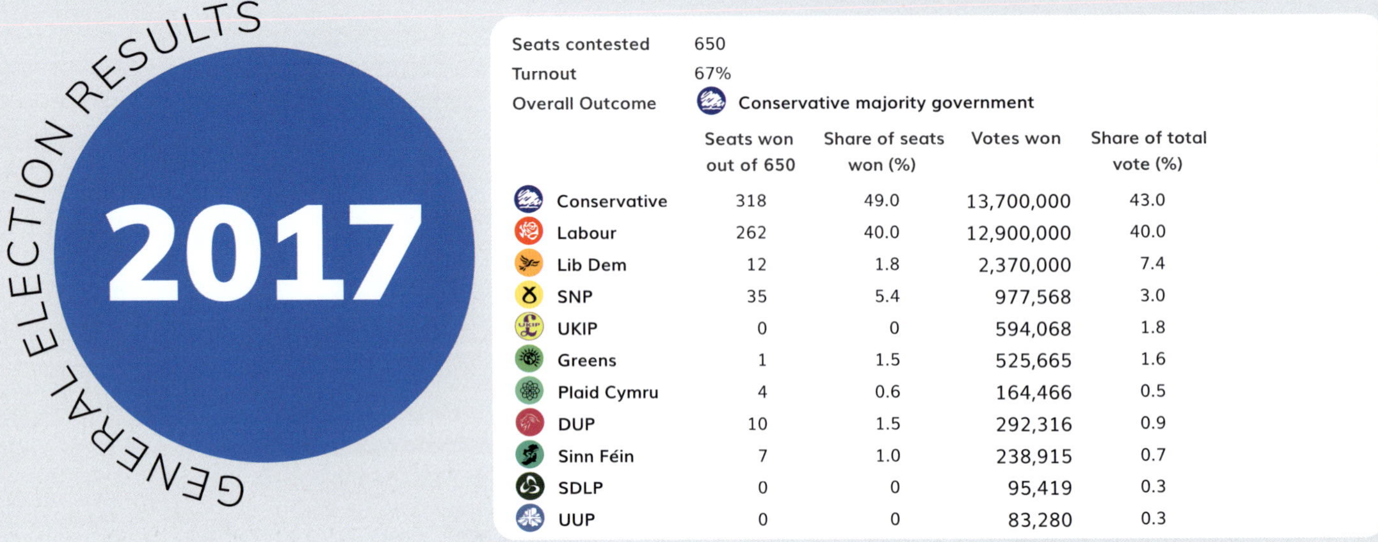

KEY STATISTICS

Seats contested 650
Turnout 67%
Overall Outcome — Conservative majority government

	Seats won out of 650	Share of seats won (%)	Votes won	Share of total vote (%)
Conservative	318	49.0	13,700,000	43.0
Labour	262	40.0	12,900,000	40.0
Lib Dem	12	1.8	2,370,000	7.4
SNP	35	5.4	977,568	3.0
UKIP	0	0	594,068	1.8
Greens	1	1.5	525,665	1.6
Plaid Cymru	4	0.6	164,466	0.5
DUP	10	1.5	292,316	0.9
Sinn Féin	7	1.0	238,915	0.7
SDLP	0	0	95,419	0.3
UUP	0	0	83,280	0.3

OTHER KEY FACTS

11% — 11% of the vote went to parties other than the Conservatives, Labour or Liberal Democrats.

13 — The Conservatives lost 13 seats but increased its vote share by 5.5%.

4 — The Liberal Democrats gained 4 seats.

21 — The SNP lost 21 seats.

30 — Labour gained 30 seats and increased its vote share by 10%.

208 — Following the May 2017 General Election, 32% of MPs were women compared to 29% in 2015, and 208 women, the highest-ever number, were elected.

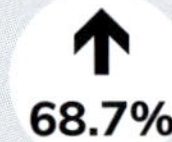
68.7% — Turnout was 68.7%, a slight rise compared to 66.2% in 2015.

Figure 4.12 Parliament in 2017

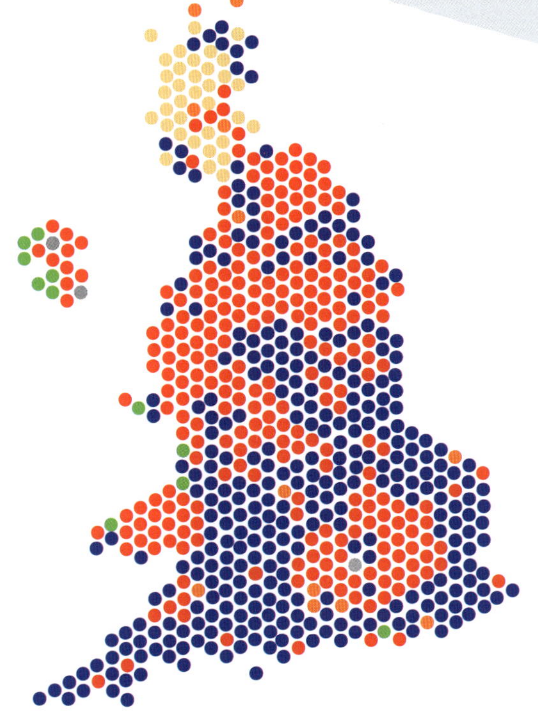

Figure 4.13 How we voted in 2017

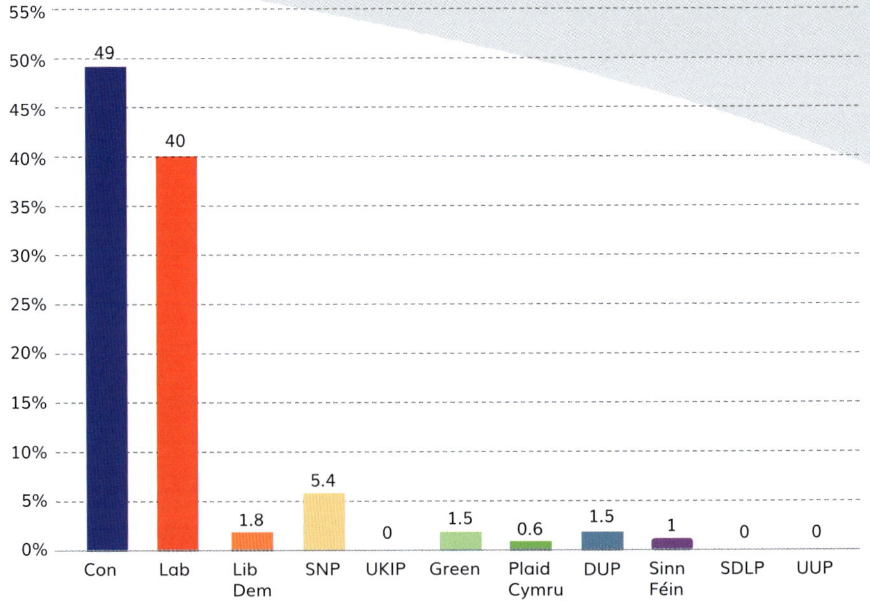

Figure 4.14 Swing analysis since 2015 Election

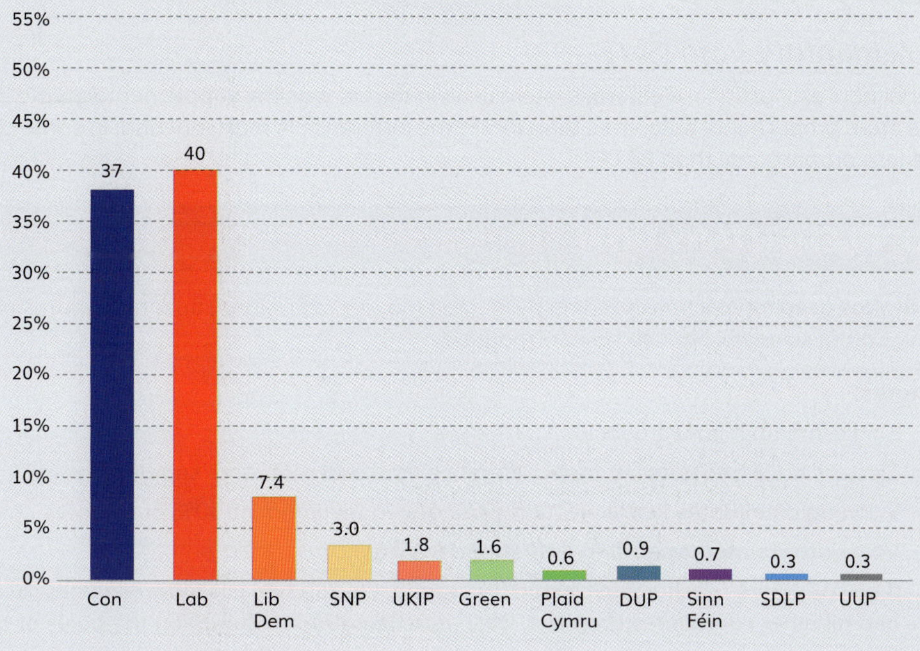
55%
50%
45%
40%
35%
30%
25%
20%
15%
10%
5%
0%
37
40
7.4
3.0
1.8
1.6
0.6
0.9
0.7
0.3
0.3
Con
Lab
Lib Dem
SNP
UKIP
Green
Plaid Cymru
DUP
Sinn Féin
SDLP
UUP

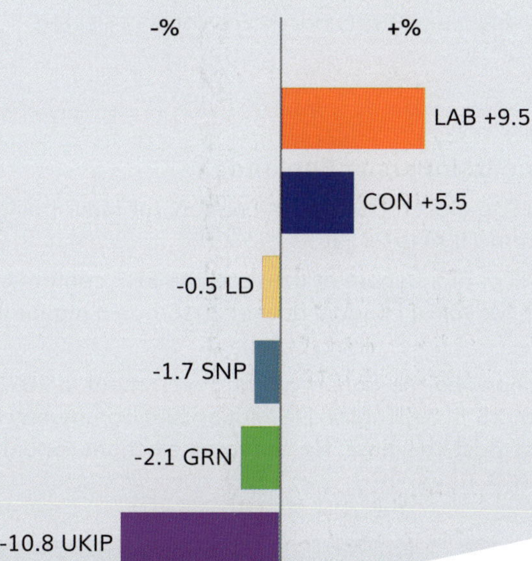
-%
+%
LAB +9.5
CON +5.5
-0.5 LD
-1.7 SNP
-2.1 GRN
-10.8 UKIP

Majority systems

Supplementary vote (SV)

The other non-proportional electoral system used in the UK was the supplementary vote (SV). Although SV has more proportional outcomes than FPTP, the difference is marginal and, in some circumstances, can be less proportional than FPTP.

SUPPLEMENTARY VOTE

Used: Was used for elections for directly elected mayors in England, and in elections for Police and Crime Commissioners. Now to be reintroduced.

Features:

» Single-member constituencies.

» Electors have two votes: a first-preference vote and a second 'supplementary' vote.

» Winning candidates in the election must gain a minimum of 50% of all votes cast.

» Votes are counted according to first preference.

» If no candidate reaches 50% in the first round, the top two candidates remain in the election and all other candidates drop out, their vote being redistributed on the basis of their second vote.

» The candidate with the most first-choice and second-choice votes is elected.

SV as used in the UK

Mayors and Police and Crime Commissioners in England

» **Supplementary vote (SV)** was used to elect the Mayor of London, for Metropolitan Mayors and Police and Crime Commissioners from 1998 to 2021.

» Despite aiming to give winners 50% or more share of the vote, the ERS confirms that 'in almost two decades of SV elections for the Mayor of London, only in 2016 has a mayor won more than 50% of the total ballots'.

» SV was abolished for mayoral elections by the Conservative Government in 2022, however the Labour Government announced in 2025, in the English Devolution and Community Empowerment Bill, that it will be scrapping first-past-the-post for mayoral elections and reinstating the supplementary vote.

Visit the companion website to see details of how SV performed in mayoral elections up to 2021 from the previous fifth edition.

Proportional systems

There are three other electoral systems used in the UK and they broadly conform to the principle of **proportional representation.** These systems are:

» The *Regional List* system which is now used for elections to the Welsh Parliament (as of 2026) when the Senedd decided to replace AMS with the List.

» The *Additional Member System* (AMS) is used for elections to the Scottish Parliament and the Greater London Assembly.

» The *Single Transferable Vote* (STV) has been used since 1998 to elect the Northern Ireland Assembly. It is also used for local elections in Northern Ireland and Scotland.

The List system

The Closed Regional List (CRL) system is a type of proportional representation (PR) electoral system used by the Senedd from 2026. Under this system, political parties present a list of candidates for each electoral region and voters vote for a party rather than for individual candidates. Seats in the legislature are then allocated to parties based on the proportion of votes they receive in each region. The party then determines which candidates from its list fill the seats.

THE LIST SYSTEM

Used: Welsh Parliament from 2026 onwards

Features:

- » The standard list system has no constituencies.
- » Each party puts up as many candidates as there are seats in a specific list order.
- » The voters have one vote and they vote for a party, not a candidate, and seats are allocated according to the percentage of votes received.
- » Under the list, 50% of the vote will typically correlate to 50% of the seats, i.e. it is directly proportionate
- » Seats are allocated based on the percentage of votes each party or independent candidate receives, using a method called the **D'Hondt** formula.
- » Candidates are selected from the top of each party's list, then depending on their percentage of the vote, they will be allocated seats.
- » There is a **closed list** where the electors have no say in the order of the politicians on the list, whereas an **open list** is when voters have some say over the order of the politicians.
- » There are also **regional lists** where the country is divided up into smaller regions allowing for some regional representation.

The D'hondt method

- » This is a very common electoral formula which is already used to allocate the regional element of AMS seats in Scotland.
- » D'Hondt works by dividing the number of votes cast for each party by the number of seats they have already won, plus one.
- » So after a party has won one seat, their votes are divided by two, after they have won two seats their votes are divided by three, and so on. Counting takes place in rounds, with the party with the highest total in each round winning the seat.

Advantages:

- » Fairer representation – it ensures that the proportion of seats each party receives in the legislature is roughly equal to the proportion of votes it gets, leading to a more accurate reflection of voters' preferences. The Welsh Government said the change would allow it to be 'better able to represent people in Wales'.
- » More diverse representation – parties can create lists that include a broader range of candidates, ensuring that minority groups have a better chance of being represented.
- » Prevents wasted votes – unlike first-past-the-post, the List System reduces wasted votes by ensuring that all votes contribute to the proportion of seats a party receives.
- » Encourages cooperation – smaller parties are more likely to be represented, which usually leads to coalitions and can encourage compromise and cooperation.
- » No tactical voting – under FPTP, voters may vote tactically, but under the List System, voters can cast their vote for their preferred party without worrying about tactical considerations.

Disadvantages:

» Party control – since parties control the candidate lists, there is a lack of democratic choice. Party leaders may prioritise loyalty over merit, and candidates who are popular with voters may be excluded if they are not favoured by party elites. This could erode trust in politicians as 'closed lists' systems put too much power in the hands of parties, with voters choosing between them instead of candidates.

» Very large constituencies – The largest geographical constituency in the new Senedd is Dwyfor Meirionnydd, Montgomeryshire and Glyndŵr. Six Members of the Senedd (MS) will serve the 1,927 sq miles. The commission admitted that it was 'not ideal to propose such a large constituency'.

» Less regional representation – as seats are allocated proportionally in each region, smaller regions may not have effective representation as it can be harder for local interests to be effectively represented.

» Limited accountability – a Closed List system can make it difficult for voters to hold individual representatives to account. If a voter dislikes a representative on their party's list, they cannot directly vote them out.

» The extra 30 Senedd members will cost around £12 million.

The D'hondt method in practice	Conservative	Labour	LibDem	Brexit	Ashfield Independent	Green	Others	Running total
Votes	258,794	204,011	33,604	15,728	13,498	10,375	9,743	
Round 1	**258,794**	204,011	33,604	15,728	13,498	10,375	9,743	1 Con
Round 2	129,397	**204,011**	33,604	15,728	13,498	10,375	9,743	1 Lab
Round 3	**129,397**	102,006	33,604	15,728	13,498	10,375	9,743	2 Con
Round 4	86,265	**102,006**	33,604	15,728	13,498	10,375	9,743	2 Lab
Round 5	**86,265**	68,004	33,604	15,728	13,498	10,375	9,743	3 Con
Round 6	64,699	**68,004**	33,604	15,728	13,498	10,375	9,743	3 Lab
Round 7	**64,699**	51,003	33,604	15,728	13,498	10,375	9,743	4 Con
Round 8	**51,759**	51,003	33,604	15,728	13,498	10,375	9,743	5 Con
Round 9	43,132	**51,003**	33,604	15,728	13,498	10,375	9,743	4 Lab
Round 10	**43,132**	40,802	33,604	15,728	13,498	10,375	9,743	6 Con
Round 11	36,971	**40,802**	33,604	15,728	13,498	10,375	9,743	5 Lab
Elected	**6**	**5**						

Source: www.electoral-reform.org.uk

As can be seen above, the Conservatives have the most votes so they win the first seat, their vote is then halved, leaving Labour as the largest party – who are then allocated the next seat. This continues until all seats are allocated.

The Closed Regional List as used in the UK

» From 2026, the Welsh Parliament will be elected by the Closed Regional List System.

» The Senedd will increase in size from 60 to 96 members.

» There will be 16 regions instead of the 40 constituencies under AMS (see Figure 4.15).

» Each region elects six politicians through party lists, using the D'Hondt formula.

» Each region is formed by pairing up the 32 seats for Westminster.

» Additionally, the fixed terms of the Senedd have been reduced from five years to four.

Figure 4.15 New Senedd regions from 2026

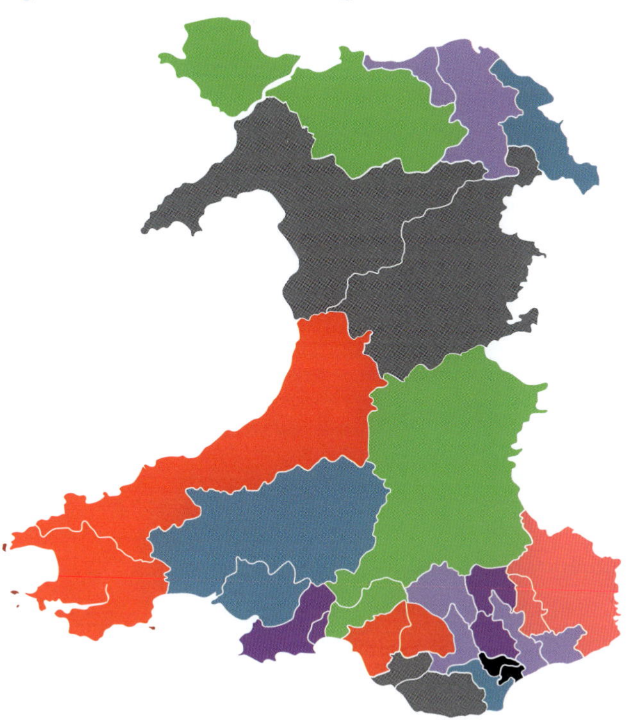

Table 4.4 Welsh Senedd Election results 2026

	Total seats	Total votes	% votes	% seats
Plaid Cymru	43	444,665	35%	45%
Reform UK	34	367,985	29%	36%
Labour	9	139,203	11%	9%
Conservative	7	134,926	11%	7%
Green	2	84,608	7%	2%
Lib Dems	1	56,012	5%	1%
Total seats	**96**			
Turnout 51.6% (+5.1)				

Additional Member System (AMS)

The **Additional Member System (AMS)** is used in the devolved region of Scotland and for the London Assembly. This system is a hybrid system, which combines the FPTP and the List system. With AMS, the voters have two completely separate votes.

Advantages:

» The mixed character of this system balances the need for constituency representation against the need for electoral fairness.

» Although the system is broadly proportional in terms of its outcomes, it keeps alive the possibility of single-party government.

» It allows voters to make wider and more considered choices. It also allows them to express personal support for a candidate, while voting for a different party with their second vote.

» Each voter has a directly accountable constituency representative.

» Every voter has at least one effective vote.

» The list element creates excellent proportionality.

Spec Key Term

Additional member system (AMS): A hybrid electoral system combining two electoral systems. There are two votes, one for a constituency using a simple plurality system, then a second vote is assigned to a party list for an 'additional' representative.

Disadvantages:

- » The retention of single-member constituencies reduces the likelihood of high levels of proportionality.
- » AMS is unfair because List members have no constituency duties.
- » List members are accountable to party leaders rather than voters, which undermines legitimacy.
- » AMS sometimes gives rise to 'overhang' seats, where a party wins more seats via the constituency vote than it is entitled to according to its proportional vote.
- » It can be complicated. People can become confused over exactly what they're supposed to do with their two votes.

ADDITIONAL MEMBER SYSTEM (AMS)

Used: Scottish Parliament, Greater London Assembly.

Features:

- » It is a 'mixed' system, made up of constituency and party-list elements.
- » A proportion of seats are filled by FPTP, using single-member constituencies.
- » The remaining seats are filled using a 'closed' party-list system.
- » Electors cast two votes: one for a candidate in a constituency election and the other for a party in a list election.
- » The party-list element is used to 'top up' the constituency results. This is done 'correctively', using the D'Hondt method to achieve the most proportional overall outcome.

AMS as used in the UK

Scotland

- » There are 129 seats in total, and voters have two votes.
- » The first vote is used to elect a constituency MSP. Out of 129 seats, 73 are chosen like this. The remaining 56 are chosen using a closed, regional list system. These additional members are elected from eight regions.

Table 4.5 Scottish Parliament Election Results 2026

Scottish Parliament Election 2026	Constituency				Regions				Total combined		
	Votes	% votes	Seats	% seats	Votes	% votes	Seats	% seats	Total seats	Total % seats	Combined vote %
SNP	877,077	38%	57	78%	625,949	27%	1	2%	58	45%	33%
Labour	440,708	19%	3	4%	368,785	16%	14	25%	17	13%	18%
Reform	361,994	16%	0	0%	383,425	17%	17	30%	17	13%	16%
Scottish Greens	52,528	2%	2	3%	321,964	14%	13	23%	15	12%	8%
Conservative	271,740	12%	4	5%	271,550	12%	8	14%	12	9%	12%
Liberal Democrats	261,408	11%	7	10%	216,224	9%	3	6%	10	8%	10%
Total seats	73				56				129		
Turnout 53.2% (-10.1)											

» The purpose of the additional members is to reduce the unfairness in the way the constituency MSPs are elected.

» In 2026, the SNP received 57 of its 58 seats from constituency MSPs and only 1 top up MSP, whereas Reform UK received 0 constituency MSPs and 17 top up MSPs (Table 4.5). Thus the top up MSPs help to ensure that the overall link between percentage of votes and the percentage of seats is fairer.

The Greater London Assembly

The Greater London Assembly comprises 25 members, 14 of which are elected directly from the London constituencies using FPTP and the remaining 11 through the list system (shown in Figure 4.16 which shows 2024 results).

Figure 4.16 **AMS and the Greater London Authority 2024**

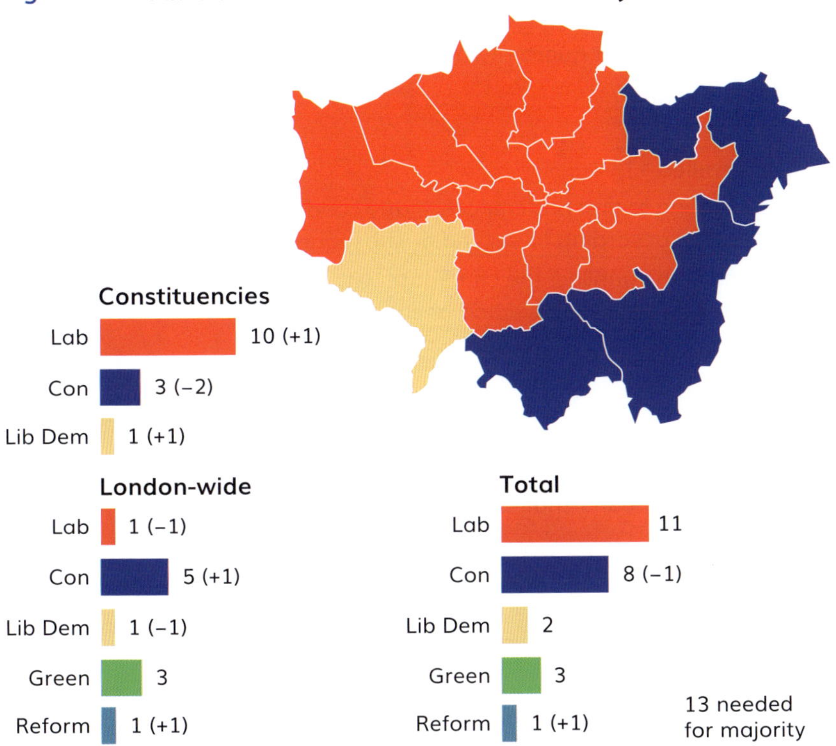

» Electors cast one vote for each aspect. The first vote goes to the constituency candidate. The List vote is cast for a voter's preferred party across London as a whole.

» Additional members are drawn from a party list depending on how many, if any, additional seats that party wins.

» Table 4.6 shows the election results since its inception in 2000.

Table 4.6 GLA Election Results 2000–24

Party	2000	2004	2008	2012	2016	2021*	2024
Labour	9	7	8	12	12	11	11
Cons	9	9	11	9	8	9	8
Green	3	2	2	2	2	3	3
Lib Dems	4	5	3	2	1	2	2
UKIP/Reform	0	2	0	0	2	-	1
BNP	0	0	1	0	-	-	-
Independent	0	0	0	0	-	-	-
Total	25	25	25	25	25	25	25

*2020 election was delayed by a year because of Covid

Single Transferable Vote (STV)

The **Single Transferable Vote (STV)** system is used in Northern Ireland Assembly elections and for Northern Irish and Scottish local council elections.

SINGLE TRANSFERABLE VOTE (STV)

Used: Northern Ireland Assembly and in Northern Ireland and Scotland for local government.

Features:

» There are multi-member constituencies.

» Political parties can put up as many candidates as there are seats to fill in each constituency.

» Electors vote preferentially.

» Candidates are elected if they achieve a quota of votes. This quota is calculated using the Droop formula, as follows:

$$\text{Quota} = \frac{\text{total number of votes cast}}{\text{(number of seats to be filled} +1)} + 1$$

» Votes are counted, firstly according to first preferences. If any candidate achieves the quota, their additional votes are counted according to second or subsequent preferences.

» If this process still leaves some seats unfilled, the candidate with the fewest votes drops out and their votes are redistributed according to second or subsequent preferences.

Advantages:

» The system can achieve highly proportional outcomes.

» The availability of several members means that constituents can choose whom to take their grievances to.

» STV gives voters more choice than any other system, which puts power in the hands of the voters.

» Fewer votes are 'wasted' under STV. This means that most voters can identity a representative that they personally helped to elect.

» There are no safe seats under STV, meaning candidates cannot be complacent and parties must campaign everywhere, and not just in **marginal seats**.

» By encouraging candidates to seek first votes, as well as lower-preference votes, the use of negative campaigning is greatly diminished.

» There is no need for tactical voting.

Disadvantages:

» Single-party government is unlikely under STV.

» Multi-member constituencies may be divisive because they encourage competition among members of the same party.

» In sparsely populated areas, such as in Scotland, STV could lead to huge constituencies where constituents feel very remote from their representatives.

» The process of counting the results takes longer under STV, meaning that results cannot usually be declared on the same night as the vote took place.

» A voting system that allows voters to rank candidates is prone to so-called 'donkey voting', where voters vote for candidates in the order they appear on the ballot.

» In large multi-member constituencies, ballot papers can get rather big and confusing. Many votes were spoilt in Scotland when it was introduced for local government.

STV – a worked example

This explains, step by step, how votes are redistributed under STV.

Figure 4.17 How votes are redistributed under STV

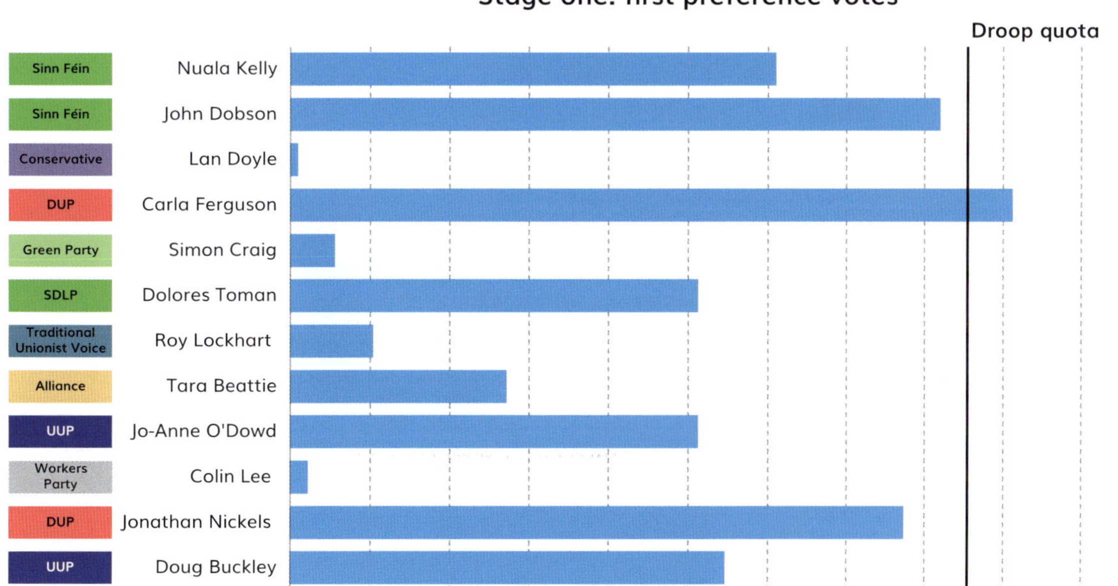

This shows where all first preference votes were allocated:

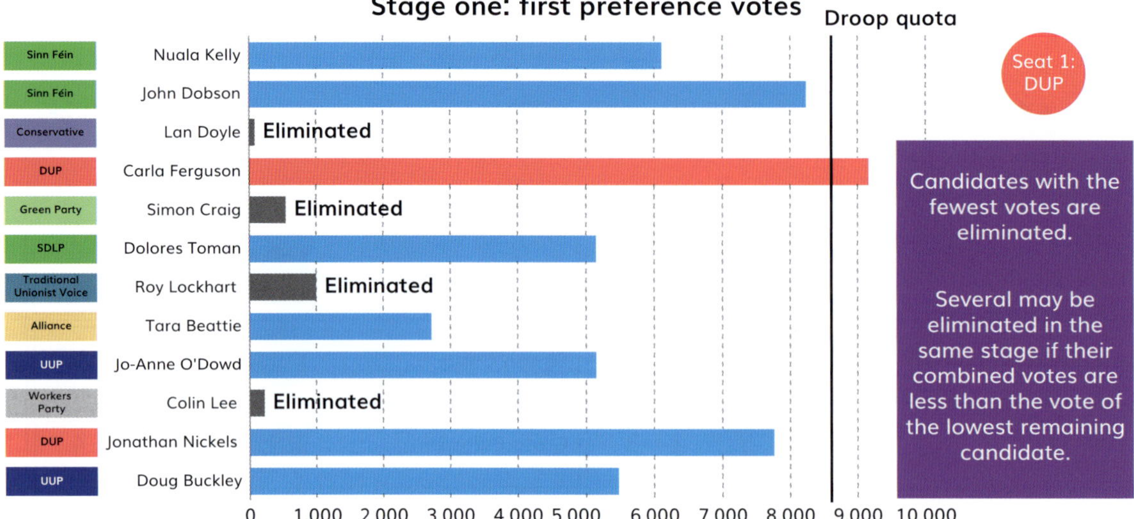

This shows the candidate who has passed the quota in pink, so has been elected, as well as the candidates who have been eliminated.

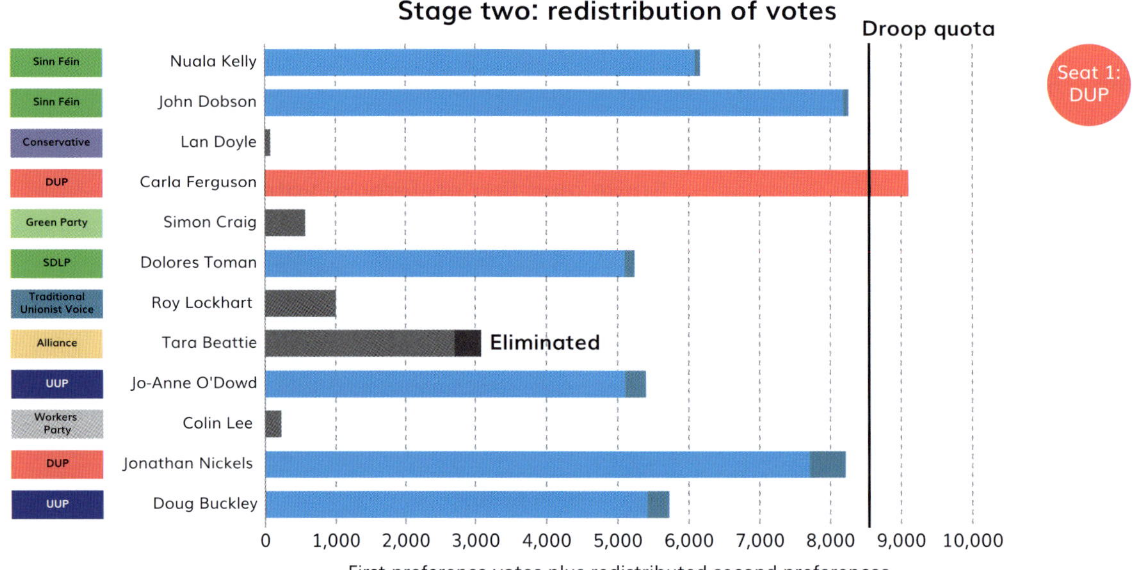

This shows where eliminated votes have been reallocated (dark grey).

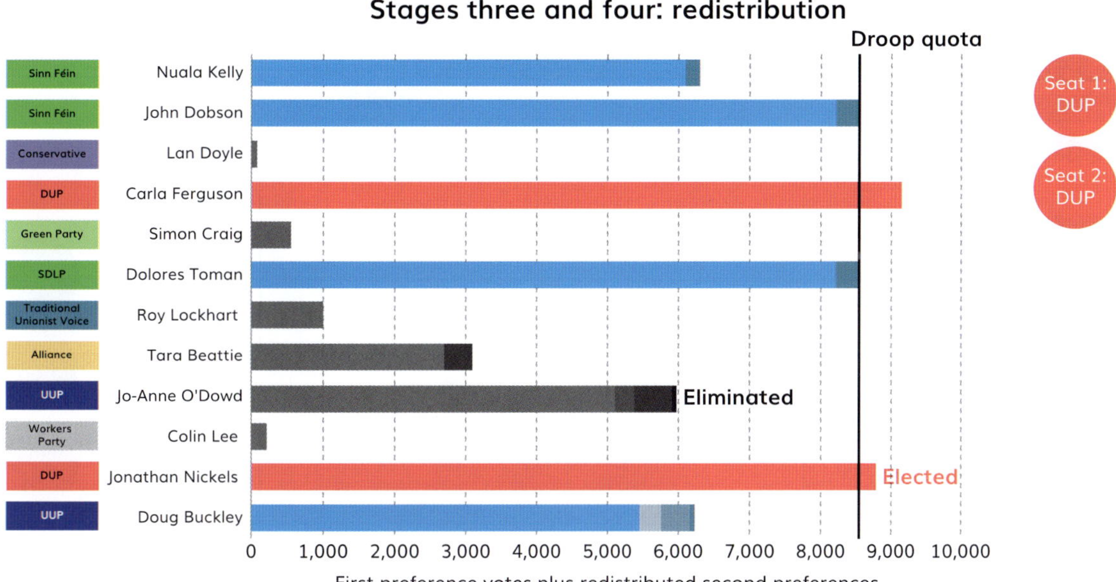

E

As more candidates are eliminated, their votes are redistributed and more candidates pass the quota and are elected.

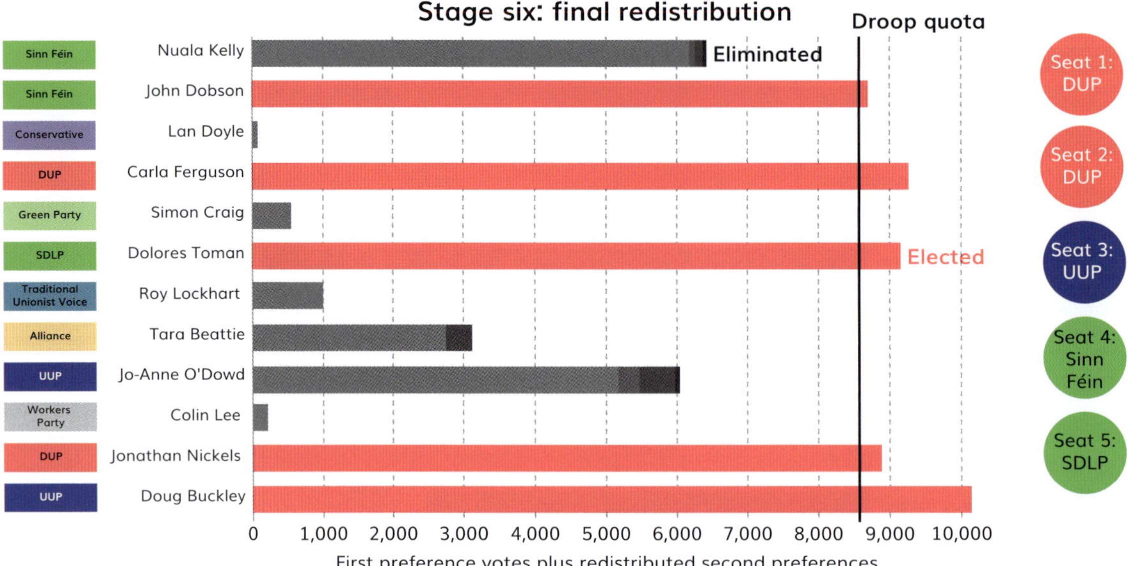

All five candidates have been elected.

STV as used in the UK

Northern Ireland

- » In the Northern Ireland Assembly, Northern Ireland is divided into 18 multi-member constituencies (the same boundaries as Westminster seats). Each of these multi-member constituencies elects five Assembly Members, to make 90 in total.
- » Each party puts forward a list of candidates. They can put forward as many as they like up to five, putting forward more where they are stronger and fewer where they have less support.
- » Voters cast their votes preferentially. There is no minimum or maximum number of preferences that can be cast; the voter just carries on until they no longer wish to express a preference.
- » A quota is then calculated in each of the 18 regions. If any candidate has enough votes to reach the quota, they are elected. Any unused portion of each vote (called a 'surplus') will be transferred to the voter's second preference. If there are still unfilled places, then the candidate with the lowest number of votes is eliminated and their votes are transferred to voters' second preferences. Any candidate who now has more than the quota is declared elected.
- » This process continues until the right number of candidates has been elected. STV has been effective in creating proportional results across Northern Ireland and enabled many different parties to be represented and to sit on the Northern Ireland Executive.

However, one of the issues with STV is complications in marking the ballot paper. According to the Electoral Office of Northern Ireland (EONI), in the 2011 NI Assembly Elections, there were more than 12,000 ballot papers rejected as 'spoilt'. The Electoral Commission introduced a new-style ballot paper for the 2016 Assembly Election to reduce the number of votes that were being accidentally wasted, which worked as they went down to 9,425. However, in 2022, the figure was back up to 11,074. Figures suggest that the number of rejected ballots used under STV is more than twice as high as in the FPTP Westminster election.

Table 4.7 Northern Ireland Assembly Election (2022)

NI Assembly Election 2022		Seats won	% of seats	First preference (votes%)	First preference votes	NI Executive seats
	Sinn Féin	27	30%	29	250,338	5
	DUP	25	27%	21	184,002	4
	Alliance	17	19%	13.5	116,681	2
	UUP	9	10%	11	96,390	1
	SDLP	8	9%	9	78,237	
	TUV	1	1%	8	65,788	
	Green (NI)	0	0%	3	16,433	
	People Before Profit	1	1%	1	9,798	
	Independents	2	2%	3	25,315	
Total		90			803,315	12
Turnout 63% **Invalid votes** 11,084						

Figure 4.18 Seats won in 2022 Northern Ireland Assembly Elections

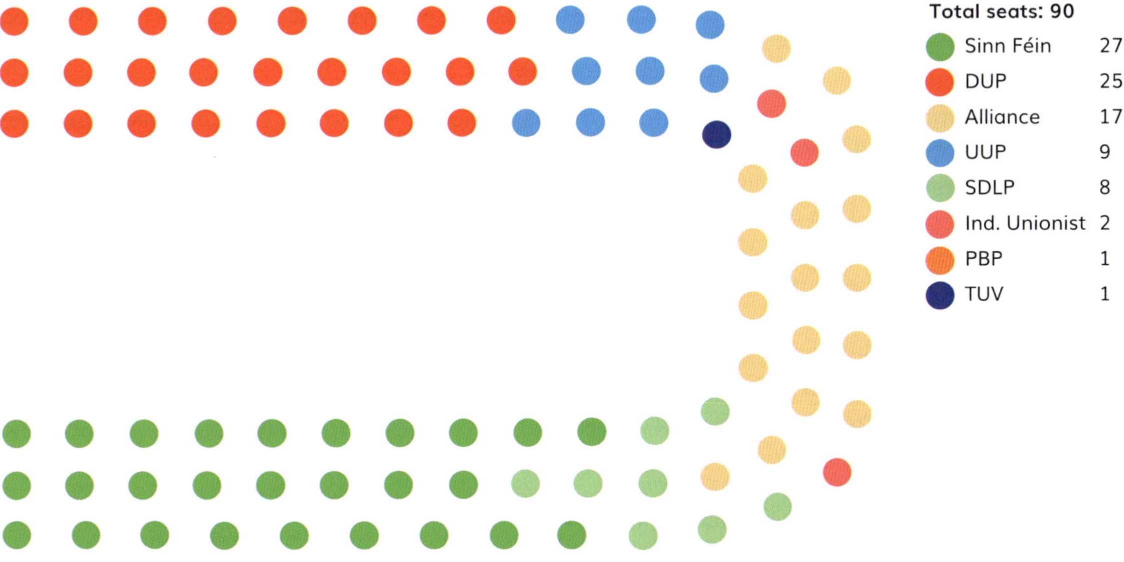

Source: Institute for Government

KEY TOPIC DEBATE: HAS THE IMPACT OF THE NEW ELECTORAL SYSTEMS MADE THE CASE FOR REPLACING FIRST-PAST-THE-POST?

The simple fact is that there is no such thing as a 'best' electoral system. Each voting system is better at achieving different things: the real question is which of these things is the most important? The electoral reform debate is, at heart, a debate about the desirable nature of government and the principles that underpin 'good' government. Is representative government, for instance, more important than effective government? There are no objective answers to these questions, only competing viewpoints. Here we identify the impact of the systems that are used in the UK.

Party representation

- **The use of PR since 1999 has allowed wider representation of political parties than FPTP in Westminster allows.** Minor parties that are denied representation by FPTP win seats when PR systems are used. This broadens the base of party representation and creates multi-party systems. Proportional electoral systems are much fairer for third parties, as the following examples illustrate:
  - The Green Party has 4 seats (0.6% of the seats) in Westminster under FPTP, but has 15 seats (12%) in the Scottish Parliament, 3 seats (12%) in the Greater London Assembly and 3 (3%) in the NI Assembly, which all use systems of PR.
  - Reform won 14% of the vote (4.1 million) but only 5 seats in the Commons in 2024. It won 17 seats in the Scottish Parliament and 34 in the Senedd in 2026.
  - In the 2026 Scottish Parliament elections, the SNP won 78% of constituency (FPTP) seats under AMS with 38% of the vote. But after AMS list seats were allocated, the SNP received 45% of the seats on 33% of the votes, making the final result more proportionate (see page 120).
  - In the same election, most AMS list seats went to Labour, Reform UK and the Greens to make the final result more proportionate. After the AMS list seats were allocated, Labour had 13% of the seats with 17% of the vote, Reform achieved 13% of the seats on a vote share of 16% and Greens achieved 12% of the seats with 8% of the vote.
  - Similarly, in the 2026 Senedd Election, the first under the Closed Regional List, Plaid Cymru gained 45% of the seats with 35% of the vote and Reform UK received 35% of the seats with 29% of the vote.
  - In Northern Ireland, STV creates a multi-party outcome with three of the larger parties all achieving significant representation in the Assembly and therefore being awarded places in a power-sharing executive. Figure 4.19 shows how disproportionate FPTP is compared to other systems used in the UK.

Figure 4.19 How proportional are elections across the UK?

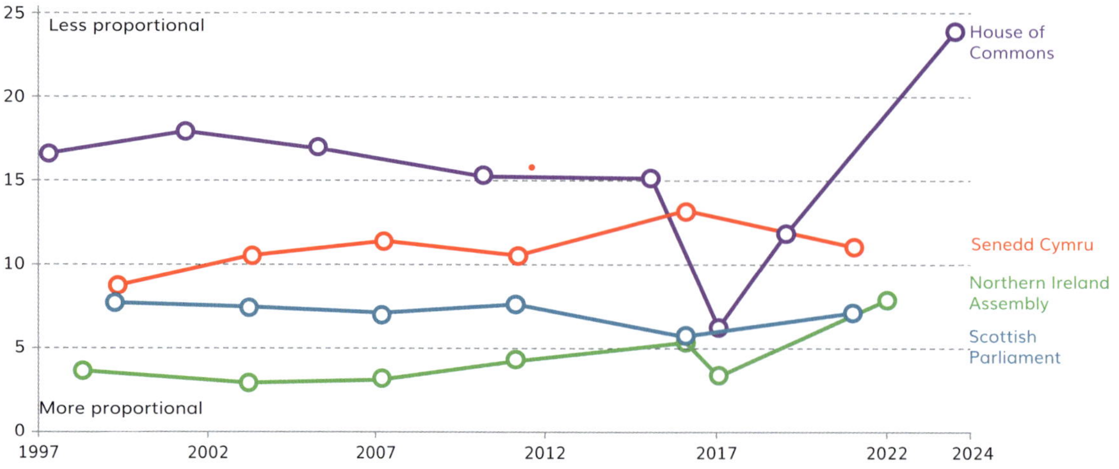

Source: Institute for Government

» The Liberal Democrats, condemned for so long by the systematic biases of FPTP, found itself represented fairly for the first time under FPTP in the UK General Election 2024, achieving 72 seats (11%) with 11.5% of the vote. In Westminster, however, this is no doubt the exception rather than the rule as typically they have greater representation where other voting systems are used.

All these examples suggest that PR has enhanced party representation in devolved bodies. Figure 4.20 outlines how Westminster would look if FPTP was replaced by three different types of PR as shown – all three systems of PR enhance the fairness and accuracy of representation of the parties, compared to FPTP.

Figure 4.20 **The 2024 General Election result and alternative projections under different voting systems**

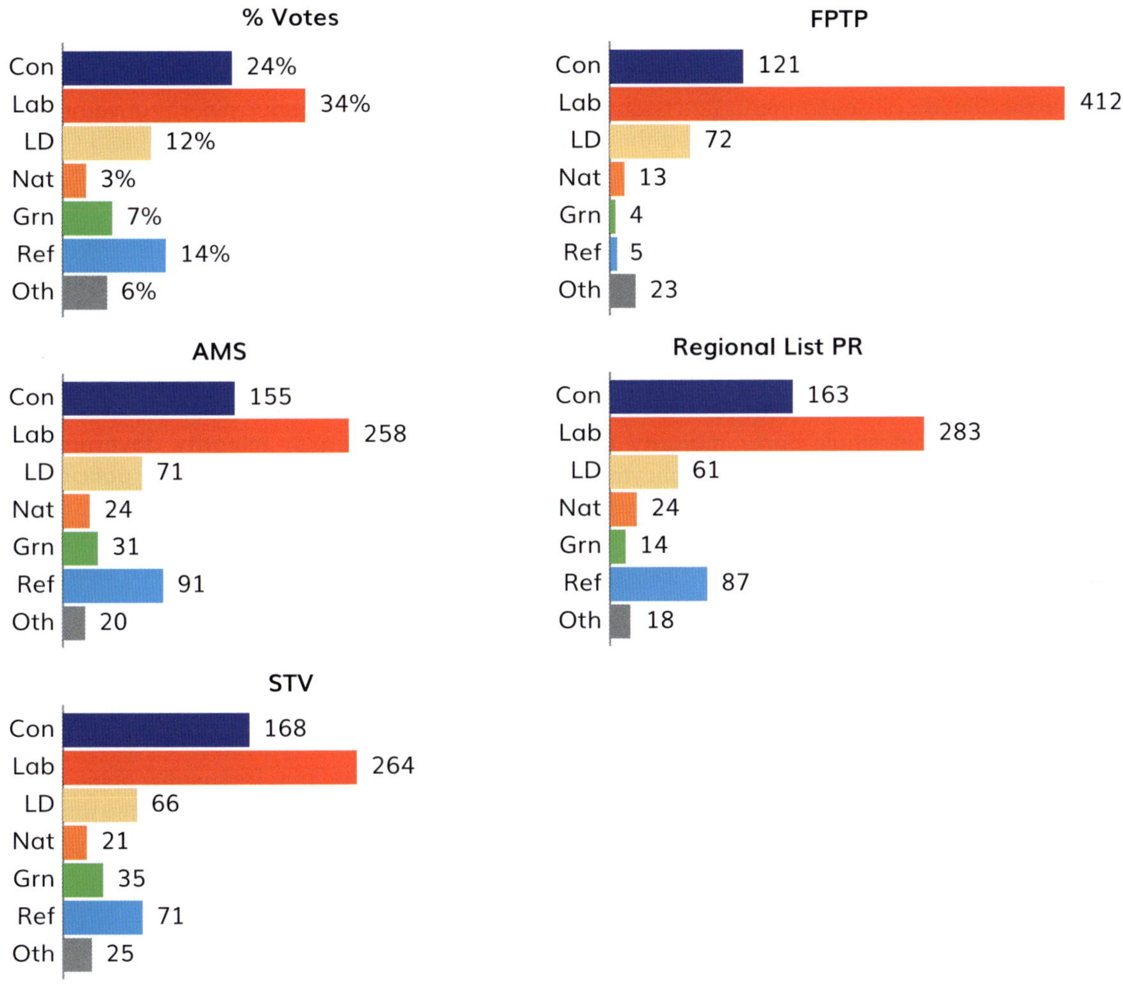

Voter choice

● **Majoritarian, proportional and hybrid systems can give voters greater choice.** FPTP requires voters to select just a single candidate. Supporters of third parties, which have very little chance of winning, can face a choice between wasting their vote on their preferred party, or tactically voting for whichever main political party they oppose the least.

» Until 2021, SV was used for mayoral elections across England and Police and Crime Commissioner elections and allowed voters to select a first- and second-choice candidate. Thus, many voters were able to vote for a preferred candidate as their first choice, and then a 'main party' candidate as their second preference. SV was replaced by FPTP in 2024, where this advantage was removed.

» AMS also allows voters to vote for different parties in the same election. In 2026, results in Scotland showed voters backing a major party in the constituency round, where third parties were unlikely to win, and then a different, perhaps smaller, party in their regional vote. The Scottish Greens won 14% of the regional vote but only 2.3% of the constituency vote in 2026.

» STV offers a great deal of voter choice and it allows voters to differentiate not only between parties, but also between candidates from the same party. STV involves fewer 'wasted' votes and offers greater potential to choose winning candidates because of its proportional character.

Type of government

● There is a tendency of more proportional voting systems to produce multi-party systems and therefore a greater likelihood of coalition or minority governments. This has tended to be found where all such electoral systems have been used in the UK. These coalitions have been largely stable and lasted the length of their term.

» In the case of the Scottish Parliament, the SNP majority government formed in 2011 is an exception as all administrations before and after were either Labour–Liberal Democrat coalitions or minority SNP government; in 2026 they achieved 58 of the 129 seats, 7 short of a majority.

» In the Senedd, all governments had been Labour-led coalitions or a Labour minority government. However, the 2026 election ousted the Labour Government dramatically giving Plaid Cymru 43 seats, 5 short of a majority, putting Labour in third place with only 9, after Reform UK with 34 seats.

» Although the Conservative–Liberal Democrat Coalition at Westminster, formed in 2010, resulted from the use of FPTP, it, in effect, provided a laboratory which enabled the implications of proportional representation to be studied.

» In the Northern Ireland Assembly, there is a complex process of power sharing intended to include both unionist and nationalist parties. After the 2022 Election, there were four parties represented in the NI Executive.

● The shift from single-party majority government to coalition or minority governments has led to a different style of policymaking and to the adoption of different policies. In particular, whereas FPTP (usually) allows majority governments to push their policies through the House of Commons, other electoral systems across the UK have fostered a policy process that emphasises the need for compromise, negotiation and consensus. The following examples demonstrate this:

» In Scotland, the SNP has been in government alone with a minority three times, and with a small majority once. It has needed to build a consensus with other parties. In 2026 they were again 7 short of a majority, while the Scottish Greens achieved 15 seats, so some sort of cooperation is likely.

» In Wales, Labour had consistently been the strongest party but frequently denied the opportunity to govern alone, except once. In 2026, Labour might find themselves in the unusual position of propping up a Plaid government, rather than the other way round.

» In Northern Ireland, the Good Friday Agreement requires that representatives of the main unionist and nationalist parties are included in the executive. The choice of STV for Assembly elections guarantees that members of the two rival communities are elected, rather than Northern Ireland submitting to single-party domination, a scenario that could risk a return to sectarian violence. The First Minister and Deputy First Minister – nominated by the two largest parties – are equal in status and share governmental responsibilities. The system of government is designed to ensure joint participation by unionists and nationalists or republicans.

» At Westminster the main parties remain in an adversarial relationship, with one major opposition party clearly playing the role of an alternative government and smaller parties having much less influence.

» However, in the case of the 2010–15 Conservative–Liberal Democrat Coalition, the parties negotiated a joint programme of government and put in place an elaborate process to reconcile policy differences between them. This appeared to work successfully for five years.

» The 2017 confidence and supply agreement was formed after tough negotiations between Arlene Foster (DUP) and Theresa May (Conservative), the most famous of which was an extra £1 billion for Northern Ireland. This was a less 'friendly' relationship than the 2010 coalition.

Key Debate Summary: Has the impact of the new electoral systems made the case for replacing first-past-the-post?

For	Theme	Against
✓ The new systems provide much better representation.	How effective are systems at providing good party representation?	✗ FPTP ensures that the party with the most votes wins the election and governs.
✓ The coalitions/minority governments in the UK devolved assemblies have been stable.	How effective are systems at providing stable government?	✗ FPTP provides stable, single-party government.
✓ The other electoral systems used in the UK all provide good MP/constituency links.	How effective are systems at providing MP constituency links?	✗ MP/constituency links under FPTP are excellent.
✓ Other systems in the UK give smaller parties much fairer representation.	How effective are systems at providing fair representation to smaller parties?	✗ Other electoral systems can allow extremist parties to get a foothold, FPTP does not.
✓ Other systems give voters the ability to choose between candidates within a party or to split their vote between a party and a candidate.	Is it better to have a slightly more complex system that produces more choice, or a simple system that is easy to understand?	✗ Other systems are complicated, but FPTP is simple and easy to operate.

Referendums in the UK

What is a referendum?

A referendum is a vote in which the electorate can express a view on a particular issue of public policy. A referendum is therefore a device of direct democracy used in representative democracies.

Referendums in the UK are not legally binding, unless Parliament indicates otherwise in the referendum legislation. This means that, legally, Parliament can ignore the results. For example, even though the result of the Brexit referendum was to leave, Parliament could have ignored it because Parliament is sovereign and the referendum in that case was 'advisory'. Up until the 1970s, referendums hadn't been used in the UK. Before Labour came to power in 1997, only four such referendums had been held (see Table 4.8).

How referendums have been used in the UK

Referendums have been held in the UK under several circumstances, which include:

1. To provide legitimacy to major constitutional changes (e.g. devolution of power to Scotland, Wales and Northern Ireland).
2. To resolve questions of major constitutional importance (e.g. referendums on Scottish independence).
3. To settle disputes within the governing party (e.g. the 1975 referendum on continuing membership of the EEC and the 2016 Brexit referendum).
4. If there are coalition negotiations, governments may agree to hold a referendum as part of the negotiations (e.g. the AV referendums in 2011).
5. To fulfil pledges made in party manifestos. In 1997, Labour promised in their manifesto to hold a referendum on instituting the position of London Mayor.

Tip: Students often incorrectly identify a flaw in Northern Ireland's government as being unstable because of STV. In fact, this instability is caused by requirements of the Good Friday Agreement which requires a complicated system of power sharing.

Table 4.8 Referendums held in the UK

Year	Issue	Yes	No	Turnout	Comment
1973	Should Northern Ireland remain part of the UK?	**99%**	1%	58%	Boycotted by the Catholic nationalists.
1975	Should the UK remain in the EEC?	**68%**	32%	64%	**NATIONAL REFERENDUM**
1979	Should there be devolution of power to Scotland?	52%	**48%**	63%	Majority was insufficient as 40% of whole electorate needed to vote yes.
1979	Should there be devolution of power to Wales?	20%	**80%**	58%	A clearly negative result.
1997	Should there be devolution of power to Scotland?	**74%**	26%	60%	A decisive yes on both questions.
	Scotland also voted in favour of tax-raising powers for the Scottish Parliament?	**63%**	37%		
1997	Should there be devolution of power to Wales?	**50.3%**	49.7%	50%	Indecisive but devolution was adopted.
1998	Should the Good Friday Agreement for Northern Ireland be implemented?	**71%**	29%	81%	Clear consent was needed and achieved.
1998	Should London have an elected mayor and assembly?	**72%**	28%	33%	A decisive result.
2011	Do you want the (Welsh) Assembly to be able to make laws on *all* matters it has powers for?	**64%**	36%	35%	Extended the law-making powers of the Welsh Assembly.
2011	Should the House of Commons use the 'alternative vote' to elect MPs?	32%	**68%**	42%	**NATIONAL REFERENDUM**
2014	Should Scotland become an independent country?	45%	**55%**	85%	Huge turnout and a clear answer.
2016	Should the UK remain a member of or leave the EU?	48%	**52%**	72.2%	A result, but not sufficiently clear for many for a decision of this magnitude.

Note: Unless otherwise stated, only voters in the affected areas took part in the referendum

CASE STUDY 4.1: EU 'IN/OUT' REFERENDUM 2016

Photo 4.2 Protesters attend anti-Brexit rallies across the UK

Source: Bloomberg / Contributor / Getty Images

Events

In 2014, David Cameron committed to holding an 'in/out' referendum on EU membership if the Conservatives won the 2015 General Election. He did so against the backdrop of growing Euroscepticism on his backbenches. By promising to hold an EU referendum, Cameron hoped to quell the rebellions over Europe and to improve the chance of a Conservative victory in 2015 by undermining UKIP. The core calculation was that the referendum would end up endorsing rather than rejecting EU membership. Cameron and his key advisers were confident of a positive outcome from the referendum for two reasons.

» The referendum campaign was expected to be an unequal struggle between, on the one hand, virtually the entire political establishment, including the leaderships of all the major parties, backed by the bulk of business leaders, senior economists and trade union bosses, and on the other hand, UKIP and 'fringe' figures in the Conservative Party.

» Despite the recognition that the EU was broadly unloved, there was an expectation that, faced with the prospect of profound and irreversible change, the electorate would 'stick with the devil they know'.

The Leave campaign was bolstered by the recruitment of senior figures such as Michael Gove and Boris Johnson, as well as by Jeremy Corbyn's unenthusiastic support for Remain. The Leave campaign also had the backing of the *Sun*, the *Daily Mail* and the *Daily Telegraph*. The 52%

victory for Leave in June 2016 showed that the prospect of change can sometimes be more attractive than the comforts of the status quo. By the morning, the UK had voted to leave the EU.

Significance

Cameron's EU referendum commitment turned into something increasingly beyond his control. Settling the issue through a referendum rather than Parliament was the only way that growing hostility towards the EU could be articulated as public opinion would have been blocked because of pro-EU majorities in each of the major Westminster parties. For the electorate, the referendum itself was a means of taking back control.

There were those who did not feel that a referendum was the best way to resolve this issue. Ken Clarke, the only Conservative Parliamentarian who voted against Cameron's referendum legislation, argued that the issue of EU membership was far too complex to expect citizens to reach a balanced and evidence-based judgement. It left them prey to misinformation and exaggeration on both sides and increased the chances that the outcome would be determined by other factors. Moreover, to boil the question of EU membership down to a simple choice between Remain and Leave was unhelpful and, in the absence of a plan for Brexit, virtually meaningless.

Parliamentarians found themselves in an impossible situation after the referendum. The vast majority had campaigned and voted to remain and now found themselves having to pass legislation to leave the EU. The Article 50 legislation went through smoothly: 498 to 114 in March 2017. However, in the following two and a half years, Parliament was unable to commit itself to fully carrying out the wishes of the electorate despite 84% of MPs being elected in 2017 on manifestos which committed them to leaving the EU. MPs were clearly frustrated that they were having to enact legislation to which they were fundamentally opposed and believed would bring devastation to the UK. This raised the issue of the role of an MP and competing theories of representation between delegate and Burkean models (discussed in more detail in Chapter 8). The result of the 2019 General Election resolved this issue, with the new Parliament passing the Withdrawal Agreement in January 2020 by 358 votes to 234.

KEY TOPIC DEBATE: SHOULD REFERENDUMS BE USED IN THE UK'S REPRESENTATIVE DEMOCRACY?

The use of referendums was historically frowned upon. They were seen as somehow 'not British' because they appeared to be in conflict with the principles of parliamentary democracy and sovereignty. It was argued that referendums diminished Parliament and undermined its legitimacy.

However, the Blair era turned those ideas on their head, making referendums part of a revolutionary constitutional reform agenda. Hence, since 1997, referendums have been much more widely used amid a growing acceptance that major changes to the way the UK is governed should be endorsed directly by the public rather than simply being left for Parliament to decide. This may have created a new constitutional convention that major constitutional changes should in future always be put to a referendum.

✔ **They enable the electorate to decide on specific issues that they might not have had the opportunity to consider at a general election.**

» This ensures that the public's views and interests are properly and accurately articulated, and not distorted by politicians who claim to 'represent' them.

» Referendums allow people to express their view on a specific issue irrespective of party connection.

» They also provide the public with a way of expressing their views about important constitutional changes: for example, all the devolved assemblies needed to be approved first via a referendum.

✖ **Referendums undermine the authority of Parliament as it may be sidelined by the overuse of referendums.**

» As suggested above, decisions made as a consequence of referendums tie Parliament's hand if it wishes subsequently to overturn these decisions. These issues go against a fundamental principle of our constitution: parliamentary sovereignty (see Chapter 10).

» Referendums also create confusion in a representative democracy because the electorate elects politicians to make decisions, but the views of politicians may run counter to the wishes of the people as expressed in the referendums. This was exactly the issue caused by the 2016 EU referendum.

» Referendums allow politicians to absolve themselves of responsibility for making difficult decisions. For example, in the EU referendum in 2016, Boris Johnson successfully campaigned to leave but without any plan to follow it through. After Cameron resigned, Johnson didn't enter the race to become leader and left it to others to resolve the ensuing chaos in the aftermath of the referendum result.

✔ **Referendums help to create a more engaged and better educated and informed electorate.**

» They make the population more active between elections, which may lead to increased turnouts. The Northern Ireland Referendum on the Good Friday Agreement had a turnout of 81%.

» Members of the public have a stronger incentive to think and act politically when they know they are going to be asked to make an important decision. It can certainly be seen as a consequence of the EU referendum that British citizens have a much greater understanding of the EU and our relationship with it.

» The media coverage of the referendum and the materials produced by referendum campaigns expose voters to further evidence and arguments to inform their decision.

✖ **However, campaigns can also be misleading or oversimplify complicated issues that are better left to elected representatives.**

» Both the Remain and Leave campaigns in the 2016 EU referendum made claims that fact checkers have found to be extremely misleading, which can make it very difficult for confused voters. Examples are the Leave campaign's infamous NHS bus claim that 'We send £350 million a week to the EU' and Cameron's suggestion that, if the UK left the EU, house prices would plummet, there would be medicine shortages and a year-long recession with the loss of half a million jobs.

» Also, the real meaning of voting 'yes' or 'no' in the 2016 EU referendum or 2014 Scottish Independence Referendum was far from clear. Did it mean staying in the single market, customs union or leaving without a deal? In Scotland did independence mean losing or keeping the pound, and did it mean staying in the EU?

» Although they might engage the electorate, this can sometimes be highly divisive, as has been illustrated by the EU and Scottish referendums. It took a significant number of voters years to accept the results of the referendum and for politics to return to a more 'normal', less toxic state.

✅ **Referendums promote participation and give everyone an equal voice.**

» Every vote cast in a referendum is worth the same no matter where you live, unlike in general elections.

» The 2014 referendum on Scottish independence had an 84.5% turnout, suggesting that people participate when they think their voice will be heard.

» They enhance participation by allowing the public to speak for themselves rather than through the distorted views of representatives.

❌ **Too regular use of referendum might result in voter apathy or fatigue.**

» There is a danger that the public becomes over-burdened with decision making and increasingly indifferent; as a result of this, decisions are made only by those who can be bothered to vote.

» In 2016, voting in Scotland on the EU referendum was slightly lower than expected for such a pro-EU part of the country: 67% turnout in Scotland compared with 72% nationally – some suggested it was due to voter fatigue.

» Low turnouts can reduce the legitimacy of referendums. The 1998 Welsh Devolution referendum had a turnout of 50% and the AV referendum turnout was 42%.

» They place political decisions in the hands of those who have limited knowledge and experience.

✅ **They can settle long-standing disputes and issues of constitutional interest.**

» The 2011 referendum on AV, which was rejected by 68% of voters, effectively kicked the discussion of replacing FPTP into the long grass for the foreseeable future.

» Scotland's long-desired Parliament of its own was established after the 1997 referendum and would be difficult to remove.

❌ **However, sometimes referendum questions can be asked more than once until the government's desired answer is received.**

» The 2014 Scottish Independence Referendum did not appear to settle the issue, and a second referendum on the matter is feasible if, at any time in the future, the SNP win an overall majority in the Scottish Parliament.

» There were huge clamours for a second referendum to overturn the 2016 EU referendum result almost immediately after the vote.

» Referendums on creating a Scottish Parliament and Welsh Parliament were both defeated in 1979. However, this did not settle the issue. Referendums were held again in 1997 and this time the devolution plans were approved.

✅ **Referendums make government more responsive by forcing them to listen to public opinion between elections.**

» As such, they provide a much-needed check on government power, because the government has less control over their outcome than it usually does over Parliament. Citizens are therefore protected against the danger of over-mighty government.

❌ **Referendums enable leaders to manipulate the political agenda.**

» The government can choose when to call them and use public resources to back their preferred outcome as happened in 2016 when £9 million of taxpayers' money was spent on a Remain leaflet issued by the government. They can control the question, the options on the ballot paper and the threshold for victory.

» The 2014 Scottish Independence Referendum was a yes/no question on independence, even though many Scottish voters wanted a third option for 'greater devolution'.

» Also, the electorate may not vote on the referendum issue and may instead use it as a vote on the government. For example, the 2011 AV referendum campaign run by Cameron centred on the fact that the Deputy Prime Minister Nick Clegg supported the reforms, rather than the actual merits of AV and FPTP. It was suggested that many voted against Clegg rather than against AV.

Key Debate Summary: Should referendums be used in the UK's representative democracy?

For	Theme	Against
✓ Referendums enable the electorate to decide on specific issues which they might not have had the opportunity to consider at a general election.	Who should decide major issues?	✗ Referendums undermine the authority of Parliament as it may be sidelined by the overuse of referendums.
✓ Referendums help to create a more engaged and better educated and informed electorate.	How effective are referendums at educating and engaging the public?	✗ Referendum campaigns can be misleading or oversimplify complicated issues. They can also be highly divisive.
✓ Referendums promote participation and give everyone an equal voice.	How effective are referendums at promoting participation?	✗ Too regular use of referendums might result in voter apathy or fatigue.

CASE STUDY 4.2: SCOTTISH INDEPENDENCE REFERENDUM 2014 AND BEYOND

Events

This was the third major referendum to have been held in Scotland, but the first to be held on the issue of independence. A referendum on Scottish devolution had been held in 1979, and successfully in 1997. Support for the Scottish National Party (SNP) grew, enabling it in 2007 to form a minority administration and then in 2011 to win an overall majority, and the SNP shifted its focus from calling for a further referendum to widen the powers of the Scottish Parliament to demanding an independence referendum. This led in 2012 to the Edinburgh Agreement, under which the Scottish and UK Governments agreed to hold an independence referendum two years later. Although David Cameron was, at the time, criticised by some in his own party for being 'over-fair' to the SNP Government in these negotiations – agreeing, among other things, that the Scottish Parliament should provide the legislative basis for the referendum, as well as determining its franchise, timing and wording – his judgement, as a unionist, was eventually proved to be correct, with 55% of the Scottish electorate voting 'no' in the eventual referendum.

Significance

One of the key consequences was a realignment of 'party politics' into 'independence politics'. Previously, you chose your politics based on a traditional left/right spectrum with a minority of Scots voting on the basis of independence from the UK. The referendum appeared to change that and voters considered independence to be a key issue. This led to a surge in support for the SNP, led by Nicola Sturgeon as the 'independence' party and the Conservatives as the flag bearer for staying in the UK; or at least this was certainly the case while Ruth Davidson was leader. For the Labour Party, the realignment was huge which was clear for all to see in the 2015 Election where Labour lost 40 of its 41 seats while the SNP won 56 out of the 59 seats in a radical realignment of party politics in Scotland.

The vote to leave the EU in June 2016 once again threw the Union into uncertainty, with Scotland voting 62%–38% to Remain. In March 2017, Sturgeon sought the powers from the UK Government to stage a fresh independence vote, which was refused by then PM Theresa May. The SNP's strong showing in the 2019 Election (winning 48 out of 69 Scottish seats at Westminster) led to a further demand by Sturgeon to hold a second independence referendum. Johnson, like May, refused.

It seemed like independence was inevitable, with Sturgeon's strong and dynamic leadership. But in February 2023, she suddenly resigned from her post and the subsequent financial scandals surrounding the arrest of the SNP CEO Peter Murrell, who was also Sturgeon's husband, plunged the SNP into turmoil. Sturgeon's replacement, Humza Yousaf, made a catastrophic error of judgement resulting in the Greens withdrawing support for them in the Scottish Parliament, leading to his resignation, leaving former leader John Swinney to take the reins. His lacklustre campaign resulted in a terrible defeat in the 2024 General Election, losing nearly 40 Westminster seats. It now seems as if another independence referendum is a long way off.

Exam Style Questions

- Evaluate the view that the performance of other electoral systems in the UK has made the case for replacing FPTP for Westminster elections (30).

- Evaluate the view that electoral systems in the UK promote multi-party systems (30).

- Evaluate the view that representative democracy in the UK is undermined by the representation provided by the electoral systems used (30).

- Evaluate the view that proportional electoral systems have fundamentally affected politics in the UK (30).

- Evaluate the view that increased use of referendums has improved democracy in the UK (30).

- Evaluate the view that referendums have more democratic legitimacy than elections in the UK (30).

Source Question

Referendums enable the electorate to decide on specific issues that they might not have had the opportunity to consider at a general election. This ensures that the public's views and interests are properly and accurately articulated, and not distorted by politicians who claim to 'represent' them. They also provide the public with a way of expressing their views about important constitutional changes; for example, all the devolved assemblies needed to be approved first via a referendum, as well as creating a more engaged and better educated electorate. Referendums encourage citizens to participate in democracy, and make them more active between elections. Unlike elections, they give everyone an equal voice as every vote cast in a referendum is worth the same no matter where you live.

On the other hand, referendums undermine the authority of Parliament because decisions made through referendums tie Parliament's hands as they cannot realistically defy the will of the public. This goes against parliamentary sovereignty. Referendums also create confusion in a representative democracy because voters elect politicians to make decisions, but the views of politicians may run counter to the wishes of the people as expressed in the referendums. This was exactly the issue caused by the 2016 EU referendum. Also, rather than educate the electorate, referendum campaigns can be misleading or oversimplify complicated issues that are better left to elected representatives. Both the Remain and Leave campaigns in the 2016 EU referendum made claims that fact checkers have found to be extremely misleading, which can make it very difficult for confused voters. Also, referendums simplify highly complex issues with the result that the real meaning of voting 'yes' or 'no' is far from clear. Lastly, although they might engage the electorate, this can sometimes be highly divisive, as has been illustrated by the EU and Scottish referendums. It took a significant number of voters years to accept the results of the referendum and for politics to return to a more 'normal', less toxic state.

Using the source, evaluate the view that referendums have a highly detrimental effect on UK politics.

In your response you must:

» *Compare and contrast different opinions in the source*

» *Examine and debate these views in a balanced way*

» *Analyse and evaluate **only** the information presented in the source.*

Chapter Summary

» FPTP, used for Westminster elections, is deeply disproportionate, but tends to provide single-party government.

» FPTP was unable to provide single-party governments between 2010 and 2019 but was able to once again provide it in the 2024 and 2019 General Elections.

» Systems of PR are used all around the UK in 'second tier' elections.

» These elections have provided results that are much more reflective of the way people have voted.

» They have also resulted in mainly coalition or minority governments which have been, largely, stable.

» Referendums have been used more widely in the UK since the 1990s.

» The most recent referendums – Scottish independence and leaving the EU – severely tested many aspects of the political system, leaving doubts in many minds as to their effectiveness as a tool for resolving contentious, complicated issues.

Further Resources

Bogdanor, V. (2009) *The People and the Party System: The Referendum and Electoral Reform in British Politics* (Cambridge: Cambridge University Press).

Curtice, J. (2015) 'A Return to Normality? How the Electoral System Operated', *Parliamentary Affairs*, Vol. 68, No. 1, September, pp. 25–40.

Denver, D., Carmen, C. and Johns, R. (2011) *Elections and Voters in Britain* (London: Palgrave Macmillan).

Farrell, D. (2011) *Electoral Systems: A Comparative Introduction* (2nd edn) (London: Bloomsbury).

Gallagher, M. and Mitchell, P. (eds) (2011) *The Politics of Electoral Systems* (Oxford: Oxford University Press).

Gallop, N. (2020) 'The 2019 General Election by Nick Gallop', *Politics Review*, Vol. 29, No. 3.

Griffiths, S. and Leach, R. (2018) *British Politics* (3rd edn) (London: Bloomsbury): Chapter 13.

Heffernan, R., Hay, C., Russell, M. and Cowley, P. (2016) *Developments in British Politics* (10th edn) (London: Bloomsbury): Chapter 3.

Moran, M. (2015) *Politics and Governance in the UK* (3rd edn) (London: Bloomsbury): Chapter 16.

Visit the companion website to access the Further Resources Booklet to explore a range of useful web links related to: case studies on UK general elections, literature from the Constitution Society and the House of Commons Library, the Electoral Reform Society and the Electoral Commission.

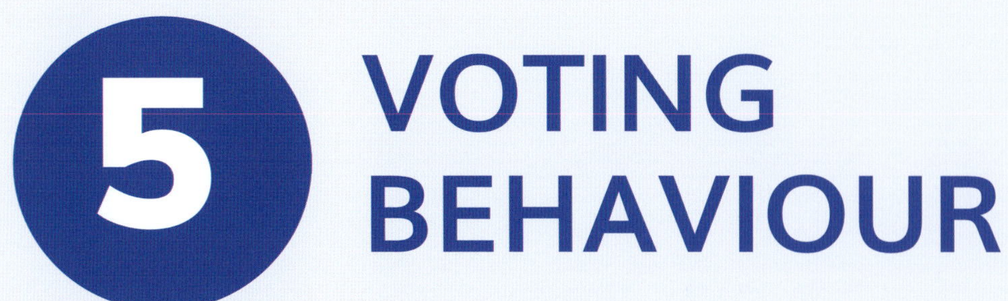

5 VOTING BEHAVIOUR

Chapter Preview

Academic interest in the study of voting behaviour grew during the 1950s and 1960s through the belief that politics can be studied scientifically if it focuses on observation and analysis of political behaviour; as a result psephology (the scientific study of voting behaviour) commands a central position in the understanding of voting behaviour. This is because voting provides one of the richest sources of information about the interaction between people and politics. By investigating the patterns and trends of voting behaviour, we are able to learn important lessons about the nature of the political system, and, in particular, the outcome of elections. Therefore, if we want to know what particular elections mean, we must start by looking at the factors that shaped how we choose to vote.

Much debate surrounds the issue of voting behaviour. Not only are there rival theories of voting, but the act of voting is also shaped by a shifting variety of long-term and short-term influences. Long-term influences affect electoral outcomes over several elections and may even be relevant to all elections. These factors include social class, age, race or ethnicity, gender, region and party loyalty. Short-term influences, by contrast, are specific to particular elections, and so do not allow conclusions to be drawn about voting patterns in general, but instead just for that election. These factors include party policies, the performance and image of parties and the effectiveness of party leaders. This chapter will explore all these areas and see how they have evolved over time.

Specification Checklist

4.1. Case studies of three key general elections

» Case studies of three elections (one from the period 1945–92, the 1997 election, and one since 1997), the results and their impact on parties and government.

» The factors that explain the outcomes of these elections, including:

- the reasons for and impact of party policies and manifesto techniques used in their election campaigns, and the wider political context of the elections
- class-based voting and other factors influencing voting patterns, such as partisanship and voting attachment
- gender, age, ethnicity and region as factors in influencing voting behaviour, turnout and trends.

» Analysis of the national voting behaviour patterns for these elections, revealed by national data sources, and how and why they vary.

Source: Paul Ellis / Contributor / Getty Images

Voting behaviour in the UK

What is voting behaviour?

How can we explain the outcome of elections? Why do people support one party rather than another? The study of voting behaviour is important because it helps us to explain the process of political change and not only changes in government, but also in parties' policies and ideological beliefs. Voting provides one of the richest sources of information about the interaction between people and politics. Voting behaviour allows us to learn about the political system, and, specifically, the outcome of elections which is shaped by a shifting variation of long-term and short-term influences.

» Long-term influences (social factors) affect electoral outcomes over several elections and may even be relevant to all elections.

» Short-term influences, by contrast, are specific to particular elections, and so do not allow conclusions to be drawn about voting patterns in general.

Long-term factors in voting behaviour (social factors)

Voting in the UK has traditionally been explained in terms of long-term social and political factors. This 'sociological model' links voting behaviour to group membership. It suggests that electors tend to adopt a voting pattern that reflects the economic and social position of the group, or groups, to which they belong. This model therefore highlights the importance of social alignment, reflecting the various divisions and tensions within society. The most significant of these are social class, gender, ethnicity, religion and region. Social classes have been categorised as shown in Table 5.1. This categorisation is based solely on occupation, and it is argued that, with up to roughly 60% of UK consumers classed as ABC1 and with much more diverse work and household patterns, the system is too blunt for modern usage. Nonetheless ABC1C2DE is still the most widely used definition. As such, the sociological model is only concerned with long-term factors. Two explanations have been advanced to explain why such factors affect voting:

» The first relies on the impact of socialisation; in other words, behaving the way you've learned to behave based on the people around you.

» The second emphasises rationality, in that people are believed to support the party that is most likely to advance the interests of their group.

Until the 1970s, voting patterns were relatively stable and predictable. Most voters could be classified as 'core' voters, with only around one-fifth being so-called **floating voters**. However, a variety of long-term factors influence voting.

> **Definition**
>
> **Floating voters:** Voters with few or no party loyalties, who therefore vote for different parties in different elections.

> **Definition**
>
> **Class alignment:** When people associate themselves with a class and firmly believe that they belong to it.
>
> **Political socialisation:** When the way you decide things politically are based on the way you've learned to behave based on the people around you.

Table 5.1 **Social classes in the UK**

Class A	Higher managerial and professional workers
Class B	Middle managers and professionals
Class C1	Clerical workers
Class C2	Skilled manual workers
Class D	Semi-skilled and unskilled workers
Class E	Unemployed, pensioners and people unable to work

Social class

Until the 1970s, class was widely seen as the key to understanding voting behaviour in the UK. Peter Pulzer (1967) famously declared: 'Class is the basis of British party politics; all else is embellishment and detail.' The stable Conservative–Labour two-party system of the 1945–70 period was largely a reflection of what was called **class alignment**. This model places a heavy stress on early **political socialisation**, seeing the family as the principal means through which political loyalties are forged. These are then, in most cases, reinforced by group membership and social experience.

Linked to this, a second factor, which explains the relatively stable voting patterns of the 1945–70 period, is that most voters had a clear and enduring identification with a particular party. This was known as **partisan alignment**. This 'party identification model' is based on the idea that people develop a sense of psychological attachment to a political party. Electors are thus seen as people who *identify* with a party, in the sense of being long-term supporters who regard the party as 'their' party. Voting is therefore a commitment to a party, rather than a product of calculation influenced by factors such as policies, personalities, campaigning and media coverage.

For example, in 1964–66, 64% of manual voters (classes C2, D and E) voted Labour, while 62% of non-manual voters (classes A, B and C1) voted Conservative. However, from the 1970s onwards, the UK has experienced an accelerating process of **class dealignment**. This does not mean that social class has become irrelevant to voting behaviour, but that the relationship between class and voting has weakened substantially. Moreover, the ABC1C2DE classification measures only occupation rather than a broader measure of social class; class may be better understood as wealth, home ownership, and income alongside occupation.

PARTISAN DEALIGNMENT

The main consequence of partisan dealignment has been greater electoral volatility. This has been reflected in increased uncertainty about electoral outcomes as 'swings' from one party to another become larger and, in the rise of new parties or the decline of old ones. A variety of explanations have been advanced for partisan dealignment:

→ **Increased education.** The expansion of education in recent decades has encouraged voters to question traditional, party-based loyalties, and perhaps to take policies and issues more seriously.

→ **Impact of the media.** Voters have access to wider sources of political information, particularly through television and more recently social media. They are therefore less dependent on party-supporting newspapers.

→ **Ideological change.** Shifts in parties' policies and ideological beliefs since the 1980s have alienated some of their traditional supporters and appealed to their non-traditional supporters.

CLASS DEALIGNMENT

Among the consequences of class dealignment has been a shift in the policies and ideas of the major two parties as they have been forced to seek votes from 'natural' supporters of other parties. Suggested explanations for class dealignment include the following:

» **Changing class system.** The manual workforce has shrunk as there has been a decline in manufacturing jobs and the 'traditional' working class has given way to the 'new' working class who work in low-paid service sector jobs, or the **gig economy**.

» **Class ambiguity.** Social class has become less clear-cut, for instance, through the decline in trade union membership and the rise in home ownership.

» **Embourgeoisement.** Growing post-war affluence encouraged some working-class voters to consider themselves middle class. Affluent workers may be more selfish.

Like social class, party loyalty has declined markedly since the 1970s, in this case through a process of **partisan dealignment.** Figure 5.1 shows just how dramatically this factor has reduced since 1992.

» By 1979, just 51% of all voters supported their 'natural' class party, and by 1987 this had fallen to 44%.

» The 2010 General Election witnessed an even weaker link between class and voting, with only 38% of electors being 'class voters'. In 2015, this rose, but only to 40%.

» In 2017, the Conservatives performed equally well among ABC1 voters and C2DE voters (44%), marginally better than Labour in both cases. Labour held 72 of the 100 constituencies with the most working-class households, the Conservatives held 13.

Figure 5.1 Votes by social class over time

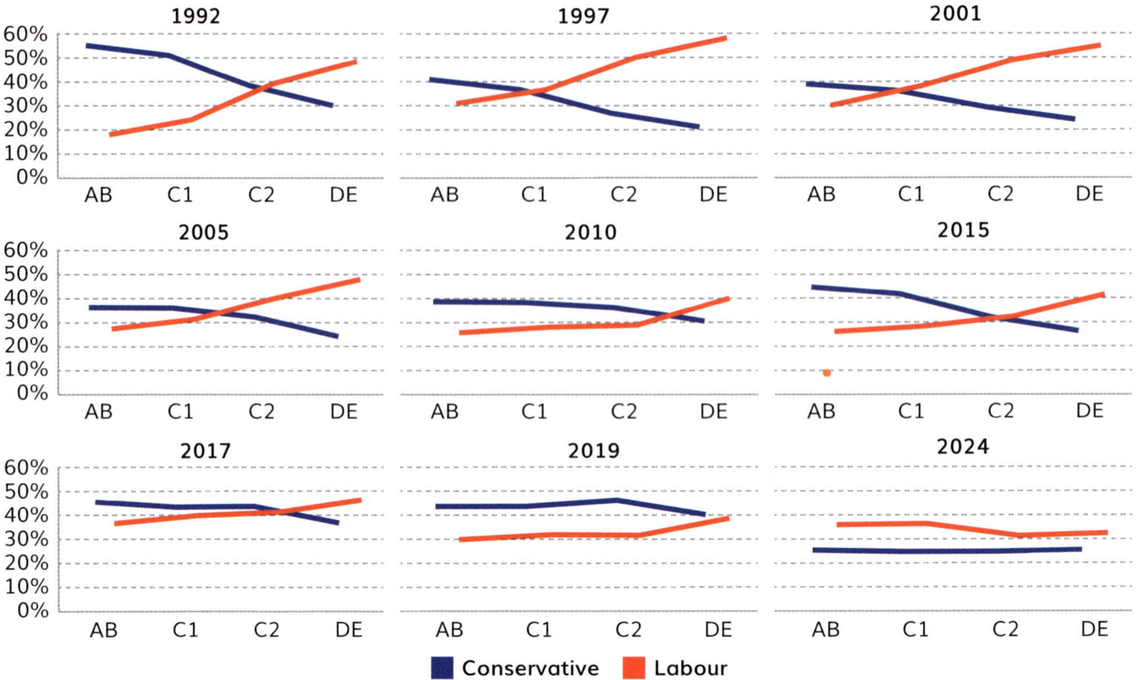

Source: © Ipsos. Reproduced with permission

» In 2019, the Conservatives comfortably outperformed Labour across all social grades. They did better among C2DE voters (48%) than they did among ABC1 voters (43%). Labour performed the same among both social grade groups (33%). In 2019, Labour held 53 of the 100 constituencies with the most working-class households and the Conservatives increased their share to 31.

Figure 5.2 Votes by social grade

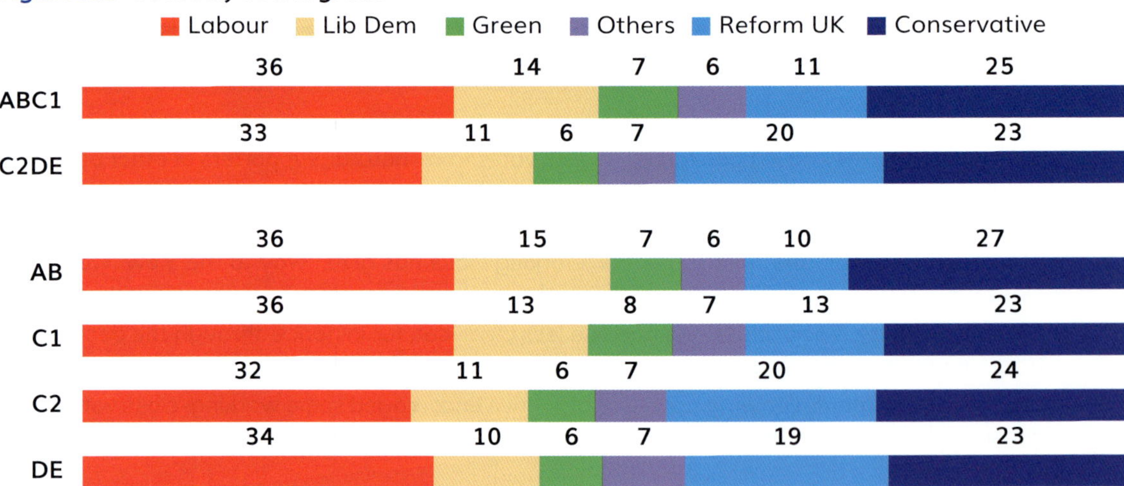

Source: YouGov, 'How Britain voted in the 2024 General Election'

» In 2024, we see a complete reversal, with Labour outperforming the Conservatives across all social grades. Interestingly, Reform UK were the equal second biggest party among C2s along with the Conservatives. Figure 5.2 shows that Reform did a lot better amongst C2DE voters (20%) than among ABC1 voters (11%), while the Liberal Democrats did slightly better with those from a higher social grade (14% to 11%).

Gender

Figure 5.3 shows that in the main, there are no fundamental differences in the way men and women vote. There is a slight gender bias for female voters to support the Conservatives. This became less pronounced under Margaret Thatcher but reasserted itself under John Major. The advent of Tony Blair and New Labour had a major impact on this gender bias, with women supporting Labour more than men, but in 2024 men and women deserted the Conservative Party in relatively equal measures.

Figure 5.3 Gender difference in voting over time

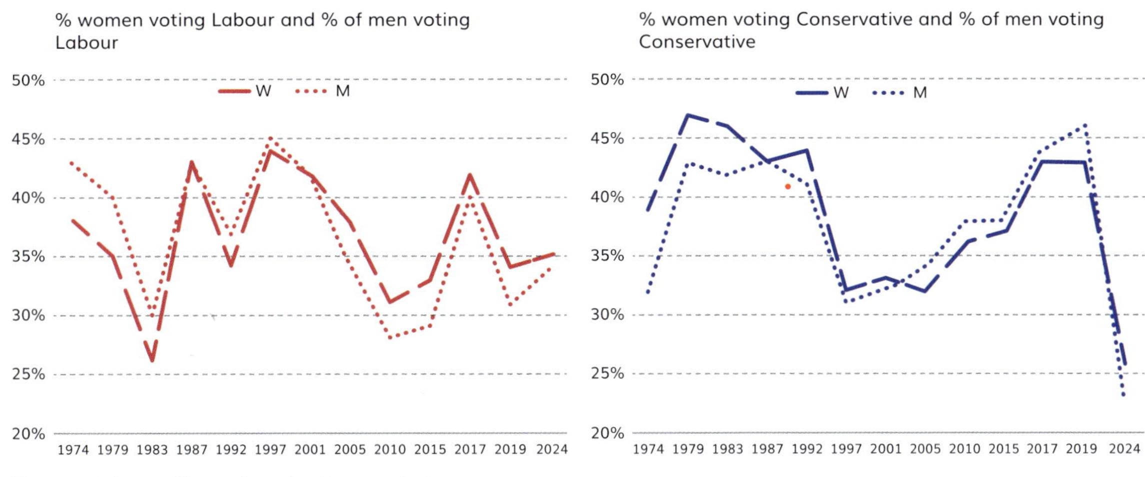

Source: © Ipsos. Reproduced with permission

» **In 1997, Labour was supported by an equal number of women and men (44%), making this the first general election that Labour would have won with an all-female electorate. This trend continued in 2001 and 2005.**

» In 2015, men were more likely to vote Conservative than women in all age groups except 50+, but the overall difference was only 2%.

» In 2019, there was a gender gap, but only among the young. The data points towards a very small gender gap, with the Conservatives on 46% among men and 44% among women, and Labour on 31% among men and 35% among women.

» In 2024, men and women voted very similarly with 34% of men and 35% of women backing Labour with the Lib Dems also receiving an almost identical vote share from men (12%) and women (13%). Slightly more women voted Conservative than men (26% to 23%) while more men voted Reform UK than women (17% to 12%).

Figure 5.4 How people voted in 2024 according to gender

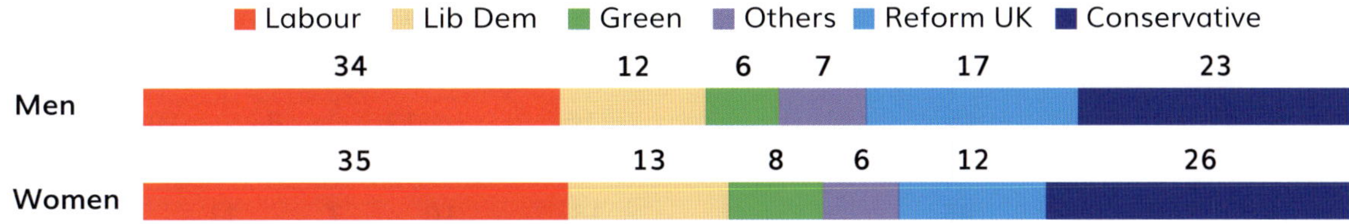

Source: YouGov, 'How Britain voted in the 2024 General Election'

Age

There has always been a general tendency for levels of Conservative support to increase with age. Even in 1997 and 2001, the Party led Labour among the over-65s. Some explain this in terms of a tendency for people to become more conservative with age, either because they are financially better-off or because they become more fearful of change. In contrast, Labour has tended to do better among young voters, a trend that increased dramatically after 2015 when Jeremy Corbyn became leader. In 2017, YouGov argued that age was the new dividing line in British politics. This notion is clearly illustrated by Figure 5.5.

Figure 5.5 Votes by age over time

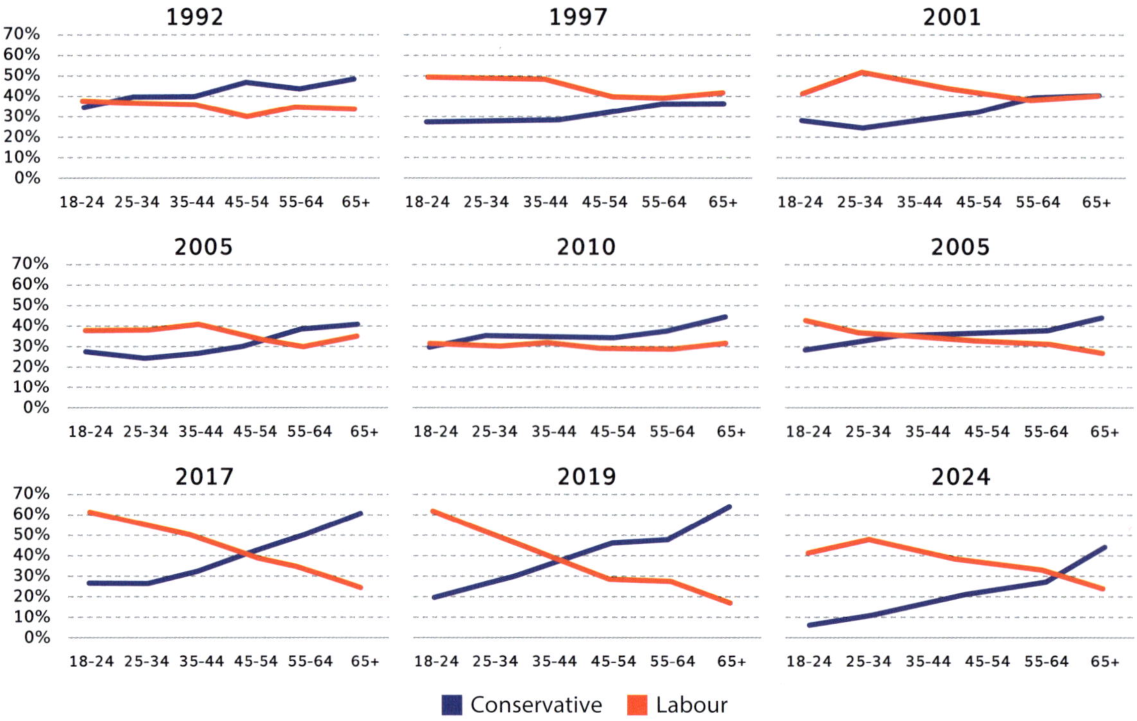

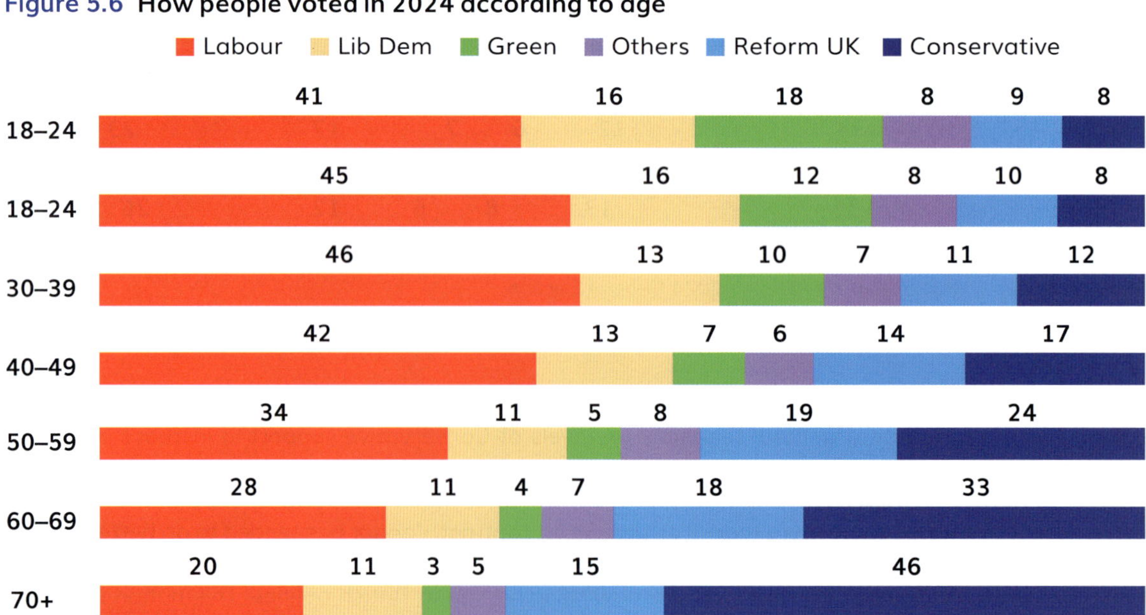

Source: © Ipsos MORI. Reproduced with permission

» Age was a major factor in the 2016 EU referendum, with support for Remain falling consistently with age while support for Leave rose. Whereas 73% of 18–24-year-old voters backed Remain, 60% of 65+ voters favoured Leave.

» In the 2017 Election, Labour had a 47% lead over the Conservatives among 18–19-year-old voters, while the Conservatives had a 50% lead among 70+ voters.

» In 2019, YouGov confirmed once more that age was still the biggest dividing line in British politics. Labour still won a majority of younger voters and the Conservatives were miles ahead among the older generations.

Figure 5.6 How people voted in 2024 according to age

Source: YouGov, 'How Britain voted in the 2024 General Election'

» In 2024, age was still a key dividing line in 2024 with younger voters being more likely to vote Labour and older voters more likely to vote for the Conservatives. However, in 2024, around the same proportion of all age groups below 50 voted for Labour. For the over-50s, the per cent voting Labour decreases more steeply with just over a third of 50–59-year-olds backing Labour, but just 20% of those 70 or older. The Green Party did a lot better with younger voters while Reform UK did better amongst older voters. The average age of a Labour voter is now 46 and a Conservative voter is 63. For the Lib Dems it is 48, Reform UK 56 and Greens 39.

Ethnicity

Black and minority ethnic (BME) voters have also usually voted Labour as can be seen by Figure 5.7. This may be because the party has been more closely associated with a pro-immigration stance historically, as well as introducing measures to support these communities. It is also the case that most ethnic minority groups experience lower income levels and higher unemployment compared to white groups. Therefore, ethnic minority support for Labour could be linked to social class.

» In 2015, Labour had a lead of 42% over the Conservatives among voters with a Black African or Caribbean heritage, and an 18% lead among voters with a South Asian heritage, although the Conservatives enjoyed a 13% lead among the much-smaller number of voters from other parts of Asia.

Figure 5.7 Votes by ethnicity in 2024

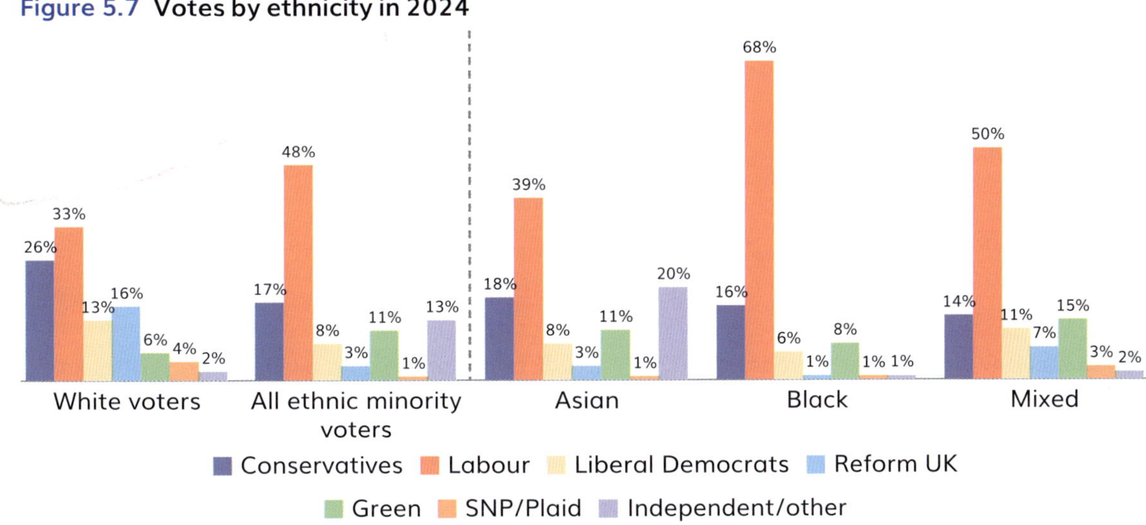

Source: © Ipsos. Reproduced with permission

» In 2017, Labour remained the most popular party among ethnic minority voters, receiving 77% of ethnic minority votes, with 20% going to the Conservatives and 3% to other parties. Labour did especially well among Muslim voters in 2015 and 2017. In 2015, Labour received 74% of votes from British Muslims – in 2017, this had risen to 87%.

» According to the Runnymede Trust, one minority group did noticeably increase its support for the Conservatives in both 2015 and 2017 – British Indians, and Hindus in particular. From 30% in 2010, the Conservatives share of the votes of British Indians went up to 40% in 2017.

» In 2019, among ethnic minority voters, Labour led the Conservatives by 64% to 20%, while among white voters the Conservatives led by 48% to 29%. However, Labour's vote share had fallen by a similar amount since 2017 among both groups, by 9% and 10% respectively. Also, Labour would have lost much of the Jewish vote due to the anti-Semitism crisis in the party, although there are only a few hundred thousand of those.

» In 2024, British Indians showed a notable inclination towards the Conservative Party, with 39% voting Conservative – significantly higher than the general population's support for the party which could well be because of Rishi Sunak being the first Hindu Prime Minister.

However, Labour experienced a substantial decline in support among Muslim voters, compared to previous elections. In 2019, over 80% of Muslim voters supported Labour. By 2024, this figure dropped to approximately 63%, with voters supporting independent candidates. This decline was attributed to dissatisfaction with Labour's handling of the Gaza conflict. In constituencies where more than 30%

of the population identified as Muslim, Labour's share of the vote fell dramatically from an average of 65% in 2019 to 36% in 2024. The election saw some Muslim voters turning to independent candidates or the Green Party, reflecting a fragmentation of the traditional voting bloc that Labour had relied upon. This is reflected in Figure 5.8.

Overall, the ethnic minority vote is increasingly fragmented. While Labour still leads overall, there are significant differences in preferences among various communities. For instance, Black voters tended to support Labour more strongly than Asian voters, who displayed more diverse political affiliations.

Figure 5.8 **Votes by ethnicity change between 2019 and 2024**

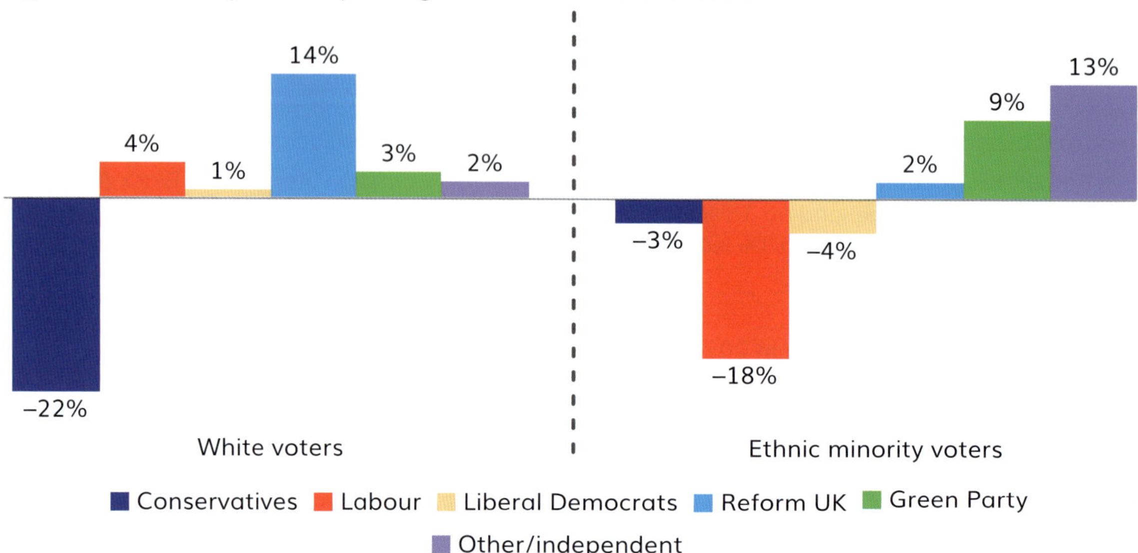

Source: © Ipsos. Reproduced with permission

Region

During the 1980s, it became increasingly topical to talk of a 'North–South divide' in UK politics linked to class-based communities in different parts of the UK. Outside London, Labour held only a handful of seats south of a line from the Bristol Channel to the Wash, while Conservative support declined in the north of England and, for a period, the party held no seats in either Scotland or Wales. However, since the Blair era, Labour began to do well in the south too.

» In 2017, there was a swing to Labour in London and the south (perhaps because these were Remain areas) as well as smaller swings in Wales, the North West and East.

» The 2019 election will be remembered as the one where the Conservatives broke the 'Red Wall', moving into many traditional Labour heartlands. The collapse of the Red Wall – safe Labour constituencies across the Midlands and the north of England – fell to the Conservatives as can be seen in Figure 5.9. However, Labour's decline in its red wall had been long term. Between 2005 and 2015, Labour's vote share fell by around 10–15% in these constituencies, this was not a dramatic overnight shift, but a decline over 20 years linked to changing demographics. There was also an urban versus rural split – Conservatives had only 21 of 73 MPs in London, and 8 MPs from 73 seats in 18 main cities outside London.

» In 2024, the question was 'Will Labour be able to rebuild the red wall?' and the answer was a categoric 'yes'. As seen in Figure 5.10, Labour regained 37 of the 38 red wall seats, with Ashfield going to Reform UK. The Conservatives lost all 28 Red Wall seats they won in 2019, dropping 24 percentage points in the process.

The 'Blue Wall' refers to a group of traditionally Conservative-held parliamentary constituencies in southern England that have historically been safe Tory seats, but have become increasingly vulnerable, particularly to Labour and the Liberal Democrats. These seats are primarily located in southern England, including the home counties and affluent suburban areas. These have been historically strong Conservative areas of support, often held for decades. In 2024 the Liberal Democrats won a majority of 'Blue Wall' seats, with the party picking up 23 of these 43 seats that were won by the Conservatives in 2019 as shown in Figure 5.11. Labour's vote share (17%) didn't move, but the party gained 9 seats, with the Conservatives reduced to just 11.

Figure 5.9 How the UK voted in 2017, 2019 and 2024

Key: • Con • Lab • Lib Dem • SNP • SF • Other

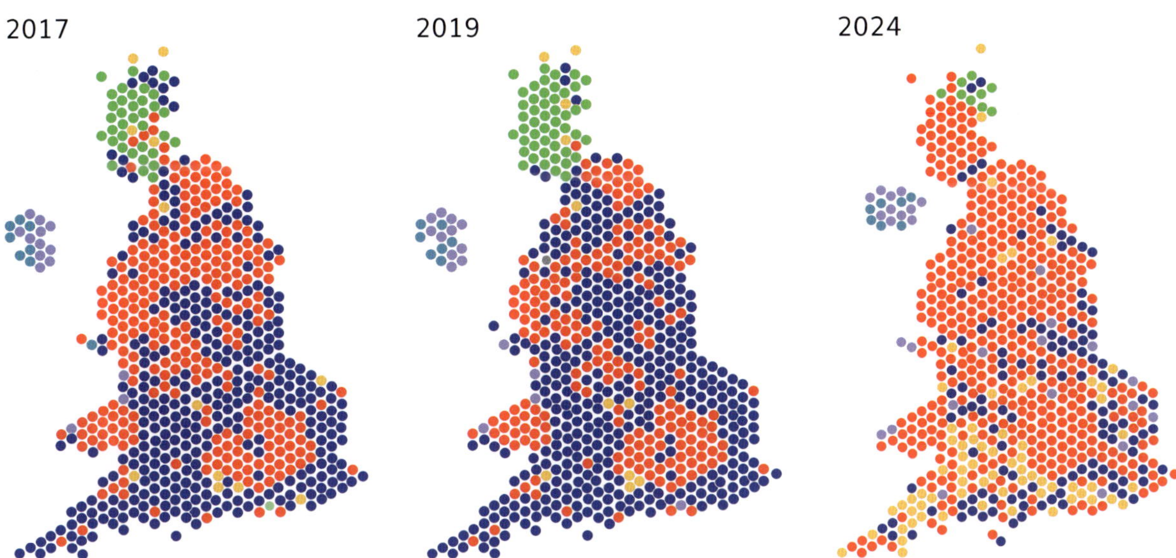

Figure 5.10 How Labour rebuilt the Red Wall in 2024

Average vote share and winners in red wall seats, 2019 vs 2024

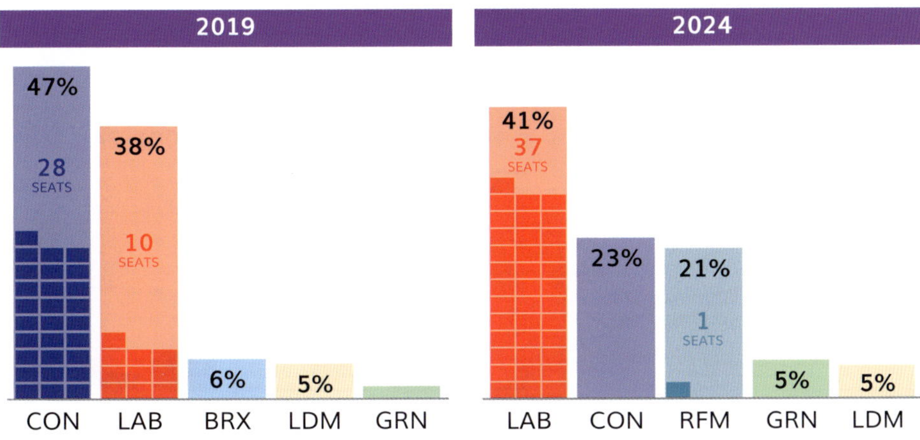

Source: Focaldata / Patrick Flynn

Figure 5.11 How the Blue Wall fractured in 2024

Average vote share and winners in 'Blue Wall' seats, 2019 vs 2024

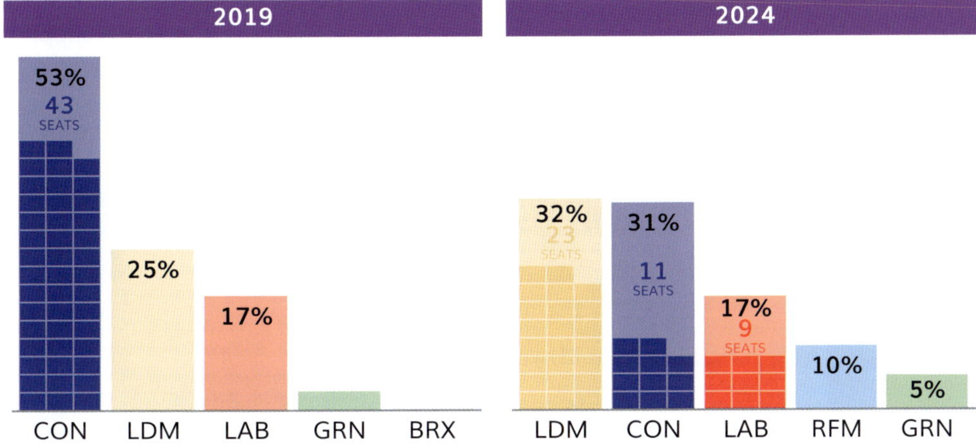

Source: Focaldata / Patrick Flynn

However, since 2014 another regional difference that has become significant is the component nations of the UK, shown by Figure 5.12.

Figure 5.12 Party representation in Scotland over time

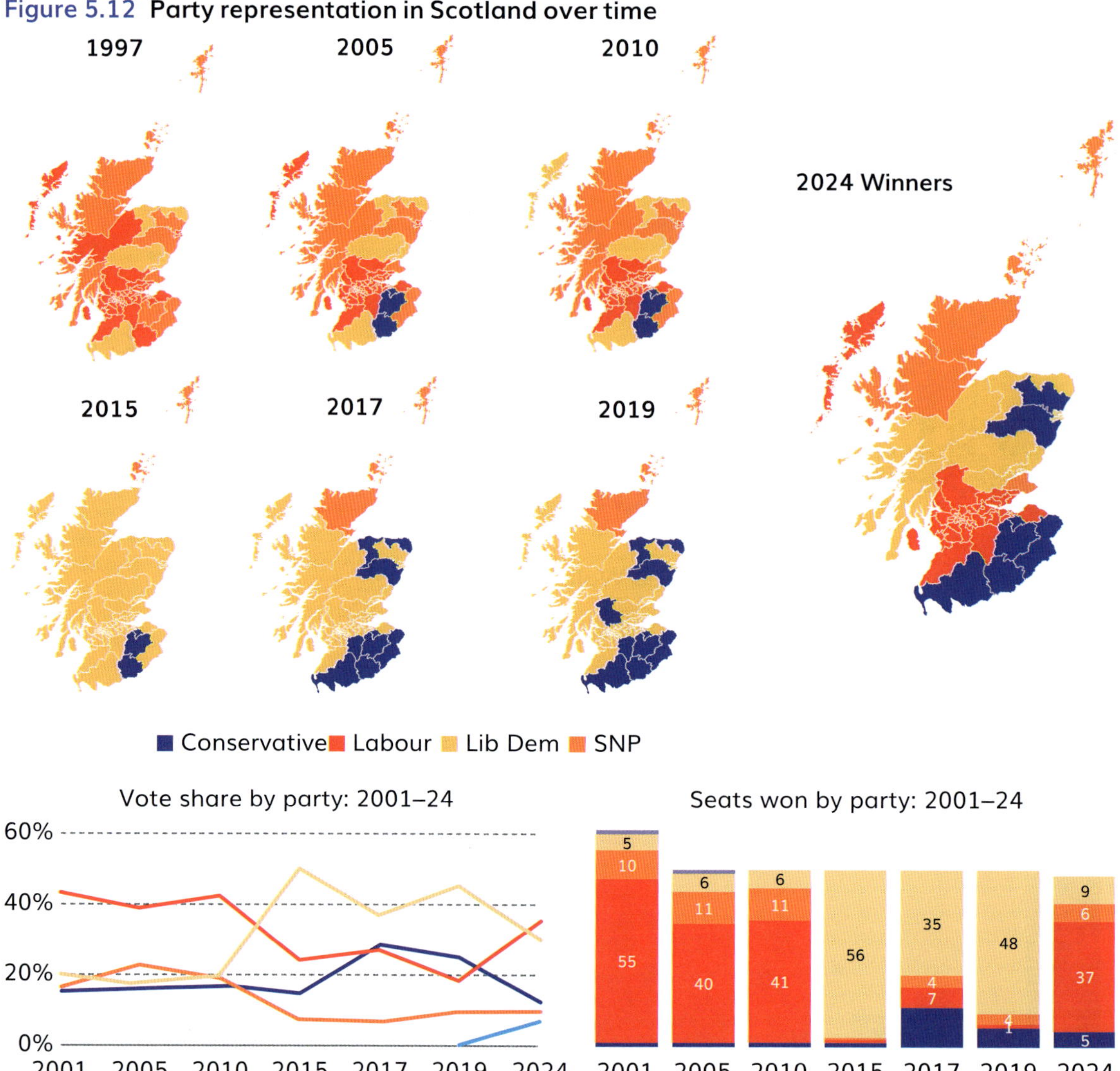

Source: Contains parliamentary information licensed under the Open Parliament Licence v3.0

Historically, Labour MPs dominated in Scotland. Although 1997 was a high-water mark, prior to this the Labour Party averaged mid-40 seats. The in-out Scottish independence referendums in 2014 radically realigned politics in Scotland, with the SNP going from 6 seats to 56 between 2010 and 2015, shown in Table 5.2. However, since the demise of Nicola Sturgeon as leader, the SNP's support collapsed and that was evident in 2024, to Labour's benefit.

Table 5.2 Scottish MPs in Westminster

	1997	2005	2010	2015	2017	2019	2024
Labour	56	41	41	1	7	1	37
Conservative	1	1	1	1	13	6	5
Liberal Democrat	5	11	11	1	4	4	6
SNP	1	6	6	56	35	58	9

In Wales, there has not been any significant realignment since the creation of the Welsh Parliament, with Labour's dominance being clear and enduring. In 2019 Labour's share of the vote was down to 41% in 2019 from 49% in 2017. However, in 2024, the Conservatives vote collapsed in Wales (following the national trend) but interestingly, Labour's share also dropped to 37%. Reform, the Greens, Plaid Cymru and the Lib Dems all increased their vote share (see Figure 5.13).

Figure 5.13 **Party representation in Wales in UK general elections**

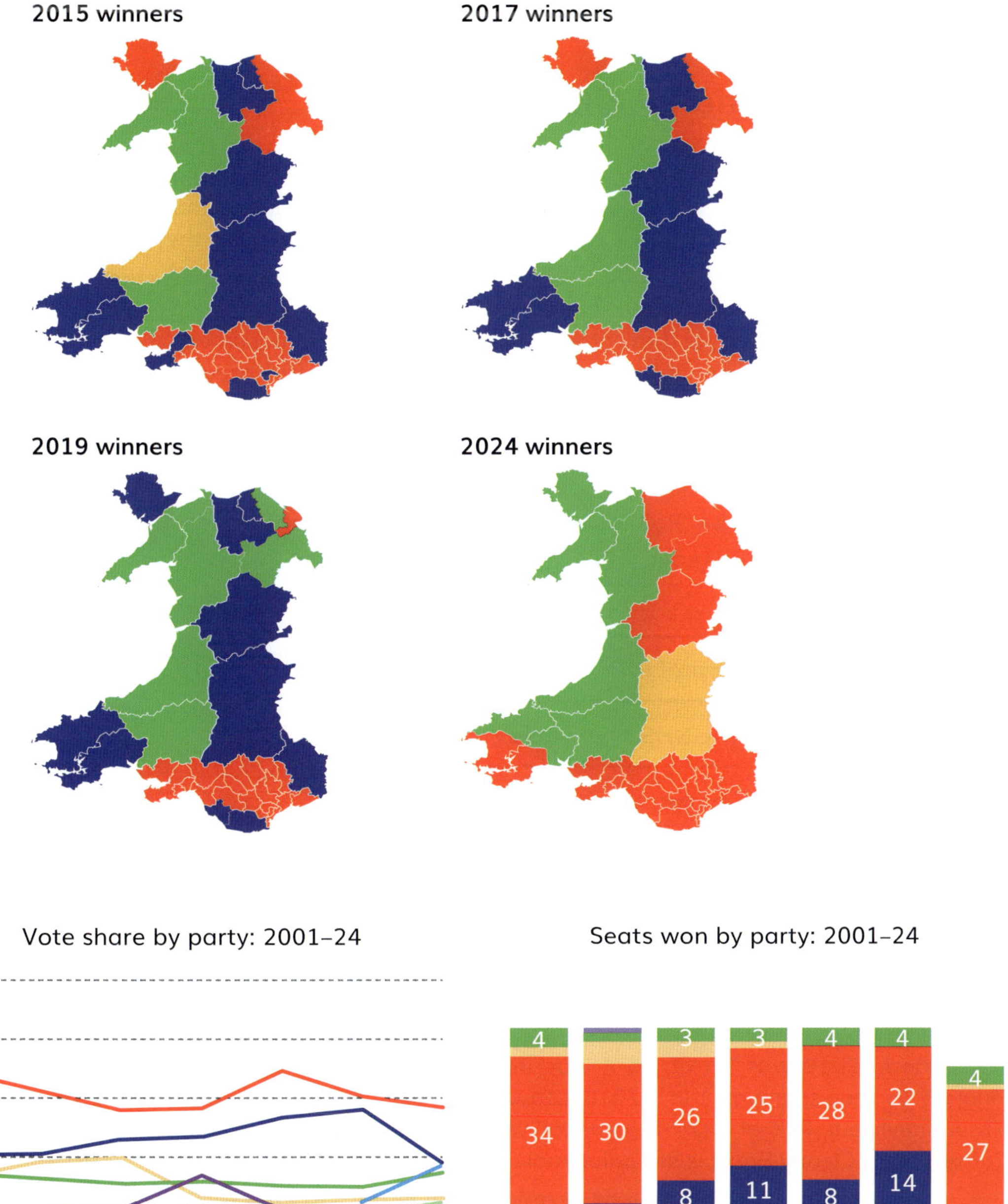

** In 2024 there were only 32 MPs elected in Wales, reduced from 40 MPs previously.*
Source: Contains parliamentary information licensed under the Open Parliament Licence v3.0

Short-term factors in voting behaviour

Electoral volatility: The degree of change in voting behaviour between elections. It is based on the idea that voters have become more willing to switch between parties as they no longer have a strong connection to any one party.

Issue voting: When voters base their decisions on political issues rather than other relevant factors, such as the party leader.

Rational choice theory: The idea that individuals make rational choices and achieve outcomes that are aligned with their own best interests.

As long-term factors became less significant from the 1970s onwards, voters reflected on several different factors when considering how to vote. Consequently, short-term factors have become more important in explaining the outcome of elections, leading to greater **electoral volatility**. A study by the British Electoral Society showed that nearly half the country (49%) switched between different parties across the three elections from 2010 to 2017. In 2024 only 58% voted Labour or Conservative down from 77% in 2019 and 82% in 2017; this is a staggering figure and suggests that voters are much more volatile than previously. A variety of short-term factors may be significant in explaining that level of volatility.

Issue voting/Rational choice theory

Parties now spend a great deal of time and effort formulating policies that will have wide electoral appeal. **Issue voting** is linked to the **rational choice** model of voting. By emphasising the importance of policies, this model stresses the importance of issue voting and suggests that parties can significantly influence their electoral performance by revising or reshaping the policies they advance.

In this model, voting is portrayed as a rational act that is undertaken on a strictly individual basis. Individual voters are therefore believed to decide their party preference based on personal self-interest. This is 'instrumental voting', in that voters behave very much like consumers, the only difference being that instead of choosing between the goods and services on offer, they choose between the policy options available. Figure 5.14 shows the key issues sconcerning voters in 2024. Overall, the three main issues were the cost of living, the NHS and immigration. With Conservatives switching to Reform, 63% of 2019 voters named immigration as the most important issue.

Figure 5.14 Poll indicating the most important issues on why people voted in 2024

All

💲	Cost of living/inflation	16%
➕	The NHS / hospitals	15%
👪	Immigration and asylum	14%
💼	The economy and jobs	9%
🧍	Having the right leadership	8%

Source: Lord Ashcroft Polls, https://lordashcroftpolls.com/

The issue of 2019 was Brexit, so it was interesting to see how significant this was in 2024. As Figure 5.15 shows, around 1 in 3 2016 'Leavers' (36%) voted Conservative, while 29% voted Reform UK. A significant 44% of 2016 'Remainers' voters Labour with 17% voting Lib Dem and 17% voting Conservative. Clearly Brexit is still influential as an issue.

Manifesto: A detailed statement of the actions and programmes that a political party would like to put in place if it is successful in the next election.

» Having the 'wrong' policies can certainly damage a party, as Labour demonstrated in 1983 when its **manifesto** contained commitments to extend nationalisation, increase taxation, boost public spending and abolish the nuclear deterrent. It was dubbed 'the longest suicide note in history'. Labour's long road back to electability started with a comprehensive policy review, which was initiated after its third successive election defeat in 1987.

» In 1997, Blair completed this shift with a commitment to maintain the privatisations of the Thatcher era as well as five other pledges, including cutting primary class sizes to 30 and no rise in income tax.

» After 2005, the Conservatives similarly tried to revive their electoral fortunes by revising their policies to reflect the need for a more compassionate conservatism which was more sympathetic to the poor, and softer on issues such as poverty and public services.

» In 2017 (as well as 2019) Brexit was a huge factor, with 55% of Remainers voting Labour and 65% of Leavers voting Conservative.

Figure 5.15 How Remain and Leave voters voted in the 2019 and 2024 General Elections

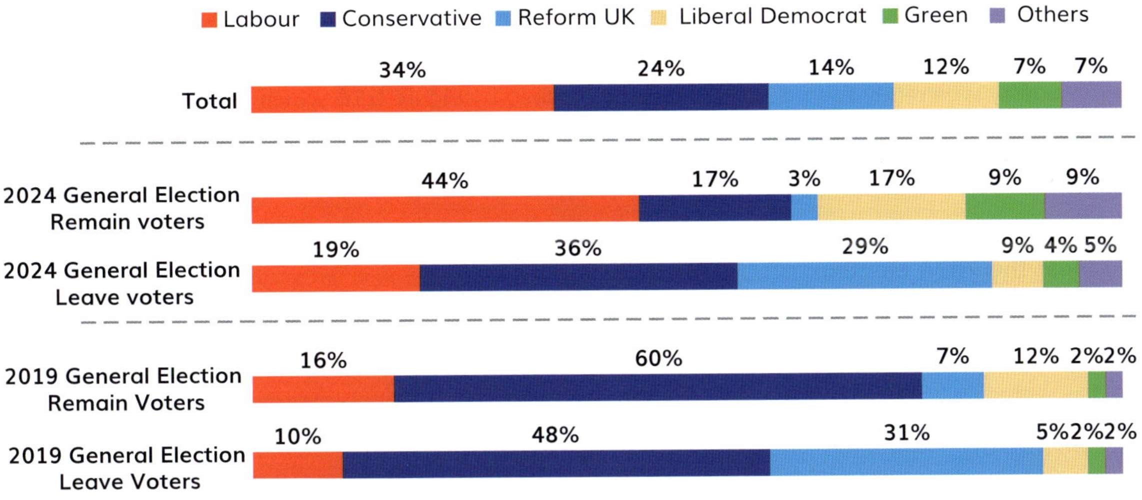

Source: Lord Ashcroft Polls, https://lordashcroftpolls.com/

- » This was also true in 2019, with Johnson's huge win being associated with his 'Get Brexit Done' slogan.
- » In 2024 the key issues were the cost of living, immigration and the NHS, but unlike in previous years, these were tightly connected to voters feeling of government incompetency.
- » However, issues are not always so significant. In 1992, 2017 and 2019, Labour's policies were more popular than the Conservatives, but in all three elections, the Conservatives prevailed.

Valence

Valence refers to issues and factors that are generally agreed upon across the political spectrum, where voters evaluate parties' perceived competence in achieving certain universally desired outcomes. It relates to issues where there is common agreement, say economic prosperity, reducing crime, improving the NHS, so the issue isn't whether a party wants to achieve economic prosperity, but rather which party is most likely to deliver it. This means that rather than focusing solely on ideological alignment, voters assess parties based on their track record, leadership qualities and ability to manage important societal challenges. In other words, voters are deciding which party *they trust* to deliver valence issues.

So, in looking at how people decide who to vote for, it is suggested that policy issues matter less than 'valence' issues. In other words, rather than looking at how closely a party's policies match their own preferences, people base their judgement on how much they believe a party will deliver. For example, in 2019, many people liked the Labour Party's manifesto but did not believe that the Party could deliver on those promises, whereas they clearly believed the Conservatives could deliver on theirs. Valence is about perceived competence, not ideology.

Governing competence

Linked to valence is **governing competence**. The conventional wisdom on elections has long been that 'governments lose elections; oppositions do not win them'. This suggests that elections are largely decided by the performance of the government of the day, and particularly by its economic performance.

- » The 1997 General Election may well have been as much about losing faith in Major's Conservative Government as it was about support for Blair's New Labour.
- » The 2010 General Election could be regarded as a 'referendum' on Labour's performance, the party was fatally damaged by the loss of its reputation for economic competence following the global financial crisis and the subsequent sharp recession.
- » In the case of the Conservatives in 2015, it was notable that the claim that their plan was working was sustained by an economic recovery that had started two years earlier.
- » In 2024 it is unquestionably the case that the country was ready to say goodbye to the Conservative Government they had first elected in 2015 under Cameron. Since then, the party (and country) had been led by May, Johnson, Truss and Sunak, with questionable legitimacy for

Spec Key Term

Governing competence: The perceived ability of the governing party in office to manage the affairs of the state well and effectively. It also applies to opposition parties and their potential governing competence.

Spec Key Term

Mandate: The successful party following an election claims it has the authority to implement its manifesto promises and also general permission to govern as new issues arise.

May in the 2017 election and a clear **mandate** for Johnson in 2019. However, it was the scandals surrounding 'Partygate' that fatefully undermined trust in the Johnson Government, followed by 49 days of a chaotic Truss Government resulting in sterling plummeting and mortgage rates surging. When Sunak replaced Truss a few weeks later, the damage was already done. The country was ready for a change. This can be seen by Figure 5.16 which showed that the main reason was that the Conservatives 'had lost people's trust' followed by 'they had not been competent', and 'Partygate and other scandals'.

Figure 5.16 Outcome of a post-election survey asking why the Conservative Party had lost the 2024 election

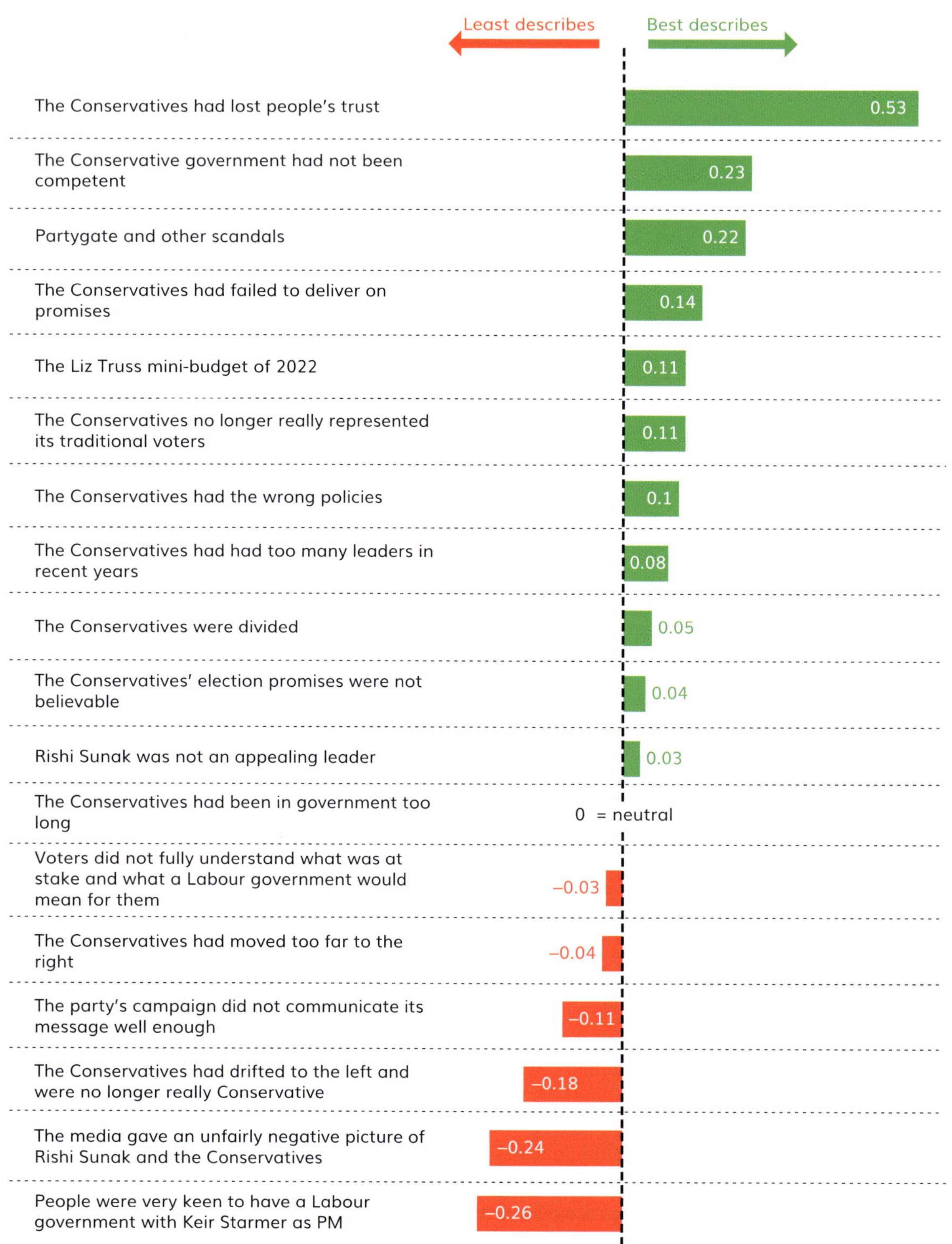

Source: Lord Ashcroft Polls, https://lordashcroftpolls.com/

CASE STUDY 5.1: THE 1983 GENERAL ELECTION

Events

On 10 June 1983, Margaret Thatcher won a remarkable victory, boosting the Conservative majority from 44 seats to 143 seats, recording the largest parliamentary landslide since Clement Attlee's in 1945.

Significance

The election was remarkable because it was fought against a backdrop of unemployment standing at over 3 million, having more than doubled since 1979. Just two years before the election, opinion polls had rated Thatcher as the most unpopular Prime Minister of modern times. Furthermore, the election was significant because Thatcher's landslide was gained despite the fact that the Conservative vote of 42.4% was 1.5% below its 1979 level. In 1983, the newly formed SDP–Liberal Alliance won only 23 seats. Their 25% share of the vote cut deep into Labour territory, helping to reduce the party's support to 28%, Labour's worst electoral performance since 1918. There is no doubt that by splitting the progressive vote, they helped the Conservatives towards their landslide win.

What long-term factors shaped the outcome of the election?

Class

Class was clearly a relevant factor in 1983, with ABC1 voters voting 55% Conservative and only 16% Labour. At the same time, 37% of the C2DE voted Conservative and only 22% for Labour. Nonetheless, it is worth noting that the most significant factor of the 1983 election across class, age and gender was the surge of support for the third party, the Alliance of the Liberals and the newly formed Social Democratic Party (SDP).

Age

In 1983, the Conservatives maintained their popularity across all age groups. It may come as a surprise to followers of elections since the turn of the millennium that the Conservatives won 40% of the vote and over across all age categories, with their highest percentage coming from the 55+ age group.

Region

In 1983, the Conservatives made further gains in London and the South while losing seats in Scotland. It is notable that the areas hardest and longest hit by the recession, namely the industrial parts of northern England and Scotland, were not areas of traditional Conservative strength, so any loss of support for them there did not affect their ability to win a landslide majority. Despite winning half a million votes less than in 1979, their majority increased from 43 to 143.

What short-term factors shaped the outcome of the election?

Leadership

Labour's dismal performance is often placed in the hands of their leader, the veteran left-winger Michael Foot, who oversaw the party's leftward shift. This led to the SDP breakaway and damaged Labour's image by associating it with splits and divisions.

Policies

Labour's 1983 election manifesto, which committed the party to wider nationalisation, an increase in government spending and withdrawal from the EEC, was famously described by a former Labour Cabinet Minister as 'the longest suicide note in history'. These policies encouraged the Party to focus its electoral appeal on the diminishing ranks of the 'traditional' working class rather than on the expanding middle class.

Media

Since the Falklands War, the press had built a 'Maggie' personality cult that prepared the way for the highly personalised 1983 election campaign. Their support was unswerving. Labour was undermined by the resolutely unsympathetic portrayal of Foot in the pro-Conservative tabloid press.

Issues

The electoral revival of Thatcher and the Conservatives is commonly seen as a consequence of the 1982 Falklands War with the 'Falklands factor' boosting Thatcher's satisfaction rating to the highest it would ever achieve (59%). Perhaps of greater significance was the UK economy returning to growth in 1982, particularly in the South of England.

Source: All statistics derived from Ipsos MORI

Leaders

In an age of class and party dealignment (see page 143), parties place increasing faith in leaders and leadership to win elections. However, what makes for an effective leader in electoral terms?

Successful leaders usually need to demonstrate several qualities:

- » *Accessibility* – leaders must be telegenic, that is, be a good media performer and demonstrate a 'relaxed likeability'.
- » *Trust* – voters need to believe that what their leaders say is true.
- » *Strength* – leaders must demonstrate that they can 'run the show'.

So how have party leaders in the UK affected the way people have voted?

<table>
<tr><td>

Definition

Electoral asset:
A leader who is very popular, possibly more popular than their party, and is a key reason why people would vote for the party.

Electoral liability:
A leader who is unpopular, and a reason why people wouldn't vote for the party.

</td></tr>
</table>

- » Tony Blair was widely believed to have been a considerable **electoral asset** for Labour in 1997 and 2001. By 2005, however, his personal appeal had diminished significantly. Nevertheless, it is difficult to argue that Blair had become an **electoral liability** as neither of his main rivals in 2005 were able to establish a lead over him, particularly on the issue of competence. In fact, Blair enjoyed a healthy 15% lead over other party leaders when respondents were asked to choose who would make the best Prime Minister. Although in 1979, 'Sunny Jim' Callaghan was significantly ahead of Margaret Thatcher in the polls, he went on to lose that year's election.

- » The importance of leaders was greatly enhanced in 2010 by the introduction of televised debates between the candidates of the three leading parties. Although the first debate appeared to transform the fortunes of Liberal Democrat leader Nick Clegg, who received an increase in his personal approval rating, this did not transform into more seats in the election. Ultimately there was only modest evidence that 'Cleggmania' shifted anyone's opinion, even though it may have had a marginal impact on turnout. Of greater significance in terms of explaining the outcome in 2010 was the poor personal standing of Gordon Brown, who consistently lagged far behind David Cameron in opinion polls.

- » An advantage that the Conservatives enjoyed in the run-up to the 2015 election was the clear and consistent opinion poll lead that Cameron maintained over Ed Miliband, who many voters struggled to see as a credible Prime Minister and was haunted by an awkward photo of him eating a bacon sandwich. He also suffered embarrassment by what became known as 'The Edstone', which was a stone tablet bearing his pledges for the 2015 General Election.

- » The 2017 Election challenged many accepted rules – none more so than the rules on leadership. Until the election, Corbyn was considered a disastrous leader and May a safe, reliable pair of hands. She certainly appeared to have two of the three criteria – trust and strength – although she was lacking in 'relaxed likeability'. However, Corbyn enthused young voters with his authentic and relaxed style, whereas May's wooden style and awkwardness turned many voters off.

- » In 2019, leadership was an issue for both parties, with neither Johnson nor Corbyn being universally liked or respected. Corbyn had lost the likeability appeal that had served him well in 2017, whereas Johnson was distrusted by many and this was not helped by his avoiding of reporters or dodging set-piece TV interviews.

- » In 2024 it is fair to say that neither leader ignited the passions of most voters. Unlike in 2019 when both leaders elicited strong feelings from voters (both positive and negative), there was no denying that they were both 'characters'. In 2024, we were faced with very different leaders. By general consensus, they were both considered decent people and honourable public servants, however neither could be considered to have the magnetic or telegenic appeal that leaders need nowadays. However, it might have been the case that after the premiership of Johnson, that was a positive attribute to many.

Figure 5.17 **Who would make the best Prime Minister in 2024**

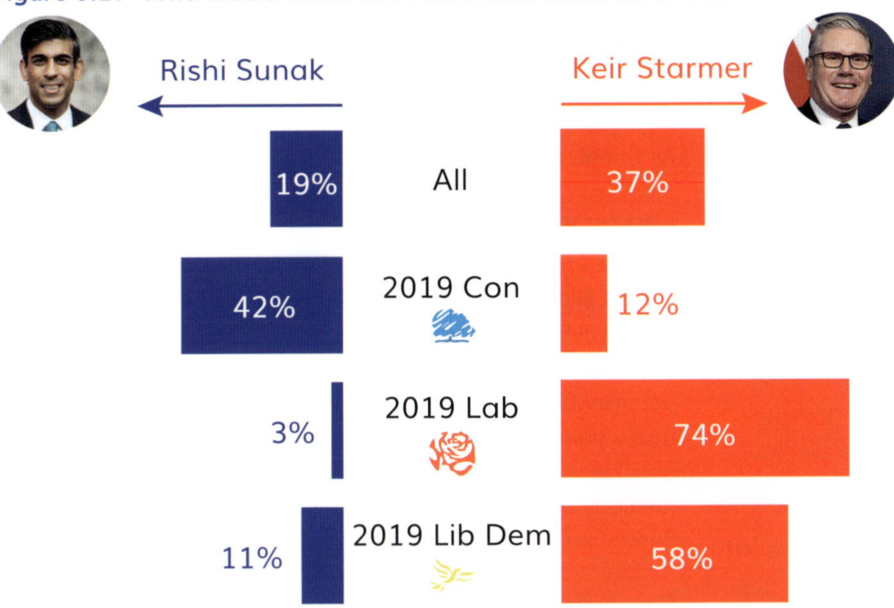

Source: Lord Ashcroft Polls, https://lordashcroftpolls.com/; Rishi Sunak photo: Samir Hussein / Contributor / Getty Images Keir Starmer photo: WPA Pool / Pool / Getty Images

CASE STUDY 5.2: THE 1997 GENERAL ELECTION

Events

The 1997 General Election resulted in a landslide Labour victory, winning 418 seats and a majority of 178, the largest since the 1930s. Labour's 1997 election success was the Party's first since 1974, and it brought to an end 18 years in opposition.

Significance

It is argued that governments lose elections, oppositions do not win them. Thus the poor state of the Conservatives, rather than the transformation of Labour, can be seen as a key reason for the outcome of the election. Conservative misfortunes began in 1992 when the UK was forced out of the Exchange Rate Mechanism, damaging the party's reputation for economic competence. Despite an economic recovery, with unemployment falling steadily, the Conservatives lost 178 seats with a 10% swing to Labour. Additionally, Major's Government was dogged throughout the 1990s by splits over Europe, which made Major appear weak and the party divided, as well as mired in 'sleaze'. They had been in power for a long time and were vulnerable to the most powerful of all electoral slogans: 'Time for a change'.

What long-term factors shaped the outcome of the election?

Class

Class can be seen as an important factor as 41% of ABs voted Conservative and only 31% voted Labour. Additionally, 50% of C2s voted Labour and 59% of DEs, compared with 27% and 21% for the Conservatives. However, the Labour share of the AB vote increased by 12% and Conservatives went down by 15%, suggesting greater evidence of class and partisan dealignment.

Gender

Although approximately 45% of men and women voted Labour, there was a larger swing to Labour amongst women (10%). It is suggested that women were impressed with Blair's commitment to public services.

Photo 5.1 **Tony Blair arriving in Downing Street after his election victory, 1997**

Source: Jeff Overs / Getty Images

Age

Age was a factor in this election, primarily amongst voters aged 25–44, although 18–24- and 45–54-year-olds weren't too far behind, with the Conservatives losing 16% of the 45–54 age bracket. In all these age groups, the Labour Party increased its share of the vote by 10%.

Region

To little surprise, in 1997, Labour dominated in Scotland, the North, North West, Yorkshire and Wales. However, what was surprising was that Labour did very well in the South, particularly in London and the South East. Its vote share increased by a minimum of 5 points across every region in the UK.

What short-term factors shaped the outcome of the election?

Policies

Having rebranded as New Labour, the party abandoned left-wing policies and began a modernisation process, adopting a centrist programme aimed at attracting support from the middle classes. This started as soon as Blair was elected leader in 1994, with the rewriting of Clause IV of the party's constitution. A policy review involved abandoning support for nationalisation and for trade unions, maintaining Conservative tax rates, while adopting Blair's mantra of being 'tough on crime, tough on the causes of crime', while Gordon Brown and Peter Mandelson wooed the business community. In order to show there was no hidden left-wing agenda, Blair produced a pledge card with Labour's five most important commitments to the electorate.

Media

Alastair Campbell and Peter Mandelson were both close to Neil Kinnock and experienced first-hand the unfair media press coverage he received. They were determined that Blair would not suffer in the same way. Under Blair, Labour launched a 'charm offensive' and assiduously cultivated the Murdoch press, flying to Australia to meet with Murdoch, and gained the endorsement of *The Sun* in the 1997 with its famous headline on election day, 'The Sun backs Blair'!

Leadership

Labour radically altered its image to win in 1997. In the late 1990s, Blair was perceived as the perfect person to lead the 'Cool Britannia' era and represented a break with the out-of-date Tories. At 43 years of age he was considerably younger than Prime Ministers were expected to be and had a young family who moved into Downing Street with him. He was an exceptional communicator, and his non-ideological approach to politics appealed to many, helping him relate to the public.

Campaign

The Conservative campaign was run against a backdrop of corruption; both for Cash for Questions (where two Conservative MPs were paid to ask questions in Parliament, which is against the rules), as well as a series of sex scandals. Perhaps the enduring memory of the campaign was former BBC war correspondent Martin Bell challenging Conservative MP Neil Hamilton (one of the MPs alleged to have received cash in return for asking questions) in 1997 for the seat in Tatton as an anti-sleaze candidate, which Bell went on to win. As one had come to expect, the Labour campaign was very slick and effective. Unsurprisingly, the campaign was presidential in style. For example, campaign literature that was disseminated both nationally and locally had Blair's picture on it. Alastair Campbell, one of the first of a new generation of exceptionally powerful 'spin doctors' was determined to control 'the message' from the centre and ensured no slip-ups during the six-week campaign.

Source: All statistics derived from Ipsos MORI

Visit the companion website for case studies of the 2010, 2015 and 2017 General Election from the previous fifth edition.

Party image and unity

Associated with a party's policies and the appeal of its leader is the image that a party has in the minds of voters. This will include how united a party is.

» For instance, Labour undoubtedly had an 'image problem' in the 1980s, being seen as a party closely linked to the unions.

» During the 1990s, the Conservative Party's splits over Europe deepened as John Major's Cabinet rebelled against him. It also developed a reputation as the 'nasty party' seen to be associated with a 'get rich quick' ethos and showing little sympathy for the weak or disadvantaged.

» In contrast, by the end of the 1990s, Labour had worked hard to change its image under Blair and the New Labour image transformed the party. It was also united behind Blair. It's interesting to note that changing a party's image requires policy changes as well as the right leader, something that is often ignored.

» After Cameron became Conservative leader in December 2005, his strategy was largely devoted to 'detoxifying' the party's image. This involved a stress on achieving a more inclusive appeal aimed at the young, women and ethnic minority voters. Such image rebranding contributed significantly to the 5% swing from Labour to the Conservatives in 2010.

» At the beginning of 2017, polls suggested that the 'strong and stable' image of May's party was just what the country wanted as she led polls by up to 20%. The party conveyed the image that they were best placed to steer the country through the Brexit process. However, that image crumbled during the election campaign and the reality was a stubborn leader with weak policies and no positive plans for the future. The Labour Party under Corbyn was positive and passionate and had a forward-looking but feasible manifesto, which enthused large swathes of young voters with their modern image.

» In 2019, both parties' image was weak. Neither leader was particularly liked nor trusted, and their manifestos were either very vague and brief (Conservative) or hugely ambitious and lacking credibility (Labour). In this period, the overriding issue was Brexit and party image was based on their position on that particular issue. Labour's image was poor, mainly because it didn't appear to have a strong and clear position, whereas the Conservative image, as the party who would 'get Brexit done', won the day in the end. Both parties were fundamentally split, with the Conservative rift being, certainly in public, much greater and deeper than Labour's.

» In 2024, the image of the Conservative Party, which had been in government since 2015, was poor. After numerous scandals and a series of leaders who had lost credibility, the image of the party was damaged. Even though Sunak had brought a period of calm credibility to the party, the spectre of Johnson and Truss's tenure was too hard to overcome. Additionally, the party was very split between those who wanted to move to the right, seeing the success of Reform UK and the one-nation wing. Conversely Starmer had succeeded in de-toxifying his party after Corbyn's time as leader and had shifted it back to the centre ground of politics. Starmer's 'Change' message resonated with the country (seen in Photo 5.2). While not hugely excited by the party, it was clear that they were a credible alternative government to the Conservatives. The scent of potential victory in 2024 and return to government after over a decade meant that divisions in the party were significantly limited.

Photo 5.2 **Labour leader Sir Keir Starmer talks at a campaign event in June 2024**

Campaigns

Traditionally it is accepted that election campaigns tend to reinforce voters' views rather than change them. Campaigns tend to focus attention on all the factors addressed above; leaders, policies, image and trust are all brought to a climax on election day. If you felt negatively towards a party on these issues before a campaign, the chances are that view was not going to change significantly. Not uncommonly, party strength on polling day is not much different from what it was at the start of the election campaign.

» In 1992, the seemingly 'grey' incumbent PM John Major was brought to life during the campaign, famously eschewing high-tech campaign strategies by standing on a soapbox to talk to voters all across the country. It was surprisingly effective and secured him a majority.

» The 2010 Conservative campaign sought to damage Labour's image by associating it with 'excessive' spending, and for wasting money when the economy was booming rather than keeping reserves for when the inevitable downturn occurred. The 2008–09 financial crisis was therefore portrayed as 'Labour's debt crisis', an allegation that Labour failed to counter effectively.

» The 2017 campaign broke all the rules and challenged traditional assumptions about election campaigns. Corbyn began the campaign 20 points behind May and by the end of it had increased Labour's vote share by 10%. It was suggested that Corbyn's ability to enthuse young people with huge rallies as well as via an excellent social media campaign was key to his success. Despite being the largest party, May was fatally wounded by her poor campaign and losing the government's majority.

» If 2017 rewrote many rules of campaigning, 2019 overturned them. Labour understandably used similar strategies that had been successful in 2017, such as an extensive manifesto filled with popular policies, a very high-profile social media campaign, and Corbyn appearing on many TV sofas and rallies packed with enthusiastic supporters. Johnson, on the other hand, dodged national events and was absent from key TV debates and interviews, and was clinically targeting key seats with his 'Get Brexit Done' message. Opinion polls seemed to suggest a closing of the gap in the run-up to election day, and many thought Corbyn had been successful in stopping Boris getting a large majority. As we now know, they were wrong. Journalists who spend a lot of time on social media platforms such as Twitter were feeling the surge of support for Corbyn and mistook it for the country at large. The surprise 80-seat majority for the Conservatives appeared to provide further evidence of the gap between the political elite and the country as a whole.

» The Conservative Party's main campaign message for 2024 was to 'stick with the plan that's working'. They campaigned hard to convince voters that there were signs of improvement and that they should stick with them. However, despite a good showing in the first debate against Starmer, Sunak's decision to leave D-Day celebrations early really damaged him. Then Nigel Farage decided to stand as MP for Clacton which was a real blow to the Conservatives' chances of retaining a significant amount of seats. In the latter days of the campaign, the revelation that some Conservative MPs and advisers had placed bets on the election date a couple of days before it was announced only reinforced the public's perception of the party as sleazy. Labour, on the other hand, carried out the '**Ming vase strategy**', which meant saying and doing nothing dramatic (or vaguely exciting) throughout the campaign to undermine their hefty lead in the polls. They left the exciting and dramatic stunts to Ed Davey who was photographed falling off a paddle board (see Photo 5.3), bungee jumping, going down a waterslide and on a roller coaster. For a leader of a party which struggles to get media attention, this was a good strategy.

Turnout

The sharp decline in electoral turnout in 2001 and 2024 (the lowest turnouts in any general election since 1918) stimulated anxiety about the state of political participation in the UK and led to a growing debate about how democracy could be 'renewed'. Although turnout increased in 2017 to 69%, it still remained below the level of the 1950s and 1960s. Figure 5.18 clearly shows considerable apathy amongst the young when it comes to voting. Partisan dealignment (see page 143) may undoubtedly be reflected in growing voter **disillusion and apathy**, as declining party identification means that people may be less concerned about the outcome of elections. Another suggestion, as identified by JK Galbraith, is the idea of the "culture of contentment", which some now refer to as 'hapathy', which is that people who are content with their circumstances, and are not under threat, don't see a need to vote. Nevertheless, partisanship started to decline in the 1970s, long before turnout levels began to cause alarm.

Figure 5.18 Turnout by age over time

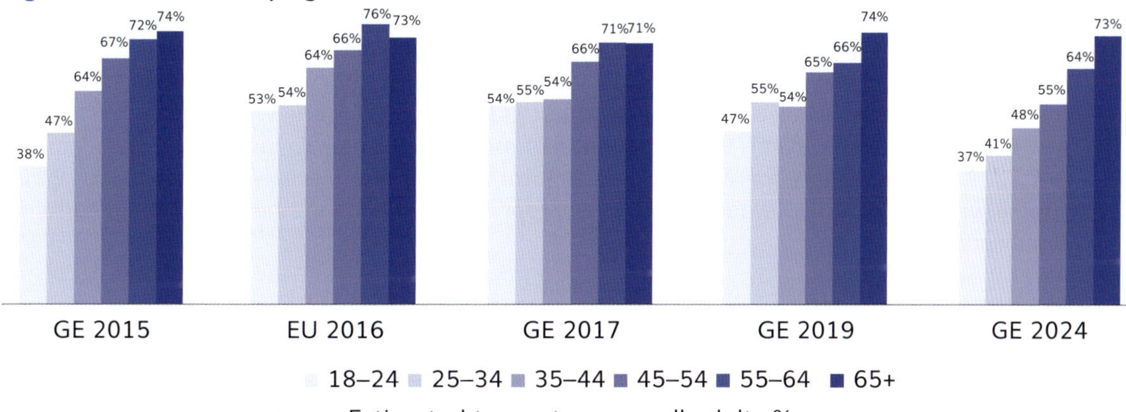

Source: © Ipsos. Reproduced with permission

There is no proven theory that adequately explains the declining turnout in 2001, 2024 and (albeit to a lesser extent) in 2005, 2010 and 2015. The answer may lie in the immediate political circumstances of these general elections.

» For example, declining turnout could be due to the simple fact that there was little in 2001 and to encourage people to vote. In 2001, a less than popular government faced an even more unpopular opposition, in 2024, the choice of a hugely unpopular government or an uninspiring opposition, and in both cases, the parties offering potential voters little choice in terms of policies or ideas.

» In 2010, an unpopular Prime Minister leading a government widely accused of economic failure, confronted an opposition that had only partially 'detoxified' its image and whose austerity package alarmed important sections of the electorate. 2015 showed a slight increase in turnout up to 66%.

» In 2017 there was an increase in turnout to 69%, suggesting that when the public feel strongly about an issue or are enthused by a leader and/or party, they vote. This rise in turnout is illustrated by Figure 5.18, which shows an increase in turnout within the youngest two age brackets.

» However, in 2019, turnout dropped down to 67% despite a huge issue at stake: the future of Brexit, but this was balanced by mistrust of both leaders. Corbyn was seen as an unsuitable leader in many ways, not helped by the allegations of anti-Semitism that had dogged the Labour Party, and Johnson was deeply mistrusted by many for alleged duplicitous behaviour during the Brexit referendum campaign and beyond. In addition, Jo Swinson led a disastrous campaign for the Liberal Democrats, which made it difficult for Remainers to feel comfortable voting for them.

» In 2024 turnout plummeted to 60%, which shocked many; this meant that approximately 40.3% of eligible voters did not participate in the election – given that Labour's share of the vote was 34%, the real 'winner' of the election were non-voters. There are several reasons which may

Figure 5.19 Which words and phrases apply to Sunak and Starmer

Source: Lord Ashcroft Polls, https://lordashcroftpolls.com/

explain the low turnout. Firstly, the 2024 election took place against a backdrop of a consistent Labour lead in polls, this can suppress turnout as supporters of both Labour and Conservative don't have a compelling reason to vote. The lack of a really popular charismatic leader could also have affected turnout as Figure 5.19 indicates. Also, the parties focused their efforts on competitive seats, which led to reduced turnout in Labour-held areas where the outcome was perceived as certain. Further, the introduction of mandatory Voter ID laws under the Elections Act 2022 posed barriers for voters. The Electoral Commission reported that at least 16,000 people were unable to vote due to lack of appropriate identification; the real figure is certainly significantly higher.

Tactical voting

Tactical voting in elections is when voters back a candidate from a party that is not their first choice to stop a less-preferred candidate from winning in their constituency. It arises from first-past-the-post, where the candidate with the most votes wins the seat, and all other votes are effectively "wasted", allowing voters to think strategically about which opponent is best placed locally to defeat a disliked party.

» Before the 2024 general election, analysts expected a rise in tactical voting to remove the deeply unpopular Conservative government. Campaign groups identified hundreds of "tactical voting seats", and post-election analysis suggested that tactical voting helped to deepen Conservative losses, particularly where Labour, the Liberal Democrats and the Greens each became clear "anti-Tory" vehicles in different areas. However, the fragmentation of the right-of-centre vote with Reform UK was also a large factor in their defeat. Commentators like John Curtice and Will Jennings described the scale of anti-Conservative tactical voting in 2024 as "remarkable" and "intense", arguing that it contributed to very large swings against Conservative incumbents.

» The 2025 Caerphilly Senedd by-election was widely seen as a textbook case of anti-Reform tactical voting. Plaid Cymru overturned over a century of Labour dominance, winning the seat for the first time as Labour's vote collapsed and smaller parties almost disappeared from the contest. Turnout was unusually high for a devolved by-election (just over 50%), and Plaid campaigners explicitly urged Labour, Liberal Democrat and Green supporters to "lend" their vote to Plaid to keep Reform UK out.

» The 2026 Gorton & Denton Westminster by-election showed similar tactical voting, but this time benefiting the Green Party rather than Labour. In 2024 Labour had won the new seat comfortably, but by early 2026 Reform UK had surged locally, and several prominent tactical voting sites indicated that the Greens, not Labour, were best placed to stop a Reform gain. Tactical voting became a central theme of the campaign. The Green Party victory pushed Labour into third place behind Reform, underlining the power of tactical voting.

Photo 5.3 **Liberal Democrat leader Ed Davey surfing during the 2024 campaign**

CASE STUDY 5.3: THE 2019 GENERAL ELECTION

Events

In another surprising result, the 2019 Election resulted in incumbent Prime Minister Boris Johnson winning an 80-seat majority, the largest his party had received since the 1980s.

Significance

In December 2019, the country went to the polls for the third time in five years. Johnson took over from May as Prime Minister in July 2019, determined to 'get Brexit done', but had been thwarted by Parliament. His ill-fated decision to prorogue Parliament, which was overturned by the Supreme Court, made him even more determined to seek an election. However, the Fixed Term Parliament Act required the consent of Parliament to call an early general election, which he finally achieved in November. Against the backdrop of ever-closing poll ratings as the campaign went on, political pundits were shocked when Johnson won an 80-seat majority.

What long-term factors shaped the outcome of the election?

Class

Class and party dealignment continued, with the Conservatives even further ahead in social classes C2DE than in 2017, while Labour lost votes amongst all social classes.

Region

The Conservatives' breaching of Labour's 'red wall' was the headline of the election. The 'red wall' stretches from the borders of north Wales to northeast England and Yorkshire, and down into the north Midlands. The Conservatives won 33 of the 63 seats in this area, with Blyth Valley electing a Conservative for the first time in its 69-year history.

Age

Age continued to be a key dividing line and had increased even further since 2017. Labour had a 43-point lead amongst voters aged 18–24, but the Conservatives had a 47-point lead amongst those aged 65+. The biggest change was amongst 35–54-year-olds, which saw a 7-point swing to the Conservatives.

Ethnicity

As in previous years, Labour had a strong lead amongst BME voters, although its vote share fell by roughly the same amount amongst both white and BME groups. Amongst BME voters, Labour led the Conservatives by 64% to 20%, while amongst white voters the Conservatives led by 48% to 29%.

What short-term factors shaped the outcome of the election?

Campaign

The Conservative campaign, led by Dominic Cummings, was tightly controlled with the 'Get Brexit Done' message at its heart. The campaign also focused on the idea of 'the people versus the establishment', with Johnson railing against Parliament and the Supreme Court ruling as examples of the establishment ignoring the will of the people. Despite a number of flash points – hiding in a fridge to avoid reporters, dodging the Andrew Neil interview and snatching a reporter's phone to avoid looking at a photo of a child waiting in a casualty corridor – Johnson's message won through.

Leadership

A YouGov poll of former Labour supporters showed that 35% turned their back on Labour because of Corbyn while only 19% cited Brexit. While he was still popular with his devoted supporters, Corbyn's image had been tarnished due to weak leadership over Brexit and the allegations of anti-Semitism. While Johnson was not universally liked or trusted, his leadership and political message were stronger.

Media

2017 showed the power of social media, but 2019 made us think again. Regular consumers of social media platforms were left with the feeling that by 12 December 2019 Corbyn might well steal the election. The result came as a stark reminder that one's social media feed is not representative of the country as a whole. The Conservatives used focus groups and polling to target swing voters and spent heavily on Facebook activity during the last week of the campaign, targeting marginal seats specifically.

Issues

Like 2017, this election was about 'Getting Brexit Done'. Johnson was relentless in pushing this slogan throughout the campaign and appeared to read the British voters better than the other parties. Unsurprisingly therefore, the Conservatives had a clear lead amongst Leave voters with a 73% to 15% lead over Labour. However, Remain voters were more split with just under half (48%) voting Labour, 21% voting Liberal Democrat and 20% voting for the Conservatives.

Source: All statistics derived from Ipsos MORI

CASE STUDY 5.4: THE 2024 GENERAL ELECTION

Photo 5.4 Rishi Sunak calls a general election outside 10 Downing Street in the pouring rain

Source: Anadolu / Getty Images

Significance

In May 2024, Rishi Sunak stunned the political establishment by calling an election for July 4th. Conventional wisdom indicated that October would be the obvious time, giving the economy the time to pick up. His announcement, in the pouring rain outside No 10 Downing Street (see Photo 5.4) was to be an omen of what was to come.

What long-term factors shaped the outcome of the election?

Age

Once again, age was a key dividing line, with younger voters favouring Labour and older voters favouring the Conservatives. The average age of a Labour voter was 46, while for a Conservative voter, it was 63, and the age at which a voter was more likely to vote Conservative than Labour was 64, a significant increase of 22 years from 2019.

Class

In 2024, social class continued to influence voting patterns, though its impact has diminished over time. The figures indicate that Labour maintained a lead among both ABC1 (36%) and C2DE (33%) classes, with a slightly higher percentage among ABC1 voters. The Conservative Party secured only 25% of the ABC vote and 23% of the C2DE vote. Of significance is Reform UK who gained 20% of the C2DE vote compared to 11% of ABC1 voters. This will have been of concern to both Labour and Conservative parties. 2024 shows us that the once-clear association between social class and party preference has diminished with other factors now playing a more substantial role in shaping voter behaviour.

Ethnicity

In 2024, Labour still led overall with minority groups, compared to other parties, yet their support decreased. While they gained 3 points with white voters, their support fell among ethnic minority voters. Labour's vote share among Asian voters fell by 13 points, and their Muslim vote also fell dramatically, with the share of Muslim voters in a constituency being strongly predictive of vote losses for Labour. The Greens and other parties gained ground for Labour. These changes can be understood by recognising that Rishi Sunak was the first Hindu Prime Minister and the Gaza issue being highly significant.

Region

If 2019 was all about the collapse of the 'Red Wall', 2024 saw it significantly rebuilt and strengthened. Labour rebuilt the Red Wall with a vote share of 41%, despite climbing just three points on 2019. It was also the case that the Conservatives heartland 'Blue Wall' fractured with the Liberal Democrats picking up 23 of these 43 seats won by the Conservatives in 2019. We also saw the collapse of the SNP vote in Scotland, with most returning to Labour, ending ten years of SNP dominance.

What short-term factors shaped the outcome of the election?

Governing Competency

Without a doubt, the 2024 election was primarily a verdict on the Conservative Government's performance and competence. They had gained a reputation for incompetence due to Johnson's scandals (Partygate) and Liz Truss's mini budget. Voters perceived the Conservatives as out of touch, uncaring, incompetent, and untrustworthy. It was clear that this was an election where voters were seeking to get rid of a government by the widespread tactical voting that occurred, with groups like Best for Britain advising center-left voters on the best candidate to defeat the Conservatives.

Issues

According to the polls, there were several key issues: the NHS, the cost of living, immigration and housing. However, these can also be connected to the widespread discontent with the Conservative Government which had been in power since 2010. When it came to immigration, the growth in support for Reform UK can be seen to correlate to this being a key issue for many voters.

Leaders

It is certainly the case that in 2024, leadership was not the push factor that we saw in 2019, but it also wasn't a pull factor either. Neither of the two main parties' leaders connected well with the public, both being described in bland terms (see Figure 5.19). However, the election was framed around the question of 'Who can you trust to govern the country?' and on this metric, Starmer positioned himself and his party as the most trustworthy.

Campaign

The Conservative Party's main message for 2024 was to 'stick with the plan that's working'. Labour campaigned with the 'Ming vase strategy', which meant saying and doing nothing dramatic (or vaguely exciting) during the campaign that might undermine their hefty lead in the polls. They left the exciting and dramatic stunts to Ed Davey who was photographed falling off a paddle board, bungee jumping, going down a waterslide and on a roller coaster. For a leader of a party which struggles to get media attention, this was a good strategy.

Moreover, as well as starting the campaign significantly behind in the polls, the Sunak campaign was widely regarded as one of the worst managed in modern times, marred by gaffes and mishaps. The image of a rain-drenched PM announcing the election outside No 10 left commentators aghast and then mid-way through the campaign, his decision to leave the commemoration of the 80th anniversary of D-Day in France early was another gaffe that offended many voters. Finally, towards the end of the campaign, the Conservatives were marred by a betting scandal involving allegations that several key aides of the PM placed bets on the date of the election before it was publicly announced. Sunak was forced to withdraw support for some candidates and pundits were left staggered by the sheer stupidity of these actions. They also hadn't accounted for the decision by Nigel Farage to return to frontline UK politics and stand as MP for Clacton. This fundamentally changed the campaign and the outcome as it meant the Conservative vote was split.

Summary

In summary, age and ethnicity appear to have been significant long-term factors in the 2024 UK General Election, but central to the outcome was governing competence – the result was primarily a verdict on the Conservative Government's performance and competence.

KEY TOPIC DEBATE: ARE SOCIAL FACTORS THE MOST IMPORTANT IN DETERMINING THE OUTCOME OF GENERAL ELECTIONS?

When looking at factors that affect the way we vote, social factors refer to class, age, gender, ethnicity and region. These are also known as long-term factors. Other factors which can affect voting behaviour at general elections are party leaders, issues, governing competence, and the media, which are known as short-term factors.

✅ **While it may no longer be true that 'class is the basis of British party politics; all else is embellishment and detail', class can still be considered a hugely significant factor in determining the way and whether people vote.**

» While this has broken down somewhat due to class and partisan dealignment, it is still possible to predict voting behaviour based on class. For example, in 2017, Labour held 72 of the 100 constituencies with the most working-class households.

» An aspect of class not considered by the ABCDE ratings are home ownership (Figure 5.20). When looking at these grouping, the most popular party among homeowners with no mortgage were the Conservatives, 37% compared to 25% who voted Labour. Only 21% of those with a mortgage voted Conservative. Amongst private renters Labour received three times the vote share of any other party at 42%.

» The fact that so many seats are traditionally considered 'safe' in UK general elections has a lot to do with the importance of class and other social factors; for example, in 2024 all five constituencies in Liverpool were strong Labour seats with approximately 63% of the vote.

Tip: Knowing about three elections is an essential part of the specification **and 1997 is Mandatory**. You can use this data to compare and contrast changes over time as part of any essay you answer on voting ehaviour.

Figure 5.20 Voting according to housing tenure

Which party did you vote for at the General Election in July 2024 %

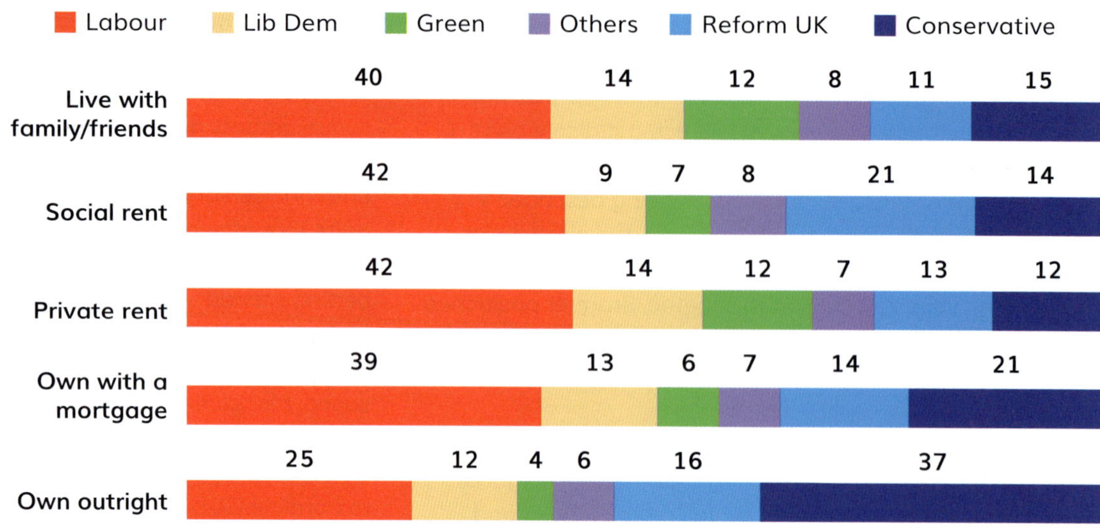

Source: YouGov, 'How Britain voted in the 2024 General Election'

❌ **Social class has lost its significance as the key social factor in determining elections.**

» In the past, working-class people generally voted for the Labour Party and middle-class people voted Conservative. For example, in the 1960s around two-thirds of the Conservative vote was made up of middle-class voters and a similar proportion of working-class voters voted for Labour. In recent years we have seen huge volatility in the way different social groups vote. In 2024, Labour outperformed the Conservatives across all social grades. It is becoming increasingly clear that partisan alignment has become a thing of the past.

» Moreover, regarding 'safe seats', in 2024 only 96 out of 650 were won on 50% or more vote share, in 2019 this figure was 229. This increased volatility indicates that class is not a reliable indicator of voting.

» Moreover, in 2017 and 2019 it can be argued that the reason for the breakdown in class voting was actually the rise of issue-based voting – Brexit. Many working-class areas had voted Leave in the 2016 Referendum. They voted Conservative because of a shift in their priorities: Brexit was more important than class. In 2024, it was about Governing competency, the public had lost complete trust in the Conservative Party and wanted them out.

» The share of the vote for Labour in Liverpool decreased from 70% to 63% in 2024, moreover, Labour dominance in Liverpool may equally be because of the age profile, the percentage of ethnic minority voters, and in response to negative representations of the city in the press: very few buy *The Sun* newspaper because of a 1989 article on the Hillsborough disaster, as well as Boris Johnson's comments about the city in a 2004 article in the *Spectator*.

✅ **Another social factor that has been a key determinant of voting is age, and this has been increasing in importance recently.**

» There has been a clear link in recent elections, showing that older voters vote Conservative and younger voters vote Labour.

» This was very evident in the 2017 election where 66% of 18–24-year-olds voted for Labour whereas the Conservatives won votes from 69% of voters aged 70+. Figure 5.11 (page 149) also shows the importance of age in the 2017 election because turnout shot up dramatically in the 18–24 age group.

» In 2019 YouGov argued that 'age was one of the most significant factors in the general election'.

» In 2024 age was still a key dividing line with younger voters being more likely to vote Labour and older voters more likely to vote for the Conservatives.

❌ **However, age may not be as significant as suggested.**

» In 2024, around the same proportion of all age groups below 50 voted for Labour. Also, the Green Party did a lot better with younger voters and Reform UK did better amongst older voters. Like class, we are seeing increased volatility amongst all ages.

» In 2019, Labour's vote share among the 18–24 age bracket dropped nearly 10 points to 56, and the age at which a voter was more likely to have voted Conservative than Labour was 39, down from 47 in 2017. Also, in 2019 in the 35–54 age group Labour's vote share fell by 11 points while the Conservatives gained 3 points.

» Moreover, age could be a function of other short-term factors. In 2017 and 2019, Labour appealed to the young with Jeremy Corbyn as leader, suggesting that it is leadership that is the significant factor. It could also be because they are less likely to own their own home, have more precarious or low paid work. In 2024 older people voting for Reform UK were probably motivated by their strong stance on the issue of immigration.

✅ **Another important social factor affecting voting behaviour is ethnicity.**

» Ethnic minorities have voted for the Labour Party because it has been closely associated with more progressive equality legislation and support for immigration. Although ethnic minorities make up around 15% of voter in the UK there are developing trends in how they vote.

» In 1997 82% of Black voters voted Labour compared with 12% who voted for the Conservatives. Similarly, the majority of Asian voters (66%) voted for the Labour Party and only 22% voted for the Conservatives.

» In 2019, not being white was the main demographic predictor of not voting Conservative. A Conservative candidate was only half as likely to secure the vote of an ethnic minority voter as of a white voter. Another way of understanding the importance of ethnicity in 2019 is that 1 in 5 Labour votes came from ethnic minority voters, whereas only 1 in 20 was for the Conservatives.

» In 2024, Labour still led overall with minority groups, although again, different groups supported Labour at different levels. Labour led the Conservatives among ethnic minority voters by 49% to 20% – a much wider lead than Labour had over the Tories among white voters (33% to 25%). However, the Conservatives' only gain of the night came in Leicester East, which had been Labour since 1987, but it has one of the largest Hindu populations of any constituency in England and, unsurprisingly, they voted for a Hindu Prime Minister, showing that ethnicity was a key driver in their vote.

❌ **However, in reality ethnic minorities are not a single homogenous group and when distinguishing between different ethnic minorities, a more nuanced picture is evident.**

» One minority group did noticeably increase its support for the Conservatives in both 2017 and 2015 – British Indians, and Hindus in particular. From 30% in 2010, the Conservatives' share of the votes of British Indians went up to 40% in 2017. In 2024 it held at 39%, which given the huge drop of support for the Conservative Party is hugely significant.

Figure 5.21 Changes in the way minority ethnic voters voted in 2024

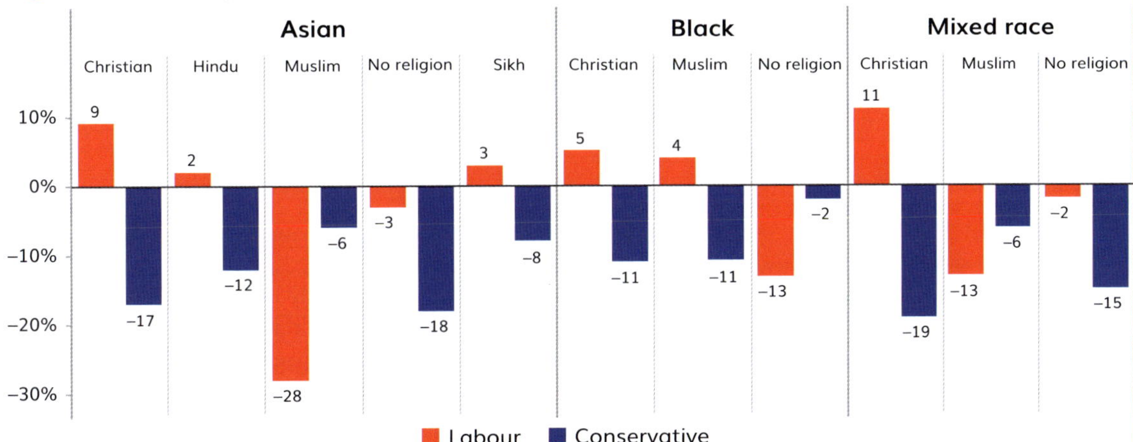

Source: FocalData / UK in a Changing Europe, July 2024

» In 2024, ethnicity did not clearly indicate a clear commitment to any one party as Figure 5.21 shows. The fall of a handful of constituencies with large Muslim populations to independents, and high-profile Labour MPs clinging on by just a few hundred votes, showed the significance of the Gaza affect. Labour support amongst Muslims dropped from 80% under Corbyn to 63%

Tip: Note that this answer is addressing two different aspects in its critique. First, it is addressing why social factors may not be so significant and then it is giving an alternative short-term factor as a reason which may explain the change in voting pattern.

in 2024. The election saw some Muslim voters turning to independent candidates or the Green Party, reflecting a fragmentation of the traditional voting bloc that Labour had relied upon.

» Additionally, once again, it could be argued that ethnic voting is a function of the short-term factor of issues and policies. Ethnic voters may vote Labour because they have better policies towards immigration or more progressive equality legislation. In 2024, a substantial minority of Muslim voters switched their vote from Labour to the Greens or independent candidates due to the Gaza conflict. This suggests that if a party changes its policies or campaigns strongly for an issue, they would be more appealing to an ethnic minority. Equally, if a party has policies or attitudes which negatively affect a minority group, e.g. Windrush Scandal, stop and search, Islamophobia or anti-Semitism, they will lose votes among this group.

✅ **Another social factor that is significant is region.**

» Since the 1980s, there has been a clear 'North–South divide': with the exception of London, Labour held only a handful of seats in the south, and Conservative support was very low in the north of England and in Scotland and Wales. This is still evident in 2024 according to Figure 5.22.

» Additionally, Labour was the party of the urban cities, Scotland and Welsh mining towns, with Conservatives dominating the rural and suburban areas.

Figure 5.22 How Britain voted in 2024

Demographic	LAB	+/-	CON	+/-	RFM	+/-	LDM
Region							
North East England	45	+3	20	−18	20	+12	6
North West England	44	−2	19	−19	17	+13	8
Yorkshire and the Humber	41	+2	23	−20	17	+11	7
East Midlands	35	+4	29	−25	19	+17	6
West Midlands	34	±0	28	−26	18	+16	9
East of England	29	+5	31	−27	17	+17	13
South East England	25	+2	31	−23	14	+14	22
South West England	24	+1	28	−25	14	+13	25
London	43	−5	21	−11	9	+7	11
Scotland	36	+17	13	−12	7	+6	9
Wales	37	−4	18	−18	17	+11	7

Source: Focaldata / Patrick Flynn

❌ **However, since the 1980s, regional changes have occurred.**

» In the Blair era, Labour began to do well in the South too, particularly in London and the South East, with their vote share increasing by 5 points across every region in the UK.

» In 2019 the Conservatives broke new ground, moving into many traditional Labour heartlands, breaching Labour's so-called 'red wall'. Across the UK, Labour's losses outweighed any gains made by the Conservatives. While the Conservatives did lose votes in the south of England and Scotland, these were balanced by gains in the rest of England and Wales.

» In 2024 the situation was reversed with Labour regaining and the Conservatives losing the red wall, showing that region is an extremely unclear and unpredictable way of determining how people will vote.

» Moreover, the demise of Nicola Sturgeon in Scotland in 2022 and a chaotic SNP led to a complete reversal of fortunes of Labour and the SNP, the latter going from 48 to 9 seats in Scotland.

» Additionally, it could be argued that patterns of regional voting have as much to do with short-term factors as long-term, social factors. It could be that the policy changes and leadership are the cause of 'regional' voting changes. In 2017 and 2019 the issue of Brexit was a key factor in the changing pattern of votes. In 2017 and 2019, the leadership of Corbyn was a factor, initially positive, then negative in 2019. Changes of leadership also explain the changes in the way Scotland voted in 2024. In 2024, there was a nationwide shift away from the Conservatives, which was reflected in regions across the whole country. Thus, it can be suggested that regions are not an important social factor, as in reality, region differences are affected by short-term factors like governing competence, leadership and policy.

Key Debate Summary: Are social factors the most important in determining the outcome of general elections?

For	Theme	Against
✓ Class can still be considered a hugely significant factor in determining the way people vote. It is still possible to predict voting behaviour based on class.	Is class still significant or does increasing electoral volatilty challenge this?	✗ Social class has lost its significance as the key social factor in determining elections. Labour has increased its vote in middle-class areas and Conservatives have increased their vote in working-class areas.
✓ Another social factor that has been a key determinant of voting is age and this has been increasing in importance recently.	Is age still significant or is it masking votes for issues or leaders?	✗ However, age may not be as significant as suggested because it could be that young people vote Labour because of their policies or leader, for example.
✓ Another important social factor affecting voting behaviour is ethnicity. Ethnic minorities tend to vote for the Labour Party.	Is ethnicity still a homogenous group?	✗ However, different ethnic minorities vote in different ways. Also, they may vote Labour because it is more closely associated with progressive equality legislation and support for immigration.
✓ Another important social factor is region. There has been a clear 'North–South divide' with Labour being successful in the North, Scotland and Wales, and Conservatives being popular in rural England and suburbs.	Is region significant or is it masking votes for issues?	✗ However, regional voting has been quite variable in the last few decades and it is suggested that regional voting is based on party policy and leadership.

Exam Style Questions

- Evaluate the view that social factors are the most significant factors in determining voting behaviour (30).

- Evaluate the view that age is the most significant factor in determining voting behaviour (30).

- Evaluate the view that volatility in UK general elections arises because of the breakdown in class voting (30).

- Evaluate the view that elections in the UK are no longer stable and predictable (30).

Source Question

Age has been increasing in importance in recent elections with older voters voting Conservative and younger voters voting Labour. This was evident in 2017 where 66% of 18–24-year-olds voted Labour whereas the Conservatives won 69% of voters aged 70+. In 2019 YouGov argued that 'age was one of the most significant factors in the general election'. Additionally, in 2024 age was still a key dividing line with younger voters more likely to vote Labour and older voters more likely to vote Conservative. Recent elections have also shown that ethnicity is an important factor in elections. In 2019, 1 in 5 Labour votes came from ethnic minority voters, whereas only 1 in 20 was for Conservatives. In 2024, Labour led the Conservatives among ethnic minority voters by 49% to 20%. Conservatives made one gain; in Leicester East, which has one of the largest Hindu populations of any constituency in England, unsurprisingly, they voted for a Hindu Prime Minister, showing that ethnicity was a key driver in their vote.

However, in 2024, around the same proportion of all age groups below 50 voted Labour, showing age was not so significant. Moreover, the reason people vote may be because of other reasons, not age. In 2017 and 2019, Labour appealed to young people with Jeremy Corbyn as leader, suggesting leadership was the significant factor, not age. In 2024 older people voted Reform, probably motivated by their stance on immigration, showing that issues were more important than age. Regarding ethnicity, one minority group that stayed loyal to Conservatives were Hindus. In 2024 the Hindu vote held at 39%, which, given the huge drop of support for the Conservative Party, is hugely significant, this is probably down to Rishi Sunak being the Conservative (and Hindu) Prime Minister – showing the importance of leadership. It could also be argued that ethnic minorities choose parties based on issues. In 2024, a substantial minority of Muslim voters switched their vote from Labour to the Greens or independent candidates due to the Gaza conflict. This suggests that if a party changes its policies or campaigns strongly for an issue, which negatively affect a minority group, e.g. the Windrush Scandal, stop and search, Islamophobia or anti-Semitism, they will lose votes among this group – hence the motivation is issues.

Using the source, evaluate the view that age and ethnicity are the most important factors in determining the way people vote in general elections.

In your response you must:

» *Compare and contrast different opinions in the source*

» *Examine and debate these views in a balanced way*

» *Analyse and evaluate **only** the information presented in the source.*

Chapter Summary

» Understanding the way people vote is very important for political parties as well as psephologists (those who study elections and trends in voting).

» There are two key indicators of voting: long-term and short-term factors.

» Long-term factors are also known as social factors. These include class, age, gender and ethnicity. These factors were considered the most significant determinants of voting behaviour, particularly class, from the middle of the last century.

» Short-term factors, those which change from election to election, became much more significant towards the end of the twentieth century and as a consequence have made elections more difficult to predict.

» Elections between 2010 and 2024 have been the most volatile in recent history.

Further Resources

IPSOS. How the voters voted in the 2024 election https://www.ipsos.com/sites/default/files/ct/news/documents/2024-07/Ipsos%20July%202024_How%20Britain%20voted_GE2024_PUBLIC.pdf

Curtice, J. (2017) '2017 General Election – return of the two-party system?', *Politics Review*, Vol. 27, No. 2, September (London: Hodder Education).

The Conservative wipeout: How the Tory party campaign came apart. 2024. https://www.newstatesman.com/the-weekend-report/2024/06/tory-collapse-conservative-party-wipeout

Whiteley, P., Clarke, H.D. and Sanders, D. (2013) *Affluence, Austerity and Electoral Change in Britain* (Cambridge: Cambridge University Press).

Visit the companion website to access the Further Resources Booklet to explore a range of useful web links related to: YouGov and Ipsos MORI statistics on voting behaviour in the past decade, online newspaper articles on topics such as party leader portrayal in the media, and much more.

6 THE MEDIA

BREAKING
Harry draws comparisons betw
QTX-81501205-channel2
QL-1
QL-2
QL-3/CONT-3
LiveU
LiveU
LiveU
LiveU 1-1
LiveU 1-2
LiveU 1-3
LiveU 2-1
INFORMER
NDI

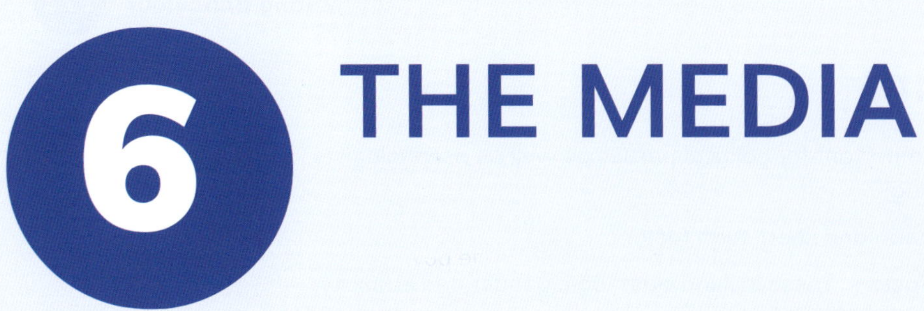

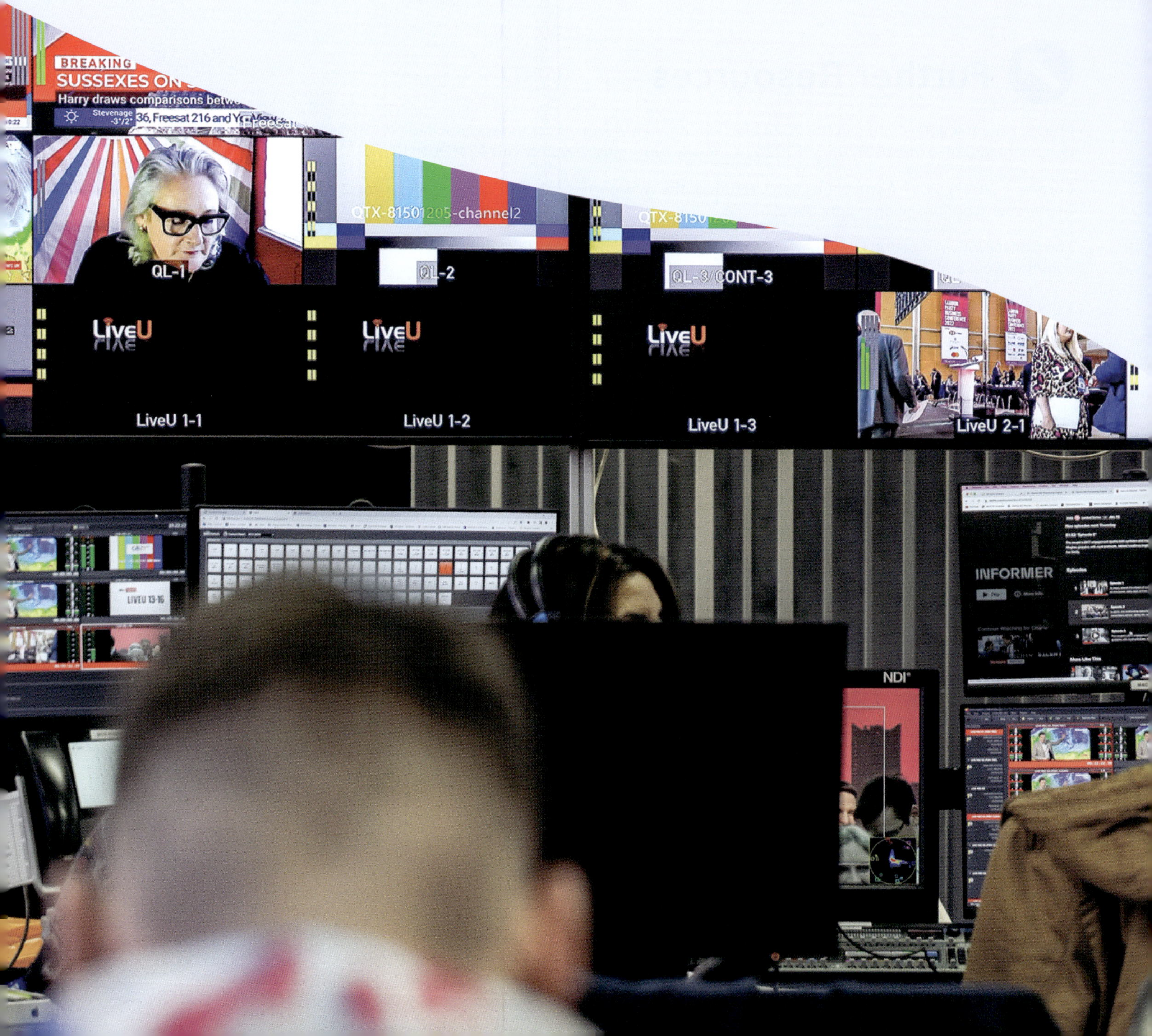

Chapter Preview

During day-to-day life, most people rely on the mass media to access the information they need to form their own political opinions; politicians rely on the media as the main tool of communication between them and the people. Because of this, the question of who owns and controls the media is highly significant. If ownership is concentrated in the hands of the few, then they may wish to use this power to push their own political agenda. However, the power and influence of the media to change voting behaviour is rejected by some, as voters are not simply empty vessels waiting to be filled by whatever messages the media send their way. It may be that the power and influence of the media is more in shaping the political debate to reflect the interests of the powerful and privileged in society.

The nature of the media has radically transformed in the UK, initially by the arrival of digital TV stations from 2000, and more recently, social media has become a key source of news. However, although it had the potential to democratise the media, the threat to democracy from fake news and disinformation, and the widespread almost immediate coverage it can achieve, are potentially an even greater threat to democracy.

Specification Checklist

4.2. The influence of the media

» The assessment of the role and impact of the media on politics – both during and between key general elections, including the importance and relevance of opinion polls, media bias and persuasion.

Source: Bloomberg / Contributor / Getty Images

The changing nature of the media

What is the media?

The media comprises organisations that are concerned with the production and distribution of all forms of knowledge, information and entertainment. The **traditional media** includes the broadcast media (television and radio) and the print media (newspapers and magazines), which has been challenged and transformed by the arrival of the **new media**, which includes a vast array of online platforms, including **social media**.

How has the nature of the media evolved?

The media has been recognised as politically significant since the late nineteenth century. Until 1945, the print media was the main way that the public could access the news. Newspapers in the UK are privately owned, free from government control and able to clearly express their political views. This gives rise to the criticism that a small number of press barons (newspaper owners) could exercise very real influence on public affairs. Since 1945, the press faced competition from the broadcast media with the birth of television. The key difference here was that unlike newspapers, the broadcast media was expected to be impartial by ensuring that a range of views was appropriately reflected; they cannot support a particular party or express a view on current affairs or matters of public policy. Since 2000, with the arrival of digital television and the internet, the media has been transformed, with a vast array of television channels and the internet's abundance of sources for news and information. This is changing the way the public is accessing the news (see Figure 6.1).

Figure 6.1 Sources of news from 2013 to 2025

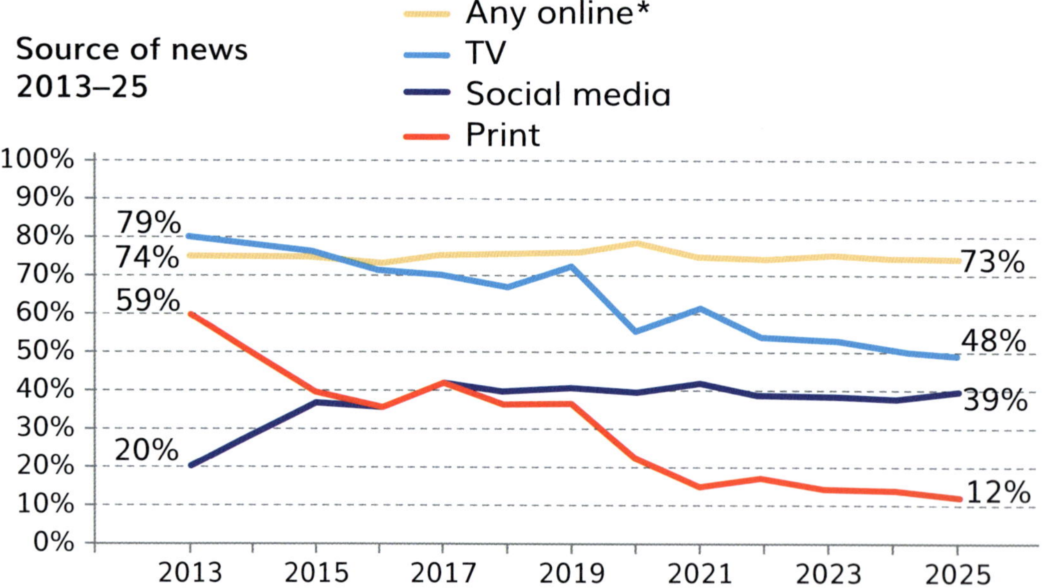

Source: Reuters Institute *Digital News Report 2025. Reproduced under the Creative Commons Attribution 4.0 International Public License*

The print media

This refers to all newspapers, whether free or paid for, local or national. Newspapers have probably suffered the most from the technological revolution with the decline in the circulation of printed papers leading to a collapse in advertising revenue, and according to YouGov data, only 12% of newspaper subscribers are aged under 25. However, it is not simply the case that the decline in readership of printed newspapers means the end of the print industry. Rather, it means its transformation.

Arguments for the decline

- ✓ UK newspaper circulation revenue fell from £2.2 billion in 2007 to £1.7 billion in 2017, then to £394 million in 2024, and advertising revenue dropped from £4.6 billion to £1.4 billion to £726.5 million in the same period. The Covid-19 pandemic accelerated these trends, further reducing print advertising and sales.

- ✓ Audiences, especially younger generations, overwhelmingly prefer digital news sources for their accessibility and convenience. Nearly half (47%) of those aged over 75 in the UK use printed newspapers as a source of news, while a third (33%) of those aged 65–74 do so. This figure dropped to just 4% of 16–24-year-olds in 2024 according to Ofcom. This does not make for good news for the printed press in the long term and suggests that a decline in readership will be a permanent feature of the future of the industry.

- ✓ Smartphones have made it easier and cheaper to access news online, leading to a sharp drop in print readership. The overall readership of the print media declined from 21.9 million in 2010 to 10.4 million in 2018, then to 6.26 million in 2025.

- ✓ The consequences for the industry have been clear as Figure 6.2 shows.

- ✓ Online news is constantly updated, making it more relevant and timely than print, which often contains information that is outdated by the time it reaches readers. This has made digital platforms the preferred source for breaking news.

- ✓ Much of the content online is free, removing the financial barrier associated with purchasing newspapers. This has made digital news more attractive to a wider audience.

- ✓ Rising costs of newsprint and concerns about sustainability make print less viable. Spiralling newsprint costs have not helped.

Arguments against the decline

- ✗ The average daily readership for newspapers in the UK shows that, although falling, papers still have considerable reach. The market remains dominated by a small number of daily papers, often with linked Sunday titles.

- ✗ The major newspapers have all adapted and moved online, operating with different financial models: *The Times* operates a subscription model, the *Guardian* looks to its readers for financial contributions, while most papers, like the *Sun* and *Daily Mail*, use a free content model and look to recoup their money from advertisers or from offering readers a premium subscription.

- ✗ Many papers have seen a large growth in online readership (see Figure 6.3), and so in some ways can be seen to have extended their reach and influence. These websites are set up in direct competition to broadcasters' websites like the BBC and online-only publications.

Photo 6.1 The newspapers' front pages of the Partygate scandal

Source: Anadolu / Contributor / Getty Images

- × Newspapers have also developed a close relationship with social media, and many journalists and papers have strong online presences, using social media to post stories as they happen and to get people to click through to their paper's online site.

- × Newspapers play a key role in financing original journalism, accounting for as much as broadcasting and online media put together. This has allowed the print media to reveal a huge number of public interest stories such as the Partygate scandal revealed by the *Daily Mirror* which led to the downfall of Boris Johnson as Prime Minister (see Photo 6.1). The Cairncross Review (2019) found that the print media still plays a central role in the generation of news.

- × The print media is still shaping the news agenda because broadcast media and social media are much more likely to carry stories that first appeared in the press rather than the other way round.

Print media is often perceived as more reliable and trustworthy than online sources, which are susceptible to misinformation and fake news. The editorial and fact-checking processes in print add to its credibility.

Broadcast media

The broadcast media includes television, radio (and now podcasts), with television remaining a key source of news as well as helping people to understand the issues of the day. The BBC, ITV and Sky News are the most significant players. The UK also has several Public Service Broadcasters (PSBs) who are the BBC, who are funded primarily by the television licence fee and publicly owned, ITV who are commercially funded, Channel 4 who are publicly owned but commercially funded, Channel 5 who are fully commercial, and S4C – the Welsh-language broadcaster – who are part publicly and part commercially funded. These broadcasters are required to deliver a range of programming that serves the public interest, including impartial news, UK-originated content and programming for diverse audiences.

Arguments for the decline

- ✓ There has been a clear generational shift towards online news, with online sources now narrowly exceeding TV as the main way UK adults access news, Ofcom suggests (70% online vs 68% TV in 2025). Among 16–24-year-olds, 88% get their news online, while only half use TV. This shift is driven by the convenience and immediacy offered by digital platforms.

Figure 6.3 2025 weekly reach of all news media, offline and online

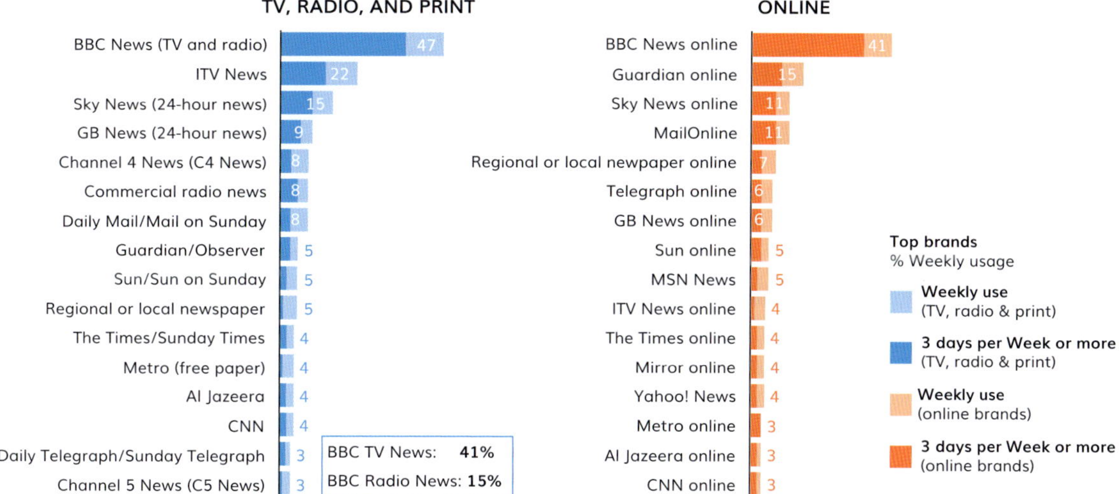

Source: Reuters Institute Digital News Report 2025. Reproduced under the Creative Commons Attribution 4.0 International Public License

- ✓ TV news reach has dropped sharply, from 79% in 2018 to 68% in 2025. Average weekly reach on TV fell from 90% in 2019 to 74% in 2025, and daily viewing dropped from over three hours pre-pandemic to under two and a half hours.
- ✓ UK broadcasters are under financial strain, with declining investment in premium content and some channels (e.g. Sky News) operating at a loss. The rise of global streaming giants like Netflix and Amazon, which outspend UK broadcasters on British-made content, intensifies competition and threatens the sustainability of traditional news operations.
- ✓ The proliferation of online news, social media and streaming platforms has fragmented audiences, making it harder for broadcasters to maintain mass reach and influence. Younger audiences, in particular, are turning to platforms like YouTube, TikTok and Instagram for news.

Visit the companion website for a brief history of the BBC, and commercial and digital stations from the previous fifth edition.

Arguments against the decline

- ✗ TV remains the most trusted news source in the UK, as shown by Figure 6.4. In an era of misinformation and deepfakes online, the regulated nature of broadcast news is seen as a safeguard for accuracy and public trust.
- ✗ While it appears that broadcasters like the BBC and Sky are losing viewers to online sources, in reality, the BBC has transferred online and is the most used website and app in the UK for news, exceeding the number of monthly reads of either the *Sun* or the *Daily Mail* reaching around 39–40 million unique monthly users in the UK, according to Ipsos.
- ✗ TV is still the leading news source for those over 55 (85% reach), ensuring that large segments of the population remain well served by broadcast news. In the 2024 Election campaign, the BBC website accounted for 28% of all time spent on news sites during the campaign, while the Mail Online made up 21%.
- ✗ Broadcasters like the BBC play a vital role in informing citizens, ensuring a shared understanding of facts. TV news remains especially important during major national events and elections, providing reliable information and uniting audiences.

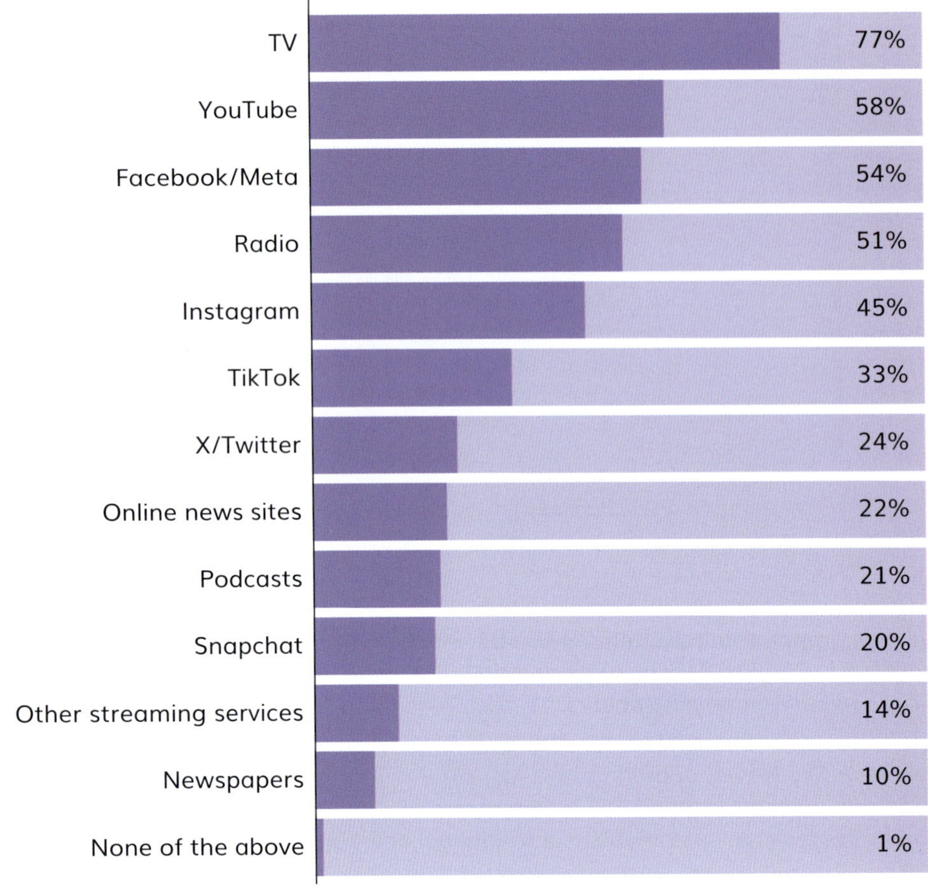

Source: Broadcast Revolution 2025, Broadcast Trends Report

- Political podcasts have become a significant force in the UK's media landscape, especially during the 2024 General Election, which many commentators dubbed 'the first podcast election'. In 2025 Lewis Goodall, in The News Agents podcast uncovered a catastrophic MoD data breach exposing 19,000 Afghans' details, which had been kept secret by a two-year super-injunction. (See Case Study on Podcasts on page 179.)
- Despite falling viewing, broadcasters are investing in digital, on-demand and streaming services to reach audiences across platforms. The BBC, ITV and others continue to innovate, offering content online and via apps, and remain among the most popular news providers across all media.
- Those aged 55 and over rely more heavily on television sources. BBC One (62%) is most used, followed by ITV (43%), the BBC News Channel (23%), BBC iPlayer (21%) and Sky News (20%). Facebook (19%) is the only social media source in the top ten sources for this group according to Ofcom.

The decline of broadcast news media in the UK is driven by shifting audience habits, financial pressures and fierce digital competition. However, broadcast news has adapted significantly and effectively to create a substantial online presence. It also remains essential for trust and is very important to older viewers and during key national moments.

CASE STUDY 6.1: THE RISE IN SIGNIFICANCE OF POLITICAL PODCASTS

The rise of political podcasts

Since 2020, political podcasts have moved from the fringes of UK media to the heart of the political conversation and election coverage. While podcasts had been steadily growing in popularity, the 2024 General Election marked a turning point, widely dubbed the UK's 'first podcast election'. Top political podcasts saw their downloads rise by more than 50% during the campaign, with platforms like Acast and Spotify reporting record growth in both listenership and total hours played. The accessibility of podcasts on demand being mobile-friendly and unregulated compared to traditional broadcast has been a key driver of this surge.

Reach and audience engagement

The reach of political podcasts has become substantial. By 2025, 51% of UK adults listened to at least one political podcast each month, with 33% of the population tuning in weekly and spending an average of between 5–9 hours per week on podcasts. Among these, political podcasts have carved out a significant niche. For example, 'The Rest Is Politics', hosted by Alastair Campbell and Rory Stewart, broke into the top three UK podcasts for the first time in 2024, achieving over 21.6 million downloads and views during the election campaign alone. Other shows, such as 'Political Currency' (Ed Balls and George Osborne), 'Electoral Dysfunction' (Sky News) and 'Political Fix' (Financial Times), all reported download increases of 40% or more during the campaign period.

Podcasts have also outperformed traditional media in some respects. 'The Rest Is Politics' commentary on televised leaders' debates, for example, attracted nearly double the audience of the debates themselves. The BBC's 'Newscast' saw a 64% growth in listenership, and Global's 'The News Agents' neared 100 million all-time downloads, with a 45% spike during the election.

Influence on UK politics

The rise of political podcasts has had several notable effects on UK politics:

» **Diversifying political discourse:** Podcasts offer a platform for in-depth discussion, nuanced analysis and cross-party dialogue. Shows deliberately pair hosts from different political backgrounds, fostering more balanced and less adversarial debate than is typical in traditional media.

» **Shaping campaign coverage:** Podcasts have become a key battleground for campaign messaging. Politicians and journalists now routinely use podcasts to break news, respond to events and explain policy in greater detail than broadcast slots allow. The Telegraph's 'The Daily T' saw its election night episode perform 45% above average, and Sky's 'Electoral Dysfunction' doubled its audience post-election.

» **Engaging new audiences:** Political podcasts are especially popular among younger, educated and politically engaged listeners, providing an alternative to both social media and the tabloid press. While this means their direct impact on overall turnout is still debated, as younger listeners are less likely to vote, their role in informing and energising these demographics is clear.

» **Challenging traditional media:** The rapid growth of podcasts has shifted some influence away from newspapers and television, with advertisers and political strategists increasingly investing in podcast sponsorships and appearances.

Top UK political podcasts 2025

Podcast name	Hosts	Achievements
The Rest Is Politics	Alastair Campbell, Rory Stewart	#1 in charts, Podcast of the Year
The News Agents	Maitlis, Sopel, Goodall	Leading daily news podcast
Pod Save the UK	Coco Khan, Nish Kumar	Popular UK spin-off, humour & analysis
Electoral Dysfunction	Rigby, Harman, Davidson	Fast-growing, cross-party debate
Political Currency	Ed Balls, George Osborne	Insider political and economic analysis
The Daily T	Tominey, Ahmed	New, right-of-centre, exclusive interviews
Newscast	BBC	Flagship BBC daily analysis
Red Box Politics	Matt Chorley	Interviews, panel discussions
Oh God, What Now?	Podmasters team	Irreverent, left-leaning analysis
Politics Weekly UK	Guardian journalists	Weekly Guardian analysis

Social media

Since 2013, social media has risen quickly in importance as a source of news in the UK.

Arguments for the significance of social media

✓ Social media has become the primary news source for over half (52%) of UK adults, overtaking both television and print, according to Ofcom. This marks a generational shift, especially among younger audiences, with 71% of 16–24-year-olds using social media for news compared to less than half who use TV, as Figure 6.5 shows.

✓ The rise of social media is a challenge to the dominance of the media by a small number of key players, so-called 'press barons'.

✓ Social media like X and TikTok enables instant access to breaking news and live updates, making news consumption more immediate and convenient.

✓ It promotes communication between large numbers of people, opening up debate and allowing for the voices of all groups to be heard.

✓ The importance of social media as a news source among young people is evident when looking at the top individual sources used. Instagram (41%), YouTube (37%), Facebook (35%), TikTok (33%) and X (27%) comprise the top five news sources used by 16–24-year-olds. BBC iPlayer (23%) and BBC One (23%) are in joint sixth position, according to Ofcom.

Figure 6.5 **Social media sources used for news 2019–25**

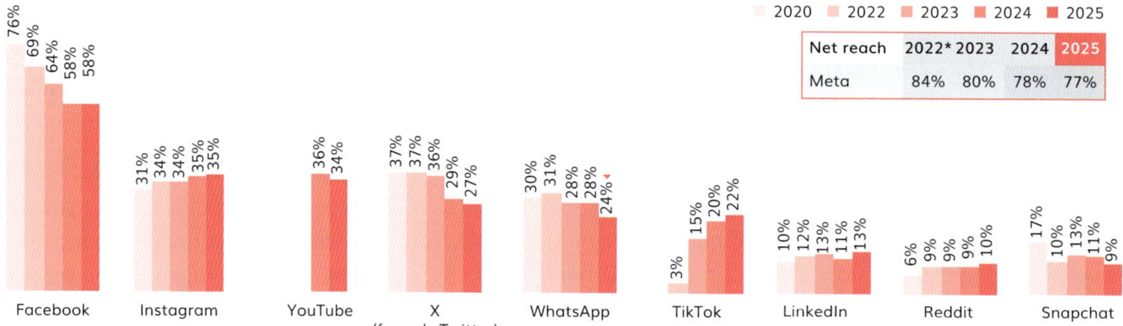

Source: News Consumption in the UK: 2025 Report © Ofcom

Arguments against the significance of social media

✗ Most social media users still get their news from the main news organisations in the UK. They click on links to the main broadcast or newspaper websites, with the BBC being the most followed news organisation in the UK on X, Instagram and Facebook, and Sky News being the most followed on TikTok.

✗ Social media is a major vehicle for misinformation. Critics argue that information that is deliberately manipulated to deceive and mislead people (**fake news**) can spread quickly and more widely through the use of social media and can be used to influence the results of elections. In a 2024 survey from Southampton Solent University, 94% of UK respondents reported witnessing misinformation on social platforms. The ease of sharing unverified or false information undermines trust in news consumed via these channels.

✗ While social media provides instant news by making any member of the public a reporter of an event as it happens, the more detailed explanations of these events are still provided by the print and broadcast media. This suggests that social media is not really changing whom the British public get their news from, just how they access it.

✗ Social media algorithms tend to reinforce users' existing beliefs by prioritising content similar to what they've engaged with before, potentially leading to **echo chambers** and reduced exposure to diverse viewpoints.

Social media has become indispensable for news consumption in the UK, especially for younger generations, due to its speed, accessibility and interactive nature. However, its rise has brought significant challenges, including widespread misinformation, declining trust and concerns about the depth and quality of news.

Definition

Fake news:
The intentional creation and sharing of false information that aims to deceive or mislead. This information is then frequently spread on purpose or inadvertently.

Definition

Echo chamber:
An environment on social media where algorithms and networks reinforce users' existing beliefs by limiting exposure to opposing views.

Key Debate Summary: Is social media now the most important type of media?

For	Theme	Against
✓ Print media is in decline in the UK with readership continuing to fall, with a limited reach with younger voters.	Has print media challenged social media by moving online?	✗ Print media is dominated by a small number of papers with a wide readership and has moved online, it has a significant reach with older voters.
✓ Broadcast news reach has dropped sharply, with broadcasters under significant financial strain. It is also being challenged by social media, especially with younger voters.	Has broadcast media challenged social media by being a more trustworthy source of news?	✗ Broadcast media remains the most important source of political information. Broadcast media has moved online and the BBC is the most used site for UK news.
✓ Social media has become the primary news source for over half of UK adults, overtaking both television and print.	Is social media really as influential on politics or is it simply a platform for broadcast and print media?	✗ Most social media users still get their news from the main news organisations in the UK; it is just changing how the public accesses the news, not whom they get it from. The surge of political podcasts also shows the importance of broadcast media

Opinion polls

What are opinion polls?

Opinion polls attempt to test the opinions of the public on a certain issue or their voting intentions.

The key types of polling used in the UK are:

- » **Voting intention polls** to gauge how people intend to vote at any one time (see Figure 6.6).
- » **Policy issue polls** that assess people's views on issues that might relate to social policy or politics, such as views on the NHS, immigration or the economy.
- » **Private polls** that are commissioned by political parties, individuals and companies, where the results are only selectively released to the public, if at all.
- » **Exit polls** which are conducted as voters leave the polling station. Exit polls are considered highly accurate because they capture actual voting behaviour rather than intentions as seen in Table 6.1. In the UK, fieldworkers at selected polling stations ask voters to fill out a mock ballot paper indicating how they voted. The results are collected and analysed to provide an early projection of the election outcome, often announced as soon as polls close at 10pm. In 2024, exit polls showed that Labour would win a landslide, Conservatives would win with a large majority in 2019, May would lose her majority in 2017 and Cameron would win a majority in 2015.

How do opinion polls work?

- » Trained interviewers ask questions of people chosen at random from the population being measured.
- » Responses are given and interpretations are made based on the results.
- » Polling companies, such as Ipsos MORI, YouGov Opinium and Survation, aim to develop reliable techniques that filter out any bias in order to give results that are as accurate as possible.
- » This involves sampling a large number of people, who are broadly representative of the social make-up of the population as a whole.

The influence of opinion polls on policy

Opinion polls significantly shaped UK policy by acting as real-time indicators of public mood, compelling both the Labour government and opposition parties to reconsider their policy profiles.

- » In 2025 Labour's Chancellor Rachel Reeves axed income tax hikes in the November Budget after YouGov data showed 64–76% opposition, a move that stemmed immediate backlash.
- » Reform's poll lead throughout 2025-26 strengthened voter focus on immigration, nudging Conservatives rightward under Kemi Badenoch and Labour toward tougher rhetoric.

» Labour responded to very poor opinion polls by shifting on welfare, while Tories under Kemi Badenoch used polls to pivot rightward on the economy and immigration.
This leads to the suggestion that, opinion polls have moved from predictors to restrictors.

Table 6.1 Exit polls vs actual results 2015–24

Election year	Party	Exit poll seats	Actual seats	Difference
2024	Labour	410	412	+2
	Conservative	131	121	-10
	Liberal Democrat	61	72	+11
	SNP	10	9	-1
	Reform UK	13	5	-8
	Green	2	4	+2
2019	Conservative	368	365	-3
	Labour	191	203	+12
	SNP	55	48	-7
	Liberal Democrat	13	11	-2
2017	Conservative	316	317	+1
	Labour	266	262	-4
2015	Conservative	316	330	+14
	Labour	239	232	-7
	SNP	58	56	-2
	Liberal Democrat	10	8	-2

The importance of a reliable method was highlighted in 2024 where opinion polls faced accuracy challenges due to huge shifts in voting patterns. According to BMG Research, a UK-based social research and analytics agency, Reflections on the 2024 Election Polling, there was a problem with the misrepresentation of undecided voters who were disproportionately 2019 Conservative voters. Consequently, many pollsters overestimated Labour's vote share. Additionally, many organisations didn't account for the huge drop in turnout which affected their predictions. Additionally, minority groups like British Muslims were underrepresented, which affected Labour's reported support in some polls. To address these issues, pollsters adopted several new methods to improve the prediction of who would actually vote. They also used different questions for undecided voters, which improved accuracy.

Figure 6.6 Example of a YouGov opinion poll in the run-up to the 2024 General Election
Voting intention (2019–24)

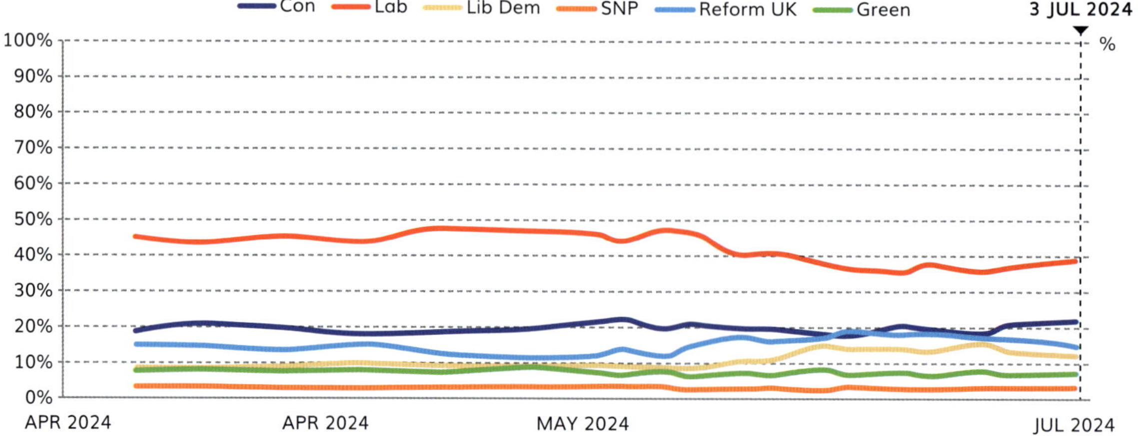

Source: YouGov plc, 2024 © All rights reserved

KEY TOPIC DEBATE: DO OPINION POLLS HAVE A POSITIVE IMPACT ON UK DEMOCRACY?

There are a number of key benefits to opinion polls in a democracy, particularly because voting in elections is such an imperfect way of measuring public opinion. A vote for a party is seen as giving support for the party's manifesto, yet most voters are unaware of the fine print in the manifesto. Opinion polls plug this gap by providing an additional way of measuring the views of the public in order to keep parties on their toes by reminding them what voters care about and think. However, there are a number of major issues for opinion polls, which can all be tied to the issue of accuracy. The failure to predict the right result can be highly consequential.

✓ **Informs policy decisions.** Parties use opinion polls to help inform policy decisions by providing the thoughts of the population. Opinion polls provide up-to-date insights into voter sentiment, helping parties and the public track shifts in support. As a result, governments can make decisions that they feel a large number of the public will support.

» In 2025, Rachel Reeves indicated that she may raise income tax, however YouGov polls revealed overwhelming public opposition (64–76%) to this policy, signalling severe political consequences. It is possible this had an impact on her decision not to raise them in the Budget.

» The 2019 Tory manifesto chimed with policy issue polls with its focus of 'Get Brexit Done' and increased spending pledges on the police, NHS and education.

» The 2017 Labour manifesto chimed with policy issue polls that showed that the public backed renationalising the railways, freezing the retirement age and building thousands of council houses.

✗ **However, inaccurate polling can lead to getting those decisions wrong.** It is also the case that opinion polls discourage parties leading (and winning) arguments in order to change the public's mind, and instead they slavishly follow the direction of opinion polls.

» In 2024, the Labour Party operated a 'Ming vase' strategy of saying very little at all, for fear of putting voters off.

» When Theresa May called the snap election in 2017, the lead over Labour in the polls was 17%. The final result was a 2.4% lead, with the Conservatives losing their majority in the Commons. Had the polls been accurate, she may not have been so keen to call an election.

✓ **Informs campaign strategy.** Polls help politicians understand the public, allowing them to adjust policies or campaign messages accordingly. This helps parties to target resources and refine their message.

» In 2024, polls showed the rise of Reform UK and the Liberal Democrats which led both Labour and the Conservatives to adjust local campaigning in marginal seats.

» In 2017, Theresa May was forced to reverse her policy to make elderly people pay more for their social care, nicknamed the 'dementia tax' by Labour, after her lead in the voting intention polls halved in a few days.

✗ **Election campaigns can become too focused on opinion polls,** and the media focuses on a 'horse race style' commentary on who is winning the race rather than focusing on interrogating the issues and policies. Equally, if the polls are wrong, this leads to the whole media narrative becoming shaped by inaccurate information.

» In 2024, many polls overestimated Labour's vote share and underestimated the Conservatives, partly because of undecided voters.

» Minority communities are often under-sampled, leading to inaccurate reflections of their voting patterns, and in 2024, most pollsters' Muslim samples were not representative, affecting Labour's projected winning margin in key constituencies.

» In 2017, polls underestimated Labour's surge; in 2019 and 2024, some polls overestimated Labour's lead and underestimated smaller parties.

✓ **Opinion polls can encourage political engagement and participation and inform public debate.**

» Polls give citizens a sense that their views matter and they can influence the debate.

» The wide publication of polling on issues such as the cost of living and the NHS keep these topics at the forefront of political discussion.

Tip: The influence of the media can be compared and contrasted to the role that long-term (social) and short-term factors play in influencing voting behaviour.

» Where the media reports a close election content, this is more likely to encourage voters to turn out. The voting intention polls were reported by the media as being close in 2010, 2015 and 2017, and all these elections showed an increase in turnout on the previous election.

❌ However, polls can also discourage participation.

» When polls predict an easy victory for one party, it can reduce turnout. Persistent predictions of a Labour landslide in 2024 may have contributed to the lowest turnout in decades as some voters felt their vote would not affect the outcome. In 2001, the polls predicted a landslide victory for Labour, the election with the lowest turnout for over 80 years.

✅ Polls can help voters make informed tactical choices.

» Polls can guide voters in marginal seats to vote tactically, influencing outcomes in closely contested areas.

» 2024 polls, such as YouGov's, provided seat-level predictions that informed tactical voting campaigns, especially in seats where Labour, Lib Dems and Greens were competing to unseat Conservatives.

❌ Polls can shape as well as reflect opinion, causing 'bandwagon' or 'underdog' effects. The most important problem with opinion polls is that they end up influencing the very outcomes they are supposed to measure. This has led countries such as France, Spain and Italy to ban all opinion polling in the period before an election. Some ways which can influence the outcomes are:

» the 'bandwagon' effect, where information from polls can influence people to alter their view to come into line with the majority

» the 'underdog' effect, when some people adopt a minority view out of sympathy

» In 2024, both YouGov and Verian found evidence of voters changing their minds after being polled, contributing to discrepancies between final polls and actual results.

Key Debate Summary: Do opinion polls have a positive impact on UK democracy?

For	Theme	Against
✓ Opinion polls informing political parties about public opinion on their policies.	How influential are opinion polls on party policy decisions?	✗ Inaccurate polling can lead to political parties making poor policy decisions.
✓ Polls help politicians understand the public, allowing them to adjust policies or campaign messages accordingly.	How well do opinion polls help politicians understand the public?	✗ Election campaigns can become too focused on opinion polls, and the media focuses on a 'horse race style' commentary.
✓ Polling can inform public debate and facilitate voter engagement and participation.	How well do opinion polls enhance public engagement?	✗ However, polls can discourage participation.
✓ Polls can help voters make informed tactical choices.	How well do opinion polls help the public make tactical voting decisions?	✗ Polls can shape as well as reflect opinion, causing 'bandwagon' or 'underdog' effects.

The influence of the media on elections

Claims that the media have affected, perhaps decisively, the outcome of elections have come not least from the media themselves. Two days after the 1992 General Election, for example, the *Sun* trumpeted, 'It's the Sun wot won it'. Despite the exaggeration involved in the *Sun*'s infamous headline, it is difficult to deny that modern election campaigns are, in a very real sense, media campaigns. Only a tiny proportion of voters attend the election rallies or meet leaders or even parliamentary candidates in the flesh during an election campaign. Instead, most people find out their information from the media.

Nevertheless, the idea that the media's influence on elections is one way is a highly simplistic view of media influence. Voters are seen as empty vessels waiting to be filled by whatever messages the media send their way. In reality, voters not only already have attitudes and beliefs of various kinds shaped by social and many other factors, but are also subject to a range of other influences, including those of their family, their friends, work colleagues and so on. It is widely argued that these attitudes and beliefs act as a filter that allows media messages to be interpreted in different ways, and, for that matter, to be accepted or rejected. A committed Conservative is unlikely to change their vote by reading the *Guardian* and a left-winger will not adjust their attitudes by reading the *Daily Express*; indeed, it is likely to only serve to reinforce their existing views.

Open bias is explicit and deliberately promoted. Most newspapers in the UK are absolutely clear about their political bias in favour of a particular party or policy, as shown by the front covers in Photo 6.2.

Hidden bias is bias that is hidden behind the mask of neutrality and allegations of hidden bias are often aimed at the broadcast media.

However, media influence is a complex process, and it is important to acknowledge that it is extremely difficult to isolate the effects of a single factor on voting behaviour, let alone the role the media plays in its entirety. Nonetheless, it is important not to dismiss the notion of media influence altogether.

Definition

Open bias: This type of bias is obvious, as it is not hidden and is clear for people to see.

Hidden bias: Is not clearly obvious, but veiled behind rationalised arguments and neutrality.

Photo 6.2 How different papers covered the historic EU Referendum result

Source: AFP / Stringer / Getty Images

Visit the companion website for case studies from the previous fifth edition on the *Sun* and its impact on public opinion.

CASE STUDY 6.2: GB NEWS

Introduction and launch

GB News launched on 13 June 2021 as the first major UK television news start-up since Sky News in 1989, with a mission to provide 'original news, opinion and debate' and to challenge what it saw as the consensus of mainstream media. Prominent hosts have included Nigel Farage, Eamonn Holmes, Michael Portillo, Jacob Rees-Mogg and Camilla Tominey.

Viewing figures and reach

GB News initially struggled with technical issues and low ratings, but by late 2023 and into 2024, it had made significant gains:

» In November 2024, GB News overtook Sky News for live TV viewers averaged over a 20-hour period (6am–2am), with 70,430 average viewers to Sky's 67,670. This trend continued into early 2025, with GB News maintaining a lead over Sky News in live TV viewership.

» By December 2024, GB News's average live views were 83% of BBC News's figures, reflecting a 21% year-on-year improvement.

» GB News's online audience has also surged, with 17.9 million unique views across its website and apps in the year to May 2024, and its reach on Facebook and YouTube rising from 37.8 million to 48 million.

» In November 2024, GB News reached 3.5 million people monthly on TV, compared to 10.9 million for BBC News and 8.2 million for Sky News.

» The GB News radio simulcast has also grown, overtaking Talk Radio's weekly reach in 2024.

» Its coverage has been particularly strong in 'Red Wall' regions, where viewership has grown fastest, reflecting its appeal to audiences outside the traditional metropolitan centres.

Impact on the media landscape

GB News has had a notable influence on the UK media environment:

» GB News claims it has forced the BBC and other rivals to adapt their output, broadening the range of views and topics covered.

» Its editorial approach, which prioritises stories and viewpoints it claims are 'overlooked' by mainstream outlets, has resonated with a segment of the public who feels disenfranchised by traditional broadcasters.

» GB News has become a key platform for right-leaning politicians and commentators, influencing the national conversation and providing a home for voices that often feel excluded from mainstream outlets.

Controversies and Ofcom complaints

From the beginning, GB News has been embroiled in controversy:

» **Ofcom complaints:** Over 4,500 complaints were lodged with Ofcom by May 2023, and some broadcasts have triggered record levels of complaints, such as a 2025 segment linking LGBTQ+ inclusion to paedophilia, which resulted in over 60,000 complaints.

» **On-air scandals:** High-profile incidents include the suspension of presenters Laurence Fox and Dan Wootton for misogynistic comments, and repeated Ofcom investigations into breaches of broadcasting standards.

» **Impartiality breaches:** Ofcom has found GB News in breach of impartiality rules on several occasions, most notably for giving Prime Minister Rishi Sunak an uncontested platform before the 2024 General Election, resulting in a £100,000 fine and a requirement to broadcast Ofcom's findings. However, GB News has also successfully challenged some Ofcom rulings in court, notably over Jacob Rees-Mogg's shows, where the High Court found Ofcom's decisions unlawful.

Neutrality and editorial stance

While GB News's editorial charter claims a commitment to impartiality and accuracy, research and monitoring consistently show a right-wing bias in both its on-air and online output, particularly in story selection and framing. The channel's opinion-led format, frequent use of Conservative politicians as presenters, and coverage that often favours right-leaning perspectives have led critics to compare it to US networks like Fox News. Ofcom has found that, at times, GB News has failed to provide due impartiality on major political controversies. GB News argues that it is simply providing a balance to the left-leaning content provided by the BBC.

Summary

GB News has rapidly become a disruptive force in the UK media landscape, growing its audience and shaping political debate, but also attracting controversy and regulatory scrutiny for its approach to impartiality. Its future will depend on whether it can sustain growth, maintain financial backing and navigate the challenges of regulatory compliance and public trust.

Broadcast media and influence

✔ **The broadcast media is seen to be incredibly influential as it is a key source of news for the public.** Despite changes in technology, the broadcast media remains dominated by a small number of very influential media outlets, such as the BBC, Sky and ITV, with large audiences.

» Political parties tailor their policy announcements, statements and public visits to get maximum visibility in the news cycle, especially during campaigns. Speeches and policies are boiled down into memorable sound bites in order to become the headline or key video clip at the top of the news shows.

» The influence of the broadcast media also means that both looking and sounding good on TV is crucial for modern political leaders. Blair's and Cameron's easy style was key to their success while May's wooden awkwardness was a significant problem in 2017. Johnson was naturally charismatic, while Starmer lacked charisma.

» Trust in broadcast media journalists remains high in comparison to the print media, suggesting a far higher level of influence (see Figure 6.6).

» The broadcast media has adapted to the arrival of online media by moving online, with the BBC as the most used source for online news in the 2024 UK Election as shown in Figure 6.7.

» The framing of news stories in the broadcast media, including which stories are selected, which are omitted, whom they choose as commentators and how they choose to construct the narrative gives them real influence. According to YouGov, during the 2024 Election campaign, TV was the most common single source of news for people in the UK. TV reached 58% and after this there is a drop to social media (43%), newspaper websites (42%) and radio (42%). A further 33% also say they get news from a news website not associated with a newspaper. Only 14% still get news from printed newspapers, while almost as many are embracing the newer medium of podcasts (13%).

» The arrival of GB News, while bound by the same neutrality guidelines as all other broadcasters, has been able to provide a clear right-wing perspective, and is growing more influential: in 2024, GB News had overtaken Sky News for the first time, averaging 70,430 live viewers to Sky's 67,670.

» The overwhelming focus of national election campaigns is still on television coverage. Manifestos are launched, policy statements are made and rallies are held, but primarily reported on and seen by voters via the TV.

» Leading politicians give frequent interviews and visit factories, hospitals and schools across the UK to raise their public profile. They do this not only to hear from members of the public but, crucially, in the hope of gaining television exposure, with speeches that are tailored and events timed and carefully staged for this purpose. The sound bite takes centre stage, with short, clear and memorable phrases, such as 'Get Brexit Done' replacing meaningful communication.

» Ed Davey took this considerably further in 2024, setting up publicity stunts of him riding a roller coaster (Photo 6.3) or falling off a paddle board on Lake Windermere. These campaign activities were designed specifically to provide great photo opportunities for the media, which is indeed what happened. This was a great strategy for a third-party leader who rarely gets any attention during election campaigns. His party received their highest vote count in 2024.

Figure 6.7 Where people sourced their news from during the 2024 campaign

Which, if any, of the following sources do you use to access news? Please select all that apply.

Photo 6.3 Ed Davey at Thorpe Park during the 2024 Election campaign

Source: Jack Taylor / Stringer

» Television coverage in election campaigns focuses far more on party leaders than their parties. Consequently, television has altered the style of election campaigning, helping to elevate personality and image over policies. In 2010, this took the form of televised head-to-head leaders' debates for the first time in UK politics, and since then they have taken place every year, but the format and participation have varied with the leaders of the two main parties not always being prepared to participate. The result is that electoral success, such as the Conservative victory in 2019, and Labour's in 2024, is claimed as a personal mandate for the party leader and used to increase the power of the Prime Minister.

Photo 6.4 Leaders' debate in the run-up to the 2024 Election

Source: Handout / Handout / Getty Images

✖ The power of the broadcast media to influence elections is limited.

» It is constrained by its obligation to impartiality, its professional standards built on neutrality and its monitoring by Ofcom. This appears to limit the ability of the broadcast media to shape how people vote.

» Trust in the broadcast media has declined in general. For example, in YouGov polling, BBC journalists were trusted by 81% and ITV journalists by 82% in 2003, but that figure has fallen significantly since then, further limiting its influence (see Figure 6.8). This decline is driven in part by the increasing belief among viewers and listeners that the broadcast media is biased.

Figure 6.8 Media trust

TRUST

Overall trust in news is stable this year, but remains more than 15pp lower than before the Brexit referendum (2016). Public broadcasters such as the BBC, Channel 4, and ITV remain the most trusted news brands along with the *Financial Times*. More opinionated news brands tend to have lower trust levels in our survey, along with tabloid newspapers.

OVERALL TRUST SCORE 2015-25

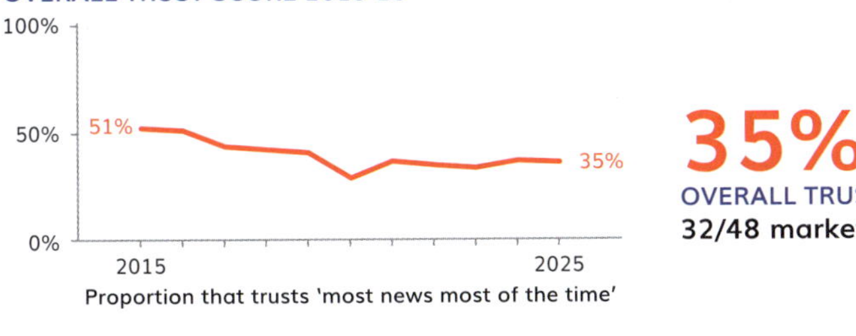

Measure of press freedom from NGO Reporters Without Borders based on expert assessment. More at rsf.org

PUBLIC OPINION ON BRAND TRUST

Only the brands listed were included in the survey. it should not be treated as a list of the most or least trusted brands, as it is not exhaustive.

Brand	Trust	Neither	Don't Trust
BBC News	60%	16%	24%
Channel 4	56%	26%	18%
Daily Mail	24%	27%	49%
Daily Mirror	22%	28%	50%
Daily Telegraph	42%	32%	25%
Financial Times	57%	30%	14%
GB News	29%	27%	44%
Guardian	57%	28%	21%
Independent	46%	36%	18%
ITV News	56%	25%	19%
MSN News	24%	43%	32%
Regional or local newspaper	51%	32%	17%
Sky News	51%	27%	22%
Sun	17%	21%	62%
The Times	47%	30%	23%

Q6_brand trust. How trustworthy would you say news from the following brands is? Please use the scale below, where 0 is 'not at all trustworthy' and 10 is 'completely trustworthy. Details: 6-10 coded as Trust', 5 coded as 'Neither, 0-4 coded as 'Don't trust. Those that haven't heard of each brand were excluded. Whether respondents consider a brand trustworthy is their subjective judgement, and the scores are aggregates of public opinion, not an objective assessment of underlying trustworthiness.

Source: Reuters Institute Digital News Report 2025. Reproduced under the Creative Commons Attribution 4.0 International Public License

» The broadcast media's influence has been challenged by social media. In particular, social media is becoming more important to younger voters.

» The broadcast media tends to follow the stories created in the printed media, rather than funding original journalism.

Print media and influence

✓ **Unlike television, the press is nakedly partisan; national newspapers usually take an explicit stance on which party, or which leader, their readers should vote for, and, in the case of the tabloid press in particular, sometimes expressing these views in strong terms.**

» The print media believes in its own power to shape elections and public opinion. The *Sun* has backed the party that has won the most seats in all elections since 1979. The shaping of the views of party leaders is particularly important: the repeated media attacks over a long period of time on leaders such as Michael Foot, Neil Kinnock, Ed Miliband and Jeremy Corbyn impacted voting behaviour. The strenuous efforts of party leaders to court the press reflects how much importance they place on the print media.

» Political parties and party leaders look to recruit journalists to serve as their directors of communications in order to manage relations with the press: Tony Blair recruited Alastair Campbell, a former political editor of the *Daily Mirror*, David Cameron followed suit, recruiting Andy Coulson, a former editor of the *News of the World*. In 2015, Jeremy Corbyn appointed ex-*Guardian* journalist, Seamus Milne, while Boris Johnson appointed another ex-journalist in Lee Cain in 2019. Keir Starmer brought in James Lyons to the Downing Street team in 2024 as his senior communications strategist. Lyons previously worked for TikTok and was deputy political editor at both the *Sunday Times* and the *Daily Mirror*.

» The print media still has extensive reach, in particular with the ABC1 voters and over-65s who are the most likely to turn out in elections. The existence of an essentially pro-Conservative press in the UK does matter, in that it makes Labour's path to power steeper and more challenging than that of the Conservatives, unless, that is, the Labour Party adopts broadly centre or centre-right policies. This, in turn, is a reflection of the impact of newspaper ownership, and of 'press barons' in particular.

» It is not just that the print media might influence voters, it's more that the printed press sets the agenda; where newspapers lead on issues, more trusted broadcasters follow. Research from Loughborough University found that issues which dominated the press also led the television news. A good example would be the *Daily Mirror* breaking the 'Partygate' scandal. This was picked up by all media and led the news agenda for many months culminating in Prime Minister Johnson stepping down.

» The print media has moved online successfully, with many print journalists using social media to direct people to stories in the papers they work for. The MailOnline, the Guardian, the Mirror and the Sun were in the top five most visited sites during the 2019 Election campaign.

» The problem of newspaper bias is exacerbated by the nature of media ownership, with much of the press now concentrated in the hands of a few press barons. In 2025, just three companies (News UK, DMGT plc and Reach plc) dominated 90% of the national newspaper market; these three companies also account for over 40% of the audience reach of the UK's top 50 online news brands (see Table 6.2). This gives huge power to the owners, to shape the media agenda and influence public opinion.

Concerns from the Media Reform Coalition and Press Gazette warned that this concentration is 'worsening the collapse of media diversity and public interest journalism across the UK media', especially at the local level, where decades of consolidation have left many areas with little or no independent local journalism. It is also noticeable that a much larger slice of the print media usually supports the Conservative Party than the Labour Party, although in 2024, more titles endorsed Labour, and in terms of market share, support was almost evenly split between Labour- and Conservative-leaning papers, with several major titles switching to Labour for the first time in decades.

✗ **While the print media exhibits clear bias, this does not mean that it has real influence.**

» The print media's impact is largely restricted to amplifying or reinforcing pre-existing sympathies or preferences and rarely extends to generating new preferences or changing established ones.

Table 6.2 Media ownership, market share and political bias

News group / Owner	Major titles	Estimated daily print circulation (2025)	2024 election endorsement(s)
DMG media	Daily Mail, Mail on Sunday, Metro, i	1,759,000	*Mail*: Conservative *i*: Neutral *Metro*: Neutral
News UK (News corp)	Sun, Sun on Sunday, Times, Sunday Times	1,620,000	*Sun*: Labour *Sunday Times*: Labour *Times*: None
Reach plc	Mirror, Express, Star, People, Sunday Mirror, etc.	617,000	*Mirror*: Labour *Express*: Conservative *Star*: Labour
Telegraph media group	Daily Telegraph, Sunday Telegraph	285,000	Conservative
Guardian media group/ Tortoise media	Guardian	60,000	Labour
Tortoise media / Guardian media group	Observer	95,500*	Labour
Financial times group	Financial Times	53,000 (UK only)	Labour
Others	Evening Standard, Independent (digital only), etc.	50,000	*Standard*: Labour *Independent*: Labour

* *Weekly figure.*

- » Newspapers are more likely to follow the opinion of their readers rather than shape it, as newspapers need to keep their readership; making the *Daily Mail* a left-wing paper would see its readership numbers collapse.
- » The readership of the print media is in serious decline. In particular younger voters are increasingly turning their backs on the print media. According to Ofcom's 2024 News Consumption Survey, just 10% of 16–24-year-olds in the UK use printed newspapers as a source of news.
- » The print media is widely distrusted, which limits its influence, in particular the journalism in the tabloid papers, such as the *Mirror* or the *Sun*, since the phone hacking scandal. This was a scandal between 2010 and 2016 about tabloid journalists illegally accessing the private voicemails of famous people and publishing articles in their papers using this information. The *Guardian* reported in 2011 that the *News of the World* had hacked the mobile phone of the murdered teenager Millie Dowler and published stories based on the information. The subsequent furore led Prime Minister Cameron to call an inquiry under Lord Leveson into the culture, ethics and practices of the press due to the public revulsion at what had happened. The *Leveson Report* was published in 2012 and called for stronger regulation of the press by a new independent body backed by legislation. This new body was never set up.
- » Despite newspapers dominating online news, in 2024, the average time people spent looking at news online was around 16 minutes per week, according to the Reuters Institute Digital News Report 2024.
- » The heavily Conservative-weighted print media was scathing in its sensationalist and aggressive coverage of Corbyn during the 2017 Election, yet the Labour Party outperformed all expectations and the Conservative Party lost its majority. This was put down to the waning influence of the print media and the rise in importance of social media.

Visit the companion website for a Case Study on the Leveson Enquiry from the previous edition.

Social media and influence

✅ **Social media is now hugely influential, challenging the dominance of the small number of broadcast and print media outlets that traditionally dominate the production of news.**

» Social media is particularly important for younger generations as a source of news. Social media gives people access to news stories and opinion shared by friends and family.

» Political parties increasingly now recognise that social media is a hugely influential way of communicating with voters. In 2017, campaigners spent nearly half (43%) of their total advertising budget on online advertising, in 2019, this increased to nearly 63% and in 2024 it is estimated at over 70%.

» The 2017 Election showed the power of social media as Labour was able to counteract negative press coverage by talking directly to voters during the campaign. Labour increased its share of the vote by 10% and significantly increased the number of young people who voted for them.

» Nigel Farage's use of TikTok in the 2024 campaign was a standout example of personality-driven digital politics. Farage's personal TikTok account outperformed all other parties, amassing more followers than Labour, the Conservatives and the Liberal Democrats combined. His short, often humorous or provocative videos – such as a five-second clip mouthing Eminem lyrics that drew over 8 million views – helped him connect with younger audiences and build a populist, anti-establishment image.

» The algorithms that select news stories for your news feed are based on your previous browsing history, meaning that it is likely that individuals will be fed a diet of news stories that confirm their existing political views. Social media has very weak regulation which means that these stories may exhibit clear bias as well as misinformation and fake news.

❌ **There is limited evidence that social media has really challenged the dominance of broadcast and print media in elections in people aged 30 and over.**

» Social media influence is not as huge as it appears as although it is changing how people access the news, it is not changing how it is generated. Much of the social media postings bring people back to the online sites of the main broadcast and print media players. In the 2024 Election, the BBC, MailOnline, Guardian, Mirror and Sun accounted for 63% of online news consumption, a reduction of just 3% since 2019.

» While powerful among the young, social media's influence is much weaker among older demographics, who are more likely to rely on TV and newspapers for political news with the figure dropping dramatically with 30-year-olds and above as shown in Table 6.3.

Table 6.3 **Influence of social media by age group in the 2024 UK General Election**

Age group	% influenced by social media	Most influential platforms
18–24	44%	Instagram, TikTok, YouTube, X
25–29	30–35% (estimate)	Instagram, TikTok, Facebook
30+	18%	Facebook
65+	19% (exposure), 10% (influence)	Facebook

Definition

Filter bubble: Happens as web companies aim to make their services more tailored to our individual tastes, meaning people do not get exposed to ideas that challenge or broaden their worldview.

» Although 2017 showed the influence of social media, 2019 was very much business as usual with Labour 'winning' the social media war, but they were unable to counter the negative impression created by the print media and were heavily beaten in the election.

» Social media reinforces views rather than changes them due to the existence of a '**filter bubble**' effect, where social media users are more likely to engage with people and media sources that share their political beliefs. This is exacerbated by the idea that social media platforms use algorithms that feed us with stories which are tailored to our views.

» The veracity of social media is further undermined as in 2025, Meta announced it was abandoning the use of independent fact checkers on Facebook and Instagram, replacing them with X-style 'community notes' where commenting on the accuracy of posts is left to users.

» While social media's reach is dramatically increasing, evidence suggests that people are not using it for news. In the 2024 campaign, the Reuters Institute for the Study of Journalism reported that approximately 3% of all users' social media time was spent on the news, and this figure had not increased since 2019, suggesting that social media's influence on elections is more limited than originally thought.

Tip: By making clear comparisons across a range of elections, parties and leaders, you can develop a higher level of analysis.

Key Debate Summary: Does the media have significant influence over elections?

For	Theme	Against
✓ Political parties and political leaders clearly feel that the media is important as they spend much of their time courting the media.	Do voters really accept the media they consume without question?	✗ The media portrayal of politics does not have a one-way impact on voters. Voters interpret the media through their own attitudes and beliefs.
✓ Modern election campaigns are very much media campaigns, with the media seeming to play a more crucial role due to electoral volatility.	Does the public fully engage with the media during campaigns or are they largely disinterested?	✗ The lack of trust in the modern media and the lack of time most people spend engaging with the news undermines the power of the media.
✓ The broadcast media has the largest reach, is the most trusted and plays a crucial role in framing political debate.	How much does broadcast media's requirement to be impartial limit its influence?	✗ The broadcast media is restricted by impartiality, falling levels of trust and is more likely to follow news stories generated in the print media.
✓ The print media has concentrated ownership, is openly partisan, and has a wide readership in print and online, with stories generated by papers tending to dominate the media.	Does print media change opinions of those who follow it?	✗ There is a serious decline in the readership of the print media, widespread distrust of print journalism, and papers tend to reflect not change the views of their readers.
✓ Social media has grown in importance in accessing the news and political information; this is reflected by the political parties spending far more on their online campaigns.	Is social media really as influential on politics as assumed?	✗ Social media is clearly changing how the news is accessed but not necessarily how it is generated.

CASE STUDY 6.3: THE INFLUENCE OF SOCIAL MEDIA ON THE UK 2024 GENERAL ELECTION

The 2024 UK General Election marked a pivotal shift in digital campaigning, with social media platforms becoming central to political strategy. While traditional media retained importance, platforms like TikTok, Instagram, Facebook and X (formerly Twitter) redefined voter engagement, particularly among younger demographics, and amplified challenges around disinformation.

Labour used TikTok's viral potential through memes and trends, such as satirical videos mocking Conservative policies, which gained millions of views. The party's followers increased to 211,000, dwarfing the Conservatives' 70,000. Reform UK, led by Nigel Farage, also thrived, with Farage's personal TikTok account outperforming all major parties combined – his Eminem clip alone drew 8 million views.

Influence across age groups

• **Younger voters (18–24):** TikTok and Instagram dominated, with 44% of 18–24-year-olds encountering election content on Instagram and 36% on TikTok.

• **Older voters (55+):** Facebook remained the primary platform, used by 69% of older adults, including 74% of Lib Dem voters. The Conservatives focused here, with Rishi Sunak's posts generating 569,000 interactions, though often these were negative reactions. Nonetheless, Facebook's reach among older demographics ensured its relevance, especially for local campaign targeting.

Disinformation

Disinformation emerged as a critical concern, with AI-generated deepfakes and manipulated media proliferating throughout the campaign. The Conservatives faced backlash for a misleading video of Keir Starmer and for relabelling their X account as 'FactcheckUK' during leaders' debates. Over half of candidates reported online harassment linked to false claims, with 65% of abuse occurring on social media. Platforms like TikTok introduced in-app election hubs with fact-checking partnerships, while Meta requires AI-content labels. Despite these measures, hostile states and partisan 'cheap fakes' exploited algorithms, particularly on X, where bot accounts flooded people's feeds with over 60,000 political messages.

Which politicians and parties went 'viral'

- **Reform UK** emerged as a social media powerhouse, focusing on Farage's populist appeal. His entry into the campaign triggered 2.12 million Facebook interactions, which accounted for 40% of all major party traffic, and Reform's TikTok following (125,500) briefly eclipsed Labour's. The party's anti-establishment messaging resonated with disaffected voters, contributing to its 14% vote share.

- **Labour** dominated engagement through relatable, youth-focused content. The #FutureIsLabour campaign increased its followers by 43%, while memes criticising Sunak's policies spread rapidly.

- **Conservatives** struggled to adapt, investing £696,000 in Facebook ads but lacking authenticity. Their polished videos underperformed against Labour's grassroots-style clips, reflecting a disconnect with younger audiences.

Conclusion

Social media's influence in 2024 was dual-edged: it enhanced engagement, particularly for younger voters, but exacerbated polarisation and misinformation. While TikTok reshaped youth outreach, Facebook retained sway among older voters. Reform UK and Labour exemplified effective digital strategies, whereas the Conservatives' reliance on older tactics were less effective. The 2024 Election emphasised the need for better regulation and accountability, but clearly shows a permanent transformation in UK political communication and that the parties that have adapted the best benefit the most.

The media and democracy

The media is seen as vital to the workings of the democratic system in the UK. It enables free speech and wide-ranging public debate, and offers a multitude of viewpoints and opinions; this is crucial because this education function enables the public to participate in local and national society. At the same time, the media plays a key public interest role by reporting on the activities of the powerful and the workings of the state at all levels. This can involve reporting on the day-to-day activities of local councils and magistrates' courts, as well as holding those in the government and Parliament accountable for their actions.

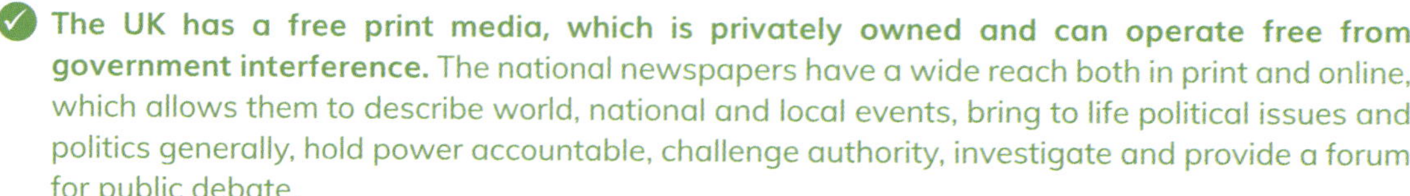

Print media and democracy

- ✅ **The UK has a free print media, which is privately owned and can operate free from government interference.** The national newspapers have a wide reach both in print and online, which allows them to describe world, national and local events, bring to life political issues and politics generally, hold power accountable, challenge authority, investigate and provide a forum for public debate.

  » The *Daily Mirror*'s Pippa Crerar broke the Partygate scandal in November 2021 when she revealed that Downing Street staff, including Prime Minister Boris Johnson, had attended parties during the 2020 Christmas lockdown, flouting the government's own Covid rules. The *Mirror*'s reporting triggered a wave of further revelations, official inquiries and police investigations into multiple gatherings. The consequences were profound: public anger eroded trust in the government, contributed to Conservative defeats in by-elections and local elections, and led to the resignation of senior staff and ultimately Boris Johnson himself as Prime Minister and MP.

» In 2017, the *Guardian* exposed the *Windrush* scandal that led to blameless British residents, who came to the UK legally from the Caribbean between 1948 and 1973, being wrongly deprived access to public services, threatened with deportation and in some cases deported.

» In May 2009, the *Daily Telegraph* broke the MPs' expenses scandal story, a public interest investigation that highlighted the misuse of taxpayers' money which resulted in some politicians going to jail and led to parliamentary reform.

(x) Ownership of the print media is highly concentrated in the hands of a few press barons with too much power to influence public opinion and election outcomes with four publishers controlling around 90% of the national newspaper market. (see Figure 6.9). Given that many of the stories that start in the main press spread on to social media and broadcast media, this concentrates power and undermines the idea of political equality.

Figure 6.9 Ownership of the print media
Combined weekly circulation by publisher (2022)

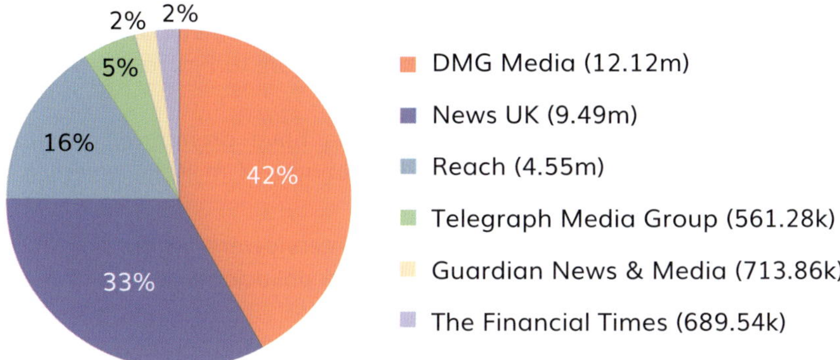

Source: Data from Press Gazette, 'Who Owns the Media' 2023

» The dominance of a Conservative print media in setting the agenda arguably makes the job of winning elections far harder for the Labour Party, while it excludes the minor parties from coverage.

» There is an accusation that the print media has dumbed down politics by concentrating more on the private lives and scandals of politicians than on their policies or ideas.

» The role of the press as a watchdog has been called into question. The Leveson Inquiry into the press found that the relationship between the press and politicians was unhealthy for democracy, leading to a lack of trust in the print media and the political process.

» The decline of local press has left a hole in local democracy. Between 2005 and 2024, nearly 300 local newspapers closed down. The collapse may partially help explain why the views of Grenfell Tower residents on the Grenfell Action Group blog about the safety of their building were not picked up by local media outlets prior to the Grenfell fire in 2017.

Broadcast media and democracy

(✓) The partisan nature of the print media is balanced by the impartial nature of the broadcast media, which is regulated by Ofcom. The broadcast media reaches the widest audience, playing a key role in educating and informing the public while creating space for all parties and different viewpoints.

» During elections in particular, the broadcast media plays the role of educating the public about how the electoral process works. In the 2024 Election campaign, Loughborough University found that 29% of the airtime was devoted to electoral processes. The BBC, in particular, is committed by its own charter 'to promote understanding of the UK political system'.

» Broadcast media remains the most trusted and used of all media sources for most groups in society, especially the BBC when you take into account its TV, radio and internet presence.

» Live TV debates during elections were introduced in 2010, and they have appeared in a range of different formats during elections since then. The first televised debate in 2010 between Gordon Brown (Labour), Nick Clegg (Liberal Democrats) and David Cameron (Conservatives) attracted 10.3 million views, so played an important educating role.

» The UK Post Office scandal was initially uncovered by a reporter for BBC Radio Surrey. Journalist Nick Wallis began investigating the wrongful prosecution of sub-postmasters while working on local news. His early coverage, and interviews with affected sub-postmasters, helped bring the issue to light. This local reporting was crucial in sustaining the story over years when national outlets showed little interest. The campaign gained momentum as *Private Eye* and other outlets picked it up, eventually leading to a landmark court case in 2018, and in 2024 there was a national outcry following ITV's dramatisation *Mr Bates vs The Post Office*. The scandal is now recognised as the largest miscarriage of justice in UK legal history, with the government forced to act and introduce legislation to exonerate hundreds of wrongly convicted sub-postmasters.

✖ The nature of the broadcast media and the increasing competition for viewers has changed the way politics is presented in ways that have been detrimental to democracy.

» The need to make news coverage more popular has led to the dumbing down of the news, where it is told through celebrity politics and a series of sound bites rather than more in-depth discussions.

» At the same time, with so many channels to choose from, those apathetic about politics can simply avoid all political news, while young people in particular are turning away from the TV news.

» Since its introduction in 2010, televised leaders' debates have dramatically reduced in popularity. In 2019, the leaders' debates received approximately 7 million viewers while in 2024 it reduced to 5 million.

» The increasing use of hostile questioning techniques by interviewers encourages the view that politicians are not to be trusted, lowering public trust in politicians, parties and political institutions and leading to apathy and disillusionment.

» This problem is matched by politicians simply refusing to engage with any broadcast media they feel is biased, as Boris Johnson did in 2019, depriving viewers of the Prime Minister's interview. Even when they are interviewed, many politicians retreat to the safety of a sound bite rather than engaging with the question in a way that informs.

» The arrival of GB News has undermined democracy by challenging the impartiality standards expected of broadcast news. In 2024, Ofcom found GB News in breach of impartiality rules for giving Prime Minister Rishi Sunak an uncontested platform before the 2024 General Election, resulting in a £100,000 fine.

Photo 6.5 **The first televised leaders' debate was held in 2010, attracting 10.3 million viewers**

Source: Handout / Getty Images

Social media and democracy

✅ **Social media has hugely increased plurality in the media as there are now many different sources of news, accessible in many different ways and controlled by a range of people so the public can be well informed and take a full part in democracy.**

» Social media can lead to communication between large numbers of people, opening up political debate and providing a space for the voices of all groups, to be heard especially those excluded from the mainstream media. This acts as a counterbalance to the concentrated ownership and power of print and broadcast media.

» Where readership of print media and viewing of broadcast media has declined, especially among the younger population, social media has become the source for political news.

» Social media has become a key tool for voter registration drives, with young people encouraging other young people to engage with the democratic process. In 2024, TikTok launched an in-app 'Local Election Centre' which was developed in partnership with fact checkers like Logically Facts and the Electoral Commission and provided users with reliable, non-partisan information about voting, registration and the electoral process. Prompts on relevant election content and searches directed millions of users, especially younger voters, to trusted resources, helping to counter misinformation and increase electoral awareness.

» Social media promotes participation in democracy because individuals can follow politicians on social media, interact with them and other political stories by commenting, retweeting, liking or signing online petitions. This allows for a far greater level of participation and the ability to hold politicians to account.

❌ **The power of the social media to enhance democratic engagement is significantly undermined by widespread disinformation and lack of regulation.**

» Social media has created a space for trolling, or online abuse, and remains a major issue that needs tackling.

» 'Filter bubbles' mean that people only follow the news and politicians that they already agree with and, more worrying, the algorithms of the social media platforms only feed people news that meets their pre-existing preferences. This lack of an alternative means that people are more vulnerable to fake news.

» Social media allows for fake news to be spread and spread more quickly, in part because the news can be created by anyone without the fact checking that is part of print or broadcast journalism.

» Owners of social media platforms wield significant and often undue power over UK politics by controlling the flow and visibility of information. For example, Elon Musk's ownership of X (formerly Twitter) has been criticised for enabling divisive content to dominate feeds, amplifying conspiracy theories and hate speech while weakening moderation. During the 2024 election, bot-like accounts on X posted over 60,000 political messages seen 150 million times, distorting debate and drowning out authentic voices. Meta owner Mark Zuckerberg, which owns Facebook, Instagram and WhatsApp, controls three of the top five platforms for news in the UK, giving it vast influence over what political content reaches voters. Ten of the top 15 online platforms used by UK audiences to access news were owned by Facebook owner Meta, Google parent Alphabet and Elon Musk's X Corp. According to Ipsos and Ofcom, 64% of the UK public use such 'online intermediaries' to access news. These individuals are undoubtedly as powerful as 'press barons' were. This concentration of power allows platform owners to shape democratic discussion, sometimes prioritising profit or ideology over factual, balanced debate.

» Technology giants can generate profiles of voters based on their preferences, and campaigning organisations can buy advertising that uses those profiles to match the message to the right people at the right time in a campaign. Dark adverts are usually targeted to appeal to the prejudices and fears of voters, and the lack of regulation of social media added to the lack of transparency over who was spending what, to target whom and how, means that much of this part of politics is shrouded in a fog.

Tip: Highlight the differences between the different types of media but also reference how the lines between social media and the more traditional print and broadcast media have become blurred.

Key Debate Summary: Does the media enhance democracy?

For	Theme	Against
✓ The print media is free, privately owned and not regulated by the government so it can hold the government to account and work in the public interest.	How effectively does print media promote democracy?	✗ The print media is not diverse enough, with too much power in too few hands leading to a view that they work in the interests of their owners not the public.
✓ The broadcast media is impartial, balances out the bias in the print media and reaches the widest audience, providing political information and a space for debate.	How effectively does broadcast media promote democracy?	✗ The broadcast media is reducing politics to a celebrity contest and sound bites while also contributing to falling trust in politicians and the media.
✓ Social media provides a much more diverse media, open to all that encourages participation and gives a voice to the voiceless.	How effectively does social media promote democracy?	✗ Social media has provided a space for trolling, fake news and dark adverts and is controlled by a few individuals, undermining democracy.

Exam Style Questions

- Evaluate the view that the media supports democracy in the UK (30).
- Evaluate the view that the media has real influence over elections in the UK (30).
- Evaluate the view that bias in the UK media has a real impact on public opinion (30).
- Evaluate the view that opinion polls make a positive contribution to democracy in the UK (30).
- Evaluate the view that the print media remains more influential than broadcast or social media in UK elections (30).

Source Question

Source 1

Political parties use opinion polls to help them make popular policy decisions by providing the views of the population. Opinion polls provide up-to-date insights into voter sentiment, helping parties and the public track shifts in support. As a result, governments can make decisions that they feel a large number of the public will support. Opinion polls also help politicians develop effective campaign strategies, allowing them to adjust policies or campaign messages accordingly, and this helps parties to target resources and refine their message during election campaigns. Opinion polls can encourage political engagement and participation and inform public debate, as when the polls reports a close contest, this is more likely to encourage voters to turn out. Opinion polls can also guide voters in marginal seats to vote tactically, influencing outcomes in closely contested areas.

Source 2

However, inaccurate polling can lead to governments getting policy and campaign decisions wrong. It is also the case that opinion polls discourage parties leading the argument to change the public's mind; instead they slavishly follow the direction of opinion polls. Election campaigns can become too focused on opinion polls and create a 'horse race style' commentary on who is winning the race rather than focusing on the issues and policies. Equally, if the polls are wrong, this leads to the whole media narrative becoming shaped by inaccurate information. Polls can also discourage participation when polls predict an easy victory for one party, as this can reduce turnout. Polls can shape as well as reflect opinion, causing a 'bandwagon' effect where voters alter their view to come into line with the majority, or 'underdog' effects when voters adopt a minority view out of sympathy. The biggest problem with opinion polls is that they end up influencing the very outcomes they are supposed to measure. This has led countries such as France, Spain and Italy to ban all opinion polling in the period before an election.

Using the source, evaluate the view that opinion polls are highly influential.

In your response you must:

» *Compare and contrast different opinions in the source*

» *Examine and debate these views in a balanced way*

» *Analyse and evaluate **only** the information presented in the source.*

Chapter Summary

» Changes in technology have meant that the media has undergone a period of rapid change in the twenty-first century.

» Newspaper readership may have declined but newspapers have moved online and utilised the power of social media. The print media is influential, partisan and ownership is concentrated in very few hands.

» The broadcast media is very influential due to its wide reach, is impartial and is the most trusted media source.

» Social media is a highly influential part of the media landscape although its influence is perhaps less than it is perceived to be.

» Opinion polls can increase the level of political communication in society but the accuracy and role of opinion polls has come under criticism.

» The media plays an important role in democracy in enabling debate, encouraging participation and holding those in power to account.

» However, the media has been accused of dumbing down politics with the focus on celebrity politics and sound bites, creating greater levels of distrust, apathy and disillusionment.

Further Resources

Griffiths, S. and Leach, R. (2018) *British Politics* (3rd edn) (London: Bloomsbury): Chapter 17: The media.

Heffernan, R., Hay, C., Russell, M. and Cowley, P. (eds) (2016) *Politics and the News Media: Messages and Messengers* (London: Bloomsbury): Chapter 10.

Leveson, Lord Justice (2012) *The Leveson Inquiry: An Inquiry into the Culture, Practices and Ethics of the Press: Executive Summary* (November).

Moran, M. (2017) *Politics and Governance in the UK* (3rd edn) (London: Bloomsbury): Chapter 15: How political communication happens.

Street, J. (2010) *Mass Media, Politics and Democracy* (2nd edn) (London: Bloomsbury).

News Consumption in the UK: 2024 Report © Ofcom Reuters Digital News Report 2025 https://reutersinstitute.politics.ox.ac.uk/digital-news-report/2025

Visit the companion website to access the Further Resources Booklet to explore a range of useful web links related to: the Leveson Inquiry, Ofcom data and reports on news consumption, the rise of fake news, the relationship between the media and austerity and more.

7 THE CONSTITUTION

Chapter Preview

Constitutions are a solution to the problem of power. As power tends to corrupt, we need to be protected from those in government. Without a constitution, the government could simply do whatever it wanted. This may mean oppressing minorities, violating freedom or even tyrannising the masses. Therefore, constitutions are vital to politics. In the UK, we have an unusual, even unique, uncodified constitution which is a collection of rules and conventions steeped in ancient traditions and customs. Since the late 1990s, there has been an upsurge in constitutional reform that is changing forever the way in which the country is governed.

One of the biggest changes has been that, instead of all the main decisions being made at the centre, they are now made at different levels through the introduction of devolution. The creation, since 1997, of a Scottish Parliament, a Welsh Parliament and a Northern Ireland Assembly has drawn power 'downwards'. To a greater or lesser degree, domestic affairs in Scotland, Wales and Northern Ireland are now decided by devolved bodies, rather than by the Westminster Parliament in London. This development has also stimulated controversy.

Specification Checklist

1.1. The nature and sources of the UK constitution, including:

» An overview of the development of the constitution through key historical documents: Magna Carta (1215); Bill of Rights (1689); Act of Settlement (1701); Acts of Union (1707); Parliament Acts (1911 and 1949); The European Communities Act (1972).

» The nature of the UK constitution: unentrenched, uncodified and unitary, and the 'twin pillars' of parliamentary sovereignty and the rule of law.

» The five main sources of the UK constitution: statute law; common law; conventions; authoritative works and treaties (including European Union law).

1.2. How the constitution has changed since 1997

» Under Labour 1997–2010: House of Lords reforms, electoral reform; devolution; the Human Rights Act 1998; and the Supreme Court.

» Under the Coalition 2010–15: Fixed-term Parliaments; further devolution to Wales.

» Any major reforms undertaken by governments since 2015, including further devolution to Scotland (in the context of the Scottish Referendum).

1.3. The role and powers of devolved bodies in the UK, and the impact of this devolution on the UK

» Devolution in England.

» Scottish Parliament and Government.

» Welsh Assembly and Government.

» Northern Ireland Assembly and Executive.

1.4. Debates on further reform

» An overview of the extent to which the individual reforms since 1997 listed in section 1.2 should be taken further.

» The extent to which devolution should be extended in England.

» Whether the UK constitution should be changed to be entrenched and codified, including a bill of rights.

What is a constitution?

A **constitution** establishes a framework of rules that are meant to constrain government power. Typically, constitutions seek to:

» Establish the duties, powers, limits and functions of government

» Regulate the relationships between the institutions

» Define the relationship between the state and the individual.

Types of constitution

Constitutions may be classified in three main ways:

1. As codified or uncodified constitutions

2. As unitary or federal constitutions

3. As entrenched or unentrenched constitutions.

Codified constitutions

A **codified constitution** is one that is based on a single document. This document lays down the core principles of the system of government. It outlines the duties, powers and functions of government and may also include a statement of citizens' rights in a bill of rights. Most liberal democratic states possess codified constitutions.

Codified constitutions have three key features:

1. The document is *authoritative*. It constitutes 'higher' law, the highest law of the land. This gives rise to a two-tier legal system, in which the constitution stands above statute law made by the legislature.

2. The provisions of the constitution are **entrenched**. Essentially, they are difficult to amend or abolish. The procedure for making and changing the constitution is more complex or difficult than for making ordinary laws.

3. It is *judiciable*. This means that all political bodies are subject to the authority of the courts, and in particular a constitutional court.

Uncodified constitutions

Uncodified constitutions are rare. Only three liberal democracies (the UK, Israel and New Zealand) have uncodified constitutions.

Uncodified constitutions have three defining features:

1. The constitution is *not absolute*. Constitutional laws enjoy the same status as ordinary laws. States that have uncodified constitutions therefore have single-tier legal systems with no higher law.

2. They are *not entrenched*. The constitution can be changed by passing a **statute law**. This is reflected in the UK in the principle of **parliamentary sovereignty** (see page 208), through which Parliament can make, unmake and amend any law it wishes, including laws that affect the constitution.

3. Uncodified constitutions are *not judiciable*. In the absence of higher law, judges do not have a legal standard against which they can declare laws as 'unconstitutional'.

Unitary and federal constitutions

Constitutions have also been classified in terms of the structure they underpin. The most widely used such classification is between unitary and federal constitutions.

» **Unitary constitutions** establish the constitutional supremacy of a central government over other bodies. This means that sovereignty exists in a single body – typically the elected legislature, meaning that it can create or abolish, strengthen or weaken all other institutions. In the UK, this is Parliament. Devolved assemblies and local authorities do not, therefore, enjoy a share of sovereignty. The exists purely on the say-so of the sovereign body.

» **Federal constitutions** divide powers between two levels of government. Both central government and regional government possess a range of powers that the other cannot encroach on. Many argue that as **devolution** has deepened, the UK's constitution has acquired a '**quasi-federal**' character.

Entrenched and unentrenched constitutions

An alternative form of classification is based on the ease with which the constitution can be changed. On the face of it, codified constitutions are relatively inflexible and **rigid**, because their provisions are in some way entrenched in higher law. By the same token, uncodified ones appear to be **flexible** and adaptable, because laws of constitutional significance can be changed through the ordinary legislative process.

However, there is no necessary relationship between codified constitutions and rigidity, or uncodified ones and flexibility. Codified constitutions can exhibit a surprising degree of flexibility, whereas some aspects of the UK's uncodified constitution have remained remarkably resistant to change, and are ingrained in our system. These include the principles of parliamentary sovereignty and the constitutional monarchy.

The UK's constitution

In summing up on the Miller ruling in 2019, the Supreme Court explained, 'Although the United Kingdom does not have a single document entitled 'The Constitution', it nevertheless possesses a Constitution, established over the course of our history by common law, statutes, conventions and practice. Since it has not been codified, it has developed pragmatically, and remains sufficiently flexible to be capable of further development.'

The UK's constitution is uncodified, unitary and unentrenched. It is less easy to understand than, for example, the US Constitution which is available to buy and read from any bookstore in the US. To understand the UK's mysterious constitution takes some effort and then the key question is, does it do its job? In order to review this question, we need to examine three issues:

» The sources of the constitution

» The principles of the constitution

» The strengths and weaknesses of the UK's constitution.

Sources of the UK constitution

The UK constitution is best thought of as a part-written and uncodified constitution. This reflects the fact that, although there is no single, authoritative constitutional document in the UK, most of the rules of the constitution are written down and many of them have a legal status. The rules and principles of the constitution, however, can be found in a variety of places. In contrast to a codified constitution, this makes the UK constitution seem confusing. The most important sources of the UK constitution are:

1. Statute law

2. Common law

3. Conventions

4. Works of constitutional authority.

Statute law

Statute law is law made by Parliament. Not *all* statute laws are of constitutional significance, however; only the ones that affect the powers and responsibilities of government or the rights and freedoms of citizens. Statute law, though, is the single most important source of the constitution.

Parliamentary sovereignty implies that statutes outrank all other sources of the constitution. If a statute conflicts with a convention or a common law, the statute will always prevail. In addition, more and more constitutional rules have come to have a legal basis, both as new constitutional statutes have been enacted and, sometimes, as conventions and common laws are turned into statutes. The Milestones timeline shows some of the key statute laws that have allowed our system to evolve.

Examples of some recent constitutionally significant statute laws include:

» Scotland Act 1998 (established the Scottish Parliament) and Government of Wales Act 1998 (established Welsh Assembly)

» Human Rights Act 1998 (translated the European Convention on Human Rights into statute law)

» House of Lords Act 1999 (reduced the number of hereditary peers sitting in the House of Lords to 92)

» Constitutional Reform Act 2005 (provided for a Supreme Court to take over the role of the Law Lords)

» The House of Lords (Hereditary Peers) Act 2026 (removed the remaining hereditary peers sitting in the House of Lords)

Common law

Common law is a body of law created by judicial rulings established over time. This has occurred through the use of precedent, where judgements in earlier, similar cases are recorded and are taken to be binding on later cases. Therefore, while statute law is made by politicians, common law (or 'case law' as it is sometimes known) is seen as 'judge-made' law. Common law therefore exists where there is no statute law. Murder is perhaps the best example of common law – it has been so well established and defined by judges over time that there is no need for Parliament to create a statute law.

Common law also occurs where statute laws may be vague or contradictory. An example of this was explored in the 1991 case R v R. Prior to this case, forced sexual activity within a marriage was not considered illegal, and a husband could enforce 'conjugal rights' on his wife without committing rape based on the belief that a wife had provided ongoing consent through the contract of marriage. However, the R v R case changed the law because the courts ruled that, even within a marriage, any non-consensual sexual activity is rape. Law Lords ruled that for modern times, marriage is a partnership of equals. Common law is therefore used to ensure that the law is constantly evolving to meet changing social attitudes.

Conventions

Conventions are customs or traditions that have endured throughout history. They are a major means by which the constitution adapts to changing circumstances and are essential to its working. Many aspects of the UK political system that one might fairly assume to be legal documents are in fact conventions. For example, it is merely a convention that a government resigns if it loses a general election, yet despite this, it has never been an issue in modern politics.

So why are conventions upheld? The answer is that they are upheld by practical political circumstances; not keeping them would result in consequences. The convention that **Royal Assent** is always granted is upheld by the monarch's desire not to challenge the 'democratic will' of Parliament, an act that would bring the future of the monarchy into question.

Examples of major constitutional conventions include:

» The powers of the Royal Prerogative are exercised by the Prime Minister, not by the monarch. These powers include the power to appoint and sack ministers, to dissolve Parliament and to ratify international **treaties**.

» Individual ministerial responsibility (Chapter 9). This broadly defines the relationship between ministers and their departments, and it defines grounds on which ministers should resign.

Definition

Quasi-federal: A division of powers between central and regional government that has some of the features of federalism without possessing a formal federal structure.

Rigid constitution: A constitution which stands above the other laws of the country and contains specific legal obstacles to be overcome before it may be amended.

Flexible constitution: A constitution that may be amended by the ordinary process of legislation and is therefore relatively easy to amend.

Spec Key Term

Common law: The legal system in England that has developed over a period of time from old customs and court decisions, rather than laws made by politicians.

Convention: Unwritten understanding about how something should be done which, although not legally enforceable, is almost universally observed, like a custom or tradition.

MILESTONES: THE DEVELOPMENT OF THE UK'S CONSTITUTIONAL SETTLEMENT

1215 **Magna Carta** – The 'Great Charter of Freedoms', imposed by rebellious barons on King John of England. In Magna Carta, the first systematic attempt was made to distinguish between monarchy and tyranny, based on the requirement that the King should rule justly and in accordance with a body of defined law and custom. Among the rights it established was the writ of habeas corpus, which allows people to appeal against imprisonment without trial.

1649 –60 **Commonwealth** – The period of English republican government between the execution of Charles I and the Restoration, when Charles II returned to England. From 1653 to his death in 1658, Oliver Cromwell ruled as the Lord Protector, refusing the offer of the crown.

1688 **Glorious Revolution** – Arguably the key moment in Britain's constitutional history. It provided the basis for the principle of parliamentary sovereignty by which monarchs William and Mary agreed to be a constitutional monarchy; they accepted that they ruled within constraints established by Parliament. This event laid the grounds for the later spread of democracy in the UK.

1689 **Bill of Rights** – Firmly established the principles of frequent parliaments, free elections and Parliamentary privilege. It also includes: no right of taxation without Parliament's agreement, freedom from government interference, the right of petition and just treatment of people by courts. The main principles of the Bill of Rights are still in force today.

1701 **Act of Settlement** – This settled the succession to the English and Irish crowns, and also disqualified anyone who became a Roman Catholic, or married one, from inheriting the throne (the disqualification was removed in 2011).

1707 **Acts of Union** – The Union with Scotland Act 1706 and the Union with England Act 1707 provided for the creation of the Kingdom of Great Britain as a single state with a single legislature. Scotland and England had previously been separate states but, since 1603, with the same monarch.

1911 and 1949 **Parliament Acts** – These Acts formally consigned the House of Lords a subordinate role to that of the House of Commons, by stipulating that the Lords can delay a non-money bill for no more than two sessions (reduced to one session in 1949), and that money bills become law one month after leaving the Commons, without the need for Lords' approval.

1972 **European Communities Act** – This Act approved and authorised the UK's membership of the European Community, which commenced at the beginning of 1973 and meant that EC/EU law became a source of the constitution.

1997 –2001 **New Labour reforms** – The first Blair Labour Government introduced a major programme of constitutional reform. Its reforms included devolution to Scotland, Wales and Northern Ireland (1998), the creation of the Greater London Authority (1999), reduced the number of hereditary peers in the Lords (2000), and the introduction of the Human Rights Act (see Chapter 2) and the Freedom of Information Act (2000).

2018 **EU Withdrawal Act** – The formal repeal of the European Communities Act 1972 and other provisions in connection with the withdrawal of the UK from the EU. It is the law that legally enforced the UK's withdrawal from the EU.

Works of constitutional authority

One of the peculiarities of the UK constitution is the need to consult works by authors who are considered to be authorities on constitutional issues. These works help to define what is constitutionally 'correct'; although they are written, they are not legally enforceable. They are needed for two reasons:

>> There are many gaps and confusions in the UK's uncodified constitution, with uncertainty about how rules and principles should be applied in practice.

>> These **authoritative works** carry out the job of interpretation – saying what the constitution *actually* means.

Nevertheless, because they lack legal authority, these constitutional works are only consulted and followed if they are considered to be relevant and their authors respected. Their status is therefore often subject to debate. Key works of constitutional authority include:

>> Walter Bagehot's *The English Constitution* (1867). Bagehot distinguished between the 'dignified' parts of the constitution (the monarchy and the Lords), from the 'efficient' parts of the constitution (the Cabinet and the Commons).

>> A.V. Dicey's *An Introduction to the Study of the Law of the Constitution* (1885). This defines the 'twin pillars' of the constitution: parliamentary sovereignty and **the rule of law**.

>> Erskine May's *Treatise on the Law, Privileges, Proceedings and Usage of Parliament* (1844). This provides the most authoritative account of the practices, procedures and rules of Parliament and was referenced by Speaker Bercow in Parliament during the Brexit crisis in 2019.

Relationship between the sources

It is clear that statute law takes precedence over all other sources. For example, the Fixed-term Parliaments Act 2011 overrode the Lascelles Convention which dealt with the circumstances in which the monarch could refuse the Prime Minister a dissolution of Parliament; when the Act was repealed, the Lascelles Convention came back into force. It can override common law because Parliament can simply pass a new law which clarifies the situation or deals with the contradiction if it doesn't like the way the judiciary has resolved the issue.

Principles of the constitution

The UK constitution may not have a written document, but it does have a set of core principles. Most important of these are:

>> Parliamentary sovereignty

>> Constitutional monarchy

>> The rule of law

>> Parliamentary government

Parliamentary sovereignty

Sovereignty defines the location of supreme constitutional power. In the UK, sovereignty is located in Parliament (see page Chapter 10 for further discussion of parliamentary sovereignty). Parliamentary sovereignty is a form of *legal* sovereignty: it means that Parliament has the ability to make, unmake or remove any law it wishes. Parliamentary sovereignty is, without doubt, the most important principle in the UK constitution.

Constitutional monarchy

Although the monarchy lost its absolute power long ago, it remains a constitutionally significant body in the UK. According to Bagehot, the 'dignified' institutions still play a vital role, specifically to serve as a symbol of political unity above party politics. According to Bagehot, the monarch has the right:

» To be informed

» To be consulted

» To warn

» To encourage.

The rule of law

The rule of law shows that in the absence of higher law, government is still subject to legal checks and constraints. Government, in short, is not 'above' the law, it is subject to the law (see Chapter 10 for a detailed discussion).

Parliamentary government

Parliamentary government exists when there is a fusion of the legislative and **executive** branches, with the leader of the largest party becoming Prime Minister (see Chapter 8 for a detailed explanation).

> **Definition**
>
> **Executive:** The branch of government that is responsible for the implementation of laws and policies made by Parliament.

KEY TOPIC DEBATE: IS THE UK CONSTITUTION FIT FOR PURPOSE?

✅ **Flexibility – One of the chief strengths of the UK constitution is that it is flexible and easy to change.**

» This occurs because of statute law, as it is easier and quicker to introduce an Act of Parliament than to amend a codified constitution. Flexibility arises because the UK constitution is not entrenched.

» The advantage of the UK's constitution is that it remains relevant and up to date. This occurs because it can adapt and respond to changing circumstances. The many constitutional reforms introduced in the UK since 1997 were easily enacted because of our uncodified constitution.

❌ **Too flexible – Critics of the UK constitution point out that it is too easy to change.**

» Being flexible is not a positive trait in a constitution. Constitutions need to be clear and relatively rigid as their job is to tell governments what they can and can't do.

» Confusion surrounds many constitutional rules because, quite simply, they are too vague. This applies particularly to the constitution's unwritten elements, like conventions.

✅ **Democratic control – In the UK's uncodified constitution, supreme constitutional authority rests in Parliament, more typically the elected House of Commons, and ultimately the people who elect them.**

» Unlike in countries with codified constitutions, constitutional decisions in the UK are not made by unelected, unaccountable judges. In the UK, Parliament has the final say, and changes to the constitution come about because of democratic pressure, not on the whim of unelected judges.

» For instance, the powers of the House of Lords were reduced through the Parliament Acts in 1911 and 1949. In recent years, under Blair in 1999 and Starmer in 2026, Acts were passed removing the right of hereditary peers to sit in the House of Lords. This was because of a growing belief that an unelected second chamber should have less power, and that hereditary peers do not belong in a modern legislature.

❌ **Ineffective checks – The UK has an over-centralised system of government with ineffective checks and balances which undermines its democratic aspects.**

» One of the key roles of a constitution is to limit government power. Without judges overseeing it, the UK constitution lacks a neutral referee which has the power to force Parliament and the Government to uphold its obligations to the people. Governments in the UK are often elected with large overall majorities in Parliament, which allows them to exercise an enormous amount of power.

» Despite the constitutional reforms introduced since 1997 having dispersed government power, many argue that they do not enable government to be effectively checked; one of the key jobs of a constitution.

✅ **Effective rights protection – The UK's constitution has evolved over time, and as rights protection has become a greater consideration of democracy, so they have evolved.**
» A key strength of the UK's uncodified constitution is that it has developed and grown over time, giving it an 'organic' character. Rights in the UK are protected by the Human Rights Act, the Equalities Act, the Supreme Court and judicial review.
» A problem with codified systems is that they codify rights that were relevant at the time into a document that is supposed to endure, whereas in the UK, this can be adapted over time.

❌ **Weak protection of rights – The organic nature of the UK's constitution provides weak protection for individual rights and civil liberties.**
» There is nothing that forces the government to respect individual freedom and basic rights, apart from the fear of not being re-elected.
» The passage of the Human Rights Act 1998 has improved rights protection. However, it stops well short of being an entrenched bill of rights because its provisions could be set aside by Parliament, as has occurred, for instance, over terrorism legislation (see Chapter 2).

✅ **Effective government – Supporters of the UK constitution often argue that it allows UK governments to carry out their election promises.**
» The UK government is able to take strong and decisive action. This is best reflected in radical governments such as Attlee's of 1945–51, which set up the NHS and nationalised a wide range of industries, the Thatcher Governments of 1979–90, which introduced privatisation and deregulated the economy, and the Blair Government's constitutional reforms from 1998 to 2005.
» These laws are also able to be amended or even abolished if the reforms turn out to be ineffective. This was seen with the Fixed-term Parliaments Act 2011 which was repealed in 2022 as it was considered ineffective.

❌ **Elective dictatorship – The most serious and challenging criticism of the UK constitution is that, in practice, it gives rise to the problem of 'elective dictatorship'.**
» Once elected, UK governments can more or less act as they please until they come up for re-election. This is because sovereign power is vested in the hands of Parliament and Parliament is routinely controlled, even dominated, by the government of the day. The Fixed-term Parliaments Act was abolished by Prime Minister Johnson because he didn't want to be restricted in when he could call an election. The repeal returned to him a prerogative power.
» In concentrating power in the hands of the executive, it allows the government of the day to shape and reshape the constitution however it wishes. This creates the impression that, in effect, the UK does not have a constitution.

Synoptic Link

The question of whether constitutions should be codified or uncodified is directly linked to the core political ideas of Conservatism and Liberalism.

Key Debate Summary: Is the UK constitution fit for purpose?

For	Theme	Against
✓ One of the chief strengths of the UK constitution is that it is flexible and easy to change.	Is flexibility desirable in a constitution?	✗ Critics of the UK constitution point out that it is sometimes difficult to know what the constitution says.
✓ Democratic rule – in the UK, supreme constitutional authority rests in the elected House of Commons. Changes often come about because of democratic pressure.	Is Parliament strong enough to protect the people from a powerful executive?	✗ The UK system lacks a neutral referee who can force Parliament to act in the interests of the people.
✓ Effective government – the UK constitution helps to make UK governments stronger and more effective.	Does lack of rights entrenchment limit the effectiveness of the Constitution?	✗ The most serious and challenging criticism of the UK constitution is that, in practice, it gives rise to the problem of 'elective dictatorship'.
✓ The UK constitution has evolved over time to provide highly effective rights protection.	Does the constitution cause or limit an 'elective dictatorship'?	✗ The UK constitution provides weak protection for individual rights and civil liberties.

KEY TOPIC DEBATE: HAVE CONSTITUTIONAL REFORMS IMPROVED THE UK POLITICAL SYSTEM?

Constitutional reform under Blair and Brown, 1997–2010

The 1997–2005 Blair Government was, without doubt, the most radical reforming government on constitutional matters of any elected in the twentieth century, with a slate of major constitutional reforms aiming to modernise, democratise and decentralise.

1 Devolution (see page 223 for details)

Devolution gave a stronger and more independent political voice to Scotland, Wales and Northern Ireland. Previously, they had been represented primarily through Parliament, where English MPs always outnumbered their MPs.

✓ Positives:

» The devolved bodies have allowed the governments to become closer to the citizens they represent, making politicians more accountable to the electorate, and ensuring their representatives are concerned with their issues.

» Devolution makes government much more region-sensitive: the devolved institutions deliver different policies to those produced by Westminster.

✗ Negatives:

» It goes too far.

» Devolution has threatened the stability of the UK. Despite a 'no' vote in the 2014 referendum, the genie was out of the bottle. When the UK as a whole, but not Scotland, voted to leave the EU in 2016, this created even greater discord. The slump in support for the SNP from 2023 may have delivered the Union a temporary reprieve, but Scottish independence is still a significant issue in Scottish politics.

» It has created regional unfairness, with different groups benefitting in the different UK regions.

It doesn't go far enough

» Devolution has left the **West Lothian Question** unresolved. While Scotland has representatives who may vote on English matters in the UK Parliament, the reverse is not true.

» The devolved bodies remain subordinate to a sovereign Parliament and can theoretically be abolished; the Northern Ireland Assembly has been prorogued six times since 1998.

Tip: almost every reform listed here has a significant section of the book devoted to it in other chapters. Please follow the page references to explore each reform in further detail.

Synoptic Link

Devolution of power is a synoptic link to the Component 1 core idea topic of Liberalism.

2 Electoral reform (see Chapter 4 for details)

Different electoral systems were introduced for the devolved bodies. This improved the representation of small parties and prevented electoral distortion.

✅ **Positives:**

» The introduction of different types of electoral systems to first-past-the-post has been successful and helps ensure that the number of seats more closely mirrors the number of votes.

» The use of AMS in Scotland and Wales (until 2021) has given many smaller parties and independents their first seats.

❌ **Negatives:**

» Participation has been disappointing. The use of PR has not resulted in a rush to polling stations.

» An unfortunate effect of the use of the top-up element in elections in Scotland is tension between the constituency and list members.

💬 **Does it go far enough?**

» There has still been no introduction of PR in the Westminster elections and 2024 was one of the most disproportionate elections on record.

3 Referendums (see Chapter 4 for details)

Since 1997 it became common practice to use referendums to consult the public on constitutional changes.

✅ **Positives:**

» Referendums have enabled representative democracy to be supplemented by a stronger element of direct democracy and brought other benefits such as improved political education.

» They have enabled voters to legitimise major constitutional changes, for example devolution or the introduction of directly elected mayors.

❌ **Negatives:**

» As the Brexit referendum showed, they undermine parliamentary sovereignty.

» They create divisions in society, as was seen by the Scottish referendum.

» Some decisions should not be put to a public vote as they are too complicated.

💬 **Does it go far enough?**

» Referendums can only be initiated by Parliament, not the people.

4 Human Rights Act of 1998 (see Chapter 2 for details)

The Human Rights Act introduced the European Convention on Human Rights (ECHR) into British law. The introduction of the HRA in 1998 gave UK citizens positive rights in UK law for the first time.

✅ **Positives:**

» Citizens now have a list of their rights, which has created a culture of rights awareness.

» This helps make clear the power of the executive and stops them from abusing the rights of the electorate.

» The role of the judiciary in protecting rights has increased as they now have the ability to declare laws incompatible.

❌ **Negatives:**

» Critics argue there has been an 'exponential expansion of rights', alongside a more litigious culture. Conservative governments were concerned at the emphasis of individual rights over collective rights which they consider to be in some way 'un-British'.

» It gives rights to the 'wrong' people. The HRA has been criticised for protecting individuals deemed threats to national security. In December 2025, the Home Office admitted that around 170 dangerous foreign nationals – more than half linked to terrorism or extremism – remain in the UK because human rights laws block their deportation.

» Judges are not elected so it is undemocratic to have them holding a democratic institution to account.

💬 Does it go far enough?

» The Human Rights Act has not been entrenched in UK law and can be abolished at any time. Cameron was only stopped from doing so by the coalition agreement in 2010. The 2019 manifesto contained a pledge to update it to ensure that there is a proper balance between the rights of individuals, our vital national security and effective government. In 2024, Robert Jenrick campaigned for the Conservative Party leadership with a pledge to withdraw from the ECHR.

» Judges cannot 'strike down' legislation, rather they can only 'declare it incompatible' with the Human Rights Act. The government has to be willing to change it.

5 The Freedom of Information Act (FOI) (see Chapter 2)

The FOI was introduced in order to create a more open government, so that individuals or groups can request papers to understand how and why decisions are made by people elected to govern on their behalf.

✅ Positives:

» The Freedom of Information Act gives citizens the 'right to know' information regarding how decisions were made, and who made decisions.

» It allows the public to access files from any governmental body or agency. The law states that any person can request information from a public body and has a right to have that information given to them.

❌ Negatives:

» It has restricted the ordinary act of governing by making ministers concerned over emails they write and minutes of meetings that are recorded.

» It has led to ministers using covert or unofficial methods to communicate controversial ideas.

💬 Does it go far enough?

» The government can reject requests if it can demonstrate that they are not in the interests of the public or national security.

» The information commissioner can't compel the government or other public bodies to release information.

» The Act is full of exemptions. Many argue it has not gone far enough with many requests being refused for a broad range of excuses including cost, inadequate information, inability to locate information etc.

6 House of Lords reform

The Lords was reformed with the 1911 Parliament Act and later the 1949 Parliament Act, which asserted the supremacy of the Commons and restricted the Lords' law-making power. In 1999, the House of Lords Act was implemented. This meant that all but 92 hereditary peers were removed. (See page 218 for the Starmer reform.)

✅ Positives:

» The Lords remains free of electoral limits and so may offer impartial advice on legislation.

» As a consequence of reform, the Lords has been much more assertive in holding government to account as it considers its legitimacy to have been renewed.

» Its composition sometimes more accurately reflects the popular vote than the Commons.

» If the chamber was fully elected, it might expect more political powers which would cause gridlock.

Synoptic Link

The Human Rights Act and Freedom of Information Act as constitutional reforms are a clear synoptic link to the Component 1 topic of Rights.

❌ **Negatives:**

» The removal of hereditary peers did not reduce the size of the chamber in the long term; there are now over 800 peers sitting in the House of Lords.

» As the Lords are now mainly appointed, this gives even more power to a Prime Minister.

💬 **Does it go far enough?**

» It remains wholly unelected, with no public accountability.

» An elected Lords would aid in preventing 'elective dictatorships', particularly as elected Lords could claim a democratic mandate in contesting legislation.

7 Judicial reform – The Constitutional Reform Act 2005 (see Chapter 10)

This Act created a clearer separation of powers at the heart of the UK system of government. The role of Lord Chancellor was split into three distinct roles and the Judicial Appointments Commission (JAC) also ensured independence in the appointment of judges. Finally, and most well known, the creation of the Supreme Court by removing the Law Lords from the House of Lords ensured a total separation of the judiciary from the two other branches of government.

✅ **Positives:**

» The newly independent judges are far more willing to be a check on the legislature and executive.

» There is better (although still limited) representation of women and minority groups via the JAC.

❌ **Negatives:**

» The position of Lord Chancellor has existed for centuries and should not have been reformed in such an ill-thought-out way.

💬 **Does it go far enough?**

» The Supreme Court is merely a geographical move from one building to another. It does not replicate the powers of the Supreme Court of the USA, and it is not Supreme.

» The Supreme Court Justices are the highest Appeal Court in the land, but as Parliament is sovereign, they have no powers to restrict it.

Constitutional reform under the Coalition 2010–15

1 Fixed-term Parliaments

The Fixed-term Parliaments Act meant that Parliaments would last for five years, removing the Prime Minister's prerogative power to call an election as they wish within a five-year limit. The only exception to this was if the government lost a vote of confidence in the Commons or if two-thirds of MPs voted for an early election.

✅ **Positives:**

» It removed the ability of the Prime Minister to manipulate a general election date for personal gains.

❌ **Negatives:**

» Five years was too long and led to a 'zombie' Parliament in 2010–15. The last year before the election in 2015 left Parliament with very little to do but wait for the election campaign to begin.

💬 **Does it go far enough?**

» The calling of the 2017 'snap election' and the 2019 Election showed the Act did not sufficiently limit a Prime Minister's power.

» The 2019 Conservative manifesto committed the party to getting rid of the Fixed-term Parliaments Act as 'it has led to paralysis at a time the country needed decisive action'. This was actioned in 2022 with the passing of 'The Dissolution and Calling of Parliament Act 2022'.

2 Wright Reforms to the House of Commons (See Chapter 8)

In May 2010, the Coalition Government agreed to bring forward the Wright Committee's parliamentary reforms in full. As a result, since 2010:

a) Chairs of most select committees are directly elected by the Commons.

b) Members of departmental and similar committees are elected by the Commons.

c) Backbenchers have an opportunity to debate issues of importance to them and the country via the newly created Backbench Business Committee (BbBC).

d) An effective e-petitions system was introduced. If an e-petition achieves over 100,000 signatures it can be considered by the BbBC to be debated in the Commons.

✅ **Positives:**
- » Select committees have been revitalised, with many highly effective chairs being more prepared to challenge the government (see Chapter 8).
- » The e-petition process has become a huge success and is used widely (see Chapter 2).
- » Backbenchers have enjoyed many debates on controversial issues, uncontrolled by the Government or whips, due to the BbBC.

Does it go far enough?
- » Not all select committees can choose their own chair, as was seen in 2020 with the Liaison Committee when the government tabled a motion to directly appoint Sir Bernard Jenkin as chair, overriding the committee's own choice. This was the first and only time the government used that power, and it sparked a backlash from other committee chairs.
- » Backbench committee debates do not compel the government to act. They are merely an opportunity for MPs to express their views.

3 Further Welsh and Scottish devolution

In 2011, the Coalition Government increased power to the Welsh Assembly following the 63% 'yes' vote in a referendum. It gave the Welsh Assembly primary law-making powers over devolved areas, and in 2014 the Assembly gained tax-raising powers.

The Scottish Parliament received more powers under the 2012 Scotland Act. As a consequence of the 2014 Independence Referendum, another Scotland Act was passed in 2016. The Scottish Parliament gained legislative powers on a range of new areas and it additionally gained new powers on tax.

4 Police and Crime Commissioners

Police and Crime Commissioners (PCC) replaced police authorities in an attempt to ensure that local police met the needs of their communities. They are in control of how an area is policed, the police budget and the amount of Council Tax charged for the police. The first elections took place in 2012. However, the Government announced in the 2026 Police Reform White Paper that their role is to be abolished after May 2028.

✅ **Positives:**
- » It creates democratic accountability at the top of the police authority.

❌ **Negatives:**
- » It can lead to decisions made with re-election in mind, not best policing practices.
- » There is a problem with low voter turnout, in some cases below 15%.

Does it go far enough?
- » It can create conflicts between PCCs and chief constables. The roles need to be more carefully defined.

5 Recall of MPs

The Recall of MPs Act 2015 introduced a process whereby an MP can lose their seat if there is a successful request to recall them. An MP can be recalled if they have been:

- » convicted of an offence and received a custodial sentence;
- » barred from the House of Commons for 10 sitting days or 14 calendar days; or
- » convicted of providing false or misleading information for allowance claims under the Parliamentary Standards Act 2009.

Petitions are triggered by MPs; members of the public cannot initiate a petition. The recall petition is open for signing for eight weeks. If at the end of that period at least 10% of eligible electors in the constituency had signed the petition, the seat would be declared vacant and a by-election would follow. The Member who was recalled can stand in the by-election. Recall has been used six times so far in the UK.

1. **North Antrim** – The first recall petition was triggered in July 2018 after the Commons agreed to suspend Ian Paisley, the MP for North Antrim, for 30 parliamentary 'sitting days'. The petition did not attract the required number of signatures to recall Mr Paisley, so he remained an MP.

2. **Peterborough** – The second recall was triggered in March 2019. Fiona Onasanya was subject to a recall process because she had been convicted with a three-month prison sentence for perverting the course of justice. The Peterborough petition was opened and was successful. A by-election was held and the Labour Party retained the seat with Lisa Forbes elected. This was the first time the recall process had been used to oust an MP.

3. **Brecon and Radnorshire petition** – In March 2019, Chris Davies, the MP for Brecon and Radnorshire, pleaded guilty to charges brought under the Parliamentary Standards Act 2009. His conviction met the third condition for the triggering of a recall petition. A by-election was held and the Conservative Party's candidate Chris Davies lost the seat to the Liberal Democrats' Jane Dodds.

4. In October 2020, the sitting MP for Rutherglen and Hamilton West, Margaret Ferrier, referred herself to the Commissioner for Standards for a breach of Covid-19 regulations in 2020. In March 2023, the Standards Committee recommended that she be suspended from the House for 30 days. A recall petition started in June 2023 and 14.7% of registered voters had signed the petition, triggering a by-election which was held in October. Ferrier didn't stand and the seat was won by the Labour Party.

5. In October 2023, the Parliamentary Commissioner for Standards upheld five allegations of bullying and one of sexual misconduct on Peter Bone, the Conservative MP for Wellingborough and recommended Mr Bone should be suspended for six weeks. The recall petition opened and the number of electors needed to sign was successful with 10,505 people signing. A by-election was held on 15 February 2024 and was won by the Labour Party.

✅ **Positives:**
- » Recall ensures that MPs stay aware of their obligations to their constituents throughout their five-year term.
- » Recall also ensures that MPs behave in a way which upholds the Standards for Public Life.

❌ **Negatives:**
- » Recall can be manipulated and used for party political ends.

💬 **Does it go far enough?**
- » Genuine recall would be started by the electorate. Recall in the UK can only occur if MPs give their permission. In 2023, Nadine Dorries announced her resignation as an MP, but ten weeks later she had not officially done so as she was waiting for a peerage from her close ally, Boris Johnson. She was under huge pressure to formally resign but MPs were unable to force a by-election. She was dubbed 'Dosser Dorries' for leaving her constituents without representation.

Visit the companion website to find examples of MPs who left Parliament before a recall petition could be called.

Constitutional reforms passed by the Conservative Government 2015–17

1 Metro Mayors

The idea of directly elected mayors has been around since the position of London Mayor was created in 1998. However, they had been overwhelmingly rejected by cities in the early 2000s and there was a lukewarm response during the 2010–15 Coalition with only three taking up the offer of their own directly elected mayor. Despite this, May's Government persevered and Metropolitan Mayors were elected for the first time in Greater Manchester, Liverpool, West Midlands, Tees Valley, West of England, and Cambridgeshire and Peterborough in 2017 and South Yorkshire in 2018. There were more new Mayors elected in 2024 and 2025. See Figure 7.7 on p.237 for full details of Metro Mayors.

✅ **Positives:**

» It gives one person overall responsibility for an area which they can fight for and plan strategically.

» It seeks to give representation to English regions, similar to the representation enjoyed by the devolved nations, which is preferable to an English Parliament.

❌ **Negatives:**

» They are often elected on a very small percentage of the vote, around 20% turnout.

💬 **Does it go far enough?**

» Some suggest that an English Parliament is the best way to give representation to the areas of England.

Constitutional reforms passed by the Conservative Government 2019–2024

1 Brexit

In January 2020, the UK formally left the EU. There is no doubt that Brexit is of profound constitutional significance, much of which may take years to unfold. Most obviously, EU law no longer takes precedence over UK law. However, the Brexit process brought up many other constitutional considerations:

» Should referendums be used to decide major constitutional issues?

» Do Prime Ministers have the right to opt out of treaties using their Royal Prerogative powers?

» Should the Supreme Court involve itself in highly political affairs?

» Should the Commons take over the role of government when the governing party is divided?

✅ **Positives:**

» Leaving the EU was the democratic will of the people, who wanted to 'take back control' from the EU.

❌ **Negatives:**

» Over 16 million people voted to stay, including a majority in Scotland and Northern Ireland. Critics suggest Brexit has done untold harm to the UK economy.

2 The Dissolution and Calling of Parliament Act

With two snap elections being called in 2017 and 2019, despite the existence of the Fixed-term Parliaments Act (FTPA), the Johnson administration decided that it was not fit for purpose and repealed it with this Act. The power to dissolve Parliament returned to a PM (with the advice and consent of the Monarch) based on the Lascelles Principles.

✅ **Positives:**

» Prime Ministers have had the power for many years and the FTPA undermined the unique British way of calling elections. Additionally, it was ineffective.

❌ **Negatives:**

» The FTPA limited the power of PMs to call elections when it suited them.

3 Judicial Review and Courts Act 2022

The aim of the Act was to create a better balance between the courts, Parliament and the Executive. It made two changes to judicial review:

» The first was to limit the ability of judges to use quashing orders over public bodies deemed to act 'ultra vires'. In addition, judges would not be able to backdate fines if an action was found unlawful.

» Secondly, the Act removed the ability of the Supreme Court to review decisions made by Upper Tribunals over employment practices, asylum cases, visa applications and requests to stay in the UK. These are known as 'cart' judicial reviews and were a power given to themselves in 2011.

✅ Positives:

» It rebalanced the relationship between the three branches to ensure the unelected branch did not have too much power over elected ones.

❌ Negatives:

» The role of the Supreme Court is to act as a check on the other branches, and this reform limited its ability to do so.

4 Elections Act 2022

The Elections Act introduced some significant changes to elections in the UK:

» a requirement for voters at polling stations in Great Britain to show photo ID to prevent fraud.

» the removal of the 15-year limit on voting rights for British citizens living overseas.

» changed Mayoral and Police and Crime Commissioner Elections from Supplementary Vote (SV) system to first-past-the-post (FPTP) (see Chapter 4 for more information).

» it also gave the government new powers over the Independent Electoral Commission which has said it was 'concerned' about its independence from political influence going forward.

✅ Positives:

» Voter ID is common across Europe and is also used in Northern Ireland.

❌ Negatives:

» The law solved a non-existent problem (of fraud) and critics suggest it was designed to disenfranchise non-Conservative voters. The *Guardian* reported that, at the 2024 General Election, of those surveyed by More In Common, 3.2% said they were turned away at least once, which if reflected across the UK would equate to more than 850,000 people. Of these, more than half said they either did not return or came back and were still unable to vote.

Constitutional reforms passed by the Labour Government 2024 onwards

1 The House of Lords (Hereditary Peers) Act 2026

This Act formally ended over 700 years of hereditary peers sitting in the Lords as all 92 hereditary peers lost their right to sit and vote in the Lords. However, as part of a political compromise to secure Conservative support and avoid prolonged parliamentary deadlock, the government offered to nominate up to 15 former hereditary peers – mostly Conservatives and some crossbenchers – as life peers, allowing them to remain in the chamber under a different status. While this means some individuals will stay, the principle of hereditary succession to Parliament is abolished, leaving the Lords composed solely of life peers and Lords Spiritual.

✅ Positives:

» The 92 remaining hereditary peers were an anomaly, left over from 1999 reforms.

💬 Does it go far enough?

» There is still not a single elected member of the House of Lords, and, with around 750 members as of March 2026, it is the second largest chamber in the world after the National People's Congress of China which has 2,977, with the third largest being the French Senate which has 348 senators.

Key Debate Summary: Have constitutional reforms in the UK improved the UK political system?

	✔ Far enough	✖ Too far	… Not far enough
Reforms that affect democracy			
Use of PR	It helps ensure that the allocation of seats more closely mirrors how the people cast their votes.	Participation has been a disappointment.	There is still no PR in the Westminster elections and FPTP has been reintroduced for Mayoral and PCC elections.
Referendums	They have enabled representative democracy to be supplemented by a stronger element of direct democracy.	Some decisions should not be put to a public vote as they are too complicated.	Referendums can only be initiated by Parliament, not the people.
Recall	Recall ensures that MPs are answerable to their constituents.	Recall can be manipulated and used for party political ends.	Genuine recall should be started by the electorate, not MPs.
Voter ID	Voter ID legislation brought the UK in line with most modern democracies.	It disenfranchised thousands of voters according to reports.	
Reforms that decentralise power			
Devolution	It has allowed the government to become closer to the people.	Devolution has threatened the stability of the UK.	Devolution has left the West Lothian Question unresolved with England unfairly treated.
Metro Mayors	It gives one person overall responsibility for an area.	They are elected on a very small percentage of the vote.	An English Parliament is the best way to give England representation.
PCC	It creates accountability at the top of the police authority.	It can lead to decisions made with re-election, not policing in mind.	It can create conflicts between PCCs and chief constables.
Reforms that enhance rights protection			
Human Rights Act	Citizens have a list of their rights, creating awareness.	The HRA has created a more litigious culture in the UK.	The Human Rights Act has not been entrenched in UK law and can be abolished at any time.
Freedom of Information	FOI gives citizens the 'right to know' information regarding how decisions were made.	It has restricted the ordinary acts of governing by making ministers concerned over emails and minutes of meetings.	It has some major exceptions; a minister has to argue it would cause 'prejudice'.

	✓ **Far enough**	✗ **Too far**	⋯ **Not far enough**
	Reforms that modernise the system		
Lords reform	Since reform, the Lords has been much more assertive in holding governments to account.	Despite the removal of hereditary peers, the Lords is too large.	The House remains wholly unelected, with no public accountability.
Judicial reform	The Supreme Court is far more willing to be a check on the legislature and executive.	The position of Lord Chancellor has existed for centuries and should not have been reformed in such an ill-thought-out way.	The Supreme Court is merely a geographical move from one building to another. It has no more powers; it is not Supreme.
Wright Reforms	Select committees have been revitalised with many highly effective independent chairs and members.	N/A	Backbench committee debates do not compel the government to act. They are merely an opportunity for MPs to express their views.

Further constitutional reforms

Despite all the constitutional reforms passed by governments since 1997, there are still a few debates that are unresolved. One of the key issues is whether or not the UK would benefit from a codified constitution. Another is whether the House of Lords should be reformed.

KEY TOPIC DEBATE: SHOULD THE UK CONSTITUTION BE CODIFIED?

✓ **Clear rules.** In a codified constitution, key constitutional rules are collected together in a single document, and they are more clearly defined than in an uncodified constitution. This creates less confusion about the meaning of constitutional rules and greater certainty that they can be enforced.

✗ **Rigidity.** Codified constitutions tend to be more rigid than uncodified ones because higher law is more difficult to change than statute law. The constitution could therefore easily become outdated and fail to respond to an ever-changing political environment. Uncodified constitutions can adapt to changing political circumstances.

✓ **Limited government.** A codified constitution would limit government power and would provide a solution to the problem of 'elective dictatorship' by ending parliamentary sovereignty. Government and Parliament would be bound by the rules enshrined in the constitution. Higher, constitutional law would also safeguard the constitution from interference by the government of the day.

✗ **Unnecessary.** Parliamentary sovereignty is at the heart of the UK political system, and changing that undermines the essence of the British system which has worked very well for centuries.

Codified constitutions may not be the most effective way of limiting government power. Improving democracy or strengthening checks and balances may be better ways of preventing over-mighty government, making a written constitution unnecessary.

✓ **Neutral interpretation.** A codified constitution would be 'policed' by senior judges. This would ensure that the provisions of the constitution are properly upheld by an independent public body. Also, because judges are 'above' politics, they would act as neutral and impartial constitutional referees.

✗ **Judicial tyranny.** Judges are not the best people to police the constitution because they are unelected and socially unrepresentative. A codified constitution could be interpreted in a way that is not subject to public accountability. It may also reflect the preferences and values of senior judges. It is better to have Parliament as the highest constitutional authority; they can be removed by the electorate.

✓ **Protecting rights.** Individual liberty would be more securely protected by a codified constitution because it would define the relationship between the state and the citizens, usually through a bill of rights. Rights would be more clearly defined and easier to enforce. Moreover, rights could not be removed on the whim of the government of the day.

✗ **Legalistic.** Codified constitutions are legal documents, created by people at one point in time. They will codify a set of rights that were deemed important at that time. If they are vague enough to incorporate change over time, they will be no better than an uncodified constitution. They will need to be interpreted by lawyers and judges who will have their own biases. The US Bill of Rights has not stopped discrimination against black people for two centuries.

Key Debate Summary: Should the UK constitution be codified?

For	Theme	Against
✓ Key constitutional rules are collected together in a single document and they are more clearly defined.	Would codification provide clarity or excessive rigidity?	✗ Codified constitutions are more rigid and could therefore easily become outdated.
✓ A codified constitution would limit government power.	How much should a constitution limit the elected government?	✗ Improving democracy or strengthening checks and balances may be better ways of preventing over-mighty governments.
✓ A codified constitution would be 'policed' by senior judges.	Is it desirable to have judges telling politicians what to do?	✗ Judges are not the best people to police the constitution because they are unelected.
✓ Individual liberty would be more securely protected by a codified constitution.	Would codification enhance rights protection or entrench outdated ideas?	✗ They would codify a set of rights that were deemed important at that time.

KEY TOPIC DEBATE: SHOULD THE HOUSE OF LORDS BE REFORMED?

Democracy

✓ **Undemocratic and Unrepresentative Composition – The House of Lords is unelected, with members appointed via patronage, undermining democratic legitimacy. The most recent reforms removing the number of hereditary peers doesn't make it more democratic.**

- Boris Johnson and Liz Truss faced criticism for packing the Lords with allies and donors. In 2023, the Institute for Government highlighted 'unregulated patronage power' as a core problem, eroding public trust.
- The Lords is the second-largest legislature globally (after China), with around 750 members, costing taxpayers £120 million annually.
- The current size of the chamber, largely because Prime Ministers seek to 'pack' the house with their supporters, is unacceptable.

✓ **Full or partial election would raise the democratic authority and legitimacy of the second chamber, and they might also inject a more 'professional' element into the Lords.**

- Every year there is criticism of many peers who turn up for their daily attendance allowance of around £300 without participating in any debates or business of the house.
- If it was elected using a system of proportional representation, the Lords could be said to more accurately represent the wishes of the people and would allow small parties to have more influence on the legislative process.

✗ **If the democratic status of the second chamber were increased it might challenge the authority of the Commons, leading to gridlock.** An elected chamber would have a new sense of legitimacy and would see no need to give way to the Commons as they currently do. This problem would be further complicated if party control in the two chambers were different.

- ❌ **The Salisbury Convention ensures the Lords does not block manifesto commitments.** This ensures that the elected Commons has the final word.
  - The House of Lords (Hereditary Peers) Act 2026 and the Illegal Migration Act (2023) are both examples of manifesto promises that the Lords upheld, despite significant opposition in the chamber.
- ❌ **Because it is appointed, the Lords has been able to closely mirror the popular vote.**
  - the Lib Dems, for example, have about 10% of the Lords.

Scrutiny

- ✅ **Ineffective scrutiny – An elected chamber would be a more effective check on the executive. A more assertive second chamber would be a good thing in a country that is often described as an 'elective dictatorship'. Critics argue that currently, the Lords' revising role is undermined by partisan loyalty and absenteeism.**
  - In 2026 the Lords tabled 2,283 amendments to the Terminally Ill Adults (End of Life) Bill, resulting in it running out of time and not passing despite a majority in the Commons having backed it. Critics argue this was not scrutiny but obstruction by a handful of Lords who were able to thwart the wishes of the elected Commons.
  - During the 2023 Illegal Migration Act debates, the Lords proposed 20 amendments, but most were overturned by the Commons; if it were elected, it might hold more sway.
  - In 2024, only 30% of peers actively participated in legislative work, while 88 peers never spoke or voted.
- ❌ **Since 1999, the Lords has proved to be a useful check on the executive-dominated Commons, suggesting there is no need for any further reform. The Lords' current role as a revising chamber balances efficiency with scrutiny.**
  - It has defeated the government hundreds of times since the bulk of hereditary peers were removed in 1997.
  - Nearly 25% of Lords are crossbenchers (or independents), which means they are unafraid to challenge the government.
  - The Lords' 400+ defeats of government bills since 2019 forced compromises on policies like the Police, Crime, Sentencing and Courts Act.

Scandals and Expertise

- ✅ **Scandals and lack of accountability – Controversies over the appointment of party donors have damaged the Lords' reputation and fuelled calls for reform. Election might inject a more 'professional' element into the second chamber.**
  - Investigations revealed that, between 2013 and 2023, nearly a quarter of party-nominated peers were major donors, with some attending the chamber infrequently and contributing little to legislative scrutiny.
  - In 2023, a Labour peer, Lord Brookman, claimed £50,000 without contributing to debates, highlighting systemic abuse.
  - In 2020, Boris Johnson overruled the security service and House of Lords Appointments Commission over warnings to grant a peerage to Evgeny Lebedev, son of a former KGB agent, in 2020. The appointment, which was made despite national security concerns, sparked accusations of cronyism, constitutional risk and vulnerability to foreign influence.
  - The Michelle Mone scandal revealed that she had financial links to PPE Medpro, a company awarded £200 million in Covid contracts via the government's VIP lane. Mone later admitted lying about her involvement; the firm is under National Crime Agency investigation for fraud, as millions of items of PPE were unusable.
  - This has led to widespread perceptions that peerages are used as rewards for political loyalty or financial contributions, undermining public trust.
- ❌ **Election would eliminate the many current professional appointed members who represent minority groups in society or are experts in their field, but who would not stand for election.**
  - All the experience of the ex-ministers and Prime Ministers in the Lords we have currently would be lost.

- Currently, the chamber contains people who have experience of something other than professional politics, which cannot be said for many MPs in the Commons.
- Appointed peers (e.g. academics, judges) provide non-partisan expertise absent in the Commons.
- Crossbenchers (independent peers) played key roles in improving the 2023 Online Safety Bill, adding safeguards for free speech.

Key Debate Summary: Should the House of Lords be reformed?

For	Theme	Against
✓ Full or partial election would raise the democratic authority and legitimacy of the second chamber.	Would an elected Lords work effectively alongside the Commons?	✗ If the democratic status of the second chamber were increased it might challenge the authority of the Commons, leading to gridlock.
✓ An elected chamber would be a more effective check on the executive.	Does the Lords need to be elected to be an effective check on the government?	✗ Since 1999, the Lords has proved to be a useful check on the executive dominated Commons, suggesting there is no need for any further reform.
✓ Controversies over the appointment of party donors have damaged the Lords' reputation and fuelled calls for reform.	Would election enhance the reputation of the Lords?	✗ Election would eliminate the many current professional appointed members who represent minority groups in society or are experts in their field, but who would not stand for election.

Devolution in the UK

Devolution is the transfer of power from central government to lower regional institutions. The term is derived from the Latin verb meaning 'to roll down'.

Devolution differs from federalism in that, although they may look the same, devolved bodies have no share in **sovereignty**. Their responsibilities and powers are determined by the central sovereign authority, which can, in theory at least, abolish them. Devolution nevertheless comes in different forms:

- » *Administrative* devolution allows regional institutions to implement policies decided elsewhere.
- » *Legislative* devolution operates through elected regional assemblies that are invested with policymaking responsibilities and, usually, have some tax-raising powers.

Devolution has been the most significant change to the UK's constitutional arrangements since 1997. The UK is made up of four component nations, as is shown in Figure 7.1.

Devolution in the UK has largely been a response to the emergence of Scottish and Welsh nationalism. The two nationalist parties, Plaid Cymru ('Party of Wales') and the Scottish National Party (SNP), grew in significance during the 1970s and unsuccessful attempts were made to introduce assemblies in Scotland and Wales in 1978 and 1979, respectively. Support for devolution waned until the 1990s when there was resurgence after over a decade of Conservative Government in Westminster despite no support for the Conservatives in Scotland or Wales.

Labour had wanted to reintroduce plans for devolution since the time of John Smith, who became leader in 1992, and worked with other parties and groups to set up a framework for Scottish devolution. Plans for Welsh devolution were drawn up, largely to complement Scottish proposals, and Labour's election in 1997 provided the basis for these plans to be implemented.

The first elections for the Scottish Parliament and the Welsh Parliament were held in 1999, following successful referendums. The Northern Ireland Assembly came into existence in 1998 as a consequence of the Belfast Agreement (also known as the Good Friday Agreement).

Devolution has quickly become a popular and established feature of UK politics, and one that all major UK parties now support. The UK has a novel form of devolution in that it operates in different ways in different parts of the UK. This is what is called **asymmetrical devolution**. Scotland, Wales and Northern Ireland therefore each have different systems of devolution.

Definition

Sovereignty: The principle of absolute and unlimited power, implying either supreme legal authority (legal sovereignty) or unchallengeable political power (political sovereignty) (see chapter 10).

Asymmetrical devolution: A form of devolution that operates differently in different regions, with no common pattern of devolved powers and responsibilities within the state.

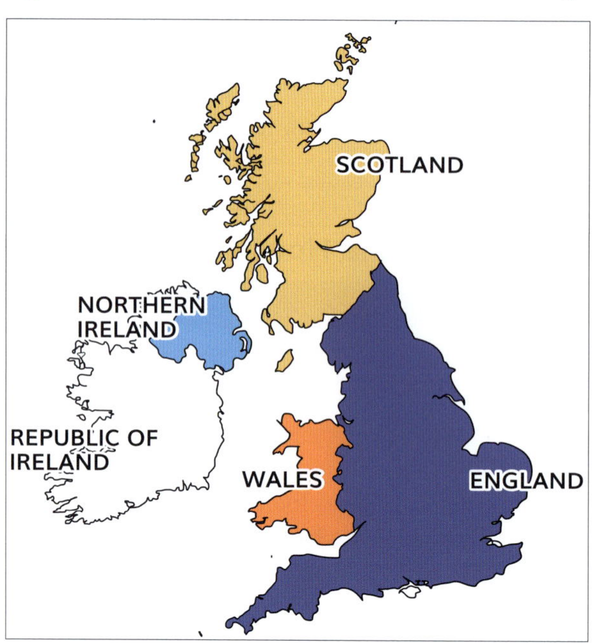

Figure 7.1 The four nations of the United Kingdom

Table 7.1 Powers of the devolved institutions

	Scottish parliament	Welsh parliament	NI Assembly
Agriculture, forestry and fishing	✓	✓	✓
Education	✓	✓	✓
Environment	✓	✓	✓
Health	✓	✓	✓
Housing	✓	✓	✓
Local government	✓	✓	✓
Justice	✓		✓
Fire service	✓	✓	✓
Economic development	✓	✓	✓
Transport	✓	✓	✓
Tax varying powers	✓	✓	
Tourism, culture heritage and sport	✓	✓	✓

Table 7.2 Powers reserved to Westminster

The constitution
Foreign affairs
Defence and national security
Immigration
The economy
Welfare**
International trade and financial markets

*** Welfare is a reserved matter in Wales, but some welfare powers have been transferred to the Scottish Parliament.*

Devolution in Scotland

The Scotland Act 1998 established the Scottish Parliament and Scottish Government. Its provisions included the following key ones:

1. Created the Scottish Parliament with powers to make laws on devolved matters.

2. Established a system of reserved and devolved powers (see Tables 7.1 and 7.2).

3. Granted the Scottish Parliament tax-varying powers.

However, the Act also included a provision for the UK Parliament to be able to legislate on all matters, including devolved ones, subject to the **Sewel Convention**.

The Act came into force on 1 July 1999, following the first Scottish Parliament elections. It marked a significant change in the governance of Scotland within the United Kingdom, devolving substantial powers while maintaining the overall structure of the UK.

The Scottish Parliament is an example of legislative devolution. It has **primary legislative powers** in most fields of domestic policy and tax-varying powers (the ability to raise or lower income tax).

As Table 7.2 shows, devolution is best described as a 'process and not an event'. Since the initial 1998 Scotland Act, there have been two additional Acts (in 2012 and 2016), increasing the scope and amount of power conferred on the Scottish Parliament and Government.

The Scotland Act 2012 introduced several key changes to expand the powers of the Scottish Parliament:

1. The Act increased the amount the Scottish Parliament was able to raise on income tax.

2. It allowed the Scottish Parliament to introduce Scottish-specific taxes to replace UK ones, for example stamp duty. It also created Revenue Scotland to manage these devolved taxes.

3. The Scottish Government gained borrowing powers of up to £5 billion.

4. It also gained some smaller additional legislative powers.

The Act sought to increase Scotland's fiscal autonomy and responsibility.

During the referendum campaign in 2014, Prime Minister Cameron promised 'devo-max' to the people of Scotland to encourage them to vote to stay in the UK, and following the 55%–45% vote to stay, the UK Parliament passed the 2016 Scotland Act. The Scotland Act 2016 significantly expanded the powers of the Scottish Parliament in several key areas:

- The Act gave the Scottish Parliament more control over income tax, air passenger duty and other levies on building supplies. Additionally, it agreed that 50% of all VAT revenues raised in Scotland would be assigned to the Scottish Government.

- It devolved control over several benefits and granted power to the Parliament to create new benefits and top up reserved benefits.

- Fundamentally, the Act declared the Scottish Parliament and Government as permanent parts of the UK's constitutional arrangements, as well as providing the ability to amend the operation of the Scottish Parliament and Government, including control of the Parliament's electoral system.

- There were also some additional, smaller areas where power was devolved, for example control over British Transport Police in Scotland, road signs, speed limits, and onshore oil and gas extraction.

These expanded powers significantly increased the Scottish Parliament's autonomy and financial accountability, making it one of the most powerful devolved parliaments in the world.

The increased range of powers for the Scottish Parliament mirrored the rise in the popularity of the SNP in Scottish and Westminster Parliamentary elections between 2011 and 2024, with increased powers offered to appease the growing thirst for independence.

At the beginning of 2023, it looked as if Scottish independence was almost inevitable, and with Nicola Sturgeon as First Minister, the SNP looked like the party that would lead this charge. However, her sudden and dramatic resignation in February 2023 changed the Scottish political landscape fundamentally.

Figure 7.2 How devolution has evolved in Scotland

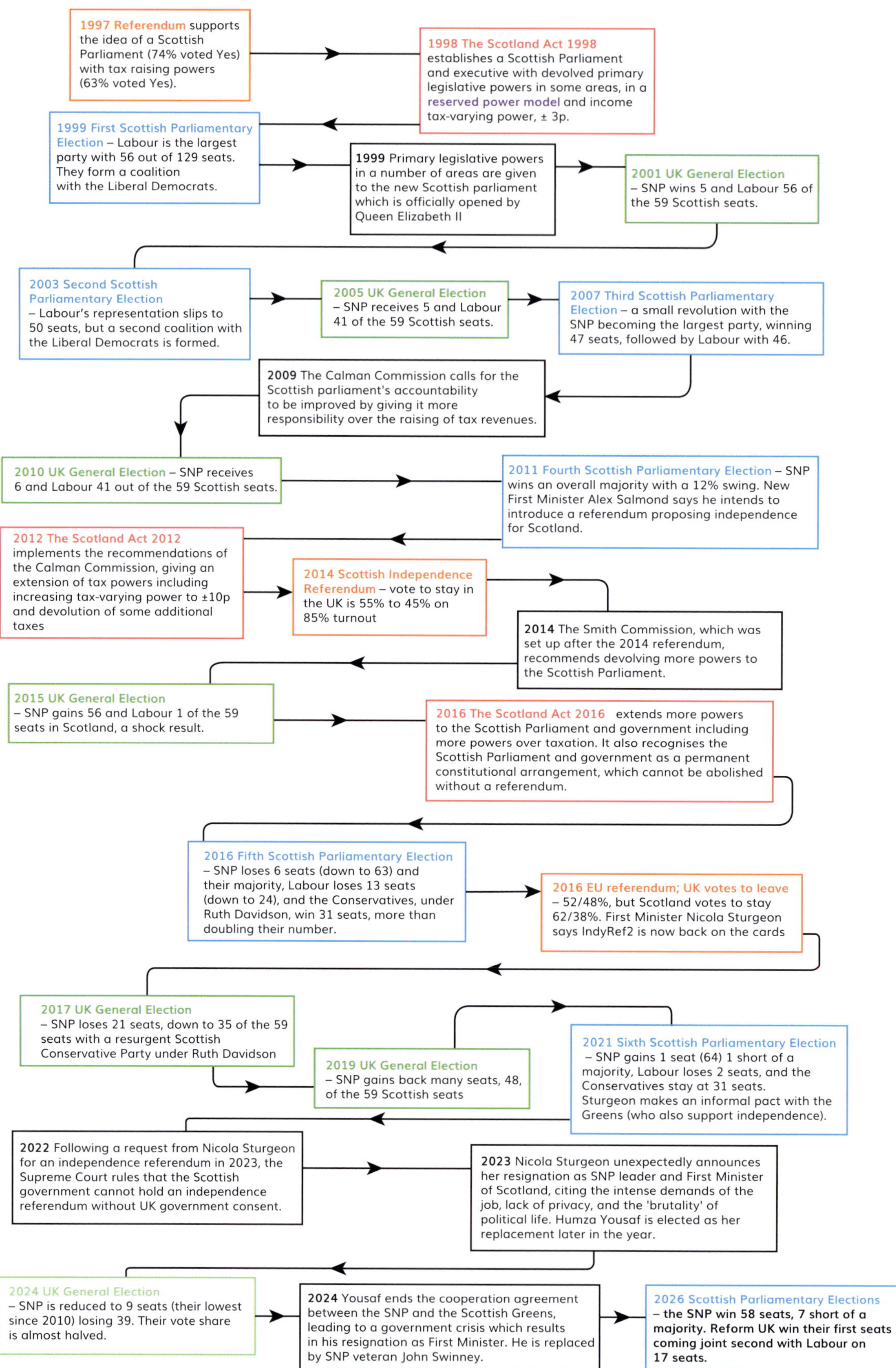

Visit the companion website for a case study on the Scottish Independence Referendum from the previous fifth edition.

CASE STUDY 7.1: STURGEON'S RESIGNATION AND THE CONSEQUENCES FOR SCOTTISH POLITICS

Nicola Sturgeon's resignation as First Minister of Scotland in February 2023 marked a pivotal moment in Scottish politics. Having led the SNP as First Minister since 2014, Sturgeon's departure raised significant questions about the future of the party and the independence movement. Her resignation came amid mounting controversies, including financial scandals involving her husband, Peter Murrell, and growing dissatisfaction with her leadership within her party, and a transgender row.

Reasons for her resignation

In her resignation speech, Sturgeon said she could no longer give her full commitment to the role, citing leadership fatigue and the personal toll the job had taken on her. This decision shocked the political establishment on both sides of the border as Sturgeon had been a central figure in Scottish politics for years, leading the SNP through major political events, notably the Brexit crisis and the Covid-19 pandemic.

Although not referenced by Sturgeon at the time, it became clear within weeks that one of the most significant factors contributing to her resignation was the scandal surrounding her husband, Peter Murrell, who had served as the SNP's chief executive until 2023. The SNP was embroiled in a series of financial controversies that had been bubbling for some time, but the situation intensified in early 2023 with allegations of financial mismanagement and concerns over party funding, raising questions about the integrity of the SNP's financial operations. Specifically, the allegations surrounded £600,000 raised in 2017 to fund a second independence referendum campaign, and concerns about its allocation and transparency. Murrell was at the centre of this controversy. The scandal put Sturgeon in an uncomfortable position. While she denied any personal wrongdoing, her association with Murrell, as both his wife and the leader of the party, made it increasingly difficult to maintain her credibility.

Another key factor in Sturgeon's resignation was the growing division within the SNP. While the party had dominated Scottish politics under her leadership, internal tensions and dissatisfaction with her leadership style were becoming evident. Some were frustrated with the lack of progress on Scottish independence, while others were unhappy with Sturgeon's handling of internal party issues. Sturgeon also faced declining popularity among the electorate. Additionally, she had become embroiled in a gender recognition controversy and faced significant criticism over the Gender Recognition Reform Bill, which led to a drop in support for independence and the SNP. Concern for the bill was compounded by a high-profile case involving a transgender woman convicted of rape being initially sent to a women's prison, which caused further controversy and forced Sturgeon into a policy U-turn.

Succession and beyond

Following Sturgeon's resignation, the SNP elected Humza Yousaf, Sturgeon's long-time ally, as leader. Yousaf became the first ethnic minority leader of the SNP. However, his leadership faced immediate challenges, including the task of addressing the fallout from the scandals surrounding Murrell.

Yousaf's tenure as Scotland's First Minister and leader of the SNP came to an abrupt end in April 2024, less than a year after he assumed office. Yousaf had unilaterally ended the power-sharing agreement between the SNP and the Scottish Greens, which he later admitted was a significant error, which left him leading a minority government without clear allies and, unsurprisingly, he immediately faced a confidence vote in the Scottish Parliament. When it became clear that he didn't have the votes to survive, Yousaf announced his resignation as First Minister and SNP leader in April 2024. Veteran SNP (former leader) John Swinney was soon elected as his replacement. In the July 2024 UK General Election, support for the SNP haemorrhaged with their vote reduced from 1.2 million in 2019 to 720,000. They lost 39 seats, down to 9 – their lowest since 2010.

Nicola Sturgeon's resignation in 2023 marked the end of an era in Scottish politics.

Devolution in Wales

The Welsh Assembly was, in origin, an example of administrative devolution, in that it had no control over taxation and only **secondary legislative powers**. However, following a referendum in March 2011, the Welsh Assembly gained primary legislative powers in all 20 areas for which it is responsible.

The story of devolution in Wales is, in some ways, even more about a 'process not an event', as in 1997 Welsh people were fairly ambivalent about devolution, yet the years following the referendum have seen the Welsh enjoying their experience of self-rule rather more than one may have predicted in 1997. Yet it would be a mistake to think that Wales is following the Scottish model. In many ways, they couldn't be more different. As Figure 7.3 shows, one key way that nationalism in Wales is different to

Figure 7.3 How devolution has evolved in Wales

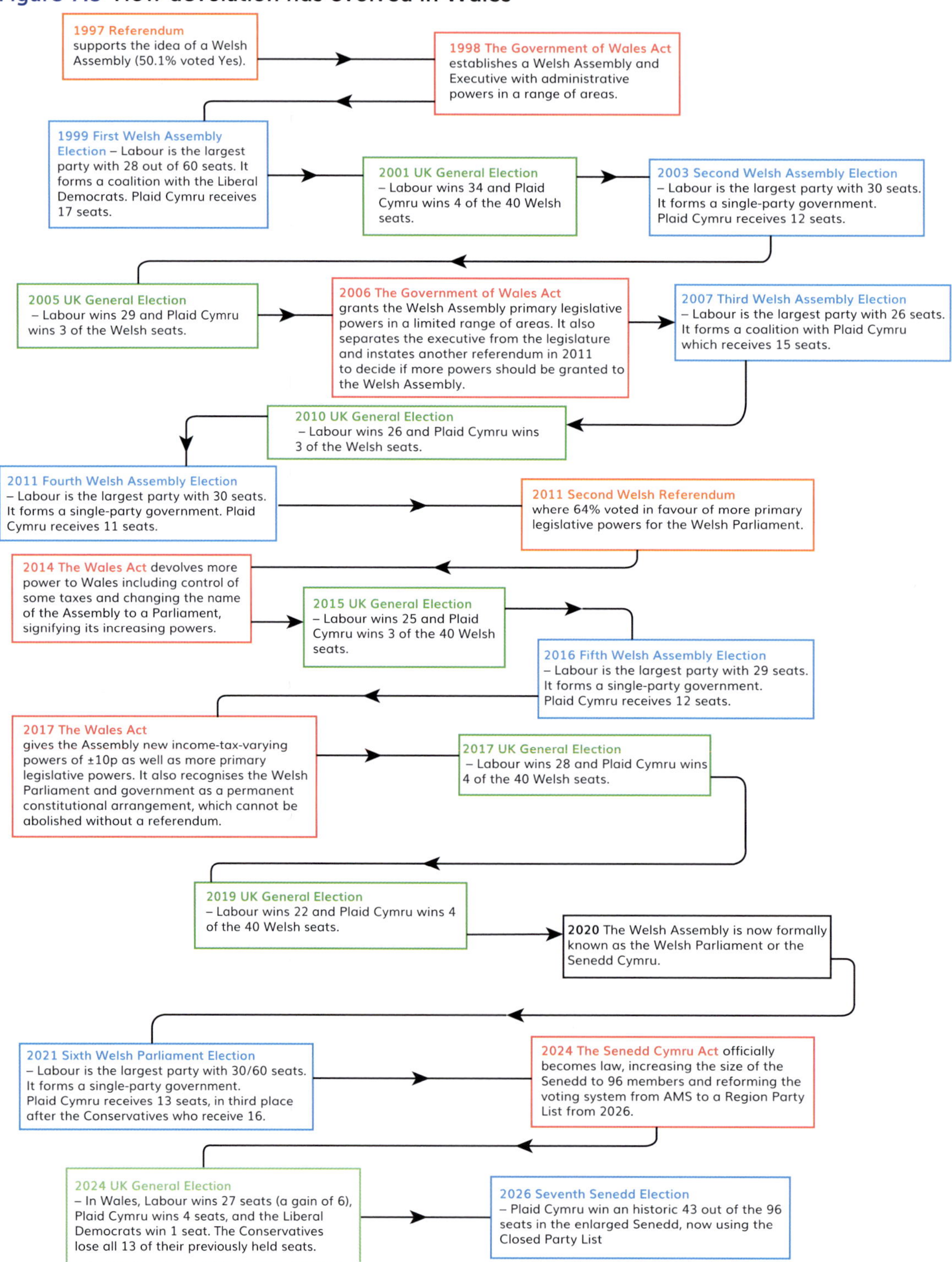

Scotland can be understood by comparing the fortunes of the SNP with Plaid Cymru. Until 2026, Plaid had not seen any real change in its fortunes and Labour had been able to hold on to around half the seats in the Senedd at each election. This may have been because nationalism in Wales took a more cultural rather than political approach. The issue of independence has not fully taken hold in Wales. However, with the election of a minority Plaid government in 2026, nothing is certain any more.

The Government of Wales Act 1998 created the National Assembly for Wales, establishing it as a body to make secondary legislation for Wales. It was initially limited to secondary legislation based on the slim majority of a 50.3% 'yes' vote in the 1998 referendum. However, since then, the Welsh Senedd has been given more power five times.

Government of Wales Act 2006:

- Gave the Assembly the power to pass 'Assembly Measures' which have the status of primary legislation. In so doing, it set the stage for the Assembly to gain full law-making powers in 20 devolved areas.
- Established a Welsh Government with powers to improve the economy and the culture of Wales.
- Formally separated the functions of the Assembly and the Welsh Government.

Following the 2011 Referendum where 64% voted in favour of more primary legislative powers for the Welsh Assembly, the Wales Act 2014 was passed.

- It devolved powers to impose taxes and allowed for a referendum on whether the Welsh Government could vary income tax.
- It extended the borrowing powers of the Welsh Government.
- It extended the Senedd term from four to five years and banned people from being Members of Parliament as well as members of the Senedd.

The Wales Act 2017 made some extremely significant constitutional changes to the status of the Welsh Assembly.

- It replaced the **'conferred powers' model** with a **'reserved powers' model**, allowing the Senedd to legislate on any matter not explicitly reserved to Westminster. This brought Wales more in line with the devolution arrangements in Scotland and Northern Ireland.
- The Act enshrined the Assembly and Welsh Government as permanent parts of the UK's constitutional arrangements, which could not be abolished without the agreement of the Welsh people.
- It transferred ten more areas to Welsh Ministers including transport regulation and Senedd and local government elections.
- The Assembly gained powers over its own internal, organisational and electoral arrangements, including the ability to change its name and voting system.

Devolution in Northern Ireland

Between the 1970s and 1990s, Northern Ireland endured a bloody conflict known as 'the Troubles' which left nearly 4,000 people dead and thousands more injured.

At the heart of the Troubles was the division between the **unionist** community, who identify as British and want Northern Ireland to remain part of the United Kingdom, and the **nationalist** community who want Northern Ireland to be part of the Irish Republic.

Devolution in Northern Ireland is tightly linked to the Northern Ireland peace process and specifically to the 1998 Good Friday Agreement. The Good Friday Agreement resulted in power-sharing governments being formed in the Northern Ireland Assembly. The division of powers between the Northern Ireland Assembly and Westminster is different to Scotland and Wales, with powers divided into three categories:

- » Transferred – issues on which the Assembly has full legislative powers.
- » Reserved – which can be transferred with cross-community consent.
- » Excepted – which cannot be transferred without primary legislation from Westminster.

Figure 7.4 How devolution has evolved in Northern Ireland

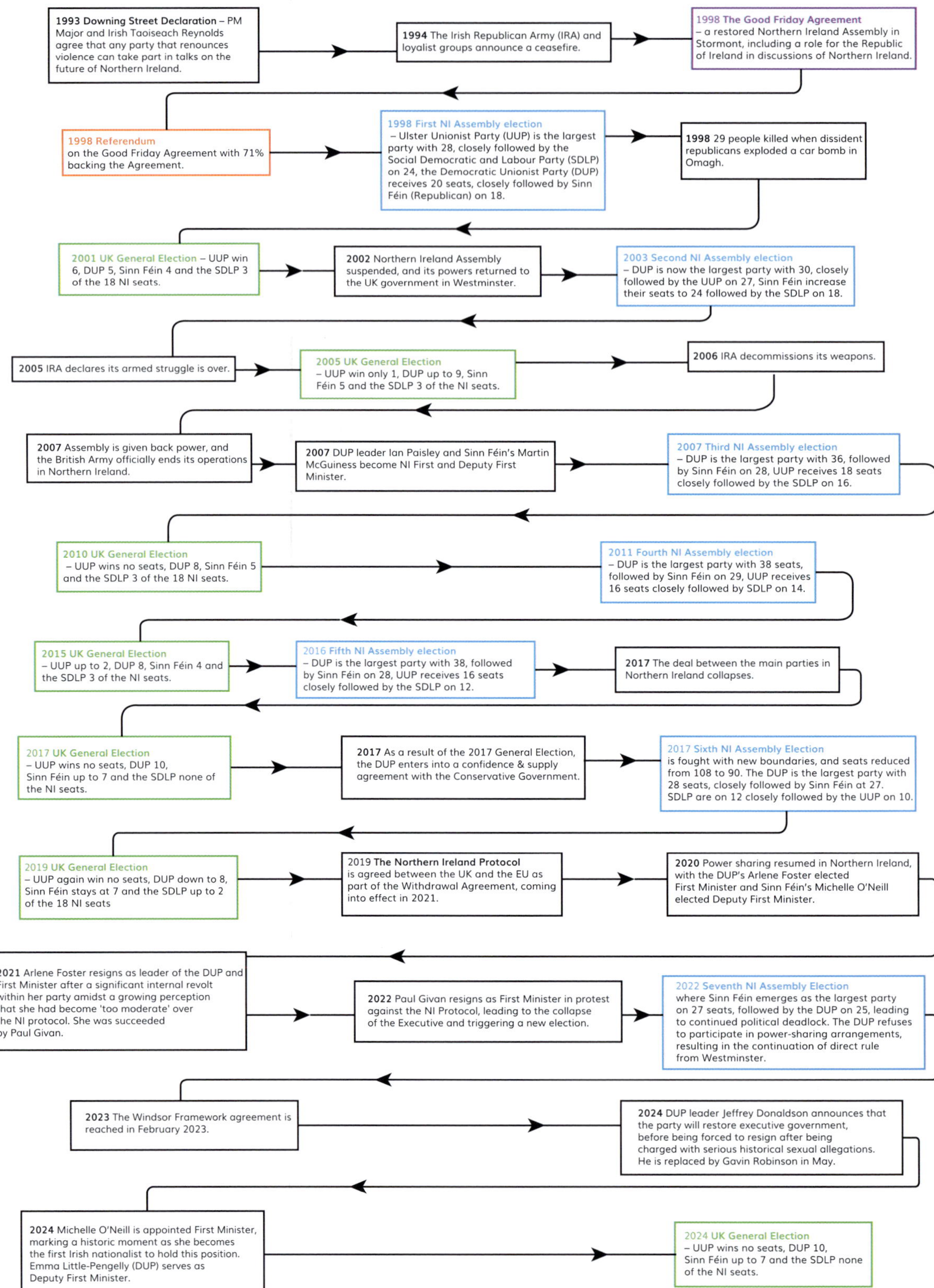

Photo 7.1 British Prime Minister Tony Blair (R), US Senator George Mitchell (C) and Irish Prime Minister Bertie Ahern (L) smiling on 10 April 1998 after they signed a historic agreement for peace in Northern Ireland, ending a 30-year conflict

Source: Getty Images / Dan Chung

The Good Friday Agreement also enshrines in law the requirement for a power-sharing agreement between the largest unionist and largest nationalist parties. However, this has not been without its difficulties and, as Figure 7.4 shows, devolution has been suspended and reinstated several times since 1998.

Devolution was suspended in 2002 because the two largest parties were unable to sustain agreement, and not returned till 2007. Following an election in May 2007, the NI Executive comprising the DUP, Sinn Féin, UUP and SDLP was finally able to take office. The First Minister Ian Paisley, from the hard-line DUP, shared power with Deputy First Minister Martin McGuinness, from Sinn Féin. It is impossible to understate the enormity of this and it was the symbol of what devolution in Northern Ireland had achieved. Not only did these former sworn political enemies manage to work together, in fact they struck up a deep friendship and seemed to enjoy each other's company so much that they were dubbed the 'chuckle brothers'. After Paisley's death in 2014, McGuinness said, 'Despite our differences, I found him to be a charismatic and powerful personality. He always treated me and those who worked with me with respect and courtesy. The peace process and I have lost a friend.' This tribute would have been inconceivable ten years earlier.

Brexit and Northern Ireland – implications for devolution

The Northern Ireland Protocol

The Northern Ireland Protocol was a complex solution aimed at balancing trade relationships post-Brexit, while maintaining peace on the island of Ireland and upholding the principles of the Good Friday Agreement. It was agreed in October 2019, between the UK and the EU. The Protocol came into effect on 1 January 2021 as part of the overall Brexit transition. However, the Protocol played a significant role in the ensuing political instability in Northern Ireland:

- The Protocol was a contentious issue for unionist parties which argued that it undermined Northern Ireland's constitutional status within the UK. It united various unionist parties (DUP, UUP, TUV) in opposition, reflecting widespread discontent within the unionist community.

- This sentiment contributed to the resignation of DUP First Minister Paul Givan in February 2022, who stated that the Protocol had disrupted the delicate political balance established by the Belfast Agreement.

- Unionists argue that it created a customs border in the Irish Sea, between the UK mainland and the island of Ireland. In other words, it treats Northern Ireland as if it is part of Ireland and not part of the UK.

Figure 7.5 **The Northern Ireland Protocol**

- They argue that it subjected Northern Ireland to EU laws and regulations without any representation, creating a democratic deficit, and that it effectively placed Northern Ireland under the jurisdiction of a foreign entity (the EU) without consent from its citizens, see Figure 7.5.
- Unionist parties argued that the Protocol undermined the principles of the Good Friday Agreement, which established that any change in Northern Ireland's constitutional status must have explicit democratic consent.
- Lastly, they argued that the Protocol undermined Northern Ireland's economic position within the UK, leading to increased costs and supply chain disruptions for businesses reliant on imports from Great Britain.

The Windsor Framework

The Windsor Framework is a post-Brexit agreement reached in February 2023 between the UK and the EU. It modified the original Northern Ireland Protocol to address concerns raised by unionists and to facilitate smoother trade between Great Britain and Northern Ireland. Its key elements are as follows:

- The Framework establishes two distinct lanes for goods arriving in Northern Ireland from Great Britain:
  - Green Lane: For goods intended to remain in Northern Ireland, which will face minimal checks and paperwork.
  - Red Lane: For goods that may enter the EU single market, which will continue to be subject to standard customs checks. This is shown by Figure 7.6.
- The Framework introduces a mechanism known as the Stormont Brake, allowing the Northern Ireland Assembly to object to new EU laws that would apply in Northern Ireland. This aims to address concerns about democratic accountability regarding EU regulations.

Figure 7.6 **The Windsor Framework**

- The agreement removed bans on specific products, such as chilled meats, entering Northern Ireland from Great Britain.
- The UK and EU committed to work together to resolve any emerging issues through dialogue rather than formal dispute mechanisms.

The new arrangements began operating on 1 October 2023.

The aim of the Windsor Framework was to alleviate the concerns of unionist parties with the Northern Ireland Protocol. The Windsor Framework did not fully satisfiy unionist concerns, particularly those of the DUP. The DUP described the Windsor Framework as representing 'significant progress' in some areas but maintained that there were still 'key issues of concern' that needed to be addressed. However, by 2024, the DUP agreed to restore devolution and in February 2024, Michelle O'Neill was appointed First Minister, marking a historic moment as she became the first Irish nationalist to hold this position. Emma Little-Pengelly (DUP) serves as deputy First Minister.

Devolution in Northern Ireland brought about through the Good Friday Agreement was able to bring an end to the Troubles and has allowed Northern Ireland's two communities to pursue their contrasting aspirations without violence.

Photo 7.2 Michelle O'Neill, appointed as First Minister, with Emma Little-Pengelly (DUP) serving as Deputy First Minister, meeting then UK Prime Minister Rishi Sunak

Source: Charles McQuillan / Stringer / Getty Images

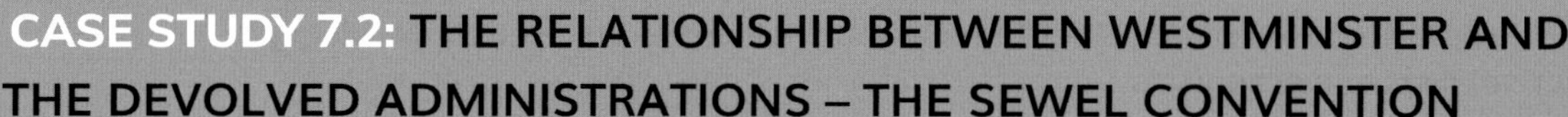

CASE STUDY 7.2: THE RELATIONSHIP BETWEEN WESTMINSTER AND THE DEVOLVED ADMINISTRATIONS – THE SEWEL CONVENTION

The Sewel Convention is a constitutional principle in the United Kingdom that governs the relationship between the UK Parliament and devolved legislatures. It states that the UK Parliament 'will not normally legislate with regard to devolved matters without the consent' of the relevant devolved legislature.

The Sewel Convention applies when the UK Parliament wants to legislate on matters within the powers of the devolved institutions. Typically, the UK Government consults with devolved administrations early in the legislative process, and following that, devolved legislatures then vote on legislative consent motions to grant or withhold consent. It aims to protect the autonomy of devolved institutions and ensure their democratic authority over devolved matters. It is a crucial element of the UK's devolution arrangements, balancing the principle of parliamentary sovereignty with respect for devolved powers.

The aim of Sewel is to safeguard the autonomy of devolved institutions, and in so doing it has become an important symbol of the political authority of devolved institutions, empowering them to influence Westminster legislation affecting devolved matters. The convention thus plays a crucial role in maintaining the delicate balance of the UK's devolved constitutional structure, though recent challenges have highlighted its limitations and sparked debates about potential reforms.

Sewel and the Supreme Court

Interestingly, even though Sewel is recognised in the Scotland Act 2016 and Wales Act 2017, the convention (like all conventions) is not legally binding. The Supreme Court confirmed this in the Miller 2017 judgement. The Court ruled that the Sewel Convention remained a political convention and is not legally binding. It said that 'policing the scope and manner of its operation does not lie within the constitutional remit of the judiciary', meaning that the courts cannot enforce the convention or resolve disputes about its application. The judgement emphasised that Parliament's recognition of the convention in statute did not make it legally enforceable. If Parliament had intended to make it justiciable, it would have used clearer language to that effect.

The Evolution of the Sewel Convention

The Sewel Convention has been used extensively since 1999, with over 450 legislative consent motions voted on in devolved legislatures. One of the biggest challenges to Sewel was Brexit, with the UK government proceeding with legislation despite devolved parliaments withholding consent. Additionally, while breaches were rare before 2016, 19 of the 28 instances of denied consent occurred in the 2019–24 Parliament. This reflects the complex dynamic of the UK's devolution arrangements and the challenges faced in balancing central and devolved powers.

Challenges to Sewel

The convention has faced challenges, and there have been several notable examples of breaches of the Sewel Convention, particularly related to Brexit legislation, when legislation was passed without consent from devolved legislatures.

1. European Union (Withdrawal) Act 2018: The Scottish Parliament refused consent, but the UK Government proceeded with the legislation regardless. This marked the first time Westminster legislated without the consent of the Scottish Parliament since devolution in 1999.
2. European Union (Withdrawal Agreement) Act 2020: All three devolved legislatures (Scotland, Wales and Northern Ireland) withheld consent, yet the UK Parliament passed the Act.

Following the EU Withdrawal Act, the Scottish Government went on a 'Sewel Strike', refusing to consent to most Brexit-related bills except in exceptional circumstances.

3. UK Internal Market Act 2020: Both the Scottish Parliament and Welsh Senedd refused consent, arguing the Act fundamentally changed and damaged the devolution settlement. However, the UK Government pushed it through.
4. European Union Future Relationship Act 2020: The UK Gvernment proceeded with legislation on the EU–UK deal without the consent of the Scottish Parliament.

These examples highlight growing tensions between the UK Government and devolved administrations, particularly around Brexit legislation. The frequency of breaches has led to concerns about the effectiveness of the convention and calls for reform from both the Scottish and Welsh Governments.

Policy differences in England, Scotland, Wales and Northern Ireland

One of the key reasons for devolution is to create local solutions to local problems. Public policy in Scotland, Wales and Northern Ireland has diverged from the rest of the UK as a result of devolution, leading to concern about the overall unity of the United Kingdom. This has led to significant policy differences:

» The Visitor Levy (Scotland) Act 2024 allows Scottish local authorities to charge a levy on overnight stays, a power not available in England.

» Scotland passed the Hunting with Dogs (Scotland) Act 2023, further restricting hunting practices beyond existing UK laws.

» In England and Wales, the minimum age for marriage is 18 years old, which was introduced in 2023. In Scotland and Northern Ireland, the minimum age remains at 16 years old. While England and Wales are implementing stricter regulations to protect young people from forced marriages, Scotland is reviewing this policy to explore a change.

» Scotland has universal free school meals for all children in primary years 1 to 5, whereas Wales is gradually phasing in universal free school meals for all primary school children. Northern Ireland only has means-tested free school meals. England has universal free school meals in reception, year 1 and year 2. Interestingly, the Mayor of London introduced universal free schools meals across London in 2023. All nations have free school meals means-tested for older children.

» Controversially, the Gender Recognition Reform Bill passed the Scottish Parliament in December 2022. However, the bill was prevented from proceeding to Royal Assent by an order under Section 35 of the Scotland Act 1998, made by the UK Government. They argued that it would have adverse effects on the operation of UK-wide equality legislation, particularly the Equality Act 2010 which protects the characteristic of 'sex', as well as on the reserved matters of fiscal and social security policy. The decision was challenged by the Scottish Government but upheld by Scotland's highest civil court in December 2023.

» Scotland's Hate Crime and Public Order Act 2021 expanded hate crime laws, including the creation of a new offence of 'stirring up hatred'. England has not introduced comparable legislation.

» Scotland passed the Period Products (Free Provision) Act in 2021, making it the first country to make period products freely available to all who need them. England has not introduced similar legislation.

» Smacking children is banned in Scotland and Wales, with children having the same legal protection from assault as adults, while it is still legal with restrictions in England and Northern Ireland.

» During the Covid pandemic, Scotland, Wales and Northern Ireland differed significantly in their approaches.

» The introduction of a minimum unit price for alcohol in Scotland was linked to the desire to tackle harmful levels of alcohol consumption in 2018. Wales introduced one in 2020.

» In 2015, Wales changed to an 'opt-out' system for organ donations. The UK Government followed and changed the law in England to start an 'opt-out' system from 2020.

» In Wales (2007), Northern Ireland (2010) and Scotland (2011), prescriptions became free, whereas in England there is still a charge.

» Scotland, Wales and Northern Ireland kept the Educational Maintenance Allowance which was abolished in England.

» The abolition of tuition fees for university students in Scotland in 2008, whereas in the UK students pay tuition fees, and they were recently raised to £9,535 from 2025–26.

» The introduction of free long-term care for the elderly in 2002 in Scotland.

However, arguably one of the most remarkable features of policymaking in Scotland under devolution has been how limited the changes have been. Devolution was supposed to free Scotland, Wales and Northern Ireland from the dead hand of decision making at a UK level, but the reality has been much more modest than the rhetoric of political leaders.

Visit the companion website for a case study on Devolution and Covid from the previous fifth edition.

Devolution in England

Instead of introducing an English Parliament, which was not supported by any major party, devolution in England is characterised by the creation of so-called 'Metro Mayors'. The introduction of Metro Mayors in England was part of a broader push for devolution of power from London to regional leaders. Metro Mayors are directly elected leaders responsible for overseeing urban areas with significant influence over regional economic, social and infrastructural development. The most prominent example of this is the Mayor of London, but Metro Mayors also govern cities like Greater Manchester, Liverpool City Region and West Midlands (see Figure 7.7).

The asymmetrical nature of English devolution

The extent of powers granted to each Metro Mayor varies, depending on the devolution deal struck with central government. In many cases, the power structures are complex, as many responsibilities (e.g. healthcare, social services and policing) are still primarily handled by local councils or are subject to national government oversight. For example, the West Midlands Metro Mayor has control over housing and transport but does not have full control over the police. On the other hand, the London Mayor has significant autonomy over policing and has been able to implement various policies in areas like air quality and green energy that mayors in other regions do not control to the same extent.

Role and powers of Metro Mayors:

1. Metro Mayors oversee several combined authorities.

2. Metro Mayors are directly elected, giving them a broad mandate.

3. Metro Mayors concentrate on strategic issues, such as transport, housing and economic development.

4. Metro Mayors tend to have high public profiles and recognition.

5. These powers give Metro Mayors influence when dealing with central government.

As of March 2026, approximately 48 million people in England live under a Metro Mayor, including the Mayor of London. This accounts for 75% of England's population. There are currently 17 combined authorities with elected Metro Mayors, plus the Mayor of London.

As the timeline below shows, devolution in England is in its infancy. Early attempts by the Blair Government to introduce Mayors were thwarted and were again rejected by the public under the coalition. However, in 2017, Metro Mayors with wider regional reach seemed to catch a mood and were successfully introduced across England. Many of these Mayors were re-elected in 2021 and again in 2024.

Advantages and disadvantages of Metro Mayors

Advantages

- ✓ Metro Mayors provide a visible, directly elected leader for their regions, offering a clear point of accountability for local issues. For example, Andy Burnham in Greater Manchester has been a prominent voice on issues like transport and homelessness since 2020.

- ✓ Metro Mayors have executive powers over areas such as transport, housing, skills and planning, allowing for more coordinated regional strategies. In London, Sadiq Khan has used these powers to implement policies like the Ultra Low Emission Zone expansion in 2021.

- ✓ The role of Metro Mayors is designed to boost economic performance in their regions. For instance, Andy Street in the West Midlands worked on initiatives to attract investment and create jobs since 2020.

- ✓ Metro Mayors have access to devolved powers and funding from central government, allowing for more localised decision making. The Greater London Authority, for example, controls a budget of £20.7 billion annually.

Definition

The Barnett formula:
The devolved administrations in Scotland, Wales and Northern Ireland receive grants from the UK Government that fund most of their spending. The Barnett formula calculates the block grant aiming to give each country the same pounds-per-person funding.

Figure 7.7 How devolution has evolved in England

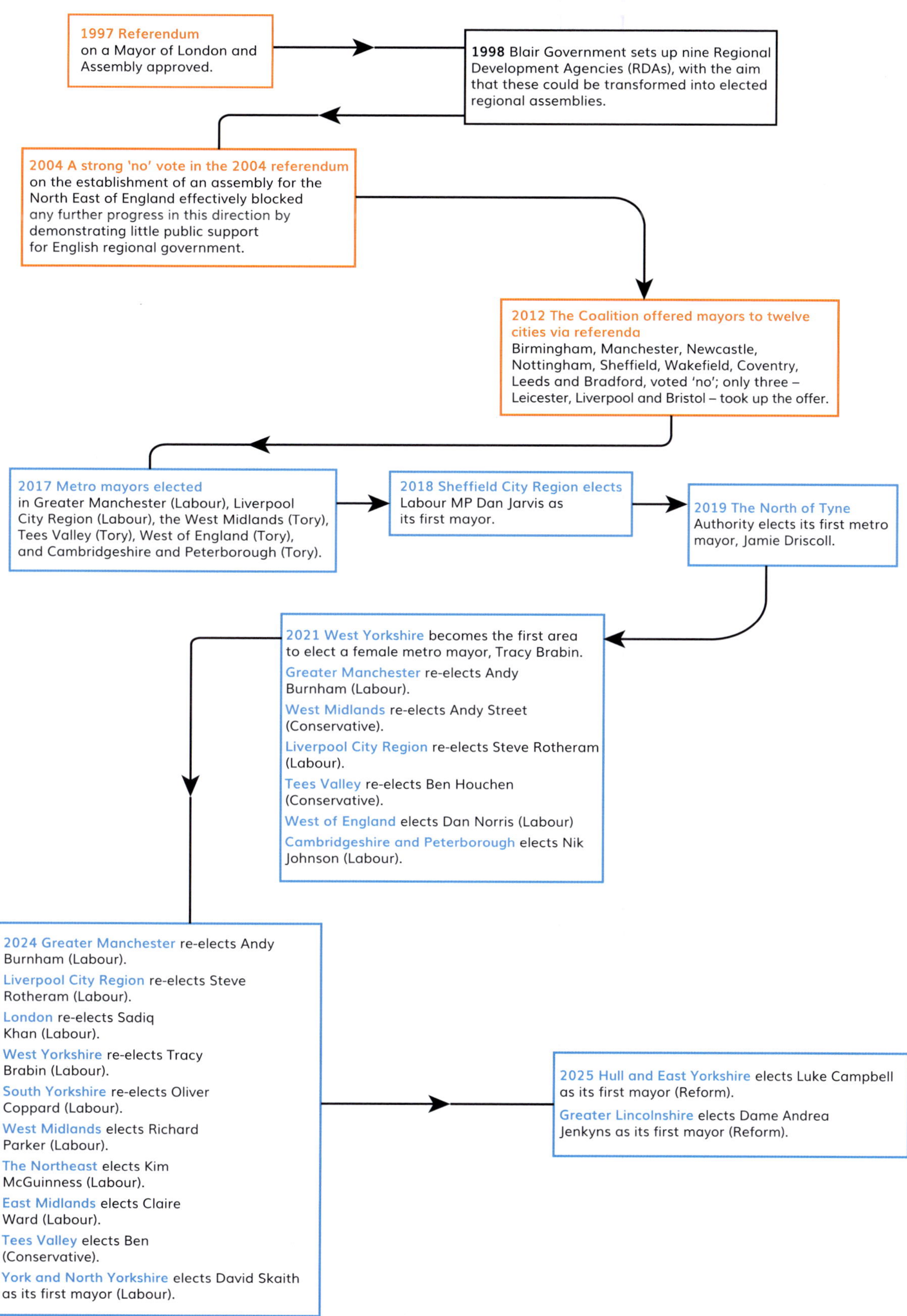

Disadvantages

✗ Despite their high profile, Metro Mayors often have limited powers and budgets compared to central government. For example, while they have some control over policing, the majority of police funding still comes from national government.

✗ The introduction of Metro Mayors can lead to tensions with existing local authorities and/or central government. This was evident in disputes between Andy Burnham and the UK Government over Covid-19 restrictions in 2020.

✗ The Metro Mayor system is not uniformly applied across England, leading to potential disparities in governance and funding between regions with and without Metro Mayors.

✗ While Metro Mayors are directly elected, there are concerns about the effectiveness of scrutiny mechanisms. The London Assembly, for instance, has limited powers to hold the Mayor of London to account.

✗ The high profile of Metro Mayors can lead to unrealistic public expectations about what they can achieve, given their limited powers and resources.

In late 2024, Angela Rayner, the then Deputy Prime Minister and Secretary of State for Housing, Communities and Local Government, introduced the English Devolution Bill, which passed the Commons in 2025 and moved up to be considered by the Lords. It proposed significant changes to devolution and Metro Mayor powers in England. The Bill gave them more direct planning powers and created 'strategic authorities' across England. It also gives all established Mayors the right to request further devolution as well as making devolution the standard position of government rather than an exception.

KEY TOPIC DEBATE: HAS DEVOLUTION BEEN A SUCCESS?

✅ **Devolution has brought democracy closer to the people.**

» The creation of the devolved institutions has allowed voters in the nations to elect representatives who are directly responsible for decisions that affect their daily lives.

» This has led to improved local responsibility as they are able to craft policies that are tailored to the specific political, cultural and social needs, which may differ from those in England.

» This is shown by the policy divergence (highlighted on page 235).

❌ **However, recently the devolved institutions have clashed with the UK Parliament, undermining democracy.**

» Breaches of the Sewel Convention between 2019 and 2024 have undermined democracy significantly, with decisions being made in Westminster without the consent of the devolved administration.

» Sunak's blocking of the Gender Reform Recognition Act, using section 35, highlighted the significant limits to the democratic notion of devolution.

✅ **Devolved institutions have increased participation and representation, helping to engage the electorate.**

» It has increased public participation and political engagement by giving citizens a greater sense of ownership over their political institutions.

» Surveys indicate that a significant majority in devolved regions support the continuation of devolution, viewing it as a preferred system of governance. This suggests that devolution has been successful in meeting public expectations.

» Devolution has improved representation for regions, particularly for women and minority groups because of the proportional electoral systems they use, compared to Westminster. This has led to more diverse political representation within devolved assemblies.

❌ **Asymmetric devolution – the differing powers of the different institutions is confusing and unfair.**

» It has moved at different speeds for each region and each region has different powers, which makes the whole process imbalanced and uncertain.

Synoptic Link

The use of proportional electoral systems in devolved assemblies are a clear synoptic link to the Component 1 topic of Elections.

» While some devolved administrations, particularly Scotland, have received wide-ranging powers, others like Wales have been given more limited authority, which has led to frustration and inconsistency across the UK. This is also true of Metro Mayors, with huge variance in their powers.

✅ **Devolution has given the component nations of the UK enormous freedom to experiment with policy to best serve their nation.**

» Devolved administrations serve as 'policy laboratories', experimenting with innovative solutions that can be adopted or adapted by other regions or the UK Government.

» Scotland, in particular, has enjoyed the freedom devolution has provided. Examples include Scotland's first smoking ban and various health initiatives.

❌ **However, rather than quench the thirst for autonomy, devolution has dramatically increased the desire for Scottish independence.**

» Since 2011, under the government of the SNP, Scotland has pushed for one and then a second independence referendum. This was further exacerbated by the different regional votes in the EU referendum and the subsequent EU legislation passed by the UK Parliament without Scotland's consent.

» Moreover rather than the freedom resulting in positive outcomes, some people criticise the Scottish Government for not managing Scotland's drug crisis effectively. Scotland continues to have the highest drug death rate in Europe, and a significant portion of drug-related deaths involves opioids.

✅ **Devolution has brought economic benefits to some regions by enabling more targeted regional economic strategies.**

» Local governments can direct investment and resources into areas such as infrastructure, industry and regional development that benefit their specific areas.

❌ **Despite the promise of devolution bringing economic benefits to regions, critics argue that it has not succeeded in addressing regional inequalities within the UK.**

» Both Wales and Northern Ireland continue to struggle with higher poverty rates and lower economic growth compared to the rest of the UK. Devolution has not provided the tools or financial autonomy necessary to tackle these deep-rooted issues effectively.

✅ **Devolution has been credited with bringing stability and peace to some regions, particularly Northern Ireland, which had endured years of violent conflict before the Good Friday Agreement and the subsequent creation of the Northern Ireland Assembly – a huge achievement.**

» The Northern Ireland Assembly has played a crucial role in fostering political cooperation between unionists and nationalists. Though the Assembly has faced challenges, it has allowed for power sharing and peace building, preventing a return to the kind of violent sectarian conflict that dominated the twentieth century.

» Devolution has achieved the unthinkable: republicans and unionists working together to secure a peaceful long-term environment in Northern Ireland.

❌ **However, the Northern Ireland Government has been suspended and the province ruled from Westminster many times.**

» Irreconcilable disagreement between the two sides has led to many years of direct rule from Westminster since 1998.

» Devolution has also been linked to increased political polarisation in Scotland. While the 2014 Referendum resulted in a "no" vote it sparked a renewed and more radical debate on Scottish independence, which remains a significant political issue.

✅ **Metro Mayors have led to greater regional identity in England.**

» Metro Mayors oversee approximately 48 million people in England.

» They provide a visible, directly elected leader for their regions, offering a clear point of accountability for local issues.

» They are able to make strategic decisions across whole city regions.

❌ **Interest in Metro Mayors is low and they have limited powers.**

» The average turnout for Metro Mayors in 2024 was approximately 30%, down from 35% in 2021.

> » Metro Mayors may have a high profile but they have limited powers and budgets.

> » Metro Mayors can lead to conflict with Westminster.

✅ **Welsh interest in devolution has increased since the very narrow referendum vote, as has the demand for greater powers for their Parliament.**

> » Despite only around 25% of eligible voters voting in favour of setting up a Welsh Assembly in 1997, the Welsh Assembly has been a great success, and the Welsh people have voted for greater powers. As a result, it is now called the Welsh Parliament, to reflect its powers.

❌ **England has been short-changed in terms of devolution.**

> » Despite the fact that 83% of the population of the UK lives in England, there is no English assembly, just Metropolitan Mayors, and a Mayor for London.

> » EVEL, introduced, in part, to resolve the West Lothian Question, was too complicated and an unsatisfactory solution, which was abolished in 2020.

Key Debate Summary: Has devolution been a success?

For	Theme	Against
✓ Devolution has brought democracy closer to the people.	Has devolution created democratic uncertainty?	✗ Recent breaches of the Sewel Convention have undermined democracy.
✓ Devolved institutions have increased participation and representation.	How effectively has devolution enhanced representation?	✗ The differing powers of the different institutions is confusing.
✓ Devolution has given the component nations of the UK enormous freedom to experiment with policy to best serve their nation.	Has devolution undermined the United Kingdom?	✗ This freedom has only reinforced the desire for self-rule.
✓ Devolution has brought economic benefits to some regions.	How effectively has devolution addressed regional inequality?	✗ Devolution has not succeeded in addressing regional inequalities within the UK.
✓ Devolution has created stability and peace to some regions.	Has devolution been good for Northern Ireland?	✗ The Northern Ireland Government has been suspended many times, and Scotland is very divided.
✓ Metro Mayors have led to greater regional identity in England.	Have Metro Mayors enhanced the governance of England?	✗ Interest in Metro Mayors is low and they have limited powers.
✓ Welsh interest in devolution has increased.	Is the West Lothian Question still a problem?	✗ England has been short-changed in terms of devolution.

Exam Style Questions

- Evaluate the view that the UK constitution is no longer fit for purpose (30).
- Evaluate the view that the UK constitution should now be codified (30).
- Evaluate the view that reforms to the UK's constitution have not gone far enough (30).
- Evaluate the view that the House of Lords should be reformed (30).
- Evaluate the view that devolution across all four nations of the UK has been a success (30).
- Evaluate the view that Devolution has been divisive in the UK (30).
- Evaluate the view that devolution has undermined the unitary status of the UK (30).

Source Question

One of the chief strengths of the UK constitution is that it is flexible and easy to change, as it is easier and quicker to introduce an Act of Parliament than to amend, for example, the US Constitution. For example, the UK's constitution has evolved over time to become highly effective at rights protection: rights in the UK are protected by the Human Rights Act, the Supreme Court and judicial review. Moreover, in the UK's uncodified constitution, supreme constitutional authority rests in the elected House of Commons, and ultimately the people who elect them, whereas with codified constitutions, decisions are made by unelected judges. Supporters of the UK constitution often argue that the UK Government is able to take strong and decisive action. If these laws turn out to be ineffective they can be amended or even abolished.

However, critics of the UK constitution point out that being flexible is not a positive trait in a constitution. Constitutions need to be clear and relatively rigid as their job is to tell governments what they can and can't do. And while it might be the case that currently the UK has effective rights protection – although critics would suggest it does not – the organic nature of the UK's constitution means there is nothing that forces the government to respect individual freedom and basic rights, apart from the fear of not being re-elected. Parliament is sovereign, the Supreme Court secondary. One of the key roles of a constitution is to check government power, but the UK constitution lacks the ability to force Parliament to uphold its obligations, and governments in the UK are often elected with large overall majorities in Parliament which allows them to exercise a great deal of power.

Using the source, evaluate the view that the UK constitution is no longer fit for purpose (30).

In your response you must:

- *Compare and contrast different opinions in the source*
- *Examine and debate these views in a balanced way*
- *Analyse and evaluate **only** the information presented in the source.*

 # Chapter Summary

» The role of a constitution is to organise a political system and keep all players in check.

» The UK's constitution is uncodified and made up of a number of sources which work together.

» There is a debate as to whether the UK constitution works effectively.

» Since 1997 there has been a plethora of constitutional changes which have transformed the UK's political system, some more than others.

» Devolution has had a transformative effect on almost all parts of the UK.

 # Further Resources

Barnett, H. (2002) *Britain Unwrapped: Government and Constitution Explained* (London: Penguin).

Bogdanor, V. (2011) *The Coalition and the Constitution* (Oxford: Hart Publishing).

Brazier, R. (2008) *Constitutional Reform: Reshaping the British Political System* (Oxford: Oxford University Press).

Griffiths, S. and Leach, R. (2018) *British Politics* (3rd edn) (London: Bloomsbury Academic): Chapters 5 and 11.

Heffernan, R., Hay, C., Russell, M. and Cowley, P. (2016) *Developments in British Politics* (10th edn) (London: Bloomsbury Academic): Chapters 1 and 13.

King, A. (2001) *Does the United Kingdom Still Have a Constitution?* (London: Sweet & Maxwell).

Moran, M. (2015) *Politics and Governance in the UK* (3rd edn) (London: Bloomsbury Academic): Chapters 3, 8, and 9.

Institute for Government paper on 'How the government can extend devolution to the whole of England' (2024) https://www.instituteforgovernment.org.uk/publication/completing-devolution-map-england

Institute for Government landing page for Devolution https://www.instituteforgovernment.org.uk/our-work/topics/devolution

Institute for Government explainer on Metro Mayors (2025) https://www.instituteforgovernment.org.uk/explainer/metro-mayors-devolution

Institute for Government explainer on the Welsh Parliament (2021) https://www.instituteforgovernment.org.uk/explainer/senedd-cymru-welsh-parliament

Institute for Government explainer of the Sewel Convention (2024) https://www.instituteforgovernment.org.uk/publication/sewel-convention-case-studies

Visit the companion website to access the Further Resources Booklet to explore a range of useful web links related to: The Good Friday Agreement, 10 things we found out when the Freedom of Information Act was introduced, further insight into devolution in the UK.

8 PARLIAMENT

Chapter Preview

Parliament is considered to be the 'debating chamber of the nation', but Parliament is much more than a place where people talk. Parliament is the UK's supreme law-making body, and it is the key institution within its 'parliamentary' system of government. This means that the government does not operate separately from Parliament, but rather it governs *in* and *through* Parliament.

Yet, the decline of Parliament has been a recurrent theme in the UK, dating back to the nineteenth century. Parliament, it seems, has lost power to many bodies – parties, the executive, lobbyists and pressure groups, the mass media, and so on. For some, Parliament has simply become an irrelevance, a sideshow to the real business of running the country. But this image is an unbalanced one. Parliament does make a difference, but a key question is: does it make *enough* difference? Although Parliament has changed significantly in recent years, there is continued and growing pressure for more radical change.

Key Questions and Debates

» What is Parliament and how is it different from government?

» How is the House of Lords different from the House of Commons?

» What are the main functions of Parliament?

» How does Parliament scrutinise the executive?

» Which is more effective: the Commons or the Lords?

Specification Checklist

2.1 The structure and role of the House of Commons and House of Lords

» The selection of members of the House of Commons and House of Lords, including the different types of peers

» The main functions of the House of Commons and House of Lords and the extent to which these functions are fulfilled

2.2 The comparative powers of the House of Commons and House of Lords

» The exclusive powers of the House of Commons

» The main powers of the House of Lords

» Debates about the relative power of the two houses

2.3 The legislative process

» The different stages a bill must go through to become law

» The interaction between the Commons and the Lords during the legislative process, including the Salisbury Convention

2.4 The ways in which Parliament interacts with the executive

» The role and significance of backbenchers in both Houses, including the importance of parliamentary privilege

» The work of select committees

» The role and significance of the opposition

» The purpose and nature of ministerial question time, including Prime Minister's Questions

What is Parliament and how is it different from government?

Although **Parliament** is often treated as a single institution, it is in fact composed of three parts:

» The House of Commons

» The House of Lords

» The Monarchy

In order to fully understand how Parliament works, it is essential to understand the difference between Parliament – the UK's **legislature** – and the government – the UK's **executive**. The function of most legislatures is to consider and pass legislation, hold the government to account and represent the people who elected them. The role of the executive – the UK Government – is to propose laws to Parliament and to run the country. This will be explored in much greater detail in the following chapter. However, the UK system is a parliamentary system which means the legislature and executive are fused together, not separated.

Figure 8.1 The fusion of power in the UK system

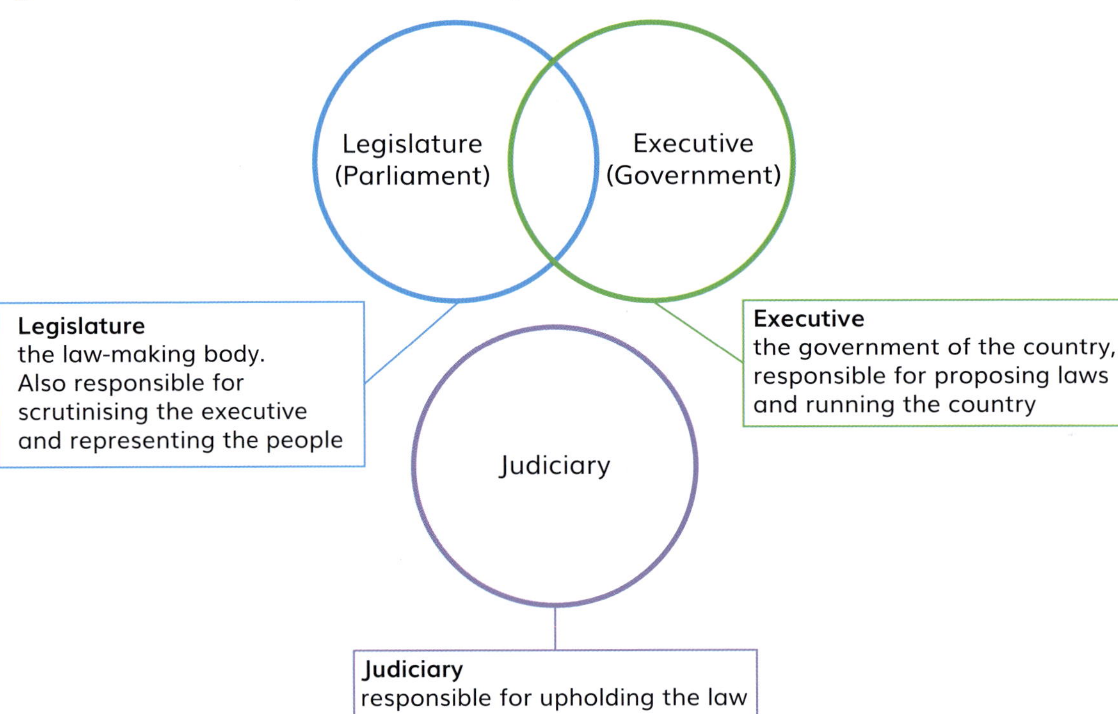

Parliamentary government

A parliamentary system is one in which government governs in and through Parliament. It is based on a **fusion of powers** between the legislative and executive branches of government, which are, therefore, overlapping and interlocking institutions (see Figure 8.1). This goes against the idea of a **separation of powers**.

The chief features of parliamentary government are as follows:

» There is a fusion of powers of the executive and the legislative branches.

» Governments are formed as a result of parliamentary elections, based on the strength of party representation in the **House of Commons**. There are no separate, direct elections for a Prime Minister.

» The personnel of government *must* come from Parliament, typically from the largest party in the Commons.

» The government is responsible to Parliament in that it can only continue to govern if it retains the confidence of the Commons and can be removed through a defeat on a **vote of confidence**. This is also known as **confidence and supply** (supply meaning support for budget, finance and spending legislation).

» Government has a collective 'face' and is based on the principle of Cabinet government (see Chapter 9) rather than personal leadership.

» The Prime Minister is head of the government but not **head of state**; these two roles are strictly separate.

The House of Commons

The composition of the Commons is made up of Members of Parliament (MPs) who need to win an election to take their seat. The composition of the Commons is as follows:

» The Commons consists of 650 MPs. This number is not fixed but only varies when changes are made to constituencies by the Boundary Commission.

» Each MP is elected by a single-member parliamentary constituency using the 'first-past-the-post' voting system (see Chapter 4).

» MPs are almost always representatives of a party and are subject to a system of party discipline.

» Most MPs are **backbenchers** while the minority, who are members of the government or Shadow Cabinet, are categorised as **frontbenchers**.

Photo 8.1 Commons Chamber, Palace of Westminster, London

Source: PA Images / Alamy

Key roles in the House of Commons

The role of MPs

» MPs represent their constituencies and deal with the grievances of individual constituents.

» They are expected to scrutinise the government.

» MPs are also expected to debate legislation and the great issues of the day.

» In general terms, MPs legitimise legislation and represent popular consent.

Definition

Vote of confidence: A motion in the Commons with the wording: 'That this House has no confidence in HM Government'. If the vote is lost, a government may have to step down and if a new government can't be formed, a general election called.

Head of state: The leading representative of a state, who personally embodies the state's power and authority.

Frontbenchers: An MP who holds a ministerial or 'shadow' ministerial post, and who usually sits on the front benches.

Spec Key Term

Confidence and supply: The right to remove the government and to grant or withhold funding. Also used to describe a type of informal coalition agreement where the minority partner agrees to provide this in exchange for policy concessions.

Backbencher: An MP who does not hold a ministerial or 'shadow' ministerial post; so-called because they tend to sit on the back benches.

Figure 8.2 Who's who in the House of Commons?

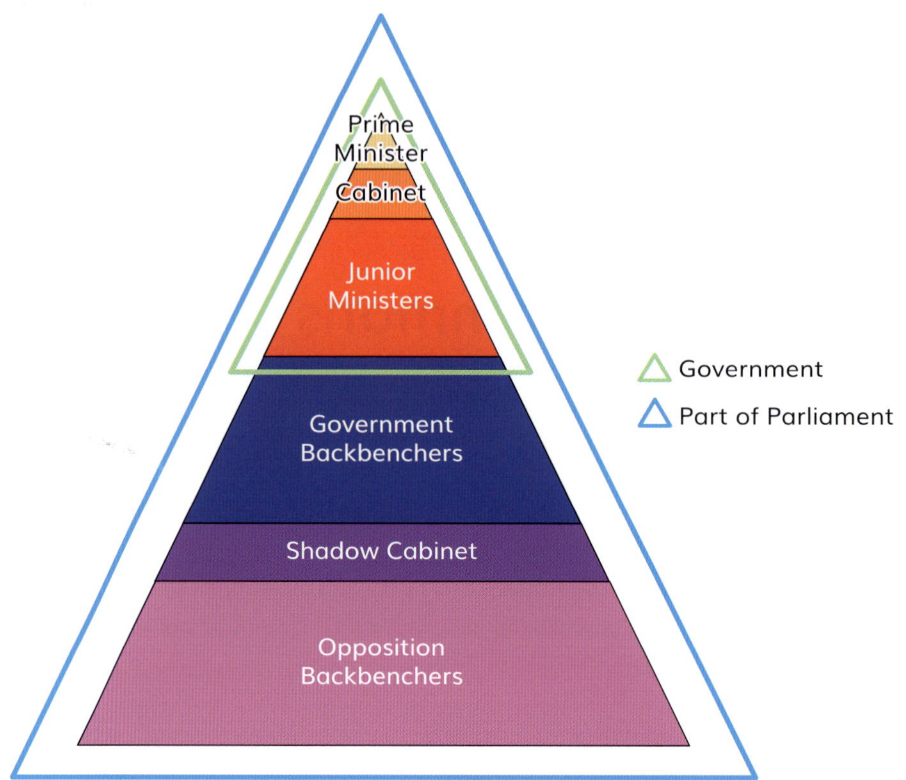

The role of backbenchers

Most MPs are backbenchers, these are MPs who are not:

- » Cabinet ministers
- » Members of the government
- » Members of the Shadow Cabinet.

It is important to distinguish between the slightly differing roles of backbenchers from the governing party and those from the **opposition**. Government backbenchers are not expected to criticise the government too strongly even when the interests of their constituency are an issue. Opposition backbenchers are expected to play a prominent part in opposing the government as well as looking after the interests of their constituency. The main opportunities for backbenchers to represent their constituents in the Commons are as follows:

- » Questioning ministers
- » Participating in debates
- » Voting on legislation
- » Participating in public bill and select committees.

These will all be analysed later in the chapter.

The role of the Official Opposition

The Official Opposition has two main functions:

1. It opposes and criticises the policies of the government.

2. In doing so, it presents itself to the electorate as an alternative government.

Even though the government dominates the Commons, the Official Opposition is an integral part of it. It is organised on broadly similar lines to the government with a Shadow Cabinet and whips. The Official Opposition has certain privileges in Parliament. For instance, the leader of the Official Opposition is called upon every Wednesday to question the Prime Minister and has more questions than anyone else. Official Opposition MPs are on all committees in the Commons and are given 20 days a year to raise issues for debate. In practice, the Official Opposition criticises the government in order to keep it on its toes and to present itself as an alternative to the government. For example, prior to the general election in July 2024, Keir Starmer and the Labour Party worked hard to present themselves as a credible alternative government to the Conservative Party.

The role of the whips

All parties have a group of officials known as whips who are responsible for ensuring that the work of the parliamentary party runs as smoothly as possible.

They have a number of roles, for example:

» They work with their opposition whip to arrange the business of the House and send out memos of business to be considered in the following week.

» They are responsible for '**pairing**' MPs who wish to be absent from the House.

» They ensure that the party leader is aware of the feelings of MPs on issues and legislation going through Parliament and vice versa.

» They have many incentives and sanctions available and can make the life of an MP difficult if they are unwilling to '**toe the party line**'.

» At times of minority and coalition government, the job of whips is considerably harder because power lies with the backbenchers rather than the government. This is because it only takes a small handful of backbenchers to rebel for the government to lose a vote. Whips work hard to ensure that all backbenchers vote with their party.

» Occasionally, an MP or group of MPs may refuse to comply with the whip's instructions, which can result in MPs being disciplined, or the ultimate sanction: the whip is withdrawn (expulsion from the parliamentary party). For example, in July 2024, merely weeks after Labour's election landslide victory, a group of seven Labour MPs rebelled against the government on an amendment to scrap the two-child benefit cap. Prime Minister Keir Starmer suspended the whip for six months, meaning that the seven MPs had to sit as independents. The whip was reinstated eventually for all but one of the seven (Zarah Sultana, who left the party to form Your Party with Jeremy Corbyn).

The role of the Speaker

The Speaker is the chair of the Commons and plays a very important part in its proceedings. The Speaker is an MP and is elected to the role by their fellow MPs. Although they are members of a particular political party, they are expected to act with absolute impartiality once they become Speaker. Normally their constituency is not contested at election time. The Speaker takes no active part in debates in the Commons.

The duties of the Speaker include:

» Calling upon MPs to speak in debates.

» Ensuring that parties receive their fair share of debating time.

» Disciplining MPs when they break the rules and procedures of the House.

» Announcing the results of votes in the House.

» Casting the deciding vote in the event of a tie (convention dictates that this is usually to uphold the government).

Definition

Pairing: An arrangement between two MPs of opposing parties to not vote in a particular division, enabling an MP to be absent without affecting the result of the vote, as they effectively cancel each other out.

Toe the party line: To support and vote with your party even if you disagree with it.

Visit the companion website for a case study on Controversy surrounding recent Speakers from the previous fifth edition.

Photo 8.2 Sir Lindsay Hoyle has been serving as Speaker of the House of Commons since 2019

Source: WPA Pool / Pool / Getty Images

The House of Lords

The composition of the House of Lords is both complex and controversial. It is complex because there are four kinds of peers, or Lords. It is controversial because none of these peers are elected. The current membership stems from the House of Lords Act 1999, which removed most (but not all) of the previously dominant hereditary peers, The House of Lords (Hereditary Peers) Act 2026 which removed the remaining 92 hereditary peers and from the 2005 Constitutional Reform Act (see page 314), which removed the Law Lords from the House of Lords and set up a Supreme Court, which came into existence in 2009.

The House of Lords consists of the following:

» **Life peers**. Life peers are entitled to sit in the Lords for their own lifetimes. The monarch formally appoints life peers on the advice of the Prime Minister, who submits nominations. Party leaders, such as those from Labour, the Conservatives and Liberal Democrats, also recommend candidates. Life peers now dominate the work of the Lords. They account for the overwhelming majority of peers (see Table 8.1).

» **People's peers**. 'People's peers' are life peers appointed to the House of Lords through recommendations made by the House of Lords Appointments Commission. These peers are selected on a non-partisan basis, based on their merit and potential contribution to the House of Lords, although their lack of resemblance to 'ordinary' citizens has been a source of criticism. There are currently 76 'people's peers' in the Lords.

» **Hereditary peers**. These peers held inherited titles which carried the right to sit in the Lords. Prior to 1999 there were over 700 hereditary peers, but since then a maximum of 92 were permitted to sit and were elected by other members of the Lords. Since 2026, hereditary peers have been entirely removed from the Lords.

» **Lords Spiritual**. These are the 26 bishops and archbishops of the Church of England. They are collectively referred to as the 'Lords Spiritual'. They are appointed by the Prime Minister on the basis of recommendations made by the Church of England.

The Monarchy

The role of the monarch is mostly ceremonial and symbolic. As the head of state, the monarch symbolises the authority of the Crown. In Walter Bagehot's formulation, the monarchy is a 'dignified' rather than an 'effective' institution. The monarch is associated with Parliament in several ways:

Photo 8.3 The King appointted Keir Starmer as Prime Minister in July 2025 following the Labour Party's landslide victory

» **Appointing a government**. The monarch 'chooses' the Prime Minister, but in practice, the monarch has little choice over this matter because the leader of the largest party in the Commons is the only person who can command the confidence of Parliament.

» **Opening and dismissing Parliament**. The monarch opens Parliament through the State Opening at the beginning of the parliamentary year. At the request of the Prime Minister, the monarch 'dissolves' Parliament to allow a general election to be held.

» **The King's speech**. This is a speech that is delivered at the beginning of each parliamentary session and informs Parliament of the government's legislative programme. It is written by the Prime Minister's office but delivered by the monarch.

» **Royal Assent**. This is the final stage of the legislative process, when the monarch signs a bill to officially make it an Act. However, this is a mere formality as, by convention, monarchs never refuse Royal Assent.

The comparative powers of the House of Commons and House of Lords

The powers of the House of Commons

The Commons is politically and legally the dominant chamber of Parliament. This applies to such an extent that the Commons is sometimes taken to be synonymous with Parliament itself. However, a distinction should be made between the formal powers of the Commons, enshrined in law and constitutional theory, and its political significance.

The key powers of the House of Commons include:

» *Supreme legislative power*. In theory, the Commons can make, unmake and amend any law it wishes, with the Lords only being able to delay these laws. The legal sovereignty of Parliament is thus exercised in practice by the Commons.

» The power to approve the government's budget and any 'money bills'.

The power to scrutinise government ministers via departmental **select committees** (see page 266) only exist in the Commons. The Lords have select committees but these are not focused on scrutinising government departments.

> **Spec Key Term**
>
> **Select committee:** Committees responsible for scrutinising the work of government departments. There are also other select committees that take on a wider remit.

Table 8.1 The composition of the Commons and the Lords (March 2026)

		House of Commons (2026)	House of Lords (2026)
		650 MPs in total	**750** Lords in total
Social representation		**385** Men	**503** Men
		265 Women	**247** Women
		90 Ethnic minorities	**55** Ethnic minorities*
		75 LGBT	**40***
Party breakdown		**409** Labour	**227** Labour
		121 Conservative	**250** Conservative
		72 Liberal Democrat	**76** Liberal Democrat
		9 SNP	**160** Crossbenchers
		5 Greens	**23** Lords Spiritual
		5 Reform	**14** Others
		7 Sinn Féin	
		5 DUP	
		19 Others	
Type		**650** MPs	**724** Life peers
			23 Lords spiritual

estimated figure as no official figure available

» The power to question government ministers and the Prime Minister. Only the Commons can do this.

» The power to represent the people and be held accountable by them.

» The legitimation of government and its legislation.

» The power to remove the government of the day. A government that is defeated in the Commons on a matter of confidence is obliged to resign and a general election be held.

The powers of the House of Lords

The Lords' legislative powers are set out in the Parliament Acts of 1911 and 1949. The Lords have the following powers:

» The Lords can delay bills passed by the Commons for up to one year.

» The Lords cannot delay **money bills**.

» The **Salisbury Convention** says that the Lords cannot defeat measures that are outlined in the government's election manifesto.

» The Lords are more independent with less loyalty to parties, with just under a quarter being **crossbenchers**. Lords tend to be less loyal because they have either joined as crossbenchers or because they are not seeking party approval.

» The Lords have Question Time and every government department has a Lords spokesperson who must respond to questions.

Photo 8.4 **The House of Lords chamber in session at the Houses of Parliament in London**

Source: WPA Pool / Pool / Getty Images

» Legislative committees in the Lords include peers who are experts in a particular field. For example:

- **Baroness Kennedy of The Shaws**: A leading barrister and human rights advocate, influential in legal and social justice matters.
- **Baroness Kidron**: Film director and advocate for children's digital rights, instrumental in shaping legislation on online safety.
- **Lord Cashman**: Co-founder of Stonewall UK and a champion for LGBTQ+ rights.
- **Lord Etherton**: Former Master of the Rolls (2016–21), providing significant legal expertise to debates on judicial reform.
- **Lord Walton** was a former president of the British Medical Association.
- **Baroness Lawrence** is a campaigner for the awareness and reform of institutionalised **racism.**
- **Baroness Grey-Thompson** is a campaigner for disability sports.

» The Lords have the time and independence to debate important issues at leisure. They also debate controversial ethical issues such as genetic engineering.

» On occasions, the Lords can provide the government with ministers, for example Lord Cameron was in Rishi Sunak's Cabinet as Foreign Secretary.

» The Lords possess some concurrent veto powers that cannot be overridden by the Commons. These can only be used with the consent of both Houses of Parliament. They include:

- The extension of the life of a Parliament (delays to general elections)
- The sacking of senior judges
- The introduction of secondary or delegated legislation.

Definition

Crossbenchers: Members of the Lords who are not affiliated to any party and have no party loyalty.

Synoptic Link

The issue at the heart of the Salisbury Convention is legitimacy: the mandate and democracy which can be linked back to the Component 1 topics of Democracy and Elections.

The legislative process

In order for legislation to pass, it must be approved by both chambers (unless the 1949 Parliament Act is invoked, which would mean a delay of one year). Most of the time, the Lords accepts bills passed by the Commons, maybe sometimes making some minor procedural changes. However, occasionally the interaction between the Commons and the Lords during the legislative process involves a lot of back and forth. This is known as parliamentary 'ping-pong'.

When a **legislative bill** has passed through the third reading in both Houses, it is returned to the House where it started for any amendments made by the second House to be considered. If the

Spec Key Term

Legislative bills: Proposed laws passing through Parliament.

Commons makes amendments to the bill, the Lords must consider them and either agree or disagree to the amendments or make alternative proposals. If the Lords disagree with any amendments by the Commons, or make alternative proposals, then the bill is sent back to the Commons – this is shown in Figure 8.3.

Bills may go back and forth between the Houses until they reach agreement; this is known as '**ping-pong**'. When agreement has been reached between the Commons and the Lords, the bill is ready for Royal Assent. Once a bill receives Royal Assent it is an Act of Parliament (the proposals in the bill become law). In exceptional cases, when the two Houses do not reach agreement, the bill falls. If certain conditions are met, the Commons can use the Parliament Acts to pass the bill, without the consent of the Lords, in the following session, after a year's delay.

> **Definition**
>
> **Ping-pong:** The colloquial term for the process by which legislation goes back and forth between the Commons and Lords to find common ground.

Figure 8.3 The stages a legislative bill goes through to become law

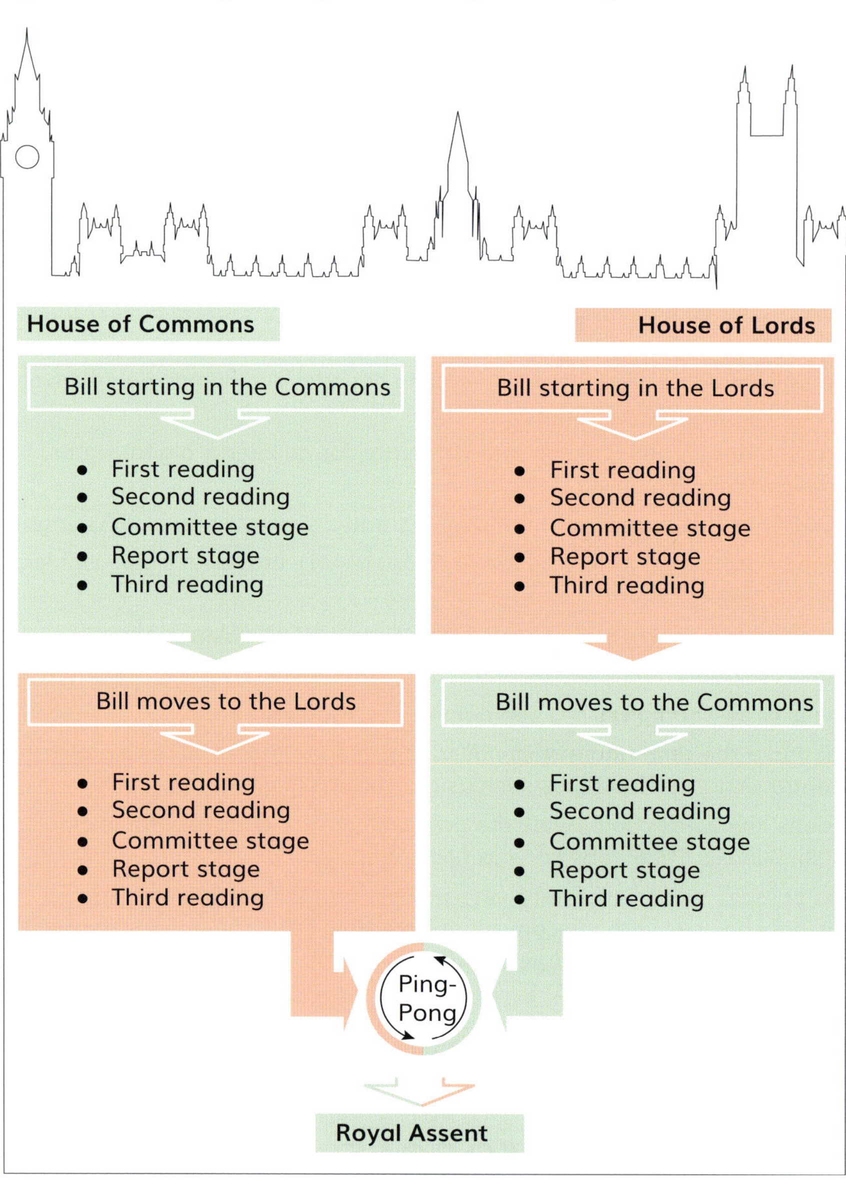

Source: Contains parliamentary information licensed under the Open Parliament Licence v3.0

HOW LAWS ARE PASSED:

➜ **Preparatory stages.** Before bills are passed, their provisions may have been outlined in a White Paper or a Green Paper.

➜ **First reading.** The bill is introduced to Parliament through the formal reading of its title and (usually) the setting of a date for its second reading. There is no debate or vote at this stage.

➜ **Second reading.** This is the first substantive stage. It involves a full debate that considers the principles (rather than the details) of the bill, followed by a vote. It is the first stage at which the bill can be defeated.

➜ **Committee stage.** This is when the details of the bill are considered line by line. It is carried out by a public bill committee (formerly known as a standing committee), consisting of about 18 MPs, but it may be considered by a committee of the whole House. Most amendments are made at this stage, and new provisions can be included.

➜ **Report stage.** This is when the committee reports back to the full House of Commons on any changes made during the committee stage. The Commons may amend or reverse changes at the report stage.

➜ **Third reading.** This replicates the second reading in that it is a debate of the full chamber, enabling the House to take an overview of the bill in its amended state, followed by a vote. No amendments may be made at this stage, and it is very unusual for bills to be defeated at the third reading.

➜ **The 'other place'.** Major bills are considered first by the Commons, but other bills may start in the Lords. Once passed by one chamber, the bill goes through essentially the same process in what is referred to as the 'other place', before finally going to the monarch for Royal Assent.

KEY TOPIC DEBATE: IS PARLIAMENT EFFECTIVE IN FULFILLING ITS FUNCTIONS?

The key functions of Parliament are:

1. Legislation

2. Representation

3. Recruiting and maintaining the government

4. Legitimacy

5. Scrutiny.

1 Legislative function

Parliament is the supreme legislature in the UK in that it can make and unmake any law it wishes, as expressed in the principle of parliamentary sovereignty (see Chapter 10). The role of Parliament is to consider the laws the government wishes to pass and, after debating and scrutinising them thoroughly, it is generally expected to pass them. Parliament is not restricted by a codified constitution, and no other law-making body can challenge Parliament's authority. Devolved parliaments, local authorities and ministers can only make laws because Parliament *allows* them to.

The bulk of Parliament's time is spent considering the government's legislative programme. Party control of the Commons means that government bills are rarely defeated, and most amendments affect the details of legislation, not its major principles. It is more accurate to say that legislation is passed *through* Parliament rather than *by* Parliament. Lastly, the Lords play a subordinate role in the legislative process. It is essentially a 'revising chamber'; most of its time is spent 'cleaning up' bills that were not adequately scrutinised in the Commons.

Only a small number of bills, known as **private members' bills**, are initiated by backbenchers, and these are usually only successful if they have government support. In 2024, Kim Leadbeater proposed a bill to legalise assisted dying in England and Wales. After consideration, this groundbreaking legislation was passed by the House of Commons. However it was thwarted by the Lords and did not pass.

Tip:
Parliament being effective in its legislative function DOESN'T mean passing all the legislation the government would want without scrutiny. In fact, this would mean Parliament was being ineffective in its legislative function.

The effectiveness of Parliament's legislative function

The way to examine Parliament's effectiveness is to see when it has challenged government legislation and when it has allowed a government to pass legislation virtually unchallenged. It is also worth noting that it is not just defeating government bills that matters; the threat of defeating government bills is also important because it can force the government to compromise and introduce amendments to win support from backbenchers.

✓ Effective

1. In early 2026, Labour's 'Hillsborough Law' Bill provoked a major threatened backbench rebellion over a national-security exemption for the intelligence services from the new duty of candour. Around 30–50 Labour MPs signalled they would vote against the government, backed by Hillsborough families, campaigners and metro mayors such as Andy Burnham. Facing near-certain defeat, ministers withdrew their amendment and then pulled the Commons debate entirely, delaying the Bill and forcing a rethink of the exemption. In 2025, The Lords inflicted four consecutive defeats on the government's **Data (Use and Access) Act 2025** over plans to let AI developers access copyrighted material. Peers voted 242–116 against so copyright holders could see when their work was being used. Despite repeated Commons rejections, the Lords refused to back down and the government ultimately passed the bill without the AI provisions.

2. **Welfare Cuts**: In July 2025, Starmer faced his biggest rebellion with over 100 Labour MPs opposing the Universal Credit and Personal Independence Payment Bill 2025. Starmer had been working behind the scenes to convince backbenchers to support the legislation and the day before it was tabled had agreed to make changes to how the bill would be implemented. Despite this, mid second reading, the Work and Pensions Minister, Sir Stephen Timms, announced another climbdown on the floor of the House as it became clear the bill would still not pass. This flagship legislation to deal with the welfare crisis failed because the government failed to read the mood of their backbenchers.

3. **The Planning and Infrastructure Act 2025** saw a notable Labour backbench rebellion in June 2025, when 15 Labour MPs defied the whip to support Chris Hinchliff's amendment imposing environmental obligations on developers. Hinchliff was suspended for repeated rebellions, but the government subsequently U-turned and incorporated his amendments.

4. **In June 2025, the Data (Use and Access) Act** was finally passed after the House of Lords passed significant amendments to this bill against the government's wishes. The government accepted some of the Lords' amendments, specifically around children's data.

5. **Winter Fuel Payments and Child Benefit Cap 2024**: 53 Labour MPs abstained on the government vote to cut Winter Fuel Payments and 40 on keeping the two-child cap on Child Benefit.

6. **Illegal Migration Act 2023**: (see Case Study on page 257). This legislation showed how effective Parliament can be in achieving concessions from a government determined to pass a piece of legislation.

7. In 2023, the government lost a vote in the Commons over a Labour amendment to the **Victims and Prisoners Act** regarding compensation for victims of the NHS infected blood scandal, 246 votes to 242 after 22 Conservatives rebelled. The amendment remained in the Bill as it later became an Act in 2024.

8. **International Aid Budget Reduction**: There is ongoing discontent regarding cuts to the international aid budget to fund increased defence spending.

✗ Ineffective

Usually, however, governments enjoy majority control of the Commons and are rarely defeated. This undermines the effectiveness of Parliament. For example, Blair did not lose a single vote in the Commons for eight whole years – from 1997 to 2005.

1. In 2026 the Lords passed 12 amendments to the National Insurance Contributions Bill seeking to exempt basic rate taxpayers, raise the £2,000 salary sacrifice cap, and protect small and medium-sized businesses, as well as graduates with student loans. The government rejected all 12, quoting their financial privilege over money bills. After a final Lords vote, peers conceded defeat.

2. **Employment Rights Act 2025**: This bill saw extensive debate during committee stages, with over 250 amendments tabled. Opposition MPs raised concerns over worker protections and trade union rights; however, all opposition amendments were rejected, with the biggest change

coming from external pressure when 'day-one' unfair dismissal rights were abolished in favour of a six-month qualifying period, and the bill went on to achieve Royal Assent in December 2025.

3. In April 2025, Parliament passed **the Steel Industry (Special Measures) Act**. Parliament was recalled from its Easter recess for an emergency Saturday sitting and the bill was introduced, debated and passed by the Commons and Lords in under seven hours. Royal Assent was granted the same evening, and the Act came into force immediately. In the Commons, eight amendments were tabled – including proposals for a sunset clause – but there was no time to debate them and none were adopted. The government provided no reasoning for the lack of post-legislative scrutiny or sunset provisions and the speed and manner of passage drew criticism from some peers and MPs, as well as from the Lords Constitution Committee, which later published a report highlighting concerns about the use of fast-track legislation for such significant powers.

4. The **Passenger Railway Services Act 2024** transferred rail services to public ownership. Future rail services must be provided by public sector companies rather than private firms and the transition occurs when current franchise agreements expire. The Act fulfilled the government's manifesto commitment to bring the railways back into public ownership, aiming to improve service reliability, accountability and reinvest profits into the network. The legislation was introduced, quickly progressed through the Commons and was passed by a large margin: 351 votes to 84. The Lords made some amendments, but the Commons ultimately disagreed with them and the bill was finalised and became a law in November 2024.

5. **The Public Order Act 2023**: Passed by the Commons but subsequently, the Lords made several key amendments. The Commons upheld an abortion clinic protest provision but rejected other Lords amendments. This led to a process of 'ping-pong', with the Lords ultimately relenting.

6. **Retained EU Law (Revocation and Reform) Act (2023)**: The Lords attempted to make several amendments to this law, particularly concerning parliamentary scrutiny of changes to retained EU law. These amendments were later overturned by the Commons, showing the power of the elected Commons.

7. **Public Authorities (Fraud, Error and Recovery) Act 2025**: which expands government powers to investigate and recover public sector fraud, faced criticism and the SNP tabled an amendment urging Parliament to reject the bill at its second reading, highlighting concerns over expanded investigatory powers and potential overreach in debt recovery measures;, however, the bill was passed by Parliament with no further amendments.

8. **Economic Crime and Corporate Transparency Act 2025**: The Lords inflicted six defeats on this bill, including amendments to limit investigatory powers and enhance safeguards; however, the Commons overturned all amendments, reinstating the government's original provisions and the Act was passed in 2025.

These examples underscore the dominant position of the Commons, particularly when the government has a majority and therefore a mandate.

CASE STUDY 8.1: THE ILLEGAL MIGRATION ACT AND PARLIAMENTARY LEGISLATIVE SCRUTINY

The passage of the Illegal Migration Act through Parliament in 2023 provides an interesting case study of the legislative process and the interplay between the House of Commons and the House of Lords.

Initial passage and Lords' scrutiny

The bill was introduced in the Commons and passed relatively quickly, with only two days of debate on the floor of the House. This limited time for scrutiny was criticised by MPs and the media. When the bill reached the Lords, it faced significant challenges:

1. The Lords inflicted a record 20 defeats on the government.

2. Peers proposed numerous amendments, including:

- Requirements for safe and legal routes into the UK
- Protections for unaccompanied children
- Safeguards for victims of modern slavery
- Maintaining existing legal detention limits

Parliamentary ping-pong

The amended bill returned to the Commons, where MPs voted against almost all of the changes proposed by the Lords. This led to parliamentary 'ping-pong', where the bill went back and forth between the two houses. The key points of contention included:

- Treatment of unaccompanied children

- Provisions for safe and legal routes

- Modern slavery protections

- Detention limits

Government concessions and final passage

Despite initial resistance, the government made some concessions to address concerns raised in both Houses. These included:

1. Exempting unaccompanied children from the duty to remove until they turn 18

2. Adding legal aid provisions for those receiving removal notices

3. Maintaining some protections for victims of modern slavery

After multiple rounds of amendments and debates, both houses eventually agreed on the final text of the bill. It received Royal Assent on 20 July 2023, becoming the Illegal Migration Act 2023.

Conclusion

The passage of this Act demonstrates the important role of the Lords in scrutinising and amending legislation, even when faced with a government determined to pass its agenda. It also highlights the process of negotiation and compromise that can occur during the legislative process, as the government made some concessions to secure the bill's passage.

2 Representative function

Representation of the people is one of the essential functions of Parliament. It is a key role of MPs to represent their constituency, individual constituents and various causes or campaigns. MPs occasionally use **parliamentary privilege** to represent issues which they feel are not being addressed sufficiently in other ways. In 2025, Louise Haigh and the Liberal Democrat MP Layla Moran both gave detailed examples of how ITN used non-disclosure agreements (NDAs) to cover up cases of harassment in the workplace to support their case. They were promoting an amendment that would ban the use of NDAs that prevents workers revealing harassment they endured.

The idea of representation in Parliament can be understood in three ways:

1. Is Parliament democratically representative?

Based on the notion of legitimacy, this concept of representation focuses on whether those in the legislature can claim a genuine mandate from the people.

✅ **Each MP in the Commons is elected in a free and fair election** and they also represent an area in the UK as they are elected by a geographical constituency. They clearly have legitimacy.

✅ **MPs raise the grievances of their constituents.** It is important that the people have a means by which their dissatisfaction with government can be expressed peacefully and democratically.

❌ **The first-past-the-post electoral system undermines the effectiveness of representation in the Commons** by distorting the representation of parties so MPs are often elected by less than half of their constituents. In 2024, only 96 out of 650 MPs received more than 50% of the vote in their constituency (Chapter 4).

❌ **Because the Lords is unelected, it carries out a limited representative role** and weakens the democratic responsiveness of Parliament.

2. Does Parliament reflect the people it represents?

This idea emphasises the importance of a representative body reflecting people's social characteristics and the groups to which they belong, also known as 'descriptive representation'. It is primarily concerned with improving the representation of people in society who have been under-represented – women, ethnic minorities and so on. The social backgrounds of MPs elected in 2024 are shown in Table 8.2. Supporters of descriptive representation believe that this will result in political bodies making better decisions because the views and interests of previously under-represented groups will be effectively represented.

✅ **The 2024 UK General Election resulted in the most diverse Parliament in British history:** 263 women MPs were elected, representing 40% of the House of Commons, a record 90 ethnic minority MPs were elected, accounting for 14% of all MPs and 64 openly LGBTQ+ MPs were elected, representing 9.8% of the total MPs.

Table 8.2 The social backgrounds of MPs

- **Social class.** MPs are predominantly middle class. Over four-fifths have a professional or business background, with the main professions being politics (23%), business (22%) and finance (15%). The manual working class is significantly under-represented (10%), even in the Labour Party.

- **Gender.** Women continue to be under-represented in the Commons, but there has been substantial progress since the 1980s, when their numbers stood at only just over 3% of MPs. The 2024 Election saw the largest-ever number of women MPs, at 263 (40% of the total).

- **Ethnicity.** Ethnic minorities remain under-represented. However, 2024 saw the highest number of non-white MPs being elected, at 90, or 14% of the whole, up from 52 in 2017.

- **Age.** MPs are predominantly middle-aged: 58% of them are aged between 40 and 59, with the average age in 2024 being 48 – three years younger than 2019.

- **Education.** MPs are better educated than most UK citizens. Over two-thirds are graduates with 20% being Oxbridge-educated and a further 34% went to an elite Russell Group university. The proportion of MPs who attended fee-paying schools is at an all-time low of 24%, down from 50% in 1979.

- **Sexuality.** There are 64 LGBTQ+ MPs (10%), which is higher than the official statistics in the UK (around 4%).

❌ **White, middle-class men still dominate Parliament with 387 out of 650 MPs being men.** Former Labour MP, Laura Pidcock, was elected as the MP for North West Durham in 2017. In her maiden speech she announced that 'the place reeks of the establishment and of power'. She also argued: 'The clothes, the language and the obsession with hierarchies, control and domination are symbolic of the system at large.'

❌ **Only approximately 6% of the Lords come from a minority ethnic background.**

3. Whom should MPs represent?

There are three different theories of representation when it comes to British MPs:

a) **The trustee model of representation**. MPs decide what they think is best for constituents, and constituents trust them to do so. An MP acts on *behalf* of others, using their supposedly superior knowledge, better education or greater experience. It is often referred to as 'Burkean representation', as its classic expression is found in the speech that the Conservative philosopher and historian Edmund Burke (1729–97) gave to the electors of Bristol in 1774. He declared: 'Your representative owes you, not his industry alone, but his judgement; and he betrays, instead of serving you, if he sacrifices it to your opinion.' This view prevailed in the UK until the 1950s.

b) **The delegate model of representation**. MPs are essentially the 'messenger' of their constituents. In this sense, they act as a **delegate** conveying the views of others, without expressing their own views or opinions. Historically, the concept of delegation has rarely been applied to MPs, however social media has had a dramatic effect on this with MPs coming under huge pressure in recent years with organised campaigns to encourage them to vote a certain way.

c) **The doctrine of the mandate**. In winning an election, a party gains a mandate to carry out the policies contained in its manifesto. This doctrine implies that it is political parties, not individual MPs, that fulfil Parliament's representative function. Such thinking provides a clear justification for party unity and party discipline. This is the most influential theory of representation in modern UK politics, although it is being challenged by the delegate model due to social media.

In UK politics, we can see evidence of these different theories:

» General elections in the UK tend to be focused on parties. Voters often don't know the name of candidates, voting instead for the party they prefer. This gives credence to the idea of the doctrine of the mandate theory.

Definition

Delegate: A person who is chosen to act for another on the basis of clear guidance or instructions; delegates do not think for themselves.

Synoptic Link

The Representative function of Parliament section links to the Democracy topic, the Parties topic and the Elections topic.

» Social media has been an effective way for constituents to express their concerns directly to their MP. They can contact MPs on X, encouraging them to act as delegates. This occurred with the war in Gaza when social media campaigns led to many MPs reconsidering their vote for a ceasefire. Jess Phillips, who resigned her position as a shadow junior minister, is on record as saying that she would have lost her seat in 2024 if she had voted with her party.

» Under the 2010–15 Coalition, Conservative and Liberal Democrat MPs supported policies that weren't in their manifesto or went against their manifesto. This went against the doctrine of the mandate.

» Free votes on issues allow MPs to have more ability to listen to the views of constituents or their conscience, supporting the trustee model. In 2025, MPs were given a free vote on the difficult moral issue of assisted dying.

» The introduction of the Backbench Business Committee in 2010 helped MPs to raise local concerns. The Committee meets weekly on Tuesdays to hear from backbench MPs who would like to put forward a particular issue for debate in the Commons.

Visit the companion website for a case study on Brexit and representation from the previous fifth edition

3 The function of recruiting and maintaining the government

In the UK, all ministers from the Prime Minister downwards must be either MPs or peers. Before they become frontbenchers, they learn the job on the back benches. In addition, a key but often insufficiently explained function of the Commons is the maintenance of the government. This means that governments can only continue with the support of Parliament.

✅ **By participating in debates, asking parliamentary questions and sitting on committees, ministers of the future learn their trade.**

» They gain an understanding of how government works and how policy is developed. Thatcher, Major, Brown, May, Johnson, Truss and Sunak all started on the back benches and held important government jobs before becoming Prime Minister.

» By needing to maintain the support of Parliament, governments must listen to their backbench MPs.

» Ultimately, the government must maintain the support of the Commons, otherwise it risks losing a vote of confidence. For example, in 1979, the Labour Government led by James Callaghan lost a vote of confidence on the floor of the Commons and was forced to call a general election, which they went on to lose. This was the last time this happened.

❌ **Ministers are recruited from a limited pool of talent: mainly the MPs of the largest party in the Commons.** Because MPs are entering the Commons at a younger age than in the last century, fewer ministers have experience of careers outside of politics.

» Parliamentarians may acquire speech-making skills and learn how to deliver sound bites, but they do not gain the management skills to run a government department.

» While it is true that governments need the support of their backbenchers, the reality is that governments with large majorities are usually able to dictate to their MPs rather than listen to them.

» While it has a majority in the Commons, the government is extremely unlikely to lose a vote of confidence. Theresa May faced a confidence vote the day after she lost her Brexit Withdrawal Agreement vote by 432 votes to 202 in 2019, yet she won the confidence vote by 325 to 306.

4 Legitimacy function

Another function of Parliament is to promote legitimacy. Governments must govern *through* Parliament and in doing so, their actions are more likely to be seen as 'rightful' and therefore more likely to be accepted as legitimate.

✅ **Parliament is essentially a representative assembly for the public. When it approves a measure, it is as if the public has approved it.**
  » Parliament gives the consent of the people to laws that they are expected to obey. Without this consent, laws would lack authority.
  » Parliament is legally sovereign so all laws that have been passed by Parliament have full legal authority.

❌ **Being unelected, the Lords has no democratic legitimacy.**
  » Prime Ministers, especially those with large majorities, use Parliament as a 'rubber-stamp' for their legislation, not allowing sufficient time or encouraging Parliament to scrutinise legislation sufficiently.
  » Respect for Parliament has been undermined by scandals like 'Partygate' and the scandal surrounding Owen Paterson, who was found to have broken paid advocacy rules with the government initially tried to block his suspension, causing public outcry.

Key Debate Summary: Is Parliament effective in fulfilling its functions?

For analysis of the scrutiny function, see page 262.

For	Theme	Against
✓ Parliament is effective in carrying out its legislative function. Since 2010 especially, Parliament has pushed governments to make changes to legislation.	How effective is Parliament in carrying out its legislative function?	✗ Parliament is only effective in encouraging governments to rethink legislation when governments have small (or no) majorities.
✓ The Lords are also effective at getting governments to rethink because it is more independent than the Commons.	How effective is Parliament in carrying out its legislative function?	✗ The Lords are not able to veto legislation, only delay.
✓ The 2019 Parliament was the most diverse ever.	How effective is Parliament in carrying out its representative function?	✗ Even though it was the most diverse, Parliament still remains seriously unrepresentative.
✓ All MPs represent a part of the UK and are answerable to their constituents.	How effective is Parliament in carrying out its representative function?	✗ Most MPs are not elected by 50% of their constituents, undermining their representative nature.
✓ The Commons are effective at maintaining the government as long it has the support of the chamber.	How effective is Parliament in recruiting and upholding the government?	✗ Partisanship takes priority in the Commons. Only one government has lost a vote of confidence. Parties prefer to change their leader mid-term rather than face a general election.
✓ Legitimising the work of the government is one of Parliament's main constitutional purposes.	How effective is Parliament in carrying out its legitimisation function?	✗ The legitimacy of Parliament is undermined by the role the Lords play in legislation.

KEY TOPIC DEBATE: IS PARLIAMENT EFFECTIVE IN SCRUTINISING THE EXECUTIVE?

Definition

Scrutiny: Examining something in a close or detailed way.

Spec Key Term

Elective dictatorship: A government that dominates Parliament, usually due to a large majority, and therefore has few limits on its power.

Parliament does not govern; its role is to check the government. Therefore, many argue that Parliament's most important function is to 'hold the government to account', which enables ministers to explain their actions and justify their policies. It does this through its **scrutiny function**.

Scrutiny involves Parliament checking how government is operating and whether it's acting in the public interest. Government must present all decisions and policies to Parliament. Government ministers have considerable power; therefore, Parliament scrutinises the use of this power in an attempt to prevent '**elective dictatorship**'.

The term 'elective dictatorship' is a phrase popularised by Lord Hailsham in 1976. His main concern was that 'the sovereignty of Parliament has become the sovereignty of the Commons, and the sovereignty of the Commons has increasingly become the sovereignty of the government.' He argued that in a parliamentary system, the legislature can be dominated by the executive and, due to the strength of the whip system, government bills are rarely defeated in the Commons. This was especially true under the Thatcher and Blair Governments which both enjoyed very large majorities, and both Prime Ministers were accused of running elective dictatorships. Although Starmer also has a three-figure majority, unlike his predecessors, he has not been able to ignore his backbenchers.

There are several ways that Parliament can scrutinise the executive.

Questioning

Prime Minister's and Ministers' Questions

Prime Minister's Questions (PMQs) is a weekly event held in the Commons where MPs can question the Prime Minister on government policies and current political issues. It is probably the best-known form of scrutiny in the Commons and takes place each Wednesday at noon and lasts for approximately half an hour. Traditionally, PMQs are dominated by clashes between the Prime Minister and the Leader of the Opposition, who can ask a number of supplementary questions (currently six). PMQs is broadcast live on TV. Ministers' Question Time means that Cabinet (and other) Ministers answer questions from MPs live in the chamber (each department features in a four-week daily cycle Monday–Thursday).

While PMQs has its critics, the benefits highlight its role in maintaining parliamentary accountability and fostering democratic debate:

✓ PMQs provides a weekly opportunity to question the Prime Minister on current affairs, serving as a 'routine check-up' that keeps the PM accountable.

✓ The open questioning style requires the Prime Minister to be well informed on various topics across government departments, enhancing accountability. In July 2025, Badenoch used PMQs to target Starmer's welfare U-turns. Hours after Starmer's government performed an 11th-hour U-turn on welfare cuts following a massive Labour backbench rebellion, Badenoch criticised him by accusing him of abandoning the most vulnerable, arguing he was "out of his depth and out of time."

✓ PMQs places the Prime Minister in the spotlight, making them personally accountable for government actions. For example, it was in response to a question about reports of parties in No 10 when Boris Johnson repeatedly denied strict lockdown rules were breached. 'All guidance was followed completely in No 10,' he told the Commons. This led to investigations by the Privileges Committee which concluded that he had deliberately misled Parliament and faced a 90-day suspension and a recall petition. This led to him stepping down as an MP, having already resigned as Prime Minister.

✓ The format allows both the Leader of the Opposition and backbench MPs to ask questions, providing broad participation in the Commons. At his first ever PMQs as opposition leader, David Cameron quipped to Prime Minister Blair, 'He was the future once.'

✓ The tradition of PMQs contributes to a political culture where it is normal and acceptable to criticise the government openly.

 ✓ PMQs allows for timely questioning on current events. In February 2026 at PMQs, Kemi Badenoch pressed Keir Starmer on whether he knew of Peter Mandelson's ongoing friendship with Jeffrey Epstein before appointing him as US Ambassador. Starmer was pressed to admit that he knew and the revelation severely damaged Starmer with calls for his resignation and huge reputational damage. This showed how PMQs can be highly effective at holding a Prime Minister to account.

 ✓ PMQs serves as a public test of leadership skills for both the Prime Minister and the Leader of the Opposition. Many opposition leaders have been highly effective at this, making a name for themselves and raising their visibility with the electorate.

The main criticisms of PMQs include:

 ✗ PMQs is often criticised for being too aggressive and noisy with MPs engaging in the worst of playground bullying behaviour to intimidate or humiliate. Around 47% of respondents in a Hansard survey, Tuned In or Turned Off, agreed that PMQs 'is too noisy and aggressive'. This can be intimidating for backbenchers, especially those less comfortable with the theatrical nature of the proceedings.

 ✗ Many MPs ask planted questions, designed to allow the Prime Minister to score party political points and reel out statistics about how the government's policies are benefitting their country. 67% of respondents agreed that 'there is too much party political point-scoring instead of answering the question' in the Hansard survey. Backbenchers are expected to support their party, which can constrain their ability to ask challenging questions or raise controversial issues.

 ✗ PMQs is often criticised for being excessively theatrical and scripted, prioritising style over substance. In the Hansard survey, Only 16% agreed that 'MPs behave professionally' at PMQs, while 48% disagreed. It is coordinated by Downing Street, where pre-prepared questions are given to backbenchers, allowing the Prime Minister to reel off statements boasting about the government's record. This wastes valuable scrutiny time.

 ✗ The format makes it easy for the Prime Minister to avoid detailed, forensic questioning. It doesn't allow backbenchers to ask follow-up questions, limiting their ability to engage in detailed, forensic questioning of the Prime Minister. In March 2026 Starmer did not answer a single question asked of him about whether he spoke to Peter Mandelson at all before appointing him as US Ambassador. so it is therefore an inadequate form of scrutiny.

 ✗ While backbenchers can use PMQs to draw attention to issues, this doesn't necessarily lead to action being taken on their concerns.

However, PMQs add to the representative nature of backbenchers by allowing them to raise constituency issues. These examples show that constituency issues are an integral part of PMQs, allowing MPs to bring local matters to national attention. In March 2026, MPs used this platform to raise local concerns:

1. Dr Andrew Murrison, MP for South West Wiltshire, used PMQs to warn that eight fire stations and 96 retained firefighters across Wiltshire and Dorset faced closure due to grant cuts and overoptimistic Treasury council tax assumptions. He asked Starmer to facilitate an urgent ministerial meeting for local MPs to discuss extending the fire precept. Starmer agreed a meeting would be arranged.

2. Brian Mathew, MP for Melksham and Devizes, raised concerns at PMQs about cuts to services at Melksham Community Hospital in his constituency, then followed up by writing to the Prime Minister demanding better provision. He used the PMQs exchange to pressure the government publicly, posting afterwards on social media to raise awareness.

Urgent questions

If an urgent matter arises, MPs may apply to ask an urgent question. If the Speaker is satisfied that the question is urgent, the request is granted, and the relevant government minister must come to the chamber to explain what the government is doing. As shown by Figure 8.4, there has been an increase in the number of urgent questions in the past decade. According to the Institute for Government, urgent questions have provided far more frequent opportunities for backbenchers to raise matters of importance and receive a timely response. The greater willingness of the former Speaker Bercow to grant urgent questions, as well as the Brexit debate between 2017 and 2019 are likely to have been the most significant drivers of the increase.

Figure 8.4 Number of urgent questions asked by session

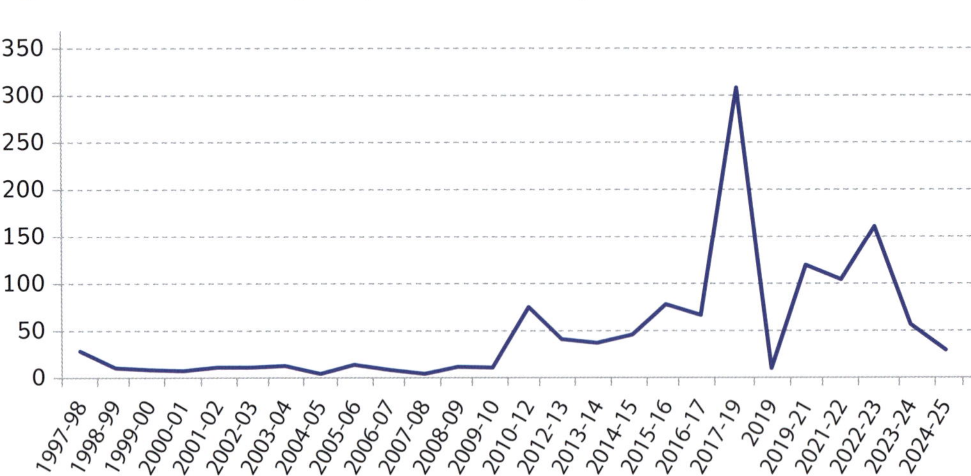

Source: Contains parliamentary information licensed under the Open Parliament Licence v3.0

Written questions and letters. Much information is provided to MPs and peers in answers to written questions, and ministers must respond to letters they receive from MPs and peers.

Humble address. This archaic procedure has been used to table motions and, among other things, to call for papers from departments. The motion can be debated, amended and voted on. Humble addresses are considered to be binding on the Commons.

» In February 2026 the Conservatives forced a humble address, compelling the government to release all documents on Mandelson's Epstein-linked ambassador appointment. This triggered disclosure of WhatsApp messages between Mandelson, Starmer's aides, and ministers – including Wes Streeting's 14-month chat history – revealing internal warnings were ignored before the appointment.

» In March 2022, Labour tabled a humble address motion requesting the release of documents related to Lord Lebedev's appointment. The motion passed requiring the government to disclose the requested documents. The government responded to the humble address by only releasing limited information citing national security concerns. Labour accused the government of a 'cover-up'. This highlighted the tension between parliamentary scrutiny and government claims of national security.

» In 2021 Labour used the procedure to compel the government to disclose documents related to Covid-19 testing contracts awarded to Randox.

Public Bill Committees

Public Bill Committees (PBC) are temporary committees formed in the Commons to scrutinise proposed legislation after second reading. They consist of at least 16 MPs, with party representation proportional to their size in the Commons.

Role in the amendment process

1. Public Bill Committees scrutinise a bill clause by clause at the committee stage of a bill.

2. They consider whether amendments should be made, new clauses added, and if existing provisions should remain.

3. Any MP can table amendments to a bill, but only members of the committee can formally move and vote on these amendments.

4. The Chair decides which amendments are debated and voted on.

5. MPs can propose amendments, and the committee debates their merits.

6. After debate, amendments may either be withdrawn or pushed to a vote.

7. If an amendment is agreed upon, it is incorporated into the bill; if rejected, it doesn't proceed.

8. Once all clauses have been considered, the committee reports the bill back to the Commons for further consideration at report stage.

Effectiveness

Public Bill Committees provide a platform for detailed scrutiny and allow MPs to propose targeted changes. However, their effectiveness is often limited by government dominance, as the governing party typically has a majority in committees. This means most opposition amendments are rejected unless they align with government priorities. Despite these limitations, PBCs occasionally influence legislation by highlighting potential flaws or unintended consequences that may lead to government concessions.

✓ Some MPs bring relevant experience to committees, making them twice as likely to table amendments.

✓ PBCs can alert ministers to necessary changes, even if most amendments come from the government.

✓ In some cases, MPs with shared policy interests work constructively across party lines. For example, in the **Tobacco and Vapes Bill 2025**, where amendments on health inequalities passed due to rare cross-party support.

Photo 8.5 A public bill committee at work

Source: PA Images / Alamy

However, Public Bill Committees face significant challenges:

✖ Lack of expertise:
  ○ The temporary nature of PBCs prevents members from building up specialised knowledge or developing strong working relationships across party lines.
  ○ Only about 8% of PBC places are allocated to MPs who sit on the relevant departmental select committees.
  ○ For example, the **Children's Wellbeing and Schools Bill 2025** faced criticism for insufficient input from education specialists, resulting in vague safeguarding provisions.

✖ Government dominance:
  ○ With whips enforcing party discipline, opposition amendments rarely succeed. In 2024–25, only 0.5% of accepted amendments originated from opposition parties.
  ○ For example, in the **Border Security, Asylum and Immigration Act 2025**, proposals to soften deportation rules were voted down along party lines, despite human rights concerns.

✖ Whip-driven appointments:
  ○ The Committee of Selection is dominated by party whips. In 2024–25, this led to committees stacked with loyal backbenchers rather than independent-minded MPs or subject specialists. This can lead to politically partisan debates rather than constructive scrutiny.

- ○ For example, during scrutiny of the **Public Authorities (Fraud, Error and Recovery) Act 2025**, the SNP proposed amendments to protect vulnerable groups, but they were overwhelmingly rejected due to the government's majority.
- ○ Whips punish dissenters by blocking promotions or removing committee positions. In 2024, several Labour MPs were excluded from PBCs after criticising the party's stance on the **Employment Rights Act 2025**.

✗ Time constraints:
- ○ PBCs often have limited time between evidence-taking and line-by-line scrutiny. The busy parliamentary timetable makes it difficult for MPs to attend committee meetings consistently.
- ○ Whips frequently impose time limits (known as a guillotine) on debates to speed up legislation. For the **Terminally Ill Adults (End of Life) Bill 2025**, even though 19 sittings were allowed, key ethical debates were curtailed to meet deadlines. Critics argued that rushed scrutiny led to poorly examined clauses, such as safeguards for vulnerable patients in assisted dying proposals. When the Bill reached the Lords it ran out of time before all the amendments could be considered.

These challenges often result in less effective scrutiny and amendment of legislation compared to more permanent, specialist committees seen in other parliaments.

Select committees

Departmental select committees are cross-party groups of MPs responsible for scrutinising the work of specific government departments. The composition of these committees reflects the party balance in the Commons, with chairs elected by fellow MPs. Typically, a committee has 11 members. Select committee chairs are now paid a significant salary increment and attract a good deal of media attention, as do their reports, and as a result, the role has grown in importance. The support staff for chairs and committee members has also increased. Each select committee shadows the work of a government department and their main functions include:

1. Examining expenditure, administration and policies of government departments and associated public bodies.

2. Conducting inquiries on specific topics within their responsibility. For example, the Environmental Audit Committee scrutinised the government's progress on achieving net-zero carbon emissions by 2050, prompting the Department for Energy Security and Net Zero to accelerate certain initiatives.

3. Gathering written and oral evidence from ministers, civil servants, experts and members of the public, known as the power to send for 'persons, papers and records'.

4. Publishing reports with findings and recommendations.

Effectiveness

Select committees are deliberately composed of MPs from different parties, fostering a more bipartisan approach to scrutiny. The **Wright Reforms** of 2010 made seemingly small changes to how chairs and members of most select committees were chosen. But these small changes had an enormous and positive impact on the way select committees work. Because of the Wright Reforms, the executive no longer controls the membership of most select committees, which means they act more independently and scrutinise departments effectively:

- ✓ Committee members decide on the areas they will investigate, allowing them to set their own agenda independently of government priorities. In December 2025, the Public Accounts Committee (PAC) considered the government's plan for mandatory digital ID cards linked to public services. They reported that the scheme would cost £2.3 billion with "no credible evidence" it would reduce fraud, concluding it was "a solution in search of a problem". The government then abandoned the scheme, with Chancellor Rachel Reeves citing "value for money concerns." PAC Chair Meg Hillier said: "This is exactly what our committee warned against."

- ✓ They can summon witnesses and gather written and oral evidence which enables them to conduct thorough, independent investigations. In February 2026 the Housing, Communities and Local Government Select Committee investigated the Government's planned delay of elections in 30 councils undergoing reorganisation, affecting 4.6 million voters. Their scathing report called the plan "undemocratic" and warned that it may not be legal. The Government U-turned, just days before a Reform UK legal challenge was due in court.

✓ They can be highly effective at reacting quickly to current events. In April 2026, the Foreign Affairs Select Committee called former senior Foreign Office civil servant Sir Olly Robbins, over the appointment of Peter Mandelson as British Ambassador to the US. In it Robbins accused No 10 of a "dismissive" attitude towards vetting and that his department faced "an atmosphere of pressure" over the process to allow Mandelson to start his role in Washington. They also called Morgan McSweeney and Sir Philip Barton.

✓ Select committee reports receive a good deal of publicity, especially when they are critical. Committees have increasingly used platforms like X and Instagram to communicate their work and gather evidence. In March 2026, the PAC found that key bodies like the Environment Agency and Natural Resources Wales were "spread too thin" due to funding cuts. The report warned that without urgent investment, regulators could not deliver the government's own environmental goals. The government then announced a £120 million emergency funding package for environmental regulators and committed to a full spending review by summer, directly accepting the PAC's central recommendation. Committees produce reports and the government is expected to respond within two months. This creates a formal mechanism for holding the government to account.

The impact of select committees on government policy has grown, with analysts like Benton and Russell arguing that they are now 'an integrated part of the policymaking process' and 'taken seriously' by the government. Recent innovations include conducting short, sharp inquiries, holding informal seminars, engaging in joint working between committees, and finding new ways to involve the public in committee work. Committees are most effective when they are strategic, timely or persistent in their enquiries. However, select committees face several limitations in holding the government to account:

✗ While committees can summon witnesses, they lack clear enforcement powers to compel attendance or testimony. In January 2025, the online fashion seller Shein refused to reassure the Business and Trade Committee (chaired by Labour MP Liam Byrne) that its products do not include cotton produced by forced Uyghur labour, prompting MPs to accuse it of 'wilful ignorance'. Charlie Maynard MP said politicians had 'asked very simple questions' and were 'not given straight answers'.

✗ The majority of committee members belong to the governing party, potentially limiting independence. Despite efforts at bipartisanship, political allegiances can still influence committee effectiveness.

✗ Government accepts only around 40% of committee recommendations, according to analysis by Benton and Russell, usually those already aligned with existing policies. In 2026, the Home Affairs Committee considered the government's Earned Settlement immigration proposals (requiring migrants to meet strict conditions before gaining indefinite leave). After 12 oral evidence sessions, the committee heard unanimous expert warnings that the government's "Earned Settlement" proposals would significantly damage public services and communities. However, the government proceeded without publishing an impact assessment, despite National Audit Office criticism.

✗ There have also been concerns about ministers taking select committees seriously. In his book *Walking the Dark Side: Evading Parliamentary Scrutiny* (2021), David Judge documented ministers failing to appear in front of select committees when requested or cancelling after they had agreed to appear.

✗ Ministers have a huge amount of research support whereas committees lack sufficient resources to conduct thorough investigations. They also struggle to examine issues due to time limitations. For example, in February 2025, the Science, Innovation and Technology Committee (chaired by Labour MP Chi Onwurah) summoned directors from Meta, TikTok and X to give evidence on misinformation and harmful algorithms. However, the session left MPs frustrated and Ms Onwurah expressed disappointment, stating that the witnesses failed to provide clear answers on their content moderation policies.

✗ Select committees only work effectively when they operate in a bipartisan manner, with MPs from different sides of the committee endorsing the same report. This is difficult to ensure because, even though whips no longer control membership of committees, they would be aware of all their deliberations.

Key differences between public bill committees and select committees

Feature	Public bill committees (PBCs)	Select committees
Purpose	Scrutinise specific bills after their second reading, focusing on clause-by-clause analysis.	Examine the policies, administration and spending of government departments or broader issues.
Formation	Temporary committees formed for each bill.	Permanent committees established for the duration of a Parliament.
Membership selection	Members are chosen by party whips via the Committee of Selection, often prioritising loyalty over expertise.	Members are elected by MPs (since 2010), increasing independence and credibility.
Independence	Limited, due to government dominance and whip control over membership.	High independence; chairs are elected by MPs and members are chosen by secret ballot.
Scope of work	Focused solely on scrutinising the content of a single bill.	Broad remit to investigate departmental policies, cross-cutting issues or public concerns.
Evidence gathering	Can take written and oral evidence from experts but rarely does so extensively.	Regularly gathers written and oral evidence from ministers, civil servants, experts and the public.
Amendment power	Can propose amendments to bills but rarely succeeds in passing opposition amendments due to government majority.	Does not amend legislation but makes recommendations in reports that the government must respond to.
Transparency	Proceedings are less publicised; debates often follow party lines.	Hearings are televised, reports are widely published, and they attract significant media attention.

Other select committees:

» **Liaison Committee** – The Liaison Committee brings together all chairs of Commons select committees to question the Prime Minister, and is an important aspect of parliamentary scrutiny.

Introduced in 2002, this committee allows for three times a year attendance of the Prime Minister where he is subject to scrutiny by some of the most senior, experienced and expert backbenchers in the Commons. In his book *Prime Ministers in Power*, Mark Bennister argues that the Liaison Committee is ideally suited to conduct scrutiny of the Prime Minister, giving it considerable legitimacy, independence and expertise.

1. In 2024, the committee questioned Rishi Sunak on strategic decision making and future-proofing ministerial decisions. MPs criticised the Whitehall culture and called for urgent reform to improve the quality of strategic thinking.

2. The March 2026 Liaison Committee was a masterclass in damage limitation for Starmer. Coming just weeks after the Mandelson scandal erupted, he successfully managed to dodge all questions on the scandal. He also deflected on the war on Iran with vague claims of inside knowledge. Starmer repeatedly closed down difficult questions by promising answers "at a later date," citing "ongoing reports or inquiries". He also committed to write to MPs with further information allowing him to avoid making any newsworthy commitments on record. This illustrated how Liaison Committee sessions can be managed by a skilled PM to avoid scrutiny rather than enable it, particularly especially when the committee's Labour majority reduces incentive to press hard.

» **Privileges Committee** – The Privileges Committee is a select committee responsible for investigating potential breaches of parliamentary privilege and contempt of Parliament.

1. It consists of seven cross-party backbench members, with a majority of Government MPs reflecting the overall composition of the House, with the chair traditionally drawn from the main opposition party, currently Conservative MP Alberto Costa.

2. The committee can only consider matters referred to it by the Commons as a whole.

3. It has the authority to summon MPs, request documents and appoint legal advisers.

In 2023, the committee investigated Boris Johnson's conduct in the 'Partygate' allegations and whether he misled Parliament about alleged breaches of lockdown rules in Downing Street. In June 2023, the committee published its final report, concluding that Johnson had deliberately misled the House, committing a serious contempt of Parliament, recommending a 90-day suspension for Johnson, and that he should not be entitled to a former Member's security pass. Johnson had already resigned as an MP a few days earlier. This example showcases the Privileges Committee's crucial role in upholding parliamentary standards and holding even the highest-ranking officials accountable for their actions in relation to Parliament.

» **Standards Committee** – As well as the Privileges Committee, there is also the Standards Committee which oversees the MPs' Code of Conduct. Between 2019 and 2024, 16 MPs were suspended from the Commons, some for up to six weeks, and in fact, a further five resigned after facing charges of serious impropriety. The increase probably has to do with 2020 reforms when a new 'independent expert panel' was established to reinforce Parliament's role, dealing with cases of misconduct independently of Parliament. Although this panel can *recommend* the suspension of MPs from the Commons, this can only be *actioned* by a vote of the House. Since the Recall of MPs Act (2015), prolonged suspensions have become a more serious concern for MPs, who may then be recalled and lose their seat.

Figure 8.5 Total suspended MPs from the Commons during each Parliament

Number of MPs suspended during each Parliament

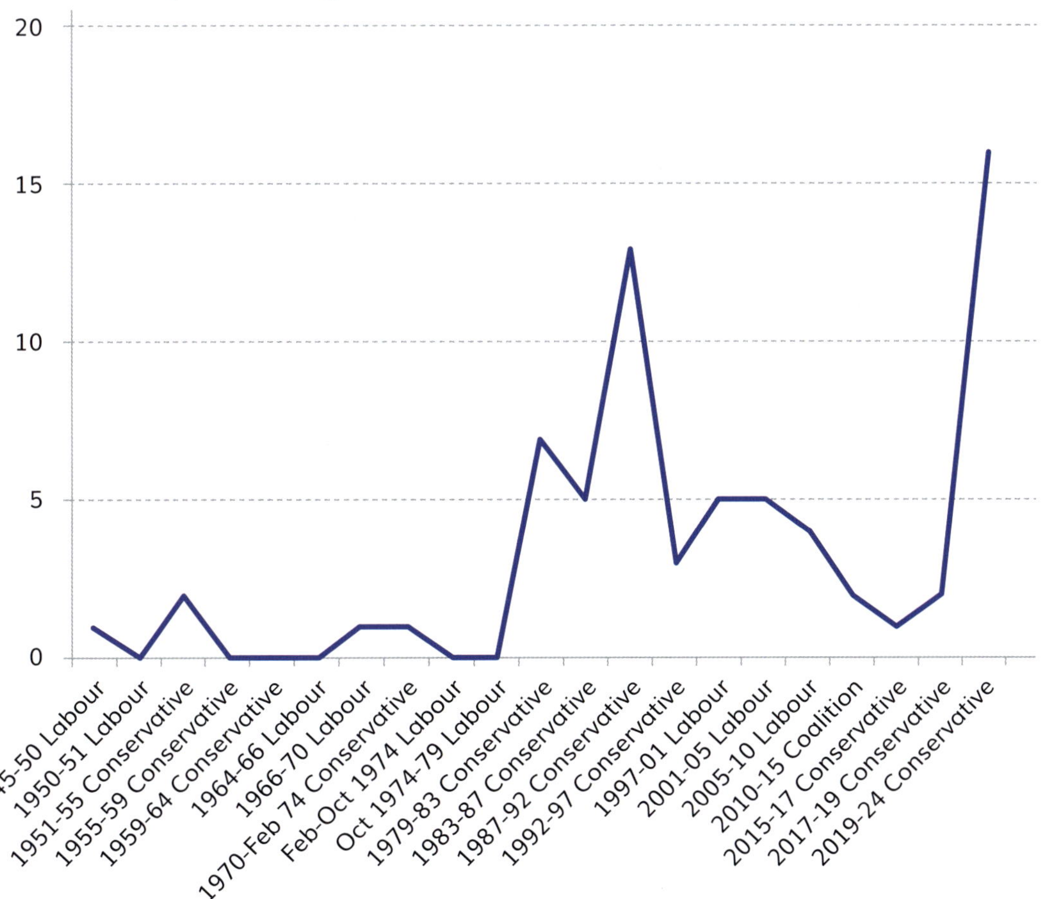

Source: Data from SW Londoner (www.swlondon.co.uk), 'MP suspensions hit record high in current Parliament', William Robinson

» **Public Accounts Committee** – The Public Accounts Committee (PAC) is a select committee responsible for overseeing government expenditures. Key functions include:

1. The PAC examines the value for money of government projects, programmes and delivery.

2. It consists of up to 16 members, with the chair traditionally drawn from the main opposition party, currently Conservative MP Geoffrey Clifton-Brown.

3. The committee looks at how public money has been spent, rather than examining the merits of government policy.

4. The PAC is assisted by the Comptroller and Auditor General and the National Audit Office.

Recently, the Public Accounts Committee has investigated several high-profile cases:

1. In March 2026, the PAC published a report highlighting a "growing financial crisis" for hospices, with many facing closure due to frozen NHS contracts and rising costs. The PAC recommended an emergency funding package as well as a statutory duty on NHS commissioners to fund hospices at sustainable rates. However, the government offered no response and the PAC publicly criticised the government for ignoring the crisis.

2. In March 2025, the PAC published a report highlighting the unprecedented high backlog of 73,105 cases in Crown Courts. The committee criticised the Ministry of Justice for failing to take urgent action to address this issue, which severely impacted victims of crime and their families.

» **Backbench Business Committee (see below)**

Debating

Debates are another way for Parliament to hold the government to account. Most debates in Parliament are to discuss government's proposals for legislation. These Bills are debated carefully in their second reading on the floor of the Commons and the Lords. An MP may also apply to the Speaker for an emergency debate when a matter needs to be discussed urgently. *Adjournment debates* are an opportunity for an individual backbench MP to raise an issue and receive a response from the relevant minister. In the past, one area where it was felt Parliament was lacking was in providing backbenchers more time to debate matters of their own choosing. This was remedied by the Wright Reforms which created the Backbench Business Committee (BbBC).

The Backbench Business Committee is responsible for deciding, on behalf of backbenchers, the business before the House for approximately one day each week. The Committee is allocated 35 days per parliamentary session. Backbenchers can add any debate they wish to a list and the committee chooses which ones to debate. Hence, the BbBC gives backbenchers an opportunity to request debates of their choosing. In addition, any e-petition on Parliament's website which gathers over 100,000 signatures is automatically added to the list for consideration.

Examples of debates held via the BbBC are:

1. In March 2026, a debate on the government response to the Mandelson-Epstein scandal and standards in public life was secured through backbench pressure via the Backbench Business Committee. Cross-party criticism forced Starmer to announce a standards review led by the Committee on Standards in Public Life. It was described as "the most heated backbench-secured debate of the session".

2. In March 2026, the Backbench Business Committee scheduled an e-petition debate on postponing local elections in 30 councils undergoing reorganisation. The petition had gathered 547,000 e-petition signatures in just 10 days. A few days later, the government announced a full reversal, although some credit this to the Reform UK-backed legal case.

3. Close the borders. Suspend ALL immigration for five years: This controversial petition was debated on 10 March 2025, highlighting ongoing discussions about immigration policy in the UK.

4. Don't apply VAT to independent school fees, or remove business rates relief: This petition, which garnered 114,997 signatures, was debated on 3 March 2025. It addressed concerns about potential changes to the tax treatment of independent schools.

5. Introduce 16 as the minimum age for children to have social media: Debated on 24 February 2025, this petition received 129,125 signatures, reflecting growing concerns about the impact of social media on young people.

6. Don't change inheritance tax relief for working farms: This petition, which gathered 152,634 signatures, was debated on 10 February 2025, addressing concerns about potential changes to inheritance tax rules for agricultural properties.

✓ **Since the advent of the Backbench Business Committee, backbenchers in the Commons have had a great deal more time to discuss the key issues of the day.**

» Allow BN(O)s ETA-free entry – Following this petition and debate, the government decided to exempt British National (Overseas) passport holders from requiring an Electronic Travel Authorisation for UK travel, demonstrating a direct policy change.

✓ **The link to e-petitions has given the public a say in what's discussed, creating greater connections between MPs and the public.**

✓ **Emergency debates have been used more often and effectively since 2010.**

» Emergency debates (sometimes referred to as 'Standing Order No 24' debates), provide a way for MPs to propose a debate at short notice on a 'specific and important matter that should have urgent consideration'. If the Speaker believes that the application for an emergency debate has merit, they will allow the MP proposing the debate three minutes to pitch the topic to the House. The Speaker then decides whether to put the application to the House for approval and if the House agrees, the debate will usually be scheduled urgently.

✓ **Prime Ministers have become reluctant to initiate military action without Parliament debating the matter first.**

» In 2014, David Cameron recalled Parliament from its summer recess to debate a motion on using air strikes against ISIS in Iraq. This motion was successful.

» In 2015, Parliament was again given the opportunity to debate the issue of air strikes in Syria. MPs voted to approve air strikes in Syria after a ten-hour debate in the Commons.

✗ **The debates initiated by the Backbench Business Committee are merely motions for discussion; the outcome of MPs' votes does not compel a government to act.**

» The petition on inheritance tax relief for working farms which gathered 152,634 signatures did not result in a change in policy.

✗ **While there is slightly more time for genuine debate, the whips control and curtail the independence of MPs.**

✗ **Prime Ministers are not obliged to consult Parliament before military action.**

» Neither Sunak nor Starmer consulted Parliament in 2024 and 2025 over the UK joining air strikes against the Houthis in Yemen.

The Official Opposition

The second largest party in the Commons is designated as 'Her Majesty's Loyal Opposition'. It is given privileges in debates, at Question Times and in the management of parliamentary business to help it carry out its role of opposing the government of the day. On 'opposition days', opposition parties choose the subject for debate and use these days as opportunities to criticise and embarrass the government.

However, the ability of the opposition to scrutinise the executive is often affected by factors beyond its control, such as the size and unity of the governing party and the length of time the government has been in office. However, oppositions can still influence the popularity and power of a government in certain circumstances.

✓ **The Starmer opposition, specifically between 2022 and 2024,** was very effective in highlighting weakness in the Johnson/Truss/Sunak Government, as well as presenting itself as a credible alternative government-in-waiting.

✓ **The Cameron opposition 2005–10** managed to underline divisions in the final years of the Blair premiership, as well as throughout the Brown one.

✗ **However, a government with a large majority can ignore their opposition,** as Blair did between 1997 and 2005.

✗ **Even if the government has a weak or no majority, a poor opposition leader may not be able to make the most of their position.**

» For example, Kemi Badenoch was criticised for being ineffective when the Starmer Government was in chaos in 2025.

Key Debate Summary: Is Parliament effective in scrutinising the executive?

For	Theme	Against
✓ PMQs and urgent questions are effective ways of scrutinising the executive, albeit in different ways.	How effective is questioning used to scrutinise the government?	✗ PMQs encourages the worst of MPs' behaviour in the Commons.
✓ Public bill committees can now call on the expertise of people outside Parliament as well as the greater expertise of their members.	How effective are public bill committees at scrutinising the government?	✗ Public bill committees are controlled by the whips and are therefore ineffective at challenging the government.
✓ Select committees are much more independent and effective now. They attract well-known politicians as their chairs.	How effective are select committees at scrutinising the government?	✗ Select committees have no enforcement powers and have limited research support compared to the departments they are checking.
✓ Since the Wright Reforms, backbench MPs have more control over parliamentary business in order to debate issues of their choosing.	Have the Wright Reforms enhanced scrutiny of the government?	✗ While they can debate more issues, these debates have no impact on government policy.
✓ The opposition is given a privileged position in Parliament which enables them to effectively scrutinise the government.	How effective is the opposition at scrutinising the government?	✗ Ultimately, if the government has a majority, it can be very difficult for the opposition to hold it to account effectively.

CASE STUDY 8.2: THE CHANGING ROLE OF PARLIAMENT

Since 2010, Parliament has undergone significant shifts in its dynamics, marked by increased backbench assertiveness, the rise of factions and the growing influence of social media on MPs' behaviour. These changes reflect an increase in parliamentary power and a change in the relationship between MPs, parties and the public.

Backbenchers challenging government

The role of backbenchers has evolved significantly since 2010, becoming more influential and relevant in the parliamentary process. The Wright Reforms of 2010 strengthened select committees, enhancing their independence and introduced the Backbench Business which gives backbenchers greater influence on the parliamentary agenda.

Perhaps unsurprisingly therefore, Parliament has seen a significant increase in backbench rebellions. Weak or minority governments since 2010 have had to consider backbenchers more carefully. The 2010–15 Coalition Parliament held the record as the most rebellious in history only to be overtaken by May's premiership (2016–19), largely driven by divisions over Brexit. Backbenchers exerted significant influence, repeatedly challenging her government and shaping the legislative agenda. She also suffered the biggest government defeat in 2019 with the historic defeat by 230 votes (202 in favour, 432 against), the largest defeat for a sitting government in UK history.

One would have expected the 2019 Johnson Government, with its 80-seat majority, to have a smooth ride with backbenchers, and that was certainly the case for the first few months with Brexit legislation passing first time with 330 votes to 231 in early 2020. However, the Covid pandemic meant that Parliament stopped meeting in person, and, far away from the eyes of whips, backbenchers (particularly the many newly elected 2019 MPs) were more likely to vote independently. Once Parliament returned to meeting in Westminster, the die had been cast and backbenchers had a taste of their independence with 44% of all Conservative MPs having rebelled at least once, and 70 MPs had rebelled at least six times. Clearly, backbenchers were becoming more comfortable voting against the government, with rebellions occurring in roughly a quarter of all divisions since the 2019 election.

Government adaptation to backbench influence

Consequently, faced with increasingly independent backbenchers, governments have been forced to engage with backbenchers over legislation. Nonetheless, governments increasingly anticipate backbench feeling during bill drafting. The Public Authorities (Fraud, Error and Recovery) Act (2025) incorporated safeguards like vulnerability checks and appeals processes to pre-empt rebellions over debt recovery measures. Similarly, the Victims and Prisoners Act (2024) saw ministers concede to Lords amendments on parole reforms after backbench pressure. This reactive approach is evident in the 'ping-pong' process, where bills like the Public Order Act 2023 underwent multiple revisions to address concerns over protest restrictions. However, an example where the government simply failed to anticipate their backbenchers' strength of feeling occurred in July 2025. Having been insistent that they would make no changes to their welfare reforms, the Starmer Government essentially lost control of the Commons which led to a humiliating U-turn. The £5 billion saving they were hoping to make disappeared as enough MPs were prepared to rebel so they would lose the vote. Starmer was criticised for taking his eye off the ball; it cost his leadership significantly and he never recovered. Backbenchers now knew that if they worked together, they could change the government's mind. Throughout 2026 it was clear that Starmer was unable to overrule his backbenchers with one U-turn after another over issues like digital ID cards, inheritance tax for farmers and a two-child benefit cap, to name a few. After disastrous election results in May 2026, the Starmer project seemed to be over.

Factional pressure and opposition strategy

Political factions within parties have also become pivotal in shaping legislation. This phenomenon, which was started by the **European Research Group (ERG)** during the Brexit process, has become a mainstay of parliamentary politics. The **Net Zero Scrutiny Group (NZSG)** exemplifies this shift, mobilising backbenchers to roll back climate policies, and the **Northern Research Group** was set up in 2020 by 'Red Wall' Conservative MPs to push the government's levelling up agenda. As Starmer's popularity took a downward turn, so did his power. The so-called "soft left" of the party organised themselves very effectively to direct him towards a more traditionally Labour agenda. Ed Miliband, his Energy and Net Zero Secretary, wielded significant power behind the scenes. From the backbenches, Angela Rayner made her leadership ambitions clear by being critical of his role in Labour's poor poll ratings.

Starmer's large majority should have meant it was harder for factions to make an impact, nonetheless he continued to face significant rebellions from the left of the party.

Social media's impact on MPs' behaviour

Another way Parliament has evolved is in response to social media. Social media has reshaped political engagement, often detrimentally. A 2024 Vuelio survey revealed 81% of MPs believe platforms like X have worsened public attitudes towards politicians, fostering distrust and misinformation, although 47% believe social media has improved political transparency. However, it has amplified grassroots campaigns, compelling MPs to respond swiftly to public sentiment. For instance:

1. A coordinated social media campaign led by LGBTQ+ rights groups and allies put pressure on MPs to support a comprehensive ban on conversion therapy. The online activism contributed to increased support for the ban among MPs across party lines.

2. Child safety campaigners used social media to highlight the need for stronger protections in the Online Safety Bill. This digital campaign influenced MPs to vote for amendments, strengthening the bill's provisions related to child safety online.

3. Throughout 2023–2025, a coordinated campaign both on social media and on the streets by pro-Palestinian groups managed to exert significant pressure on MPs to vote for various anti-Israel policies.

This process has been criticised as 'policy by viral trend' dynamics, where complex issues are overshadowed by simplistic online narratives with 42% believing social media has negatively affected the policymaking process. Moreover, MPs are now increasingly fearful of online abuse, which may result in them feeling pressurised to give in to small but highly active groups which can subvert democracy.

Legislative function

✅ **Party discipline in the Lords is weaker than in the Commons, so it is more independent.** Because approximately a quarter of Lords are crossbenchers, peers are more able to express their own views. Moreover, since the removal of hereditary peers in 1999 and 2026, the Lords have been more willing to challenge the government:

» **Planning and Infrastructure Act 2025** enhancing democratic accountability and environmental protections.

Synoptic Link

It is often suggested that the 1999 Lords reform reinvigorated the Lords as they felt more legitimate. One can say the same about the 2025 reforms. This links to the Democracy topic.

» Strengthened the **Online Safety Act 2023** by adding protections for journalism and encrypted messaging.

» Enhanced the reporting requirements of the **Retained EU Law Act (2023)** to demand clearer safeguards for environmental standards.

» Inflicted **14 defeats in a single day on the Police, Crime, Sentencing and Courts Act (2022),** forcing the government to reconsider several controversial provisions.

» The Lords defeated key clauses of the **Nationality and Borders Act (2022)** multiple times.

» The House of Lords inflicted a total of 12 defeats on the UK Government's **Rwanda Act** during 2024:

  – The Lords voted through five amendments aimed at ensuring compliance with domestic and international law. These changes significantly challenged the bill's core objectives.

  – The Lords inflicted a further seven defeats, including amendments requiring 'due regard' for international law, exempting victims of modern slavery and unaccompanied children from deportation, and allowing courts to intervene if Rwanda's safety was questioned.

✅ **The Lords is a revising chamber** and between November 2023 and May 2024 it made 2,377 amendments across 67 bills, often improving legislative detail.

✅ **The Lords spend significantly more time debating bills** – over half its sitting hours – compared to about a third in the Commons. There are no guillotines or timetabling restrictions, allowing for thorough examination, whereas in the Commons there are strict timetabling limits, often leading to rushed scrutiny in committee stages or shortened debates. The leisurely timetable in the Lords enabled ministers to respond to early-stage concerns during debates on bills like the **Online Safety Act**, resulting in significant amendments.

✅ **Ad hoc committees conduct post-legislative scrutiny** – inquiries into specific laws' effectiveness after implementation. This systematic approach ensures laws remain fit for purpose. The Lords conducted inquiries into Covid-related legislation in 2024, identifying areas needing improvement. In the Commons, post-legislative scrutiny is less systematic and typically occurs through departmental select committees.

❌ **The legal restraints on the Lords remain, as demonstrated by the Commons overturning various Lords amendments to legislation.** The Parliament Act 1949 makes the Lords less powerful than the Commons because it prevents them from vetoing legislation and only allows them to delay for a year. The Commons has responded to recent defeats in the House of Lords in the following ways:

1. Although the Lords inflicted defeats on the **Police, Crime, Sentencing and Courts Act (2022),** most amendments were overturned by the Commons.

2. The Lords defeated key clauses of the **Nationality and Borders Act (2022)** multiple times, but most amendments were rejected by the Commons.

3. The House of Lords inflicted six defeats on the **Economic Crime and Corporate Transparency Act (2023),** however the Commons overturned all six defeats.

4. The Lords voted to exempt care providers, small businesses and charities from a National Insurance increase during the report stage of the **National Insurance Act (2025),** but the Commons rejected all 21 Lords amendments when it returned to the Commons.

5. The Lords repeatedly challenged and amended the **Illegal Migration Act** during its passage in 2023. However, the government ultimately succeeded in passing it after overturning all 12 Lords' amendments.

6. With the **Retained EU Law (Revocation and Reform) Act in 2023,** the Commons overturned amendments made by the Lords, specifically those concerning parliamentary scrutiny of changes to retained EU law.

❌ **The Salisbury Convention means the House of Lords doesn't oppose measures in the manifesto of the elected government.**

» Lord Kinnoull spoke in the Lords regarding the Salisbury Convention and the Rwanda Bill, arguing that asylum and immigration featured on the 2019 campaign trail and the subject 'was widely covered and spoken about by the parties and the candidates'. He noted that the government has passed several tough asylum and immigration bills since 2019, which have 'all enjoyed conventional protection'. 'The pattern of behaviour could be argued as being an example where a general election campaign trail gave significant support in providing conventional protection to a bill, and that that bill became a Manifesto Bill.' In other words, he is arguing that the Salisbury Convention be widened to widely discussed issues in election campaigns as well as policies specifically in the manifesto.

Aspect	Lords strengths	Commons strengths
Depth of scrutiny	Detailed line-by-line examination	Swift passage of priority legislation
Expertise	Specialised knowledge from experienced professionals	Constituency-focused representation
Independence	Less partisan; members not bound by party whips	Democratic legitimacy through elected representatives
Time allocation	No guillotines; ample time for debate	Timetabled debates ensure efficiency
Post-legislative scrutiny	Systematic ad hoc inquiries	Departmental select committee oversight

Scrutiny

✓ **The government majority in the Commons means the government is rarely checked effectively,** but because the government doesn't have a majority in the Lords, scrutiny is much more effective.

✓ **The Lords are more independent and so issues may be looked at in a non-partisan manner,** especially by crossbench peers. Because Lords are there for life, whips have limited power over them.

✓ **The Lords has a system of select committees.** These do not mirror government departments as in the Commons, but are set up to look at particular issues. There are permanent committees on the economy and on science and technology which reinforces the Lords' ability to specialise in certain areas. In 2025–26, the House of Lords select committees published 63 reports on topics ranging from water regulation and environmental enforcement to AI in weapons systems, hospice funding, digital ID proposals, and the constitutional implications of the Mandelson–Epstein affair.

✓ **The Lords benefits from members with specialised knowledge, allowing for more informed debates and amendments.** In contrast, the Commons' scrutiny is often constrained by time pressures and party politics.

✗ **The Lords are less effective in scrutinising the government.**
  » PMQs and MQs allow the Commons to directly scrutinise government by making it accountable for its actions; this direct scrutiny is not possible in the Lords.

✗ **The Commons select committees have grown in influence and authority since being reformed in 2010. The lack of departmental select committees in the Lords limits their ability to scrutinise effectively.**
  » Since 2010, select committee chairs have been elected by backbenchers, not whips. Members of these committees tend to serve for the full parliamentary term, meaning that they develop significant expertise in their area. The expertise provided by the Lords is now matched by these committees.
  » Also, the Commons have the Liaison Committee which questions and checks the Prime Minister, something the Lords cannot do.

✗ **The Lords cannot bring down the government, unlike the Commons.**
  » The Commons can vote in a motion of no confidence, and if a government loses this motion, convention dictates they must resign.

Representation

✅ **While the Lords cannot claim democratic legitimacy, as an unelected house they may be more willing to represent people and issues that an elected house may be less inclined to.**

» For example, asylum and protection of human rights issues are not as electorally popular as other issues and the Lords can highlight these concerns without fear of losing popularity. In both the **Nationality and Borders Act (2022)** and the **Illegal Migration Act (2023)**, the Lords attempted to push the Commons to protect the rights of asylum seekers more effectively.

✅ **The Lords represents areas of expertise outside of politics** – in areas such as medicine, law, business, the arts, science, sports, education, the armed forces, diplomacy and public service – which is lacking in the Commons.

1. **Baroness Willis of Summertown** is a British biologist and Oxford University professor who studies the relationship between long-term ecosystem dynamics and environmental change.
2. **Baroness Vere of Norbiton** sits as a Conservative peer and was executive director of the Girls' Schools Association.
3. **Baroness Tyler of Enfield** is a Liberal Democrat peer and is CEO of Relate – a counselling service.
4. **Baroness Vadera** is an investment banker and economist – she is chair of Prudential plc, former chair of Santander UK and former government adviser.
5. There are also four presidents of the Supreme Court, including the current president, **Lord Reed of Allermuir**.
6. **Lord Vallance of Balham** serves as minister for science and was previously the government's chief scientific adviser during Covid.
7. **Lord Patel** is a former president of the Royal College of Obstetricians and Gynaecologists.

✅ **While the upper chamber is unelected and not representative of public choice, it is sometimes claimed that the Lords does a better job of addressing representational deficits as the appointment system helps to directly address imbalances.** Also, MPs often focus on constituency concerns rather than technical expertise, limiting their ability to scrutinise complex legislation effectively.

❌ **The Commons is elected, allowing MPs to represent their constituents.**

» It can do this collectively by speaking against something happening in their area which will have a negative effect on their constituents.

» It can also represent them individually via adjournment debates, raising issues at PMQs or MQs or raising it privately with a member of the government.

❌ **The political appointment of life peers has become problematic in the Lords, undermining their role.**

» Recently the Lords has been in the spotlight for scandals involving its own members. Most infamously, Michelle Mone hit the headlines when it was alleged that a company associated with her made a lot of money from supplying faulty PPE equipment to the government during the Covid pandemic.

» Lord Alli hit the headlines in 2024 for the gifts and money given to the Starmer family.

» Russian Oligarch, Lord Lebedev, was appointed to the Lords by Boris Johnson despite allegations that the House of Lords Appointment Commission took advice from the intelligence services and advised Boris Johnson not to proceed.

» The Lord Mandelson scandal involving Jeffrey Epstein in 2026 highlighted again the difficulty in removing peers immersed in scandal.

Key Debate Summary: Is the House of Lords as effective as the Commons in fulfilling its functions?

For	Theme	Against
✓ Party discipline in the Lords is weaker than in the Commons, so it is more independent and much more able to challenge the government on their legislative agenda.	Who is more effective in the legislative function?	✗ The limit to the legal powers of the Lords, i.e. it can only delay laws, means that it cannot effectively hold the government to account.
✓ As there is no government majority in the Lords, the Lords are often more able to scrutinise the government.	Who is more effective in the scrutiny function?	✗ The Lords have no direct ability to challenge the Prime Minister or government departments, unlike in the Commons.
✓ The Lords are able to represent the people via the expertise on offer, as well as representing more vulnerable members of society.	Who is more effective in the representative function?	✗ Because they are unelected, the Lords cannot hope to fulfil a representative function as effectively as the Commons.

Visit the companion website for a bonus case study on Parliament and the Brexit process from the previous fifth edition.

Exam Style Questions

- Evaluate the view that Parliament now carries out its functions effectively (30).

- Evaluate the view that Parliament is the most powerful of all the branches (30).

- Evaluate the view that the power of Parliament has been radically enhanced by constitutional reforms since 1997 (30).

- Evaluate the view that power has now fundamentally shifted from the government to Parliament (30).

- Evaluate the view that backbenchers are now highly effective in holding the government to account (30).

- Evaluate the view that the House of Lords now performs a meaningful role in the UK system of government (30).

- Evaluate the view that the power exerted by the Lords is now too great for an unelected body (30).

Source Question

Within Parliament, there are many ways to scrutinise the government. One of the most famous is Prime Minister's Questions which is a weekly event held in the Commons where MPs can question the Prime Minister on government policies. It is probably the best-known form of scrutiny in the Commons and the open questioning style requires the Prime Minister to be well informed on various topics across government departments, enhancing accountability. Another are Public Bill Committees which provide a platform for detailed scrutiny of legislation and allow MPs to propose changes. They can influence legislation by highlighting potential flaws or unintended consequences. In some cases, MPs with shared policy interests work constructively across party lines in Public Bill Committees. Departmental select committees are cross-party groups responsible for scrutinising the work of government departments. They can summon witnesses and gather evidence which enables them to conduct thorough, independent investigations. Because MPs tend to stay in the same committee for the whole parliamentary term, they build up expertise. Select committees can also appoint independent specialist advisers to assist in their work.

However, these areas of scrutiny are limited in several ways. PMQs is often criticised for being too aggressive and noisy with MPs engaging in behaviour designed to humiliate. Also, many government MPs ask friendly planted questions, allowing the Prime Minister to score party political points. The format also makes it easy for Prime Ministers to avoid forensic questioning as it doesn't allow for follow-up questions. Public Bill Committees' effectiveness is limited as the governing party typically has a majority in committees, which means they are stacked with loyal backbenchers rather than independent-minded MPs or subject specialists. This means most opposition amendments are rejected unless they align with government priorities. Moreover, the temporary nature of Public Bill Committees prevents members from building up specialised knowledge or developing strong relationships across party lines. While select committees can summon witnesses, they lack clear enforcement powers to compel attendance or testimony and despite efforts at bipartisanship, political allegiances can still influence committee effectiveness; whips may not control appointments, but the proceedings of committees are all public. Lastly. The government accepts only around 40% of committee recommendations, showing their lack of effectiveness.

Using the source, evaluate the view that Parliament is ineffective at scrutinising the government (30).

In your response you must:

- » *Compare and contrast different opinions in the source*

- » *Examine and debate these views in a balanced way*

- » *Analyse and evaluate **only** the information presented in the source.*

Chapter Summary

» The role of Parliament and the government are fundamentally different.

» Within Parliament, the two chambers of the Commons and Lords have very different compositions.

» Parliament has a number of functions and is more effective at some than others.

» There are a number of ways Parliament scrutinises the executive, and some are more effective than others.

» Within the chambers of Parliament, the Commons and the Lords have different ways of holding the government to account.

Further Resources

The UK Parliament education website is an excellent resource with many videos and explainers as well as links to arrange visits or speakers. https://learning.parliament.uk/en/

The Constitution Unit. Should we be worried about Parliamentary Scrutiny (2025) https://constitution-unit.com/2025/02/17/should-we-be-worried-about-the-decline-of-parliamentary-scrutiny/

Ethnic diversity in politics and public life (2023) https://commonslibrary.parliament.uk/research-briefings/sn01156/

How Committees Work https://www.parliament.uk/about/how/committees/

Bennister, M. (2012) *Prime Ministers in Power* (London: Palgrave Macmillan).

Griffiths, S. and Leach, R. (2018) *British Politics* (3rd edn) (London: Bloomsbury Academic): Chapter 6.

Heffernan, R., Hay, C., Russell, M., Cowley, P. (eds) (2016) *Developments in British Politics* (10th edn) (London: Bloomsbury Academic): Chapter 6.

Moran, M. (2015) *Politics and Governance in the UK* (3rd edn) (London: Bloomsbury Academic): Chapter 7.

Thompson, L. (2015) *Making British Law: Committees in Action* (London: Palgrave Macmillan): Chapter 1: The role and function of bill committees.

Visit the companion website to access the Further Resources Booklet to explore a range of useful web links related to: how various leaders fared at their first PMQs, whether the Commons' committee systems effectively scrutinise government policymaking and more.

9 THE PRIME MINISTER AND EXECUTIVE

Chapter Preview

The executive is the powerhouse of government. It is the part of government that provides political leadership, makes decisions and enforces those decisions. This is why it is so important to ensure that executive power is carefully checked or constrained as the executive needs to be held accountable for its actions. Without checks and adjustments, government might become a tyranny against the people. However, attention also falls on who has power within the executive. Who exactly wields executive power?

Prime Ministers are certainly the best-known figures in politics. When we vote, our main thought is generally who will be the Prime Minister. When major events happen, it is the Prime Minister who speaks for the government or on behalf of the nation. The impression is that the Prime Minister, in effect, 'runs the country'. Nevertheless, the Prime Minister does not govern alone. In fact, at least in theory, the UK executive is collective rather than personal.

Key Questions and Debates

- » **What is the executive?**
- » **What is the role of the Prime Minister, the Cabinet, junior ministers and civil servants?**
- » **Where does power lie within the executive?**
- » **What makes a Prime Minister powerful?**
- » **How important are the conventions of ministerial responsibility?**

Specification Checklist

3.1. The structure, role and powers of the executive

- » **Its structure, including Prime Minister, the Cabinet, junior ministers and government departments.**
- » **Its main roles, including proposing legislation, proposing a budget and making policy decisions within laws and budget.**
- » **The main powers of the executive, including Royal Prerogative powers, initiation of legislation and secondary legislative power.**

3.2. The concept of ministerial responsibility

- » **The concept of individual ministerial responsibility.**
- » **The concept of collective ministerial responsibility.**

3.3. The Prime Minister and the Cabinet
3.3.1. The power of the Prime Minister and the Cabinet

- » **The factors governing the Prime Minister's selection of ministers.**
- » **The factors that affect the relationship between the Cabinet and the Prime Minister, and the ways they have changed and the balance of power between the Prime Minister and the Cabinet.**

3.3.2. The powers of the Prime Minister and the Cabinet to dictate events and determine policy

- » **Students must study the influence of one Prime Minister from 1945 to 1997 and one post-1997 Prime Minister.**
- » **Students may choose any pre-1997 and any post-1997 Prime Minister, provided that they study them in an equivalent level of detail, covering both events and policy, with examples that illustrate both control and a lack of control.**

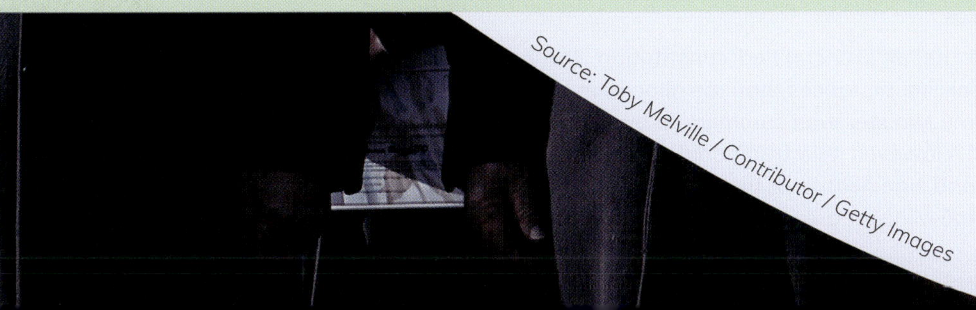

Source: Toby Melville / Contributor / Getty Images

What is the executive?

The **executive** is responsible for implementing government policy. It is the chief source of political leadership and, most importantly, decides on policy. In short, the role of the executive is to 'govern'. There are two parts to the executive:

- » The *political* executive, also known as 'the government'. This is composed of approximately 100 elected ministers and its job is to take overall responsibility for the direction and coordination of government policy.
- » The *official* executive, or **bureaucracy**. This is composed of a small elite of senior civil servants (sometimes known as 'mandarins') and its job is to provide policy advice and to implement government policy.

This chapter will focus on the political executive, known as 'the government'.

Figure 9.1 The structure of the executive

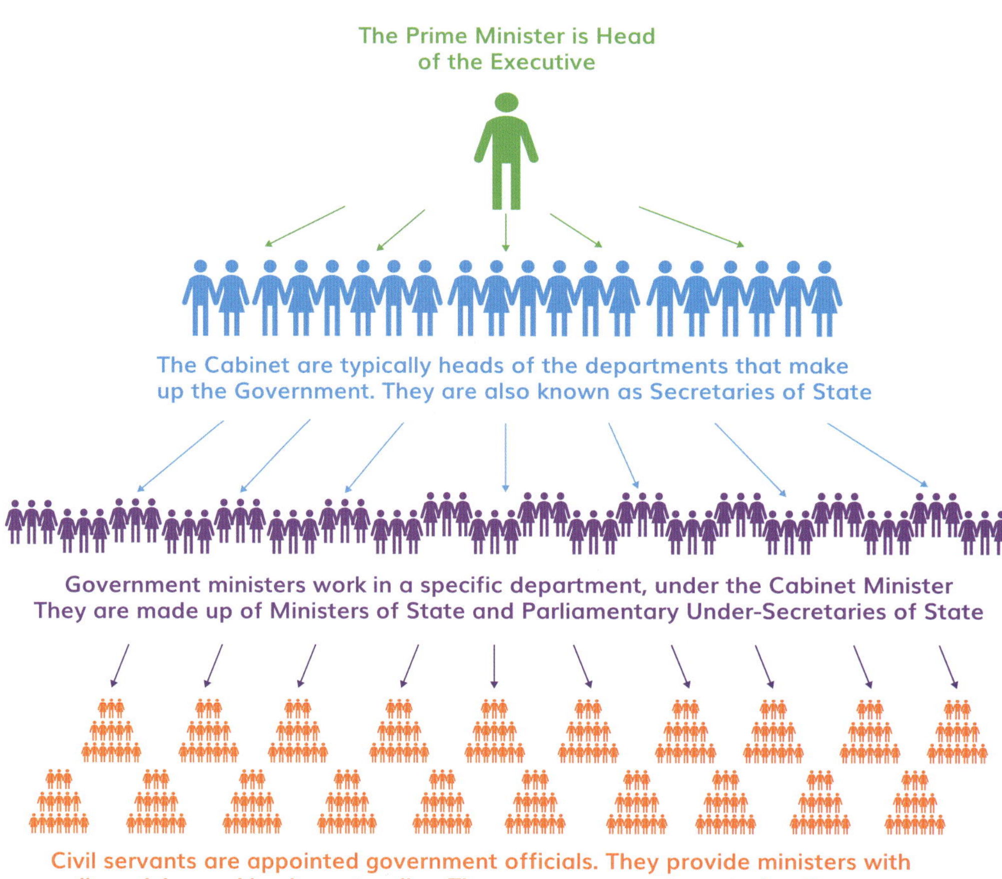

The Prime Minister

The Prime Minister is the single most important figure in the UK political system. They are usually the leader of the party which has majority control of the House of Commons and they are the UK's 'chief executive'.

Due to the UK's uncodified constitution, the role of the Prime Minister has been shaped more by practical circumstances than the allocation of formal responsibilities. The traditional view of the role of the Prime Minister was summed up by Walter Bagehot (1867) as '*primus inter pares*', or 'first among equals'. However, this traditional formulation has ceased to be accurate. It fails to capture the full range and significance of the role of the modern Prime Minister. The key aspects of the modern role of the Prime Minister are:

» **Forming a government.** Prime Ministers appoint all other members of the government. This power to 'hire and fire' is known as patronage and extends to the Cabinet and other ministers. It gives the Prime Minister substantial control over the careers of their party's MPs.

» **Directing government policy.** The Prime Minister sets the overall direction of government policy and defines its strategic goals. In doing so, they can interfere in any aspect of policy, although economic policy and foreign policy tend to be the major concerns of most Prime Ministers.

» **Managing the Cabinet system.** The Prime Minister chairs Cabinet meetings, determines their number and their length, and also sets up Cabinet committees.

» **Organising government.** Prime Ministers are responsible for the structure and organisation of government. This involves setting up, reorganising and abolishing government departments, as well as being responsible for the Civil Service.

» **Controlling Parliament.** As leader of the largest party in the Commons, the Prime Minister effectively controls it and governs through Parliament. Prime Ministers may make use of their control of Parliament to introduce secondary legislation which enables laws to be amended by government ministers without requiring the authority of Parliament.

» **Providing national leadership.** The Prime Minister's authority is based on being elected by the people, and Prime Ministers provide national leadership, particularly at times of national crisis, war or in response to major events.

The Cabinet

The Cabinet is a committee of the leading members of the government. It comprises approximately twenty formal members (although a larger number may be allowed to attend), most of whom are secretaries of state responsible for running Whitehall departments (see Figure 9.1).

Within the Cabinet there are the four great offices of state, which alongside the Prime Minister are the Chancellor of the Exchequer, Foreign Secretary and Home Secretary; in 2026 three of these four positions were held by women for the first time. This may also mean that these ministers form an inner circle of ministers who are consulted more frequently by the Prime Minister, known as an inner Cabinet.

Government ministers, civil servants and special advisers

A minister is a person appointed to perform a government function. Whereas Cabinet ministers are responsible for the work of their whole department, ministers are responsible for an area within their department. For example, Yvette Cooper was a Cabinet minister serving as the Secretary of State for Foreign and Commonwealth and Development Affairs. She was responsible for the whole department, whereas Stephen Doughty MP was the Minister of State for Europe, North America and Overseas Territories within the Foreign Office.

All ministers are supported by civil servants:

» Civil servants are permanent post-holders in the government. They remain in post while ministers and governments come and go.

» Civil servants are bound by the principle of *neutrality*. In other words they are expected to be loyal and supportive of any minister and any government, whatever their political views.

» Finally, they are anonymous, meaning that they are 'nameless' in the sense that they work in the background to support the public figure – the minister.

Ministers are also supported by special advisers, known as 'spads'.

» Unlike a civil servant, spads will only stay in a government department as long as the minister they serve does.

» Spads give party political advice and support to their minister in a way that it would be inappropriate for the Civil Service to provide. They can be policy experts, recruited for their expertise in a particular field, or media advisers who present their minister's views and influence how policy is communicated to the public. These media advisers are also known as 'spin doctors'.

» While few could name a top civil servant of Tony Blair, Boris Johnson or Keir Starmer, many know the name of their top spad, namely Alastair Campbell, Dominic Cummings and Morgan McSweeney.

Factors taken into account when appointing ministers

Convention dictates that Prime Ministers are free to select anyone they wish from Parliament to be **ministers** in their Cabinet. However, there are various factors that they have to take into account.

» Often, Prime Ministers choose people who are close allies. They may have been long-time close friends, joined Parliament at the same time, or supported each other's careers through Parliament.

  ○ Keir Starmer and Rachel Reeves became close as they worked together to formulate their policy approach while in opposition.

  ○ George Osborne and David Cameron had been friends since university and built up their relationship from then.

» **'Big beasts'** are usually difficult to leave out from the Cabinet. Big beasts have a significant power base within the party – among backbenchers, ministerial colleagues inside and outside the Cabinet, as well as in the party more widely. Therefore, Prime Ministers might feel compelled to appoint them.

  ○ Keir Starmer included Angela Rayner in his Cabinet and made her Deputy Prime Minister because of her popularity in the wider Labour Party and also among the left of his party.

» Without a doubt, Prime Ministers appoint MPs to their Cabinet who have displayed exceptional ability.

  ○ Keir Starmer chose Wes Streeting for Health Secretary because Streeting brought a combination of experience, communication skills and a clear commitment to NHS reform that matched Starmer's priorities for government.

  ○ Rishi Sunak kept Jeremy Hunt as Chancellor as he had navigated the post-Truss economic crisis well and was trusted by the markets.

» Prime Ministers are wise to balance the 'wings' of their party in their Cabinet to ensure effective party management.

  ○ Starmer balanced his Cabinet by having people from the centre-left – Angela Rayner, Ed Miliband and Lisa Nandy – alongside more centre-right figures like Wes Streeting.

  ○ Theresa May had to ensure Leavers and Remainers were balanced in her Cabinet.

  ○ It's worth noting that after winning an 80-seat majority in December 2019, Boris Johnson did not feel the need to balance his Cabinet in this way.

» Surprisingly, Prime Ministers often include their rivals in their Cabinet in order to 'silence' them by making them subject to collective responsibility.

  ○ Sunak initially kept Suella Braverman in her position of Home Secretary, as well as Penny Mordaunt as Leader of the House of Commons.

» They might wish to have a socially balanced Cabinet.

  ○ Starmer's 2024 Cabinet was the most socially balanced ever in terms of education and gender and improved class representation. This included 11 women including a female Chancellor for the first time and a woman as Home Secretary. However, it is less ethnically diverse at the top than recent Conservative Cabinets, despite Parliament as a whole becoming more diverse.

  ○ Sunak was the first Hindu Prime Minister of the UK and his Cabinet also included five ethnic minority members.

Who has power in the executive?

Debate about executive power has been one of the recurrent themes of UK politics. Different views have been fashionable at different times, but the question has remained the same – who runs the country? It would be a mistake, however, to treat these contrasting models of executive power as simply 'right' or 'wrong' because none of these models fully explains who has power in all cases and in all circumstances. Each of the models, nevertheless, captures some 'truth'. The main theories of executive power are:

» Cabinet government

» Prime-ministerial government

» Presidentialism.

Cabinet government

This 'traditional' view of the UK executive emphasises that power is collective, and as such is located in the Cabinet rather than the Prime Minister. Moreover, within the Cabinet, all ministers are equal. Each of them has the capacity to influence government policy and shape the direction in which the government is going.

The theory of Cabinet government is underpinned by the convention of collective responsibility, in which all ministers are expected to publicly support decisions made by the Cabinet, or resign from the government. This helps to ensure Cabinet unity, in the sense that disagreement or dissent is only ever expressed within the secrecy of the Cabinet room and never in public. However, Cabinet government in its formal sense is clearly outdated. Nonetheless, it provides a reminder that, despite the growth in Prime Ministerial power, no Prime Minister can survive if they lose the support of their Cabinet.

Prime Ministerial government

The belief that Cabinet Government had been replaced by Prime Ministerial Government was first made by Richard Crossman (1963) in a new introduction to Bagehot's *English Constitution* when he said, 'The post-war epoch has seen the final transformation of Cabinet Government into Prime Ministerial Government.'

The key feature of this view is that it is the Prime Minister, and not the Cabinet, who dominates both the executive and Parliament. They make major government decisions and exert influence over all policy areas. The move towards Prime Ministerial Government highlights the huge growth in Prime Ministerial power, acknowledging that the Cabinet is not a policymaking body, but a source of advice and support for the Prime Minister.

Presidentialism

Since the 1990s, some commentators have drawn attention to what they have seen as the growth of presidentialism in the UK (Foley, *The Rise of the British Presidency* 1993, 2001). This suggests that UK Prime Ministers increasingly resemble Presidents, with Prime Ministers such as Wilson, Thatcher and Blair usually being seen as key examples. To a large extent, this view overlaps with the Prime Ministerial Government model. Most importantly, both views emphasise the dominance of the Prime Minister over the Cabinet (see page 295 for a debate on presidentialism).

KEY TOPIC DEBATE: HOW IMPORTANT IS THE CABINET?

The importance of Cabinet can be seen in the key functions it fulfils and their limits.

✗ A Prime Minister with a united Cabinet behind them is enormously powerful.

» The Prime Minister's ability to dominate the Cabinet usually results in their Cabinet being united behind them.

» Prime Ministers now have considerable sources of their own advice which makes them less reliant on their Cabinet. Recent Prime Ministers have had a Policy Unit at No 10 and a range of special advisers who report directly to them.

» The growth of special advisers has meant that Cabinet acts as little more than a 'rubber stamp' for decisions made elsewhere, meeting for less time than in the past.

✓ Prime Ministers are ultimately only as powerful as their Cabinet allows them to be.

» No Prime Minister can survive, long term, without broad Cabinet support. The Cabinet can overrule or even remove a Prime Minister, as happened to Thatcher, Blair, May, Johnson, and Truss.

» Although Starmer lost the support of much of the parliamentary party throughout 2025–26, it was only when Cabinet Ministers like Wes Streeting resigned that his position became very difficult.

✗ The Prime Minister has significant powers of patronage.

» The Prime Minister appoints, promotes, demotes and sacks all members of the Cabinet and government. This enables Prime Ministers to choose people who are either personally loyal or ideologically sympathetic to them.

» Patronage powers also promote loyalty in Cabinet members as a Prime Minister can make or break their political careers.

» The doctrine of collective responsibility gives the Prime Minister power to silence dissenters in Cabinet (see page 299).

✅ **Some Cabinet ministers are very powerful in their own right, so it would be difficult for a Prime Minister to sack a 'big beast'.**

» These 'big beasts' have important power bases in the party. They provide a balance to the overarching power of the Prime Ministers and are hard to silence. Their sacking or resignation can erode the Prime Minister's authority.

» Suella Braverman was included in Sunak's Cabinet even though she was clearly a rival for his job.

» Wes Streeting was in Starmer's Cabinet even though he was a big rival.

✅ **Prime Ministers need to be careful how they use their patronage powers as a poorly planned reshuffle can erode confidence in their leadership.**

» For example, May was unable to reshuffle her Cabinet as she wished since Jeremy Hunt refused to accept her offer to move from the Health Department.

❌ **Prime Ministers control the workings of Cabinet and may be able to manipulate the outcome of policy discussion through bilateral meetings with ministers (sofa government) and bypass the Cabinet (see Figure 9.2).**

» Blair was particularly keen on this. Cameron also liked a degree of informality, but his experience of coalition government meant he had to formalise meetings and decisions. Prime Ministerial domination has marginalised Cabinet.

» Prime Ministers use smaller groups of Cabinet ministers, called Cabinet committees, to control the debate and remove discussion from full Cabinet to a group of hand-picked ministers they can rely on. Pat McFadden was one of Keir Starmer's closest and most trusted allies in government and part of Starmer's informal 'quad' of top decision makers, alongside Rachel Reeves and Ed Miliband.

» The Prime Minister shapes the Cabinet's agenda and chairs Cabinet meetings, giving them the ability to sum up Cabinet conclusions and maintain control over Cabinet discussions.

✅ **In some circumstances the Cabinet still makes key decisions.**

» The Cabinet still gives authority to government policy. Even though meaningful debate and the formulation of policy decisions effectively takes place elsewhere, these decisions must be brought to and approved by the Cabinet to become official government policy.

» For example, in 2024, the Cabinet approved the decision to build 1.5 million homes in England as well as the policy to create a new 'grey belt' category and allow more flexible developments.

» The Cabinet is involved with the management of emergencies or crises.

» This happens via COBRA (Cabinet Office Briefing Room A). The Cabinet convenes immediately to address the emergency and decide how to deal with the problem.

» In March 2026 Keir Starmer chaired COBRA meetings over the UK's response to Iranian strikes and the impact on energy prices, also concentrating on the wider economic impact of the war.

Definition

Bilateral meeting: A meeting between the Prime Minister and one other Cabinet minister to discuss and sometimes decide policy.

Key Debate Summary: How important is the Cabinet?

For	Theme	Against
✔ No Prime Minister can survive without the support of their Cabinet. Cabinet needs to approve all policies.	Can PMs dominate without their cabinet behind them?	✖ A dominant Prime Minister is usually deferred to by their Cabinet and Cabinet is a rubber stamp for decisions made elsewhere.
✔ Patronage powers must be handled carefully to maintain authority and big beasts are hard to silence.	How much is the PM able to use patronage and collective ministerial responsibility (CMR) to keep the Cabinet in line?	✖ The Prime Minister has significant powers of patronage and can use collective ministerial responsibility (CMR) effectively.
✔ Some key decisions are still made by Cabinet, and management of emergencies.	Are all decisions made by the PM, without Cabinet discussion?	✖ Prime Ministers can manipulate Cabinet by the use of bilateral meetings and Cabinet committees. The Prime Minister controls the workings of Cabinet.

Figure 9.2 How decisions are made in the executive

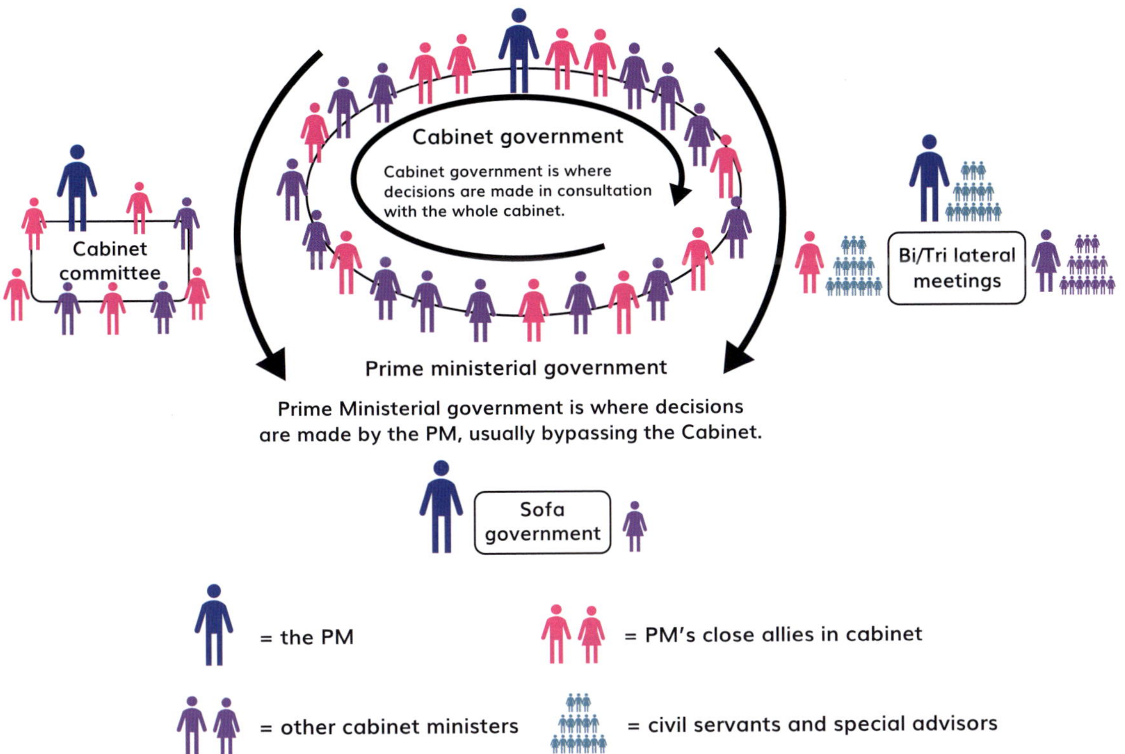

Prime Minister's prerogative powers

The formal powers of the Prime Minister are relatively modest, and are derived from the **Royal Prerogative**. Royal Prerogative powers are powers exercised 'on behalf' of the monarch by the Prime Minister. They do not require the permission of Parliament. Such prerogative powers have existed over a long period of time and are therefore traditional in nature. Prerogative powers allow the Prime Minister to:

» Appoint ministers and other senior figures

» Dissolve and recall Parliament

» Sign treaties

» Grant honours

» Declare war and command the armed forces

» Annex and yield territory

» Control the workings of the Civil Service.

However, this list of formal powers does not capture the full significance of the post of the Prime Minister. Prime Ministers are much more important than their 'constitutional' role suggests.

Spec Key Term

Royal Prerogative:
A set of powers and privileges belonging to the monarch but normally exercised by the Prime Minister or Cabinet, such as the granting of honours or legal pardons.

KEY TOPIC DEBATE: ARE PRIME MINISTERS STILL AS POWERFUL AS THEY ONCE WERE?

The powers of the Prime Minister and their limits

All Prime Ministers have many powers at their disposal; however, as Figure 9.3 shows, those powers come with limits. The key resources available to the Prime Minister are:

» The power of patronage and other prerogative powers

» Their control over the wider executive

» Leadership of the party, both in and outside of Parliament

Figure 9.3 The powers and limits of the Prime Minister

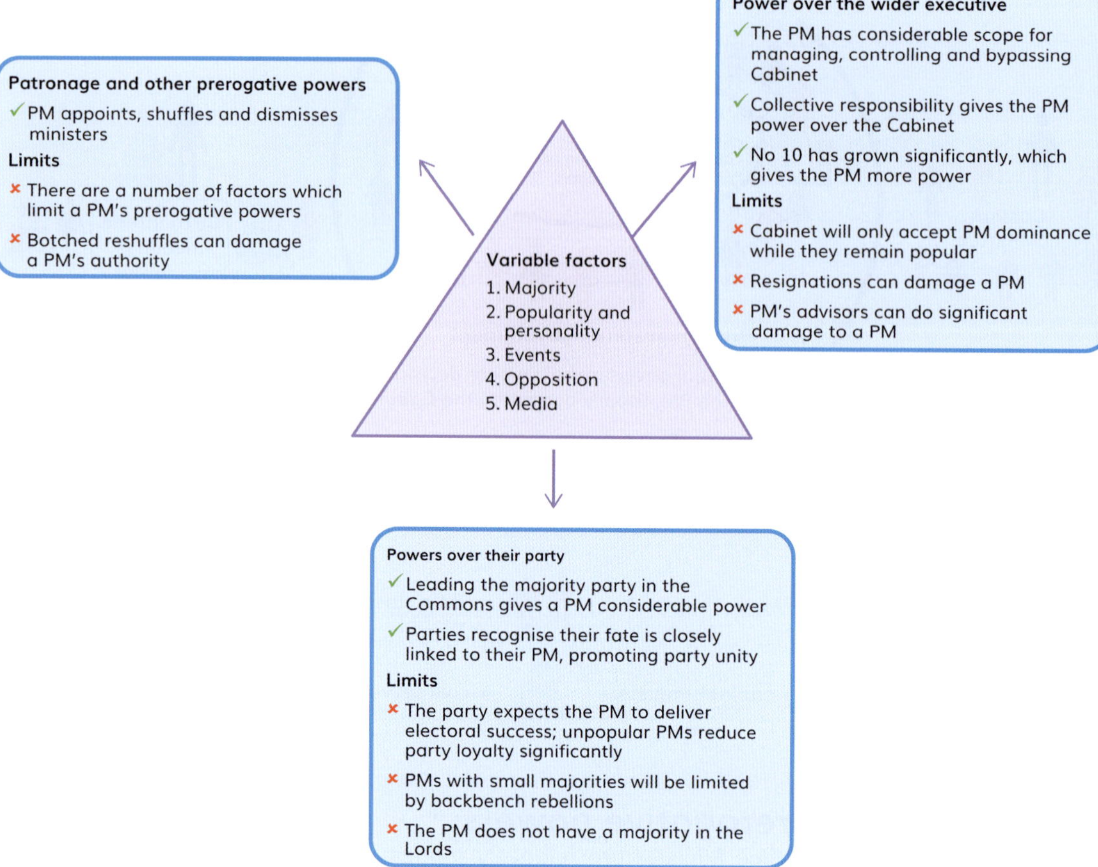

Tip: The Specification requires knowledge of TWO PMs, one from 1945–97 and one post-1997. However, it is probably the case that using examples of several PMs would be even more effective.

1 Patronage and other prerogative powers

The key power of the Prime Minister is the power of patronage. This strengthens the Prime Minister in two important ways:

The Prime Minister can ensure the appointment of loyal supporters who share their ideological preferences. Equally, rivals and critics can be kept out.

» As the Prime Minister controls their political career, this ensures that both ministers and the vast majority of backbenchers remain loyal and supportive.

» Keir Starmer's first Cabinet in July 2024 was largely comprised of his close allies keeping his top team from opposition virtually intact. This included key allies like Pat McFadden (Chancellor of the Duchy of Lancaster), Rachel Reeves (Chancellor), Yvette Cooper (Home Secretary) and Shabana Mahmood (Justice Secretary). This was unsurprising considering the extent of his election victory.

» Similarly, Blair in 1997 appointed a Cabinet based on his New Labour values, after his landslide victory.

» Thatcher consolidated her position after 1983 by transforming her Cabinet from one dominated by 'wets' (One Nation Conservatives) to one in which all the key economic posts were in the hands of 'drys' (Thatcherites).

Limits to the Prime Minister's power of patronage

However, the power of patronage has its limits. In hiring and firing ministers, Prime Ministers must take account of the following considerations:

» Prime Ministers need to weigh up a whole range of factors when appointing their Cabinet. Party unity requires that the major wings in their party feel they are represented, as well as a social balance.

» Prime Ministers need to pick the top talent from their party if they want to be successful and often Prime Ministers decide to include their rivals or critics; these so-called 'big beasts' may be less dangerous inside government (where they are subject to collective responsibility) than outside.

» Lastly, a botched reshuffle can undermine the Prime Minister's credibility.

  – In a 2025 reshuffle, Starmer reportedly asked Ed Miliband to leave the energy brief and take over the Housing, Communities and Local Government role vacated by Angela Rayner. Miliband allegedly refused to move, insisting on staying at Energy Security and Net Zero, where he has been the key architect of the government's net zero agenda.

  – Rishi Sunak's 2023 reshuffle was criticised for the appointment of David Cameron as Foreign Secretary, particularly as he was made a Lord to take up the position. The sacking of Suella Braverman deepened party divisions, and consequently, all four great offices of state were held by men.

  – Theresa May's 2018 reshuffle was intended as a relaunch to assert her authority, but it quickly descended into chaos with Jeremy Hunt, Health Secretary, refusing to move, while Education Secretary Justine Greening rejected a move to Work and Pensions and instead quit the government. The reshuffle was widely branded a failure, leaving May looking weak and unable to control her own ministers.

2 Their control over the executive

✅ **Prime Ministers have considerable scope for managing and controlling the Cabinet, government and the wider executive.**

» Prime Ministers have enormous control over Cabinet meetings and use their powers to chair and manage the agenda to head off disagreement. They also control the creation and membership of Cabinet committees, which gives them opportunities to move decisions away from full Cabinet.

  – In Starmer's operation, Pat McFadden (a very close ally) chaired two Cabinet committees and sat on five more, while the Prime Minister himself chaired five committees. Between them, there were only two committees that they didn't control – Europe and the Future of Work.

  – Liz Truss and her Chancellor, Kwasi Kwarteng, did not tell or consult the Cabinet on key elements of her ill-fated mini-budget before it was announced, including the controversial abolition of the 45% top rate of income tax. Even Truss's closest Cabinet allies were unaware of some major measures until the night before the announcement, and several ministers, including her Levelling Up Secretary Simon Clarke, expressed surprise and frustration at being left out of the decision-making process.

» Collective responsibility gags dissenters and brings awkward ministers into line. It means the Prime Minister can lead a government with a united front.

» 'No 10' has grown significantly because of the increase of bodies and advisers who support the Prime Minister. This includes:

  – the **Prime Minister's Office** (including the Policy Unit) which has developed into the centre of the UK executive. It is staffed by a mix of civil servants who advise on policy and special advisers to help with communication and strategy.

  – Since Blair, the number and significance of special advisers who report directly to the Prime Minister has increased markedly, 50 compared to eight during Major's time; additionally, Blair became the first Prime Minister to give senior special advisers formal control over civil servants.

  – This means that the Prime Minister has the resources to work independently of the Cabinet. It was alleged that Starmer's Chief of Staff, Morgan McSweeney, had more influence than any Cabinet Minister.

  – During the Covid-19 pandemic, it was alleged that Johnson made most decisions with his 'quad' of ministers: Dominic Raab, Matt Hancock, Rishi Sunak and Michael Gove, avoiding wider Cabinet participation.

Limits to the Prime Minister's control over the executive

❌ **However, the Prime Minister's ability to manage and control the executive has its limits.**

» Most importantly, the Cabinet's support for the Prime Minister is conditional on the Prime Minister being popular and successful.

- When Starmer was first elected on a landslide in 2024, he was dominant. However, as his popularity plummeted throughout 2025–2026, and elections and by-elections were lost, often with Labour in 3rd place, his Cabinet flexed its muscles to insist he pursue their agenda, and even consider stepping down.
- When the economy was booming and the UK had been successful in the Falklands War, Thatcher was hugely popular, and she had her Cabinet's support. By the 1990s her Cabinet were frustrated by her mistakes over the Poll Tax and intransigence over Europe and in 1990 they turned on her, leading to her resignation.

» Cabinet resignations, particularly the resignation of senior figures, can damage political support for the Prime Minister.

- When Sunak and Javid resigned from Johnson's Cabinet in 2022, it was clear that his days were numbered.

» Compared to other world leaders, the support available to a UK Prime Minister is meagre, limiting their ability to deliver on their promises.

» Additionally, the weaknesses of some of the people who support PMs have been evident with recent Prime Ministers' top advisers courting significant controversy. The following top advisers all became the main story during their time advising the Prime Minister costing their Prime Minister considerable support:

- In February 2026 Starmer lost two key advisers as fallout from the Mandelson-Epstein affair. First, Morgan McSweeney, Starmer's Chief of Staff and then Tim Allan, Director of Communications, resigned after facing intense criticism over their roles in the mishandled Mandelson appointment and ensuing scandal.
- Sue Gray was appointed as Keir Starmer's Chief of Staff in opposition, causing controversy as she had led the critical inquiry into Boris Johnson's Partygate allegations. The controversy didn't stop there, as when in government, there was internal criticism over her management style, with headlines dominated by her; she resigned less than 100 days into Labour's Government and was replaced by Morgan McSweeney.
- Dominic Cummings was infamous for the role he played in the EU referendum alongside Johnson. His dictatorial attitude towards ministers, civil servants, advisers and MPs when he came to No 10 with Johnson in 2019 made him particularly unpopular amongst ministers. When he broke lockdown rules in April 2020, many were gleeful that he got his comeuppance. By the end of 2020 he had resigned.
- Alastair Campbell, Blair's chief 'spin doctor', became a liability for the Blair Government's ability to achieve its aims and he resigned after the death of Dr David Kelly who was caught up in the search for weapons of mass destruction in Iraq.

3 Leadership over the party

✅ **Party leadership underpins all other aspects of Prime Ministerial power. It gives them wide control.**

» The Prime Minister has considerable power as the leader of the majority party in the Commons. The bigger the majority, the greater the power of the Prime Minister. It allows them to control Parliament through commanding a disciplined majority in the House of Commons.

- Even though Boris Johnson faced a number of challenges during his time as Prime Minister, he did not lose any votes on legislation after he secured an 80-seat majority in 2019.
- Despite some substantial backbench revolts, Blair did not suffer a single Commons defeat between 1997 and 2005 as he had a three-figure majority.

» Party members recognise that the party's fortunes are closely linked to the Prime Minister's personal standing. This tends to discourage party splits and public criticism of the Prime Minister.

- Throughout 2025, Starmer announced difficult policy decisions on welfare and immigration which many in the party found difficult. There were significant abstentions from backbenchers and initially only muted criticisms.
- After he won the 2019 Election with an 80-seat majority, Johnson's party quickly supported his EU Withdrawal Agreement legislation, despite refusing to do so for May for the two years she tried to get it through Parliament.

» The Prime Minister and other government ministers are also MPs and sit and vote in Parliament. This gives the government a head start in support for its legislation because it is unlikely that members of the government will oppose government bills as they would lose their government position.

Limits to the Prime Minister's power over their party

❌ **However, the benefits that flow from party leadership are limited in several ways.**

» As the party leader, the Prime Minister is meant to deliver electoral success. If the government becomes unpopular, and especially if the Prime Minister is viewed as an electoral liability, party loyalty can evaporate very quickly.

- Starmer's poor opinion poll ratings throughout 2025–2026, alongside heavy election losses, resulted in him losing his authority within his party with leadership challenges from Wes Streeting and other key figures in the party.

- Despite only being chosen as party leader (and therefore Prime Minister) by her party in September 2022, after her infamously disastrous mini-budget, Lis Truss's popularity plummeted, alongside her party's, and within 45 days of becoming Prime Minister, she was forced to resign in the October.

- Although seeming invincible after winning an 80-seat majority in December 2019, revelations of parties in 10 Downing Street during Covid lockdowns fundamentally damaged Johnson in the public's eye, and his popularity never recovered. His party made it clear that they did not want him as their leader, and he stepped down as Prime Minister in July 2022.

» Prime Ministers with small majorities will be limited by Parliament because backbench rebellions can destabilise their position. They need to ensure party unity to get things done.

- May lost her party's majority in the 2017 snap election and had to form an agreement with the DUP to sustain her party in Westminster. George Osborne described her as 'a dead woman walking', indicating the almost impossible situation she found herself in. His predictions were accurate and May's time as Prime Minister was one of the most tumultuous in modern history.

» The Commons can effectively remove a government by forcing a vote of confidence in the government.

- James Callaghan's administration fell in 1979 after losing a vote of confidence by a single vote: 311 to 310. This was the first time a British Government had lost such a vote since 1924.

» The House of Lords is a limit on the Prime Minister's leadership because the governing party does not have majority control of the Lords. For example, the Lords rejected Rishi Sunak's Rwanda legislation a total of ten times during its passage through Parliament. Peers inflicted five defeats in one session, followed by five further defeats in another, amending the bill on issues such as legal challenges, judicial oversight and protections for vulnerable groups.

Elastic band theory: Variable factors that determine the power of the Prime Minister

As can be seen in the section above, Prime Ministers have many ways to exercise power, but there are also significant limits to consider. Nevertheless, the extent of their power fluctuates not only from Prime Minister to Prime Minister but also at different times within the same premiership. In an article titled 'The Prime Minister's Power' (1985), George Jones argued that Prime Ministerial power was dependent upon many 'variables' which affect their ability to exercise their powers. The term 'elastic band theory' was coined to describe this phenomenon.

Size of majority

The ability to command a large majority is a pivotal factor in Prime Ministerial power. The larger the government's majority, the stronger a Prime Minister will usually be.

» Starmer's 2024 three-figure majority should have enabled him to govern comfortably for his full term. However, his majority was a "shallow" one with many Labour MPs winning their seats by a small margin and this therefore made them conscious of opinion poll ratings and election losses. Consequently, Starmer found himself unable to command his majority throughout

Tip: for more examples of Lords defeats of the government, see the Parliament Chapter.

Synoptic Link

A Prime Minister's popularity is crucial to their ability to control their party, and this is typically judged through opinion polls (a Component 1 topic).

2025–2026 and made U-turn after U-turn as his party refused to support him. After the May 2026 elections, they found it difficult to support his leadership any longer.

» May's lack of majority after 2017 meant that it was impossible for her to be a dominant Prime Minister. Instead she had to rely on DUP support and as her party was fundamentally divided over Brexit, she found her time as Prime Minister extremely difficult.

» Landslide majorities in 1997 (178) and in 2001 (167) enabled the Blair Government to suffer no defeats in the House of Commons in its first two terms. Once Blair's majority had fallen to 65 after the 2005 Election, this could be done by around 30 MPs, and he lost two votes in the Commons. The contrast between small and large majorities can be stark.

» When Margaret Thatcher had majorities of over 100, her position was secure. However, John Major's majority was only ever 21 at its height and this caused him issues throughout his premiership.

Popularity and personality of the Prime Minister

The Prime Minister's popularity with the public underpins all the other constraints on them and their personality can have a significant effect on this. When Prime Ministers are popular and their governments are riding high in the polls, their authority over the Cabinet and the party is assured. However, when the government's popularity dips, and its chances of winning the next election are thrown into doubt, life becomes much more difficult for the Prime Minister.

» Starmer won a landslide majority in 2024 primarily due to the collapse of the Conservative vote, and his popularity was never as high as previous, more charismatic prime ministers. Throughout 2025–26 his poor decision making resulted in the public losing faith in him and as opinion polls nose dived, so did his power.

» Blair's declining personal popularity leading up to the 2005 General Election persuaded him to pre-announce his resignation. This left him as a 'lame duck' Prime Minister for the rest of his two years in office.

» Johnson had always been seen as an ebullient figure. He was able to win the London mayoral election twice, which was considered impossible for a Conservative. He also confounded expectations in 2019 by winning many seats in Labour heartlands. This led many in his party to give him the benefit of the doubt more than once. However, as his premiership progressed and his popularity faded, the party's confidence in him lessened, leading to his demise.

» May, on the other hand, was never particularly popular as Prime Minister and the more the public saw of her the less they liked. She lacked charisma on a national stage, and her 2017 election campaign highlighted her personality flaws all too clearly. Her backbenchers, needing any excuse not to support her Brexit position, exploited her lack of popularity.

» In the early years of her premiership, Thatcher's personality was a vote winner; she was strong and strident with a clear vision for the country. Her popularity was high as many voters liked what they saw. However, as the 1980s progressed, the positive character traits became negatives; she was difficult, inflexible and unwilling to listen to colleagues. Thatcher's vulnerability in the late 1980s coincided with declining poll ratings and early signs of improved support for the Labour Party.

The pressure of events

When Harold Macmillan was Prime Minister from 1957–63, somebody asked him what worried him most. Famously, he replied: 'Events, dear boy, events.' In other words, Macmillan was highlighting the limited control that Prime Ministers have over 'what happens'. In theory, Prime Ministers 'run the country', but in practice surprises come along that demonstrate how little control they actually have.

» Starmer was already unpopular at the start of 2026 when the Epstein-Mandelson scandal nearly unraveled his premiership for good. At the heart of the issue was the PM's judgment, something most PMs struggle to come back from.

» There can be no bigger 'event' that immediately derailed a premiership than the Truss mini-budget. Within hours there was financial market turmoil, a sharp rise in government borrowing costs, a fall in the pound and mortgage chaos. Within 45 days, she was no longer Prime Minister.

» Even though Johnson was riding high in January 2020, the Covid-19 global pandemic impacted on his government in a number of different ways. His mishandling of the pandemic significantly dented his credibility, but the vaccine rollout later in his premiership was a huge success, gaining him authority. But in 2022, 'Partygate' revelations dealt him a fatal blow from which he never recovered.

» For May it was all about Brexit. Her inability to unite her party around her Brexit vision was a personal and political failure.

» As far as Cameron is concerned, he may not have been so willing to commit his party to holding a referendum on EU membership had he known the outcome.

» The biggest 'event' for the Blair Government was Iraq, which changed his premiership forever.

» Victory in the Falklands War of 1982 considerably benefitted Thatcher. Ultimately, however, the introduction of the Poll Tax and divisions over the EU ended Thatcher's premiership.

Opposition

The opposition is another important variable. If a Prime Minister is facing an effective opposition with a charismatic leader, they may find this undermines their own position whereas if the opposition party is divided or the leader ineffective, the Prime Minister may find their position bolstered.

» The Conservative opposition under Kemi Badenoch, recovering from one of their worst electoral defeats as well as significant challenges from Reform UK, made it harder to present an effective challenge to the Starmer Government. Although Badenoch's performance improved in 2026, there was no significant uplift in the opinion polls.

» Labour in opposition under Starmer (2020–24) was a time of mixed fortunes. Initially, Starmer found it very difficult to 'cut through' to the public, with many voters having no idea who he was. However, as Johnson's premiership unravelled, followed shortly after by Truss's and then the lacklustre Sunak period in office, Starmer was able to take advantage of the chaos and lead his party to a huge victory in 2024.

» The Corbyn-led Labour opposition (2015–19) was divided and ineffective. Even though the party did well in the 2017 Election, increasing their vote share by 10%, the party's splits over Brexit enabled the Conservative Government to pass key legislation and survive confidence votes as Labour could not present a united alternative or clear policy. Corbyn himself was dogged by negative press which made his position even more difficult.

» David Cameron was highly effective as Leader of the Opposition from 2005 to 2010. He immediately set himself apart as a Conservative leader by cycling to work and was pictured riding huskies on a visit to the Arctic to highlight climate change, broadening his appeal. He capitalised on Labour's weaknesses during the 2008 financial crisis, criticising Gordon Brown's record and weakening Brown's position. Famously, at his first Prime Minister's Questions in 2005, David Cameron said to Tony Blair: 'He was the future once.' This sharp line highlighted the generational shift in British politics and quickly became one of the most memorable PMQs moments. The phrase encapsulated the sense that Blair's era was ending and marked Cameron as a rising political force. He led the Conservatives to significant electoral gains, ultimately returning them to government in 2010.

The media

Although not included in the original thesis by Jones, the media has an enormous effect on the power of a Prime Minister. The 24/7 news cycle and social media has not only increased the flow of political information to the public, but also reordered power relationships within the executive.

» The media's obsession with personality and image guarantees that media attention focuses primarily on leaders, and especially on the Prime Minister. Thatcher, Blair, Cameron and Johnson were highly effective media performers and were able to use the media to their advantage.

» Appointments such as that of Alastair Campbell under the Blair Government and Dominic Cummings and Lee Cain under Johnson's Government gave rise to an emphasis on 'spin' and 'news management'.

Definition

Spin: The biased or distorted presentation of information so as to gain a desired response; being 'economical with the truth'.

However, media attention does not always work to the benefit of the Prime Minister. Bad news stories such as policy blunders and ministerial resignations are often hyped by the media, turning a problem into a crisis. Also, if Prime Ministers are poor media performers, it can overshadow many other positive qualities.

» While Johnson was a skilled media performer, as things went downhill for him, he faced relentless media focus, particularly over Partygate.

» May was not a skilled media performer, seeming to lack humour and charisma. She appeared wooden and lacklustre in interviews and did herself no favours by admitting to a TV interviewer that the naughtiest thing she ever did was 'running through a field of wheat' when younger.

» The relationship between the Prime Minister and the media reached a low under Gordon Brown, who lacked the presentational skills to be a successful modern leader. Brown's media image was poor from the start, and then went downhill. Memories of a disastrous YouTube appearance and being infamously caught on mic referring to Gillian Duffy as a 'bigoted woman' are just two examples of a disastrous media image.

Key Debate Summary: Are Prime Ministers still as powerful as they once were?

For	Theme	Against
✓ Prime Ministers have the hugely significant power of patronage. » **Popular** Prime Ministers and those with **large majorities** are often able to exercise this power greatly, e.g. Blair and Thatcher at their height were able to appoint anyone they wanted to their Cabinet.	Why are some PMs able to wield their patronage powers fully and others not?	✗ Prime Ministers must be careful to consider many factors when appointing their Cabinet. » Weaker Prime Ministers who are **unpopular** in their party and/or with the public like Brown or May must carefully balance their Cabinets to ensure support.
✓ Prime Ministers have the ability to control the executive. » **Charismatic** Prime Ministers can bypass or dominate their Cabinet to get the outcomes they want. » The growth of No 10 as a policy unit has increased the power of the Prime Minister. » Good 'spin doctors' can ensure **positive media coverage** for a Prime Minister which will enhance their power. » When Prime Ministers are **popular**, their Cabinet is more likely to give them significant flexibility.	Why are some PMs able to control their Cabinet and others not?	✗ Prime Ministers need to ensure they maintain the support of their Cabinet. » All Prime Ministers need to ensure over the longer term that they keep their Cabinet behind them and not take them for granted. » Sometimes, overzealous 'spin doctors' become the story and Prime Ministers face the political fallout, denting their **popularity** with the public. » Unforeseen **events** meant that even once-strong Prime Ministers like Johnson, Blair and Thatcher eventually lost the support of their Cabinet and were forced out of office.
✓ A Prime Minister's party is naturally loyal to their leader. » Almost every Prime Minister begins their time in office with the support of their backbenchers, a so-called 'honeymoon period'. This is because they have a mandate and are **popular** with the electorate.	Why do some PMs get their party's full support and others not?	✗ Party loyalty is completely dependent on the possibility of electoral success. » Equally, if Prime Ministers don't respond well to **events** or have a skilled Leader of the **Opposition** and see their **popularity** diminish, they will soon lose the support of their party.

Michael Foley's theory of **Presidential Government** in the UK, (*The Rise of the British Presidency* 1993, 2001) argues that UK Prime Ministers increasingly resemble US Presidents, relying on personal leadership, direct media engagement and appeals to the public, often bypassing Cabinet and parliamentary constraints. However, while UK Prime Ministers have adopted many presidential characteristics, the parliamentary system and parties continue to impose significant limitations.

> **Spec Key Term**
>
> **Presidential government:** The tendency for political leaders to act increasingly like executive presidents, through the rise of personalised leadership.

Photo 9.1 Are Prime Ministers becoming more presidential?

Source: Stefan Rousseau / Contributor / Getty Images

✅ Spatial Leadership

» **Growth of 'spatial leadership'.** This is the tendency of Prime Ministers to distance themselves from their parties by presenting themselves as 'outsiders' or developing their own ideological stance with Prime Ministers positioning themselves above party politics.

- Thatcher dominated Cabinet discussions, sidelined dissenting 'wets' and promoted 'Thatcherism' as a personal ideology. Her leadership style resembled a CEO centralising authority.
- Blair relied on 'sofa government', making key decisions (e.g. the Iraq War) with a small inner circle, marginalising Cabinet input.
- Cameron painted himself as a 'moderniser' – reformed his party by advocating for policies such as legalising gay marriage.
- Truss rapidly launched her own economic agenda ('Trussonomics'), sidelining Cabinet input and expert advice e.g. dismissing the Treasury's top civil servant and bypassing the Office for Budget Responsibility.

❌ Accountability Mechanisms

» **Parliamentary system.** The UK does not have a separation of powers between the legislature and executive; instead, parliamentary scrutiny and party mechanisms keep presidential tendencies in check.

- May lost control of her party when she accepted that junior ministers could vote with their consciences over Brexit processes.
- Despite Blair and Thatcher distancing themselves, they were eventually ousted by their parties.
- Truss's commitment to her economic policy meant there was nowhere to hide when the markets collapsed.
- Starmer's premiership was significantly limited throughout 2025–2026 by his parliamentary party's refusal to support his agenda due to election losses and poor opinion polls.

> **Tip:** It is important to be able to discuss the relevance of presidentialism in relation to Prime Ministerial power in UK politics.

» **Prime Ministers need their Cabinet** as they need their Cabinet's support to survive.

- In 2022, mass resignations from Johnson's Cabinet – including his Chancellor and Home Secretary – led to his resignation as he had lost his authority over his party.

- In May 2026 Wes Streeting resigned from the Cabinet saying he has "lost confidence" in Starmer's leadership. This resignation was a signal to others who felt the same to join him in challenging Starmer to the leadership.

✅ **Populist Outreach and Quasi Head of State**

» **Tendency towards 'populist outreach'.** This is the tendency of Prime Ministers to try to 'reach out' directly to the public by claiming to articulate their deepest hopes and fears. There is a growing tendency for the Prime Minister to speak *for* the nation in major events. They increasingly use media to craft a presidential image, employing spin doctors and staged events to connect directly with the public.

- Blair used spin doctors like Alastair Campbell to help him control media narratives. He also framed the Iraq War as a moral imperative, guided by his personal values. His 'people's princess' speech after Diana's death highlighted emotional communication, reaching out directly to the people.

- Boris Johnson used televised updates to appeal directly to the people to stay at home and accept all Covid guidelines. He also held daily Covid-19 briefings, which were presidential in style.

» **Head of State:** Prime Ministers increasingly act as heads of state in international diplomacy, overshadowing the monarchy (see Photo 9.1).

- Starmer initially worked hard to have a very close relationship with President Trump. But in 2026 Starmer refused to let President Trump use UK air bases in Diego Garcia or to join in offensive actions against Iran which soured their relationship.

- Starmer also led the European 'coalition of the willing' in early 2025 by supporting Ukraine after President Zelensky's disastrous visit to the White House, which led to a public argument between him, Trump and Vance. Starmer organised a summit which pledged military aid for Ukraine, uniting over 30 countries. He received very positive media coverage for his proactive diplomacy and leadership.

- Johnson played a prominent role at G7 and NATO summits, and he also took an international lead on support for Zelensky during the Ukraine war.

- May gave the green light to military intervention in Syria without following the convention to ask Parliament.

❌ **Leadership Style limitations**

» **Not all Prime Ministers are able to embrace a presidential style**; some are restricted by external factors, while others prioritise consensus.

- May tried to make the 2017 General Election about her 'strong and stable leadership'; however, this spectacularly backfired as her campaign fell apart and she ended up losing seats. Her rigid leadership on Brexit led to parliamentary gridlock.

- Major chose to seek consensus in his party during the early stages of his premiership after Thatcher's combative style.

» **Some prime ministers are unable to dictate foreign policy** like a president.

- Cameron was unable to persuade the Commons to approve air strikes in Syria.

✅ **Policy Centralisation at No 10**

» **Strengthened Cabinet Office.** Presidentialism centralises decision making within the Prime Minister's office, reducing reliance on Cabinet or Parliament. In the UK, we have seen the size and resources available to the **Cabinet Office** grow significantly, turning it into a Prime Minister's department responsible for co-ordinating the rest of Whitehall.

- Tony Blair was accused of surrounding himself with special advisers and not consulting his Cabinet. Cabinet meetings were short and advisory, with decisions being made elsewhere. This is known as a **sofa government**. Tony Blair was also accused of downsizing the importance of Parliament because, except for once a week at PMQs, he rarely attended.

- Truss used her powers of patronage to appoint only loyalists to her Cabinet, and infamously she relied heavily on advisers from the Institute of Economic Affairs think tank.

Definition

Cabinet office: Responsible for supporting the Prime Minister and ensuring the effective running of government. It is composed of various units which take the lead in certain critical policy areas and coordinate the delivery of government policy.

Sofa government: An informal decision-making style within government, stemming from the idea that politicians would be sitting on sofas discussing potential policy ideas. This term was coined to describe Blair's style of government.

» **Wider use of special advisers.** Prime Ministers increasingly rely on hand-picked political advisers rather than on Cabinets, ministers and senior civil servants. These advisers often have a personal loyalty to the Prime Minister rather than to the party or government.

- Boris Johnson appointed Dominic Cummings as his Chief of Staff after he helped him win the Brexit referendum and then the 2019 General Election, and Cummings had a huge influence over the machinery of government.
- During the Blair years, Alastair Campbell was known as the real Deputy Prime Minister.
- Starmer relied heavily on Morgan McSweeney as his Chief of Staff who supported him through his 2020 leadership election, manifesto design and general election win in 2024 before having to resign in 2026.

❌ Party and parliamentary limits

» **Unlike Presidents,** Prime Ministers must navigate their party rebellions and the various factional interests that arise.

- Starmer found it increasingly difficult to control the left and right wings of his party.
- Truss's downfall demonstrates the limits of presidential-style leadership in the UK. Despite her initial autonomy, she quickly lost authority when her policies triggered market turmoil, party rebellion and public criticism. The lack of a personal mandate, internal party dissent and external pressures (media, Bank of England) forced her resignation, showing that UK Prime Ministers cannot escape parliamentary and party constraints.
- During his time in office, Johnson had to adapt and amend policies to avoid backbench rebellions.
- Cameron's Coalition with the Lib Dems required compromise, diluting his agenda.

» **Personalised election campaigns.** The media increasingly portrays elections as personalised battles between the Prime Minister and the Leader of the Opposition. The leader becomes the 'brand image' of their party or government, meaning that personality and image have become major determinants of political success or failure.

✅ Personal mandates.

As a consequence of personalised election campaigns, Prime Ministers claim a mandate on the basis of *their* electoral success. Prime Ministers have therefore become the chief source of their party or government's policy direction.

- Johnson framed Brexit as a personal mandate with 'Get Brexit Done', using populist rhetoric to override party dissent.
- In 2022, when the Conservative Party were trying to oust Johnson, Jacob Rees-Mogg argued that the UK had 'moved to an essentially presidential system' and that any new leader would need to seek their own mandate.
- Labour's 2024 campaign deliberately adopted a presidential style, putting Starmer at the centre of messaging and media appearances, echoing US presidential campaigns and focusing on his personal leadership and vision.

❌ Structural Constraints

» In the UK, Prime Ministers derive authority from Parliament, not direct elections, limiting their ability to act as presidents.

- In 2017, May lost her majority, weakening her ability to govern unilaterally.

» Prime Ministers do not have a separate mandate; they become Prime Minister by simply being the leader of the largest party. This means they can be removed without calling an election.

- Truss, Johnson and May were all removed by their parties.
- Thatcher, despite having a landslide majority, was removed by her party as a result of the decision to implement the Poll Tax.
- Sunak's premiership was shaped by party divisions, parliamentary arithmetic and the need to compromise – factors that limit presidentialism in practice.
- Despite campaigning in a presidential manner in 2024, Starmer soon found himself limited by his parliamentary party, as so many Prime Ministers do.

Key Debate Summary: Are UK Prime Ministers becoming Presidential?

For	Theme	Against
✓ The growth of 'spatial leadership' when Prime Ministers distance themselves from their parties, developing their own ideological stance.	How effectively are Prime Ministers able to exercise spatial leadership?	✗ The UK does not have a separation of powers between the legislature and executive; instead, parliamentary scrutiny and party mechanisms keep presidential tendencies in check.
✓ Tendency towards 'populist outreach' when Prime Ministers try to 'reach out' to the public by claiming to articulate their deepest hopes and fears.	How effectively are Prime Ministers able to exercise populist outreach?	✗ Not all Prime Ministers are able to embrace a presidential style; some are restricted by external factors, and others prioritise consensus.
✓ Centralisation of decision making with No 10 and heavy reliance on special advisers rather than Cabinet.	How effectively are Prime Ministers able to ignore their cabinet, relying instead on special advisors?	✗ Unlike Presidents, Prime Ministers must navigate their party rebellions and the various factional interests that arise.
✓ Personalised election campaigns where the leader becomes the 'brand image' of their party.	How effectively are Prime Ministers able to become the brand of their party?	✗ Prime Ministers do not have a separate mandate; they become Prime Minister by simply being the leader of the largest party. This means they can be removed without calling an election.

The significance of ministerial responsibility

Individual ministerial responsibility

Individual responsibility is the convention that defines the relationship between ministers and their departments. It has two main features:

> **Ministers are responsible for and accountable to Parliament for the policies and actions of their departments.** This is reflected in an obligation to inform and explain, but it may extend to resignation in the event of blunders or policy failures. In theory, individual responsibility implies that ministers take responsibility for the mistakes made by junior ministers and civil servants, but in practice they now only resign as a result of blunders that they have made personally.

> **It also implies that civil servants are responsible to their ministers.** This suggests that civil servants should be loyal and supportive to their minister no matter which party is in government, although if they have ethical concerns about a minister's conduct, they should refer these to the **Cabinet Secretary**.

According to the Cabinet Manual 2011, 'Ministers are individually responsible to Parliament for (i) departmental matters and (ii) for their own conduct in office. … Ministers hold office as long as they have the confidence of the Prime Minister.' This shows that there are two strands to individual ministerial responsibility.

1. **Legal responsibility.** Individual ministerial responsibility refers to the convention that ministers are responsible for all that goes on within their own department, whether or not they are directly involved. In extreme cases they may be required to resign, but normally have to account to Parliament and face criticism. A historic example of this convention in action was the resignation of Lord Carrington in 1982 due to the invasion of the Falkland Islands. As Foreign Secretary, he felt it a matter of honour that he should resign, despite protestations from his Prime Minister. However, in the modern era, this is rarely the case.

The ministerial code is part of the Cabinet Manual and stated that ministers were expected to offer their resignation to the Prime Minister if they knowingly misled Parliament. For other breaches, there was a strong expectation – both in convention and public perception – that ministers should resign

---

Spec Key Term

Individual responsibility: The principle by which ministers are responsible for their personal conduct and for their departments.

Definition

Cabinet Secretary: The most senior Civil Service adviser to the Prime Minister and Cabinet. They often act as one of the Prime Minister's senior advisers on the working of government and on major policy decisions.

or be dismissed for any violation of the code. In 2018, Amber Rudd was forced to resign when it was revealed that she had inadvertently misled Parliament when answering questions over the existence of targets regarding the *Windrush* scandal. She explained in her resignation letter that she had 'not been sufficiently aware' of them. This resignation serves as a reminder that ministers must be aware of actions and decisions made in their department.

However, in 2022, the then Prime Minister, Boris Johnson, made significant changes to the ministerial code. Johnson added the caveat that only 'knowingly misleading Parliament' would automatically require resignation, while other breaches could result in lesser sanctions such as a public apology, remedial action or temporary loss of salary. Ultimately, the Prime Minister is the final arbiter of whether a minister should resign for a breach of the code. Johnson's changes made it less likely that ministers, like Rudd, would have to resign for breaching standards, allowing for more flexible and less severe responses to breaches.

2. **Political responsibility**. This aspect covers ministers' personal conduct, unrelated to how effective they are at their job. The media is only too eager to pick up on any event which might suggest that the MP has been dishonest and/or hypocritical. Ministers are forced to resign because of some personal failing which is not necessarily related to their performance as head of a government department. A clear example of this was Chris Pincher, who resigned as Conservative deputy chief whip in July 2022 after admitting he 'drank far too much' and 'embarrassed myself and other people' during a drunken night out, which led to allegations of sexual misconduct.

Collective ministerial responsibility

According to the Cabinet Manual: 'The roles of the Prime Minister and Cabinet are governed largely by convention; decisions made at Cabinet and Cabinet committee level are binding on all members of the government, save where collective agreement is expressly set aside, and any minister who cannot accept them is expected to resign.' **Collective responsibility** is a convention that extends to *all* government ministers based on the view that ministers have responsibility, as a group, for all the policies of the government. Collective responsibility is important because:

» It ensures that the government is collectively responsible to Parliament and ministers present a united front, with the government collectively shouldering responsibility for government actions and policies.

» It means that discussions inside Cabinet remain private and conflict remains confidential. Any member of the Cabinet who feels unable to accept this restraint is expected to resign.

» It can underpin Prime Ministerial power by silencing critics within the government.

» It also creates a **payroll vote** in Parliament and helps ensure that potential rebels in government can be silenced. An example of this occurred in 2025 when International Development Minister Anneliese Dodds resigned over cuts to the aid budget. This shows the convention is working well.

However, collective ministerial responsibility has come under strain historically with ministers disagreeing but not resigning. The past 50 years have witnessed several internal battles within Cabinet and some of these have led to the ultimate downfall of a Prime Minister. Also, the fact that collective responsibility can be, and has been, set aside has led some academics to argue that it is a rule enforced by Prime Ministers when it suits them and discarded when it does not. The lesson from history is clear – a Prime Minister must maintain at least the semblance of Cabinet unity if they wish to lay claim to be the leader of the country at large.

The best example of a collapse of collective responsibility came during 2018–19 of the May Government. During this time, ministers publicly disagreed with May's policy and didn't resign. This had the effect of fundamentally destabilising the government. In 2019, 13 Conservative ministers – including four Cabinet ministers – abstained on ruling out a no-deal Brexit in all circumstances despite a three-line whip for them to oppose it. Extraordinarily, it later emerged that they had been given permission to do so without being sacked by the Prime Minister. Power visibly ebbed away from May as her divided Cabinet openly discussed alternatives to her EU deal and voted against it while staying in her Cabinet. She was too weak to sack them, and they knew it. Collective responsibility was dead and without it, the appearance of a united government died too.

Referendums and coalitions can also be a challenge to collective responsibility. In the 2016 Brexit Referendum, Cameron suspended collective responsibility, allowing ministers to campaign for either side, and under the 2010 Coalition, the notion of collective ministerial responsibility was viewed differently with the Coalition Agreement outlining a number of policy areas where internal disagreements were permitted.

Spec Key Term

Collective responsibility: The principle by which ministers must support Cabinet decisions or leave the executive.

Definition

Payroll vote: Used to describe MPs who hold positions in the government which they would have to resign from in order to oppose the government.

Figure 9.4 Number of ministerial resignations outside reshuffles, 1979–2026

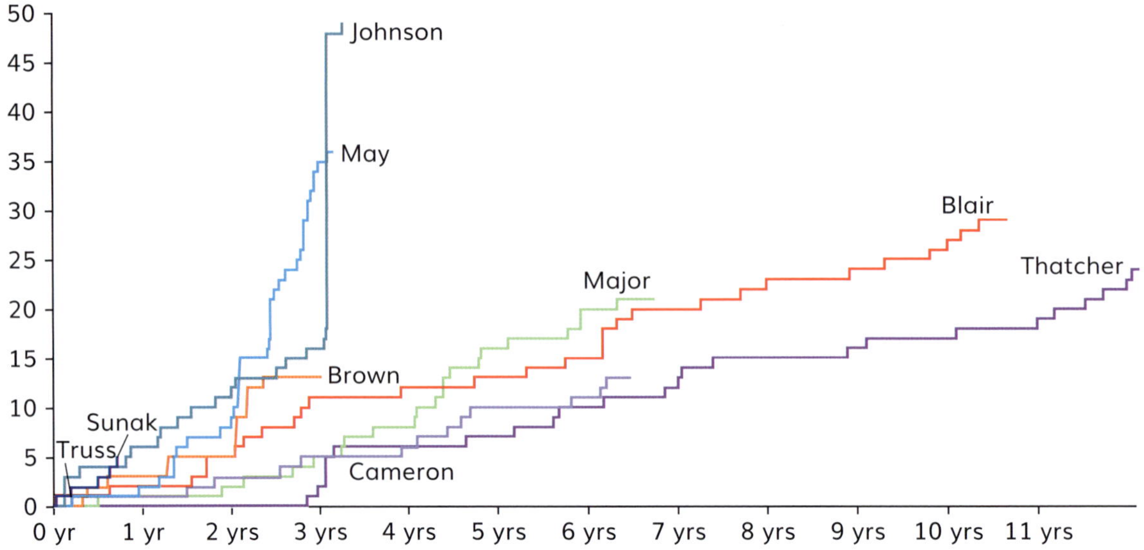

Source: Institute for Government

KEY TOPIC DEBATE: ARE THE CONVENTIONS OF MINISTERIAL RESPONSIBILITY STILL IMPORTANT?

✓ **Collective ministerial responsibility is a key element of government unity and the Cabinet is still held to account through it. Ministers resign or are sacked if they can't support the government's policy.**

» In May 2026, Wes Streeting resigned from the Cabinet saying he had "lost confidence" in Starmer's leadership.

» In June 2025, Labour MP Vicky Foxcroft resigned as a whip over the government's plans to cut disability benefits. She was unable to support the policy.

» In 2023, Suella Braverman was sacked as Home Secretary after publishing an article criticising police handling of protests, defying No 10's requests for changes before publication.

» In 2023, Zac Goldsmith resigned as Minister for Energy, Climate and Environment after disagreeing with the government's climate and environment policy.

» In 2022, Sajid Javid and Rishi Sunak both resigned in protest at Boris Johnson's handling of the Chris Pincher scandal and broader concerns about the Prime Minister's integrity and leadership. Johnson's premiership had been in danger for months after several scandals, but it was the Pincher scandal that led to the resignations. Considered the 'last straw' for many, the scandal arose after it was revealed that Johnson had promoted Pincher, who was publicly facing multiple allegations of sexual assault, to the position despite knowing of the allegations beforehand. Their resignations triggered 62 further departures, ultimately forcing Johnson to resign as Prime Minister.

✗ **However, collective ministerial responsibility has come under strain with ministers disagreeing but not resigning. A Prime Minister must maintain Cabinet unity if they wish to lead with conviction.**

» In March 2026, Culture Secretary Lisa Nandy called the government's situation "unforgivable" because scandals like the Mandelson–Epstein affair left Labour looking self-absorbed and chaotic instead of fixing the crises facing the public who trusted them. Criticising a government you are a part of is certainly a breach of CMR, yet she did not resign.

» In 2025, David Lammy warned that aid cuts could allow China to step in and further its global influence, saying that the aid cut was regrettable but also one of 'the hard-headed decisions you make when you are in government'. Cabinet Energy Secretary Ed Miliband also raised concerns. Neither minister resigned.

» Throughout 2018–19, Prime Minister May had many senior ministers disagreeing and not resigning, which was very destabilising to her government. Chancellor Philip Hammond and Brexit Secretary David Davis publicly challenged each other regarding the ending of free movement, but neither resigned despite openly contradicting one another.

✓ **Collective responsibility is a flexible convention which can be temporarily suspended when issues that transcend party politics are to be considered by the government.**
» In 2025, CMR was waived for the Terminally Ill (Adults) End of Life Bill.
» In 2016, May announced that Cabinet ministers who disagreed with the decision to grant Heathrow an extra runway would be given a 'derogation' from collective responsibility.
» On the 2016 referendum on the UK's membership of the European Union, Cameron suspended collective responsibility, allowing ministers to campaign for either side.
» Under the 2010–15 Coalition, collective responsibility was suspended in certain policy areas.
» In 1975, ministers in the Labour Government were allowed to disagree publicly during the referendum campaign on the EC. This historic decision was known as 'the agreement to differ'.

✗ **The fact that collective responsibility can be, and has been, set aside has led some to argue that it is a rule enforced by Prime Ministers when it suits them and discarded when it does not.**
» All the examples above occurred to resolve party management difficulties. In other words, collective responsibility *had* to be suspended on these occasions because the Prime Minister could not make their Cabinet support them.
» This shows that collective responsibility is not effective in making ministers support the policies of their government.

✓ **Ministers take responsibility by being answerable and accountable for the work of their departments. Only when they are clearly personally to blame will they resign.** The resignation of a Cabinet minister due to individual ministerial responsibility depends on the severity of the issue, the Prime Minister's response and the role of the media. It is unreasonable to suggest every minister should resign due to a small failure in their own department, but on key issues individual ministerial responsibility does still occur.
» In 2022, Kwasi Kwarteng was sacked as Chancellor by Liz Truss after 38 days in post, making him responsible for the mini-budget fiasco.
» In 2022, Suella Braverman resigned as Home Secretary under Liz Truss after she sent an official government document from her personal email to a parliamentary colleague, which breached the ministerial code. In her resignation letter, Braverman accepted responsibility for this 'technical infringement' and stated that resigning was the right thing to do.
» In 2018, Amber Rudd resigned as Home Secretary when she inadvertently misled MPs over whether she knew about targets to remove illegal immigrants.
» It is also worth noting that Individual Ministerial Responsibility (IMR) applies to the highest office, that of the Prime Minister. David Cameron resigned the morning after the EU referendum, acknowledging his failure to achieve the result he wanted. Boris Johnson was forced to step down as Prime Minister after his role in the Partygate scandal.

✗ **Individual ministerial responsibility is clear, but ministers seek to shift the blame to others to deflect bad publicity.** There is no formal mechanism for enforcing it, meaning that today ministers frequently use ignorance of misbehaviour as an argument for lack of culpability. Often, it is the media who are the ultimate deciders of when ministers resign, not the conventions.
» In 2025, an Ethiopian asylum seeker and convicted sex offender was mistakenly released from HMP Chelmsford while Justice Secretary David Lammy was responsible for prisons. Lammy was then forced to admit that a total of 91 prisoners were freed in error between April and October 2025. He did not resign.
» In August 2021, Foreign Secretary Dominic Raab was on holiday when Kabul fell to the Taliban. Raab faced intense criticism for not returning to the UK immediately. Despite reports that Downing Street had told him to come back, he stayed until after the capital had already fallen. Raab delegated critical phone calls to a junior minister, and there were widespread calls for his resignation. Prime Minister Johnson, however, continued to express confidence in Raab, who remained in post despite the controversy.
» In 2020, Priti Patel was found to have broken the ministerial code with regards to allegations of bullying civil servants in her department. Yet Johnson stood by her and refused to sack her, leading the Institute for Government to say that the ministerial code had been fatally undermined.

✓ **Individual ministerial responsibility is an important aspect of governance as it ensures that those involved at the top of public life maintain the correct standards of behaviour.**
» In September 2025, Angela Rayner resigned as deputy prime minister, housing secretary and Labour deputy leader after an ethics adviser found she had underpaid stamp duty on

> **Tip:** When writing essays, it's not enough to list examples like this; it is better to take a couple of examples and explain HOW they show that the convention is/isn't working.

her £800,000 Hove flat, breaching the ministerial code despite claiming it was an honest mistake.

» In August 2025, Homelessness and Democracy minister Rushanara Ali resigned after it emerged she had evicted tenants from her east London property and then re-listed it with the rent increased by about £700 a month, prompting accusations of hypocrisy.

» In 2025, Economic Secretary to the Treasury, Tulip Siddiq, resigned after intense media scrutiny over her family ties and property ownership abroad. Although cleared of wrongdoing, she stepped down because the controversy risked distracting from government work.

» Andrew Gwynne was forced to resign as a government minister in February 2025 after a series of offensive and inappropriate messages posted in a WhatsApp group. These messages included derogatory and prejudiced remarks about constituents, Labour colleagues and antisemitic slights.

» In 2024, Transport Secretary Louise Haigh resigned after revelations about a past criminal conviction.

» In 2023, Dominic Raab resigned as Deputy Prime Minister and Justice Secretary after a bullying investigation upheld complaints against him.

» In 2023, Nadhim Zahawi was sacked as Conservative Party Chairman and Minister without Portfolio for breaching the ministerial code over seven breaches of his tax affairs.

» In 2022, Deputy Chief Whip Chris Pincher resigned after reports surfaced that he drunkenly groped two men at the Carlton Club.

❌ **As ministerial responsibilities are merely conventions and not legally binding, their application is inconsistently applied. Hence, they do not result in securing the accountability of ministers.**

» In 2022, Prime Minister Boris Johnson took the step of updating the ministerial code from 'misleading parliament' to '*knowingly* misleading Parliament' as a reason to resign. It is particularly hard to prove this additional aspect. It is also worth noting that this occurred whilst Johnson himself was under investigation for misleading parliament about Partygate allegations.

» In the case of Raab in 2023, the allegations of bullying had been around for many, many months, yet Raab hung on. He finally resigned because an independent investigation upheld complaints that he had bullied civil servants while serving as Foreign and Justice Secretary. The inquiry found Raab had acted in an 'intimidating' and 'persistently aggressive' manner, including abusing or misusing power in ways that undermined or humiliated officials.

Key Debate Summary: Are the conventions of ministerial responsibility still important?

For	Theme	Against
✓ Collective ministerial responsibility is still important as it is a key element of government unity and the Cabinet is still held to account through it.	How effectively is CMR upheld by ministers?	✗ However, collective ministerial responsibility has come under great strain with ministers disagreeing but not resigning.
✓ Collective responsibility is a flexible convention that can be temporarily suspended for issues that transcend party politics.	How effectively is CMR upheld by ministers?	✗ The fact that collective responsibility can be, and has been, set aside has led some to argue that it is a rule enforced by Prime Ministers when it suits them and discarded when it does not.
✓ Individual ministerial responsibility is an important aspect of governance as it ensures that Ministers are fully focused on the work and actions of their department.	Do Ministers resign when they make a mistake in their work as a Minister?	✗ Because they are merely conventions, and not legally binding, their application is inconsistently applied, hence they do not result in securing the accountability of ministers.
✓ Individual ministerial responsibility also ensures that those involved at the top of public life maintain the correct quality of behaviour.	Do Ministers resign when they behave inappropriately in their personal life?	✗ Individual ministerial responsibility is clear, but ministers seek to shift the blame to others to deflect bad publicity.

CASE STUDY 9.1: THATCHER AS PRIME MINISTER 1979–90

Photo 9.2 US President Ronald Reagan and UK Prime Minister Margaret Thatcher, 1981

Source: Bettmann / Getty Images

In January 1979, Prime Minister James Callaghan famously predicted a 'sea change' in British politics, sensing the public was ready for a dramatic shift: one that would soon be embodied by Margaret Thatcher. Callaghan's prophecy proved accurate: the modern era of British politics is often considered to have begun with Thatcher's general election victory in May 1979. Thatcher's rise to Conservative leadership in 1975 was itself unexpected, making her the first female leader of a major British party and, four years later, the first woman Prime Minister winning the 1979 General Election with a majority of 43. She was determined to turn the economy around with her monetarist economic policies.

Uncertain early years as Prime Minister

Thatcher's early years as Prime Minister were marked by economic hardship and social unrest. Unemployment soared above 3 million and riots erupted in cities across England. Despite mounting criticism, Thatcher, alongside Chancellor Geoffrey Howe, pressed on with monetarist economic policies designed to curb inflation and reduce the state's role in the economy. At the 1980 Conservative Party Conference, she famously declared, 'You turn if you want to. The lady's not for turning.' Her resolve was soon tested by the 1982 Argentine invasion of the Falkland Islands. Thatcher's decisive leadership during the conflict, culminating in the recapture of the islands, transformed her public image into the 'Iron Lady'. The victory, coupled with an improving economy and a divided Labour opposition, paved the way for a landslide Conservative win in the 1983 General Election, with a majority of 144 seats.

After the Falklands

With her authority strengthened, Thatcher pushed forward her transformative agenda. 'Thatcherism'

became synonymous with rolling back the state: major privatisations of British Telecom, British Airways and British Gas; the sale of council houses to tenants; and significant tax cuts for individuals. While rooted in monetarist theory, Thatcherism quickly evolved to reflect her personal convictions and leadership style. Her second term saw the defeat of the year-long miners' strike, which she framed as a battle against the 'enemy within'. This victory further cemented her reputation for toughness.

Thatcher's premiership was also shaped by external threats, notably the 1984 IRA bombing of the Grand Hotel in Brighton during the Conservative Party Conference. Surviving the attempt on her life, she delivered her speech the next day, reinforcing her image as resolute and courageous. However, the Troubles in Northern Ireland persisted, with little progress towards peace during her time in office.

On the world stage, Thatcher's profile soared. She forged a close ideological partnership with US President Ronald Reagan, sharing a commitment to free-market economics and anti-communism. She also recognised the reforming potential of Soviet leader Mikhail Gorbachev, playing a prominent role in the West's response to the end of the Cold War. Many argue that her influence on global affairs exceeded the UK's declining international standing.

Thatcher secured a third term in 1987 with a reduced but still commanding majority. However, her leadership style became increasingly autocratic. She surrounded herself with loyalists and became estranged from key colleagues like Geoffrey Howe and Nigel Lawson. Her political instincts, once finely attuned to public sentiment, began to falter. The introduction of the deeply unpopular Poll Tax alienated both the public and many within her own party. Her combative approach led to mounting tensions within her Cabinet, particularly over Europe, resulting in the resignations of Howe and Lawson.

The decline

Ultimately, the Conservative Party's instinct for survival prevailed. After more than 11 years in power and three election victories, Thatcher's MPs decided her time was up. Michael Heseltine challenged her leadership in 1990; although she won the first ballot, it was not decisive enough to avoid a second. Cabinet colleagues advised her that victory was unlikely, and she resigned, leaving Downing Street after a dramatic and divisive tenure. Margaret Thatcher died in 2013, but her legacy of economic transformation, political polarisation and a reshaped Conservative Party continues to shape British politics.

CASE STUDY 9.2: BLAIR AS PRIME MINISTER 1997–2007

Source: Adrian Dennis / AFP / Getty Images

Photo 9.3 British Prime Minister Tony Blair poses for a photo with troops at Shaiba Logistics Base in Basra, Iraq in December 2004

Tony Blair became Prime Minister in 1997, ending 18 years of Conservative rule and leading Labour to a landslide victory with 419 out of 650 seats. This overwhelming majority not only secured Blair's position for a full term but also made it likely he would serve at least two terms.

The powerful years

Blair's early years in office were marked by a prolonged honeymoon period, high personal popularity and a largely united party. He responded deftly to national moments like the death of Princess Diana, managed the media with skill, and effectively countered opposition leader William Hague. With such a commanding majority, Blair kept his Cabinet at arm's length, relying instead on a close circle of advisers: Peter Mandelson, Alastair Campbell and Jonathan Powell. This 'sofa government' approach allowed him to shape policy informally, persuading key figures in private rather than through formal Cabinet meetings.

However, Blair's relationship with his Chancellor, Gordon Brown, was fraught with tension. Brown believed Blair had promised to step aside after one term – a pact Blair later denied. This led to a power struggle, with Brown controlling the Treasury and withholding support for policies he viewed as too 'Blairite'. Deputy Prime Minister John Prescott often had to mediate between the two camps, and eventually, the 'Brownites' became a powerful force within Labour.

Blair's Government delivered a sweeping programme of constitutional reform, as promised in the 1997 manifesto. This included devolution to Scotland, Wales and Northern Ireland, the Human Rights Act, reform of the House of Lords, and the separation of the Law Lords from Parliament. He also introduced significant reforms to education and the NHS, often through public-private partnerships. Blair's involvement in the Northern Ireland peace process was a lasting achievement, helping to secure an end to decades of violence. In foreign affairs, Blair's early interventions in Kosovo and Sierra Leone were widely praised and boosted his confidence on the world stage.

Afghanistan, Iraq and beyond

However, the aftermath of the 11 September 2001 terrorist attacks marked a turning point. Blair was the first world leader to visit President George W Bush in the US, pledging to stand 'shoulder to shoulder' with America. This close alliance led to British involvement in the wars in Afghanistan and, more controversially, Iraq. In 2003, despite widespread opposition and inconclusive evidence of weapons of mass destruction, Blair supported the US-led invasion of Iraq. The toppling of Saddam Hussein was followed by years of violent insurgency and instability. No weapons were found, and Blair's reputation was permanently damaged by accusations that he had misled Parliament and the public.

Blair's dominance over Cabinet and government, built on Labour's electoral successes in 1997 and 2001, allowed him to prevail over internal opposition for much of his tenure. However, the Iraq War revealed the limits of prime ministerial power. Blair's popularity plummeted, and Labour's majority was slashed to 65 seats in the 2005 Election and he had already promised not to seek a fourth term. The later years of his premiership were marked by backbench rebellions over issues such as tuition fees, foundation hospitals and anti-terror legislation. Blair, who had never lost a Commons vote between 1997 and 2005, now faced a more assertive Parliament. Ultimately, mounting opposition within his party and the legacy of Iraq forced Blair to announce a timetable for his departure, and he stepped down in June 2007, handing over to Gordon Brown. Blair's legacy is one of dramatic transformation for Labour and the UK, but also of controversy and division, particularly over Iraq.

CASE STUDY 9.3: BORIS JOHNSON 2019–22

Boris Johnson's time as UK Prime Minister was one of extraordinary drama, marked by major political achievements, deep controversies and ultimately a spectacular collapse driven by scandal and backbench revolts.

The highs

Johnson entered Downing Street in July 2019 after winning the Conservative leadership with a promise to 'Get Brexit Done'. At the time, the UK was hindered by parliamentary deadlock over Brexit, having repeatedly failed to ratify a withdrawal agreement under May. Johnson's assertive style and willingness to take risks – such as unlawfully proroguing Parliament to force through his agenda – set him apart from his predecessor, Theresa May.

His first major achievement was securing a revised Brexit deal with the EU and then calling a snap general election in December 2019. The result was a historic Conservative landslide, delivering an 80-seat majority – the party's best result in three decades. With this mandate, Johnson swiftly passed his Brexit deal, ending the UK's formal EU membership in January 2020. This 'got Brexit done', fulfilling a central campaign promise.

Another high point was the UK's Covid-19 vaccine rollout. Under Johnson, Britain became one of the first countries to approve and distribute vaccines, outpacing most of Europe and the world. This success was widely credited with saving lives and enabling a faster reopening of society.

Johnson's Government also increased public sector spending; it pledged 20,000 new police officers and launched major infrastructure projects like HS2, aiming to 'level up' the country.

The lows

Despite these achievements, Johnson's premiership was beset by controversy and mismanagement. In August 2019, Boris Johnson's Government advised The Queen to prorogue Parliament for five weeks, just ahead of the Brexit deadline. Critics noted the timing would severely limit Parliament's ability to scrutinise Brexit, especially efforts to block a no-deal exit. The Supreme Court ultimately ruled the prorogation unlawful, finding the government failed to provide reasonable justification and that the move unjustifiably interfered with parliamentary sovereignty. Parliament was reconvened immediately, and the episode marked a serious constitutional crisis.

His handling of the Covid-19 pandemic drew criticism for delays in imposing lockdowns, confusion over restrictions, and the costly failure of the NHS Test and Trace system. The government's messaging was often muddled.

Johnson's leadership style, which was charismatic but often chaotic, led to accusations of a lack of focus and clear philosophy. His former adviser Dominic Cummings branded him an 'out-of-control shopping trolley', and critics pointed to frequent U-turns and policy reversals. It was often suggested that he would adopt the policy of the last person he spoke to, which led to confusion within government.

In 2021, the Owen Paterson affair, where he attempted to block Paterson's suspension by ordering Conservative MPs to vote for an overhaul of the standards system, sparked widespread outrage, with accusations of 'sleaze' and undermining parliamentary standards which forced Johnson into a rapid U-turn. This damaged his authority and credibility, triggering unrest within the Conservative Party and eroding trust in his leadership. This marked the beginning of a series of crises that ultimately contributed to Johnson's downfall as Prime Minister.

The 'Partygate' scandal (revelations that Johnson and senior officials attended parties in Downing Street during Covid lockdowns) proved especially damaging. Johnson became the first sitting prime minister found to have broken the law while in office, receiving a police fine. The scandal eroded public trust and triggered a parliamentary inquiry into whether he misled Parliament.

Backbench unrest and rebellion

Johnson's approach frequently alienated his own MPs. Early in his premiership, he expelled 21 Conservative MPs – including senior figures – for rebelling on Brexit, a move that deepened party divisions. Later, as the pandemic wore on, he faced major backbench rebellions over Covid restrictions, at times with nearly 100 Tory MPs voting against him. He also faced dissent over free school meals and other policy areas.

As scandals mounted, Johnson's authority weakened. By-elections in Conservative heartlands and a string of ministerial resignations signalled growing discontent. His handling of the Chris Pincher affair in July 2022, when he appointed him as Deputy Whip despite knowing that he had been accused of sexual misconduct, then misleading colleagues about what he knew, was the final straw.

Downfall: mass resignations and collapse

The Pincher scandal triggered a tidal wave of resignations: first Sajid Javid and Rishi Sunak, then more than 60 ministers and aides within 72 hours. Johnson tried to cling on, insisting he had a mandate to govern, but the resignations made his position untenable. By July 2022, Johnson announced his resignation as Conservative leader, though he stayed on as caretaker prime minister until September.

Conclusion

Boris Johnson's premiership was defined by dramatic highs and lows, from delivering Brexit and a landslide election win to presiding over scandals and mass resignations. His downfall was ultimately self-inflicted, the product of a leadership style that inspired loyalty and resentment in equal measure, and a disregard for rules that, in the end, cost him the support of his own party.

CASE STUDY 9.4: THE PREMIERSHIP OF LIZ TRUSS 2022

Photo 9.4 Liz Truss's beleaguered premiership

Source: Mark Kerrison / Contributor / Getty Images

Liz Truss's premiership, from 6 September to 25 October 2022, stands as the shortest and one of the most tumultuous in British history. Lasting just 49 days, her time in office was defined by economic upheaval, political miscalculation and a rapid loss of authority, culminating in her resignation amid party and public pressure.

Rise to power and early challenges

Truss became Prime Minister after winning the Conservative Party leadership contest, succeeding Boris Johnson at a time of significant instability. The UK was facing a cost of living crisis, soaring energy prices and the ongoing war in Ukraine. Within days of her appointment, the nation was plunged into mourning by the death of Queen Elizabeth II, briefly suspending government business and delaying her policy agenda.

The mini-budget and economic crisis

Truss's defining policy moment came on 23 September when her Chancellor, Kwasi Kwarteng, unveiled a 'mini-budget' featuring £45 billion of unfunded tax cuts, including abolishing the top rate of income tax and cancelling planned rises in National Insurance and corporation tax. This package, designed to stimulate growth and signal a new economic direction, was not accompanied by an assessment from the Office for Budget Responsibility (OBR), breaking with established practice and alarming financial markets.

The reaction was immediate and severe. The pound plummeted to historic lows, government borrowing costs soared, and the Bank of England was forced to intervene to stabilise the bond market. The International Monetary Fund, foreign leaders and senior Conservative MPs voiced strong criticism. The chaos undermined confidence in the government's economic competence and led to a dramatic loss of support within her own party.

Political fallout and Cabinet turmoil

Truss's political authority quickly eroded. Her refusal to appoint ministers who had not supported her leadership bid left her with a narrow base of support and a lack of experienced talent in her Cabinet. As the crisis deepened, she sacked Chancellor Kwarteng and replaced him with Jeremy Hunt, who swiftly reversed almost all the mini-budget measures in an effort to restore market confidence.

Further instability followed with the resignation of Home Secretary Suella Braverman, who cited a breach of ministerial rules and criticised the government's direction in her resignation letter. On 19 October, a chaotic parliamentary vote on fracking descended into confusion, with allegations of bullying and manhandling of MPs further damaging the government's reputation and exposing deep divisions within the Conservative Party.

Backbench unrest and loss of authority

Truss's support among Conservative MPs collapsed as her economic strategy unravelled and her authority was openly challenged. The party, already fatigued by years of internal conflict and leadership changes, was unwilling to rally behind a leader seen as responsible for economic turmoil and public outrage; calls for her resignation grew louder by the day. Amid the turmoil, the *Daily Star* ran a viral livestream to see if an iceberg lettuce would outlast her time in office. The lettuce became a symbol of her political fragility.

Resignation and legacy

On 20 October, after just 44 days in office, Truss announced her resignation as Conservative leader and Prime Minister, acknowledging she could not deliver the mandate on which she was elected by her party. She was succeeded by Rishi Sunak, who reversed many of her policies while retaining Jeremy Hunt as Chancellor.

Truss's premiership is widely regarded as a case study in the dangers of radical economic policy without broad support or institutional backing. Her rapid downfall was driven by market panic, poor political judgement and a lack of party unity. It remains a cautionary tale about the limits of ideological zeal and the importance of political and economic stability in government leadership.

CASE STUDY 9.5: THE PREMIERSHIP OF RISHI SUNAK 2022–24

Rishi Sunak's tenure as Prime Minister of the United Kingdom (October 2022–July 2024) was marked by efforts to restore economic stability after the turmoil of Liz Truss's brief leadership, persistent internal party divisions, and a struggle to reconnect the Conservative Party with the electorate amid mounting crises. His time in office ultimately ended with a landslide defeat to Labour.

Rise to power and immediate challenges

Sunak became Prime Minister on 25 October 2022 following the resignation of Liz Truss after her 'mini-budget' sparked financial chaos, and was the first British Asian and Hindu to hold the office, a historic milestone. He inherited a country facing a cost of living crisis, high inflation and low public trust in government after years of Conservative infighting and scandal.

His initial priority was to steady the economy and government. He reversed many of Truss's policies, restored a sense of fiscal discipline, and kept Jeremy Hunt as Chancellor. Sunak's Government was seen as a return to 'sensible policymaking', with a focus on stability and competence.

Five key pledges and policy record

In January 2023, Sunak outlined five key pledges, with halving inflation as his top priority. By the end of 2023, he achieved this goal, providing some relief to households facing rising costs. Additionally, the economy showed slight growth, although modest by historical standards. Despite these successes, Sunak's progress on his other pledges – cutting NHS waiting lists, getting debt falling and stopping small boat crossings – was less successful. Waiting lists remained stubbornly high, the Rwanda deportation plan was repeatedly blocked by the courts, small boat arrivals remained a contentious and unresolved issue, and debt reduction was not achieved as hoped. Nonetheless, delivering on the inflation pledge was a central achievement of his premiership, demonstrating his commitment to economic stability and responsible governance.

Leadership style and party management

Sunak's leadership was defined by caution and pragmatism. He sought to restore standards in public life after the Johnson and Truss eras, but was criticised for lacking vision and failing to inspire the public or his party.

Party management proved a persistent challenge. Sunak inherited a fractious Conservative Party, with deep divisions between centrist and right-wing factions. His attempts to balance these interests – such as reappointing rivals like Suella Braverman and Penny Mordaunt to senior roles – kept the party together in the short term but did not resolve underlying tensions. Backbench unrest grew as the party's poll ratings failed to improve. Sunak faced repeated rebellions over migration, tax policy and social issues. The Rwanda plan, in particular, exposed deep splits, with MPs on both the right and left threatening to vote against the government.

Downfall and election defeat

By 2024, Sunak's Government was beset by by-election losses, continued cost of living pressures and a sense of drift. Labour maintained a commanding lead in the polls, and Sunak's personal ratings remained low. Despite speculation he might delay, Sunak surprised everyone by calling a general election for July 2024. The result was a historic defeat for the Conservatives, with Labour winning a landslide majority. Sunak immediately resigned as Prime Minister and party leader, accepting responsibility for the loss and pledging to remain as an MP.

Conclusion and legacy

Rishi Sunak's premiership was defined by crisis management rather than transformation. He succeeded in restoring a measure of stability after Truss's chaos and delivered on inflation, but failed to revive Conservative fortunes or address the deeper challenges facing the UK. His legacy is one of competence in adversity, but also of missed opportunities and a party unable to renew itself after 14 years in power.

Exam Style Questions

- Evaluate the view that Prime Ministers have become too powerful in recent years (30).
- Evaluate the view that the personalities and leadership styles of Prime Ministers have the biggest influence on the power they wield (30).
- Evaluate the view that Prime Ministers are only as powerful as their parties allow them to be (30).
- Evaluate the view that the limitations provided by the other branches on the Prime Minister now ultimately outweigh the Prime Minister's powers (30).
- Evaluate the view that the power of the executive has been severely undermined by constitutional reforms since 1997 (30).
- Evaluate the view that it is the Cabinet that can shape policy and control the power of the Prime Minister, not Parliament.
- Evaluate the view that the UK Government's control over Parliament has reduced in recent years (30).

Source Question

Source 1

The Prime Minister's ability to dominate the Cabinet usually results in their Cabinet being united behind them. Nowadays, Prime Ministers have considerable sources of their own advice which makes them less reliant on their Cabinet. Recent Prime Ministers have had a Policy Unit at No 10 and a range of special advisers who report directly to them. This growth of special advisers has meant that Cabinet acts as little more than a 'rubber stamp' for decisions made elsewhere, meeting for less time than in the past. The Prime Minister also has significant powers of patronage, which enables Prime Ministers to choose people who are either personally loyal or ideologically sympathetic to them. Patronage powers also encourage loyalty in Cabinet members as a Prime Minister can make or break their political careers, and collective responsibility enables a Prime Minister to silence dissenters in Cabinet. Lastly, Prime Ministers can control the workings of Cabinet and may be able to manipulate the outcome of policy discussion through bilateral meetings with ministers and bypass the Cabinet through the use of Cabinet committees, to control debate and remove discussion from full Cabinet to a group of hand-picked ministers they can rely on.

Source 2

Prime Ministers are ultimately only as powerful as their Cabinet allows them to be; no Prime Minister can survive, long term, without broad Cabinet support. The Cabinet can overrule or even remove a Prime Minister, as has happened a number of times. Some Cabinet ministers are very powerful in their own right and it would be difficult for a Prime Minister to sack 'big beasts' who have important power bases in the party. They provide a balance to the overarching power of the Prime Ministers and are hard to silence. Prime Ministers need to be careful how they use their patronage powers as a poorly planned reshuffle can erode confidence in their leadership. In some circumstances the Cabinet still makes key decisions, and it still gives authority to government policy. Even though meaningful debate and the formulation of policy decisions takes place elsewhere, these decisions must be brought to and approved by the Cabinet to become official government policy. Lastly, the Cabinet is involved with the management of emergencies or crises via COBRA. The Cabinet meets immediately to address the emergency and decide how to deal with the problem.

Using the source, evaluate the view that Cabinet is still important (30).

In your response you must:

- *Compare and contrast different opinions in the source*
- *Examine and debate these views in a balanced way*
- *Analyse and evaluate **only** the information presented in the source.*

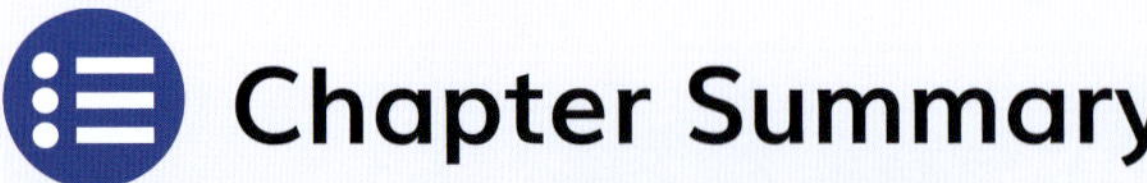

Chapter Summary

» There are different groups within the executive, all with different roles.

» The power balance between the Prime Minister and the executive is constantly changing.

» Prime Ministers have many powers, but also many limits to those powers.

» The ability of Prime Ministers to exercise their powers depends on a range of variable factors.

» The conventions of ministerial responsibility are hugely significant in underpinning the work of government.

Further Resources

Dunleavy, P (2024) Starmer's core executive reveals a centralisation of power LSE Blogs https://eprints.lse.ac.uk/126473/1/politicsandpolicy_2024_11_5_starmers-core-executive-reveals-a-centralisation-of-power.pdf

The Ministerial Code https://www.gov.uk/government/publications/ministerial-code/ministerial-code

Partygate illustrates the fundamental constitutional responsibility of government MPs, The Constitution Unit Blog https://constitution-unit.com/2022/04/14/partygate-illustrates-the-fundamental-constitutional-responsibility-of-government-mps/

Bennister, M. (2012) *Prime Ministers in Power* (London: Palgrave Macmillan).

Gimson, A. (2018) *Gimson's Prime Ministers. Brief Lives from Walpole to Johnson* (London: Penguin Random House).

Seldon, A. (2007) *Blair's Britain, 1997–2007* (Cambridge: Cambridge University Press).

Seldon, A. and Lodge, G. (2011) *Brown at 10* (London: Biteback Publishing).

Seldon, A. (2016) *Cameron at 10: The Verdict* (London: William Collins Publishers).

Seldon, A. (2019) *May at 10* (London: Biteback Publishing).

Seldon, A. and Newell, R. (2023) *Johnson at 10: The Inside Story* (Atlantic Books).

Seldon, A. (2024) *Truss at 10: How Not to be Prime Minister* (Atlantic Books).

Visit the companion website to access the Further Resources Booklet to explore a range of useful web links related to: government reshuffles, an LSE blog post on Boris Johnson's Cabinet reconstruction, the power of the Prime Minister and more.

10 THE SUPREME COURT, THE EU AND SOVEREIGNTY

Chapter Preview

The study of government has traditionally meant the study of central government at a national level. The study of UK Government therefore focused primarily on bodies such as the Westminster Parliament, the Prime Minister and the Cabinet. However, in light of changes to the UK constitution, it is important to understand the impact of the Supreme Court and Brexit on the UK and how the nature of sovereignty has changed.

Law and politics are supposed to be different things. When judges administer the law, they are meant to act in a strictly non-political way. Being neutral as well as independent from the other institutions of government, judges are 'above' politics. Furthermore, the law does not speak for itself; it is interpreted by judges who may be influenced by their own beliefs and prejudices. Recent years have seen major changes within the judiciary. In particular, the introduction in 2009 of a Supreme Court tends to strengthen the tendency for senior judges in the UK to act as policymakers, threatening to give them a role similar to that of US judges. At the same time, it has served to strengthen the principle of the separation of powers.

On 23 June 2016, the UK voted to leave the EU and there is little doubt that politics has been transformed by that vote. Therefore, it is important to understand the UK's politically contentious relationship with the EU and how this has impacted the UK. It also raises the question of what the relationship with the EU looks like with the UK on the outside and the impact on UK politics.

Specification Checklist

4.1 The Supreme Court and its interactions with, and influence over, the legislative and policymaking processes

» The role and composition of the Supreme Court.

» The key operating principles of the Supreme Court, including judicial neutrality and judicial independence and their extent.

» The degree to which the Supreme Court influences both the executive and Parliament, including the doctrine of ultra vires and judicial review.

4.2 The aims, role and impact of the European Union (EU) on the UK Government

» The aims of the EU, including the 'four freedoms' of the single market, social policy, and political and economic union, and the extent to which these have been achieved.

» The role of the EU in policymaking.

» The impact of the EU, including the main effects of at least two EU policies and their impact on the UK political system and UK policymaking.

4.3 The location of sovereignty in the UK political system

» The distinction between legal sovereignty and political sovereignty.

» The extent to which sovereignty has moved between different branches of government.

» Where sovereignty can now be said to lie in the UK.

The Supreme Court

Constitutional Reform Act 2005

The Constitutional Reform Act 2005 (CRA) introduced a series of reforms that have had major constitutional and judicial significance. At the heart of these reforms was the creation of a UK Supreme Court. The court opened in October 2009. The 12-strong court replaced the Law Lords as the highest court in the land. Its members are known as justices of the Supreme Court. Although they are known as Lord or Lady, the title is purely honorary and does not confer membership of the Lords or any legislative role.

The Constitutional Reform Act and the Supreme Court have made a number of changes to the way that the UK constitution works:

» The CRA substantially strengthened the separation of powers between the legislature, the executive and the judiciary (see Figure 10.1).

» Over time it was becoming increasingly clear that the judiciary was being asked to adjudicate upon constitutional issues which it was not appropriate for members of the Lords to decide.

Figure 10.1 Changes to the Law Lords and Lord Chancellor by the Constitutional Reform Act

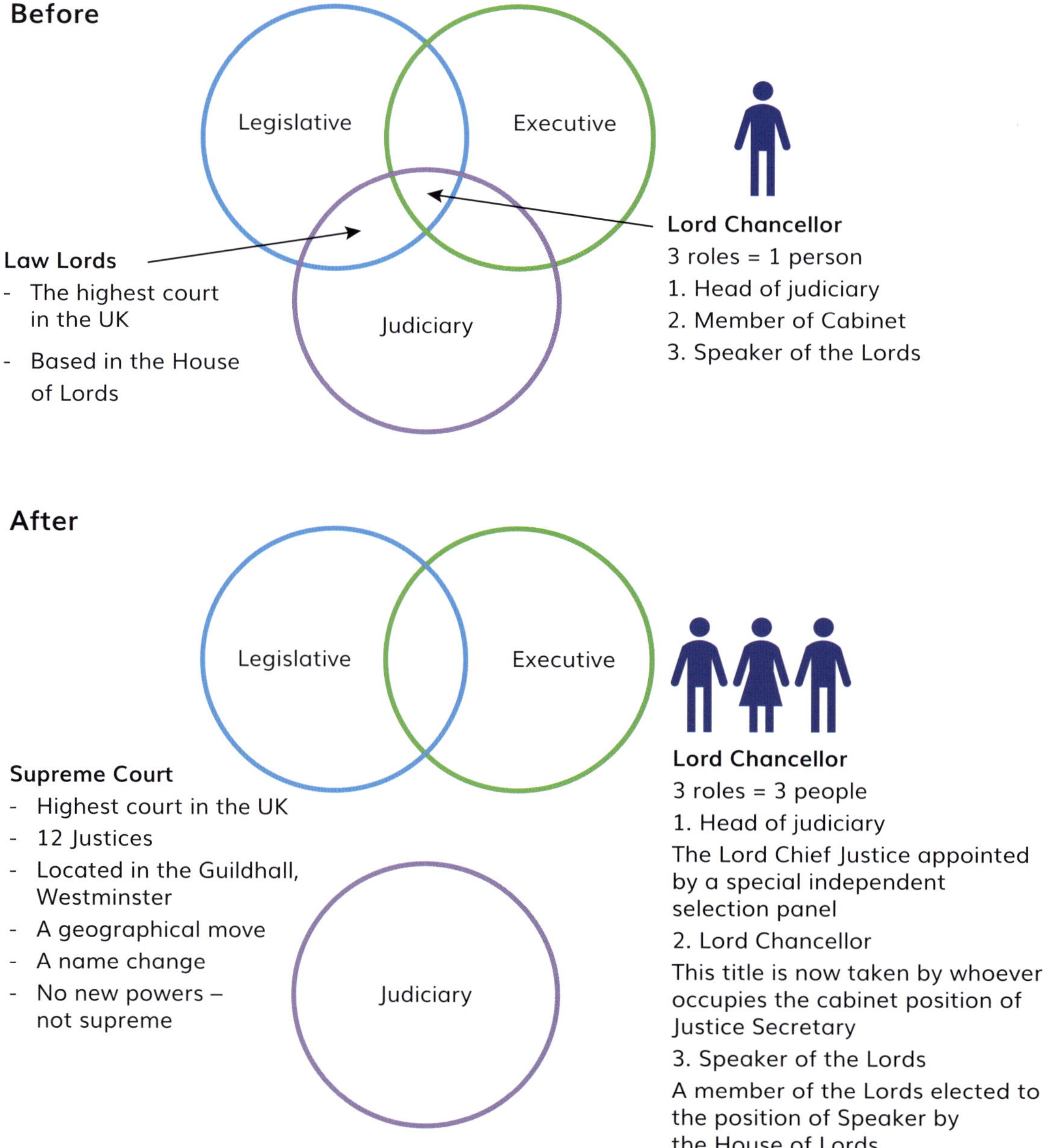

» In the case of *R (Jackson) v Attorney-General* (2005), the Law Lords had to resolve a dispute between the Commons and Lords in relation to whether the use of the Parliament Acts of 1911 and 1949 by the House of Commons was valid to pass the Hunting Act 2004, which banned fox hunting. Yet the judges hearing the case were, by definition, members of the Lords.

» With such cases continuing to arise, the Supreme Court ensured the need for independence and judicial neutrality to determine the constitutional limits of governmental power.

» The second anomaly arose from the office of Lord Chancellor which, uniquely, fused judicial (head of the judiciary), legislative (presiding officer of the House of Lords) and executive (Cabinet Minister) roles. This system did not appear to uphold the principle of judicial independence. As a result, the roles of the Lord Chancellor's office were split to maintain the separation of powers. The post of Lord Chancellor was merged with that of Secretary of State for Justice, and the post was no longer to be held by a sitting judge or peer but by an MP. The Lord Chief Justice became the head of the judiciary, and the presiding officer of the House of Lords is now the Lords Speaker who is elected by members of the Lords.

» The CRA addressed long-term concerns about the independence of the judiciary that arose from the control that ministers exercised over the process of judicial appointments by creating the Judicial Appointments Commission (JAC).

» Previously, the Law Lords were appointed by the Crown, on the advice of the Prime Minister. Other judges were appointed by the Crown, on the advice of the Lord Chancellor, who in turn was appointed by the Prime Minister and was a member of the Cabinet.

» The JAC was created to select candidates, free from political interference while encouraging diversity in the range of people available for selection; candidates are chosen based on merit, through free and fair competition. The JAC appoints judges to courts and tribunals but *does not* select Justices for the Supreme Court.

» A new process was set up for appointments to the Supreme Court based on the creation of an independent selection commission for any vacant seat that arises.

» The Supreme Court is a court for the whole United Kingdom to resolve key constitutional questions.

Spec Key Term

Judicial neutrality: Absence of any form of partisanship or commitment; a refusal to 'take sides' so that the decisions that are taken are objective; impartiality.

Judicial independence: The constitutional principle that the actions and decisions of judges should not be influenced by pressure from other branches of government. This allows the Supreme Court to protect citizens from the unjustified use of power by government and resolve disputes, whether between individuals or between individuals and the state.

Photo 10.1 The Supreme Court is located in Middlesex Guildhall. Its physical separation from Westminster acts as reinforcement of the principle of the separation of powers

» In the case of *R (Miller) v Prime Minister and Cherry v Advocate General for Scotland* (2019) UKSC 41, the Supreme Court was asked to rule on whether it was within the prerogative powers of government to advise the Queen to prorogue Parliament in the run-up to the deadline for leaving the EU.

» The Divisional Court of England and Wales ruled the case was non-judiciable so could not be resolved by legal principle or the courts, while the Court of Session in Scotland decided it was judiciable and an unlawful exercise of power by the government. Both courts could not be right, and only a Supreme Court for the whole UK could resolve the issue.

The role of the court

The court:

» Hears appeals on points of law of public importance.

» Concentrates on cases of the greatest public and constitutional importance.

» Acts as the final court of appeal for all UK civil cases, and criminal cases from England, Wales and Northern Ireland.

» Has assumed the role of adjudicating on whether the devolved legislatures and governments had acted within or exceeded their devolved powers.

How Supreme Court Justices are appointed

The judicial appointments process prior to the Constitutional Reform Act (CRA) made appointments appear as if they were subject to political interference and compromised the principle of the separation of powers. Under the CRA, the appointment process for Supreme Court judges works in the following way:

» When a vacancy appears on the court, a selection commission is created. Any potential candidates must apply for the job and are then interviewed by the Selection Commission.

» Candidates must have held judicial high office for at least two years or satisfy the 15-year eligibility condition in terms of their work as a barrister or solicitor.

» The commission is chaired by the incumbent President of the Supreme Court, who also nominates a senior judge who is not on the Supreme Court to sit.

» In addition, it includes a representative from the separate Judicial Appointments Commission for England and Wales, Scotland and Northern Ireland; one of these representatives must be a non-lawyer.

The Commission largely does its job its own way and while the Minister for Justice can ask the Commission to think again if the Minister feels the candidate they have nominated is not appropriate, or reject the candidate outright, this ministerial power has never been used. It is even questionable whether this ministerial power could ever be used as it would almost certainly involve the Minister of Justice declaring they have no faith in a candidate who is very likely to be a senior serving judge.

The powers of the Supreme Court

Historically, the key power of the courts has been to strike down decisions by public bodies, including government ministers where those decisions were considered to be **ultra vires**.

Judicial review

Judicial review and the Executive

The Supreme Court exercises the power of judicial review, allowing the court to rule on whether a decision or action taken by a public authority, including a minister, is ultra vires. In the UK, the court can uphold an application for **judicial review** where a decision is deemed to be illegal, irrational or due to procedural impropriety.

It stops public authorities from doing something that the law forbids or acting where they have no legal authority. In doing so, it acts as a check on the executive branch. If a judicial review is upheld, then the court can quash a government decision and award damages in certain situations. This enables the court to uphold the rule of law.

Spec Key Term

Ultra vires:
Literally, 'beyond the power'; this applies when public bodies have acted illegally because their actions have no statutory authority.

Judicial review:
The power to review actions taken by public bodies on the grounds that they are ultra vires and to review Acts of Parliament to see if they are compatible with the Human Rights Act.

The fundamental principle of the rule of law is that all are subject to the law; so ministers and public bodies are expected to act within the law. Where they act beyond the law, citizens have the right to challenge that action in the courts and seek redress for their grievances. To support this fundamental principle, there are a number of key ingredients to make this work:

» All must be equal before the law.

» The law must clear and accessible.

» The law must provide protection of basic human rights.

» There must be a clear legal mechanism for resolving disputes.

» The state will comply with its obligations in international as well as national law.

The Human Rights Act came into effect in 2000 and it makes it unlawful for a public authority to act in a way that is incompatible with it (unless authorised to do so by an Act of Parliament). The UK courts can hear cases on whether a decision by a public authority, including government departments, has infringed on rights under the ECHR. If ruled unlawful, the courts can cancel a decision, send the decision back to the public authority to make the decision again and/or award compensation where it is necessary, just and appropriate. This type of judicial review has particularly come into the limelight with the number of cases regarding immigration and deportation and the Home Office.

The case of *National Council for Civil Liberties (Liberty) v Secretary of State for the Home Department* (2024) involved a challenge by Liberty against the then Secretary of State regarding the legality of regulations made under the Police, Crime, Sentencing and Courts Act 2022. In June 2023, the Secretary of State used a statutory instrument to give police powers to restrict protests which cause 'more than minor' disruption – a significantly lower threshold than the previous definition of 'serious disruption'. This was despite the fact that an amendment attempting to do the same thing was voted out by Parliament in 2023. Liberty argued that these regulations were ultra vires as they altered the definition of 'serious disruption' in a manner not authorised by Parliament. Additionally, the consultation process was criticised for being procedurally unfair as it mainly involved law enforcement agencies and excluded other stakeholders. The High Court ruled in favour of Liberty, finding the regulations to be ultra vires and the consultation process to be flawed. In 2025, the Court of Appeal dismissed the Government's appeal, upholding the High Court's conclusion that the regulations were unlawful. The ruling removed the "more than minor" test and restored a higher "serious disruption" threshold. The ruling also signalled that ministers cannot use secondary legislation to rewrite key thresholds Parliament chose to keep.

The Liberty court case is an example of an outsider pressure group using the courts to protect the rights of its members.

CASE STUDY 10.1: R (ON THE APPLICATION OF MILLER AND ANOTHER) (RESPONDENTS) V SECRETARY OF STATE FOR EXITING THE EUROPEAN UNION (APPELLANT)

Photo 10.2 Gina Miller speaks outside the Supreme Court on 24 January 2017 following the ruling on Article 50

Source: WPA Pool / Pool / Getty Images

Events

Following the Brexit Referendum in 2016, the government proposed to use its prerogative powers to withdraw from the EU by serving an Article 50 notice, as laid out in the 2009 Treaty of Lisbon, to withdraw the UK from the EU Treaties. The constitutional issue that was raised was whether the government could use its prerogative powers to trigger Article 50 without prior authorisation by an Act of Parliament. The case brought by Gina Miller and Deir Dos Santos against the Secretary of State for Exiting the European Union argued that there was a well-established principle that prerogative powers could not be applied to Acts which might lead to a change in domestic law. Because the withdrawal from the EU would change domestic law, then the government needed an Act of Parliament to give it the authority to trigger the withdrawal. The case was originally heard in the High

Court in October 2016 before being brought to appeal in the Supreme Court later that year.

Significance

This Supreme Court case was the most constitutionally significant in the UK for decades. This is because it reasserted the authority of Parliament and defined the boundaries of executive power; the principle stands that government can make and unmake treaties, but only Parliament can change the law. By a majority of eight to three, the court ruled that an Act of Parliament was required to authorise ministers to give notice of the decision of the UK to withdraw from the European Union. The key reason given was that the European Communities Act 1972 authorised the process of EU law becoming UK law and taking primacy over UK domestic law. Leaving the EU will clearly change UK law, so the withdrawal requires an Act of Parliament.

The judges, moreover, always insisted theirs was not a political decision. They were merely applying the law. This was a constitutional, legal matter and nothing to do with the political issues of the benefits of the withdrawal decision, the timing of the decision or the nature of the terms for departure or the future arrangement with the EU. Nevertheless, the High Court case in particular attracted sometimes vitriolic criticism. Branded by one national newspaper 'Enemies of the People' for having, supposedly, blocked the popular will as expressed in the Referendum, the judges concerned were also condemned by some Brexiteers for unwarranted judicial activism (meddling in matters that should have been left to politicians) and for allowing alleged Europhile sympathies to affect their professional judgements. In the build-up to the Supreme Court decision, much of the media speculated about the pro-EU positions of the individual judges, based on investigations into their backgrounds and social media postings by members of their families. The Lord Chancellor, Liz Truss MP, was quick to defend the judiciary stating that: 'Our independent judiciary is the cornerstone of the rule of law and is vital to our constitution and our freedoms. The reputation of our judiciary is unrivalled the world over, and our Supreme Court justices are people of integrity and impartiality.' However, in the end, while the judgement was important constitutionally, it had little impact on the Brexit process as Parliament quickly passed an Act authorising the government to trigger Article 50. The government still triggered Article 50 within its original deadline of the end of March 2017.

Tip: Although older than you would normally seek to use, the Miller Rulings are still vital to understanding the role of the Supreme Court in holding the executive to account.

Tip: The ECHR is not related to the EU, except that all EU member states must have signed the Convention.

Judicial review and Parliament

The Supreme Court works within the existing framework of parliamentary sovereignty so it cannot strike down legislation as unconstitutional. The Human Rights Act (HRA), which came into effect in 2000, incorporated the European Convention on Human Rights (ECHR) into UK law. The Act was a major constitutional reform in that it marked a shift in the UK in favour of an explicit and codified legal definition of individual rights allowing individuals to bring cases for breaches of their rights to UK courts. In doing so, it substantially widened the capacity of the judiciary to protect civil liberties and act as a check on the exercise of executive power and, in certain respects, legislative power. It also meant that these rights were available in UK courts rather than only in Strasbourg – the location of the European Court of Human Rights.

The UK Supreme Court also interprets all existing legislation so that it is compatible with the ECHR insofar as it is possible to do so. If the court decides it is not possible to interpret legislation so that it is compatible with the HRA, it will issue what is known as a 'declaration of incompatibility' under Section 4 of the HRA. Although a declaration of incompatibility does not place any legal obligation on the government to amend or repeal legislation, it sends a clear message to legislators that this piece of legislation is incompatible, and that they now need to decide what to do about it. This means that Parliament can, of course, choose to do nothing, although this remains highly unlikely. An instance of Parliament changing the law due to a declaration of incompatibility was in 2022 when the Abortion (Northern Ireland) Regulations 2022 was introduced. This legislation addressed the incompatibility identified by the Supreme Court regarding Northern Ireland's abortion laws as they prohibited abortion in cases of rape, incest and fatal foetal abnormality. Another example occurred in 2019 when the court ruled that the Civil Partnership Act 2004 for opposite-sex couples to enter into a civil partnership was incompatible with human rights law, so the government remedied the situation via the Civil Partnership (Opposite-sex Couples) Regulations 2019.

Between 2000 and 2026, the various courts in the UK issued 52 declarations of incompatibility. Twelve declarations were overturned on appeal, leaving 40 declarations. However, it is suggested that most of these cases are relatively uncontroversial, and only the controversial ones hit the headlines.

The Judicial Review and Courts Act 2022

In 2022, the government made one of the most significant changes to judicial review in recent years. The government introduced the Judicial Review and Courts Act 2022 which made several important changes to how people can challenge government decisions and how courts work in the UK.

» **New Types of Court Orders:** Courts can now delay when their decisions take effect (called 'suspended quashing orders') or rule that decisions only apply to future cases ('prospective-only remedies'). This means when the government makes a mistake, courts have more flexibility in how they fix it.

» **Removed Certain Appeals:** The Act stopped people from challenging decisions of the Upper Tribunal that refuse permission to appeal from the First-tier Tribunal (known as 'Cart judicial reviews'). This mainly affects immigration, asylum and welfare cases.

The Act also modernised court procedures by introducing online options for minor offences as well as making it easier to move cases between magistrates and Crown Courts and lastly it expanded the use of virtual hearings and online processes to make courts more efficient.

The government argued that these changes made the justice system more efficient and practical. However, critics were fearful that they would make it harder for people to challenge unfair government decisions and could have left vulnerable people without proper legal protection.

> **Synoptic Link**
>
> The HRA increases the power of the Supreme Court to act as a protector of citizens' rights.

Judicial independence and neutrality

The Supreme Court is made up of 12 unelected and unaccountable judges. This raises the question of why the public is willing to accept decisions made by the judiciary. The answer lies in ensuring that all parts of society have confidence that the decisions taken by the Supreme Court are independent and neutral.

Judicial independence – The principle of judicial independence is one of the key parts of the constitution. Judicial independence refers to the ability of courts and judges to perform their duties without interference or influence from external sources, such as the government, private interests or the media. Judges can therefore apply the law as their own experience and legal training dictates, rather than as ministers, civil servants or Parliamentarians would wish. As such, judicial independence is a vital guarantee of the rule of law. Law cannot act as a constraint on government if the executive and Parliament can influence judges in how they interpret and apply the law. This concept is crucial for ensuring that judges can decide cases based solely on the law and the facts presented in court.

Judicial neutrality – Judicial neutrality refers to the principle that judges must remain impartial and free from political or other bias when making decisions. This means judges should apply and interpret the law without allowing personal opinions, prejudices or political preferences to influence their rulings. While it is challenging to achieve complete neutrality due to the inherent biases of judges, efforts are made to maintain impartiality through practices such as avoiding political activity and ensuring decisions are grounded in legal justifications. Judges are meant to be neutral in the sense that they are able to ensure that their own views and beliefs do not *affect* their professional behaviour. Personal preferences and beliefs must be left at the court door.

This is made all the more difficult when the Supreme Court takes cases about issues where public opinion is deeply divided. This can lead to assumptions that decisions are based on the individual political or moral positions of the judges rather than deciding legal questions by using their legal expertise.

KEY TOPIC DEBATE: IS THE SUPREME COURT INDEPENDENT AND NEUTRAL?

✖ **The biggest threat to judicial independence in the UK was the way the judicial function was entangled with the executive and legislative function.**

» The highest court of the land was the Law Lords, fusing together the legislative and judicial functions.

» The three functions of the state were fused together in the office of the Lord Chancellor.

» The power of elected politicians over the appointment of judges made appointments appear to be open to political influence.

✔ **These threats were largely neutralised by the passage of the CRA in 2005, while independence was already protected by rules around pay and tenure.**

» **Constitutional commitment.** Since the passing of the CRA, judicial independence instead of being a convention is now guaranteed by an Act of Parliament. The CRA details that the Lord Chancellor, and all ministers, must uphold the continued independence of the judiciary.

» **An independent appointments process.** The CRA established the Judicial Appointments Commission to ensure that there were no concerns about political interference in the appointments process.

» **Separation of powers.** The CRA made a clear separation of powers by establishing the Supreme Court and splitting the roles of the Lord Chancellor.

» **Pay.** Judges must be paid sufficient salaries to ensure their integrity and impartiality. Judges should receive appropriate pay, and changes to their salaries and pensions must not be used as a means of influencing judicial decision making. In 2026, Supreme Court justices were paid £280,311,with the President of the Supreme Court paid £290,213. The Senior Salaries Review Body, a non-political body, currently makes recommendations to the government on the remuneration of the judiciary. However, it remains the case that these recommendations need to be voted on in Parliament and are not always passed, especially in times of austerity.

» **Security of tenure.** Security of tenure means that once they are appointed, judges cannot be sacked. They remain in office until their retirement age of 75. The possibility of removal or demotion cannot therefore be used to affect their decision making. Senior judges can only be removed by an address of both Houses of Parliament, something that has not happened since 1830.

✅ **Judicial independence relies on the commitment of ministers to uphold the independence of the judiciary and relies on them respecting constitutional conventions.**

» There are conventions that protect independence such as the government should not use its contacts with the judiciary to influence decisions, and ministers should exercise restraint when commenting on decisions, whether or not those decisions favour the government and the **sub judice rule** that prohibits parliamentary debate of matters currently before the courts.

❌ **A serious concern about judicial independence stems from a growing willingness of ministers to publicly criticise the courts.**

» The separation of the judicial and legislative functions leads to the risk that over time, the understanding between politicians and judges of their respective roles in our constitution will grow weaker.

» Ministers, in being increasingly willing to make public statements about how the courts should address issues related to public order and civil liberties, and in expressing disappointment at the stance that judges have taken, have tested the principle of judicial independence. In 2025, Kemi Badenoch said a decision to grant a Palestinian family the right to live in the UK through a scheme designed for Ukrainians, was 'completely wrong'. Starmer agreed, adding: 'It should be Parliament that makes the rules on immigration.'

» The rulings around Article 50 and the prorogation of Parliament both saw a growing willingness of politicians to publicly criticise the courts.

✅ **Judges recognise the limits to their role to rule on the lawfulness of actions and not to make decisions on policy so that they ensure that they do not become players in the political process.**

» In essence, this is the practice of judicial restraint, The Supreme Court President, Lord Reed, has frequently advocated for judicial restraint, emphasising that judges should respect the roles of Parliament and the executive, avoid overreach in judicial review, and uphold constitutional balance amid populist pressures. In a 2025 speech on the role of the judiciary, he cautioned courts against pushing boundaries that might provoke backlash, urging mutual restraint between branches of government. He also praised self-restraint in cases like Shamima Begum, where the Supreme Court deferred to executive discretion on national security rather than expanding review powers.

❌ **Judges appear to be taking a more judicially active role as they seem more prepared to challenge the executive and Parliament.**

» The HRA has brought more political questions before the court which has placed judges at the heart of political decisions.

» Interestingly, in the second Miller ruling, the lower court had argued that the case was non-judiciable, and could not be resolved by legal principle or the courts. Yet the Supreme Court decided it was judiciable and went on to overrule the government. This suggests judicial activism.

» There has been a rise in the number of cases of judicial review because the public seems more willing to challenge the lawfulness of the decisions of public bodies, including government, than ever before. The number of cases rose from 4,240 in 2000 to around 15,600 in 2013, with the vast majority of these cases being immigration and asylum cases. However, the

---

Judicial Review and Courts Act 2022 made changes to how people can challenge government decisions in an aim to reduce the number of cases. In 2025 there was a sharp rise in judicial review applications from previous years, with 3,700 applications. The 2024 figure was 730.

Figure 10.2 Judicial review cases since 2020

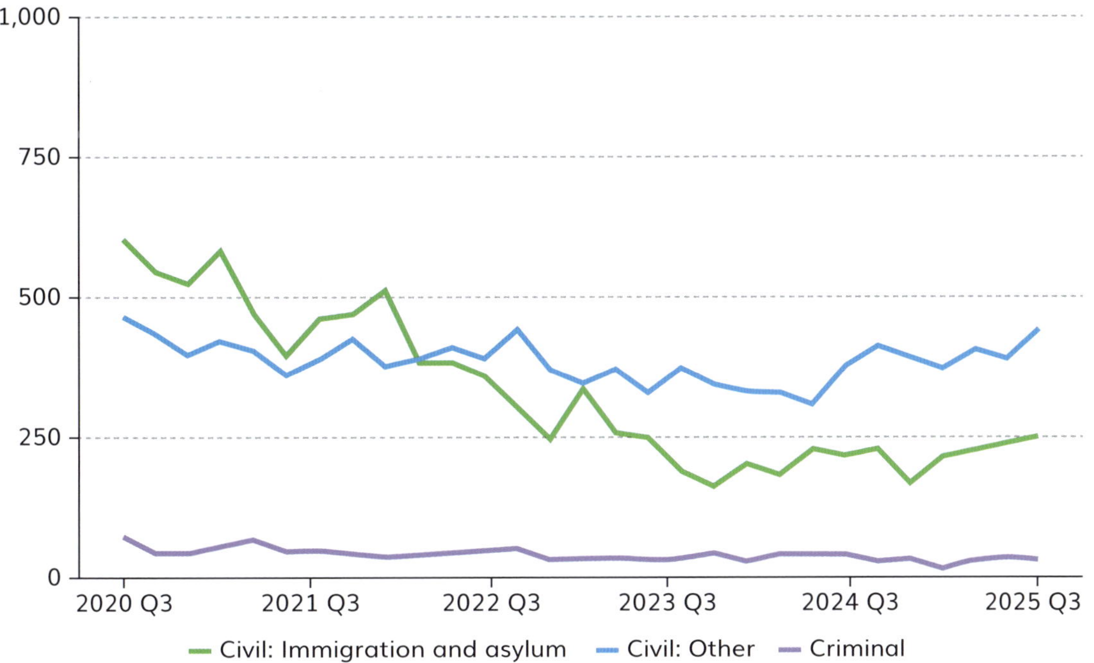

Source: Contains public sector information licensed under the Open Government Licence v3.0

✓ **Judges sign up to the principle of neutrality and acknowledge that they are accountable to the law, and should behave in such a way to enhance the confidence of the public in their personal impartiality and that of the judiciary.**

» Judges are expected to refrain from any activities, including political activities, which might create the impression of bias or a conflict of interest. Judges must stick to legal topics, not engage in political debate or controversy.

» The judicial oath sums up this point: 'I will do right to all manner of people after the laws and usages of this Realm, without fear or favour, affection or ill-will.'

» The Supreme Court is live streamed so that it is accessible to everyone. This creates a level of accountability as senior judges must explain their rulings, highlighting, in the process, the points of law that have affected them. Those watching either the Article 50 or prorogation cases could see that the court was tackling legal questions about the constitutional issues of the balance of power between legislature and executive, not a debate about the pros and cons of membership of the EU.

✗ **Increasing attacks by the media on the character of judges rather than their decisions, as well as the increasing visibility of judges as public figures, undermines impartiality.**

» The media, in particular over the Article 50 case, was seen by some to have attacked the views of the judges making the decision, questioning their neutrality on the issue of Brexit. However, the media argues that, given its role, the Supreme Court is fair game for public scrutiny.

» Lord Neuberger, the President of the Supreme Court at the time, publicly criticised some of the attacks by the media, claiming that they undermined the rule of law and the reputation of the legal system, and was critical of the government for not being quicker and clearer in defending the judiciary.

✗ **It is argued that there is a bias within the senior judiciary, which stems from the fact that judges are predominantly male, white, upper-middle class and public-school and 'Oxbridge' educated.**

» This argument that the Supreme Court is not neutral, but naturally pro the establishment, has been traditionally made from the left of politics, but is increasingly a view taken by the right.

Synoptic Link

Link together the idea of judicial neutrality with the media reporting on key Supreme Court cases.

The left has tended to attack impartiality in terms of bias against minority groups in society due to their lack of social representation. The right has attacked the judiciary for its inbuilt liberal attitudes in favouring individual rights over the public interest and being anti-Brexit.

» The Supreme Court in 2026 had only two female justices out of twelve and no justice from an ethnic minority background, while the majority of justices were Oxbridge-educated. There have only ever been five women Supreme Court Justices since its inception.

» In the *Radmacher v Granatino* case, regarding a pre-nuptial agreement, Lady Hale, in her dissenting judgement, raised concerns about potential gender bias in the Supreme Court's decision. She noted that the court, composed of eight men and one woman, might be ill-suited to decide on an issue with a clear 'gender dimension'.

» In 2014, 6% of court judges were from ethnic minority backgrounds, by 2020 it had only improved to 8% and in 2025 it was 12%. While ethnic minority representation has increased among barristers (17%), solicitors (19%) and Chartered Legal Executives (11%) from 2014 to 2024, ethnic minorities remain underrepresented. Underrepresentation is particularly pronounced in senior judicial positions; Black judges make up only 1.09% of the judiciary by 2025 compared to 1.02% in 2014. At the current rate, it would take over a hundred years for the proportion of Black judges to match the general population.

✅ **The judiciary is slowly becoming more diverse, and this will increase the diversity of the Supreme Court over time.**

» In 2023, Dame Sue Carr was appointed the first Lady Chief Justice – the top judge for England and Wales.

» In 1984, only 5% of court judges were women, by 2014 it was 24% and by 2025 it was 39%. In 2025, 28% of senior court posts (High Court and above) are held by women, 54% of tribunal judges are women and women make up 62% of the most senior tribunal roles.

Photo 10.3 Baroness Hale of Richmond was the first woman to have served as President of the Supreme Court

Source: Dan Kitwood / Staff / Getty Images

» Recent initiatives have sought to address ethnic minority underrepresentation, with the Judicial Diversity and Inclusion Strategy 2020–2025 aiming to increase diversity in the judiciary, including measures to encourage more people from BAME backgrounds to apply for judicial roles and the Judicial Diversity Forum is focusing on the appointment of Black judges as a priority.

» The extensive process of legal training (senior judges have usually worked as barristers or junior judges for between 20 and 30 years) is designed to enable judges to focus entirely on legal considerations. Their ability to act impartially and objectively is strengthened by the requirement that court proceedings are conducted fairly and that judgements are based on evidence.

Key Debate Summary: Is the Supreme Court independent and neutral?

For	Theme	Against
✓ The CRA enforced a strict separation of power by moving the judicial function from the Lords to the Supreme Court.	Did the CRA enhance judicial independence?	✗ The biggest threat to judicial independence in the UK has been the lack of a strict separation of powers.
✓ Judicial independence relies on the commitment of ministers to respecting the independence of the judiciary.	Do ministers respect the independence of the judiciary?	✗ Judicial independence is threatened by a growing willingness of ministers to publicly criticise the courts.
✓ Judges recognise the limits to their role.	Are judges becoming more political?	✗ Judges are argued to be taking a more judicially active role.
✓ Judges need to ensure the confidence of the public in their personal neutrality and that of the judiciary.	Are judges now seen as less neutral?	✗ Increasing attacks by the media on the character of judges rather than their decisions plus the more public role of senior judges undermines impartiality.
✓ The judiciary is slowly becoming more diverse.	Is diversity happening quickly enough?	✗ It is argued that a bias tends to operate within the senior judiciary based on their background.

CASE STUDY 10.2: R (ON THE APPLICATION OF MILLER) (APPELLANT) V THE PRIME MINISTER (RESPONDENT) CHERRY AND OTHERS (RESPONDENTS) V ADVOCATE GENERAL FOR SCOTLAND (APPELLANT) (SCOTLAND) (2019) UKSC 41

Events

In 2019, Prime Minister Boris Johnson requested that Parliament be prorogued (suspended) from a date between 12 and 14 September and for a Queen's Speech on 14 October. The government argued that this was about the new Prime Minister being able to set out his own priorities in the Queen's Speech while critics argued it was an attempt to stop MPs debating Brexit and passing law to stop a no-deal Brexit by the 31 October cut-off date. Separate appeals were brought in the High Court of England and Wales and the Court of Session in Scotland. The High Court dismissed the appeal, claiming it was non-judiciable, while the Court of Session ruled the appeal judiciable and the prorogation unlawful. Given the decisions, it was clear that both courts could not be right and given the importance of the case, the Supreme Court convened a panel of 11 justices, the maximum number of judges allowed to sit, to hear the appeal.

Significance

The judgement issued was a unanimous verdict from all 11 judges. The court ruled that the appeal was justiciable as it was ruled that the courts have the jurisdiction to rule upon the existence and the limits to a prerogative power. The court then ruled that the limits to the use of the prerogative power to prorogue Parliament were the principles of parliamentary sovereignty and the principle of parliamentary accountability; the ability of Parliament to hold the Prime Minister and ministers collectively responsible and accountable to Parliament.

In issuing its judgement, the court ruled that the prorogation was unlawful and should be quashed because the prorogation had the impact of preventing Parliament from carrying out its constitutional functions without any reasonable justification. In the opening paragraph of their judgement, the 11 justices wrote: 'It is important, once again, to emphasise that these cases are not about when and on what terms the United Kingdom is to leave the European Union.'

The ruling dominated the newspapers with headlines such as 'Boris Blasts: Who Runs Britain?' and 'What's Lawful about Denying 17.4m Brexit?' Allegations swirled that the Prime Minister had declared war on the judiciary and that the Commons Leader, Jacob Rees-Mogg, had described the ruling as a 'constitutional coup'. Richard Ekins, head of think tank Policy Exchange's Judicial Power Project argued the court needed to be reminded of the limits to its judicial power and the ruling was yet another example of those who lose the political debate using the courts to achieve their political goals. The Lord Chancellor, Robert Buckland MP, had to publicly defend the court, stating that 'we must all remember that our world-class judiciary always acts free from political motivation or influence and that the rule of law is the basis of our democracy, for all seasons. Personal attacks on judges from any quarter are completely unacceptable.'

KEY TOPIC DEBATE: DOES THE SUPREME COURT HAVE TOO MUCH POWER?

The twenty-first century has seen a growing debate in the UK about the power and role of the Supreme Court. In particular, judicial review has come under increasing scrutiny given the rise in cases and the high-profile decisions in the two 'Miller' rulings. This raises the issue of whether the court has too much power over the executive and the legislature.

✔ **Judicial Review gives unelected judges too much power to limit the executive as the courts can declare actions of the executive to be 'ultra vires' or in contravention of the Human Rights Act, and quash them.**

» Although judicial review acts to ensure that the public have the ability to challenge the lawfulness of the actions of the government, critics argue that recently, this has placed too much power in the hands of the judiciary. Elected politicians should be able to make decisions and then be held accountable for those decisions to the public at election time, rather than unelected judges.

» In 2023, the Supreme Court ruled unanimously that the government's policy to send asylum seekers to Rwanda was unlawful on the grounds that asylum seekers sent to Rwanda would face a real risk of refoulement (being returned to their home country where they could face ill treatment); this is despite the fact that according to a Savanta opinion poll, 47% of the public supported it (26% opposed it).

✘ **The court rules on the lawfulness of an action on cases that are brought before it. It can only work within what the law states, and the executive has the power to place a new bill in front of Parliament to change the law.**

» Despite the 2023 Rwanda ruling, the government introduced, and Parliament passed, the Safety of Rwanda Act in 2024. It required all decision makers, including courts and tribunals, to 'conclusively treat Rwanda as a safe country' for asylum seekers. It also prohibited legal challenges based on the argument that Rwanda is unsafe, by disapplying sections 2, 3, and 6 to 9 of the Human Rights Act. It did allow individual challenges based on 'compelling evidence relating specifically to the person's particular circumstances' that Rwanda is not safe for them specifically. It declared that removing someone to Rwanda complied with all relevant international law. This Act significantly removed the power of courts to challenge the government's Rwanda policy. See the Case Study on the Safety of Rwanda Act in Chapter 2.

» The Supreme Court is also bound by the fact that it cannot initiate cases; it can only rule on cases that are brought before it.

✅ **The Supreme Court has the power to declare Acts of Parliament as incompatible with the Human Rights Act.**

» By ruling that a law is incompatible with the HRA, the Supreme Court is essentially pushing Parliament to take action to amend or remove the law in question, undermining their sovereignty.

» In the case of *Secretary of State for Business and Trade v Mercer* (2024), the Supreme Court declared that Section 146 of the Trade Union and Labour Relations (Consolidation) Act 1992 was incompatible with Article 11 of the ECHR (freedom of assembly and association) which failed to protect workers from dismissal for participating in lawful strike action. This case acknowledged workers' rights under Article 11 highlighting legislative shortcomings. The The Employment Rights Act 2025 addressed these issues, and specifically, it included provisions to ensure compatibility with Article 11 of the ECHR, which protects the right to strike.

» Perhaps still the most controversial declaration that illustrates the power of the Supreme Court in this area was made by its predecessor, the Law Lords, in 2004. In *A and others v Secretary of State for the Home Department* in 2004 (*Belmarsh* case), it was ruled that the clause of the Anti-terrorism, Crime and Security Act 2001 allowing indefinite detention without trial of foreign nationals suspected of international terrorism was incompatible with Articles 5 and 14 of the ECHR. Despite being highly critical of the judgement, the government introduced the Prevention of Terrorism Act 2005, which replaced indefinite detention with control orders, and this was passed by Parliament.

❌ **A declaration of incompatibility works within the principle of parliamentary sovereignty. The court cannot strike down an Act of Parliament or force Parliament to take action.**

» When introducing the Illegal Migration Act 2023, the Home Secretary used section 19(1)(b) of the Human Rights Act to state that she was unable to confirm compatibility with rights. The Act expressly disapplies section 3 of the HRA, which normally requires courts and public authorities to interpret legislation compatibly with Convention rights where possible. This removed a key protection against human rights violations. This showed that Parliament can pass any law it chooses, even if it is incompatible with the HRA.

✅ **The Supreme Court is becoming more activist, making decisions that take the court beyond its legal role into the heart of the political debate.**

» Given that the court is unelected and unaccountable, it is seen as unacceptable that the court is involving itself in political decision making. Political decisions are the reserve of democratically elected politicians in the executive and legislature.

» The two Miller rulings created a dangerous precedent that saw the Supreme Court step into the highly charged political arena of Brexit. Remainers applauded their ruling and Leavers were appalled by it showing very clearly the political nature of their ruling. Critics argue that the rulings undermined the court's credibility, which is something they need to be mindful of.

» More recently, the court has been at the heart of rulings regarding asylum and illegal migration, limiting the government's ability to carry out its policies, who would argue that they have a mandate for these policies and the Supreme Court does not.

❌ **The Supreme Court is simply fulfilling its role as the constitutional court for the UK, resolving key constitutional and legal questions.**

» The Human Rights Act 1998 was passed by a democratically elected Parliament. In so doing, it voted to give the Supreme Court a greater role in protecting civil liberties in the UK and checking the executive.

» The huge levels of constitutional change brought about by Brexit, asylum, immigration, human rights and devolution have created a situation where the Supreme Court has been placed at the heart of these key constitutional issues.

» In 2022, the Supreme Court was called upon by Nicola Sturgeon to rule on who had the power to call a second Independence Referendum in Scotland. The court ruled unanimously that the Scottish Parliament did not have the power to unilaterally call a second referendum on Scottish independence without the consent of the UK Government. The court emphasised that measures questioning the integrity of the United Kingdom fall outside the Scottish Parliament's competence. The court was simply resolving a constitutional issue between the Westminster and Scottish Parliaments.

» In both Miller rulings, the Supreme Court was resolving key constitutional questions about the separation of powers in the UK.

» In the Miller 2017 ruling, the court also ruled that the Sewel Convention was not legally binding. The judgement emphasised that Parliament's recognition of the convention in statute did not make it legally enforceable. If Parliament had intended to make it justiciable, it would have used clearer language to that effect. This shows the court acting with restraint.

Key Debate Summary: Does the Supreme Court have too much power?

For	Theme	Against
✓ The power of judicial review is a powerful check on the executive branch.	Is the court effective at checking the executive?	✗ The court can't initiate its own cases and can only interpret the law, while the executive can place a new law in front of Parliament.
✓ The Supreme Court has the power to declare Acts of Parliament as incompatible with the Human Rights Act.	Is the court effective at upholding rights?	✗ Due to parliamentary sovereignty, the court cannot strike down an Act of Parliament or force Parliament to take action.
✓ The Supreme Court is becoming more judicially activist.	Is the court becoming too political?	✗ The Supreme Court is simply fulfilling its role as the constitutional court for the UK.

The impact of the EU on the UK

Photo 10.4 Does Brexit mean Brexit?

Source: Peter Dazeley / Getty Images

Spec Key Term

European Union (EU): The European Union is the term adopted after the Maastricht Treaty of 1992 to describe the political and economic union that fosters cooperation between member states.

The aims of the EU

The **European Union** is an economic and political union between 27 member nations that span much of the continent of Europe.

The main aim of the founders was to foster closer economic ties in the belief that countries that trade together become economically interdependent, making peace far more likely than conflict.

The European Economic Community (EEC) was established by the Treaty of Rome, 1957 by six countries: Belgium, France, Italy, Luxembourg, Germany and the Netherlands. This was purely an economic relationship at this stage. The UK was not interested in joining, seeing its more significant relationship as that with the USA. However, in 1973 the UK joined the then EEC.

The signing in 1986 of the Single European Act envisaged an unrestricted flow of goods, services, capital and people – a 'single market' throughout Europe's 12 members (Denmark, United Kingdom, Ireland, Greece, Portugal and Spain had now joined). This was an economic union to enable member stages to prosper by working together. However, the Maastricht Treaty 1993 led to the creation of the European Union (EU). This committed the EU's 15 members (including Austria, Finland and Sweden) to both **political union** and **monetary union**.

During this period, the UK's commitment to Europe was always somewhat equivocal. Europe was seen as an economic union and the issue of deeper political integration was of little interest, while the widening of membership raised concerns about the free movement of people. Overall public opinion remained largely indifferent to Europe and membership remained politically controversial within the two main political parties.

> **Visit the companion website for a detailed history of the development of the EU from the previous fifth edition.**

The 'four freedoms'

The Treaty of Rome in 1957, which established the European Economic Community, set out the **four freedoms**: the freedom of movement of goods, services, capital and people. These freedoms were further strengthened by future treaties as the Community moved from a **customs union** towards a single market.

The freedoms are the foundation of the single market and were established with the aim of benefitting member states by generating trade, improving productivity and offering workers better opportunities. For a state to be part of the single market, it must sign up to all four freedoms.

> **Visit the companion website for details on the four freedoms of the EU from the previous fifth edition.**

The single market

The single market is seen by the EU as one of its greatest achievements as it is said to have fuelled economic growth and made the life of European businesses and citizens easier. It removed tariffs, quotas or taxes on trade and included the free movement of goods, services, capital and people. It is argued that it stimulates competition and trade, improves efficiency, raises quality and helps cut prices.

Political and economic union

Economic union

The Maastricht Treaty 1993 laid out plans for an 'ever closer union' built around the single market and member states adopting a single currency – the euro – by 2002 and handing over regulation to a European Central Bank. The UK secured an opt-out from the euro under John Major and remained outside the eurozone.

The global financial crisis of 2007–09 left Portugal, Ireland, Italy, Greece and Spain in a position where they would be unable to pay their debts. This presented a threat to the survival of the euro, so consequently, these states received a huge European bailout to keep them afloat at eye-watering costs to other eurozone states. Moreover, these states had to accept stark 'conditions' to reforms to their economies in return for the bailout. These reforms were deeply unpopular and showed that economic unity comes with a loss of sovereignty. Post-Covid there has been sluggish growth in the eurozone which has further weakened the case for other states to join the euro.

Political union

The widening membership of the EU has had a significant impact on the decision-making processes of the EU, with a wide range of national interests that have to be satisfied. The loss of **national vetoes** and move to **Qualified Majority Voting** has further highlighted tensions. The problems within the EU have been exposed by the migrant crisis, which began in 2015 and is still causing significant concerns over ten years later. It triggered deep political divides, both north–south and east–west, as member states could not agree on a migration policy.

KEY TOPIC DEBATE: HOW MUCH IMPACT DOES THE EU HAVE ON THE UK?

Policy

Since the UK's departure from the EU, the EU continues to influence UK policy in several areas:

- The **Trade and Cooperation Agreement** (TCA) governs trade relations between the UK and EU, and it includes:

  - Agreements on fishing policy which address shared fish stocks, quotas, access rights and sustainability measures. The TCA also allows mutual access for UK and EU vessels to fish in each other's waters under specific licensing systems.

  - The UK is no longer part of the EU's Common Agricultural Policy (CAP), which previously provided substantial subsidies to farmers. However, the TCA allows for tariff-free and quota-free trade in agricultural goods between the EU and the UK, provided products meet rules of origin requirements. This ensures that goods produced primarily in either region can move without additional tariffs. However, goods face non-tariff barriers like checks, customs declarations and compliance with EU standards for food safety and labelling.

- When Starmer became Prime Minister, he sought a 'reset' in EU–UK relations, with proposed agreements to include a veterinary deal, emissions trading linkage and youth mobility facilitation, and for the UK to rejoin the Erasmus student exchange programme.

- In 2025, Starmer attended a summit with EU leaders to discuss collaboration on security and defence amidst global instability.

- In 2025 the so-called "Coalition of the Willing", led by the UK and France, was agreed which was a multinational initiative to support Ukraine against Russia, focusing on security guarantees, military aid, and post-ceasefire peacekeeping plans. It includes over 30 countries from the EU and NATO as well as Ukraine. While this was not a UK-EU agreement, it showed that the UK was able to work very closely alongside the EU and other partners.

- In May 2025, a wide-ranging deal was struck at the Lancaster House Summit which included:

  - A defence pact as the first step towards securing British access to a new EU rearmament fund, though the UK will pay into the fund.

  - Faster access for travellers who will be able to use e-gates at airports on the continent.

  - A landmark emissions-trading deal, meaning UK exporters avoid £800 million of carbon border taxes.

  - Closer cooperation on crime and migration, including access to the EU facial recognition data.

  - Further collaboration on tackling illegal migration and improving border management.

  - The deal paves the way for the UK's return to the Erasmus university exchange programme, and the creation of a youth mobility scheme, which was agreed at the end of 2025 for an initial one year period.

  - The deal included the removal of restrictions from agrifood trade which paved the way for the removal of checks on British food exports, allowing many foods to be sold again with ease in the EU.

  - Controversially, the deal granted EU fishers access to British waters for an additional 12 years.

- **Critics of Brexit** argue that it has permanently altered the UK's economic landscape:

  - Reduced trade efficiency due to regulatory barriers.

  - Shifting business models to mitigate Brexit's impact, such as establishing EU-based subsidiaries.

  - Loss of access to the single market's benefits, such as streamlined financial services regulations.

Political parties

The impact of Brexit on political parties in the UK has been profound, reshaping their strategies, internal dynamics and electoral prospects. Since the 2016 Referendum, Brexit influenced party alignments, voter bases and policy priorities in various ways:

1. Conservative Party

Brexit initially united the Conservatives under the 'Get Brexit Done' slogan in 2019, which secured a large parliamentary majority. However, post-Brexit, the party struggled to maintain cohesion as factions debated the future direction of Brexit-related policies. Hardline Brexiteers pushed for a more complete break from EU regulations, while moderates advocated pragmatic cooperation with the EU. The party's long-standing internal split over Europe, which Brexit was intended to resolve, has still left divisions. The focus on Brexit helped the Conservatives win Leave voters in 2019, but alienated some traditional supporters, particularly in Remain areas.

2. Labour Party

Labour adopted a cautious approach to Brexit since Starmer became Prime Minister, seeking to appeal to both Leave and Remain voters by promising to 'make Brexit work'. The party does not advocate rejoining the EU or single market to avoid alienating Leave voters and reigniting divisive debates. Labour must appeal to both pro-Brexit voters in 'Red Wall' constituencies, which largely supported Leave in the 2016 Referendum, and pro-EU voters concentrated in urban areas and among party members. This balancing act is critical to maintaining electoral support, particularly given the rise of Reform UK as a competitor in Leave-leaning regions. Labour's Brexit strategy focused on incremental changes, resetting the UK's relationship with the EU, and by reintroducing popular schemes like the Erasmus student exchange scheme which are unlikely to address the broader economic damage caused by Brexit. Also, although Starmer sought a reset in UK–EU relations, he also worked hard to establish strong ties with President Trump.

Synoptic Link

Link together the EU to the nature of the party system in the UK and its impact on party unity.

Photo 10.5 **PM Keir Starmer meets with Ursula von der Leyen, President of the European Commission, to discuss a reset in UK–EU relations**

Source: Thierry Monasse / Contributor / Getty Images

3. Other parties

- The Liberal Democrats propose rejoining the single market as a step towards eventual EU membership.
- The SNP has tied its pro-EU stance to its push for Scottish independence, arguing that an independent Scotland could rejoin the EU.

Synoptic Link

Link together the EU and voting behaviour in the UK, both in elections and referendums.

- The Green Party uses Brexit as a platform to promote broader issues like environmental sustainability while supporting a closer relationship with the EU.
- Reform UK advocates scrapping remaining EU laws and renegotiating post-Brexit agreements.

Sovereignty

- The European Union (Withdrawal) Act 2018 repealed the European Communities Act 1972, which had given EU law supremacy over some UK law. This marked a formal return to the principle that Parliament can 'make or unmake any law'. By leaving the EU, the UK is no longer bound by EU law or the jurisdiction of the Court of Justice of the European Union in most areas. Parliament now has the ability to legislate in ways that were previously restricted by EU membership, such as setting its own rules on trade and regulatory standards. It is now free to diverge from EU rules if it chooses to do so.
- While Brexit has restored significant sovereignty to the UK, it remains bound by various obligations and constraints stemming from its agreements with the EU. These include:
  - regulatory alignment in Northern Ireland
  - trade-related provisions under the TCA
  - new administrative requirements for travel and immigration
  - lost 'passporting' rights for financial services after Brexit
  - future cooperation which may require further alignment with EU rules.

These limits reflect a balance between sovereignty and maintaining practical ties with the UK's largest trading partner.

Impact on devolution

Tip: See Devolution section of Chapter 7 for a detailed analysis of the impact of Brexit on devolution.

Brexit has complicated relationships between Westminster and devolved administrations in Scotland, Wales and Northern Ireland.

- Most significantly, Northern Ireland remains aligned with EU single market rules for goods to avoid a hard border with the Republic of Ireland. This means EU regulations on product standards, customs and VAT continue to apply in Northern Ireland. Moreover, the Court of Justice of the European Union (CJEU) retains jurisdiction over disputes related to EU law in Northern Ireland. UK courts can refer cases to the CJEU for preliminary rulings in these areas. Consequently, Brexit has intensified political divisions in Northern Ireland. Unionist parties like the DUP oppose the Northern Ireland Protocol as a threat to UK sovereignty, while nationalist parties like Sinn Féin view it as a step towards Irish unification and rejoining the EU. This destabilised the power-sharing institutions established by the Good Friday Agreement. The devolved government at Stormont was suspended for significant periods due to disagreements over the Northern Ireland Protocol (see Devolution section for more information).
- In Scotland, Brexit has fuelled calls for independence, given that Scotland voted overwhelmingly to remain in the EU (62%), with the Scottish National Party (SNP) arguing that Brexit represents a material change in circumstances justifying another independence referendum.
- Although Wales voted to leave (52.5%), its devolved government opposed Brexit's form and outcome, highlighting concerns over economic impacts and loss of EU funding for agriculture and structural projects.
- Brexit removed EU frameworks that regulated many devolved policy areas, such as agriculture, fisheries and environmental standards. The UK Government retained control over some of these powers through mechanisms like 'retained EU law', which has been contentious among devolved administrations. The devolved governments argue this undermines their authority as they expected these powers to return directly to them. For example, the Scottish and Welsh Governments claim their powers have been reduced without their consent with UK ministers acting in a devolved area. Devolved governments felt excluded from key decisions during Brexit negotiations. Consequently, trust between Westminster and the devolved administrations was significantly eroded.

Key Debate Summary: How much impact does the EU have on the UK?

For	Theme	Against
✓ The TCA and other agreements have a significant impact on UK policy.	How much freedom does the UK have in policymaking?	✗ The UK is now free to determine all aspects of policy in a post-Brexit world.
✓ The EU created divisions in the main parties, and has seen the rise of new parties.	Are divisions over the EU still creating problems for political parties?	✗ Post Brexit, the divisions within the parties are less significant.
✓ The UK is still bound by many agreements with the EU.	Does the ECJ still have too much power over the UK?	✗ The UK left the EU and took back control by repealing the European Communities Act and leaving the jurisdiction of the Court of Justice of the European Union.
✓ Northern Ireland is still in the single market and under the jurisdiction of the Court of Justice of the European Union.	Is the situation in Northern Ireland a challenge for the UK?	✗ This is to ensure frictionless movement of goods across the UK, and is not political.

Sovereignty

What is sovereignty?

Sovereignty, in its simplest sense, is the principle of absolute and unlimited power. As such, sovereignty is the defining feature of a state, emphasising the state's supreme authority over its internal affairs (sometimes called 'internal sovereignty'). The location of internal sovereignty largely determines the constitutional make-up of a state. The United Kingdom is a unitary state (see page 205), with sovereignty located in the Westminster Parliament.

Parliamentary sovereignty (legal sovereignty)

Parliamentary sovereignty has long been seen as a key principle of the constitution of the United Kingdom. What parliamentary sovereignty means in practice is that Parliament has no legal limits on its law-making powers. This principle is most closely associated with A.V. Dicey's 1885 work, *Introduction to the Study of the Law of the Constitution*, in which he states that 'Parliament has the right to make or unmake any law whatever; and further no person or body is recognised by the law of England as having the right to override or set aside the legislation of Parliament.' The concept of parliamentary sovereignty that Dicey is describing is **legal sovereignty** as there are no legal limits on Parliament's powers to make or unmake law. It is worth unpicking A.V. Dicey's definition to find the rules that underpin parliamentary sovereignty.

» Firstly, this means that statute law, passed by Parliament, is supreme over all other kinds of law, such as common law.

» Secondly, no other body, such as another legislature or the Supreme Court, can challenge or set aside any statute law passed by Parliament.

» Thirdly, the principle includes the idea that no Parliament can bind its successors, meaning no Parliament can pass laws that future Parliaments cannot change. Any power which has been transferred either upwards or downwards can be reversed by a simple Act of Parliament.

» Lastly, the absence of a codified constitution ensures that there is no higher authority than Parliament.

However, there are non-legal limits on Parliament; these limits are the practical and political realities of the world in which Parliament operates.

In this case, it makes more sense to discuss power in terms of **political sovereignty** as this focuses on where power lies in the real world rather than where power lies in a strictly legal sense.

» Political sovereignty refers to the location of real power – who makes decisions in reality. It ignores where legal sovereignty may lie and concentrates on who realistically can exercise power within the state.

» In reality, the electorate are sovereign only at times of elections and Parliament is only really answerable to the people once every five years.

Spec Key Term

Legal sovereignty: Refers to supreme legal authority: that is, an unchallengeable 'right' to establish any law one wishes. (Parliament is sovereign in a strictly legal sense.)

Political sovereignty: Sovereignty refers to absolute political power: that is, an unrestricted 'ability' to act however one wishes.

» When the government is able to dominate Parliament, i.e. when it has a secure majority in the Commons, it could be said to have political sovereignty.

» The transfer of many powers to Scotland, Wales and Northern Ireland under devolution law could be said to have transferred political sovereignty as it seems inconceivable that these powers will ever be reclaimed by the UK Parliament, even though legally they could.

Parliament is not, and has never been, politically sovereign. Parliament has the legal right to make, amend or unmake any law it wishes, but does not always have the political ability to do so.

There has been a long-running contradiction in representative democracy in the UK between parliamentary sovereignty and **popular sovereignty**, by which supreme power is seen to lie with the people. Popular sovereignty is the principle that supreme authority is entrusted in the people. Parliament receives its authority from the electorate, and when Parliament passes laws that are in conflict with the views of the people, then tension arises and Parliament's power can be challenged. It refers to those circumstances when the people's decisions are binding. It is suggested that the people have sovereignty as:

1. they elect Parliament

2. they give a mandate to the government

3. referendum results are typically accepted even though they may not be legally binding.

4. ultimately Parliament rules for the people and therefore all laws require the acceptance or active support of its citizens for its policies.

Thus, the real source of power lies with the people. As Dicey says, 'Behind the legal sovereign that the lawyer recognises, there is another sovereign to whom the legal sovereign must bow. This is the political sovereign. In democracies, the legal sovereign receives its authority from the electorate, whatever be the basis of the right of vote, and is answerable to it for the exercise of its powers.'

The other main political constraints on parliamentary sovereignty include powerful pressure groups, especially major business interests; public opinion; electoral pressures; the views of major trading partners, notably the USA and the EU; and the policies of international organisations, such as the EU, the World Trade Organization (WTO) and the UN.

KEY TOPIC DEBATE: IS PARLIAMENT SOVEREIGN?

Over recent years, Parliament has passed an increasing number of statutes that appear to provide practical limits on parliamentary sovereignty, including the Devolution Acts, the Human Rights Act and the Constitutional Reform Act. In addition to this, the wider use of referendums – a form of popular sovereignty – has placed further limits on the legal sovereignty of Parliament. Finally, it has been argued that sovereignty has been drifting from Parliament to the executive branch as the executive has become more dominant.

However, these developments do not essentially weaken the principle of parliamentary sovereignty, since, legally at least, only Parliament can make law. Parliament can repeal any of the laws that appear to provide practical limits and could choose to ignore the outcomes of a referendum if they are not legally binding.

Devolution

Legally, the power of Westminster is unaffected by the passage of the Devolution Acts, yet in a practical sense, Parliament has lost the power to make law in many areas of domestic law, particularly in Scotland.

❌ **It is almost impossible to imagine the reversal of devolution in Scotland and Wales without the support of the majority of the populations in those countries, suggesting Parliament is not politically sovereign.**

» The Sewel Convention states that the UK Parliament 'will not normally legislate with regard to devolved matters without the consent' of the relevant devolved legislature. It is recognised in the Scotland Act 2016 and Wales Act 2017 by stating that the devolution settlements can only be reversed via referendum. This appears to recognise that the UK has moved to a quasi-federal system of government and all the political pressure is now for more devolution of powers not less.

✅ **There is no loss of legal sovereignty because even devolution (or even quasi-federalism) is not the same as federalism.**

» Even though Sewel is recognised in the Scotland Act 2016 and Wales Act 2017, the convention (like all conventions) is not legally binding. The Supreme Court confirmed this in the Miller 2017 judgement ruling. It said that that 'policing the scope and manner of its operation does not lie within the constitutional remit of the judiciary'. The judgement emphasised that Parliament's recognition of the convention in statute did not make it legally enforceable. If Parliament had intended to make it justiciable, it would have used clearer language.

» There have been a number of occasions when Sewel has been ignored by the UK Government between 2019 and 2024 with decisions being made in Westminster without the consent of the devolved administration (see Devolution chapter for more details).

» Furthermore, Sunak's blocking of Scotland's Gender Reform Recognition Act, using section 35, highlighted the significant limits to devolution.

Human Rights Act

The Human Rights Act and the creation of the Supreme Court, via the Constitutional Reform Act 2005, do not give the courts the ability to strike down legislation passed by Parliament. However, the balance between Parliament and the judiciary has been altered because Parliament feels the responsibility to respond to decisions by the court that declare statutes incompatible with the Human Rights Act.

❌ **While Parliament remains legally sovereign, it is clear that Parliament feels obliged to respond to judicial decisions regarding the Human Rights Act.**

» In the cases of abortion in Northern Ireland, civil partnerships and the police keeping fingerprints and DNA on file, Parliament has amended the law in response to judicial decisions, showing that there are real restrictions on the sovereignty of Parliament.

» When Parliament had managed all the hurdles imposed on the Rwanda policy that the UK Supreme Court had requested, flights were stopped by a ruling of the ECtHR. This suggests Parliament is not sovereign.

✅ **Parliamentary sovereignty means that the Supreme Court cannot strike down statutes and, while the court is part of the discussion about rights, Parliament has the final say.**

» When introducing the Illegal Migration Act 2023, the Home Secretary used section 19(1)(b) of the Human Rights Act to state that she was unable to confirm compatibility with rights. The Act expressly disapplied section 3 of the HRA, which normally requires courts and public authorities to interpret legislation compatibly with Convention rights where possible. This showed that Parliament can pass any law it chooses, even if it is incompatible with the HRA.

✅ **Ultimately, Parliament is legally sovereign and has the power to repeal, replace or amend the Human Rights Act, and it can also withdraw from the European Convention on Human Rights.**

» There is real debate in the UK about the need to withdraw from the ECHR to give Parliament the ability to Act as it wishes without wider interference.

Wider use of referendums

Since the referendum on continuing European Community membership in 1975, the UK Government has increasingly used referendums on important constitutional issues, including multiple referendums on devolution as well as Scottish independence and continued membership of the EU. This raises the question as to whether popular sovereignty through referendums is a challenge to parliamentary sovereignty.

❌ **Referendums limit Parliament as it is politically unrealistic for Parliament to ignore a clear result in a referendum where there has been a reasonable turnout.**

» In the 2016 Brexit Referendum, while a majority of both the House of Commons and House of Lords supported Remain, as did the leaders of the three main parties heading into the Referendum, in the end, popular sovereignty won out over the will of Parliament in the triggering of Article 50 and the passing of the EU Withdrawal Act of 2018.

Tip: See Case Study on the ECHR in Chapter 2.

Synoptic Link

Link together the protection of rights in the UK and parliamentary sovereignty.

✅ **Referendums in the UK can only be granted via an Act of Parliament, and the result of a referendum is typically advisory and not legally binding.**

» In 2022, the Supreme Court ruled unanimously that the Scottish Parliament did not have the power to unilaterally call a second referendum on Scottish independence without the consent of the UK Government. The court emphasised that measures questioning the integrity of the United Kingdom were for the Westminster Parliament to decide.

» Many MPs continued to campaign against Brexit after the referendum; in fact, Parliament tried to take over the entire proceedings of withdrawal in an attempt, many suggest, to thwart it. This shows that Parliament does not always feel the need to abide by the outcome of referendums.

Dominance of the executive

It has been argued that there has been a drift in power from Parliament to the executive branch. However, it remains the case that Parliament has the legal power to make or unmake any law.

❌ **In the UK, the fused executive and legislative branches mean that, in practice, political sovereignty has passed from Parliament to the executive when a Prime Minister has a large majority in the House of Commons.**

» Johnson passed his Brexit legislation in December 2019 by 358 votes to 234, a majority of 124. This is despite the fact that the majority of MPs in Parliament had voted to remain in the UK. Johnson's majority ensured that his MPs voted with him.

❌ **The Royal Prerogative, including the power of patronage and the party whip system, helps ensure the Prime Minister's dominance over Parliament.**

» Starmer withdrew the whip from seven Labour MPs when they voted against his child benefit policy in 2024. This showed his party that he was not prepared to tolerate any dissent.

» In the case of the two Thatcher Governments of 1983 and 1987, and the Blair Governments of 1997 and 2001, where both Prime Ministers enjoyed a majority of over 100 seats, executive dominance was the norm. Blair did not lose a vote in the House of Commons from 1997 to 2005, suggesting that political sovereignty resides in the executive.

✅ **Ultimately, only Parliament has the power to make or unmake any law.**

» Whatever the size of the government's majority, the executive still has to rely on Parliament to pass legislation.

» While Parliament may rarely exercise its power to veto legislation proposed by the executive, its ability to use this power means that the executive often must compromise with Parliament by amending the legislation in order to get it passed. During 2025, Starmer faced significant rebellions by normally loyal MPs over welfare reform, winter fuel payments and climb downs over some business rates and inheritance tax on farms. These led to significant U-turns showing the power of Parliament.

✅ **The relationship between Parliament and the executive is constantly changing.**

» When the Prime Minister is weak, Parliament is more dominant, such as during the period Theresa May was in power where she suffered 33 defeats in the Commons.

» However, even when there is a dominant Prime Minister, such as Blair, Parliament can still exercise its powers, as it did in 2005 when Blair was defeated on his proposal to allow the police to detain terror suspects for up to 90 days without charging them.

Key Debate Summary: Is Parliament sovereign?

For	Theme	Against
✓ Parliament is and always has been legally sovereign as there are no legal limits on its ability to make or unmake any law.	Does political and popular sovereignty override legal sovereignty?	✗ Parliament has never been politically sovereign; it is limited by popular sovereignty and a range of other real-world, political limits.
✓ Parliament remains legally sovereign because devolved powers can be recalled.	How much does devolution challenge Parliamentary sovereignty?	✗ Politically, power has now passed to the devolved assemblies because the UK is increasingly a quasi-federal system.
✓ The judiciary cannot strike down a statute for breaking the HRA and Parliament can repeal the HRA if it chooses, so Parliament remains legally sovereign.	How much does the HRA challenge Parliamentary sovereignty?	✗ Parliament feels obliged to respect and respond to judicial decisions suggesting there are limits to Parliament's political sovereignty.
✓ Only Parliament can call a referendum and the result is advisory so Parliament remains legally sovereign.	How much do referendum results challenge Parliamentary sovereignty?	✗ Politically, it is unrealistic for Parliament to ignore a clear result on a decent turnout in a referendum.
✓ Parliament is legally sovereign, and the executive has to rely on it for all its legislation.	How much does a dominant executive challenge Parliamentary sovereignty?	✗ Politically, the executive, particularly when it has a large majority, dominates Parliament and so controls the law-making process.

Exam Style Questions

- Evaluate the view that the Supreme Court is neither independent nor neutral (30).

- Evaluate the view that the Supreme Court is an effective check on the executive and legislative branches (30).

- Evaluate the view that the UK Supreme Court has too much power for an unelected and unaccountable body (30).

- Evaluate the view that sovereignty no longer lies in Parliament (30).

Source Question

Source 1

Judicial review gives unelected judges too much power to limit the executive as the courts can declare actions of the executive to be 'ultra vires' or in contravention of the Human Rights Act and quash them. As well as that, the Supreme Court also has the power to declare Acts of Parliament incompatible with the Human Rights Act. By ruling that a law is incompatible with the HRA, the Supreme Court is essentially making Parliament take action to amend or remove the law in question, undermining its sovereignty. Consequently, the Supreme Court is becoming more activist, making decisions that take the court beyond its legal role into the heart of the political debate. Given that the court is unelected and unaccountable, it is unacceptable that the court is involving itself in political decision making. Political decisions are the reserve of democratically elected politicians in the executive and legislature.

Source 2

The court only rules on the lawfulness of an action on cases that are brought before it. It can only work within what the law states, and the executive has the power to place a new bill in front of Parliament to change the law. Moreover, declarations of incompatibility work within the principle of parliamentary sovereignty as the court cannot strike down an Act of Parliament or force Parliament to take action, merely identify an incompatibility with the HRA. The Human Rights Act was passed by a democratically elected Parliament, and in so doing, it gave the Supreme Court a greater role in protecting rights and checking the executive. It is simply fulfilling its role in resolving key constitutional and legal questions. The huge levels of constitutional change brought about by Brexit, asylum, immigration, human rights and devolution have created a situation where the Supreme Court has been placed at the heart of these key constitutional issues.

Using the source, evaluate the view that the Supreme Court has too much power for an unelected body.

In your response you must:

- » *Compare and contrast different opinions in the source*
- » *Examine and debate these views in a balanced way*
- » *Analyse and evaluate **only** the information presented in the source.*

 # Chapter Summary

» The Constitutional Reform Act reinforced the separation of powers in the UK through the transfer of the House of Lords' judicial function to a new Supreme Court.

» All parts of society need to have confidence that the decisions taken by the Supreme Court are independent and impartial, but question marks remain over whether this is the case.

» The Supreme Court plays a key role in upholding the rule of law through judicial review. However, there is controversy over whether the court has too much power over the executive and the legislature.

» There has been a process of closer political and economic union in Europe and this has impacted on the UK's relationship with the EU.

» The impact of the EU on the UK despite Brexit remains a dynamic and contested debate.

» The nature of sovereignty remains contested in the UK, with contested debates both about where sovereignty lies and where it should lie.

 # Further Resources

Visit www.supremecourt.uk/ to learn more about the role of the Supreme Court, the justices and its decided cases.

Lady Hale, *The Supreme Court of the United Kingdom – Lessons from our First Ten Years*, transcript of lecture (12 December 2019). Available at www.supremecourt.uk/docs/ten-year-anniversary-lecture-lady-hale.pdf (accessed 14 December 2020).

Visit the companion website to access the Further Resources Booklet to explore a range of useful web links related to: diversity and the Supreme Court, the relationship between the judiciary and Parliament, the aims and role of the EU, Brexit and the constitution and more.

11 EXAM FOCUS

Introduction

The aim of this chapter is to unpick the Assessment Objectives (AOs) that are crucial to understanding how to do well in your A-Level Politics exams. We'll help you to understand what they mean and, most crucially, how to incorporate them into your answers to both essay and source questions. We will lead you step by step through all the elements that make up the skills and knowledge needed to do well, including how to incorporate the AOs, how to answer a source question, and how to organise your paragraphs in essay and source questions. We'll then bring all of this together with a full worked example at the end of the chapter. Throughout this book, when we have considered the key debates within a topic, we have provided matched, paired points for both sides of an argument. In this chapter, we will explain how to use these points when writing essays.

Before going into more detail, we first provide an initial overview of some of the key things you need to know about the exams covering UK Politics: the exam papers and question types, the three AOs, the idea of 'synopticity', the breadth of questions, caps on marks and the need to provide balanced answers.

The exam

The UK content of the course is assessed in two separate exams. Component 1 is the UK Politics element and Component 2 is UK Government. (Both Components 1 and 2 also include questions relating to the Political Ideas part of the course.)

In each UK section of the exam you will have to answer:

» ONE source question from a choice of TWO
» ONE essay question from a choice of TWO

The types of questions

Components 1 and 2 each have an identical range of questions. They both have three question types:

» UK source questions – 30 marks
» UK essay questions – 30 marks
» Ideas essay questions – 24 marks

This chapter is concerned only with the first two types of question (the UK questions).

UK source questions

Questions for UK source questions will typically begin with the stem 'Evaluate the view that…', followed by a statement. The source, of approximately 300 words, will give two opposing views to the statement outlined in the title. Your job is to read the source, consider both sides of the arguments presented in the source and then compose an answer which argues throughout that one side of the argument is stronger than the other.

For example, in the Edexcel Pearson 2025 Component 1 A-Level exam, one source title was, 'Using the source, evaluate the view that rights in the UK are poorly protected.' It was followed by a source outlining both sides of the debate with a number of points included in each side.

Source questions are marked out of 30 which are allocated as follows: AO1 – 10 marks, AO2 – 10 marks, AO3 – 10 marks.

UK essay questions

Questions for UK essays will also typically begin with the stem 'Evaluate the view that …' and follow with a statement for you to consider. Here, you have to consider both sides of the argument and then compose an answer which argues throughout that one side of the argument is stronger than the other. For example, in the Edexcel Pearson June 2025 Component 2 A-Level exam, one essay question was, 'Evaluate the view that Prime Ministers now have too much power.'

Essay questions are marked out of 30 which are allocated as follows: AO1 – 10 marks, AO2 – 10 marks, AO3 – 10 marks.

Introduction to the Assessment Objectives (AOs)

AO1

> **'Demonstrate knowledge and understanding of political institutions, processes, concepts, theories and issues.'**

(See page 342 for more details)

AO1 is probably the AO that everyone is most familiar with because it relates to 'knowledge and understanding'. This is what is taught in classrooms day in, day out. Everything in the chapters of this book begins with AO1: knowledge and the understanding that flows from it. Without good knowledge and understanding, there is a limit to how effectively you can utilise the other two AOs.

AO2

> **'Analyse aspects of politics and political information, including in relation to parallels, connections, similarities and differences.'**

(See page 343 for more details)

AO2 is about analysis, but what does this actually mean? Dictionary definitions include 'detailed examination' or 'the process of examining' something. So, what do we have to do to improve our AO2 marks?

» Firstly, we have to be solid in our AO1 because analysis (AO2) flows from and is grounded in knowledge and understanding.

» Secondly, we have to explore our AO1 point in more detail, probing, investigating and exploring the knowledge we have stated as AO1.

» Thirdly, AO2 also requires comparative analysis, which means exploring AO1 points to tease out similarities and differences, or to compare how they've changed over time.

AO3

> **'Evaluate aspects of politics and political information, including to construct arguments, make substantiated judgements and draw conclusions.'**

(See page 349 for more details)

To evaluate, according to dictionary definitions, is to 'judge the importance or value of something' or to 'make a judgement about them, for example about how good or bad they are'. AO3 is all about judgements; it requires you to not just **know** information (AO1) and to **explore** and **compare** information (AO2), but also to consider all of that and then decide which side of the argument is stronger i.e. **judge** (AO3).

The above provides a basic introduction to the AOs. Later in the chapter we will be exploring ways to incorporate them into answers and looking at good (and not so good) practice.

Synopticity in the two UK papers

Synopticity in A-Level Politics refers to being able to tie things together or connect things from different Components. By doing this, you are demonstrating a wider understanding of how different elements of the course relate to each other, illustrating that you understand the subject in a more holistic way. Synopticity in the UK papers occurs in Component 2, but only in UK 30-mark essays.

In these essays you are required to draw on relevant knowledge from Component 1 UK and/or the Core Ideas. For example, a question asking whether a Prime Minister is too powerful may include references to the role of first-past-the-post in creating large majorities, as well as the role of the party and policies in keeping a Prime Minister popular and in power. A question on whether the UK should have a codified constitution could make a connection with the contrasting traditions of liberalism and conservatism in their view of this debate, as well as discussing the role of constitutions in rights protection, all of which are found in Component 1.

STUDENT EXTRACT – 'Evaluate the view that Parliament is able to sufficiently limit the power of the Prime Minister' – looking at Synopticity

Despite the fact that Johnson still had a significant majority in 2023, his popularity took a nosedive after Partygate scandals were revealed by the Daily Mirror newspaper. Poor opinion poll ratings continued for months, which led to his party realising that they could not continue with him as their leader.

By linking Johnson's demise to revelations by the media and poor opinion poll ratings, the student is making an effective synoptic link back to Component 1.

It's important to know that there is a cap in place here – if no synoptic skills are addressed in the essay, you can't achieve the best marks. Also, it's worth noting that good synoptic links can add to the overall AO1 marks achieved and this gives you a chance to draw from all the UK politics and ideas content from Component 1 in answering the questions.

Caps on the UK papers

Throughout the two UK papers, there are a number of caps to be aware of. It's important to know where they exist to make sure you don't fall foul of them.

1. All 30-mark questions (both sources and essays) will be capped at Level 2 if answers don't consider both sides of the argument.
2. If a source answer (in either Component 1 or 2) does not use the information in the source, it can be capped at Level 2.
3. Essays in Component 2 must have synoptic links back to topics in Component 1 otherwise they will be capped at Level 4.

'Consideration of both views' and balance

The 30-mark Source questions in Components 1 and 2 ask students to 'examine and debate these views in a balanced way', and the 30-mark Essay questions ask students to 'consider this view and the alternative to this view in a balanced way'.

So, what does 'balance' mean? While it's not necessary to ensure that you have an even word count of arguments in favour to arguments against in your answer, it is also important to ensure that both sides of the argument have been fairly considered. So, a 60:40 split is probably fine, but anything significantly less than that may not be considered balanced.

Another issue which students find difficult is the need to reconcile the need for 'balance' with the AO3 need to 'make substantiated judgement'. The answer to this conundrum is not as complicated as it may first appear. If you are answering a question on whether FPTP should be reformed, and you are taking the viewpoint that it should be reformed, you must still ensure that nearly half your answer is exploring the benefits of FPTP, even if you then go on to criticise these benefits to justify your view.

STUDENT EXTRACT – 'Evaluate the view that the only parties that matter are Labour and Conservative' – looking at balance

Command	Evaluate the view
Topic	Labour & Conservative Parties
Keyword(s)	Only

Smaller parties such as the SNP and Reform UK (and UKIP) have had the ability to push politics in a certain direction, meaning that Labour and the Conservatives are not always the only parties that matter. The SNP was the third largest party in Parliament between 2015 and 2024, so consequently they had greater influence in Parliament and used its presence to call for debates and ask questions that unsettled the government. In 2024, Reform UK only had five MPs, including Nigel Farage. Farage was able to influence UK immigration politics hugely, affecting both the Labour and Conservative Party. Previously, Farage's UKIP was the single most significant reason why the Brexit referendum was called and won. All these examples clearly show that smaller parties, not only Labour and the Conservatives, matter. On the other hand, the power of the SNP is limited due to the fact that Labour is unwilling to work with them as the SNP have taken away many Scottish seats from Labour.

> This is a very unbalanced answer, merely paying lip service to the other side of the argument.

STUDENT EXTRACT – 'Evaluate the view that Parliament is able to sufficiently limit the power of the Prime Minister' – looking at balance

Command	Evaluate the view
Topic	Labour & Conservative Parties
Keyword(s)	Only

EXTRACT 1:

Another argument is that although PMs may be able to control the Commons, they have less control of the Lords. This is because party loyalties are weaker in the Lords and the government does not have an inbuilt majority. The House of Lords defeated the government ten times over the Rwanda bill during its passage in early 2024, amending the bill to address concerns about Rwanda's safety, legal rights and protections for specific groups. May's 'Brexit' Bill in 2019 faced 15 defeats in the Lords.

> Here the student is outlining one side of the argument.

However, defeats in the Lords are usually overturned in the Commons showing that Prime Ministers are not really limited by the Lords. Often the Lords relent due to the undemocratic nature and their lack of legitimacy because they are unelected and recognise their constitutional role as secondary to the elected Commons. After the Rwanda bill was defeated in the Lords with a series of amendments, the Commons repeatedly rejected the Lords' changes and maintained the government's original position, voting down all amendments. May's Brexit Bill was also ultimately passed by the Lords. Additionally, the Lords are constrained by the Salisbury Convention, a reminder of their secondary nature as an unelected house.

> This paragraph argues the other side and rejects the arguments from the paragraph above. Overall this is a balanced argument which comes to the view that PMs aren't limited by Parliament. It's also worth noting here that this question references 'Parliament' and the student has done well to discuss both the Commons and the Lords. When a question uses the term 'Parliament', it is expected that students discuss both Houses of Parliament in their answer.

Assessment objectives in detail

AO1 in detail

> **'Demonstrate knowledge and understanding of political institutions, processes, concepts, theories and issues.'**

We introduced the AOs at the beginning of the chapter, but now we are going to look at them in more detail. To recap, **AO1** is about what you know, what you've been taught and the level at which you understand it.

- When answering a question, you have to begin with **AO1** and the key is to **carefully select** the information you think will best help you to answer the question. What are the key points you need to discuss to answer the question? Knowledge selection is a much-underrated skill when considering **AO1**, but it's included in the exam board mark scheme for **AO1**. This means you must choose very carefully which information you are going to write about in your answer. Sometimes, students write 'everything they know' about a topic and hope that their teachers can sift the important bits from the unimportant bits. It's worth noting that higher **AO1** marks require students to do the sifting, not their teachers!

- Another area where **AO1** can cause issues is **if students focus predominantly on AO1** to the exclusion of the other two AOs. An outstanding student, who can write reams of detail about an issue, can only ever get 10 out of 30 for it because there are only 10 marks available for **AO1** knowledge and understanding. **AO1** requires students to know and understand their knowledge *and* how to use it, remembering that the key to writing a really good answer is to balance all three AOs.

- **A final aspect of AO1 is the use of examples**. Examples, used well, lift ordinary **AO1** to really good **AO1**, like seasoning a plate of food. Some students underuse their examples, often punctuating an essay with little more than 'e.g. Just Stop Oil'. While lots of detail about who Just Stop Oil are and what they stand for is not needed, using relevant details, about whether Just Stop Oil's methods were effective or counterproductive to enhance and explain your point, can really lift an answer.

STUDENT EXTRACT **'Evaluate the view that the only parties that matter are Labour and Conservative' – looking at AO1**

Command	Evaluate the view
Topic	Labour & Conservative Parties
Keyword(s)	Only

EXTRACT:

It could be argued that the only political parties that matter in our political system are the Conservatives and Labour. Since 1922, with few coalitions, the Conservatives and Labour have battled it out to be our governing party. For example, if we look at the results of the 2019 Election, the Conservatives won 43.6% of the vote and Labour won 32.2% of the vote. Coming in third was the Liberal Democrats with 11.5% of the vote. Seats wise, the Conservatives had 365 seats, Labour 203 and Lib Dems 11. This data tells us that both in percentage of votes and seats, the Conservatives and Labour are the two dominant parties (by a landslide) and therefore it could be argued that they are the only two that matter.

> Here the student is giving too much statistical information about seats won etc., which is overshadowing the point they are making. Just below it they summarise the data and begin to make (and end) their point.

STUDENT EXTRACT – 'Evaluate the view that the only parties that matter are Labour and Conservative' – looking at AO1

Command	Evaluate the view
Topic	Labour & Conservative Parties
Keyword(s)	Only

It can be argued that the Conservative and Labour Parties are in fact the only political parties to matter within UK politics due to their continuous domination at all general elections because they are the only two parties to ever win majorities in Westminster. In fact, the UK has at times been described as having a dominant party system where for a prolonged period of time between 1979 and 1992, 1997 and 2010, and then 2019 and 2024 saw Conservative and Labour Governments with large majorities. The repetitive pattern of political power exchanging hands between the Conservative and Labour Parties highlights their supremacy over the UK political climate, providing them with the greatest opportunity to influence UK politics. As a result, this may lead to conclusions that due to their political dominance they are the only two parties to matter.

> Here the student gets straight to the point they are making in the opening sentence. The student uses key words like 'dominant party systems' very effectively. They use examples very effectively to develop their point, without overdoing it. Throughout their whole answer, they have not lost sight of the question and selected **AO1** effectively to answer it.

AO2 in detail

> **'Analyse aspects of politics and political information, including in relation to parallels, connections, similarities and differences.'**

AO2 requires students to analyse in two distinct ways:

- » Firstly, to examine and explore **AO1** in more detail, or as the Level Based Mark Scheme puts it, to make 'logical chains of reasoning'.
- » Secondly, to 'draw on similarities and differences' to make 'cohesive and convincing connections'. Making these comparisons also relates to changes over time.

The first aspect of AO2 requires students to explore and probe **AO1** points that they have raised. This is often a challenge to understand.

Sometimes, students add **AO1** detail, thinking this is the same as analysing a point; they often make the same point in different ways, rather than develop their point.

STUDENT EXTRACT – 'Evaluate the view that devolution has been successful in the UK' – looking at AO2

Command	Evaluate the view
Topic	Devolution
Keyword(s)	Successful

It can be argued that devolution has not been successful because it has seen an asymmetric amount of power devolved to each country. The main features of devolved power in the UK are legislative, financial and administrative. Devolution has arguably been asymmetric because Scotland has been provided the most power, followed by Wales and then Northern Ireland. This is asymmetric as it provides different powers to the different regions. This means that some parts have more powers than others.

> This paragraph doesn't really move on from the initial point that devolution is asymmetric.

Sometimes it's easier to use phrases which naturally lend themselves to analysis:

» this means that

» therefore

» this leads to

» this is because

» this shows that

» as a consequence

» as a result.

You can try to use one of these phrases after you've written a couple of sentences at the beginning of your paragraph to help you analyse your point. Using 'signposts' like these helps to flag to your teacher that you are analysing.

STUDENT EXTRACT 'Evaluate the view that devolution has been successful in the UK' – looking at AO2

Command	Evaluate the view
Topic	Devolution
Keyword(s)	Successful

> Here the student has started the point with asymmetric devolution but extended it to show why it caused problems, before concluding that, as a result, devolution has not been successful.

It can be argued that devolution has not been successful because it is asymmetric, with different powers devolved to each country, but with Scotland having more power than the other two nations. This has led to tensions within the UK and calls for greater regional balance with Wales fighting for, and gaining, more power subsequently. Another consequence of the asymmetrical nature of devolution in the UK is that some English cities have been given their own Mayors; however, ironically this has caused its own issues of asymmetry with many regions of England feeling overlooked as they don't have an elected Mayor. Hence it can be seen that as a result of the asymmetric nature of devolution, it has not been successful in the UK.

STUDENT EXTRACT – 'Evaluate the view that social factors determine voting behaviour' – looking at AO2

Command	Evaluate the view
Topic	Social factors
Keyword(s)	Determine

> The phrase 'no longer' here shows change over time which is an important element of AO2.
>
> Here the student is developing their AO2 by developing an example to explore the point more deeply.

Class division is no longer as pronounced as it was due to class dealignment. This has happened because society has generally become more affluent and some of the working class aspire to be middle class as they want to earn more and own property. This is shown by Thatcher's policy of the sale of council homes to tenants to help get them on the property ladder, so those who were working class can feel like they have something to aspire to be rather than just sitting at the bottom of the pecking order.

While examples are primarily a feature of AO1, the way they are used can allow them to improve a student's AO2.

STUDENT EXTRACT 'Evaluate the view that wealth is the key factor in pressure group success' – looking at how to develop examples

Basic example – *As well as wealth, celebrity endorsement can make pressure groups more successful, such as Marcus Rashford and the free school meals issue during Covid.*

> This demonstrates **AO1** only.

Explained example – *As well as wealth, celebrity endorsement can make pressure groups more successful, such as Marcus Rashford and the Free Meal vouchers in the summer holidays during the Covid crisis. By publicly talking about his own experiences of growing up in poverty, and how necessary the vouchers were to his family, he was able to create empathy and support for the scheme among the wider public and was successful in making the government do a U-turn. Rashford's involvement in this campaign made it successful because it raised the media profile of the campaign, helping it to gain public sympathy and in turn put pressure on the government.*

> This demonstrates **AO1** and **AO2**.

The second aspect of AO2 requires students to analyse opposing aspects of a debate. This form of analysis is a key part of essay writing. This means looking at two different features and then comparing and contrasting them to see where there might be similarities and/or differences. It also relates to comparing how one thing may have changed over time, for example, the power of a Prime Minister, or the effectiveness of Parliament. Students often don't understand how to construct comparative analysis as opposed to just writing about two different things.

A very useful way to enhance comparative analysis is by using comparative language. This will enable you to draw comparisons and contrasts between different arguments. Some simple ways to incorporate comparative analysis is by using words like:

- » whereas
- » despite
- » however
- » similarly
- » although
- » not only
- » but also
- » in contrast
- » both
- » as well as
- » instead
- » no longer
- » still

As mentioned earlier, using 'signposts' like this helps to flag to your teacher that you are analysing.

There is a simple way to understand the difference between comparative analysis and simply discussing two different things. Take the following example.

Here are two bottles. Let's start off describing them both.

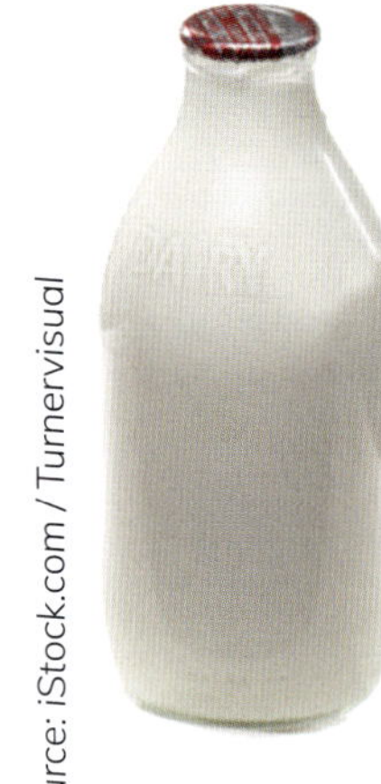

Source: iStock.com / Turnervisual

This container holds milk and is designed in a way to keep the milk fresh. It is made from glass, which is transparent. This bottle is cylindrical and has a tapering neck to allow easy pouring of the milk. It has a coloured foil lid which has been heat sealed on. Milk in glass bottles is usually delivered to the door and the bottles are collected so they can be sanitised and reused, almost immediately.

This is knowledge – AO1

Source: iStock.com / bahadir-yeniceri

This container holds milk and is made of plastic. It has been designed to keep milk fresh. It has an opaque finish and a different coloured plastic lid. Under the lid, it has a heat-sealed foil cap to keep the milk fresh. This bottle is rectangular in shape and is tapered at the top to make pouring the milk easier. The design of the container also incorporates a handle to make holding and pouring even easier. Milk in plastic containers like this is normally sold in shops. The container can be recycled.

This is knowledge – AO1

Above are correct facts about both containers but there is no comparison. Now we are going to take these facts and turn them into comparative paragraphs.

'Both containers hold milk. While they are both designed to help keep the milk fresh, the way they do this is different. The glass bottle just has a heat-sealed foil lid, whereas the plastic bottle has a heat-sealed foil lid as well as a plastic screw cap too which makes the bottle easier to reseal once the foil lid has been removed.'

One clear way they are different is that one is made of glass and the other of plastic. This also means that while one is transparent, the other is opaque. In addition, because one is made of plastic, it has been shaped to incorporate a handle which makes it easier to carry. Their shape is another area of difference; one is cylindrical in shape whereas the other one is rectangular. However, despite this difference, both are tapered at the top in order to make it easier to pour the milk.

One final comparison is their ability to be reused. While it's clear that both can be recycled, only the glass bottle can be almost instantly reused, simply requiring sanitising after use to enable it to be reused. The plastic bottle, on the other hand, needs a lengthier process of recycling before the plastic can be reused.'

This is analysis – AO2

Tip: Note that using the word 'easier' is comparative, using the word 'easy' would not be.

This type of technique can be used in essays and source answers when discussing the relative merits of one side over another.

AO2 and 'paired' points

One highly effective way to create effective analysis is to match your arguments 'for' and 'against', in the book, we refer to this as 'pairing'. Throughout this book we have provided matched, paired points for you to consider when writing essays.

If you look at the example above, the comparisons are made between two related aspects of the containers; lids are compared with lids, and shape is compared with shape. The comparison would not be effective if we compared the lid of one with the shape of the other; it would be an inadequate comparison. This is true when comparing arguments – they need to relate to each other.

Try this technique when comparing different electoral systems. For example:

- Compare whether different electoral systems provide local representation; another theme might be whether they fairly reflect the way people have voted.

- Equally, when looking at similarities or differences between party policies, it would be wise to compare their foreign policies, their welfare policies and their policies on law and order. You wouldn't compare one party's foreign policy with another's welfare policy; it would not really enable you to make effective comparisons.

Throughout the book, the Key Topic Debates have been laid out in this way, pairing and comparing arguments. There are also summary tables at the end of each debate so you can use them when revising a topic.

STUDENT EXTRACT – 'Evaluate the view that the differences between the political parties are greater than the similarities' – looking at AO2 analysis

Command	Evaluate the view
Topic	Political parties
Keyword(s)	Differences **greater than** similarities

For the three major parties, economic policy is an area of similarity as all three parties support capitalism as their primary economic policy. All three parties support the principle of equality of opportunity and this principle can be seen in many of their policies: support for the NHS and state-funded education. As well as this there is a genuine mutual support for international trade.

> Here the student is identifying and drawing on similarities between the parties.

STUDENT EXTRACT – 'Evaluate the view that the differences between the political parties are greater than the similarities' – looking at AO2 analysis

Command	Evaluate the view
Topic	Political parties
Keyword(s)	Differences **greater than** similarities

Despite similarities in their support for capitalism, the parties disagree when it comes to the role of the economy in several key ways. Labour and the Conservatives differ on National Insurance as Labour increased employer NI to 15% and lowered the threshold to £5,000, significantly raising business costs. The Conservatives, on the other hand, oppose these changes and seek to cut employee NI and pledge not to raise it for workers either. Additionally, the Labour Government introduced changes to inheritance tax on farms which the Conservatives are fundamentally opposed to.

> Here the student is looking at differences, comparing views and making effective use of comparative language.

STUDENT EXTRACT – 'Using the source, evaluate the view that the use of proportional representation would not improve elections to the Commons' – looking at comparative analysis AO2

Command	Evaluate the view
Topic	Proportional representation
Keyword(s)	Not improve

While it is true that FPTP is unfair to smaller parties as it requires a high concentration of votes in a constituency, this 'problem' leads to a positive outcome, as usually one of the two major parties is able to form a strong and stable government, and hence more able to make coherent and conclusive decisions on key matters.

> In this small extract from a longer paragraph, the student is effectively referencing an earlier argument that FPTP is unfair to smaller parties but then challenging this argument with another one. This is an effective example of comparative analysis.

STUDENT EXTRACT – 'Evaluate the view that Parliament is able to sufficiently limit the power of the Prime Minister' – looking at comparative analysis AO2

Command	Evaluate the view
Topic	Parliament, Prime Minister
Keyword(s)	Sufficiently limit

While it has been argued that previously Parliament was unable to challenge the power of Prime Ministers, more recent times have shown this view to be inaccurate. Since 2010, and especially in the 2017–19 Parliament, Prime Ministers have been very effectively challenged by Parliament. Reduced majorities and more rebellious backbenchers have made life difficult for more recent Prime Ministers. Theresa May went down in history for the biggest government defeat, losing by 230 votes. This is a far cry from Blair not losing a single vote between 1997 and 2005. Even Prime Ministers with larger majorities, like Johnson, Truss and Sunak, as well as Starmer, have faced considerably more rebellious MPs, often leading them to reconsider their policies.

> This student is comparing the past with the present, making highly effective comparisons.
>
> They are also using their examples effectively to enhance their point.

AO3 in detail

'Evaluate aspects of politics and political information, including to construct arguments, make substantiated judgements and draw conclusions.'

This AO requires you to evaluate. This means weighing up the evidence on both sides and coming to a reasoned judgement. You must come down on one side; you must conclude that one side of the argument is better than the other. It doesn't matter which side as all perspectives are equally valid. Additionally, your conclusion can be that one side wins hands down, or that one side is marginally more convincing than the other, as long as you conclude that it is the 'better side'.

However, the AO requires you to make a 'substantiated judgement', in other words you can't just present both sides equally throughout the essay and then, in your conclusion, argue that side X is *stronger than side Y*. A substantiated judgement is one which is argued throughout the answer. This should begin in the introduction, continue throughout the essay and be reasserted in the conclusion. This means that answers need to be carefully thought out and planned to ensure that AO3 is embedded throughout your answer.

In addition, **AO3** marks can be improved by weighing up the importance of the point you are making, for example by using phrases such as: 'this argument is very compelling', 'this point may be of less importance than', 'this view fails to recognise'.

Incorporating AO3 in introductions

STUDENT EXTRACT – 'Using the source, evaluate the view that UK democracy is in crisis' – looking at AO3 in introductions

Command	Evaluate the view
Topic	UK democracy
Keyword(s)	In crisis

In this essay I will consider the source's view on the low participation at the ballot box and how it demonstrates UK democracy in crisis. In contrast, I will also consider the view that participation outside the ballot box is on the rise, demonstrating a democracy that is not in crisis. I will consider the source's view that the levels of trust and confidence in the government are low, and in contrast I will consider how its impact is minimised as it is caused by short-term factors, not long-term ones. In my essay I will argue that UK democracy is not in crisis.

> Although this introduction unnecessarily outlines all the points it will make, it does set out clearly in the final sentence the line of argument to the question.

STUDENT EXTRACT – 'Using the source, evaluate the view that the use of proportional representation would not improve elections to the Commons' – looking at AO3 in introductions

Command	Evaluate the view
Topic	Proportional representation
Keyword(s)	Not improve

The current electoral system used for elections in the Commons is the system of First-Past-the-Post (FPTP). This electoral system is a simple plurality electoral system whereby constituents elect one candidate from a political party to represent them in the House of Commons. First-past-the-post is the current electoral system used in Westminster. There are flaws with the system, however it is extremely unlikely that there would be an entirely flawless system. Hence, this essay will argue that the use of proportional representation would not improve elections to the Commons.

> While this introduction could be reduced in length a bit, from an **AO3** perspective it nails the key aspect of outlining the way it is going to argue.

STUDENT EXTRACT – 'Evaluate the view that the only parties that matter are Labour and Conservative' – looking at AO3 in introductions

Command	Evaluate the view
Topic	Labour & Conservative Parties
Keyword(s)	Only

I agree with the view to some extent; however, I do not think that Labour and Conservatives are the only parties that matter. I think that they are the dominant parties but other parties matter in order to secure Britain as a democracy. However, some would agree with the view due to the first-past-the-post voting system, who actually votes for them and why. But some would disagree due to the ability of smaller parties to influence politics and discussions in Parliament.

> This student is not answering the question in their introduction – they are giving all the possible options of what they might think. This is to be avoided.

Incorporating AO3 throughout the essay

One of the most important things to understand about all three AOs is that they don't work in isolation. AO2 feeds off AO1 and AO3 feeds off AO2 and hence in turn, AO1. In other words, in order to enhance AO3, it is necessary, firstly, to know the arguments on both sides of the debate (AO1), and then to have developed and compared both sides with each other (AO2). If this has been done, you are then able to come to a 'substantiated judgement' about which side of the debate you think is stronger.

While it's important for AO3 to top and tail answers with effective introductions and conclusions, this is not enough. To achieve a Level 5 in AO3, the Pearson Level Based Mark Scheme requires students to:

> *'Construct fully relevant evaluation of political information, constructing fully effective arguments and judgements, which are consistently substantiated and lead to fully focused and justified conclusions.'*

This can be interpreted to mean that your AO3 must occur throughout the answer. We're now going to look at ways this can be achieved.

Let's assume a student has argued in one paragraph in favour of a point and in the following paragraph they've argued against it. How then can they add evaluation to this? One way is to add an 'interim judgement'. This is a third paragraph after the two described above which evaluates which side of the argument is stronger.

STUDENT EXTRACT – 'Evaluate the view that the only parties that matter are Labour and Conservative' – looking at AO3 via interim judgements

Command	Evaluate the view
Topic	Labour & Conservative Parties
Keyword(s)	Only

All of this evidence does, however, suggest that the view that the Labour and Conservative Parties are the only parties that matter in our political system is valid. This is because they are the two most powerful parties in the UK right now, as they have the most elected MPs in Parliament who have the ability to influence decisions.

STUDENT EXTRACT – 'Evaluate the view that the only parties that matter are Labour and Conservative' – looking at AO3 via interim judgements

Command	Evaluate the view
Topic	Labour & Conservative Parties
Keyword(s)	Only

Overall, although it is valid to conclude that the Conservative and Labour Parties have the most important influence over UK politics, it is unjust to claim they are the only parties to matter. Nevertheless, the importance of minor parties must not be exaggerated because, although the Liberal Democrats were able to form a government in the Coalition, they have failed to ever gain a majority within the Commons. Furthermore, following the Coalition their influence over UK politics declined, highlighting that although important, minor parties still fail to compare to both the Conservative and Labour Parties who in comparison matter more.

This paragraph is relatively brief, but does manage to provide a judgement, enhancing AO3 marks.

This longer paragraph is much more detailed in its evaluation, considering both sides and balancing one view against the other before concluding that Labour and Conservatives matter more.

It's also useful to note that this response is more nuanced in its evaluation. It is not arguing that smaller parties don't matter at all, but that ultimately, despite their importance in a number of ways, they don't matter as much as the two main parties, fulfilling the requirement to make a judgement, but suggesting that it is a marginal one. This is completely valid.

This is completely valid.

Another way of incorporating AO3 into answers is by integrating AO3 into the two-paragraph model mentioned earlier.

STUDENT EXTRACT – 'Evaluate the view that Parliament is able to sufficiently limit the power of the Prime Minister' – looking at AO3 judgements incorporated into paragraphs

A less convincing argument is that the opposition is ineffective at holding the government to account as PMQs is a weak form of scrutiny. The official opposition uses PMQs to question the government and force them to justify policy action. This has proved to be ineffective because PMQs are typically coordinated by Downing Street, with backbenchers asking pre-prepared questions so the Prime Minister is able to boast about the government's current situation rather than being scrutinised. For example in May 2024, Conservative backbencher Fay Jones asked Prime Minister Sunak a question praising the government's record on rural broadband rollout, giving the Prime Minister an opportunity to highlight Conservative achievements.

The more persuasive argument is that PMQs remain one of the most visible and impactful means of parliamentary scrutiny. The official opposition is given a unique opportunity to confront the Prime Minister directly, exposing weaknesses, forcing public justification of policies, and shaping political narratives. A clear demonstration of this came in 2025, following the Supreme Court's ruling on the legal definition of a woman. During PMQs, Leader of the Opposition Kemi Badenoch put Labour leader Keir Starmer on the defensive by accusing him of lacking 'moral courage' and branding him a 'weathervane' for shifting his stance on whether a transgender woman is a woman. She asked him to publicly apologise to MP Rosie Duffield, an MP who left Labour over the party's stance on gender issues. Her piercing challenge forced Starmer to address internal divisions revealing his vulnerability on the issue as he was put on the defensive. This exchange not only captured headlines but also spotlighted internal Labour tensions, prompting a national debate on gender policy. Such moments illustrate that PMQs, far from being ineffective, are a powerful mechanism through which the opposition can hold the government accountable. By commanding public attention and framing political discourse, PMQs helps ensure transparency and keeps political leaders answerable. By forcing the government to publicly defend its decisions, the opposition, through strategic use of this platform, plays a vital role in upholding democratic scrutiny and challenging those in power.

This integrated second paragraph above shows how the student is evaluating by incorporating their view into the paragraph. In this type of method, they are presenting the argument they don't agree with in the first paragraph, but then arguing against it, expressing their view, in the second. While this way is more complex, it might be less time-consuming than adding a third paragraph.

Either of these methods are highly effective ways of incorporating AO3 into your answers and ensuring that judgements are demonstrated throughout your answer.

Incorporating AO3 in conclusions

While your introductions begin the process of AO3, your conclusion should simply bring your whole argument together and end the journey. What a conclusion should not do is contain *all* your evaluation in one place; evaluation must be spread throughout your essay.

STUDENT EXTRACT – 'Evaluate the view that devolution has been successful in the UK' – looking at AO3 in conclusions

Command	Evaluate the view
Topic	Devolution
Keyword(s)	Successful

Overall, despite devolution leading to anger from some due to its asymmetric nature, devolution has clearly been successful because it has led to devolved government making key decisions regarding their country. Moreover, although nationalism is rising in the devolved regions, devolution has not led to any sort of break-up of the United Kingdom. Therefore, it is clear to see that devolution has been successful in the United Kingdom.

Here the student is bringing their essay to a close with a summary of their points and reinforcing the view from their whole essay that devolution has been successful.

STUDENT EXTRACT – 'Evaluate the view that the only parties that matter are Labour and Conservative' – looking at AO3 in conclusions

Command	Evaluate the view
Topic	Labour & Conservative Parties
Keyword(s)	Only

To conclude, Labour and Conservatives are the two biggest parties and they are the only two that are likely to form a government (largely due to FPTP), however this doesn't mean that they are the only parties that matter. Smaller parties have the ability to influence politics and they represent the views of many that are lost within the voting system. Minor parties matter but don't receive the same representation, which leaves the impression that Labour and Conservatives are the only parties that matter. However, I disagree.

> This is a conclusion which asks as many questions as it answers. Although it ends the paragraph with 'I disagree', it has taken so many twists and turns, it is uncertain what they disagree with. It is always best to keep conclusions simple and simply restate the view argued through the essay.

STUDENT EXTRACT – 'Evaluate the view that Parliament has become more effective' – looking at AO3 in conclusions

Command	Evaluate the view
Topic	Parliament
Keyword(s)	**Become more** effective

In conclusion, it is correct to argue that Parliament is indeed highly effective. Via three crucial elements – the House of Commons, the House of Lords and select committees – Parliament is able to successfully deliver its function of ensuring legislation is compatible with public and national interest, that the government is held to account, and democracy is subsequently upheld. These three elements are clearly done successfully, therefore Parliament is clearly highly effective.

> This is a detailed conclusion which reinforces at the beginning and end of the paragraph what it has been arguing throughout the answer.

Focusing on the actual question asked

In the exam, the most common reason for underperformance is not answering the question asked or not fully answering it. Throughout this chapter you will have seen that each essay title has a box identifying the Command word, the Topic and (very importantly) the Keyword(s). It is essential for students to fully focus on the question asked.

STUDENT EXTRACT – 'Evaluate the view that the only parties that matter are Labour and Conservative' – looking at balance

Command	Evaluate the view
Topic	Labour & Conservative Parties
Keyword(s)	Only

In the question above, the key aspect of this essay is the phrase "**the only** parties that matter", it's not asking whether minor parties have had some sort of impact, or whether Labour and Conservatives have lost support. It is asking whether they are **the only** parties that matter. This is different to asking whether the two main parties are still powerful, therefore any pre-prepared essay plans <u>must be adapted</u> to reflect the actual question asked. The keyword box usually (but not always) has a phrase that needs clarifying, for example, what does "sufficiently" mean in practice, or "successful" or "in crisis" or "only".

STUDENT EXTRACT – 'Evaluate the view that Parliament is able to sufficiently limit the power of the Prime Minister' – looking at comparative analysis AO2

Command	Evaluate the view
Topic	Parliament, Prime Minister
Keyword(s)	Sufficiently limit

In the above question, it is easy to answer the question by debating whether Parliament can limit the powers of the Prime Minister. However, this question is asking whether it **sufficiently limits** the PM's powers, in other words, does it limit it enough? (You could even argue that it limited it too much during May's premiership.) Top-level answers will see, understand and address this, most others will miss this nuance. The best answers will normally start by explaining what 'sufficiently' means in practice.

Source questions

Question 1 of both UK papers are source-based questions. Like the essay questions they are worth 30 marks and you should think about spending 40–45 minutes on them. Source questions can be asked about any aspect of the Component 1 or Component 2 UK specification and can be made up of text, a table, graphs or charts or a combination of these. They could be presented as one source or two separate sources. They will usually have the stem 'Using the source, evaluate the view that ...'.

The source (or sources) will have the two sides of an argument to a debate and the question will be about this debate. For example, if the question is, 'Using the source, evaluate the view that Parliament no longer fulfils its functions', the source will put forward the views that it does AND it does not fulfil its functions. Your job is to use the points raised in the source to formulate your answer.

The source below is from the June 2025 Component 1 Edexcel paper.

Instructions on the exam paper

There are some clear requirements about what you need to do in a source question. On the exam paper, after the source question, there will be a short list to guide you, as follows:

'*In your response you must*':

- » '*compare and contrast the different opinions in the source*'
  - This means you must use the points in the source to construct your essay, finding areas of agreement and disagreement.
- » '*examine and debate these views in a balanced way*'
  - This means that you must look at both sides discussed in the source and give both fair consideration (see section on balance on page p340).
- » '*analyse and evaluate only the information presented in the source*'
  - This piece of advice relates to the fact that AO2 and AO3 can only be awarded to points derived from the source. In other words, you can mention points not included in the source, but you will get no AO2 or AO3 marks from them. Students often find this advice quite complicated and follow the simpler advice to not introduce any new points that are not in the source.

Provenance

Another area of confusion for students (especially students of A-Level History) is the issue of the provenance of the source, i.e. its origins, or its authors. While it is expected that A-Level History students consider the source's origin and what that may mean with regards to the source's bias or its reliability, this is NOT the case with sources in A-Level Politics. There is no need to do this and students will waste valuable time if they choose to ignore this advice.

Look at Source 1(a) in the Source Booklet.

1 (a) Using the source, evaluate the view that rights in the UK are poorly protected.

In your response you must:

- *compare and contrast the different opinions in the source*
- *examine and debate these views in a balanced way*
- *analyse and evaluate **only** the information presented in the source.*

(30)

SECTION A

Political Participation

Source 1(a)

In the following paragraphs Colm O'Cinneide, Professor of Constitutional and Human Rights Law at UCL, considers the current strengths and weaknesses of the protection of rights in the UK.

Strengths

Current legislation provides strong legal protection for civil and political rights with the Human Rights Act, the European Convention on Human Rights and the Equality Act 2010. In addition, common law has long protected civil liberties such as the freedom of speech and jury trial. These are protected by the judiciary. There is an effective institutional framework protecting rights.

In UK civil society, there is a strong commitment to rights, values and activism. Human rights and civil liberties enjoy relatively strong political support from political parties and also from pressure groups, younger age groups and in the devolved regions. As such the public have the freedom to protest in order to protect and advance rights.

Weaknesses

The existing framework of UK legal rights protection (based on the HRA and European Convention) is vulnerable to political attack, with Conservative calls for a 'British Bill of Rights' to replace them. Whatever our opinion of Brexit, leaving the EU has made weaker the protection for certain migrant and labour rights formerly provided by EU law. The EU's Fundamental Charter of Rights no longer applies.

UK governments have been repeatedly able to introduce legislation weakening rights, especially in areas of national security, immigration and criminal justice.

Legal rights protection in the UK is limited. Social and economic rights (for example, to receive appropriate healthcare) are the most poorly established and protected. There is confusion between collective and individual rights. For now, the place of legal rights protection within the UK's constitutional culture remains uncertain. The major source of the problem is that little political consensus exists on the nature and meaning of human rights and how they should be guaranteed.

(Source: adapted from https://www.democraticaudit.com/2018/11/28/how-well-does-the-uks-democracy-protect-human-rights-and-civil-liberties/)

Source: Pearson Edexcel Level 3 GCE: Politics (Advanced), Paper 1: UK Politics and Core Political Ideas (2025) (9PL0/01)

Preparing to answer the source

Source answers should be structured in exactly the same way as essays. The only difference is where your points come from. In theory, you have 45 minutes to answer a source question, but in reality, you will have less than this. Below are some suggestions for how to prepare your answer.

1. It's essential to read the source thoroughly as your answer must be based on it. Read it through once first.

2. Read through it a second time and now use two different coloured highlighters to highlight the **arguments in favour** in one colour and the **arguments against** in another colour.

3. Make a simple grid plan (see below). Write down very briefly – one or two words is fine – the arguments for each side as outlined in the source. These, and only these, will form the basis of your answer (if you are really struggling with time you could miss this step out).

4. Pair up the arguments and counterarguments as much as possible (see the red arrows below).

5. Use these points as outlined throughout this chapter (although you do not have to use them all, just use the ones you feel are the most important and you are most confident writing about).

FOR	AGAINST
1	a
2	b
3	c
4	d

'Using the source'

The phrase preceding the question in source questions is 'Using the source …' and this is the most important aspect of answering a source question. As you can see in the first bullet on the top of page 354, you are being told to '**compare and contrast the different opinions IN THE SOURCE**'. You must not ignore this advice.

The whole point of the source is that you should read, understand and then debate the source's views on the question and not hijack the question to answer it in the way you want to. (This is the point of the essays [Question 2] where you can freestyle with the points you choose to answer the question.) In many ways, the source can be seen as easier because it is giving you the points to discuss, you don't have to think of them yourself!

So, for example, if a source says that, 'Current legislation provides strong legal protection for civil and political rights', you could use that point in your answer in two ways:

1. 'According to the source, "Current legislation provides strong legal protection for civil and political rights." This can be seen because governments have introduced the Human Rights Act and the Equality Act, both of which have had a huge impact on rights protection in the UK.'

   OR

2. 'The source suggests that one way rights have been protected in the UK is by the commitment by consecutive governments to introduce legislation which has provided significantly effective rights protection for UK citizens, namely the Human Rights Act and the Equality Act.'

Option 1 directly quotes the source before continuing to discuss it, whereas option 2 paraphrases the point made in the source. Both of these are excellent ways of fulfilling the criterion of 'using the source'. What you should avoid, however, is writing out large chunks of the source, like below, which is both time-consuming and unnecessary. The answer below is a simple rewrite of the source showing limited understanding of the points raised.

Rights in the UK are poorly protected because 'the existing framework of UK legal rights protection is vulnerable to political attack'. This is because the 'Conservatives call for a "British Bill of Rights" to replace' the Human Rights Act. Also 'leaving the EU has made the protection for certain migrant and labour rights weaker as the EU's Fundamental Charter of Rights no longer applies.' Another point from the source is that 'UK governments have been repeatedly able to introduce legislation weakening rights, especially in areas of national security, immigration and criminal justice.'

The '9 source rule'

One easy way to make sure you are showing that you are using the source is to remember the '9 source rule'. This is the suggestion that you use the word 'source' nine times in your answer. It focuses you to ensure that you are showing evidence of using the source throughout your answer. So, when are the nine times:

- Twice in the introduction – 'Source 1 suggests that rights are well protected, whereas source 2 disagrees arguing that rights are inadequately protected in the UK.'
- Once at the beginning of your 'point' paragraph and once at the beginning of your 'counterpoint' paragraph. 'The weaker argument from the source is that …' 'The stronger argument in the source…' (you do this for each paragraph so six times).
- Once in the conclusion – 'Therefore it is clear that according to both sources/the source ….'

However, remember the word 'source' must be followed by information from the source and then you must develop and analyse it using your own knowledge to be successful. Just using the word is not enough. The 'rule' is a reminder to use the source, and to show you are using the source to formulate your answer.

Interpreting AO1 for source answers

As previously discussed, the three AOs are worth one-third each of the 30 marks available in your source answer. While AO2 and AO3 are the same in essays and source questions, students can sometimes get confused about how to achieve good AO1 marks in sources. In a source, AO1 marks generally begin from points within the source, i.e. by identifying a key AO1 point made in the source. In addition, you can improve your AO1 mark by adding an explanation of the point raised in the source. Using examples and evidence to explain the point also adds to AO1 marks.

Source 1 suggests that legislation in the UK 'provides strong legal protection for civil and political rights' as the Human Rights Act has been revolutionary in upholding rights. The Act has been used countless times since it was introduced to ensure that rights were being upheld, and governments were held accountable. For example, it ruled that Rwanda was not a safe country to send illegal immigrants to, decimating the government's Rwanda plan.'

Here the student has taken a point from the source and then explained it before adding an example.

Debating not describing

One other issue with the source is to make sure you are not simply describing what the source says. Sometimes, students simply outline what the source is saying in their answers.

The source suggests that there is protection for rights in the UK because of the HRA and ECHR. It also suggests that common law and the courts are very good at upholding rights, particularly freedom of speech and the right to a jury trial. It also argues that parties and pressure groups are very effective at protecting rights and making sure the public have the freedom to protest.

This doesn't meet the basic purpose of what is required. The source answer needs to debate the issues raised in the source, not simply explain the source in your own words.

Structuring answers

Introductions and conclusions

Introductions play an important role in source and essay answers. They should usually fulfil two to three functions.

- » First, you should **define** anything that MAY need defining. (This one depends on the title and can be ignored in some cases – if it's a word or phrase that would be commonly understood, e.g. elections, then it probably doesn't need defining, but if it's a less well-known phrase or concept, e.g. democratic deficit, then it probably does.)

- So, if a question is asking whether the UK is suffering from a participation crisis, it would be useful to provide a brief definition of what this phrase means. Equally, however, if the question is whether the UK is a democracy, the term 'democracy' probably does not need defining in the introduction (although you may choose to outline the criteria for judging throughout the essay).

» The second purpose an introduction should serve is to provide **context** to the question/answer; to 'frame the debate'.

- This is usually a summary of the two perspectives of the debate and/or changes over time. It's important to note the word 'summary'. Too often students list all the arguments they are going to debate throughout their essay, both for and against, in their introduction. This is unnecessary and a waste of precious words (and hence time). A couple of sentences which sum up the key views of each side are more than sufficient.

- In a source answer, you should follow the advice above but also use this as an opportunity to reference the source, i.e. 'according to the source'. Again, it should still be a summary, but you should refer to something in the source. This shows that you are fully engaged with it (see 9 source rule on page 357).

» A final, but key, function of an introduction is to express a **line of argument**.

- This is crucial to your AO3 analysis. It needs to be clear.

- Often students end their introduction by stating their intention to investigate both sides and come to a view. It is better, at this stage, to outline the view that you are going to take to signal that you are fully aware of the AO3 demands. This is why it is so important to plan your answer fully before you start writing – you need to know your destination.

Visit the companion website and navigate to the section about how to plan your revision and effectively prepare for your exam.

Conclusions are crucial because they play a parallel role to introductions. The role of a conclusion should not be underestimated.

» A good conclusion should be brief; it should not be rambling.

» It is the culmination of your essay and the last thing to be read. Its objective is to reassert your view.

» You need to briefly bring all the arguments together and clarify your line of argument by making your point of view clear.

» You need to be convincing and persuasive without being overly strident or dismissive. Remember, it's OK to argue that the perspective you are arguing has only marginally 'won'.

How to organise your sections

One of the most challenging aspects of exam questions is bringing everything you've learned together to answer the question asked of you while making sure you are hitting the requirements of all three AOs. Here we are going to look at ways you can organise your answers to be as effective as possible. This advice applies equally to sources and essays. The only difference between the two is (a) where your points come from and (b) ensuring you reference the source. Apart from that, the structure of essays and sources can be identical because the AOs they need to hit are the same.

Firstly, it goes without saying that you need to know your stuff. No amount of organising paragraphs can drastically improve the quality of a student's answer if it doesn't show good knowledge and understanding of the content. As was outlined on page 342, AO1 is the foundation of everything else; without it, there is a limit to what can be achieved. On the assumption that AO1 knowledge is solid, it's important to know how you can ensure that the structure of your answer is set up to address the different needs laid out in this chapter.

We've covered introductions and conclusions, so that leaves the main body of the essay. The first step when considering the content you need to answer a question is to select the best arguments to discuss. In the source, this has already been done for you. Once you've decided on the best content, how then do you organise this, and which structure would best enable an answer to address all three AOs?

Tip: A 'section' includes a for and against paired point and also needs to include substantiated judgements.

The answer is clearly one that pairs 'for' and 'against' arguments and which facilitates comparative analysis, consequently enabling substantiated judgements to be made.

Once you've selected your arguments, the next stage is to organise your arguments into pairs, ideally matching the 'for' and 'against' pair (this is discussed in more detail on page 347). Throughout this book, we have laid out the arguments to Key Topic Debates according to this structure. This is important because this is the key to both AO2 comparative analysis and AO3 evaluation. It's not enough to pair any 'for' argument with any 'against' argument – they have to be related to each other.

How many sections?

The most frequent question asked by students is 'how many sections do we need to write?'. Annoyingly, there is no simple answer. On the assumption that you have no more than 45 minutes in the exam, it is fair to say that the answer is more than one and fewer than four! But the *length and amount of development within a section is as important as the number of points*. For example, if Student A has written three well-developed sections and Student B has written two well-developed sections, then Student B would probably achieve fewer marks than Student A. However, if Student C writes two highly detailed, developed and analytical sections, then they could achieve similar marks to Student A. However, in reality it is probably *more difficult* to do two significantly more detailed paragraphs than it is to do three well-developed ones. Figure 11.1 shows this.

Figure 11.1 Different layout of section lengths

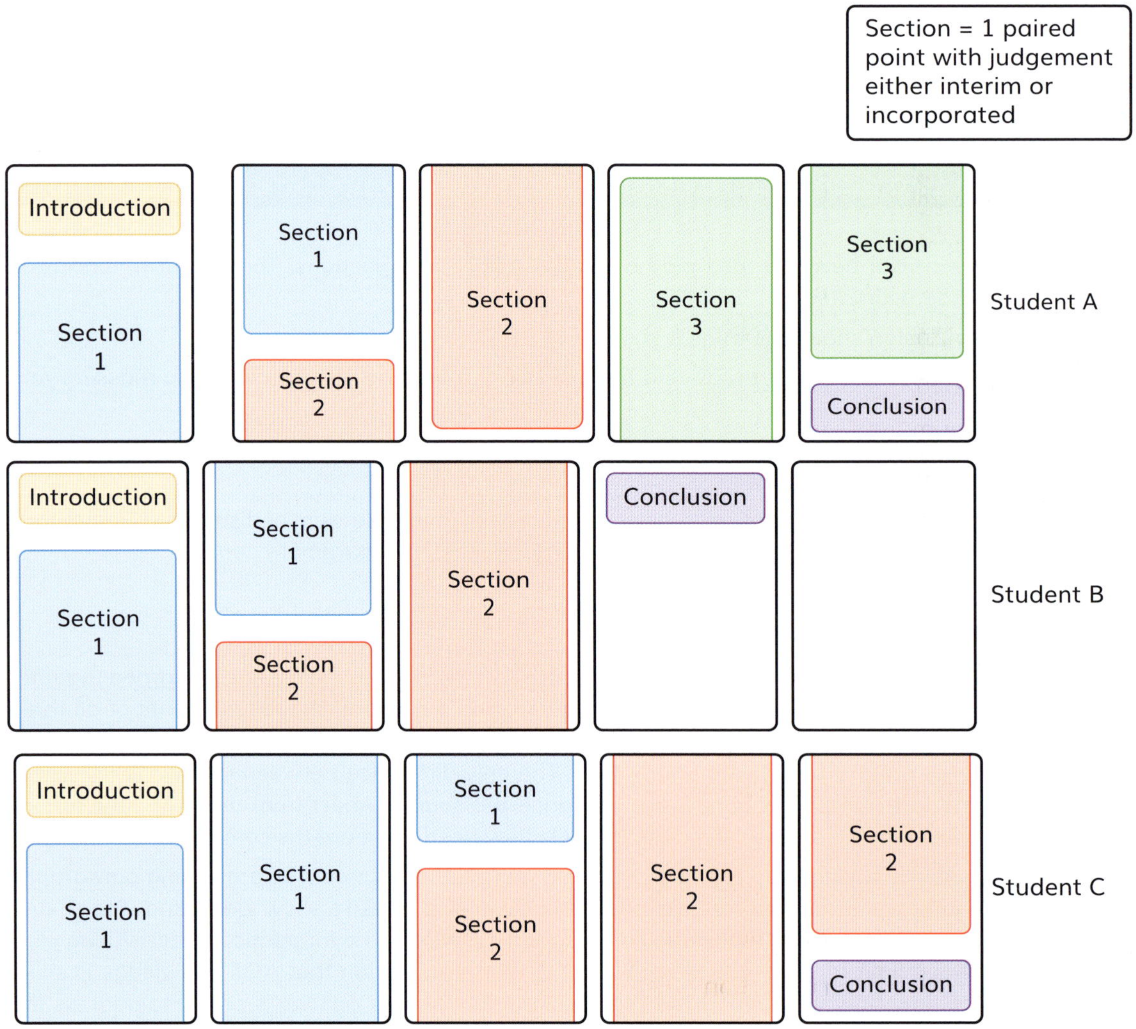

The structure in Figure 11.2 covers **AO1** and **AO2**, but still leaves **AO3** to be included. We know that **AO3** must be included throughout the answer, not just left to the end, or even just the beginning and end. This is therefore NOT an advisable structure.

The diagram to the right shows the layout of one section.

Figure 11.2 Structure 1 – not recommended

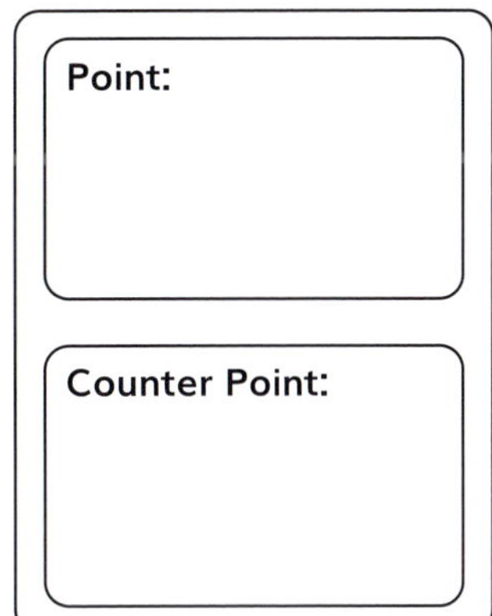

Two possible ways of including **AO3** in the answer are considered below.

This first option includes an interim judgement after both views are taken into consideration. The structure would look something like Figure 11.3.

Figure 11.3 Structure 2 – interim judgements

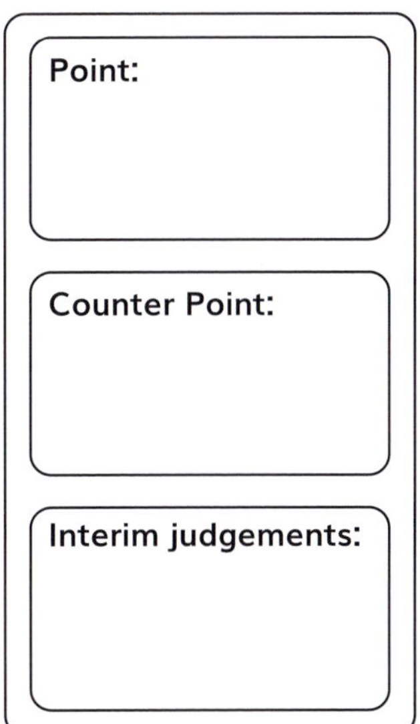

Here there is a paired point and counterpoint but the judgement is left to the end of the section.

STUDENT EXTRACT – 'Evaluate the view that the UK is experiencing a participation crisis' – looking at structure 2 – interim judgements

Command	Evaluate the view
Topic	Democracy
Keyword(s)	Participation crisis

Section 1

Argument in favour

It can be argued that there is a participation crisis because the public have limited interest in engaging with and participating in politics. This is suggested by the decreasing voter turnout. Since 1945 there has been much fluctuation, however the

Here in the opening paragraph of the section the student is outlining the arguments agreeing with the essay title by looking at voter turnout *statistics are troubling for many politicians considering that voter turnout is lower in the present day than it was 50 years ago. Average voter turnout during 1945 to 1997 General Elections was 76% compared to 60% voter turnout in the 2024 General Election. This is significant as it brings the legitimacy of the governing body into question. This is because fewer people voting means that the government will be elected on a smaller share of the vote. The lower voter turnouts suggest that fewer people are showing an interest in politics and are less concerned if their opinions are not represented in Parliament.*

Argument against

Alternatively, others may argue that there is not a participation crisis and the low voter turnout is simply due to lack of interest when things are not of huge significance, or in the case of 2024 when there was no appetite for another Conservative Government, but equally Starmer's Labour Party was not hugely popular. Consequently, turnout was low. The public do not want to vote on issues that will not make a major difference in their lives or in 'second order' elections like those held for the bodies in Scotland, Wales and Northern Ireland. This is because these smaller bodies are seen by some as less powerful and influential. Voter turnout is more likely to increase if the matter is something that will affect vast amounts of the public who feel passionately about the issue or if the issue is viewed as controversial. For example, there was a huge turnout of 72.2% for the controversial EU referendum as the outcomes of this referendum would have a significant impact on almost everyone across the country.

Interim judgement

However, this counterargument is weak because turnout is still relatively low in most, if not all, general elections. The outcomes of general elections always affect people, as the result determines which party will govern the country. This is a matter that one would think the public would be concerned about, yet the majority of people seem to be uninterested. This proves that the UK is experiencing a participation crisis as the public aren't involving themselves in matters that will affect them the most and they seem unaffected by this.

In the counter paragraph of the section, the student is giving the alternative arguments, crucially, related to voter turnout.

Finally in this section, the student is giving their judgement.

An alternative structure is the one shown in Figure 11.4. This is a slightly more complex structure but with the advantage of saving words (and hence time) as there is no separate judgement paragraph because the judgement is incorporated into the second paragraph. For this structure to work effectively, the order that you argue the 'for' and 'against' points is important. Let's say you are going to agree with the essay title; for this structure to work, you would begin with the 'against' argument (i.e. the one you DON'T agree with). You would then follow this with the one you do agree with and as part of your analysis in this paragraph you would include your critical judgement.

Figure 11.4 Structure 3 – incorporated judgements

	Introduction	
Section One	Argument against the view you're arguing	
	Argument in favour of the view you're arguing, including substantiated judgement	
Section Two	Argument against the view you're arguing	
	Argument in favour of the view you're arguing, including substantiated judgement	
Section Three	Argument against the view you're arguing	
	Argument in favour of the view you're arguing, including substantiated judgement	
	Conclusion	

Point:

Critique-incorporating A03

Here the student is incorporating the judgement throughout the second paragraph of the section, turning the counterargument into a critique of the first paragraph.

STUDENT EXTRACT 'Evaluate the view that the UK is experiencing a participation crisis' – looking at structure

Section One

Argument against the view you're arguing

A reasonable but less convincing view is that the UK is not experiencing a participation crisis. This is because low voter turnout in recent years is simply due to a lack of interest in things that are not of huge significance. This suggests that the public don't want to vote on issues that will not make a major difference in their lives or in 'second order' elections, like those held for the bodies in Scotland, Wales and Northern Ireland. This is because these smaller bodies are seen as less powerful and influential. They suggest that voter turnout is more likely to increase if the matter is something that will affect a vast number of the public who feel passionately about the issue or if the issue is viewed as controversial. For example, there was a huge turnout of 72.2% for the controversial EU referendum as the outcomes of this referendum would have a significant impact on almost everyone across the country.

> In the first paragraph of the section, the student is outlining the argument they don't agree with. Note that the language is relatively passive, and they are presenting a view rather than arguing it.

Argument in favour of the view you're arguing, including substantiated incorporated judgements

The claim that there is no participation crisis in the UK fails to withstand scrutiny, particularly when we examine long-term trends in voter turnout. In reality, turnout has been consistently low, not just in 'second order' elections, but even in general elections – arguably the most important democratic event in the political calendar. *This pattern strongly suggests that the UK is indeed facing a serious participation crisis.* General elections determine who will govern the entire nation and shape public policy, yet public engagement continues to decline. Since the 1970s, voter turnout has dropped dramatically; while the average turnout between 1945 and 1997 stood at 76%, it fell to just 60% in the 2024 General Election. *This stark decline* is not a mere statistical variation – it is a clear indication that fewer citizens are interested in, or feel represented by, the political process. *This disengagement is profoundly troubling.* In a democracy, legitimacy rests on the active participation of its citizens. When fewer people vote, *it raises serious questions about whether elected governments truly represent the will of the people.* Apathy towards voting is not just a passive choice; it erodes democratic accountability and undermines the very foundation of representative government. *Therefore, far from being a minor concern, declining turnout is a symptom of a broader democratic dissatisfaction. The evidence is compelling: the UK is not just experiencing a participation crisis – it is deep in the midst of one, and the consequences for democratic legitimacy and public engagement cannot be ignored.*

> In this second paragraph, they are proposing the alternative view but ALSO arguing in favour of that view. They are critiquing the arguments above and suggesting that this side of the argument is stronger. By doing this they are incorporating their **AO3** into the paragraph.

Factors questions

Another type of question which can be asked is a 'factors question'. This is where the question will reference one 'factor' and then ask if it the most important/significant one. A question like this is inviting you to compare the named 'factor' with other factors of your choosing. It is essential that you consider the named factor throughout your answer, not just in one section before moving on.

For example, if asked to "Evaluate the view that **select committees** are the most effective way for the Commons to hold the Executive to account", select committees must be looked at and compared to other forms of scrutiny. Remember, you can look at different types of select committees – Departmental, Liaison, Public Accounts, Privileges, etc. What would not be as effective would be to compare, for example, select committees to select committees, PMQs to PMQs, and Public Bill Committees to Public Bill Committees.

Putting it all together

We have now looked at all the different elements of an answer to an essay and a source question. Let's now look at a whole essay and how to combine these elements to make a good answer.

KEY

AO2 DEPTH

AO2 DIRECT COMPARISONS

AO2/AO3 COMBINED

AO3

SYNOPTIC LINK

Evaluate the view that the UK constitution is no longer fit for purpose

Command	Evaluate the view
Topic	UK Constitution
Keyword(s)	**No longer** fit for purpose

Draft 1

A constitution is the set of political principles by which a state or organisation is governed, especially in relation to the rights of the people it governs. In the UK there is an uncodified and unentrenched constitution based on the principle of parliamentary sovereignty. Many argue that the UK constitution is fit for purpose as it is flexible, and supreme constitutional authority rests in the elected House of Commons and it allows the government to be stronger and more effective. However, many disagree with this as they believe the UK constitution is no longer fit for purpose as its flexibility can result in uncertainty, and the UK has a centralised system of government with weak checks and balances, which can lead to the problem of 'elective dictatorship'. This essay will consider both views and come to a judgement.

On the one hand, some argue that the UK constitution is fit for purpose as it is flexible. This is due to parliamentary sovereignty resulting in Parliament being unable to bind its successors; similarly a source of the UK constitution is statute law which means that it is easy to introduce an Act of Parliament. This means that the UK constitution is able to reflect the ever-changing needs of the population, ensuring the constitution is timeless and constantly relevant. An example of this is the introduction of devolution by Tony Blair in 1998 as a response to rising nationalism in Scotland and Wales. A further example of this is his House of Lords reforms where the population resented hereditary peers, resulting in the number of hereditary peers being reduced to 92 in the House of Lords Act (1999), and also the Human Rights Act that enshrined the ECHR in UK law. Moreover,

A very long introduction which explains what a constitution, and the UK constitution is, unnecessarily lists all the arguments for and against the essay, but doesn't come to a view, which is crucial.

There are a number of examples mentioned rather than just picking one and analysing it. Or referencing a few and analysing them.

the flexibility of the constitution ensures that old ideas are not entrenched, which means that outdated ideas are removed, ensuring the constitution stays current and effective. An example of this is in 2022 where the Conservative Government introduced legislation to repeal the Fixed-term Parliaments Act. This means that the UK's current needs and wants are being expressed in the constitution and old ideas are removed.

The opposing argument is that the UK constitution is not fit for purpose as it is flexible which can lead to uncertainty; this is because flexibility can be interpreted in various ways leading to confusion for the population, with many arguing a constitution should be clear in order to guide the government. This means that the nature of the constitution is a threat to individual freedom and the basic nature of rights. An example of this is the Police, Crime and Sentencing Act 2022 which allowed the Home Secretary to ban 'unacceptable' protests and created the offence of 'public nuisance' when protesting. A further example of this is the Human Rights Act 1998 which is not legally binding, meaning the government can ignore the Act if an incompatibility is declared. This means that the flexibility of the constitution has allowed core ideas that protect rights and individual liberties to be ignored and left unprotected as there is not a strict guideline for government's actions and ways to protect these rights.

> ✓ In this section, we see a good pairing of points, and synoptic link made (HRA and rights protection).
>
> ✗ However, it lacks any **AO3** judgement, and also arguments have not been fully developed which limits **AO2** marks.

Another argument is that the constitution is fit for purpose as it allows for the government to be stronger and more effective. This is because the uncodified and unentrenched constitution allows governments to clear decisions during crises. The constitution means that government decisions can be backed by statute law, which are sovereign and can't be struck down. This means that governments can make strong and decisive actions. An example for this is Attlee during 1945–51 when setting up the NHS and nationalising the Bank of England in response to damage caused by the Second World War. This means that governments can be effective with their policy and ensure that their actions are beneficial to the current time, with few roadblocks to decisive and effective action.

The opposing view is that the UK constitution gives rise to the problem of an 'elective dictatorship'; as if elected with a large overall majority, the government is able to do as they please. An example of this is the Asylum and Immigration Act 2024 which aimed to send illegal immigrants to Rwanda. A further example of this is the Elections Act 2022 which requires photo ID when voting, discouraging voter fraud and ensuring better party representation. This means that the governing party with a large majority is essentially free to do as they want in shaping the constitution, regardless of liberties and rights. The constitution has allowed a concentration of power which has allowed the government of the day to shape the constitution, leading to an all-powerful government.

> ✓ In this section, we see good pairing of points again, and the reference to the Elections Act 2022 is synoptic.
>
> ✗ However, the examples used here are problematic. They are either far too old or are inaccurately explained. The reference to a large majority could have been linked to FPTP to add another synoptic link, and it also lacks any AO3 judgement.

The example of the Fixed Term Parliament Act is a really good one, but the essay doesn't explore it in any detail to consolidate their point.

This is a good example of a synoptic link back to Paper 1 (which is a requirement in Paper 2 essays), but could be developed more.

This is a really key point, but it isn't developed enough.

A really, really old example. There are much newer examples that could have been used.

This is a great example, but inaccurate, as the Act, better known as the 'Safety of Rwanda Act' made Rwanda a safe country despite the Supreme Court ruling to the contrary. Consequently, the key issue of the Act (that Government worked around a Supreme Court ruling) has been missed.

While there is **AO2** development here, it is quite general as opposed to picking up the point made by the (very good) example.

This isn't quite right, it lies in Parliament.

This point is quite vague, and the point they are making is unclear.

This point is too similar to the elective dictatorship point above.

This is not AO2 development, it's repetition of the opening sentence.

A good example which has some development.

This is quite a weak point, because it is widely recognised that the opposite is true; the Lords became more effective after the removal of hereditary peers. While it is completely fine to argue from either side of the debate, it is crucial that the argument is credible. Also, Life Peers have always been appointed by the PM, amongst others.

A final argument is that supreme constitutional authority rests in the elected House of Commons. This is because there is an uncodified constitution, and this means that democratic rule is in the Commons, which results in changes to the constitution stemming from democratic pressures as the Commons is elected. An example of this is where powers of the House of Lords were reduced from the Parliament Acts in 1911 and 1949, which occurred from a popular belief that an unelected second chamber shouldn't have the right to block policy from an elected government. This means that changes to the constitution are democratic as they occur from the elected House of Commons, which each represent a constituency, ensuring that changes are directly wanted by the electorate.

The opposing argument is that the UK constitution is not fit for purpose as it has led to an over-centralised system of government with weak checks and balances. This is because of the uncodified constitution leading to a high concentration of power and an over-mighty executive branch located mainly in Westminster with weak checks and balances. An example of this is the Environment Act 2021, which allowed ministers to alter environmental regulations through secondary legislation. This means that the executive has been able to consolidate power at the expense of oversight and accountability of the overly-centralised executive. Similarly, due to the current constitution there are very weak checks and balances on the government. This may be because the House of Lords Act in 1999, which cut down the number of hereditary peers, has resulted in power being shifted to Westminster and increased centralised power as Lords are now appointed and approved by the Prime Minister, giving them more power. This means that the checks of the Lords on the government have become ineffective as it is often loyal supporters who are appointed as Lords, leading to the government being unchecked and increasing the centralisation of power. An example of this is in 2022 when Johnson selected a dozen of his close allies to be appointed to the Lords, including Lord Lebedev, with close KGB ties, and being advised not to approve his appointment.

> ✅ It has a good, recent example in the counterpoint, and has some AO2 development.
>
> ❌ In this section, the first point is unclear, and the counterargument is too similar to the point made above about elective dictatorship. It also lacks any AO3 judgement.

A very long conclusion, which restates all the arguments and does, finally, include a clear line of argument.

To conclude, there are many arguments that the constitution is and isn't fit for purpose. As outlined, many argue that the constitution is fit for purpose as it allows flexibility, ensuring old ideas aren't entrenched in the constitution. Supreme constitutional authority rests in the elected House of Commons, ensuring changes to the constitution are democratically accountable and allows the government to be stronger and effective by taking decisive action. However, these arguments should be rejected as the UK constitution is no longer fit for purpose as flexibility can lead to uncertainty which threatens rights, which has led to an over-centralised system of government with weak checks and balances, allowing the government to threaten individual liberties that can give rise to an elective dictatorship which allows the government of the day to reshape the whole constitution and do as they please. It must be considered that the governing party's ability to change the constitution is restricted by the size of their majority, popularity of their party and the electorate's opinions on the matter. Despite this, overall, the UK constitution is no longer fit for purpose, which is the strongest argument here.

Evaluate the view that the UK constitution is no longer fit for purpose

Command	Evaluate the view
Topic	UK Constitution
Keyword(s)	**No longer** fit for purpose

DRAFT 2

The UK has an uncodified and unentrenched constitution based on the principle of parliamentary sovereignty, which sets out the principles of governance, and the rights of the people. Many argue that the UK constitution is fit for purpose as its flexibility ensures that it remains relevant and effective. However, the stronger argument is that the UK constitution is no longer fit for purpose as its flexibility can result in uncertainty, and the problem of an 'elective dictatorship'. Thus, this essay will argue that the constitution is no longer fit for purpose.

An argument that is reasonable but unconvincing is that the constitution is fit for purpose, as it is flexible. This is due to parliamentary sovereignty which means that it is easy to make changes by passing an Act of Parliament. The UK constitution can thus reflect the ever-changing needs of the population, ensuring the constitution is timeless and relevant. This ability to make changes organically is crucial to the success of our evolutionary constitution. Examples of this are the constitutional reforms introduced by Blair in the 1990s. These reforms revolutionised and modernised the UK system, considerably enhancing its democratic nature. Rights were considerably protected by the HRA and devolution and the Lords Reform decentralised and democratised our system. Moreover, the ability to leave the EU without any significant constitutional constraints reinforces this point. This indicates that the flexibility of the UK's constitution ensures outdated practices are not entrenched, and can be removed, and that decisions backed by the people can be enacted, ensuring the Constitution stays current and effective. It also ensures ineffective practices can be removed with little fuss. An example of this is in 2022 where the Conservative Government introduced legislation to repeal the Fixed-term Parliaments Act 2011; the Act was clearly not working, with two snap elections called in 2017 and 2019, highlighting just how ineffective it was.

However, this view fundamentally fails to recognise that the UK constitution is not fit for purpose as it is too flexible. Being flexible is not a strength in a constitution; clarity and rigidity are essential to define and limit government power, and protect citizens' rights. In the UK, the constitution is whatever a majority in the Commons says it is as Parliament is unable to bind its successors. This means no legislation – no matter how vital – can be entrenched. To take the example of Brexit from above, this is an example of the weakness of our constitution, not a strength. On a small margin of 52:48, there were no constitutional safeguards to restrain such a profound change; instead it was powerless, and even though Parliament clearly sought to thwart Brexit, they had no clear mechanisms to do this. This vulnerability is further exposed by the Police, Crime and Sentencing Act 2022 which introduced sweeping protest restrictions. The Act was used to silence Steve Bray's peaceful anti-Brexit demonstrations – first through the seizure of his equipment, then by banning him from all streets surrounding Parliament, after disrupting Sunak's General Election announcement, reflecting the expanded protest control powers granted by the Act. Such actions highlight how easily

---

A brief reference to both sides - framing the debate as the detail will come throughout the essay.

Importantly, it ends with a clear view.

Did you know that you can use the core ideas from paper 1 to make synoptic links? Here the student is expressing the Conservative view of organic change.

The reforms are now referred to and analysed rather than explained in detail.

Now with added analysis, the point is well made.

Identifying the directly opposing point (pairing arguments), is a key way of addressing this aspect of **AO2**, and 'too flexible' is a clear **AO3** judgement.

Directly critiquing a point from the opposing paragraph is another excellent way to address this aspect of **AO2**.

the government can expand its powers with little constitutional resistance. Constitutions are meant to restrain authority; ours enables it. These points demonstrate convincingly that the significantly stronger argument is that the UK constitution is not fit for purpose.

> ✓ This section above shows a point and a critique with a clear line of argument. Examples are current and are used well to illustrate and develop the point being made. There are synoptic links throughout and the critique is analytical and evaluative, arguing its case throughout.

A plausible but still flawed argument is that the constitution is fit for purpose as it allows for the government to be stronger and more effective. This is because the uncodified and unentrenched constitution allows governments to make clear decisions during crises. This means that government decisions can be backed by statute law, which can't be struck down by any higher body and governments can take strong and decisive actions. An example of this is during the Covid pandemic in 2020 when the government were able to quickly pass laws to lock down the country to protect lives. This showed that governments can act quickly when necessary and not have any lengthy processes to go through. They can act decisively and ensure that their actions are beneficial, without being restricted by a codified constitution.

However, this view is short-sighted because in reality, the absence of formal constraints in the UK constitution enables what Lord Hailsham termed an 'elective dictatorship'. This is because FPTP tends to provide a 'winner's bonus' to the winning party, often giving them a very large overall majority, with considerably fewer votes, allowing the government to exercise unchecked power, which shows that the stronger argument is that the UK constitution is clearly not fit for purpose. An example of this is the Environment Act 2021, which allowed ministers to alter environmental regulations through secondary legislation, bypassing full parliamentary scrutiny and weakening accountability. This means that the executive has been able to consolidate power at the expense of oversight and accountability. Similarly, the Safety of Rwanda Act 2024 followed a Supreme Court ruling that Rwanda was unsafe for asylum seekers. Rather than accepting judicial oversight, the government responded by legislating that Rwanda must be treated as safe, effectively nullifying legal checks. This was a clear abuse of power, undermining an important check on a powerful executive, yet it was completely legal and constitutional due to our uncodified system which allows significant power to be held by a government with a majority in the Commons. The UK constitution promotes a dangerous concentration of power which allows governments with large majorities to be free to do as they want. It is therefore undoubtedly the case that the UK constitution is no longer fit for purpose.

> Again, this is a paired argument, it is critiquing the points raised in the opening paragraph of a section.

> By adding a little bit of information, the point now becomes synoptic.

> ✓ In the section above we see clearly paired points and excellent examples. Importantly, these examples are **used** to develop the point being made and are an integral part of the answer. In the critique paragraph we see effective use of AO2 and AO3 being combined.

A final argument, which is ultimately flawed, is that the UK constitution is fit for purpose because it has evolved over time to provide improved rights protection. Rights protection was enhanced by the passage of the Human Rights Act, the Freedom of Information Act and the Equalities Act. Consequently, there have many significant cases since then where the law has been used to uphold and protect the rights of its citizens. In 2025, the Supreme Court ruled that, under the Equality Act 2010, the legal definition of 'woman' refers to biological sex only, not to acquired gender. This decision clarified that sex-based legal protections apply exclusively to biological women, while reaffirming that transgender people remain protected from discrimination under separate provisions of the Equalities Act. This ruling, while controversial to some, helped to clarify how institutions should protect the spaces of biological women. The FOIA played a significant role in uncovering details about the Post Office Horizon scandal, which involved wrongful convictions of sub-postmasters due to faults in the Horizon IT system. These cases highlight that an uncodified constitution can change and reform organically so that it serves its citizens well.

However, the far stronger and more compelling argument is that the UK's uncodified constitution fundamentally fails to protect rights. The Human Rights Act cannot be entrenched as Parliament cannot bind its successors, as such. We have seen parts of the Conservative Party and Reform UK saying that they wish to withdraw from the ECHR and limit the ability of the HRA to prioritise individual rights over collective rights. Such proposals highlight the fragility of rights under the current system, showing it is not fit for purpose. Additionally, the constitution has not stopped the government from significantly undermining citizens' rights in the UK. The right to protest has been significantly curtailed by the Police, Crime and Sentencing Act 2022. In 2022, Just Stop Oil protesters were jailed under this offence and received lengthy custodial sentences for organising and carrying out disruptive protests, such as blocking the M25 motorway. This was an excessive response that undermines the historic and democratic right to protest. This is because the Human Rights Act is ineffective and not legally binding on the government. A further example is the Elections Act 2022 which required photo ID when voting, under the guise of preventing fraud, but was widely seen as an effort to suppress turnout among demographics less likely to support the government. Despite serious implications for the right to vote, Parliament passed it with limited checks. In the 2024 General Election, 16,000 voters were turned away, however broader research suggests the real impact was likely to be in the hundreds of thousands. All these cases can leave no room for doubt that a constitution which permits governments to restrict fundamental rights with such ease, is clearly no longer fit for purpose.

> ✅ The final paired section above, we once again see excellent use of examples, which illustrate and develop the points being made. There is a very clear line of argument throughout and the whole section is synoptic as it is discussing rights protection.

> By addressing failures in rights protection, this is a paired point, reinforcing comparative **AO2**.

To conclude, it is abundantly clear that the UK Constitution is not fit for purpose as its flexible, organic nature, has led to an over-centralised system of government with weak checks and balances allowing the government to undermine rights and give rise to an elective dictatorship which allows the government of the day to reshape the constitution and act as they please.

 Final thought

On our companion website you will find a lot of helpful advice on how to prepare for your exam, but before we end the chapter, remember this ...

Perhaps the most important piece of advice is worth reiterating: answer the question set, NOT the one you wish had come up. This means that the time you spend selecting a question and wondering what, exactly, the question is asking, is the **most valuable time** you spend in the examination – that is, the bit **before** you start writing.

Around two-thirds of candidates underperform to some degree in every examination because, anxious to start writing and believing (foolishly) that quantity is more important than quality, they ignore this advice. Make sure that, for this purpose at least, you are in the minority. Good luck!